Learn at Home
Grade 5

From the Editors of American Education Publishing

Table of Contents

Table of Contents

Welcome!

Congratulations on your decision to educate at home! Perhaps you are a bit nervous or overwhelmed by the task ahead of you. *Learn at Home* will give you the guidance you need to provide your child with the best fifth-grade education possible. This book is only a guide, however, and you are encouraged to supplement your child's curriculum with other books, activities and resources that suit your situation and your child's unique interests.

Create an inviting learning environment for your child. It should be comfortable and attractive, yet a place in which your child can work without distractions. Your child's work area should include a desk or table, a chalkboard or dry-erase board, an easel, appropriate writing and art materials, a cozy area for reading (perhaps with pillows or a bean bag chair), a bulletin board for displaying work and shelves for books and storage. Hang a clock and a calendar in the room as well. Collect inexpensive materials from around your home for your child to use in art projects, as math manipulatives or for language activities. Bottle caps, cardboard tubes, dried pasta and beans, old magazines, egg cartons, small tiles and wooden cubes are certain to come in handy throughout the year.

The Learn at Home Series

The *Learn at Home* series is an easy-to-use line of resource guides for parents who have chosen to teach their children at home. The series covers grades K through 6, one volume per grade level. Each book in the series is organized the same. An introductory section called **Background Information and Supporting Activities** provides general information and activity ideas for each area of the curriculum. This section is then followed by thirty-six weeks of instruction in six curricular areas. At the fifth-grade level, these areas include Language Skills, Spelling, Reading, Math, Science and Social Studies.

Each of the thirty-six weeks is then further divided into three sections: **Lesson Plans, Teaching Suggestions and Activities** and **Activity Sheets**. Each week's **Lesson Plan** includes lessons and activity suggestions for all six curricular areas. Though divided into separate areas of the curriculum, many of these activities are actually cross-curricular in nature. The lesson plans are brief, but further explanations are often provided in the next section, **Teaching Suggestions and Activities**. This section generally contains detailed directions for activities mentioned in the lesson plans, as well as background information and a variety of suggestions for related activities and extensions. **Activity Sheets** round out each week's materials. These sheets are grouped by subject and arranged in the order in which they appear in the lesson plans. Activity sheets are referred to by name and page number and are highlighted by **bold** print throughout this book.

Background Information and Supporting Activities

LANGUAGE SKILLS

▶ BACKGROUND

Language skills should be taught in real context and in all subject areas. Whenever possible, integrate your teaching of grammar, handwriting and writing skills into other areas of the curriculum, such as science or social studies. Ask your child to write on a science topic he/she is currently investigating or to answer a question in writing about a historical event.

▶ GRAMMAR

The following language skills are taught at the fifth-grade level. Incorporate these skills into your curriculum using the activities provided in the lesson plans as well as your own original ideas.

Vocabulary Development	Antonyms, homonyms and synonyms Analogies Similes and metaphors Correct word usage
Parts of Speech	Nouns, verbs, adjectives, adverbs, prepositions, conjunctions and interjections Kinds of phrases Appositives
Punctuation	Punctuation marks Capitalization with punctuation
Sentence Structure	Complete sentences Types of sentences Subject and predicate Subject/verb agreement
Paragraphs	Paragraph organization Topic sentences Recognizing details Types of paragraphs
Editing	Writing process Proofreader's marks
Other	Writing business letters and friendly letters Alphabetical order

▶ HANDWRITING

The weekly language lessons in this book do not include activities for practicing handwriting. Depending on your child's needs, however, you may wish to purchase an alphabet desk tape or an alphabet chart or banner to hang on the classroom wall. These can be found at most parent/teacher stores. Since there is more than one style of cursive handwriting, you should choose one that is compatible with the printing style taught at younger grades.

► THE WRITING PROCESS

Engage your child in meaningful writing activities each week. Use a writing lesson as an opportunity to stress a newly learned grammatical skill. While the focus of some writing activities will be correctness, others will encourage fluency. Devote at least thirty minutes each day to writing, whether it be creative writing or writing in other areas of the curriculum. The writing process is ongoing but generally includes these steps:

Prewriting   The writer brainstorms ideas, gathers and organizes information.

Drafting   The writer composes or writes a rough draft using prewriting ideas. He/she should not worry about mistakes at this stage. The emphasis here is on fluency, not accuracy. The writer dates the drafts and keeps them in a writing folder.

Revising   The writer rereads the draft, checking to see that it is fluent, interesting and stays on topic. Then, he/she reads the rough draft to another person to gather feedback on word choice, fluency, clarity and interest. The writer makes changes as needed.

Editing   The writer proofreads, then edits, the revised piece of writing for proper spelling, capitalization and grammar.

Publishing   The writer copies the corrected proof and prepares to present it.

► PUBLISHING OPTIONS

The purpose of publishing your child's written work is to present his/her material to a real audience. Most of the writing we do as adults has a real or intended audience. Writing with a reader in mind will motivate your child to write, and he/she may take more care to express him/herself clearly and accurately.

- Reproduce your child's completed and edited story in book form, complete with illustrations and a cover. Start a "library" of your child's work.

- Arrange for your child to read a completed story to an audience.

- Submit one of your child's completed and edited written pieces to a children's magazine such as *Cricket, Stone Soup* or *Highlights for Children*.

- Create a quarterly literary magazine to publish your child's favorite poems, stories, articles and essays. Each week, ask your child to select a written piece to save for the magazine. Once you have collected several pieces of writing, help him/her edit and arrange the pieces to form an interesting magazine. He/she may want to supplement the pieces with pictures, ads, puzzles, riddles and editorials. Make copies of the magazine and send to relatives and friends.

► WRITING OPPORTUNITIES

Create opportunities to get your child writing. The more often your child writes, the more fluent he/she will become. Listed below are ten ideas to help you motivate your child to write.

Letter Writing   Arrange for your child to write letters on a regular basis to a relative, friend or pen pal. Encourage a prompt response to the letters he/she receives.

Diary/Journal   Have your child write in a journal every day. Let your child write about anything. Occasionally you may need to suggest journal topics. Your child's journal can be a place for personal reflection, current events, lists, jokes and riddles, descriptions of wonderful or terrible things, ideas for stories and much more.

Learn At Home, Grade 5

Story Starter	Write an intriguing sentence on the chalkboard. **Example:** *Elliot ran into the house, slamming the door behind him.* Ask your child to reflect on the sentence for a few minutes, then write a story based on the sentence. Use the same sentence on more than one occasion to inspire several different stories.
Descriptive Paragraph	Suggest a topic or situation for your child to describe in writing, using adjectives and descriptive phrases. Ask him/her to explain the subject clearly enough that the reader can visualize the subject.
Character Description	Have your child write a descriptive paragraph about a character. Ask your child to choose a favorite (or least favorite) character from a book, a person in history, a relative or another person. You may also suggest that your child write a riddle about the character. The riddle would include descriptive sentences that do not mention the character's name. The purpose of writing the riddle would be to have someone else guess who the character is. (The character must be familiar to the person guessing.)
Answering Questions	Write a question on the chalkboard each day or one day each week. Ask your child to reflect on the answer before writing. Alternate questions that require no research, such as *What did you do Saturday?* with questions that may require a bit of research, such as *Where and when was the first Thanksgiving celebration?*
Expressing an Opinion	Discuss a current topic of debate with your child. Then, have your child write his/her opinion on the issue, citing evidence or examples that substantiate his/her view. You may wish to use the format of a letter to the editor for this activity.
Feelings	Have your child write about his/her feelings in different situations. *How does it feel to lose a game? How would you react to a growling dog? How do you react when you open a present you don't like?*
Writing Directions	Have your child write detailed directions for completing a task he/she knows how to do very well, such as making a capital S, folding a sweater, making a bed or finding a specific phone number. Focus on clarity and conciseness.

SPELLING

▶ BACKGROUND

Spelling is applicable to all areas of study, so work to integrate it into all areas of the curriculum. As your child encounters new terms in social studies, science and math, add that vocabulary to the weekly spelling lists. Add words from your child's own writing as well. Repeating spelling words during the week will help your child memorize words for a test, but it will not help him/her retain the words for the long term. The most effective technique for retaining accurate spelling is to use the words in context. Each week, engage your child in a writing activity using the spelling words. Steady exposure to words through reading will also improve your child's ability to spell.

▶ TEACHING SPELLING SKILLS

Each weekly lesson plan contains a list of 18 vocabulary words for your child to learn. Review weeks are the only exceptions—the spelling lists for weeks 9, 18, 27 and 36 are generated by you and your child based on words from previous weeks' lists that need to be reviewed. Follow the schedule below for each week's spelling lessons.

Monday

1. Give your child a pretest of the new word list. Read each word, use it in a sentence, then read the word again. Enunciate each word clearly to avoid confusion.

2. Have your child correct his/her own pretest as you read the word aloud and spell it. Ask your child to make a check mark next to each word that is spelled correctly and circle each word that is misspelled. Have your child write each misspelled word correctly next to the incorrect spelling. These words will comprise the study list for the week.

3. Add words to the list from your child's written work or from other curriculum areas. Keep the list at around 18 words. Have your child copy the study list twice: once for him/herself and a second time for your records.

4. Discuss any spelling rules that apply to the words in the list.

Tuesday

1. Have your child complete the provided activity sheet. Ask your child to name any additional words that fit in the spelling category.

2. Have your child practice spelling each word aloud through games and physical activity. Play games such as "Hangman," "Boggle" and "Scrabble."

Wednesday

1. Have your child use each spelling word in a meaningful sentence.

2. Have your child read the completed sentences aloud.

Thursday

1. Have your child complete an activity that involves writing, forming, tracing or reading the spelling words repeatedly. Several activity suggestions are included on pages 9 to 10.

2. Have your child practice using the spelling words orally.

▶ READING JOURNAL

Have your child keep a Reading Journal. Encourage your child to write in the journal on a regular basis. Assign questions to answer in the journal or allow your child to write on other topics related to the book. The best questions will ask your child to express an opinion, make a recommendation, criticize a decision or debate an issue presented in the book.

▶ BOOK PROJECT IDEAS

After reading a book, engage your child in an activity that requires imagination and creativity, as well as an understanding of the story just read. Several suggestions for follow-up activities are listed below. These activities may accompany or replace the traditional written book report. Display these choices on a chart and keep posted all year.

- Design and create a diorama.
- Write a poem about a character.
- Retell a poem in story form.
- Retell a story in poem form.
- Write a sequel.
- Write a critique of the book.
- Illustrate a favorite scene.
- Write a new ending.
- Make a filmstrip of the events.
- Prepare and perform a puppet show.
- Rewrite a scene from the book in play form.
- Compare two characters using a Venn diagram.
- Illustrate a fable and write out the moral.
- Write three questions to ask the subject of a biography.
- Design and create a commercial to sell the book.
- List things a character might say in given situations.
- Draw a comic strip with characters from the book.
- Write a sensational news story about an event in the book.
- Build a mobile representing attributes of a character.

▶ INCENTIVES

Reading can be its own reward, but your child may need a little encouragement at times. Choose an incentive that fits your child's interests and your own philosophy.

1. Make a record sheet like the one shown here. After your child finishes a book, have him/her complete one line on the chart. When each line of the chart is filled—you decide how many lines it should have—let your child choose an activity as a reward. You could play a game together, bake cookies or go ice-skating.

Title	Author	Main Idea	Rating
Through the Looking Glass	Lewis Carroll		
Mr. Popper's Penguins	Richard and Florence Atwater		

2. Set a reading goal. Choose a theme that will motivate your child. Design a bulletin board display around the theme. For each book your child reads, add something to the display. When the display is full, your child earns a reward related to the theme.

   Example: Draw a large pizza. Your child gets to add a mushroom or piece of pepperoni to the pizza for each book he/she reads. Have your child write the title of a completed book on each mushroom or piece of pepperoni. When the pizza is full of toppings, your child earns a pizza lunch with someone special.

▶ THEMATIC UNIT

A thematic unit is a way of organizing lessons from more than one subject area around one theme. For example, if you are reading a novel about the American West, design math story problems related to that theme. In science, you could set up experiments by growing different plants in sand. In social studies, you could study the geography of the West. In spelling, add words from the novel or theme-related vocabulary to the spelling list. Teaching thematically takes imagination and planning, but lessons can be more meaningful to your child if they are taught in an interesting context.

MATH

▶ BACKGROUND

The fifth-grade math curriculum is filled with activities and exercises designed to help your child comprehend the logic behind math operations. Your child will review the fundamental concepts of place value, addition, subtraction, multiplication and division, and will learn to apply these concepts to rounding, estimation, geometry, graphing, tangrams, fractions, decimals, percents and ratios. Your child will also learn how to work with numbers in different bases, such as base ten or base two. Whatever the topic, look for opportunities to relate math to your child's own world. Show your child the practical applications of mathematics.

▶ PROGRESS CHART

Have your child practice graphing skills while keeping a record of personal progress each quarter. Using a sheet of graph paper, have your child design a graph to record the name of each skill or assignment, the date and a range of scores (from 0 to 100 in increments of 5). For each assignment completed, your child will color in his/her score. Set a standard of excellence, such as 90%, that your child should strive to attain. Provide opportunities for your child to improve low scores, whether it be repeating an assignment after further instruction or completing a related assignment.

▶ BOOK OF SITUATIONAL PROBLEMS

Provide a notebook for creating and solving situational problems, or word problems. Have your child design two or three situational problems using current math concepts each week. Encourage your child to relate the math concept to his/her own experience—daily activities or themes from other curricular areas. This activity will stress the importance of the math concepts and teach that they have practical applications. Have your child leave the problems unsolved until the review week. Use the term *situational problem* rather than *word (or story) problem* to encourage your child to see math in real-life situations. You may also wish to act out, draw or model problems in order to increase your child's understanding.

▶ VOCABULARY

As new vocabulary is introduced in the math lessons, have your child record and define them in his/her Book of Situational Problems. During review weeks, have your child define the terms and provide examples when appropriate. You may also choose to add some of these terms to your child's weekly spelling lists.

SCIENCE

▶ BACKGROUND

Fifth-grade science covers a wide range of topics. This year, your child will learn about the plant and animal kingdoms, as well as living organisms that do not belong to either of these categories. Your child will also investigate earth science, specifically various landforms, bodies of water and climate. Finally, your child will study physical science, conducting experiments to explore the concepts of force, motion and work.

▶ THE SCIENCE LEARNING CYCLE

Encourage your child to follow the science learning cycle whenever he/she has a question related to science or when exploring a new idea.

1. Begin with a question. **Example:** *What will happen if I leave this half-eaten apple on the counter?* State a possible hypothesis.

2. Follow up the question with an exploration that involves observation, play, experimentation, debate and other methods of inquiry. Encourage your child to use descriptive language, measure when appropriate and keep a journal of observations.

3. Propose explanations and solutions for the initial question. An explanation may prove or disprove the earlier hypothesis. This is a time of writing, talking and evaluating. After this step, you may need to return to the second step of the cycle, exploring the topic further.

4. Apply the knowledge to real life. Ask: *Where have you seen this happen before? What will you do differently because of the experiment?* This fourth step may also spark a new question that will begin the cycle again.

Do not worry if you don't have answers to all of your child's questions. The science learning cycle promotes exploration and prompts your child to construct his/her own knowledge, based on experience. The more experience you provide, the clearer and more accurate your child's understanding will be. If your child presses you for an answer, you can say, *Let's find out, What do you think?* or *Where have you seen something like that?* Your child will not always be satisfied, but keep in mind that your vocabulary-filled answers are not always easy to comprehend. Science is a process of wondering. Keep the wondering alive. A good scientist asks a lot of questions!

▶ SCIENCE PROCESS SKILLS

1. Observing
2. Classifying
3. Using numbers
4. Measuring
5. Using space-time relationships
6. Communicating
7. Predicting
8. Inferring
9. Formulating hypotheses
10. Controlling variables
11. Interpreting data
12. Defining operationally
13. Experimenting
14. Formulating models

▶ SCIENCE LOG

Have your child keep a folder of record sheets, activity sheets and other lab notes from each unit of study. Provide your child with a notebook, or Science Log, for recording observations and writing about each lesson. At the end of the unit, the folder and Science Log will serve as excellent resources for review.

Learn At Home, Grade 5

SOCIAL STUDIES

▶ BACKGROUND

In the fifth grade, your child will explore American history in-depth, including culture, geography and economics from the time of Columbus through the Civil War. Other topics of study include physical features, natural resources, regions, famous Americans and the nation's capital. Seek a variety of resources to teach social studies, such as textbooks, posters, videotapes, films, magazines, books, audiotapes, computer software and resource books. Check your area for historians, archaeologists, geographers, inventors and politicians who might be available to speak with your child.

▶ COMMUNITY INVOLVEMENT

Get your child involved in your community this year. Each Friday, have your child perform some sort of community service. Here are some suggested activities:

1. Tutor a young child in the primary grades.

2. Read aloud to a young child or to an older adult.

3. Volunteer at the local library to straighten shelves, dust or make photocopies.

4. Help out Habitat for Humanity in some way to build a home for a needy family.

5. Organize a fund-raising project such as a book fair, garage sale or bake sale to raise money for a community organization.

6. Help out at the humane society.

7. Volunteer at a community organization and learn more about their work.

8. Plan and prepare a warm meal for someone who is ill, elderly or busy with a new baby.

9. Run errands for someone who is ill, elderly or busy with a new baby.

10. Collect clean, used clothing and nonperishable food items for someone in need. Take the donations to a shelter, church or mission.

11. Work in a food pantry or other type of distribution center.

12. Pick up litter in a park or other public area.

▶ SOCIAL STUDIES CENTER

Set up an area in the classroom as a Social Studies Center. If possible, put the center near a bulletin board where you can mount a large map of the United States and some of your child's work. Suggested supplies and materials for the center include maps, a globe, an atlas, books about U.S. history, almanacs, encyclopedias, video- and audiotapes, pictures of times past, copies of historical documents, games and biographies of famous people.

Language Skills	Spelling	Reading
Monday Discuss different reasons for writing. Brainstorm ideas with your child and create a chart for future reference. *See* Language Skills, Week 1, number 1. Then, introduce the writing process. Have your child choose a topic, make a plan for writing and begin working on a rough draft today. Guide your child through the writing process over the course of this week. For more on the writing process, see page 6.	Pretest your child on these spelling words: amaze daydream matriarch anyway delay nature basic dismay place brace essay raisin braid faint rate daisy hasten wage Have your child correct the pretest. Add personalized words and make two copies of this week's study list.	Ask your child to read fairy tales this week, some new and some familiar. Keep a chart of the story elements so your child can compare the fairy tales and make general observations. Include the following headings on the chart: *title, good characters, evil characters, elements of magic, problem, solution* and *significant numbers* (3 and 7 are common). Discuss the story elements several times over the next four days.
Tuesday **Vocabulary Development:** Review homophones with your child. *Homophones* are words that sound alike but differ in meaning and spelling. Have your child complete **Homophones** (p. 22).	Review this week's spelling words. Have your child complete **Amazing a** (p. 24).	**Quotation Marks:** Seek out a passage in one fairy tale in which someone is speaking. Ask your child to read the passage aloud with lots of expression. Then, discuss the format of quotations and the use of quotation marks. *See* Reading, Week 1, number 1. Have your child write a quotation following the format of a quotation from the fairy tale.
Wednesday Review *synonyms* and *antonyms*. Write several sentences on the chalkboard, underlining a key word in each. *See* Language Skills, Week 1, number 2 for examples. Ask your child to copy the sentences and replace each underlined word with a synonym or an antonym. Then, have your child read the new sentences aloud. Have your child complete **Synonym or Antonym?** (p. 23).	Have your child use each of this week's spelling words correctly in a sentence.	Ask your child to browse through several fairy tales, looking for synonyms to replace the word *said*. Help your child make a list of the words he/she finds, as well as any others you two can think of. Precise words such as *whispered, replied, yelled* and *exclaimed* convey an author's meaning more accurately than the word *said*.
Thursday Review similes, *metaphors* and *personification*. *See* Language Skills, Week 1, number 3. Write several sentences on the board containing similes and metaphors. Ask your child to name the two things being compared in each case. Have your child browse through books and other materials looking for other examples of figurative language. Can your child find examples of similes, metaphors and personification? Ask your child to write his/her own figures of speech.	Have your child study this week's spelling words. For activity ideas, see pages 9 and 10.	Discuss the chart made on Monday. Ask your child to predict elements of an unfamiliar fairy tale. Then, read the tale. How accurate were your child's predictions? Teach your child the difference between direct and indirect quotations. *See* Reading, Week 1, number 2. Select five direct quotations from a fairy tale and ask your child to change them into indirect quotations.
Friday Write several sentences containing similes, metaphors or personification. **Examples:** *The trees' shadows danced in the moonlight. The meat was as tough as a piece of leather.* Ask your child to identify and name the different types of figurative language. Then, ask him/her to describe to you the meaning of each phrase. Finally, have him/her select one sentence and draw a humorous, literal interpretation of it.	Give your child the final spelling test. Have your child record pretest and final test words in his/her Word Bank.	Select a few dialogues from a favorite fairy tale. Allow your child to choose one role while you play the other. Read each scene together with expression and discuss what happens.

18

Math	Science	Social Studies
Place Value Discuss the usefulness of a place-value chart. Use the pattern found in Math, Week 1, number 1 to help your child create his/her own place-value chart to use. Explain the names of the places and periods on the chart. Encourage your child to use the chart to practice reading large numbers through the millions. *See* Math, Week 1, numbers 2 and 3.	**Animal Kingdom** Explain to your child that all living things are classified into five kingdoms. The two most familiar to your child will be the plant and animal kingdoms. Gather plenty of resource materials on all five kingdoms. Allow your child some time to look through these materials. Copy **The Animal Kingdom** (p. 26) for your child. Read together and discuss the information presented.	**European Settlers** Introduce the topic of American history and European settlement. *See* Social Studies, Week 1. Ask your child to interview several family members and neighbors about what it means to them to be Americans. Discuss each person's response, and have your child write a paragraph summary.
Discuss the use of large numbers with your child. Ask him/her to flip through magazines, newspapers, almanacs and other materials and point out any large numbers he/she finds. *What kinds of things are these numbers used to describe? Why is it important to understand the magnitude of these large numbers?*	Ask your child to make a glossary of terms related to the animal kingdom. *See* Science, Week 1, number 1 for a list of terms. Add these words to spelling lists as they are discussed. Have your child use information from a pie chart to create a bar graph comparing the number of species in different phyla. *See* Science, Week 1, number 2. Have your child use a different color for each bar and name three animals from each group.	Discuss why people travel to new places. *What reasons did the early European explorers have for traveling to the New World?* Have your child research the motivations of such European explorers as John Cabot, de La Salle, Columbus, Magellan, Balboa, Ponce de León, Coronado and Vespucci. Ask your child to consider the influence of the family, the church and the state on these explorers' journeys.
Have your child read the book *How Much Is a Million?* by David Schwartz. Then ask, "How much is a billion?" Try to help your child gain a sense of one billion using the counting activity described in Math, Week 1, number 4.	Collect pictures of animals from nature magazines and old books. Try to find representatives from several different phyla. Ask your child to sort the animals into meaningful categories. Discuss similarities and differences among the categories. Have your child try to name the phylum in which each animal belongs. Have your child complete **Phyla Match** (p. 27), looking up each term to determine the answers.	Help your child organize the information from his/her research on a time line, using a long sheet of butcher paper and a black marker. Draw a horizontal line along the center of the paper. Beginning at the year 1490, make a mark for each 10 years up to 1870. Label centuries and half-centuries (1500, 1550, etc.). Write events on index cards and tape or glue to the time line, or write events directly on the time line. Continue to add to the time line over the next several weeks.
Help your child practice reading and writing large numbers. *See* Math, Week 1, number 5. Write 10–12 numbers (ranging in size) on the chalkboard. Ask your child to read the numbers aloud. Then, read aloud 10–12 different numbers and ask your child to write them on the board. If your child has trouble, let him/her use the place-value chart to write out the numbers.	Choose two animals from the same phylum (chordates, arthropods, mollusks, echinoderms, flatworms, etc.). Help your child make a Venn diagram to compare the two animals. Discuss the comparisons made by your child on the diagram. Explain that scientists classify and name groups of animals using a similar process. Ask your child why it is helpful (to scientists) to classify animals.	At the time of Columbus's travels, the most important navigation tool was the *astrolabe*. What was an astrolabe and what did it do? What eventually replaced the astrolabe? Have your child find out what other tools navigators use today.

Teach your child the following rules for writing large numbers in words:
  1. Place commas between periods just as if you were writing numerals.
  2. Always include a hyphen between the tens and ones, as in *ninety-four*.
Copy **Checks** (p. 25). Let your child write out checks for large amounts to imaginary people or companies. Explain that a check must show the amount both in numerals and in words.
	Have your child make a folder to organize his/her work from the animal unit. Provide supplies for making a science folder. Your child may decorate the outside of the folder with animals. Inside the folder, have your child keep completed activity sheets and a Science Log, as well as other information and completed projects related to the animal kingdom.	Discuss the meaning of the term *community service*. Explain the importance of serving the community. Help your child brainstorm and plan some possible activities to help out in your community.

19

TEACHING SUGGESTIONS AND ACTIVITIES

LANGUAGE SKILLS (Vocabulary Development)

▶ 1. Write *Why Write?* on a piece of chart paper. Brainstorm reasons for writing. Write the reasons on the chart and keep the chart as a reference. Use the following reasons for writing to get you started: to explain (recipes, definitions), to persuade (advertisements, job applications), to entertain (stories, jokes), to relate information (letters to family and friends, journal), to inform (instructions, news, reports), to question (interviews, scientific observations) and to voice opinions (editorials, postcards).

▶ 2. Use sentences like the following for Wednesday's activity.

Tommy's words were <u>inaudible</u>.
The <u>raging</u> water of the stream carried our raft <u>swiftly</u> toward the rocks ahead.
The fire marshal ruled that the old theater was <u>dangerous</u> for further use.

▶ 3. Figurative language allows a writer to emphasize or dramatize an idea in a sentence.

Similes compare two things directly using the words *like* or *as*.
Example: The bumblebee is like a ballerina when it demonstrates the location of the nectar.

Metaphors state that one thing *is* another thing. A metaphor can create a more dramatic image than a simile.
Example: The bumblebee is a dancing, twirling ballerina as it demonstrates the location of the nectar.

Personification attributes human qualities to nonhuman things for dramatic or humorous effect.
Example: The bee performed a honey opera for its adoring fans.

READING (Quotation Marks)

▶ 1. Give your child a sentence containing a direct quotation. Ask him/her to read aloud *only* the words spoken by the character. Look at the relationship among the quotation marks, commas and other words in the sentence. *Who is speaking? How can you tell? To whom is the character talking?* Have your child find other examples of direct quotations.

▶ 2. Collect examples of direct and indirect quotations. Discuss the differences with your child.

Direct: Thomas said, "My sister Gina was sick yesterday."

Indirect: Thomas said that his sister Gina was sick yesterday.

MATH (Place Value)

▶ 1. Reproduce the place-value chart below one of the following ways: draw the chart on the chalkboard; enlarge, copy and laminate the chart, allowing your child to write on it with marker; or recreate the chart on a large piece of poster board, and write the digits 0–9 on individual index cards to place on the chart.

BILLIONS			MILLIONS			THOUSANDS			ONES		
Hundreds	Tens	Ones	Hundreds	Tens	Ones	Hundreds	Tens	Ones	Hundreds	Tens	Ones

▶ 2. Ask your child to study the place-value chart. Discuss the elements of the chart and our numbering system.

    a. Numbers are composed of ones, tens and hundreds.

    b. Each group of ones, tens and hundreds is called a *period*.

    c. *Periods* are separated by a comma (,).

    d. The first period (on the far right) is called the *ones*, the second is called the *thousands*, the third the *millions* and the fourth the *billions*. The periods can follow the same pattern infinitely toward the left.

Learn At Home, Grade 5

▶ 3. Ask your child to write a given number in a given place on the place-value chart. Then, have him/her read the resulting number out loud. Tell your child to assume there are zeros in the places not mentioned. **Examples:** *Write a 3 in the tens place. (30) Write an 8 in the ones place of the millions period. (8,000,000)* Repeat several times, then increase the difficulty. If the activity is too hard, spend a few days building experience with the concept of place value. Build smaller numbers using manipulatives to teach the place-value pattern.

▶ 4. Numbers as large as one billion are often difficult to comprehend, since most people will never have or even see this much money. Use the following activity to help illustrate the concept of a billion for your child.

Collect or make 60 play dollars (or use real money if you can). Ask your child to predict how long it will take to earn a billion dollars if you give him/her a dollar every second. Watch the clock and give your child a dollar a second. After one minute, ask your child to count the bills. Then, continue to count using the calculator. (Push "+ 1" every second.) When your child grows tired of this activity, have him/her propose a method for determining how many days it will take to get to a billion seconds (and a billion dollars). There is more than one way to figure it out.

▶ 5. When reading large numbers, have your child picture the numbers on the place-value chart. Have your child read the number to the left of the first comma as if nothing followed, then name the period to which it belongs. Do the same for each succeeding period. **Note:** The word *and* is not used. As will be discussed later in this book, the word *and* is used to designate a fraction or decimal portion of a number. The number 900,016,047,245 is read as: nine hundred *billion*, sixteen *million*, forty-seven *thousand*, two hundred forty-five.

SCIENCE (Animal Kingdom)

BACKGROUND

Animals' ability to move around distinguishes them from other types of living things. There are more than 1.5 million known kinds of animals. The animal kingdom is subdivided into 33 major groups called *phyla*. Each phylum is then further divided into categories that group animals according to similar features.

▶ 1. Add the following words to this week's spelling list. Have your child look up each word in a dictionary or science resource. Discuss the meaning. Have your child make a glossary of animal kingdom words. Have him/her arrange the entries in alphabetical order and write a definition for each word.

phylum	endangered	vertebrates	coelenterate	chordate
ecosystem	characteristics	invertebrates	cnidarian	endoskeleton
habitat	survival	flatworm	mollusk	exoskeleton
population	adaptation	segmented worm	echinoderm	arthropod

▶ 2. Enlarge or recreate the pie chart shown here. Have your child use the information from the chart to create a bar graph comparing the number of species in different phyla.

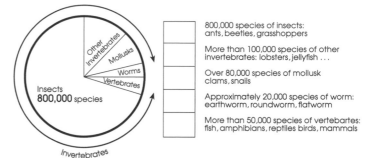

800,000 species of insects: ants, beetles, grasshoppers

More than 100,000 species of other invertebrates: lobsters, jellyfish ...

Over 80,000 species of mollusk clams, snails

Approximately 20,000 species of worm: earthworm, roundworm, flatworm

More than 50,000 species of vertebartes: fish, amphibians, reptiles birds, mammals

SOCIAL STUDIES (European Settlers)

BACKGROUND

The discoveries of Columbus and others paved the way for Europeans (especially the British) to cross the Atlantic and settle along the east coast of the future United States of America. They lived in small settlements (located between modern-day Maine and Georgia) under British rule until they could no longer bear the demands of the king. It was then that independence from Britain was declared, a war was fought and the United States was born. From that time on, immigrants from many countries have come to the U.S. in search of a better or freer life. The settlements spread westward as the population increased.

Homophones

Homophones are words that sound alike but have different spellings and meanings.

Write the correct homophone in the blank.

_____*Their*_____ house is around the corner from us. (their, there)

1. We couldn't decide _____ to visit Boston or St. Louis. (weather, whether)

2. We chose to visit Boston, the _____ of Massachusetts. (capital, capitol)

3. We drove _____ the city in _____ days. (to, too, two)

4. Our _____ was over interstate highways. (route, root)

5. We _____ many signs along the way. (read, red)

6. My brothers couldn't hide _____ excitement. (their, there)

7. We found that _____ an exciting city. (its, it's)

8. It was interesting to _____ the accent of the people. (hear, here)

9. Many people related interesting _____ to us about the city's history. (tales, tails)

10. We appreciated the _____ and quiet of the parks. (peace, piece)

11. We walked up and down _____ of houses in the historic district. (rows, rose)

12. I wore a _____ in one of my shoes from _____ much walking. (whole, hole) (so, sew)

13. Luckily, this caused me _____ _____. (know, no) (pain, pane)

14. I had to have the _____ of the shoe repaired. (soul, sole)

22

Synonym or Antonym?

Draw a green circle around each word that is a synonym of the first word.
Draw an orange box around each word that is its antonym. Use a dictionary to look up any words you do not know.

forfeit	choose	generous	gain	lose
adjacent	sudden	nearby	clean	remote
pompous	modest	festive	noisy	proud
nosegay	unhappy	bouquet	puncture	weeds
exquisite	careful	beyond	hideous	delightful
impeccable	flawed	perfect	scarce	painful
wary	alert	brittle	unguarded	tired
harry	furry	attract	annoy	soothe
despondently	happily	elegantly	crazily	unhappily
interrogate	cross-examine	dislike	persecute	hush
cull	answer	charge	select	scatter
elude	confront	scold	avoid	frighten

23

Amazing a

Write each spelling word in the appropriate spelling pattern category.

Long a

ay

_____
_____
_____
_____

a-e

_____
_____
_____
_____

a

_____
_____
_____

ai

_____
_____
_____

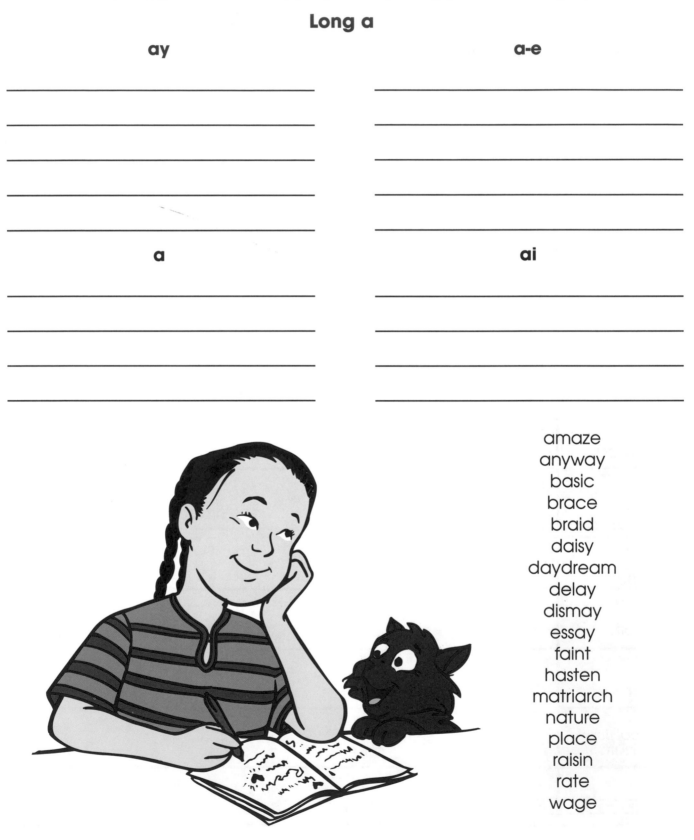

amaze
anyway
basic
brace
braid
daisy
daydream
delay
dismay
essay
faint
hasten
matriarch
nature
place
raisin
rate
wage

24

Learn At Home, Grade 5

Fill in each check completely. Invent who you will write it to and why.

Name _____   Date _____   6389A
Address _____
_____

Pay to the Order of _____ $ _____
_____ Dollars

School Bank
5555 Fifth Street
Fifthville, GA 32132

For _____   _____
                                        Signature

Name _____   Date _____   6390A
Address _____
_____

Pay to the Order of _____ $ _____
_____ Dollars

School Bank
5555 Fifth Street
Fifthville, GA 32132

For _____   _____
                                        Signature

Name _____   Date _____   6391A
Address _____
_____

Pay to the Order of _____ $ _____
_____ Dollars

School Bank
5555 Fifth Street
Fifthville, GA 32132

For _____   _____
                                        Signature

The Animal Kingdom

The animal kingdom can be divided into two main groups. Animals with backbones are called **vertebrates** and those without are called **invertebrates**.

It's All in the Name! Every living thing is given a scientific name made from two Greek or Latin words. The first is the *genus* name, and the second is the *species*.

human = *Homo sapiens*
dog = *Canis familiaris*
cat = *Felis domesticus*

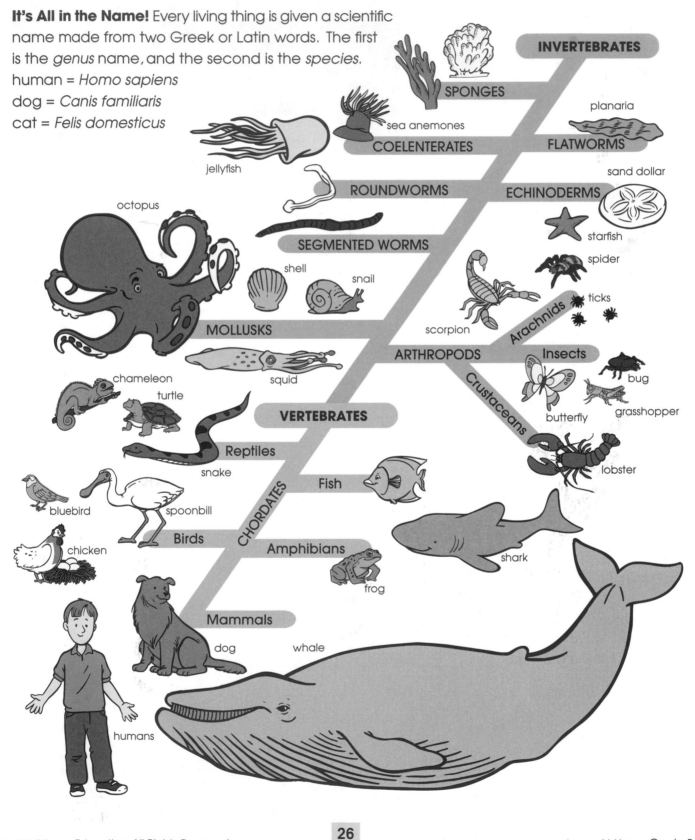

INVERTEBRATES

SPONGES

sea anemones

planaria

COELENTERATES

FLATWORMS

jellyfish

ROUNDWORMS

ECHINODERMS

sand dollar

octopus

SEGMENTED WORMS

starfish

shell

snail

spider

ticks

MOLLUSKS

scorpion

Arachnids

ARTHROPODS

Insects

bug

Crustaceans

chameleon

squid

butterfly

grasshopper

turtle

VERTEBRATES

Reptiles

snake

Fish

lobster

bluebird

spoonbill

CHORDATES

Birds

Amphibians

chicken

shark

frog

Mammals

dog

whale

humans

Learn At Home, Grade 5

Phyla Match

Scientists separate animals according to their differences and group them according to their likenesses.

Draw a line from the phylum in the first column to the correct picture and then to the related characteristics. The first one is done for you.

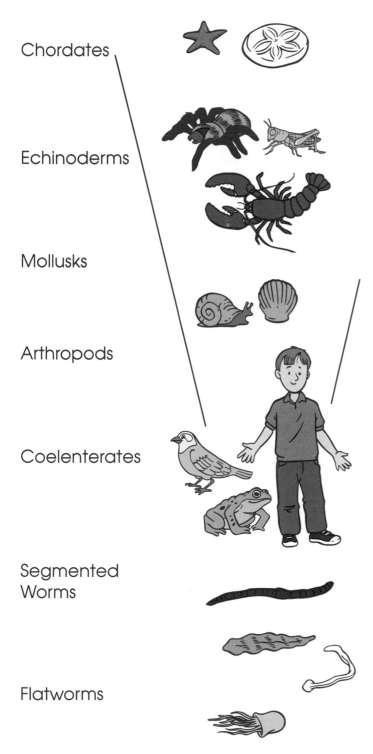

Chordates

Echinoderms

Mollusks

Arthropods

Coelenterates

Segmented Worms

Flatworms

The bodies of these marine animals have limy plates with spines.

These animals have a head, thorax, abdomen and three or more pairs of legs.

These animals have a notochord (a rod-like structure) down the middle of their backs.

These radially symmetrical animals contain a jellylike material between two layers of cells.

These soft-bodied animals are usually covered by a limy shell.

These animals have soft, thin, flat bodies made of three layers of cells.

These animals have long bodies divided into many segments.

Language Skills	Spelling	Reading
Monday **Vocabulary Development** Give your child a writing topic for this week, such as a fiction or nonfiction story about an animal. Encourage your child to incorporate figurative language into his/her writing. Guide your child in making a plan for writing. Are there any questions he/she needs to answer before writing the piece? Have your child do any necessary research, then begin work on a rough draft.	Pretest your child on these spelling words: breathe hockey respond breeze kidney screech crease lease sleeve delight plead squeak donkey queen steam eager recent zebra Have your child correct the pretest. Add personalized words and make two copies of this week's study list.	**Story Elements** Introduce *The Girl Who Loved Wild Horses* by Paul Goble. For a weekly reading plan and other ideas, see pages 12–13. What does your child know about horses and Native Americans? Choose vocabulary from the book that you think your child may not know. Discuss the vocabulary, then read the story. *See* Reading, Week 2, number 1. Have your child complete **Story Organizer** (p. 33).
Tuesday Review *idioms* and *hyperbole*. Have your child look up and define these terms. Discuss the similarities and differences between these two kinds of figures of speech. *See* Language Skills, Week 2, number 1. Have your child write a short story about an imaginary superhero. Have your child come up with an apt name for the hero. The story should contain hyperbole and other figurative language.	Review this week's spelling words. Have your child complete **Breezing Through e** (p. 32).	Help your child create a character web about the girl who loved wild horses. *See* Reading, Week 2, number 2.
Wednesday Ask your child to look up the words *anagram* and *palindrome* in a dictionary. Discuss their meanings. Can your child name some examples? **Anagrams:** star/arts, paste/tapes, teach/cheat **Palindromes:** level, noon, radar Ask your child to write sentences that contain pairs of anagrams and palindromes.	Have your child use each of this week's spelling words correctly in a sentence.	Ask your child to write a descriptive paragraph about the special relationship the girl had with horses before the storm separated her from her family.
Thursday Encourage your child to liven up his/her writing with the use of alliteration, the repetition of a beginning sound in two or more words or syllables. *Alliteration* is often used in poetry and advertising. Using alliteration can help develop vocabulary since it will challenge your child to seek help from a dictionary. Ask your child to write a creative, yet coherent, tongue twister using alliteration.	Have your child study this week's spelling words. For activity ideas, see pages 9–10.	Introduce another book by Paul Goble. Before reading, ask your child to predict some similarities between this book and *The Girl Who Loved Wild Horses*. Have your child read the second book by Paul Goble. Have your child compare and contrast the main character in the story to the girl in *The Girl Who Loved Wild Horses*.
Friday Help your child understand the concept of *analogy*. *See* Language Skills, Week 2, number 2 for activities to help teach about analogies. Have your child write six analogies.	Give your child the final spelling test. Have your child record pretest and final test words in his/her Word Bank.	Discuss the representation of nature in both books. How does the solution in each story relate to the earth?

Learn At Home, Grade 5

Math	Science	Social Studies
Place Value and Addition Understanding place value is key to aligning large numbers for addition. Show your child that it is important to write addition problems neatly for the sake of accuracy. *See* Math, Week 2, number 1. Have your child complete **Dog's Best Friend** (p. 34).	**Invertebrates** Discuss the differences between invertebrate animals and vertebrate animals. Discuss the purpose of a backbone, then compare the backbones of different vertebrates. Have your child feel his/her own backbone or your backbone. If you have a pet such as a cat, hamster or snake, have your child feel its backbone, too. How do the animals' backbones differ? Why? Have your child complete **Sort 'Em Out** (p. 39).	**Colonial America** Introduce your child to life in Colonial America. *See* Social Studies, Week 2. Have your child read about the Pilgrims and the Plymouth Colony. *Why did the Pilgrims come to America? When did they arrive?* Have your child add this date to the time line. Discuss the legend of Plymouth Rock.
Review rounding with small numbers. **Examples:** *Round 33 to the nearest ten.* *Round 125 to the nearest ten.* Then, teach your child to round to a given place. *See* Math, Week 2, number 2. Have your child complete **Rounding** (p. 35).	Provide materials about flatworms and roundworms for your child's reference. Name and show examples of each. *Where do these worms live?* Introduce the terms *parasite* and *scavenger*. Ask your child to take notes on flatworms and roundworms in his/her Science Log. Have him/her draw and label an example of each type of worm.	Discuss aspects of colonial life in America. *What were some of the hardships the early settlers faced? How did they dress? Where did they live? What did they eat?* Have your child read about the colony at Jamestown. Ask your child to think of an appropriate symbol for Jamestown, then make a flag bearing the symbol to be flown over the fort there.
Review rounding numbers to a given place. Have your child complete **Number-Line Rounding** (p. 36). Then, ask your child to do some mental math. Give him/her numbers to round without using paper. Can he/she do it?	Provide reference materials about segmented worms and ribbon worms. Obtain a living earthworm from outside or from a bait shop. Ask your child to observe the worm's appearance and behavior. Ask him/her *What type of worm it is?* When you are done observing, return the earthworm to the soil. *How do earthworms benefit gardeners?* Ask your child to take notes and draw illustrations of segmented worms and ribbon worms in his/her Science Log.	Have your child read about the Virginia Company of London. The Virginia Company tried to encourage the Jamestown men to stay in the struggling colony by sending young women from England to marry colonial bachelors. Ask your child to imagine that he/she is a young woman traveling to America or a young man living in Virginia waiting for his bride. Have the child write a journal entry expressing his/her feelings about the future.
Teach your child how to use rounding to estimate the solution of an addition problem. *See* Math, Week 2, number 3. Give your child two addition problems to estimate, then solve. Have your child compare his/her answers with the estimates. If the numbers are not close, ask your child to double-check his/her addition. Have your child complete **Estimating Sums** (p. 37).	Work with your child to create a mealworm habitat. Then, observe the mealworm's life cycle. *See* Science, Week 2, number 1.	Have your child read about the winter of 1609–1610 at Jamestown. Have your child read *The Serpent Never Sleeps* by Scott O'Dell.
Quiz your child on place-value concepts. Have your child complete **Place Value** (p. 38). Reteach any concepts, if necessary.	Discuss coelenterates. *See* Science, Week 2, number 2. Ask your child to take notes and draw illustrations of coelenterates in his/her Science Log.	Arrange for your child to perform some community service.

29

TEACHING SUGGESTIONS AND ACTIVITIES

LANGUAGE SKILLS (Vocabulary Development)

▶ 1. Read each sentence below out loud. Ask your child whether the sentence contains hyperbole or an idiom. Then, have your child paraphrase the sentence to demonstrate its meaning.

The suitcase weighed a ton!   *The money was burning a hole in her pocket.*
Don't cry over spilled milk.   *We could hardly see the street over the mile-high snowdrifts.*
Mike and Liz are two peas in a pod.   *Rita was on pins and needles the day before her new job began.*

▶ 2. Use the following activities to help teach your child about analogies.

a. Write several analogies on the chalkboard. Ask your child to underline the key elements in each one.

Examples: A <u>foal</u> is to a <u>horse</u> as a <u>calf</u> is to a <u>cow</u>.
<u>Yellow</u> is to <u>sun</u> as <u>blue</u> is to <u>water</u>.
A <u>staple</u> is to <u>paper</u> as a <u>nail</u> is to <u>wood</u>.

b. Write incomplete analogies on the board for your child to complete.

Examples: Leaf is to _____ as knife is to knives.
Gas is to car as _____ is to person.
Women are to _____ as men are to boys.

c. Write groups of four words (in any order) on the chalkboard. Ask your child to use the four words in each group to write an analogy that makes sense.

Examples: nests, squirrels, people, homes   *Nests are to squirrels as homes are to people.*
listening, seeing, eyes, ears   *Ears are to listening as eyes are to seeing.*
hands, fingers, toes, feet   *Toes are to feet as fingers are to hands.*

READING (Story Elements)

▶ 1. Most stories contain five basic elements: setting, characters, problem, events and solution. The *setting* is when and where a story takes place. Setting can range from specific (12:00 noon at a café in downtown Chicago) to vague (springtime on a faraway island). Though not always obvious, the setting is usually identifiable. *Characters* are the people who appear in the story. There is usually one main character and sometimes several other characters with whom the main character interacts. The main character typically encounters a *problem* or series of problems in the story that he/she must address. These problems eventually lead to a climax. There are usually a series of *events* in a story as well. These events may be the main character's attempts at solving the problem. And finally, there is a *solution*. This is how the problem is solved (or *not* solved) or the goal is achieved (or *not* achieved). Sometimes the solution is different than you'd expect. Be sure your child understands these elements before asking him/her to fill out **Story Organizer** (p. 33). Use the **Story Organizer** with other stories read throughout the year.

▶ 2. Ask your child to write the main character's name in the center of a sheet of paper, then write adjectives that describe the character all around his/her name. Draw a line connecting the character's name to each adjective. Then, draw a line out from each adjective and write an incident from the story that demonstrates that adjective.

MATH (Place Value and Addition)

▶ 1. Maintain the place value of numerals when adding numbers of several digits. If the number 35 were carelessly written in the hundreds and tens place, it would be 350, causing a gross error in the addition.

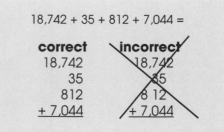

$$18,742 + 35 + 812 + 7,044 =$$

correct	~~incorrect~~
18,742	18,742
35	35
812	8 12
+ 7,044	+ 7,044

Learn At Home, Grade 5

▶ 2. Teach your child the following steps to round numbers to a given place. Draw number lines so your child can see where a number actually lies between two others. Encourage your child to do the same when practicing rounding on his/her own.

Step:

a. Locate and highlight the place to which the number is to be rounded.

b. Look at the digit to the right of the designated place. If this number is 5 or greater, round *up* the highlighted number. If this number is 4 or less, round the highlighted number *down* by keeping the digit the same.

c. Rewrite the original number with the amended digit in the highlighted place and change all of the digits to the right to zeros.

Example:

Round 3,163 to the nearest 100.

The number to the right is 6. Six is greater than 5, so round the number in the hundreds place up.

The rounded number is 3,200.

▶ 3. To estimate the answer to an addition problem, round each of the addends to the same place. Round to the highest place of the smallest number.

Example:

Problem	Highlight the thousands place	Round to estimate
27,345	27,345	27,000
3,529 (smallest number)	**3**,529	4,000
+ 12,001	+ 12,001	+ 12,000

SCIENCE (Invertebrates)

▶ 1. Help your child create a mealworm habitat. Obtain some mealworms from a pet or bait shop. The mealworm is the *larval* stage of the mealworm beetle. The mealworm changes first into a *pupa*, then into an *adult*. The adult beetle lays eggs, beginning the life cycle all over again. Mealworms can be kept in any cardboard or plastic container. Line the bottom of the container with about an inch of bran flakes, add a few scraps of apple or potato and cover the worms with a wet paper towel. During the next seven weeks, have your child remove the towel and observe the mealworms each day. The mealworm habitat can be maintained as long as you wish.

▶ 2. Provide reference materials about coelenterates (also known as cnidarians). Show your child colorful pictures of hydra, jellyfish and sea anemones and discuss the characteristics of these animals. Explore the habitats of these animals and their protective devices. *Why is the sting from (some of) these animals so painful?*

SOCIAL STUDIES (Colonial America)

BACKGROUND

The colonial period in America began in 1607 with the founding of Jamestown and ended in 1775 with the start of the Revolutionary War. While the majority of colonists were English, settlers also came from other western European countries. At that time, much of western Europe was engaged in a fierce competition for power. Colonies in the New World could provide their mother countries with valuable materials and help bolster trade. Many new arrivals, however, came for entirely different reasons. Some came because life was intolerable at home; others came purely for adventure. Still others were brought against their will. Nevertheless, they all brought skills that helped forge a new nation.

Breezing Through e

On the flags, **write** the spelling words according to the **long e** spelling patterns. Indicate the spelling pattern to the right of each flag.

Spelling Pattern

breathe
breeze
crease
delight
donkey
eager
hockey
kidney
lease
plead
queen
recent
respond
screech
sleeve
squeak
steam
zebra

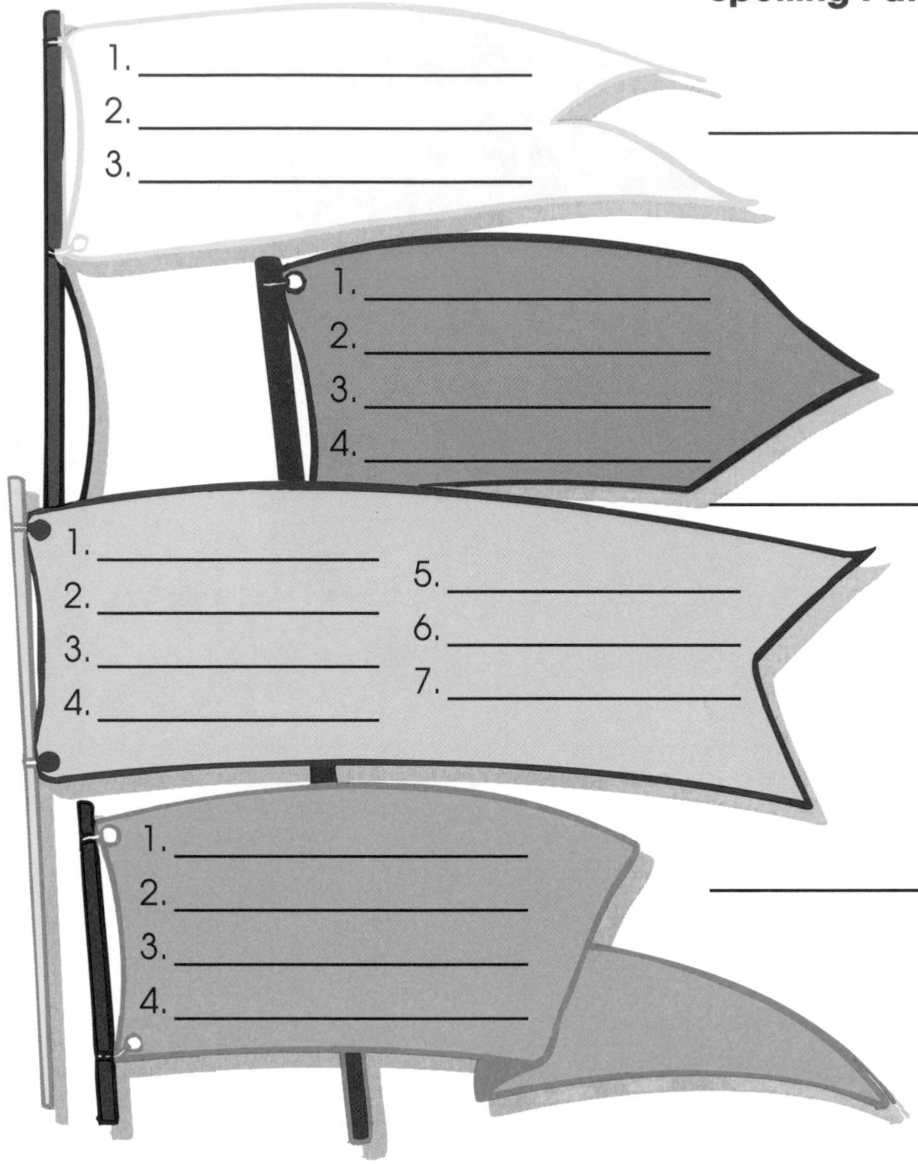

1. _____
2. _____
3. _____

_____

1. _____
2. _____
3. _____
4. _____

1. _____   5. _____
2. _____   6. _____
3. _____   7. _____
4. _____

1. _____
2. _____
3. _____
4. _____

_____

_____

Write four generalizations about words with the **long e** sound.

1. _____
2. _____
3. _____
4. _____

Learn At Home, Grade 5

Story Organizer

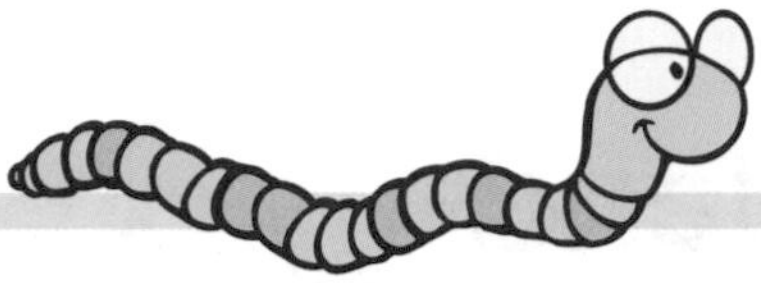

Week 2

Date ____________ Title ____

Vocabulary | **Definitions**

____________________ ____

____________________ ____

____________________ ____

____________________ ____

____________________ ____

Setting: ____

Characters: ____

____

Problem: ____

____

Events: ____

____

____

____

____

Solution: ____

____

____

Did you enjoy this story? 1 2 3 4 5 6

Not at all … Very much!

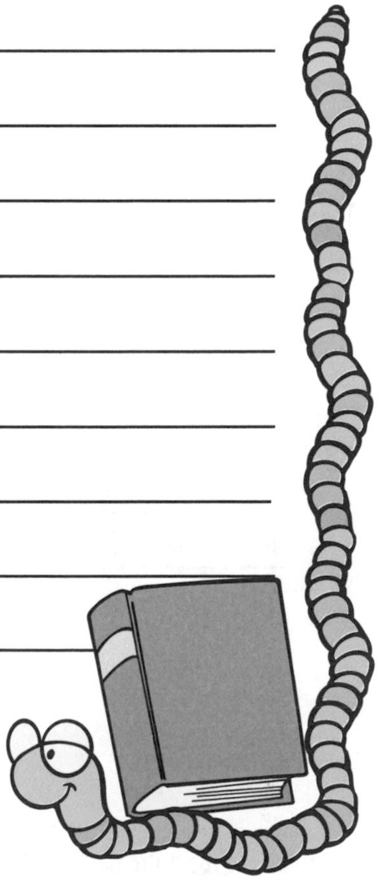

Dog's Best Friend

Bob the butcher is popular with the dogs in town. He was making a delivery this morning when he noticed he was being followed by two dogs. Bob tried to climb a ladder to escape from the dogs. Solve the following addition problems and shade in the answers on the ladder. If all the numbers are shaded when the problems have been solved, Bob made it up the ladder. Some answers may not be on the ladder.

1. 986,145 621,332 + 200,008	2. 1,873,402 925,666 + 4,689	3. 506,328 886,510 + 342,225
4. 43,015 2,811,604 + 987,053	5. 18,443 300,604 + 999,999	6. 8,075 14,608 + 33,914
7. 9,162 7,804 + 755,122	8. 88,714 213,653 + 5,441,298	9. 3,244,662 1,986,114 + 521,387
10. 4,581 22,983 + 5,618,775	11. 818,623 926 + 3,260,004	12. 80,436 9,159 + 3,028,761
13. 25,004 862,010 + 9,302	14. 5,043,666 4,589,771 + 8,711,229	15. 432,188 900,000 + 611,042

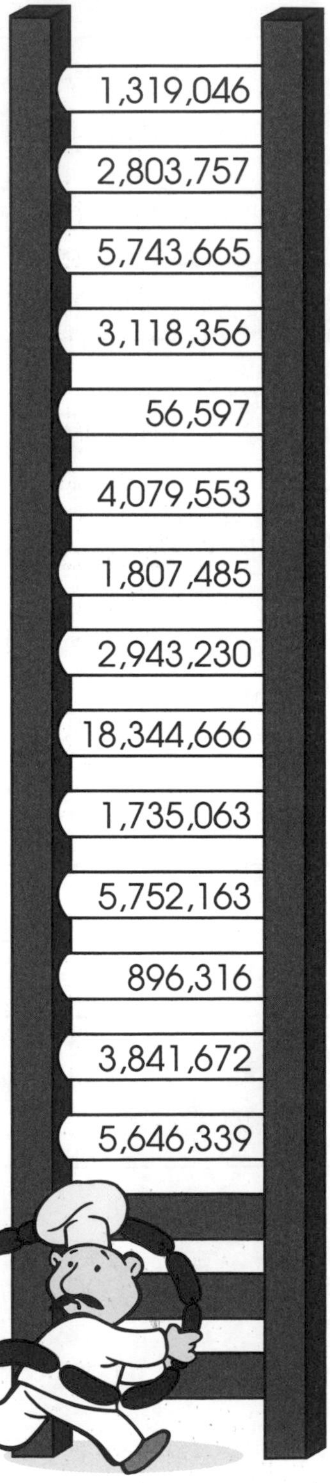

Ladder:
1,319,046
2,803,757
5,743,665
3,118,356
56,597
4,079,553
1,807,485
2,943,230
18,344,666
1,735,063
5,752,163
896,316
3,841,672
5,646,339

Does Bob make it? _____

Learn At Home, Grade 5

Rounding

Follow these steps to round numbers to a given place.

Example: Round 35,634 to the nearest thousand.

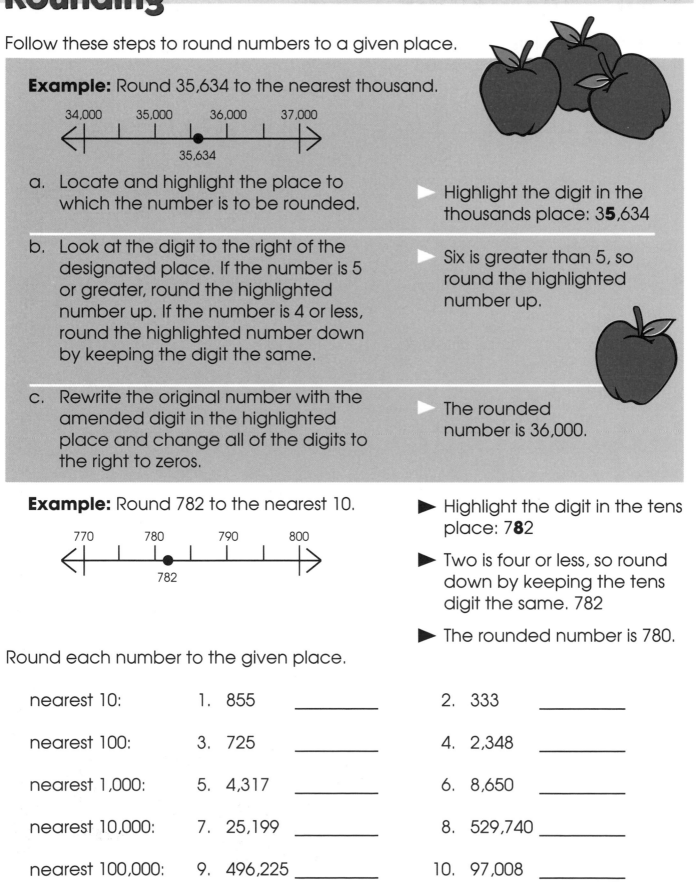

a. Locate and highlight the place to which the number is to be rounded.

▶ Highlight the digit in the thousands place: 3**5**,634

b. Look at the digit to the right of the designated place. If the number is 5 or greater, round the highlighted number up. If the number is 4 or less, round the highlighted number down by keeping the digit the same.

▶ Six is greater than 5, so round the highlighted number up.

c. Rewrite the original number with the amended digit in the highlighted place and change all of the digits to the right to zeros.

▶ The rounded number is 36,000.

Example: Round 782 to the nearest 10.

770   780   790   800
782

▶ Highlight the digit in the tens place: 7**8**2

▶ Two is four or less, so round down by keeping the tens digit the same. 782

▶ The rounded number is 780.

Round each number to the given place.

nearest 10:   1. 855 _____   2. 333 _____

nearest 100:   3. 725 _____   4. 2,348 _____

nearest 1,000:   5. 4,317 _____   6. 8,650 _____

nearest 10,000:   7. 25,199 _____   8. 529,740 _____

nearest 100,000:   9. 496,225 _____   10. 97,008 _____

Number-Line Rounding

Label the endpoints. **Plot** the given number. **Circle** the closer endpoint. The first three have been done for you.

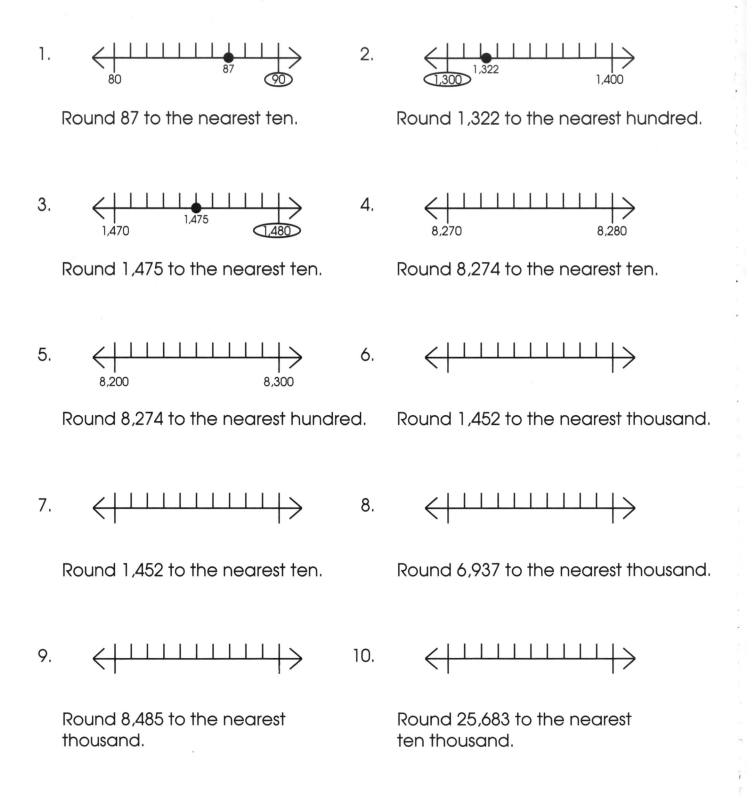

1.

    80   87   90

Round 87 to the nearest ten.

2.

   1,300   1,322   1,400

Round 1,322 to the nearest hundred.

3.

   1,470   1,475   1,480

Round 1,475 to the nearest ten.

4.

   8,270   8,280

Round 8,274 to the nearest ten.

5.

   8,200   8,300

Round 8,274 to the nearest hundred.

6.

Round 1,452 to the nearest thousand.

7.

Round 1,452 to the nearest ten.

8.

Round 6,937 to the nearest thousand.

9.

Round 8,485 to the nearest thousand.

10.

Round 25,683 to the nearest ten thousand.

Learn At Home, Grade 5

Estimating Sums

Estimate by rounding before you add.

Nearest Ten	**Nearest Hundred**	**Nearest Thousand**

$$88 \rightarrow 90$$
$$+\ 51 \rightarrow +\ 50$$
$$\overline{139} \qquad \overline{140}$$

Actual = 139
Estimated = 140
Difference = 1

$$244 \rightarrow 200$$
$$+\ 776 \rightarrow +\ 800$$
$$\overline{1{,}020} \qquad \overline{1{,}000}$$

Actual = 1,020
Estimated = 1,000
Difference = 20

$$4{,}566 \rightarrow 5{,}000$$
$$+\ 3{,}320 \rightarrow +\ 3{,}000$$
$$\overline{7{,}886} \qquad \overline{8{,}000}$$

Actual = 7,886
Estimated = 8,000
Difference = 114

When you do not have to be exact, estimating can be easy and close to the actual sum.

Estimate the sums. Round numbers to the highest place value of the smaller number.

1. $52 \rightarrow 50$
     $+\ 66 \rightarrow 70$

2. 618
     $+\ 384$

3. $3{,}477$
     $+\ 8{,}611$

4. 44
     $+\ 91$

5. 222
     $+\ 479$

6. $1{,}190$
     $+\ 7{,}625$

7. 36
     $+\ 19$

8. 566
     $+\ 818$

9. $4{,}533$
     $+\ 7{,}498$

Place Value

Read and solve.

1. Write the number 2,058,763 in words. _____

   _____

2. Write the following in numerals: eight billion, two hundred thirty-seven
   million, eighty-five thousand, three hundred four.

   _____

3. In the number 9,876,543,210 . . .

   which digit is in the hundred thousands place? _____

   which digit is in the ones place? _____

   in what place is the 9? _____

4. Add.

   3,259 + 32,769 + 305 = _____

   8,759,233 + 3,410 + 655,200 = _____

5. Round . . .

   84,239 to the nearest ten. _____

   7,857,355 to the nearest ten thousand. _____

6. Estimate the sum.

   34,396 →
   + 5,875   + _____

Sort 'Em Out

Vertebrates are animals with backbones. Animals without backbones are called **invertebrates.** At the bottom of the page are pictures of both kinds of animals. **Write** the name of each animal under the correct heading below.

Vertebrates	**Invertebrates**
1. _____	1. _____
2. _____	2. _____
3. _____	3. _____
4. _____	4. _____
5. _____	5. _____

Color and **cut out** all the vertebrates. On a separate sheet of paper, make a background using felt-tip markers for your vertebrate animals and **glue** them on it. Label your drawing: **Vertebrates**.

39

	Language Skills	**Spelling**	**Reading**
Monday	A writer's intention determines the type of paragraph he/she will write. Teach your child to recognize *descriptive, expository, narrative* and *persuasive* paragraphs. *See* Language Skills, Week 3, number 1. Seek out examples of each type of writing to show your child. Ask your child to write a descriptive paragraph about a favorite place. Encourage your child to use all the senses when describing the place.	Pretest your child on these spelling words: arrive fighting spying childhood grind style chime ideal thigh climate prize timing delight sight title digest silence violin Have your child correct the pretest. Add personalized words and make two copies of this week's study list.	Introduce *Farmer Boy* by Laura Ingalls Wilder. For a weekly reading plan and other ideas, see pages 12–13. Ask your child to draw a picture of Almanzo based on Wilder's description of him in chapter 1.
Tuesday	**Parts of Speech:** People often confuse the words *good* and *well, bad* and *badly. Good* and *bad* are adjectives that should be used to describe nouns. *Well* and *badly* are adverbs that should be used to modify verbs. Teach your child to use these words correctly. Include several examples. *See* Language Skills, Week 2, number 2. Have your child complete **Good, Bad; Well, Badly** (p. 44).	Review this week's spelling words. Have your child complete **Mile-High i** (p. 45).	The characters in *Farmer Boy* face a series of problems. Have your child write a plot profile for each problem or obstacle as he/she reads. Each profile should include the character(s), the problem, the events leading to the solution and the solution. It may be presented as a list, paragraph, chart or line graph of excitement levels. Have your child read 2–3 more chapters of *Farmer Boy* and write a plot profile for a problem in the story.
Wednesday	Teach your child to recognize *demonstrative* and *interrogative* pronouns. *See* Language Skills, Week 3, number 3. Ask your child to scan *Farmer Boy* for examples of demonstrative and interrogative pronouns. Have your child copy the sentences from the book onto the chalkboard and underline the pronoun(s) in each one.	Have your child use each of this week's spelling words correctly in a sentence.	Have your child read 2–3 more chapters of *Farmer Boy* and write a plot profile for a problem in the story.
Thursday	Teach your child the correct usage of *who* and *whom*. Provide sentences for your child to complete with the correct form. *See* Language Skills, Week 3, numbers 4 and 5. Have your child write a persuasive paragraph using the correct forms of *who*.	Have your child study this week's spelling words. For activity ideas, see pages 9–10.	Have your child read 2–3 more chapters of *Farmer Boy* and write a plot profile for a problem in the story.
Friday	Ask your child to compose a narrative paragraph about something that happened this week. Remind your child to tell about the events in the order that they occurred.	Give your child the final spelling test. Have your child record pretest and final test words in his/her Word Bank.	Have your child read 2–3 more chapters of *Farmer Boy* and write a plot profile for a problem in the story.

Learn At Home, Grade 5

Math	Science	Social Studies
Introduce your child to the commutative property of addition. The *commutative property* states that a series of numbers can be added in any order and results in the same sum. **Example:** 4 + 3 + 2 = 9, 3 + 4 + 2 = 9, 2 + 3 + 4 = 9, 4 + 2 + 3 = 9 *See* Math, Week 3, number 1. Have your child complete **Commutative Property of Addition** (p. 46).	**Arthropods** Have your child continue to observe the mealworm habitat created in Week 2 and record observations in his/her Science Log. Select an outdoor study site near your classroom to conduct a population study. Follow the directions on **Animal Population in a Study Site** (p. 48). Ask your child to predict what the ground will look like at the end of the week.	**Colonial America** Ask your child to classify the American colonies by region. Have your child make a simple chart with three columns, labeled *New England Colonies, Middle Colonies* and *Southern Colonies*. Have him/her name each colony and write it in the appropriate column. *How did life compare in the three areas?* Ask your child to find out. Have your child complete **The New World** (p. 49).
Review the concept that addition is simply the reverse of subtraction. Make counters for this activity. Have your child measure and cut out 80 1-inch squares from a sheet of white poster board. Use the counters to model adding two sets together. Then, remove (subtract) one of the sets from the total to show that the other set remains. Have your child complete **Opposite Operations** (p. 47).	Discuss the phylum of arthropods. *See* Science, Week 3, number 1. Provide picture books and other resources about arthropods for your child's reference. Ask your child to take notes about arthropods in his/her Science Log, describing the characteristics (and contributions) of spiders, insects, lobsters and crabs. Encourage your child to include illustrations as well.	Help your child gather resources from the library about the early American colonies. Ask your child to read about the different colonies and write a summary about each. (This may take 2 or 3 days to complete.) Have your child include a visual with each summary, such as a picture, diagram or graph relating information about the colony.
Variables: Introduce the basics of algebra by showing your child how to use a letter as a variable in an addition sentence. Replace the blank in an addition problem with a letter or *variable*. The letter stands for an unknown. **Example:** 3 + 6 = ___ $a = 9$ 3 + 6 = a Give your child addition problems to solve containing variables. *See* Math, Week 3, number 2.	Discuss the insects common to your area. Have your child read about moths and butterflies in an encyclopedia or in nature magazines such as *Ranger Rick, National Geographic* or *National Wildlife*. Ask your child to draw and label a moth and butterfly, listing the similarities and differences between them.	Allow your child to continue working on the research and writing project begun yesterday.
Chip Trading: Play a chip-trading game to help your child prepare for regrouping bases other than base 10. You will need 80 colored chips, a die and a sheet of white poster board. Color the 80 1-inch squares made on Tuesday. Color 20 squares of each color: yellow, green, blue and red. *See* Math, Week 3, number 3 for information on making the game board and playing the game.	Discuss the types of insects that live inside your home. Show your child how to collect data on the number and type of arthropods in your house. *See* Science, Week 3, number 2.	Have your child complete the colony project begun on Tuesday. Ask your child to assemble the summaries, pictures, diagrams and graphs into one book about the first colonies. Then, have him/her create a cover and bind together. Many trade routes were established from the New World to Europe and Africa. Some settlers were single people seeking to make money through trade. Discuss what was carried in each leg of the trade routes.
Play the chip-trading game from yesterday, this time using base 5 instead of base 10. In this version of the game, chip values are as follows: yellow chip = one (1) green chip = five yellow chips (5) blue chip = five green chips (25) red chip = five blue chips (125) Play this game throughout the year, using a variety of different place values (base 10, base 5, base 2, etc.).	Return to the animal population study site established on Monday. Ask your child to remove the cardboard and any rocks and boards from the study site. What kinds of organisms does your child observe at the site? Can he/she identify them? How many of each type of organism are present? Ask your child to record his/her findings in the Science Log. *See* Science, Week 3, number 3 for more questions and research ideas.	Arrange for your child to perform some community service.

TEACHING SUGGESTIONS AND ACTIVITIES

LANGUAGE SKILLS (Parts of Speech)

▶ 1. A *descriptive* paragraph provides details about something to create a vivid image in the mind of the reader.
An *expository* paragraph provides facts, gives directions, explains something or defines terms.
A *narrative* paragraph tells about an event in story form.
A *persuasive* paragraph expresses an opinion and tries to persuade the reader of that opinion.

▶ 2. Write the following sentences on the chalkboard, underlining the words *good* and *bad*.

Toby was a <u>good</u> dog because he brought the newspaper in every morning.
Elm Avenue was a <u>bad</u> street to live on because there was so much traffic.

Write the following sentences on the chalkboard, underlining the words *well* and *badly*.

Jay did not kick the soccer ball <u>well</u>, and it went out-of-bounds.
Jennifer had a sore throat and sang <u>badly</u> at her recital.

▶ 3. A demonstrative pronoun is used to point out people or things. The demonstrative pronouns are *this*, *that*, *these* and *those*.

Examples: *This* is Carrie's hat.   Give me *that*.
Those are my shoes.   *These* are the books I told you about.

Interrogative pronouns are used in questions. They are *who*, *whom*, *which*, *what* and *whose*.

Examples: *Who* owns that car?   *Whom* do I ask for help?
Which socks should I wear?   *Whose* pen is this?

▶ 4. The word *who* is used as the subject of a sentence or clause. **Example:** *Who left the party early?* In this case, *who* is the subject. Try replacing the word *who* with *he*. (He left the party early.) If it still makes sense, the correct form is *who*. The word *whom* is used as the object of a sentence or phrase. **Example:** *Whom did Farhad see?* In this case, *whom* is the object of *did see*. Try replacing the word *whom* with *him*. (Farhad did see him.) If it still makes sense, the correct form is *whom*. *Whom* usually follows a preposition as in *to whom*, *for whom* and *with whom*. Copy the following sentences and allow your child to practice using these words.

Who/whom do you think let the dog out?
Several people who/whom came to the party wore red.
From who/whom did this package come?
I do not know for who/whom this note is intended.

▶ 5. Copy the following sentences. Have your child fill in the correct form of *who*.

There was no card to show to _____ the package should be delivered. (whom)
Did you see _____ got the prize? (who)
With _____ did Mike go to the party? (whom)
Can you read _____ signed up to play baseball? (who)

MATH (Variables / Chip Trading)

▶ 1. The commutative property of addition is helpful to know when faced with adding a series of numbers, such as $2 + 2 + 2 + 9 + 2 + 1 + 2 =$ ___. The easiest way to add this set of numbers is to add the 2's first, then the 9, then the 1. You can also apply the commutative property when adding columns of numbers.

▶ 2. Write 10–15 addition problems with variables on the chalkboard. Ask your child to solve them. Be sure to use different letters as variables, change the number of addends and the size of each addend in the problems.

Examples: $13 + 4 = b$ $325 + 43 + 12 = r$ $3 + 2 + 1 + 10 = k$ $75,432 + 3,700 = x$

Learn At Home, Grade 5

3. *Making the game board:* Make one game board for each player. Have your child cut a rectangle measuring 15" x 18" from the sheet of poster board. Ask him/her to divide the sheet into four columns across the 18" side, then label the columns from left to right: *Red, Blue, Green* and *Yellow.* Have your child color the columns accordingly using markers or crayons. Laminate the board for durability—it will be used often.

Object of the game: To be the first to have a red chip (counter).

How to play:

a. Place the 80 colored squares in a pile between the players. Roll the die to determine who goes first.

Chip values for the **first** game (in base 10) are as follows: yellow chip = one (1)
green chip = ten yellow chips (10)
blue chip = ten green chips (100)
red chip = ten blue chips (1,000)

b. Player 1 rolls the die and places that number of yellow chips in the yellow column of his/her game board.

c. Player 1 must read and write down the value of his/her chips before play passes to Player 2. To read the value, the player tells how many chips lie in each colored section of his/her game board. Later in the game it may read, "2 blue, 4 green and 3 yellow." (You may wish to create a record sheet that looks like a small version of the game board for the players to record the value of their chips.)

d. Players take turns repeating steps b and c, each time adding chips to their game boards.

e. Each time a player has enough yellow chips (10 in this game), he/she must trade for a green chip. The player returns the (10) yellow chips to the center and places the equivalent green chip in the green column of the game board. When a player has enough green chips, he/she must trade them for a blue chip. Blue chips are traded for a red. The first player to get a red chip wins the game.

SCIENCE (Arthropods)

1. The phylum *Arthropoda* includes invertebrates such as insects, arachnids and crustaceans. An arthropod is characterized by an *exoskeleton* and segmented body. Review the terms *antennae, head, thorax* and *abdomen.* Insects make up the largest group of arthropods. Ask your child to name as many kinds of insects as he/she can. Discuss the harmful and beneficial effects of insects. Next, show your child pictures of spiders, mites, ticks and scorpions. Compare these arachnids to insects. How are they similar? How are they different? Much of the seafood we eat—including crab, crayfish, shrimp and lobster—is also from the phylum *Arthropoda.* Explore the habitats and habits of these creatures with your child.

2. Help your child conduct a search for arthropods at home. Have your child record his/her findings on a simple chart like the one shown here.

number of legs	number of body segments	color	type of movement	insect or spider
6	3	black and green	walks and flies	insect (housefly)

3. Ask your child to respond to the following questions and directions. Some may require further research.

a. Give a description of your study site.

b. What types of organisms did you find under the wet cardboard?

c. How many were there?

d. Describe the organisms and their movements.

e. Did you accurately predict the types of organisms that might be found at the site?

f. What conditions do you think the organisms prefer?

g. Why would scientists want to map a study site and know the number of organisms at that site?

Good, Bad; Well, Badly

Good and **bad** are adjectives that modify nouns or pronouns. **Well** and **badly** are adverbs that modify verbs.

Examples:
A guitar is a **good** instrument to play on a hayride.
Bringing a piano along would be a **bad** choice.
It's hard to play the accordion **well** while you're dancing.
I played **badly** because my arm was sore.

Complete each sentence below with the correct adjective or adverb found in parentheses. In the blank at the end of the sentence, **write** whether an adjective or adverb has been used.

1. Michele used to play the clarinet _____ (bad, badly) when she first started. _____

2. I felt Mark's choice to learn how to play the piano was a _____ (good, well) one. _____

3. Curt sang very _____ (good, well) at the graduation ceremony last night. _____

4. Alan made a _____ (bad, badly) choice when he quit music class before the session ended. _____

5. Debra made a _____ (good, well) decision when she brought the music home to practice over vacation. _____

6. Mr. Sutton said that I display _____ (good, well) rhythm. _____

7. Leaving an expensive instrument out where it can get damaged is a _____ (bad, badly) thing to do. _____

8. Gwen performed the trumpet solo _____ (good, well) because she practiced every day. _____

Learn At Home, Grade 5

arrive
childhood
chime
climate
delight
digest
fighting
grind
ideal
prize
sight
silence
spying
style
thigh
timing
title
violin

These planes have sighted four spelling patterns for the **long i** sound. **Write** each spelling word in the correct category.

y

_____

_____

i-e

_____

_____

_____

igh

_____

_____

i

_____   _____   _____

_____   _____   _____

_____   _____   _____

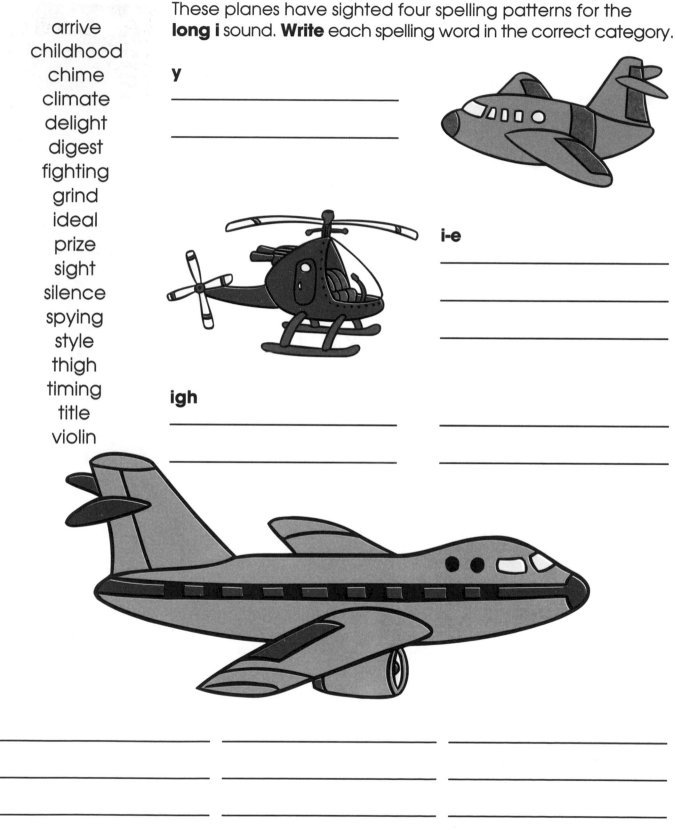

Commutative Property of Addition

An easy way to add a column of single-digit numbers is to find all those that equal ten first. Show how you would group these numbers, then add them to find the sums.

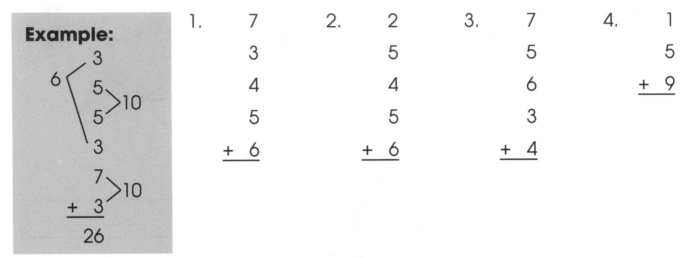

Example:

```
    3
 6 ⟨
    5
    5 ⟩10
    3
    7
    7 ⟩10
 +  3
   26
```

1.	7	2.	2	3.	7	4.	1
	3		5		5		5
	4		4		6		+ 9
	5		5		3		
	+ 6		+ 6		+ 4		

When a number shows up several times, add those digits first.

Example:

```
 2    (four 2's = 8)
 2
 5        8
 2      + 5
+ 2      13
```

5.	4	6.	3	7.	5
	2		7		4
	2		7		5
	2		+ 7		4
	+ 2				+ 4

8. As Jean walked through the woods, she turned over 6 rocks and counted the number of insects under each. She found 4, 6, 6, 4, 8 and 2 insects under the rocks. How many insects did she count?

9. The number of Atlanta Braves batters in the nine innings were 3, 3, 4, 5, 5, 3, 3, 3 and 6. How many Braves batters were there in the game?

Learn At Home, Grade 5

Opposite Operations

5 + 4 = 9

■■■■■ ■■■■

■■■■■■■■■

5 = 9 - 4

10 + 3 = 13

■■■■■
■■■■■   ■■■

■■■■■
■■■■■ ■■■

10 = 13 - 3

10 + 3 = 13

■■■■■
■■■■■   ■■■

■■■■■
■■■■■ ■■■

13 - 10 = 3

Complete the addition and subtraction sentences.

1. 8 + 6 = ___

    ___ - 8 = 6

2. 7 + ___ = 11

    ___ - ___ = ___

3. 12 + ___ = 20

    ___ - ___ = ___

4. 12 + ___ = 18

    ___ - ___ = ___

5. ___ + 108 = 200

    ___ - ___ = ___

6. ___ + 13 = 226

    ___ - ___ = ___

7. 22 - ___ = 12

    ___ + ___ = ___

8. 144 - ___ = 68

    ___ + ___ = ___

9. ___ - 8 = 17

    ___ + ___ = ___

10. 14 = ___ - 7

    ___ = ___ + ___

11. 39 = ___ - 12

    ___ = ___ + ___

12. 11 = ___ - 9

    ___ = ___ + ___

13. After 6 more people walked into the museum, there were 14 people inside. How many people were inside before the 6 entered?

14. When I added 11 more rocks to my collection, I had 37 rocks. How many rocks did I have before?

15. On a Sunday afternoon, we drove to the lake to view the fall colors. We drove a total of 58 miles. If the return trip was 29 miles, how far was the trip there?

47

Animal Population in a Study Site

In a natural environment, many small organisms will seek out those conditions most favorable to their survival. Wet leaves, compost piles, grass cuttings and garden mulch will attract a variety of small organisms, such as isopods, snails, spiders, insects, slugs, ants and worms.

You will need:

wet pieces of corrugated cardboard, potato slices, knife

Directions:

1. Locate an outdoor study site that is shaded and contains loose, rich soil.

2. Slice a raw potato into thin slices. Place these slices on top of the soil in your study site.

3. Thoroughly wet pieces of a small corrugated box, and place the pieces over the potato slices. (Rocks or boards may be used to keep the cardboard in place.)

4. Do not disturb the study site for several days.

5. After several days, remove the cardboard pieces (and the rocks and boards if they were used).

6. Observe any small organisms at the site. Try to identify and count the different organisms.

The New World

Label and **color** the first American colonies on the map below. In the blocks, **write** the names of the groups of people who were settling there and their reason(s) for coming to the New World.

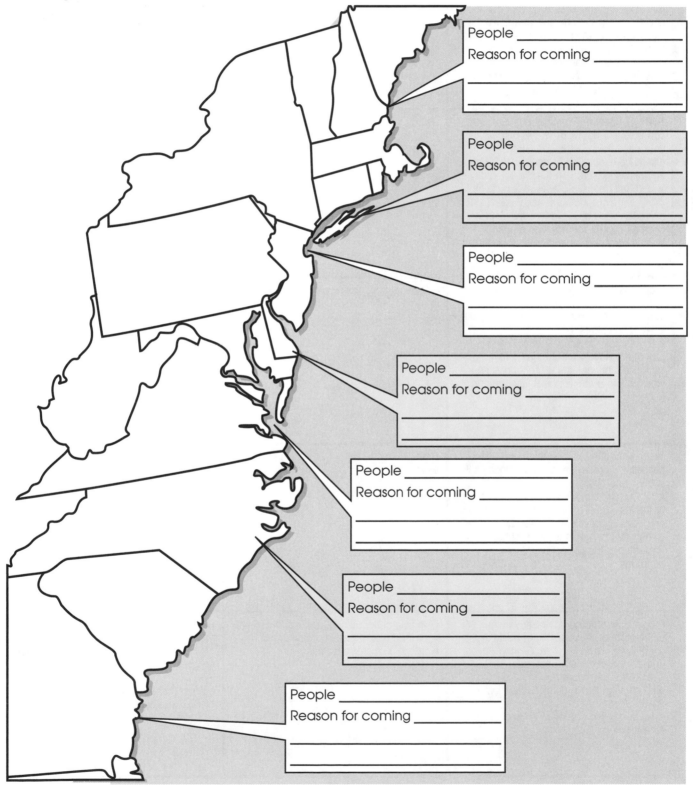

People _____
Reason for coming _____

_____
_____

People _____
Reason for coming _____

_____
_____

People _____
Reason for coming _____

_____
_____

People _____
Reason for coming _____

_____
_____

People _____
Reason for coming _____

_____
_____

People _____
Reason for coming _____

_____
_____

People _____
Reason for coming _____

_____
_____

	Language Skills	Spelling	Reading
Monday	Have your child read some of Aesop's fables. Discuss how animals are used in the stories to teach practical lessons. Have your child write an original story that teaches a lesson. First, help your child decide on a lesson he/she would like the story to teach. Then, encourage your child to choose an animal character to help illustrate that lesson. Once a topic is chosen, have your child make a plan and start a rough draft for the fable.	Pretest your child on these spelling words: arrow compose loan buffalo cove loaves burro foam roast chose gopher rows chrome grown soak cloak knowing solo Have your child correct the pretest. Add personalized words and make two copies of this week's study list.	Have your child read 2–3 more chapters of *Farmer Boy* and write a plot profile for a problem in the story.
Tuesday	**Parts of Speech:** Explain that some words can be either nouns or verbs. Discuss with your child how he/she can tell the difference by looking at the context. Write the following words on the chalkboard: *bat, watch, felt, mind, hit, answer, wash, pinch, drop, border, bark, laps*. Ask your child to use each word in two different sentences: once as a verb and once as a noun. He/she may add an ending or change the tense if needed.	Review this week's spelling words. Have your child complete **Honing Long o Skills** (p. 55).	Discuss the concept of reading for details. We can breeze through a story just to catch the meaning of the story line or we can read carefully and make mental pictures of the characters and settings along the way. Wilder is very good at writing detailed descriptions. Have your child read 2–3 more chapters of *Farmer Boy*. Ask your child to draw a picture of an image created by the author.
Wednesday	Pronouns can take different forms. Teach your child to distinguish subject pronouns from object pronouns. *See* Language Skills, Week 4, numbers 1 and 2. Ask your child to scan *Farmer Boy* for pronouns. Have your child read aloud a sentence that contains a pronoun, then tell whether it is a subject or object pronoun. Repeat with other sentences.	Have your child use each of this week's spelling words correctly in a sentence.	Have your child read 2–3 more chapters of *Farmer Boy*. Ask your child to recall details as he/she describes aloud what happened in those chapters. Listen carefully to your child's description and ask questions to encourage him/her to fill in more details from the reading.
Thursday	Teach your child to recognize and use possessive pronouns. *See* Language Skills, Week 4, number 3. Ask your child to write about his/her family or friends, using as many of the possessive pronouns as possible. Review the finished piece with your child to see that he/she understands the correct usage of the pronouns.	Have your child study this week's spelling words.	Have your child read 2–3 more chapters of *Farmer Boy*. Ask your child to write a detailed description of Almanzo's character. Encourage your child to avoid a merely physical description.
Friday	Proper nouns name a specific person, place or thing. A proper noun is always capitalized, as in *Ms. Lee, Grand Canyon* and *Smithsonian*. A proper adjective is formed from a proper noun and should also be capitalized, as in *English tea* or *Italian dressing*. Have your child complete **Proper Adjectives** (p. 54).	Give your child the final spelling test. Have your child record pretest and final test words in his/her Word Bank.	Have your child read 2–3 more chapters of *Farmer Boy*. Ask your child to write in his/her Reading Journal about what he/she has read so far, including details about the lives of the characters, a list of major events, an opinion about an event and a prediction of what is yet to come.

50

Math	**Science**	**Social Studies**
Addition and Subtraction Examine a ruler with your child. Brainstorm a list of situations in which you measure things in inches and feet. Measure the height of your child. Then, create math problems in which your child has to add inches to his/her height. Since a foot is equal to 12 inches, this may be a difficult exercise. *See* Math, Week 4, number 1. Have your child complete **Adding Inches and Feet** (p. 56).	**Echinoderms** Continue to record observations of the mealworm habitat from Week 2. Provide materials (on echinoderms) for your child's reference. *See* Science, Week 4, number 1. Ask your child to take notes on echinoderms in his/her Science Log. Have him/her draw and label three favorite echinoderms.	**Colonial Life** Have your child read about the responsibilities and daily lives of Puritan children. *See* Social Studies, Week 4, number 1. Ask your child to read the following proverbs and rewrite them in his/her own words. *Lost time is never found again.* *Don't throw stones at your neighbor's house if you live in a glass house.* *Don't throw the baby out with the bathwater.*
Today, brainstorm a list of situations in which you measure things in ounces and pounds. Measure the weight of a package to be mailed. Then, create math problems in which your child has to add ounces to the package weight. Since a pound is 16 ounces, your child will be adding and subtracting in base 16. Play the chip-trading game in base 16. Have your child complete **Adding Ounces and Pounds** (p. 57).	Visit a local aquarium, if possible. Many aquariums and zoos have tide pool exhibits where people can touch and see echinoderms and other marine creatures up close. If such a trip is not feasible, show your child color photographs of echinoderms such as starfish, brittle stars, sand dollars, sea cucumbers and sea urchins. Explain *radial symmetry* and other unusual physical characteristics of echinoderms. *See* Science, Week 4, number 2.	Read about crafts and toys from the colonial period. *What is a sampler? Who made them and why?* Look at pictures of colonial toys and discuss how they were made. Ask your child to make a sampler or to design a simple toy, instrument or game board. Provide needle and thread, corncobs, material scraps, yarn, markers, glue, pieces of balsa wood, small stones, boards and wire for the project.
Look at a clock with your child and ask him/her to tell you the current time. Then, create math problems in which your child has to add minutes to the current time. Since there are 60 minutes in an hour, your child will be adding in base 60. Play the chip-trading game in base 60. Have your child complete **Adding Minutes and Hours** (p. 58).	Have your child continue to read about echinoderms in encyclopedias, books and nature magazines or explore these creatures on CD-ROM or via the Internet. Ask your child to make identification cards for several types of echinoderms. Each card should include a picture of the animal, as well as a description of its habits, habitat and usefulness to humans.	Arrange to visit a historical museum where some of the tools, instruments, toys and clothing of the early settlers are on display. Take a close look at the kitchen utensils and tools used by the colonists. Back at home, read about some of the foods prepared by the early settlers. Help your child prepare a dish as the colonists did. *See* Social Studies, Week 4, number 2.
Review regrouping in subtraction, which is also called *borrowing*. Ask your child to explain the steps of borrowing as he/she works a problem with regrouping in the tens or hundreds place. Make sure your child understands the process and is not merely following a procedure without comprehension. Reteach with manipulatives if necessary. Give your child several subtraction problems with regrouping to solve.	Give your child the following list of terms related to echinoderms: *radial symmetry, endoskeleton, regeneration, vascular system, tube feet, rays* and *detritus.* Ask your child to create a word game that incorporates these terms as well as names of specific echinoderms. The game can be any format—crossword, word search, riddle, etc. Encourage your child to be creative!	Have your child read about the relationship between the early American settlers and the Indians. Discuss. *See* Social Studies, Week 4, number 3. Have your child read about Pocahontas and Squanto, two famous Native Americans who helped the settlers. *In what ways did they help the settlers? How might the settlers have fared, had these two people not helped them?*
Quiz your child on the addition concepts covered so far. Have your child complete **Addition** (p. 59). Reteach concepts if necessary. Teach your child how to subtract with regrouping when there are zeros in the minuend. *See* Math, Week 4, number 2.	Provide books and articles on sponges for your child's reference. Explore the structure and habits of the sponge. Where in the home are sponges most useful? Ask your child to take notes on sponges in his/her Science Log. Have your child include a labeled illustration as well.	Arrange for your child to perform some community service.

TEACHING SUGGESTIONS AND ACTIVITIES

LANGUAGE SKILLS (Parts of Speech)

▶ 1. *Pronouns* can replace nouns in any part of a sentence, so they can be subjects or objects. A pronoun may take a different form, depending on the case. If a pronoun acts as the subject, it is in the nominative case. If a pronoun acts as the object, it is in the objective case. The following pronouns are used in each case:

Nominative case (subject)	Objective case (object)
I	me
you	you
he	him
she	her
it	it
we	us
they	them

Ask your child to use each of these pronouns correctly in a sentence. Then, write or read aloud several sentences, omitting the pronouns. Have your child complete each sentence with the correct pronoun.

▶ 2. People sometimes use the incorrect pronoun when the pronoun appears in a compound subject or object. To determine the correct case, try reading each subject (or object) separately in the sentence. You will need to make the verb singular when you do this.

Example: *Mark and me like to skate.*
　　　　　　Try *Mark likes to skate.* and *Me like to skate.*
　　　　　　Since that doesn't sound right, try *I like to skate.*
　　　　　Correct: Mark and *I* like to skate.

▶ 3. The *possessive pronouns* are *my, mine, your, yours, his, her, hers, its, our, ours, their* and *theirs.* Some of these possessive pronouns are used to modify nouns, as in *my house.* In this case, the possessive pronoun is also considered to be an adjective.

MATH (Addition and Subtraction)

▶ 1. Adding inches and feet involves working in base 12. We usually work in base 10, which means we carry to the next place when we reach 10. Use last week's chip-trading game to practice this skill. *See* Math, Week 3, number 3. For today's game, a green chip is equal to 12 yellow chips (i.e., yellow chips are inches, green chips are feet).

▶ 2. Teach your child how to borrow when there are zeros in the minuend. If the adjacent place has a value of 0, continue to move to the left until you arrive at a place with a number from which you can borrow. Borrow one unit from that place and regroup it to the right. This changes the value of that zero to a value of 10 units for that place. Continue until you reach the place that originally required a number to be borrowed.

Example:

$$
\begin{array}{r}
\overset{0\ 9\ 9\ \ 9\ 14}{\cancel{100{,}043}} \\
-\ 64{,}261 \\
\hline
35{,}782
\end{array}
$$

Learn At Home, Grade 5

SCIENCE (Echinoderms)

▶ 1. Gather pictures, articles and reference materials on echinoderms to place in your science center. *Echinoderms* are often called "spiny-skinned" sea animals. If possible, check out a collection of preserved starfish, sand dollars and other echinoderms from a local museum or nature center. Have your child examine the textures and external features of the animals by touch and with the use of a magnifying glass. Discuss the symmetry of these animals and the patterns formed on the outer skin. Have your child sketch illustrations of some of the echinoderms in his/her Science Log. Point out the tiny tube feet on the underside of the animals. These act as suction cups and enable the animals to move and to grasp their prey. Use an eyedropper to demonstrate how the suction of the tube produces a grasping action. Ask your child to depress the rubber bulb, place the tip of the eyedropper on his/her hand and release the bulb.

▶ 2. Illustrate the terms *radius* and *radial symmetry* with the following demonstration. Cut a circle from construction paper. Ask your child to indicate the center of the circle with a dot. Fold the circle into halves, quarters or eighths. As the circle is unfolded, observe the lines made by the folds. These lines are the radii (plural of *radius*) of the circle. They extend from the center of the circle to its outer edge. The design made by the folds demonstrates radial symmetry. Have your child look again at the photographs of echinoderms. Can he/she see the radial symmetry in some of the animals?

SOCIAL STUDIES (Colonial Life)

▶ 1. Puritans raised their children to follow the word of God, respect those in authority and work hard to live a clean, useful life. Once they reached the age of six, Puritan children were dressed as miniature adults and were expected to act like adults. They were given jobs such as feeding chickens, cleaning the fireplace, making soap or spinning wool. Reading was very important to Puritans because they needed to be able to read the Bible. Children learned to read from an early school book, called a primer. A horn book was also used for lessons because paper for books and writing was scarce. Many early lessons came from familiar proverbs that taught the children how to behave.

▶ 2. Some staples of the early settlers' diet included succotash, hominy, mush, hoecakes, johnny cakes, beef jerky and corn pone. Native Americans helped the early settlers survive by introducing them to three main crops: corn, beans and squash. Make one or more of the following recipes with your child.

   a. **Succotash**

   1 can of whole kernel corn
   1 can of lima beans
   2 tbsp. of butter or margarine
   $\frac{1}{2}$ cup light cream

   Combine ingredients and add salt and pepper. Heat gently in a saucepan.

   b. **Hoecakes**

   In a mixing bowl, stir together cornmeal and water to make a thick mixture. Add salt to taste. Spoon about $\frac{1}{4}$ cup of the mixture onto a hot, greased griddle. Turn with a spatula until browned on both sides.

   c. **Buffalo or Beef Jerky**

   Slice meat into strips that are 1" wide and $\frac{1}{8}$" thick. Gently stretch each strip as you place it on a baking rack over a pan. Place the rack in the oven on a low setting. Dry overnight, keeping the oven door open. For added flavor, soak the meat slices in a bit of soy sauce before drying them. Jerky will keep for three months in an airtight container (or longer if frozen).

   3. Ask some of the following questions in a discussion about the colonists and Indians.

▶   *When the settlers arrived, in what ways were they inconsiderate of the people already living there?*
   How did the Indians feel about the new settlers? Why?
   In what ways did the Indians and settlers get along?
   How were the Indians helpful?
   When did the Indians and settlers not get along?

Proper Adjectives

Adjectives are words that describe nouns. **Proper adjectives** are formed from proper nouns, and they must be capitalized. Other adjectives are called **common nouns**.

Examples:
> proper adjectives: *French* toast, *American* flag
> common adjectives: *cold* toast, *waving* flag

Circle all the adjectives in the sentences below.

1. Camels have carried loads across desert sands for centuries.
2. They were once the only means of transporting goods across the Sahara Desert and Middle Eastern deserts.
3. The Sahara Desert is in the North African desert region.
4. The Arabian camel has one hump, while the Bactrian camel has two humps.
5. The Bactrian camel got its name long ago from a Central Asian country known as Bactria.
6. Both types of camels are used in some Asian regions.
7. In wars, fighting men have ridden the faithful camel.
8. The camel Napoleon rode during his Egyptian campaign was later put in an exhibit.

Write each circled adjective under the proper heading.

Proper Adjectives	Common Adjectives
1. _____	1. _____
2. _____	2. _____
3. _____	3. _____
4. _____	4. _____
5. _____	5. _____
6. _____	6. _____
7. _____	7. _____
8. _____	8. _____
9. _____	
10. _____	

54

Honing Long o Skills

Write each **long o** word in the appropriate category.

Classy Long o Categories

o	oa	o-e	ow

arrow
buffalo
burro
chose
chrome
cloak
compose
cove
foam
gopher
grown
knowing
loan
loaves
roast
rows
soak
solo

Now, **write** each word, indicating the part of speech in the parentheses. Use these abbreviations: N = noun, V = verb, A = adjective.

1._____ ( )   10._____ ( )

2._____ ( )   11._____ ( )

3._____ ( )   12._____ ( )

4._____ ( )   13._____ ( )

5._____ ( )   14._____ ( )

6._____ ( )   15._____ ( )

7._____ ( )   16._____ ( )

8._____ ( )   17._____ ( )

9._____ ( )   18._____ ( )

Adding Inches and Feet

When adding inches, regroup 1 foot for every 12 inches.

Example:

a.
    1 ft. 8 in.
  + 1 ft. 8 in.
      16 in.

16 in. = 1 ft. 4 in.

b.
        1
    1 ft. 8 in.
  + 1 ft. 8 in.
        4 in.

c.
        1
    1 ft. 8 in.
  + 1 ft. 8 in.
    3 ft. 4 in.

1.
    2 ft. 4 in.
  + 1 ft. 9 in.

2.
    12 ft. 10 in.
  + 1 ft.   5 in.

3.
    12 ft. 7 in.
  + 8 ft. 8 in.

4.
    1 ft. 5 in.
  + 3 ft. 6 in.

5.
    1 ft. 6 in.
  + 1 ft. 6 in.

6.
    7 ft. 4 in.
  + 5 ft. 5 in.

7.
    28 ft. 8 in.
  + 4 ft. 9 in.

8.
    8 ft. 9 in.
  +   7 in.

9.
    3 ft. 3 in.
  + 6 ft. 7 in.

Learn At Home, Grade 5

Adding Ounces and Pounds

When adding ounces, regroup 1 pound for every 16 ounces.

Example:

a.
```
    8 lb. 12 oz.
 + 1 lb.  8 oz.
        20 oz.
```

```
          1
b.   8 lb. 12 oz.
  + 1 lb.  8 oz.
          4 oz.
```

```
          1
c.   8 lb. 12 oz.
  + 1 lb.  8 oz.
   10 lb.  4 oz.
```

20 oz. = 1 lb. 4 oz.

1.
```
    2 lb.  7 oz.
 + 1 lb. 11 oz.
```

2.
```
    3 lb. 11 oz.
 + 1 lb. 11 oz.
```

3.
```
   27 lb. 12 oz.
 +  9 lb. 12 oz.
```

4.
```
  114 lb.  8 oz.
 + 59 lb. 10 oz.
```

5.
```
    1 lb.  8 oz.
 + 1 lb.  8 oz.
```

6.
```
    1 lb.  2 oz.
 + 1 lb. 14 oz.
```

7.
```
    7 lb. 12 oz.
 +       13 oz.
```

8.
```
          15 oz.
 + 3 lb.  5 oz.
```

9.
```
   15 lb.  6 oz.
 + 17 lb.  9 oz.
```

10. Twins were born at St. Vincent Hospital today.
One weighs 5 lb. 8 oz.
The other weighs 5 lb. 12 oz.
How much do the babies weigh together?

Adding Minutes and Hours

When adding hours and minutes, regroup 1 hour for every 60 minutes. The first one has been done for you.

1.
   1
   2 hr. 34 min.
   + 3 hr. 31 min.
   6 hr. 5 min.

2.
   5 hr. 24 min.
   + 7 hr. 19 min.

3.
   2 hr. 39 min.
   + 5 hr. 41 min.

4.
   16 hr. 51 min.
   + 4 hr. 8 min.

5.
   3 hr. 43 min.
   + 2 hr. 51 min.

6.
   3 hr. 14 min.
   + 6 hr. 72 min.

7.

+ 50 minutes

Time: _____

8.

+ 1 hour 5 minutes

Time: _____

9.

+ 30 minutes

Time: _____

10.

+ 4 hours 35 minutes

Time: _____

11. Geneva worked on her sculpture this week.

Monday:	2 hr.	14 min.
Tuesday:		30 min.
Wednesday:	1 hr.	16 min.
Thursday:	3 hr.	25 min.
Friday:	1 hr.	45 min.

Sum total: _____ _____

Learn At Home, Grade 5

Addition

Solve.

1. 3,256,289 + 17 + 2,569 = _____

2. 3 + 7 + 5 + 4 + 6 + 5 + 3 = _____

3. 15 + ___ = 27

4. ___ + 19 = 23

5. 209 + 327 = ___

6.   8 ft.   11 in.
    + 2 ft.   5 in.

7.   16 lb.   14 oz.
    + 5 lb.   12 oz.

8.   4 hr.   44 min.
    + 5 hr.   33 min.

9.

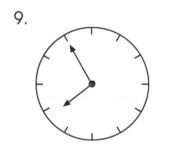

+ 2 hours 20 minutes

Time: _____

10. The Grant family is having a large crowd for Thanksgiving dinner. They bought two turkeys for dinner. One turkey weighs 15 lbs. 8 oz. The second turkey weighs 19 lbs. 10 oz. How much turkey do they have?

	Language Skills	Spelling	Reading
Monday	For this week's writing activity, have your child write and perform a radio commercial. *See* Language Skills, Week 5, number 1 for more information on this project. Once your child has chosen a topic, have him/her make a plan for writing and work on a rough draft of the commercial.	Pretest your child on these spelling words: argue excuse rude blue include statue confuse issue tissue due museum truth duke plume tube dune ruby tulip Have your child correct the pretest. Add personalized words and make two copies of this week's study list.	**Vocabulary** Have your child continue to read 2–3 chapters of *Farmer Boy* each day. As your child reads this week, have him/her copy unfamiliar words or phrases, as well as the pages on which they're found, into the Reading Journal. Discuss the meaning of the words and phrases with your child. Encourage your child to reread sections of the book containing these words/phrases to increase comprehension.
Tuesday	**Verbs:** Discuss verb conjugation. Explain that each verb has an infinitive. The infinitive begins with the word *to*, as in *to eat, to drive* and *to smell*. The infinitive is considered the basic form of the verb from which all the tenses and persons are formed. *See* Language Skills, Week 5, number 2. Give your child a list of five regular verbs to conjugate in all the persons and tenses.	Review this week's spelling words and how to divide words into syllables. (*See* Language Skills, Week 23, number 1 for rules on dividing syllables). Have your child complete **The Truth About u** (p. 66).	Have your child read 2–3 more chapters of *Farmer Boy*. Have him/her make notes of any unfamiliar vocabulary.
Wednesday	Review linking verbs with your child. *See* Language Skills, Week 5, number 3. Have your child complete **Linking Verbs** (p. 64).	Have your child use each of this week's spelling words correctly in a sentence.	Some words and phrases are considered archaic or obsolete and are no longer used in common speech or writing. Discuss these words in their original context and find background information whenever possible. For example, discuss the event of the butter-buyer coming to test the butter that Almanzo's mother made. Have your child read 2–3 more chapters of *Farmer Boy*.
Thursday	Review helping verbs with your child. Demonstrate how they can be used to change the action in sentences. *See* Language Skills, Week 5, numbers 4 and 5. Have your child complete **Forms of Be, Do and Have** (p. 65).	Have your child study this week's spelling words.	Have your child finish reading *Farmer Boy*. Choose a final book project that will allow your child to synthesize his/her learning. For book project ideas, see page 13.
Friday	Review subject/verb agreement. Write several sentences on the chalkboard, some with errors in agreement. Ask your child to read each sentence aloud, then underline the simple subject and circle the verb. *Do the subject and verb agree?* If not, ask your child to make the correction. Then, have your child write a story, focusing on subject/verb agreement. Give him/her 10 subject and verb pairs (e.g., waves/to splash) to make sentences to include in a story.	Give your child the final spelling test. Have your child record pretest and final test words in his/her Word Bank.	Discuss *Farmer Boy* with your child. Engage in a dialogue in which you both express your opinions about the story and compare the story and characters to similar stories.

60

Math	Science	Social Studies
Subtraction *Rounding* can be used to estimate answers in subtraction problems, just as in addition problems. *See* Math, Week 5, number 1. Give your child two subtraction problems to estimate, then solve. Have your child compare his/her answers with the estimates. If the numbers are not close, ask your child to double-check his/her subtraction. Have your child complete **Estimating Differences** (p. 67).	**Mollusks** Have your child continue to record observations of the mealworm habitat established in Week 2, Thursday. Provide books and other resources on mollusks for your child's reference. *See* Science, Week 5, number 1. Ask your child to take notes on mollusks in his/her Science Log. Have your child illustrate and label at least two animals that belong to this group.	Ask your child to imagine that a group of humans goes to another planet to establish a colony. When they arrive on the planet, they encounter a civilization that is already established there. How should the humans approach this civilization? How might both parties avoid conflict and foster a positive relationship with each other? Ask your child to imagine and describe in writing the initial encounter and subsequent events.
Use manipulatives to model the relationship between subtraction and addition. *See* Math, Week 5, number 2. Have your child complete **Opposite Operation of Subtraction** (p. 68).	Have your child write and illustrate an imaginative poem or short story about his/her favorite kind of mollusk.	**Southern Colonies:** Have your child research the reasons people went to the South and the challenges they met there. The Southern Colonies were populated by farmers vying to get rich through trade, Africans brought to the New World against their will and those enticed to come through gifts of land or promises of freedom. Have your child compare the Southern Colonies with the New England Colonies. *See* Social Studies, Week 5.
Show your child how to use a letter as a variable in a subtraction sentence. Replace the blank line in a subtraction problem with a letter (a variable). The letter stands for what is unknown. **Example:** $9 - 4 = b$ Have your child complete **Variables in Subtraction** (p. 69).	Seashells come in many colors, shapes and sizes. Observe actual shells or pictures of shells. *See* Science, Week 5, number 2. If you have a seashell collection at home, have your child make a chart outlining specific characteristics of each type. Make four columns: *Name, Appearance, Length* and *Mass*. Help your child measure each shell with a centimeter ruler and gram weights. Have your child fill in the chart.	In what ways did the Africans teach and influence the white settlers? Ask your child to write about the beginnings of African-American heritage.
Have your child practice subtraction by providing change from a purchase. Help your child create a "store." Use pictures from a grocery store advertisement or put price tags on household objects. You play the role of customer, while your child plays salesclerk. Choose one or two items (total under $5) and pretend to pay with a $5 bill. Have your child calculate the change using subtraction. Use real money, if possible, for making the change. Repeat with other items.	Ask your child to identify mollusks that live in the sea. Have him/her describe their physical characteristics. What do they eat? How do they move? How do they fend off predators? Have your child read articles from nature magazines about these animals and about occupations that depend on these animals.	Ask your child to write about the Southern Colonies. Have your child write about the contributions (or impact) of two key figures in the history of the Southern Colonies, describe how the colonies might have developed without the existence of slavery or examine the history of the House of Burgesses. If your child has another idea, let him/her research and write about that topic.
Today, have your child make change by counting *up* from the purchase price to $5. Use the same materials as yesterday. Teach your child to say the amount of the purchase and then count the change up to $5. *See* Math, Week 5, number 3.	Set up a freshwater snail habitat. *See* Science, Week 5, number 3. Have your child continue to observe the habitat over the next several weeks.	Arrange for your child to perform some community service.

TEACHING SUGGESTIONS AND ACTIVITIES

LANGUAGE SKILLS (Verbs)

▶ 1. Record a radio commercial for a product that will appeal to your child (movie, sporting event, food, music, etc.). Listen to the tape together and discuss the selling techniques of the commercial. Use the following questions and comments to guide your discussion:

> *Was the commercial easy to understand?*
> *Did the commercial make the product or event seem appealing?*
> *Were the voices pleasant?*
> *Was the commercial too noisy?*
> *What did you notice about the timing?*

Encourage your child to incorporate some of the selling techniques used in the commercial into his/her own ad. Ask your child to write and design a persuasive commercial for a familiar product. The commercial should last about 30 seconds when read aloud.

▶ 2. Verb *tense* indicates when the action of the sentence occurred—in the past, present or future. The *person* indicates the subject of the sentence. Review the following conjugation of the verb *to laugh*.

	Present	Past	Future
First Person (singular)	I laugh	I laughed	I will laugh
Second Person	you laugh	you laughed	you will laugh
Third Person	he/she/it laughs	he/she/it laughed	he/she/it will laugh
First Person (plural)	we laugh	we laughed	we will laugh
Second Person	you laugh	you laughed	you will laugh
Third Person	they laugh	they laughed	they will laugh

▶ 3. A linking verb joins or *links* the subject of a sentence to a word in the predicate. The most common linking verbs include *am, is, are, was* and *were*. A linking verb may be followed by a predicate noun, which renames the subject, or a predicate adjective, which describes the subject.

Examples: Clarissa is a singer. (*singer* (noun) renames Clarissa)
Clarissa is talented. (*talented* (adjective) describes Clarissa)

Give your child practice in recognizing predicate nouns and predicate adjectives. Write the following sentences (or make up your own) on the chalkboard. Ask your child to circle the linking verb in each sentence and write *adjective* or *noun* after the predicate. The first one has been done for you.

The children (were) sleepy. (adjective)   The hallway is narrow.
My mother is a doctor.   The kitten was a stray.
The cinnamon rolls are warm.   Jesse's shoes were muddy.
I am hungry!   Her brother is an actor in New York.

▶ 4. A *verb phrase* is made up of a main verb and one or more helping verbs. The helping verb helps the main verb express action.

Some common helping verbs:

am	has	are	had	will be	can be	will have been
were	did	do	is	will have	has been	might have
can	was	may	have	can have	could be	must have

Have your child use each of these helping verbs in a sentence.

▶ 5. Write the following unfinished sentences on the board. Direct your child to use a helping verb and a form of the verb shown to write the action in either the past or present.

bark
The dogs _____ . (present)
The dogs _____ . (past)

run
The horse _____ . (present)
The horse _____ . (past)

laugh
The crowd _____ . (present)
The crowd _____ . (past)

cry
The baby _____ . (present)
The baby _____ . (past)

Learn At Home, Grade 5

MATH (Subtraction)

▶ 1. To estimate the solution to a subtraction problem, round both numbers to the highest place of the smaller number. In the following example, the numbers are rounded to the hundreds place.

$$
\begin{array}{r}
4,279 \\
-\ \mathbf{3}12 \\
\end{array}
\longrightarrow
\begin{array}{r}
4,300 \\
-\ 300 \\
\hline
4,000
\end{array}
$$

▶ 2. Use manipulatives to demonstrate the subtraction problem 56 – ___ = 21. Build the first number (minuend) on a place-value chart. This is the total, the largest number in the equation. The second number (subtrahend) is missing. The solution (difference) is the part of the total remaining when the subtrahend is removed. Use the manipulatives to separate the total number into the two parts: the known difference and the unknown subtrahend. Give your child the manipulatives and ask him/her to solve the problem ___ – 4 = 5. your child should discover that by adding the subtrahend and difference, he/she can solve for the minuend.

▶ 3. To make change by counting up, follow this example:

The customer gives you $5.00 for a $2.43 purchase.
1. Say the purchase price, $2.43.
2. Put down one penny and say, $2.44.
3. Put down one penny and say, $2.45.
4. Put down one nickel and say, $2.50.
5. Put down one quarter and say, $2.75.
6. Put down one quarter and say, $3.00.
7. Put down one dollar and say, $4.00.
8. Put down one dollar and say, $5.00.

SCIENCE (Mollusks)

▶ 1. Look at pictures of snails, slugs, clams, oysters, octopuses and other examples of mollusks. Discuss the physical characteristics and habitats of these creatures. Have your child observe and describe some snail, oyster or clam shells. Direct your child to research the values and uses of some of these animals. Observe the movement of a snail or slug. Discuss the damage to gardens and plants caused by snails and slugs.

▶ 2. Gather and display a large collection of seashells or use a seashell picture guide. Have your child observe the various patterns, shapes and colors of the shells. Ask your child to use the guide to identify the shells: cowrie, cone, whelk, conch, scallop, etc. Discuss the different uses of seashells throughout history as money, jewelry, buttons and collectibles.

▶ 3. Help your child set up a freshwater snail habitat. Purchase some freshwater snails from a pet shop. Place some gravel in the bottom of a large clear jar or an aquarium. Add some aquatic plants and fill with water. Use a magnifying glass to observe the snails over a period of several weeks. Notice the egg sacs that are deposited on the container. Observe any damage to the plants. Have your child record his/her observations in the Science Log.

SOCIAL STUDIES (Southern Colonies)

Use these questions to guide a discussion comparing the New England Colonies with the Southern Colonies.

How did their reasons differ for coming to the New World?

How did their crops differ?

How did family life differ?

Both suffered from disease. How were the diseases the same? different?

Who were the workers in the South?

Where were there more wealthy people? Why?

How did education differ in New England and the Southern Colonies?

Where would you rather have grown up? Why?

What role did religion play in the lives of both groups?

Linking Verbs

Linking verbs link the subject to a word in the predicate. The linking verbs most often used are **am**, **is**, **are**, **was** and **were**.

> **Example:**
> *We **were** happy about the outcome.*

A linking verb may be followed by a **predicate noun**, which renames the subject, or a **predicate adjective**, which describes the subject.

> **Examples:**
> *Harry is a **teacher**.* (predicate noun)
> *Harry is **confident**.* (precicate verb)

Complete each sentence with a predicate noun.

1. Sarah is a _____ . 2. Her best friend is a _____ .

Circle each predicate noun. **Underline** the noun or pronoun in the subject that is renamed.

1. The children were actors.
2. The setting of the play was a garden.
3. Butterflies are main characters in the play.
4. Ralph is the star.

Complete each sentence with a predicate adjective.

1. Today's weather is _____ . 2. Tom will be _____ .

Circle each predicate adjective. **Underline** the noun or pronoun in the subject that is described.

1. The trap-door spider is clever.
2. Its building skills are amazing.
3. The webs covering the walls were soft and silky.
4. The trap was invisible.

Learn At Home, Grade 5

Forms of Be, Do and Have

Some forms of the verb **be** can be used as linking or helping verbs. Three forms of **be** cannot be used alone as verbs: **be**, **being** and **been**. These must always be used with helping verbs.

Examples:
*Polar bears **are** carnivores. (**be** as linking verb)*
*The polar bear **is** hunting the seal. (**be** as helping verb)*
*A polar bear **has been** seen near here. (**be** with helping verb)*
Forms of **be**: **am**, **is**, **are**, **was**, **were**, **be**, **being**, **been**

Complete each sentence below with the correct form of the verb **be** found in parentheses. Add helping verbs where needed.

1. Polar bears _____ excellent swimmers. (is, are)

2. The polar bear _____ seen running at a speed of 35 miles per hour. (was, being)

3. I _____ sure I saw a polar bear swimming in the water. (am, are)

4. Polar bears _____ seen swimming many miles from shore. (been, have been)

The verbs **do** and **have** can be used as main verbs or as helping verbs.

Examples:
*I **have** traveled to Canada to see polar bears. (helping verb)*
*I **did** my report on polar bears yesterday. (main verb)*
Forms of **do**: **do**, **did**, **done**   Forms of **have**: **have**, **has**, **had**

Complete the story below using the correct forms of the verbs **do** and **have**.

I _____ believe polar bears are very beautiful. I _____ seen them along the coast of Alaska. I _____ see one come up to our tour bus. By the age of 10 years, a male polar bear _____ grown to its full size. Countries around the Arctic have _____ a very good job of trying to save the polar bear from extinction. Polar bears _____ beautiful coats which _____ attracted hunters. Now the bears _____ protection from hunters by law.

The Truth About u

argue
blue
confuse
due
duke
dune
excuse
include
issue
museum
plume
ruby
rude
statue
tissue
truth
tube
tulip

The words in the list have the o͞o or yo͞o sound. **Write** each word in the appropriate category.

Classy o͞o Categories

u–e	ue	u
_____	_____	_____
_____	_____	_____
_____	_____	_____
_____	_____	_____
_____	_____	
_____		
_____		

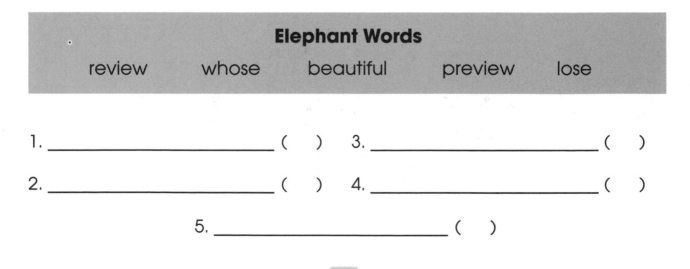

Oops! We have elephant words. Just like elephants, we must remember that a few words make the o͞o or yo͞o sound spelled with **iew**, as in **review**, **o-e**, as in **lose**, or **eau** as in **beauty**. **Write** the five elephant words in alphabetical order. Note the number of syllables each word contains in the parentheses ( ).

Elephant Words

review   whose   beautiful   preview   lose

1. _____ (   )   3. _____ (   )

2. _____ (   )   4. _____ (   )

5. _____ (   )

66

Estimating Differences

To estimate differences, round the numbers and then subtract. This skill can be used daily. An example of this would be when you travel by car. If you have a distance of 862 miles to travel and you've gone 381, you can round and subtract in your head—900 – 400 leaves approximately 500 more miles to go.

Nearest Ten	**Nearest Hundred**	**Nearest Thousand**

$$
\begin{array}{rr}
48 \rightarrow & 50 \\
- 13 \rightarrow & - 10 \\
\hline
35 & 40
\end{array}
$$

Actual = 35
Estimated = 40
Difference = 5

$$
\begin{array}{rr}
841 \rightarrow & 800 \\
- 289 \rightarrow & - 300 \\
\hline
552 & 500
\end{array}
$$

Actual = 552
Estimated = 500
Difference = 52

$$
\begin{array}{rr}
6,780 \rightarrow & 7,000 \\
- 1,912 \rightarrow & - 2,000 \\
\hline
4,868 & 5,000
\end{array}
$$

Actual = 4,868
Estimated = 5,000
Difference = 132

Keep in mind that these answers are approximate, so this method should not be used if you want an exact answer.

Subtract by estimating.

1. $\begin{array}{r} 93 \rightarrow 90 \\ - 68 \rightarrow 70 \\ \hline \end{array}$

2. $\begin{array}{r} 571 \\ - 139 \\ \hline \end{array}$

3. $\begin{array}{r} 4,899 \\ - 1,916 \\ \hline \end{array}$

4. $\begin{array}{r} 88 \\ - 19 \\ \hline \end{array}$

5. $\begin{array}{r} 912 \\ - 778 \\ \hline \end{array}$

6. $\begin{array}{r} 8,211 \\ - 5,928 \\ \hline \end{array}$

7. $\begin{array}{r} 71 \\ - 28 \\ \hline \end{array}$

8. $\begin{array}{r} 622 \\ - 266 \\ \hline \end{array}$

9. $\begin{array}{r} 6,935 \\ - 2,899 \\ \hline \end{array}$

Opposite Operation of Subtraction

Write the missing number in each subtraction sentence. Check your answer with addition. The first one shows you how.

1. __ – 10 = 5   2. __ – 12 = 24   3. __ – 8 = 40

    5 + 10 = 15

4. __ – 8 = 9   5. __ – 12 = 20   6. __ – 10 = 37

Two subtraction problems can be made from the same model. **Complete** the subtraction sentences below. **Write** a second subtraction sentence for each based on the same model.

■■■■■■■☒☒☒☒   ☒☒☒☒☒☒☒■■■■

     11 – 4 = 7   11 – 7 = 4

7. 12 – __ = 7   8. 33 – __ = 11   9. 87 – __ = 56

   12 – __ = 5

10. 20 – __ = 12   11. 85 – __ = 25   12. 187 – __ = 122

13. After I gave my friend 12 rocks from my collection, I still had 15 rocks. How many rocks were in my collection before I gave some away?

14. The bag of cookies had 20 cookies in it. Joe took some out for his lunch and left 12 in the bag. How many cookies did Joe take for lunch?

Learn At Home, Grade 5

Variables in Subtraction

A **variable** is a letter in an equation that stands for what is not known. **Solve** for the missing number. The first one has been done for you.

1. $25 - 13 = x$

    $x = $ <u>12</u>

2. $17 - 13 = p$

    $p = $ _____

3. $85 - 50 = y$

    $y = $ _____

4. $27 - 13 = z$

    $z = $ _____

5. $109 - 88 = n$

    $n = $ _____

6. $69 - 54 = h$

    $h = $ _____

7. $356 - 89 = r$

    $r = $ _____

8. $2,859 - 1,765 = k$

    $k = $ _____

9. $26,251 - 287 = c$

    $c = $ _____

10. $5,222 - 133 = a$

    $a = $ _____

11. $22,041 - 1,850 = s$

    $s = $ _____

12. $23,001 - 1,243 = w$

    $w = $ _____

13. $57,005 - 36,996 = f$

    $f = $ _____

14. $11,221 - 11,221 = m$

    $m = $ _____

15. $865,397 - 356,286 = b$

    $b = $ _____

16. $5,322 - 1,451 = e$

    $e = $ _____

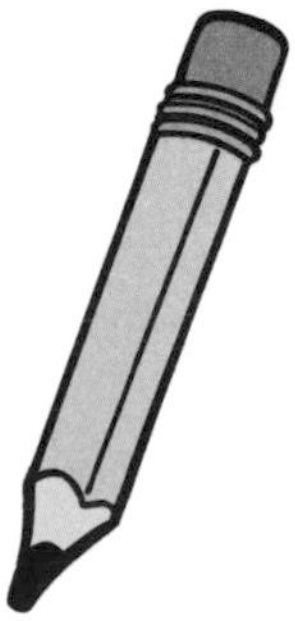

	Language Skills	**Spelling**	**Reading**
Monday	Brainstorm ideas for this week's writing topic. Use some of this week's spelling words as a starting point. Once your child has chosen a topic, have him/her make a plan for writing and start working on a rough draft for a story.	Pretest your child on these spelling words: barnyard homesick seagull blastoff ice skate snowstorm brand-new jack-o'-lantern topsy-turvy chairperson peanut butter town crier cupboard polar bear yardstick hide-and-seek post office zip code Have your child correct the pretest. Add personalized words and make two copies of this week's study list.	**Compare and Contrast** Introduce *To Walk the Sky Path* by Phyllis Reynolds Naylor. While reading this book, your child will have several opportunities to compare his/her world with the traditional world of the Seminole Indians. Have your child read chapters 1 and 2 of *To Walk the Sky Path*, then compare Billie's family life with his/her own. Have your child list similarities and differences, then combine the list into an organized paragraph.
Tuesday	**Verbs:** *Regular* verbs take the *ed* ending to show the past tense. **Example:** help/helped. *Irregular* verbs are verbs that do not add *ed* in the past tense but do undergo a change in spelling. **Example:** sleep/slept. Can your child think of other examples of irregular verbs? Have your child complete **Irregular Verbs** (p. 74).	Review this week's spelling words. Have your child complete **Conquering Compounds** (p. 76).	Have your child read chapters 3 and 4 of *To Walk the Sky Path*. Ask your child to use a Venn diagram to compare and contrast the ways of the Tommie family with the ways of the non-Indian people they encounter.
Wednesday	**Adverbs:** Review adverbs. *See* Language Skills, Week 6, number 1. Write ten sentences containing adverbs on the chalkboard. Ask your child to underline the adverb in each sentence and circle the word it modifies. Have your child sort the adverbs into three categories: those that tell when, those that tell how and those that tell where.	Have your child use each of this week's spelling words correctly in a sentence.	Have your child read chapters 5 and 6 of *To Walk the Sky Path*. Ask your child to describe Billie's experience staying overnight at Jeff's house. Include Billie's feelings and impressions.
Thursday	Adverbs can modify adjectives and other adverbs, as well as verbs. *See* Language Skills, Week 6, numbers 2 and 3. Have your child complete **Adverbs Modify** (p. 75).	Have your child study this week's spelling words.	Have your child read chapters 7 and 8 of *To Walk the Sky Path*. Ask your child to write in his/her Reading Journal about Billie's life. *Do you think Billie will have a better life than his grandfather and brother? Support your opinion with examples from the book.*
Friday	Teach your child how to use the endings *er* and *est* to form comparative forms of adjectives and adverbs that do not end in *ly*. Explain that the words *more, most, less* and *least* can also be used to indicate a comparison. *See* Language Skills, Week 6, number 4.	Give your child the final spelling test. Have your child record pretest and final test words in his/her Word Bank.	Have your child read chapters 9 and 10 of *To Walk the Sky Path*. Ask your child to answer the following question in his/her **Reading Journal:** *Can Billie be a true Indian in the white man's world? Support your answer with passages from the book and predict what Billie's life will be like when he grows up.* Review the literary device *onomatopoeia*. *See* Reading, Week 6.

Learn At Home, Grade 5

Math	Science	Social Studies
Chip Trading With Subtraction Play the chip-trading game from Week 3. Play the game in base 10, this time using subtraction. *See* Math, Week 6, number 1 for more detailed instructions.	**Vertebrates** Discuss the differences again between invertebrates and vertebrates. Then, look together with your child at the information sheet, **Vertebrates** (p. 79). Gather a variety of pictures of different vertebrates (fish, amphibians, reptiles, birds and mammals) and have your child sort the pictures into the five groups. Discuss the important characteristics of each group. *See* Science, Week 6, number 1.	Ask your child to do some research on colonial careers. Have him/her find resources at the library in which to read about the following careers: *blacksmith, barber, miller, cooper, tailor* and *wheelwright*. Ask your child to choose one occupation and write a brief report on it. Have your child include an illustration of the proper attire worn by the worker, as well as some of the tools of his/her trade.
Play the chip-trading game again today. Play with subtraction, but this time using a base other than base 10. Try base 12 or base 5.	Explore the meaning of the terms *warm-blooded* and *cold-blooded* with your child. *See* Science, Week 6, number 2. Encourage your child to continue taking notes on vertebrates in his/her Science Log.	**Middle Colonies:** The Middle Colonies were settled from the mid-1600s through the mid-1700s. Colonists were attracted to the area's temperate climate, rich soil, fertile land and the religious freedoms offered there. The Middle Colonies became known as "the bread colonies" because they farmed grains and milled flour for bread. The flour was then sold to all the colonies. Ask your child to do some research, then draw a picture or diagram of a mill.
In Week 4, you showed your child how to add inches and feel using base 12. Review your discussions from that day. Then, create subtraction problems involving inches and feet, days and weeks. Have your child complete **Subtracting Different Units** (p. 77).	Ask your child to identify some of the fish and mammals that live in the sea. Have your child read about these unique animals. Ask your child to choose one fish and one sea mammal and compare them using a Venn diagram. Next, read about the economic value of some of these creatures to humans. Several ocean-dwelling mammals are in danger of extinction. Discuss some of the laws that have been instituted to protect them.	Ask your child to read about William Penn, the founder of Pennsylvania. *What was Penn's background? What kind of a relationship did he establish with the Indians? What did he hope to accomplish in Pennsylvania? Was he ultimately successful?*
In Week 4, you showed your child how to add ounces and pounds. Now teach your child how to subtract ounces and pounds. There are 16 ounces in a pound, so use base 16 for subtraction. Create several practice problems involving pounds and ounces, minutes and seconds. Guide your child in solving the problems. Have your child complete **Subtracting in Different Bases** (p. 78).	Create a word search or crossword puzzle for your child to solve. Use the following terms: *gills, scales, cartilage, fins, spawning, swim bladder, lamprey* and *roe*. Ask your child to write a poem or short story about fish or fishing. Encourage your child to include some of these new terms in his/her poem or story.	The people who settled in the Middle Colonies came from varied backgrounds. What impact did this have on life in these colonies? How did it make the Middle Colonies a better place to live?
Quiz your child on subtraction concepts. *See* Math, Week 6, number 2 for a sample quiz. Reteach concepts if necessary.	If possible, take your child fishing or plan a trip to a fish hatchery. *What kinds of fish are common to your area? What kinds do you see?* Help your child become familiar with the categories of scientific classification: *kingdom, phylum, class, order, family, genus* and *species*. Explain that each category is more specific than the one before it—i.e., *species* is the most specific category.	Arrange for your child to perform some community service.

TEACHING SUGGESTIONS AND ACTIVITIES

LANGUAGE SKILLS (Verbs / Adverbs)

▶ 1. An adverb can tell when, how or where, indicating time, manner or place. An adverb can be used to modify a verb, an adjective or another adverb.

Adverbs of time tell *when* or *how often*. They usually modify verbs.
Example: I went to the dentist *yesterday*.

Adverbs of place tell *where*. They usually modify verbs.
Example: Sue decided to go *back*.

Adverbs of manner tell *how* or *in what manner*. They usually modify verbs.
Example: My parents taught me to look *carefully* before crossing the street.

▶ 2. Compare adjectives and adverbs. Write the sentences below on the chalkboard. Have your child underline the adjectives and circle the adverbs in each sentence. Discuss the words as your child works. Ask your child to tell whether the adverbs tell time, manner or place.

The lumbering bear is a large, fur-bearing mammal.
The huge animals are found mainly in northern countries.
A surprised bear can be a dangerous animal.
Bears have long, strong claws that handily provide food.
Hungry bears will eat almost anything voraciously.
Thick, shaggy fur easily protects bears from the stings of angry bees.

▶ 3. Adverbs are often formed by adding *ly* to an adjective. If the adjective ends in *y*, change the *y* to *i*, then add *ly*.

Examples: sad ⟶ *sadly*   exact ⟶ *exactly*
          busy ⟶ *busily*   remote ⟶ *remotely*

Have your child copy the following adjectives on the chalkboard. Then, have him/her rewrite each one as an adverb: *eager, happy, quick, wary, angry, speedy, glad, hungry, lazy, close, neat, easy.*

▶ 4. Adjectives and adverbs may change form to show comparison. The endings *er* and *est* are added or the comparison words *more, most, less* and *least* are used. Do not use comparison words **and** *er* or *est* words. The following comparison examples are incorrect. The corrected sentences follow in italics.

I have the most best dog in the world.   He ran more slowlier than she did.
I have the best dog in the world.   *He ran more slowly than she did.*

Copy the following sentences on the chalkboard. Have your child rewrite each sentence correctly.

Masks can be made more easilier from paper bags than from cloth.
The most cheapest masks are made of bags.
Find a position where the bag rests most comfortabliest on your shoulders.
More better features can be drawn on the bag by your friend.
The most best circles can be drawn by tracing around a coin with a crayon.
Use markers to color the features on your mask more brightlier.
The most perfectest use for yarn on the mask is as hair.
After finishing, we laughed most hardest at the mask I made.

READING (Compare and Contrast)

To Walk the Sky Path contains several examples of onomatopoeia. Words that imitate the sounds they are associated with—such as *quack* or *whir*—are considered onomatopoetic. We can hear a lot of the sounds of Billie's camp through the author's choice of words. **Example:** "the kachung of the bull frogs." Have your child write a descriptive poem using onomatopoeia. Here are some words to get him/her started:

beep	buzz	clink	crash	ding-dong	hiss	ping	squeal
blip	chirp	clomp	creak	grind	honk	rustle	squish
bow-wow	chug	crack	cuckoo	growl	moo	smack	thump

Learn At Home, Grade 5

MATH (Chip Trading With Subtraction)

▶ 1. Each player will begin the game with one red chip. On the first roll, each player will need to trade the red chip for 10 blue chips, 1 blue chip for 10 green chips and 1 green chip for 10 yellow chips. Each turn, the player will roll the die and remove the number of yellow chips indicated. As a player runs out of yellow chips, he/she can trade in another green chip for 10 more. The object of the game is to be the first player to subtract all of his/her chips.

▶ 2. Here is a sample quiz:

Subtract.

1. 356,710
    − 247,356

2. 86,044
    − 15,852

Estimate the answer.

3. 3,457
    − 1,135

Subtract.

4. ___ − 29 = 12

5. 16 − ___ = 7

6. 58 − 19 = r
    r = ___

7. 11 min. 34 sec.
    − 9 min. 40 sec.

8. 4 lb. 8 oz.
    − 3 lb. 11 oz.

9. 3 weeks 5 days
    − 1 week 6 days

Solve.

10. A grocery store cashier was given a five-dollar bill to pay for $3.37 in groceries. How much change should the customer receive? _____

SCIENCE (Vertebrates)

▶ 1. The phylum *Chordata* is made up of animals with backbones. The name *vertebrates* comes from the vertebrae, the bone segments that make up the spinal column. There are five classes of vertebrates: fish, amphibians, reptiles, birds and mammals. Find a resource book that shows the skeletons of some of these animals. Discuss the function of the backbone and vertebrae in the support and protection of an animal's body. Have your child sort the pictures of vertebrates into those that live in the air, in water and on land. Encourage your child to glue or tape some of the pictures in his/her Science Log or to sketch some of the animals.

▶ 2. Ask your child to look up the terms in the dictionary. A *cold-blooded* animal is one whose body temperature changes with the temperature of its environment, and a *warm-blooded* animal is one whose body temperature remains constant. Can your child think of examples of each type of animal? Have your child describe the actions of a snake, lizard or salamander when it wants to become warmer or cooler. Ask your child to write his/her own definitions of *warm-blooded* and *cold-blooded* in his/her Science Log. Have your child also include an illustration of one animal from each category.

Irregular Verbs

Verbs that do not add **ed** to show the past tense are called **irregular verbs**. Irregular verbs change in spelling in the past tense.

Examples:

Present	Past	Past with helpers
begin	*began*	*(has, have) begun*
see	*saw*	*(has, have) seen*
drive	*drove*	*(has, have) driven*

Fill in the blanks on the chart. You may refer to a dictionary.

Present	Past	Past with helpers
speak		
		taken
		ridden
choose		
	rang	
	went	
drink		
		driven
	drew	
know		
		eaten
do		

Underline the correct verb in each sentence below.

1. Martha has (began, begun) her research project.

2. First, she (chose, chosen) the topic.

3. She (drove, driven) many places to locate information.

4. Martha made a list of the interviews she had (did, done).

5. She (spoke, spoken) to people of many ages.

6. Many (knew, known) a great deal about the subject.

7. While interviewing people, Martha had (took, taken) notes.

8. Diagrams were (drew, drawn) for the project.

Learn At Home, Grade 5

Adverbs Modify

You have learned that adverbs modify verbs. An **adverb** can also modify **adjectives** and **other adverbs**. These adverbs usually tell **how much** or **to what degree**.

Examples:
> The eagle's descent was **very** steep.
> (modifies "steep," an adjective)
> The eagle attacked the fish **quite** suddenly.
> (modifies "suddenly," an adverb)

Underline only the adverbs in the sentences below that modify an adjective or another adverb. **Draw** an arrow to the word that each modifies. In the blank, **write** if the modified word is an adjective or an adverb.

1. The eagle spread its wings <u>very</u> wide. __*adverb*_____

2. It had to fly quite far to the lake. _____

3. The eagle is an extremely graceful bird. _____

4. It is much larger than most birds. _____

5. Its hooked beak is rather sharp. _____

6. The eagle watched the lake very carefully. _____

7. A large trout is really tasty food for the eagle. _____

8. A beautiful rainbow trout jumped quite suddenly out of the water. _____

9. The eagle has extremely sharp eyesight. _____

10. It swooped almost instantly toward the fish. _____

Complete each sentence with an adverb that modifies the adjective or adverb.

1. The eagle flew _____ low over the water's surface.

2. Then, it flew _____ high into the blue summer sky.

3. It landed in its nest _____ gently.

4. The eagle is a _____ majestic bird.

5. It has to be _____ patient as it hunts for food.

Conquering Compounds

barnyard
blastoff
brand-new
chairperson
cupboard
hide-and-seek
homesick
ice skate
jack-o'-lantern
peanut butter
polar bear
post office
seagull
snowstorm
topsy-turvy
town crier
yardstick
zip code

There are three types of compound words: (1) **closed compound**—two separate words joined together, that create a new meaning and written as one word; (2) **open compound**—two separate words create a new meaning, but the two words are not joined together; (3) **hyphenated compound**—two or more words, written separately but connected by a hyphen, create a new meaning.

Add a word or words to each word below to form a compound word from the spelling list.

1. cup _____

2. snow _____

3. home _____

4. barn _____

5. chair _____

6. yard _____

7. sea _____

8. hide- _____

9. brand- _____

10. polar _____

11. ice _____

12. peanut _____

13. blast _____

14. post _____

15. topsy- _____

16. town _____

17. zip _____

18. jack- _____

Learn At Home, Grade 5

Subtracting Different Units

Subtract the units. Regroup the feet and inches.

Example:

					+ 12 in.		2	
				2				
3 ft.	5 in.		3̶ ft.	5 in.		3̶ ft.	17 in.	
– 1 ft.	8 in.		– 1 ft.	8 in.		– 1 ft.	8 in.	
						1 ft.	9 in.	

Cannot take
8 from 5, so
regroup 1 foot.

1. 5 ft. 8 in.
   – 3 ft. 9 in.

2. 17 ft. 3 in.
   –   5 in.

3. 11 ft. 5 in.
   – 8 ft. 6 in.

4. 20 ft. 4 in.
   – 6 ft. 8 in.

5. 17 ft. 0 in.
   – 1 ft. 6 in.

6. 115 ft.
   – 7 ft. 8 in.

7. The carpenter's board was 8 ft. 8 in. long. She cut off 1 ft. 10 in. to use on a bench. How much of the board was left?

_____

Subtract the units. Regroup the days and weeks.

Example:

			2	+ 7 days		2	
3 weeks	1 day		3̶ weeks	1 day		3̶ weeks	8 days
– 1 week	5 days		– 1 week	5 days		– 1 week	5 days
						1 week	3 days

Cannot take 5 from 1,
so regroup 1 week.

8. 4 weeks 2 days
   – 2 weeks 5 days

9. 3 weeks 5 days
   – 1 week 2 days

10. 11 weeks 4 days
    – 7 weeks 4 days

Subtracting in Different Bases

Subtract the units. Regroup the pounds and ounces.

Example:

	17 lb.	3 oz.
−	12 lb.	5 oz.

16   + 16 oz.

	1̸7̸ lb.	3 oz.
−	12 lb.	5 oz.

16

	1̸7̸ lb.	19 oz.
−	12 lb.	5 oz.
	4 lb.	14 oz.

1.   5 lb. 8 oz.
   − 3 lb. 8 oz.

2.   17 lb. 3 oz.
   − 12 lb. 11 oz.

3.   9 lb. 11 oz.
   − 3 lb. 14 oz.

4.   2 lb. 5 oz.
   −   8 oz.

5.   1 lb. 8 oz.
   −   9 oz.

6.   7 lb.
   − 1 lb. 9 oz.

Subtract the units. Regroup the minutes and seconds.

Example:

	3 min.	25 sec.
−	1 min.	45 sec.

2   + 60 sec.

	3̸ min.	25 sec.
−	1 min.	45 sec.

2

	3̸ min.	85 sec.
−	1 min.	45 sec.
	1 min.	40 sec.

7.   7 min. 46 sec.
   − 3 min. 29 sec.

8.   4 min. 47 sec.
   − 3 min. 28 sec.

9.   9 min. 23 sec.
   − 8 min. 51 sec.

10.   4 min. 21 sec.
    − 2 min. 53 sec.

11.   12 min. 19 sec.
    −   8 min. 42 sec.

12.   16 min. 42 sec.
    −   8 min. 25 sec.

Learn At Home, Grade 5

Vertebrates

Vertebrates are animals with a backbone. Most vertebrates have a bony backbone, called a spinal column. The spinal column is made of bones called **vertebrae**.

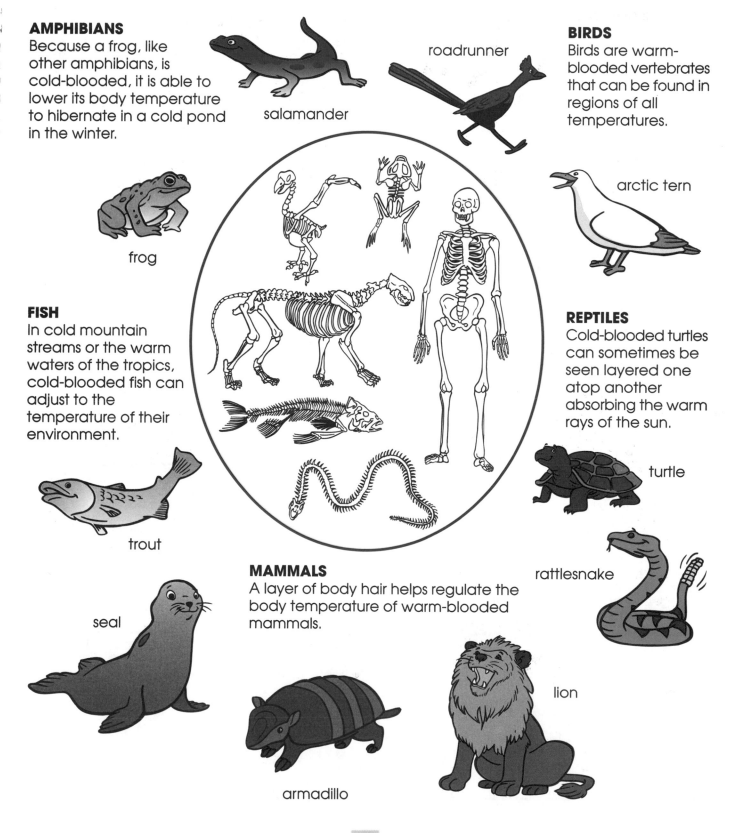

AMPHIBIANS
Because a frog, like other amphibians, is cold-blooded, it is able to lower its body temperature to hibernate in a cold pond in the winter.

salamander

frog

roadrunner

BIRDS
Birds are warm-blooded vertebrates that can be found in regions of all temperatures.

arctic tern

FISH
In cold mountain streams or the warm waters of the tropics, cold-blooded fish can adjust to the temperature of their environment.

trout

REPTILES
Cold-blooded turtles can sometimes be seen layered one atop another absorbing the warm rays of the sun.

turtle

rattlesnake

seal

MAMMALS
A layer of body hair helps regulate the body temperature of warm-blooded mammals.

lion

armadillo

	Language Skills	Spelling	Reading
Monday	Have your child choose a topic to write about in the form of a newspaper article. See today's Reading lesson. Then, have your child make a plan for writing and begin working on a rough draft of the story.	Pretest your child on these spelling words: baseball flagpole playhouse basketball harmless railway breakfast knickknack switchboard classroom lifetime taxicab driftwood motorcycle textbook firefly paperback tiptoe Have your child correct the pretest. Add personalized words and make two copies of this week's study list.	**Reading the Newspaper** Have your child read the daily newspaper this week. You will find daily activity suggestions listed here in the lesson plan. See also Reading, Week 7, numbers 1–7. Ask your child to read several short articles out loud today. Review the basic elements of a news story: *headline, byline, lead* and *body*. Have your child go back through the articles read today and highlight and label each of these elements.
Tuesday	**Prepositions:** Review prepositions and prepositional phrases. See Language Skills, Week 7, number 1. Play a game like "Simon Says." Direct your child with commands containing prepositional phrases. If you say *Simon says*, your child must repeat the prepositional phrase and perform the action. **Example:** You say, *Simon says put your hand on the table.* Your child says, *on the table* and then puts his/her hand on the table.	Review this week's spelling words. Have your child complete **Puzzling Compounds** (p. 85).	Cut out several articles and headlines from the newspaper. Put the articles in one pile and the headlines in another. Then, have your child try to match each article with the correct headline. Cut out another article from the front page of the newspaper. Leave off the headline. Have your child read the article, then dream up a headline that is catchy and expresses the main idea of the article.
Wednesday	Teach your child that prepositions may act as adjectives or adverbs. See Language Skills, Week 7, number 2. Have your child complete **Prepositional Phrases** (p. 84).	Have your child use each of this week's spelling words correctly in a sentence.	Use the newspaper to test your child's sorting and sequencing abilities. Cut apart several comic strips, frame by frame. Mix up the frames in one large pile. Have your child first sort the frames by comic, then arrange the frames of each comic in a sequence that makes sense.
Thursday	Have your child write directions for someone else to follow. Each sentence should contain a preposition, and the directions should lead to a hidden prize. Have your child give the directions to another person to follow. **Example:** *Stand at the back door. Walk two steps into the entry and turn to the left. Jump over the shoes lying on the floor. Walk around the dining room table. Look next to the bowl on the kitchen counter. Find the surprise hidden under the towel.*	Have your child study this week's spelling words.	Look at the editorial page in your local newspaper. Have your child read some of the letters to the editor and look at the political cartoons. Discuss an issue that your child feels strongly about. Then, have him/her write a brief letter to the editor on that topic. If there is time, have your child also draw a political cartoon on the same subject. If the topic is relevant, help your child submit his/her letter and cartoon to your local paper.
Friday	Give your child a list of common prepositions: *about, above, across, against, around, at, before, behind, below, beside, between, by, down, for, from, into, of, on, over, through, toward, under, up, with.* Then, have your child write ten original sentences containing prepositions. Once he/she has written the sentences, have your child tell you a story based on the sentences.	Give your child the final spelling test. Have your child record pretest and final test words in his/her Word Bank.	Look at the national and world news in your local newspaper. Have your child read several articles. For each one, have your child locate the cities, states and countries mentioned.

Learn At Home, Grade 5

Math	Science	Social Studies
Multiplication Review the multiplication facts. *See* Math, Week 7. Have your child complete a five-minute timed test, **Timed Multiplication** (p. 86). *See* Math, Week 7, number 1. Reteach, if necessary, until your child has memorized the multiplication facts. Record the time it took your child to complete the test, as well as his/her accuracy. Give your child the test again later this week or next week. Compare the results.	**Amphibians and Reptiles** Provide books and other resources on amphibians and reptiles for your child's reference. *See* Science, Week 7, number 1. Have your child take notes on amphibians and reptiles in his/her Science Log. Have him/her list examples of each type of animal and describe their characteristics. *How are these animals useful to humans?*	**Revolutionary War** Many events and government acts in the mid-1700s fueled the colonists' resentment of the British. Have your child read about the Boston Massacre and Boston Tea Party. *What government acts led to these events? See* Social Studies, Week 7, number 1. Have your child continue to add events to the time line begun in Week 1.
Review the commutative and associative properties of multiplication. *See* Math, Week 7, numbers 2 and 3.	Have your child create a chart or diagram to compare and contrast amphibians and reptiles. Have him/her select one representative from each category as an example for the comparison. Have your child take the information from this chart and write an organized paragraph that explains the similarities and differences.	Have your child read about Parliament's "Intolerable Acts." Have your child think about the struggle between the British and the American colonists in terms of *cause and effect*. Have your child write a cause and effect statement about the "Intolerable Acts."
Teach multiplication with regrouping. When a product is 10 or more, the value of the ones place is written in the product, but the value of the tens place is carried over to the next place to be added to that product. **Example:** 　　　　1 　　　25 　　　x 3 　　　75 Have your child complete **Multiplication (One-Digit Multiplier)** (p. 87).	Discuss reasons why certain amphibians and reptiles have become endangered. What measures have been taken to help protect these animals? Discuss the many theories about the extinction of animals, such as dinosaurs. *See* Science, Week 7, number 2.	Have your child read about the significance of Paul Revere's ride. *See* Social Studies, Week 7, number 2. Discuss the events of the battles at Lexington and Concord. Have your child find Lexington and Concord on a current map of Massachusetts. Have your child read "Paul Revere's Ride," a poem written by Henry Wadsworth Longfellow.
Show your child how easy it is to multiply by tens. To multiply by 10, simply add a final zero to the other factor. **Example:** 42 x 10 = 420 To multiply by 20, multiply the other factor by 2, then add a final zero. **Example:** 3 x 20 = 60 When multiplying by a multiple of ten, bring down the same number of zeros and multiply by the remaining single digit. *See* Math, Week 7, number 4.	If possible, arrange a trip with your child to a nearby zoo or nature center to observe amphibians and reptiles. *See* Science, Week 7, number 3.	Have your child read about and discuss the men who were pivotal in relations between the colonies and England from 1754 to 1775. *See* Social Studies, Week 7, number 3. Have your child begin a chart (arranged in chronological order) of famous Americans. *See* Social Studies, Week 7, number 4. Allow your child to personalize the chart with pictures or other information, if desired. Keep the chart posted in the room for quick reference.
Teach your child how to use estimation in multiplication problems. To estimate a product, round the factors. Round both factors to the highest place of the smaller number. **Example:**　176 → 180 　　　　　　x 24 → x 20 　　　　　　　　　3,600 Give your child a series of multiplication problems to estimate, then solve. Have your child check his/her work if the answer and estimate are not close.	Have your child write "What-Am-I?" riddles about amphibians or reptiles. Possible subjects for the riddles might include frogs, salamanders, alligators, dinosaurs, crocodiles, turtles, boa constrictors, rattlesnakes, coral snakes, garter snakes and cobras. Encourage your child to be creative!	Arrange for your child to perform some community service.

TEACHING SUGGESTIONS AND ACTIVITIES

LANGUAGE SKILLS (Prepositions)

▶ 1. *Prepositions* are words that show relationships between other words, such as *above*, *between*, *over* and *under*. A preposition never stands alone; it always appears in a phrase. This phrase is called a prepositional phrase. **Examples:** *in* the doghouse, *after* a huge dinner, *before* noon

▶ 2. Prepositional phrases may act as different parts of speech, such as adjectives and adverbs. When a prepositional phrase modifies a noun, it acts like an adjective. **Example:** The house <u>around the corner</u> is red. When the phrase modifies a verb, it acts like an adverb. **Example:** The dog ran <u>around the tree</u>.

READING (Reading the Newspaper)

▶ 1. Have your child look through the newspaper without any discussion at first. Then, talk about the way the paper is organized by section and page number. Refer to the index to find various features. Point out the headline, byline and body of an article. Ask your child to find given sections or features by using the index.

▶ 2. People do not usually read a newspaper from cover to cover—they scan the headlines and read first paragraphs to determine which stories might interest them. The first paragraph contains the who, what, where, when and why of the article. This piques the reader's interest and "leads" him/her into the story. For that reason, it is called the lead. Have your child read several leads and list the who, what, when, where and why of one article.

▶ 3. Use a black marker to black out every tenth word in an article before you give it to your child to read. Have your child fill in the missing words using context clues.

▶ 4. Send your child on a newspaper scavenger hunt. Prepare questions that can be answered by searching in the newspaper. Think of questions that will lead your child to look in different areas of the newspaper.

    Examples: What store is having a 50% off sale?
                 What team won the game played in Los Angeles yesterday?
                 What European leader met with the U.S. president today?
                 What will the weather be like on Tuesday?
                 What chemical gained approval from the FDA last week?

▶ 5. Have your child locate parts of speech and special types of words. For example, tell your child to circle all the nouns in an article in red, the adjectives in yellow and the verbs in blue. Or, tell your child to underline possessives and circle compound words and contractions.

▶ 6. Have your child write a newspaper article about an event from a familiar book of fiction.

▶ 7. If an article in the newspaper captures your child's interest, find a book in the library on that same topic.

MATH (Multiplication)

BACKGROUND
Memorizing multiplication facts is an important basis for success at higher math. Being able to quickly solve simple multiplication problems will allow your child to consider the meaning and application of a lesson, rather than concentrating on the routine operation of multiplication.

▶ 1. Provide your child with a few tips on how best to approach a timed test.
    a. Quickly review the problems and solve those you have memorized.
    b. On a second pass, solve the problems which take a little more concentration.
    c. On a third pass, make an educated guess on those with which you are having greater difficulty.

        Learn At Home, Grade 5

Watch your child complete the problems on **Timed Multiplication** (p. 86). Observe the facts that are difficult for your child. Note his/her strategies for solving the facts that are not memorized. Discuss your observations with your child. Then, focus your teaching on the areas your child finds most challenging.

▶ 2. The commutative property of multiplication asserts that the factors in a multiplication problem may be arranged in any order and still produce the same product.

Examples:
4 x 3 = 12   2 x 6 x 4 = 48   3 x 275 = 825
3 x 4 = 12   4 x 2 x 6 = 48   275 x 3 = 825

▶ 3. The associative property of multiplication asserts that the factors in a multiplication problem may be grouped in different ways and still produce the same product.

Example: (6 x 7) x 2 = 6 x (7 x 2)
                 (42) x 2 = 6 x (14)
                     84 = 84

▶ 4. When multiplying by a multiple of 10, multiply by the single digits and add a zero.
When multiplying by a multiple of 100, multiply by the single digit then add two zeros.

Examples: 12 x 30 = 36**0**   4 x 200 = 8**00**

SCIENCE (Amphibians and Reptiles)

▶ 1. Both amphibians and reptiles are cold-blooded animals. Have your child compare amphibians to reptiles. *How are they alike? How are they different?* Have your child describe their habitats, skin, movement, appearance, diet and means of reproduction. Introduce the term *metamorphosis*. If possible, obtain some frog eggs or tadpoles. Create a frog habitat with a large jar and some pond water. Have your child observe the frog eggs in the water for several weeks, recording any changes in the Science Log. Once the tadpoles begin to develop, transfer them to a large, shallow container with a rock for the frog to sit on. Feed the tadpoles tiny bits of cooked vegetables or meat. Have your child review his/her observations and draw a diagram of the frog's life cycle.

▶ 2. Obtain a list of endangered animals. Ask your child to read through the list and highlight the names of those animals that are amphibians or reptiles. Discuss the various reasons why animals have become endangered or extinct: destruction of habitat, change in climate, loss of food source, disease, domination of other animals, overkill by humans, catastrophic events (earthquakes, volcanoes or meteor collisions), natural selection. Discuss efforts being made to protect endangered animals. How can your child help in these efforts? Encourage him/her to find out!

▶ 3. Have your child prepare a list for the trip to the zoo or nature center. The list may contain predictions about what he/she will see or questions for caretakers. Call ahead to check on feeding times and shows. Ask if special programs on amphibians or reptiles are offered.

SOCIAL STUDIES (Revolutionary War)

▶ 1. Have your child research one of the following acts of British Parliament: the Sugar Act, the Quartering Act, the Stamp Act, the Townshend Acts, the Tea Act. Have him/her write an organized paragraph about the events leading up to the act and those following it.

▶ 2. Have your child read a biography or biographical sketch of Paul Revere from an encyclopedia or reference book. Then, have your child list some key facts about him in chronological order.

▶ 3. Your child should know the following names: John Adams, Samuel Adams, John Hancock, Patrick Henry, Thomas Paine and George Washington. Have your child do research to become familiar with the contributions of these men.

▶ 4. Have your child make a chart with five columns. Write *Early Settlers/Colonists* at the top of column one and *Believers in Freedom (1754–1775)* at the top of column two. Have your child list names of men and women studied so far who fit into each of these categories. Leave the remaining columns open for now.

Prepositional Phrases

A **prepositional phrase** is a group of words that begins with a preposition and ends with the object of the preposition.

Example: *Water makes up about 65 percent of the human body*.

Circle the prepositional phrases in the sentences.

1. An adult skeleton consists of about 200 bones.

2. The body of a 160-pound man contains about 5 quarts of blood.

3. People who live in high altitudes may have more blood flowing in their veins.

4. Our skin helps protect our inner tissues from the outside world.

If a prepositional phrase modifies a noun or pronoun, it acts as an **adjective**.
If a prepositional phrase modifies a verb, it acts as an **adverb**.

Examples: *Fluids **in the inner ear** help us maintain our balance.* (adjective)
*The doctors talked **in loud voices**.* (adverb)

Circle the prepositional phrase in each sentence. Then, identify it as an **adjective** or **adverb** on the line.

1. The muscles in the human body number 600. _____

2. All adults should brush their 32 teeth with great care. _____

3. Our skin might burn in the hot sun. _____

4. Every person on the earth is warm-blooded. _____

5. The man went through the hospital doors. _____

6. The temperature inside the body is about 98.6°. _____

7. The dentist looked inside my mouth. _____

Learn At Home, Grade 5

Puzzling Compounds

baseball	basketball	breakfast	classroom	driftwood	firefly
flagpole	harmless	knickknack	lifetime	motorcycle	paperback
playhouse	railway	switchboard	taxicab	textbook	tiptoe

Write a spelling word that matches each clue.
Then, read down the boxed letters to solve the riddle.

1. a place to learn ☐ _ _ _ _ _ _ _ _
2. the morning meal _ ☐ _ _ _ _ _ _ _
3. not capable of hurting _ ☐ _ _ _ _ _ _
4. game played with a bat and a ball ☐ _ _ _ _ _ _ _
5. to walk softly ☐ _ _ _ _ _ _
6. sometimes called a lightning bug _ _ ☐ _ _ _ _
7. one's entire period of existence _ _ ☐ _ _ _ _
8. it supports Old Glory _ _ _ _ _ _ _ ☐

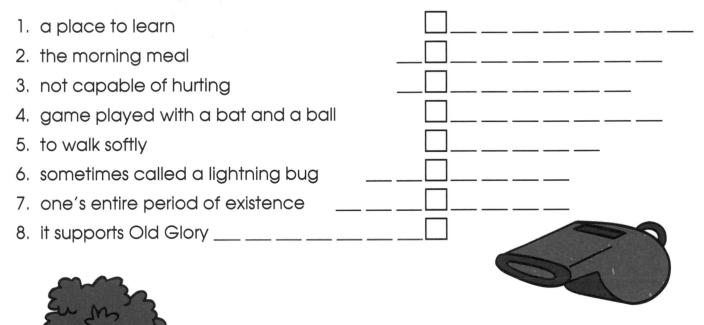

Riddle: *Which tree is the most difficult to get along with?*

Answer: _____

Write a spelling word that belongs in each group.

1. hoop, whistle, _____
2. tracks, railroad, _____
3. school, subjects, _____
4. toys, games, _____
5. wood, ashore, _____

6. circuit, panel, _____
7. read, novel, _____
8. 2-wheeled, helmet, _____
9. fare, driver, _____
10. trinket, decoration _____

Timed Multiplication

1	9	4	8	2	5	7	12
x 1	x 3	x 10	x 3	x 10	x 7	x 4	x 3

10	12	10	4	7	11	6	3
x 3	x 9	x 5	x 9	x 5	x 2	x 6	x 2

5	10	9	3	5	9	8	6
x 8	x 4	x 4	x 3	x 9	x 6	x 5	x 7

4	11	12	1	7	10	2	4
x 8	x 3	x 5	x 4	x 7	x 6	x 7	x 7

3	6	9	5	11	3	10	1
x 4	x 8	x 5	x 10	x 9	x 5	x 7	x 5

2	8	9	4	9	8	7	4
x 6	x 7	x 2	x 6	x 8	x 8	x 9	x 5

10	3	6	11	9	2	12	7
x 8	x 6	x 10	x 6	x 7	x 5	x 10	x 10

Learn At Home, Grade 5

| **Example A** (no regrouping) | 234 x 2 / 468 | **Step 1** Multiply ones. 2 x 4 = 8 **Step 2** Multiply tens. 2 x 3 = 6 **Step 3** Multiply hundreds. 2 x 2 = 4 |

| **Example B** (regrouping) | 2 1 / 563 x 4 / 2,252 | **Step 1** Multiply ones. 4 x 3 = 12 ones = 1 ten 2 ones. Carry the 1. **Step 2** Multiply tens. 4 x 6 + 1 = 25 tens = 2 hundreds 5 tens. Carry the 2. **Step 3** Multiply hundreds. 4 x 5 + 2 = 22 hundreds = 2 thousands 2 hundreds. |

| **Example C** (regrouping and zeros) | 7 5 / 7,086 x 9 / 63,774 | **Step 1** Multiply ones. 9 x 6 = 54 ones = 5 tens 4 ones. Carry the 5. **Step 2** Multiply tens. 9 x 8 + 5 = 77 tens = 7 hundreds 7 tens. Carry the 7. **Step 3** Multiply hundreds. 9 x 0 + 7 = 7 hundreds. **Step 4** Multiply thousands. 9 x 7 = 63 thousands = 6 ten-thousands 3 thousands. |

Multiply.

1. 323
    x   8

2. 1,132
    x   2

3. 789
    x   5

4. 4,008
    x   7

5. 2,580
    x   3

6. 888
    x   6

7. 4,234
    x   4

8. 589
    x   9

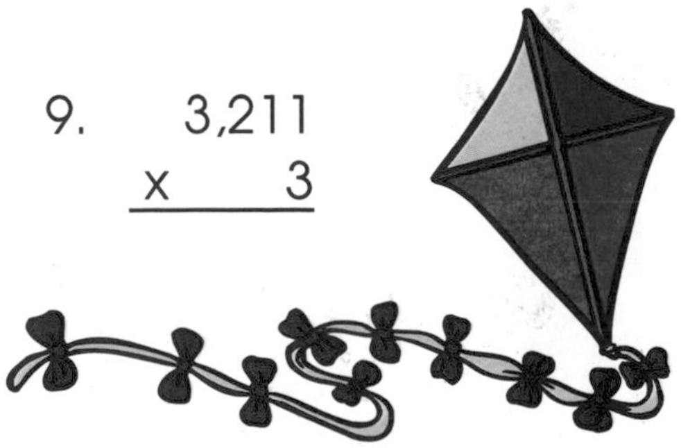

9. 3,211
    x   3

Learn At Home, Grade 5

Language Skills	**Spelling**	**Reading**
Monday Have your child write a plot summary for an episode of his/her favorite television show. The summary should include the names of the characters, the setting and the main idea of the episode. To plan the writing, have your child list ideas for the problem, events leading to the climax and the solution to the problem. Once your child has mapped out the plot, have him/her begin work on a rough draft for the story. *See* Language Skills, Week 8, number 1.	Pretest your child on these spelling words: aren't I'd wasn't can't isn't weren't couldn't let's we've didn't shouldn't wouldn't hasn't they're you'd he's they've you're Have your child correct the pretest. Add personalized words and make two copies of this week's study list.	**Pronouns** Introduce *Addie's Dakota Winter* by Laurie Lawlor. Have your child read chapter 1, then write in his/her Reading Journal about Addie's changing feelings as she walked to school. Teach your child about the different cases of pronouns. *See* Reading, Week 8, number 1.
Tuesday **Conjunctions:** Teach your child how to use conjunctions to join words, phrases or sentences. The most common conjunctions, which your child should already recognize, include *and, but* and *or.* Other conjunctions include *unless, because, neither/nor, while* and *as if.* Have your child complete **Conjunctions** (p. 92).	Review this week's spelling words. Have your child complete **Contraction Action** (p. 95).	Have your child read chapters 2 and 3 of *Addie's Dakota Winter.* Then, have him/her answer the following questions in his/her Reading Journal: *Why do you think finding a friend is so important to Addie? Do you believe Tilla's stories?*
Wednesday **Interjections and Direct Address:** Teach your child the proper use of interjections. Also discuss the use of direct address in a sentence. *See* Language Skills, Week 8, number 2. Have your child complete **Interjections and Direct Address** (p. 93).	Have your child use each of this week's spelling words correctly in a sentence.	Have your child read chapter 4 of *Addie's Dakota Winter.* Review similes. *See* Language Skills, Week 1, number 3. Write ten similes related to the story. **Example:** *Tilla's brother is as strong as an ox.* Have your child underline the two things being compared in each sentence. Then, give your child a list of partial similes. **Examples:** *Miss Brophy is... , ...as red as a fire engine.* Have your child finish each phrase.
Thursday Teach your child to distinguish between definite and indefinite articles. *See* Language Skills, Week 8, number 3. Have your child complete **Articles** (p. 94).	Have your child study this week's spelling words.	Have your child read chapters 5 and 6 of *Addie's Dakota Winter.* Then, have him/her answer the following questions in his/her Reading Journal: *Do you think Miss Brophy was right to whip the Connolly brothers? Explain. Tell about the incident from the Connolly brothers' point of view. What would you have done about the antelope if you were George and Addie's parents?*
Friday Help your child publish a piece of his/her writing. For more information on publishing your child's work, see page 6.	Give your child the final spelling test. Have your child record pretest and final test words in his/her Word Bank.	Have your child read chapter 7 of *Addie's Dakota Winter.* Review pronouns. Introduce the term *referent.* Explain that a referent is the word to which a pronoun refers. **Example:** *Billie visited the Miller family. He thought they ate unusual food.* In this case, the pronouns *he* and *they* refer to *Billie* and *the Miller family,* respectively. *See* Reading, Week 8, number 2.

Learn At Home, Grade 5

Math	**Science**	**Social Studies**
Teach your child how to perform multiplication with a two-digit factor. *See* Math, Week 8, number 1. Have your child complete **Multiplication (Two-Digit Multiplier)** (p. 96).	**Birds** Provide books, field guides and other resources on birds for your child's reference. *See* Science, Week 8, number 1. Have your child take notes on birds in his/her Science Log. Have him/her list examples of different types of birds (waterfowl, flightless, etc.) and describe their characteristics. *In what ways are birds useful to humans? What kinds of products come from birds?*	**Revolutionary War** Have your child read about George Washington's role in the Revolutionary War. Then, have your child write a persuasive article about why George Washington was the right leader for the Americans. Have your child continue to add dates and events to the time line begun in Week 1.
Teach your child how to multiply with a three- or four-digit multiplicand. **Examples:** $\begin{array}{r} 3{,}492 \\ \times\ 23 \end{array}$ $\begin{array}{r} 176 \\ \times\ 19 \end{array}$ Have your child complete **Multiplication Maze** (p. 97).	If possible, arrange to attend an Audubon Society meeting or a bird-watching event. Discuss the equipment needed for bird-watching. Have your child prepare a list of questions to ask one of the members or naturalists concerning birds and the member's interest in birds. You could also plan to visit an aviary or wetland preserve.	The Declaration of Independence was penned by Thomas Jefferson. The Americans wanted the world to know why they were breaking away from England. Read the Declaration of Independence with your child and discuss. *See* Social Studies, Week 8, number 1. Have your child write a summary of the important points of the Declaration of Independence. *See* Social Studies, Week 8, number 2.
Assess concepts that your child is having trouble with and review. If you have time, take a few minutes to review basic multiplication facts with the activity sheet, **Timed Multiplication** (p. 86). Memorizing these basic facts will help your child with the more complex multiplication problems being discussed this week.	Introduce bird-watching as a hobby. Teach your child how to use a field guide and binoculars. Select an outdoor study site for bird-watching. You're bound to see many different types of birds at a location where two habitats meet (e.g., a field near a lake or stream). Have your child bring along and fill out the **Bird-Watcher's List** (p. 99).	Discuss the signing of the Declaration of Independence. Use the following questions to guide your discussion: *How many delegates signed the Declaration of Independence? Why is John Hancock's signature at the top and so large? Why didn't George Washington sign it? Did this document signal the beginning or the end of the Revolutionary War? Where is the Liberty Bell located? Why did it ring on July 4, 1776? Why is its name so appropriate?*
Teach multiplication with a three-digit multiplier. *See* Math, Week 8, number 2. Have your child complete **Puzzling Cross Number** (p. 98).	Have your child identify your state bird. Then, give your child an outline map of the U.S. You may use **United States Map** (p. 205). Have your child fill in the name of each state's state bird. Several states may have the same state bird. Once finished, have your child write a story or poem from the perspective of his/her favorite bird. The story may be funny or serious. Have your child include an illustration with the story or poem.	Have your child consider the significance of July 4. How might life be different today had the Declaration of Independence not been signed? Have your child write an essay on the importance of Independence Day.
Give your child a lesson in economics. Help him/her design a project that requires shopping for large quantities of different products. (You do not need to carry out the project.) Project suggestions include setting up a lemonade stand, planning a family picnic or building a fort. Have your child determine the price and quantity of each item needed for the project. Using multiplication and addition, have your child estimate, then figure the actual cost of the project.	Have your child build a simple bird feeder from a paper or plastic milk carton. *See* Science, Week 8, number 2. Keep a field guide near the window so that you and your child can identify the species of any visitors.	Arrange for your child to perform some community service.

TEACHING SUGGESTIONS AND ACTIVITIES

LANGUAGE SKILLS (Conjunctions / Interjections and Direct Address)

▶ 1. Have your child continue to work on writing and editing the television script all week. For a creative way to publish this script, have your child make a mini-television from a cardboard box. Let your child draw several scenes from the story and tape them together in a long horizontal strip, then pull the strip through the mini-television set while narrating the episode.

▶ 2. An *interjection* is a word or phrase that expresses emotion and is set apart from the rest of the sentence. Interjections are separated from the rest of the sentence by commas, or they can stand alone. Strong interjections are separated by exclamation points; mild ones are separated by commas. When someone is addressed directly, the name is set off by a comma.

   Direct address is when someone is being spoken to directly. The person's name is set apart by a comma.

   Examples: *Wow!* Did you see that?
   Please, I have asked you twenty times to stop cracking your knuckles.
   Hurry! Look over there!
   Suzanne, here is a note for your dad.

▶ 3. There is just one definite article: *the*. *The* refers to a particular person, place or thing. Indefinite articles, on the other hand, are less specific. The articles *a* and *an* do not identify a particular object, but rather any of that type of object. Demonstrate this difference with the following pair of sentences: *I ate the apple. I ate an apple.* Ask your child which sentence is more specific. Why? Write the following noun phrases on the chalkboard and discuss why each article is used. Ask your child to use each phrase in a sentence.

a rainy day	an ugly duckling	a white rabbit
the tall boys	a house	a wonderful dinner

READING (Pronouns)

▶ 1. There are three cases of pronouns. Teach your child to recognize when to use each case. Have your child look for examples of each in *Addie's Dakota Winter*.

   a. *Subjective Case:* The pronoun is the subject, as in **I** *rode my bike on the bumpy sidewalk.* Subjective pronouns include *I, you, he, she, they* and *it.*

   b. *Objective Case:* The pronoun is the direct object, as in *Addie rode with* **me**. Objective pronouns include *me, you, him, her, us, them* and *it.*

   c. *Possessive Case:* The pronoun shows possession, as in *Felix borrowed* **my** *pencil.* Possessive pronouns include *my, mine, your, yours, his, her, hers, our, ours, their, theirs* and *its.*

▶ 2. Gather (or write your own) sentences that contain pronouns and their referents. In each case, have your child underline the pronoun, circle its referent and draw a line to connect the words. Then, have your child use pronouns to write five or six sentences about *Addie's Dakota Winter* (or other favorite story). Have your child underline each pronoun and circle its referent.

MATH (Multiplication)

▶ 1. A two-digit number can be written as the sum of two parts: tens and ones.

   Examples: 39 = 30 + 9   42 = 40 + 2   77 = 70 + 7

   In a multiplication problem with a two-digit multiplier, the tens and ones are multiplied separately. The products are then added together.

```
  42           42            42           42
x 21    =    x  1     +    x 20     =   + 840
  42         840          882
             840
```

Learn At Home, Grade 5

2. A three-digit number can be written as the sum of three parts: hundreds, tens and ones.

Examples: 127 = 100 + 20 + 7   348 = 300 + 40 + 8   777 = 700 + 70 + 7

In a multiplication problem with a three-digit multiplier, the hundreds, tens and ones are multiplied separately. The products are then added together.

$$
\begin{array}{ccccccccc}
246 & & 246 & & 246 & & 246 & & \mathbf{246} \\
\underline{\times 321} & = & \underline{\times\ 1} & + & \underline{\times\ 20} & + & \underline{\times\ 300} & = & \mathbf{4{,}920} \\
& & \mathbf{246} & & \mathbf{4{,}920} & & \mathbf{73{,}800} & & \underline{\mathbf{+\ 73{,}800}} \\
& & & & & & & & \mathbf{78{,}966}
\end{array}
$$

SCIENCE (Birds)

1. There is a great variety of bird species. Read the different characteristics below. Have your child name one or two birds that are known for each characteristic. The first one has been done for you.

small (*hummingbird, wren*)	large	has few enemies
brightly colored	dull color	has large wingspan
lives in cold climates	lives in warm climates	has small wingspan
cannot fly	can swim	endangered
predatory	scavenger	extinct
kept as pets	noisy	lives along the seacoast
dives into water	never found near water	lives in forests
eats mostly fish	eats mostly insects	likes to wade in water
eats mostly worms	eats mostly seeds	likes to swim
eats mostly nectar	eats mostly berries	can mimic human voices
migrates over long distances	does not migrate	sings beautiful songs
builds nests on the ground	builds nests in trees	has long legs
has a long neck	has a short neck	has short legs

2. Cut a hole in the side of a milk carton. A bird should be able to perch on the edge of the hole and reach inside. Fill the carton with seeds up to the bottom of the hole. Hang the feeder from a tree branch just outside a window. If you have pine cones in your area, you can make another bird treat. Cover a cone with a peanut butter and suet mixture, then roll the sticky cone in birdseed. Hang from a tree branch.

SOCIAL STUDIES (Revolutionary War)

1. Through reading and discussion, your child will come to recognize the people and events surrounding the writing and adoption of the Declaration of Independence. Discuss the importance of self-government as opposed to the monarchy of England and other European countries. Richard Henry Lee proposed that the colonies should be free and independent of England, and an agreement was made at the Continental Congress to write a document in which this expression of freedom would be known to the world. Have your child read about the writing and debating of the Declaration of Independence.

2. Obtain a copy of the Declaration of Independence. The original document is preserved in a special case in the National Archives Building in Washington, D.C. The Declaration of Independence can be divided into four main parts: the Preamble (which gives the reasons for writing the document), a Declaration of Rights (a description of rights summarized below), a Bill of Indictment (27 statements of abuse from the king), and a Statement of Independence (the king left them no other option than to declare independence). Some of the most important rights that the document declared were these: all people are created equal, and all people are born with certain rights that no one can take away, including life, liberty and the pursuit of happiness.

Conjunctions

A conjunction joins words, groups of words or entire sentences. The most common conjunctions are **and**, **or**, **but**.

Examples:

*Christian Huygens **and** Jean Cassini made discoveries about Saturn.* (joins subjects)

*The Italian astronomer Galileo first saw Saturn's rings through a telescope, **but** the rings weren't very clear.* (joins sentences)

*He discovered the rings in the early 1600s **and** thought they were large satellites.* (joins predicates)

Add a conjunction to each sentence below.

1. Did you know that Saturn takes about $29\frac{1}{2}$ Earth-years to orbit the Sun, _____ are you still looking up that fact?

2. Saturn _____ Earth have very different day lengths.

3. Earth's day is about 24 hours, _____ Saturn's is only about $10\frac{1}{2}$ hours.

4. Saturn has 23 satellites that have been discovered, _____ Earth has only one.

5. Saturn's natural satellites all have different names, _____ Earth's satellite is just called "the Moon."

6. Saturn has many rings that surround it, _____ Earth has none.

Add a conjunction to each phrase below that describes Saturn.

1. beautiful _____ majestic

2. far away, _____ gigantic

3. larger than Earth, _____ lighter in comparison

4. shorter days than Earth _____ faster rotation

5. atmosphere of mostly hydrogen _____ helium

6. beautiful rings _____ not the only planet with them

Interjections and Direct Address

Strong interjections, which show great feeling, are followed by exclamation points.

Mild interjections, such as **now**, **well** and **yes**, are set apart by commas.

A comma or commas are used to set apart the name of a person being directly spoken to, or addressed, in a sentence. This is called **direct address**.

Examples:
*   **Ugh!** *That soup is horrible.* (strong interjection)
*   **No**, *I haven't finished my homework yet.* (mild interjection)
*   **Sue**, *please hand me the pencil.* (direct address)
*   *Thank you,* **Jean**, *for your contribution.* (direct address)

Add commas and exclamation points where they are needed in the following sentences.

1. Yes we will finish the science project soon.
2. Wow I forgot that it must be completed by Friday.
3. Oh I forgot that the materials for the experiment are at home.
4. Jim bring the microscope to the science lab.
5. Now Leonard it's your turn to work on the experiment.
6. Will the research for the project be completed soon Amy?
7. No Mrs. Clarke it will take at least another week.
8. Yikes That was a scary experiment you did Mark.

Add commas and exclamation points where they are needed in the following sentences. In the blank, **write** the letter of the reason each punctuation mark is used. Some have two answers.

A. Interjection   **B.** Direct Address

1. _____ Lewis will you attempt this experiment on air pressure?
2. _____ No I need to work on my electricity project Sam.
3. _____ I need some help Mr. Johnson with my electrical circuit.
4. _____ The science lab is too crowded to set up the project Ms. Chang.
5. _____ Cool I would love to use the other lab.
6. _____ Yes I'll try to set up the project in that room Sarah.
7. _____ Well that solved my problem.

Articles

A, **an** and **the** are special kinds of adjectives called **articles**.

Use **a** before singular nouns that begin with a consonant sound.
Example: *a* lizard

Use **an** before singular nouns that begin with a vowel sound or a silent **h**.
Examples: *an* insect   *an* hour

Use **the** before singular or plural nouns beginning with any letter.
Examples: *the* lizards   *the* branch

Write a, **an** or **the** in the blanks to complete the paragraph.

There are nearly 3,000 different kinds of lizards. _____ lizard may have _____ tail that is much longer than its body. _____ lizard may even leave its tail behind when escaping from _____ enemy. _____ lizard then grows _____ new tail. *Dinosaur* is _____ word that means "terrible lizard." But _____ dinosaur and _____ lizard are not in _____ same family. Most lizards hatch from _____ leathery egg. _____ chameleon is _____ type of lizard that actually changes color for many different reasons. _____ chameleon may change color if it is frightened. It also changes color in response to _____ change in temperature or light. _____ chameleon gets close enough to shoot out its tongue to capture _____ insect to eat. _____ chameleon's tongue may be as long as its body. Lizards are truly _____ interesting type of animal!

Complete each sentence below using **a**, **an** or **the**.

1. _____ insect would not taste as good to me as it does to lizards!
2. _____ lizard could lose its tail while escaping from its enemies.
3. _____ chameleon's eyes can move in two different directions at once.
4. Some geckos make _____ loud sound.
5. _____ claws of some gecko lizards can be drawn in like a cat's.

94

Learn At Home, Grade 5

Contraction Action

aren't
can't
couldn't
didn't
hasn't
he's
I'd
isn't
let's
shouldn't
they're
they've
wasn't
weren't
we've
wouldn't
you'd
you're

Write the correct contraction for each word pair.

you are _____   should not _____

would not _____   did not _____

I had _____   could not _____

let us _____   was not _____

we have _____   are not _____

you had _____   is not _____

has not _____   they have _____

he is _____   can not _____

they are _____   were not _____

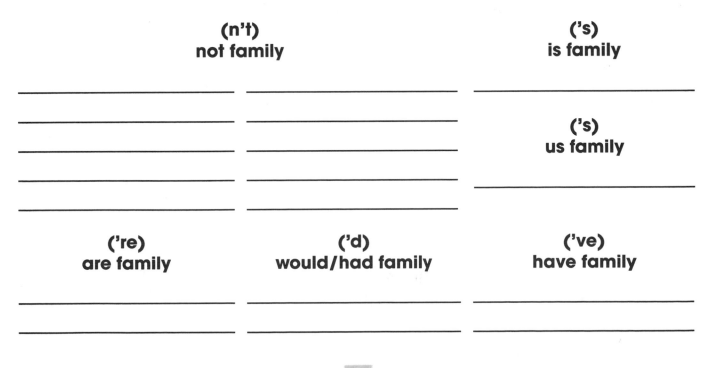

Now, put the contractions into word families.

(n't)
not family

_____   _____

_____   _____

_____   _____

_____   _____

_____

('s)
is family

_____

('s)
us family

_____

('re)
are family

_____

_____

('d)
would/had family

_____

_____

('ve)
have family

_____

_____

Multiplication (Two-Digit Multiplier)

Example A
(no regrouping)

```
    21
x   44
    84
+  840
   924
```

Step 1 Multiply by ones.
$4 \times 1 = 4$
$4 \times 2 = 8$

Step 2 Multiply by tens.
Add zero in the ones column.
$4 \times 1 = 4$
$4 \times 2 = 8$

Step 3 Add.
$84 + 840 = 924$

Example B
(regrouping)

```
     67
x    58
    536
+ 3,350
  3,886
```

Step 1 Multiply by ones.
$8 \times 7 = 56$ (Carry the 5.)
$8 \times 6 + 5 = 53$

Step 2 Multiply by tens.
Add zero in the ones column.
$5 \times 7 = 35$ (Carry the 3.)
$5 \times 6 + 3 = 33$

Step 3 Add.
$536 + 3,350 = 3,886$

Multiply.

1.
```
    43
x   33
```

2.
```
    55
x   46
```

3.
```
    78
x   68
```

4.
```
    39
x   27
```

5.
```
    21
x   87
```

6.
```
    77
x   24
```

7.
```
    44
x   16
```

8.
```
    80
x   71
```

9.
```
    65
x   49
```

Learn At Home, Grade 5

Multiplication Maze

These multiplication problems have already been done, but some of them are wrong. Check each problem. **Connect** the problems with correct answers to make a path for Zerpo to get back to his ship. Then, **correct** each wrong answer.

```
   863          904        6,520
 x  24        x  93       x   74
 21,712       85,072      582,480
```

```
                                         199
   663                                 x  98
 x  54          392          485       19,502
 53,802       x  28        x  53
              11,976       24,605        925
                                       x  68
   566                                 62,900
 x  74        2,576         466
 35,884       x  92        x  18        4,516
              236,992      8,388       x   22
                                       98,352
  5,563                     1,530
 x   35                    x   93
 194,705        719        152,290
              x  82          239                534
              69,958       x  15              x  34
                           4,585              28,156
  1,344                      329
 x   49                    x  16
 65,856         671        5,624
              x  68          793                861
              45,628       x  81              x  57
                           64,233             50,077
                             651
                           x  83
                           34,738
                 1,524
               x   43                          819
  2,316        64,532                        x  76
 x   27                     4,110            52,244
 62,532                    x   28
                           125,080
```

Learn At Home, Grade 5

Puzzling Cross Number

Solve the multiplication problems below. **Write** the answers in the puzzle.

Across

1.	462	5.	234	7.	926
	x 212		x 101		x 815

8.	624	11.	832
	x 783		x 458

13.	336	14.	801
	x 817		x 101

Down

2.	634	3.	208	4.	672
	x 755		x 422		x 833

6.	547	9.	926
	x 900		x 950

10.	698	12.	111
	x 741		x 111

Learn At Home, Grade 5

Bird-Watcher's List

Almost every bird-watcher keeps a list of the birds that he/she sees. Use the chart below to record the species of birds that you see, as well as the date, time and place that you see them. Accurate identification may also be made by identifying the sound of a bird. If a species is only heard and not seen, place an "**H**" after its name.

Observer _____

Date _____

SPECIES	DATE	TIME	LOCALITY

What bird did you see?
Look at the following.

1. Size

Is it bigger or smaller than a sparrow? robin? crow?

2. Shape

of head

of wings

of tail

3. Color and Marks

on body

on tail

on head

on wings

4. Habitat and Behaviors

What was it doing?

Where was it?

How does it fly?

Language Skills	Spelling	Reading

Monday

Review
Teach your child how to use a picture as inspiration for a writing topic. *See* Language Skills, Week 9, number 1. Give your child a picture for inspiration. Have your child follow the steps discussed to choose a topic, make a plan for writing and start working on a rough draft for a story.

Select words from the past eight weeks for this week's pretest.
Have your child correct the pretest. Add personalized words and make two copies of this week's study list.

Have your child read chapters 8 and 9 of *Addie's Dakota Winter*. Then, have your child construct a story map for these two chapters. A story map should include the following elements: characters, setting, problem, events and solution. Have your child present this information in a creative way.

Tuesday

Review vocabulary-building activities. Create a word puzzle for your child to solve. Then, have your child create his/her own word puzzle around a given topic. *See* Language Skills, Week 9, number 2 for another fun word game.

Write several pairs of guide words on the chalkboard. **Examples:** dairy – desert
mercury – monster
sleep – summer
Have your child find all the spelling words from the past eight weeks that fall between each pair of guide words. Have your child write the words in alphabetical order beneath the appropriate set of guide words.

Read ahead of your child (chapters 10–11) and write a list of questions (a study guide) for him/her to answer in writing. Include questions that ask your child to recall details and some that require personal reflection.
Have your child read chapters 10 and 11 of *Addie's Dakota Winter* and answer the prepared questions.

Wednesday

Review figurative language. Have your child define the terms *simile, metaphor, hyperbole* and *idiom*. Can he/she give an example of each? *See also* Language Skills, Week 9, number 3.

Have your child sort this week's spelling words by number of syllables. Which category contains the most words? Which category contains the fewest?

Have your child read chapters 12 and 13 of *Addie's Dakota Winter*. *See* Reading, Week 9 for a related activity on identifying proper nouns.

Thursday

Review regular and irregular verbs, action verbs and state-of-being verbs. Have your child complete **Review of Verbs** (p. 104). Reteach verb tenses or helping verbs, if necessary.

Have your child write a silly story using as many of the past eight weeks' spelling words as possible. Then, have him/her go back through the story and underline each spelling word. Further test your child's comprehension of the spelling words by asking him/her to replace some of the words with synonyms.

Have your child read the final chapters of *Addie's Dakota Winter*. Discuss your child's impressions of the book. Did he/she like it? What was his/her favorite part? What didn't he/she like about the book? Then, have your child compare *Addie's Dakota Winter* with another book he/she has read. How are the two books similar? How are they different?

Friday

Have your child write a story about a favorite mammal. The story can be fiction or non-fiction, but should include the different parts of speech studied so far. Provide your child with a detailed list of elements to include, such as adjectives, adverbs, linking verbs, helping verbs, interjections, prepositions, conjunctions and figurative language. Assess whether your child understands the proper use of each of these elements.

Give your child the final spelling test.

Have your child write a review of *Addie's Dakota Winter* as if for a newspaper. The review should include a summary of the story as well as your child's own opinions. Discuss who might be the audience for this piece of writing. Encourage your child to keep the audience in mind when writing. Edit the article and have your child proofread it carefully. You may wish to submit the finished piece to a children's magazine.

Learn At Home, Grade 5

Math	Science	Social Studies
Multiplication and Division Introduce your child to division. Show your child that division is the opposite operation of multiplication, and thus can be used to solve for missing factors in multiplication. *See* Math, Week 9, number 1. Have your child complete **Multiplication's Opposite** (p. 105).	**Mammals** Have your child make final observations of the mealworm and freshwater snail habitats. Have him/her write a paragraph summary of the changes observed in each animal. Provide materials on mammals for your child's reference. *See* Science, Week 9, number 1. Have your child take notes on mammals in his/her Science Log.	**Revolutionary War** Have your child add dates and events related to the war to the time line begun in Week 1. Have your child read and discuss the events of the Revolutionary War: *Where were battles fought? Who was involved? What were the outcomes of these battles? See* Social Studies, Week 9, number 1. Have your child draw a picture of Valley Forge. What was the "Winter of Despair"?
Teach your child how to use a letter as a variable in a multiplication sentence. Simply replace the blank in a multiplication problem with a letter (a variable). The letter stands for what is unknown. **Example:** $4 \times 6 = c$ *See* Math, Week 9, number 2.	Brainstorm a list of mammals that live in fields, grasslands and meadows. Have your child read about different prairie mammals, then look at pictures to identify them and note the characteristics of each. Have your child complete **Endangered** (p. 107).	Help your child empathize with the colonists who sought independence. Discuss the concept of independence and why people hold it so dear. *See* Social Studies, Week 9, number 2. Have your child write about a time when he/she felt his/her rights were being violated.
Review basic multiplication facts. Have your child complete **Timed Multiplication** (p. 86). Compare your child's time and score with earlier tests taken Monday, Week 7 and Wednesday, Week 8. Review multiplication concepts taught so far. Have your child practice multiplication with multiple digits. Give him/her several relevant story problems to solve.	Brainstorm a list of mammals that live in the sea. Have your child read about different sea animals, then look at pictures to identify them and note the characteristics of each. Have your child complete **A Whale of a Story** (p. 108).	Have your child read about weapons used in the Revolutionary War. *How accurate were muskets?* Have your child compare them with the weapons used in today's battles.
Test your child's understanding of material learned in the first nine weeks. Have your child complete **First Quarter Test** (p. 106).	Brainstorm a list of mammals that live in forests and jungles. Have your child read about different forest mammals, then look at pictures to identify them and note the characteristics of each. Have your child categorize mammals by given characteristics. *See* Science, Week 9, number 2.	*What role did women play in the Revolutionary War? How did they help the Continental Army?* Have your child choose one of the following female war heroes to research: Molly Pitcher, Sybil Ludington, Margaret Corbin or Deborah Sampson. Have your child read about her life and accomplishments. Then, have your child prepare a speech praising the woman's achievements and recommending her for a special honor.
Reteach any concepts that your child had trouble with on the test.	Review the different phyla of the animal kingdom. Reteach concepts, if necessary. Discuss the interdependence of animals in the world. Review the concept of a food chain or food web. Have your child complete **The Prairie Food Web** (p. 109). Discuss with him/her that the arrows point to the consumer.	Arrange for your child to perform some community service.

TEACHING SUGGESTIONS AND ACTIVITIES

LANGUAGE SKILLS (Review)

▶ 1. Show your child an interesting picture. First, have your child describe the mood or feeling that the picture inspires. Then, have your child make a list of things he/she sees in the picture. Have your child imagine what has just happened (or what is *about* to happen) in the scene. How are the lives of the characters connected? Finally, have your child map out a story by using these observations to piece together the elements: setting, characters, problem, events and solution.

▶ 2. Give your child a pair of 4-letter words. Challenge him/her to change the first word into the second word in as few steps as possible. your child may change only one letter in each step, and each change must produce a new word.

Examples: *skit* to *play*   *horn* to *yard*
      skit—slit—slat—slay—*play*   *horn*—born—barn—yarn—*yard*

Have your child try with the following word pairs: *hark* to *bird*   *pill* to *gate*   *wash* to *mist*
                    sink to *hand*   *goal* to *lost*   *joke* to *palm*

▶ 3. Have your child write the following sentences on the chalkboard. Then, have him/her underline each figure of speech and indicate whether it is an example of a metaphor, simile, hyperbole or idiom.

> The hen laid a million eggs.
> The man turned red as a beet.
> That topic was too hot to discuss.
> The donkey was as slow as molasses.
> The wind was a locomotive.
> My feet grew like weeds over the summer.
> It was raining cats and dogs last weekend.

READING (Proper Nouns)

Test your child's understanding of proper nouns. Give your child the following sentences, as written. Have your child find and circle the proper nouns in each, then rewrite the sentence with correct capitalization.

> Miss brophy grew up in lake champlain, new york.
> Addie had to visit the settlement of ree heights to see tilla.
> Addie carried her doll ruby lillian everywhere she went.
> your children really enjoyed the stories mr. fency told them when he visited.
> Addie and her family were living in hutchinson county.
> Malcolm and daniel connolly were very mischievous boys.
> The mills had moved from sabula to oak hollow.
> Miss brophy often recited poetry written by henry wadsworth longfellow.
> Addie wrote a poem titled "the wild prairie rose."
> tilla, katya, addie and nellie all went on a picnic down by the creek.

MATH (Multiplication and Division)

▶ 1. Multiplication and division are complementary processes, just like addition and subtraction. In a multiplication sentence, the *multiplicand* is the number of items in a group. The *multiplier* is the number of groups. The *product* is the total number of items. If you know the product and the multiplicand, you can use division to solve for the multiplier; if you know the product and the multiplier, you can use division to solve for the multiplicand. Use manipulatives to demonstrate several multiplication and division relationships. Then, have your child work through several problems with you. This will help solidify the concept for your child.

Learn At Home, Grade 5

▶ 2. Substitute a letter variable for a factor or product in a multiplication sentence. Then, solve for the letter.

Examples:

$3 \times 5 = a$	$3 \times b = 6$	$c \times 4 = 16$
$a = 15$	$b = 2$	$c = 4$

Now, have your child solve these multiplication problems for the variables.

Exercises:

$15 \times 29 = p$	$b \times 29 = 4,495$	$12 \times y = 744$
$p = \_\_\_$	$b = \_\_\_$	$y = \_\_\_$
$1,223 \times 23 = r$	$863 \times 39 = n$	$t \times 22 = 352$
$r = \_\_\_$	$n = \_\_\_$	$t = \_\_\_$

SCIENCE (Mammals)

▶ 1. All mammals share the following characteristics: mothers nurse their young with milk they produce, mammals nurture and protect their young more than other animals, all mammals have hair at some time in their lives, they are warm-blooded and they have larger brains than other animals. Most mammals give birth to live young, although some species give birth to poorly developed offspring that develop in a pouch. Still other species lay eggs.

▶ 2. Read aloud the characteristics below, one at a time. Have your child name one or two mammals that are known for each characteristic. The first one is done for you.

flies (*bat*)	swims
lays eggs	has a pouch for developing young
lives in cold climates	lives in a warm climate
burrows in the soil	has sharp claws
has no teeth	travels in herds
is kept as a pet	is endangered
eats plants	eats meat
has horns	has tusks
hibernates	migrates
is nocturnal	has a beak
has a long neck	has a short neck
lives in trees	eats insects
gnaws	is a common food source for humans

SOCIAL STUDIES (Revolutionary War)

▶ 1. Some of the key battles in the Revolutionary War took place at Lexington, Concord, Saratoga, Valley Forge, Trenton, Philadelphia, Yorktown, Fort Ticonderoga, Bunker Hill and Charleston. Have your child locate these sites on a map of the colonies. Have him/her research some of these battles to find out how many soldiers were on each side, which side was better equipped and trained and which side eventually won the battle. Discuss the hardships the Americans endured. Have your child find out why the French and Spanish were willing to help the American cause.

▶ 2. Have your child think about what life would be like if the government controlled where we lived, what we paid for goods and who could pass laws. Compare life in America with that in other countries today that do not have the same freedoms we have. Discuss the meaning of *independence*. Ask your child to define independence and name several examples of how he/she is independent.

Review of Verbs

Underline the complete verb in the following sentences. Be sure to include any helping verbs. **Write** if the verb is an **action** verb or **being** verb and whether the main verb is **regular** or **irregular**.

<u>_action_</u>   <u>_regular_</u>   **He <u>stepped</u> onto the plane.**

_____ _____ 1. Black soot and brilliant diamonds are both carbon.

_____ _____ 2. Diamonds are crystals of carbon.

_____ _____ 3. The carbon must be pressed very hard.

_____ _____ 4. It must be heated very hot at the same time.

_____ _____ 5. Miners usually find diamonds deep in the ground.

_____ _____ 6. For centuries, most diamond mines were in India.

_____ _____ 7. Now the biggest diamond mines are found in Africa.

_____ _____ 8. One day in 1866, some children saw a pretty pebble in a river near Hopetown, South Africa.

_____ _____ 9. It looked like frosted glass.

_____ _____ 10. The children brought it home with them.

_____ _____ 11. One day a neighbor offered money for it.

_____ _____ 12. The children gave it to him for nothing.

_____ _____ 13. The children did not know the value of the stone.

_____ _____ 14. It was a diamond.

_____ _____ 15. Word about this discovery spread quickly.

_____ _____ 16. Other people hunted for diamonds nearby.

_____ _____ 17. Many of them were disappointed.

_____ _____ 18. However, some people found diamonds in the area.

_____ _____ 19. They were blessed with good fortune.

_____ _____ 20. Diamonds were discovered in other parts of Africa as well.

Learn At Home, Grade 5

Multiplication's Opposite

Use the multiplication problem to help solve the division problems.

Example:
6 x 7 = 42
42 ÷ 7 = 6
42 ÷ 6 = 7

1. 4 x 8 = 32
    32 ÷ _____ = 4
    32 ÷ _____ = 8

2. 9 x 9 = 81
    81 ÷ 9 = _____

3. 7 x 8 = 56
    ____ ÷ 8 = 7
    56 ÷ ____ = 8

4. 22 x 12 = 264
    _____ ÷ 12 = 22
    264 ÷ 22 = ____

5. 37 x 19 = 703
    ____ ÷ 37 = 19
    703 ÷ 19 = ____

Solve the following problems and **write** two related division problems for each.

6. 22 x 17 = _____

7. 45 x 29 = _____

8. 19 x 82 = _____

9. 671 x 63 = _____

10. 663 x 54 = _____

11. 719 x 73 = _____

First Quarter Test

1. Write 4,507,039,005 in words. _____
   _____

2. Write in numerals: sixty-nine million, one hundred twelve thousand, two hundred seven. _____

3. Round 3,760 to the nearest hundred.   Round 28,343 to the nearest ten.
   _____   _____

4. $3 + 7 + 4 + 5 + 5 = a$

   $a =$ _____

5. $26,309 + 811 = x$

   $x =$ _____

6. $59 +$ _____ $= 78$

7.   22 ft. 7 in.
   +   3 ft. 6 in.

8.   7 lbs. 10 oz.
   +   3 lbs. 10 oz.

9.   8,345,246
   −   46,239

10. _____ $- 42 = 39$

11. $87 -$ _____ $= 53$

12.   17 min. 12 sec.
    −   5 min. 20 sec.

13. Provide change from $5.00 for a $2.59 purchase. _____

14. $37 \times 85 =$ ___ $\times 37$

15. $(8 \times 7) \times 6 =$ _____

16. $75 \times 7 = x$

    $x =$ _____

17. Multiply: $126 \times 100 = y$ $y =$ _____

18. Estimate: $79 \times 9 = c$ $c =$ _____

19. Solve: $39 \times 48 =$ _____

    _____ $\div 48 = 39$

Endangered

Many of the animals in the grassland community are very rare, and some are in danger of becoming extinct. The American buffalo was once one of those animals. In 1889, only 551 of them remained. Today, after laws were established to protect them, there are about 15,000 buffalo in the U.S.

The black-footed ferret, which lives in the western Great Plains of North America, is an endangered species. Complete the chart below and color the picture. You will need to find information from an encyclopedia or other source to help you.

Name: **Black-Footed Ferret** (*Mustela nigripes*)

Size: _____

Color: _____

Habitat: _____

_____

Diet: _____

_____

Conditions leading to its endangered status: _____

_____

_____

_____

A Whale of a Story

Read the following information about whales. Make a glossary of the terms in bold, writing a definition for each word based on the context. Then, use as many of the words as possible to write a poem or story.

Whales belong to a group of animals called **cetaceans.** There are two major types of whales: **baleen whales** and **toothed whales**. Baleen whales have no teeth, but they have hundreds of thin plates made of material similar to human fingernails. These **baleen plates** filter out food from the water. Small, shrimplike animals, called **krill** are the main food source of baleen whales. There are ten kinds of baleen whales. These are further divided into three groups. One group, the **rorquals**, is distinguished by long grooves on their throats and chests and contains the largest of all whales, the blue whale.

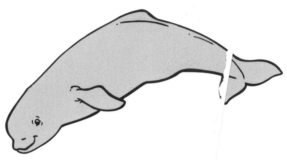

Toothed whales have teeth. There are about 65 kinds of toothed whales which are divided into five groups. One group, called the **beluga**, measures 10–15 feet long. Belugas are milk-white when fully grown and are often called white whales.

Whales are shaped like torpedoes. Every whale has a **blowhole** or a nostril on top of its head, through which it breathes. A **dorsal fin**, located on top of the body, stands upright and helps whales steer; **flippers** are also used for steering and for balance. **Flukes** are two triangular lobes that are part of the whale's tail. The flukes beat up and down to move the whale through the water. Beneath their skin, whales have a layer of fat called **blubber**. Blubber helps keep whales warm, and when food is scarce, they can live off their blubber for a long time.

Whales are some of the most intelligent animals. They communicate with one another through a variety of sounds called **phonations**, also called **whale songs**. These songs consist of groans, moans, roars, sighs, high-pitched squeaks and chirps.

There are many more interesting facts about whales. For example, whales perform impressive leaps from the water called **breaching**. Many also **migrate** thousands of miles every year to spend the winter in warm water and the summer in cold water. Whales use a method of navigation called **echolocation**. Based on an echo or reflection of sound, whales can determine the distance and direction of an object.

Whaling has become so efficient that some whales have become **endangered**. **Whalers**, people who hunt whales, realized that some species were almost extinct. In 1946, the International Whaling Committee (IWC) was formed to protect the future of whales.

The Prairie Food Web

In complex grassland communities like the prairie, the flow of food and energy cannot be described by a simple food chain. Instead, it is represented by a series of interconnected food chains called a **food web**. The many kinds of producers and consumers in the prairie community provide a wide variety of food sources.

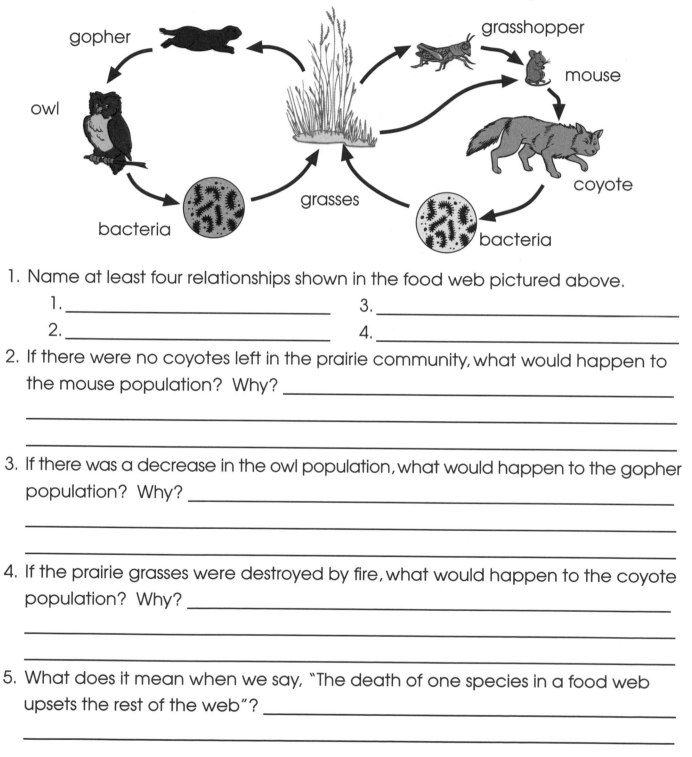

1. Name at least four relationships shown in the food web pictured above.

    1. _____   3. _____

    2. _____   4. _____

2. If there were no coyotes left in the prairie community, what would happen to the mouse population? Why? _____

    _____

    _____

3. If there was a decrease in the owl population, what would happen to the gopher population? Why? _____

    _____

    _____

4. If the prairie grasses were destroyed by fire, what would happen to the coyote population? Why? _____

    _____

    _____

5. What does it mean when we say, "The death of one species in a food web upsets the rest of the web"? _____

    _____

    _____

109

	Language Skills	**Spelling**	**Reading**
Monday	Provide 3–5 interesting pictures for your child to contemplate. Have your child choose a writing topic based on one of the pictures, make a plan for writing and begin work on a rough draft for a story.	Pretest your child on these spelling words: additive gathering sassafras badge kangaroo standard chapter magazine tacks daffodil pasture thankful dragon patches transplant fraction rapid traveler Have your child correct the pretest. Add personalized words and make two copies of this week's study list.	**Dictionary Skills** This week, engage your child in activities to help him/her learn to use the dictionary effectively. Introduce *The Cay* by Theodore Taylor. Have your child read chapter 1. Have your child note unfamiliar words (and the pages where found) in his/her Reading Journal. Have your child look up each word, write a definition and reread the passage containing the word. *See* Reading, Week 10, numbers 1 and 2.
Tuesday	**Sentences:** Review the four types of sentences: *declarative, imperative, interrogative* and *exclamatory*. *See* Language Skills, Week 10, number 1. Have your child complete **Kinds of Sentences** (p. 114).	Review this week's spelling words. Have your child complete **Managing Short a** (p. 115).	Have your child read chapters 2 and 3 of *The Cay,* noting any unfamiliar vocabulary. Prepare a vocabulary activity related to dictionary skills. *See* Reading, Week 10, number 3.
Wednesday	Review capitalization and punctuation. Have your child write two examples of each kind of sentence, focusing on correct capitalization and punctuation. Have your child label each completed sentence as declarative, interrogative, imperative or exclamatory.	Have your child use each of this week's spelling words correctly in a sentence.	Have your child read chapters 4 and 5 of *The Cay.* Have your child complete **To Know and Understand** (p. 116). Make a list of words containing 1–5 syllables. Have your child divide the words into syllables, then look up each word in the dictionary to check his/her work. How did he/she do? Reteach syllabication rules, if necessary. Have your child make a list of 10 three-, four- and five-syllable words from today's reading.
Thursday	Teach your child the words that name the four kinds of sentences: *statement, question, command* and *exclamation.* Can your child name the descriptive words that correspond to these sentence types? (*declarative, interrogative, imperative* and *exclamatory*) Have your child make four different kinds of sentences from a single group of words. *See* Language Skills, Week 10, number 2.	Have your child study this week's spelling words.	Have your child read chapters 6 and 7 of *The Cay.* Have your child draw a picture of the island and surrounding area based on descriptions in the story. Give your child a list of words to look up in the dictionary. Have him/her write down the guide words from the top of the page on which each word appears.
Friday	Demonstrate for your child how to write a statement based on a question. **Example:** Where is your brother? *My brother is at school.* Generate a list of questions for your child. Have your child respond to each question in writing with a complete statement.	Give your child the final spelling test. Have your child record pretest and final test words in his/her Word Bank.	Have your child read chapters 8 and 9 of *The Cay.* Review cause and effect. Have your child name three things that happened in the story and the effects or causes of those events.

Learn At Home, Grade 5

Math	Science	Social Studies
Division Review the process of division with your child. Using manipulatives, teach division as repeated subtraction. *See* Math, Week 10, number 1.	**Plant Kingdom** Gather several resources for your child's reference on plants, flowers, trees, forests and seeds. *See* Science, Week 10. Have your child begin a glossary of plant terms. Have him/her add to the glossary as new terms are discussed. *See* Science, Week 10, number 1.	**Revolutionary War** Have your child read about famous Americans who were associated with events of the war. <table><tr><td>Ethan Allen</td><td>Benedict Arnold</td></tr><tr><td>John Paul Jones</td><td>George Washington</td></tr><tr><td>Paul Revere</td><td>Marquis de Lafayette</td></tr><tr><td>Crispus Attucks</td><td>Friedrich von Steuben</td></tr></table>Have your child title a column *Revolutionary War* on the chart of famous Americans and write these names on it. *See* Social Studies, Week 7, number 4.
Review division facts. Remind your child to think of known multiplication facts to help solve unknown division facts. Give your child five minutes to complete **Division Facts** (p. 117). Did he/she finish all of the problems? If not, note which problems he/she found difficult. Review those facts.	Discuss the benefits of classification. Introduce your child to the different ways plants may be classified. *See* Science, Week 10, number 2. Have your child sort a set of pictures of plants into meaningful categories. Have your child give his/her particular classification system an original name.	Cornwallis surrendered to Washington on October 19, 1781. The Treaty of Paris was signed on September 3, 1783. Have your child add these dates to the time line. Read about the Treaty of Paris. *What was gained by the war? What was lost?* Have your child draw a map of the thirteen original states. *What were the borders set forth by the Treaty of Paris?*
Teach division with a one-digit divisor. *See* Math, Week 10, numbers 2 and 3. Have your child complete **Artifact Facts** (p. 118).	Help your child conduct the experiment described in **Do Plants Need Light?** (p. 120). Maintain the bean plants for several weeks to use in another experiment in Science, Week 14.	Have your child read about the government established immediately following the war. In 1781, Congress laid down basic laws for the new country. *Why didn't these laws work?* Discuss the fact that each state was declared independent of the others. Each state issued its own currency. *What kinds of problems did the independence of the states create?*
Using the same procedures as on Monday and Wednesday, teach your child how to perform division with remainders. To check a solution, your child should multiply the quotient by the divisor, then add the remainder. This total should equal the dividend. Give your child 10–15 division problems with remainders to solve. Have your child check his/her answers.	Help your child identify the main parts of a plant and their functions. *See* Science, Week 10, numbers 3 and 4. Have your child complete the puzzle on **Photosynthesis** (p. 121).	The poorly organized government led to the creation of the Constitution. The Constitutional Convention met in 1787 to write this important document that still organizes our government today. Discuss the Constitutional Convention—the key delegates and states involved, the key issues that were addressed and the process of the Constitution's eventual ratification.
Teach your child how to perform division with a zero in the quotient. Explain that the zero acts as a place holder. See the top of **Zeros in the Quotient** (p. 119) for an example. Have your child complete the problems on **Zeros in the Quotient**.	Begin the construction of a leaf/flower press. *See* Science, Week 10, number 5.	Arrange for your child to perform some community service.

TEACHING SUGGESTIONS AND ACTIVITIES

LANGUAGE SKILLS (Sentences)

▶ 1. Provide several written examples of each type of sentence for your child to identify.

Examples: *Declarative*—It was 100° F on Wednesday.   *Imperative*—Please clean up your room.
Interrogative—Where were you yesterday?   *Exclamatory*—What an awful smell!

After your child has correctly identified several written sentences, test his/her ability to *hear* different types of sentences. Say several sentences (vary the type) out loud. Can your child hear the difference? Finally, have your child give you examples of each kind of sentence.

▶ 2. Give your child the word lists below along with the following directions:

Use the words in each group to write four different kinds of sentences: statement, question, command and exclamation. Use as many of the words as you can in each sentence, but do not add any others. Some sentences will use more words than others. Words may be used more than once, but not within the same sentence. Each word in the list must be used in at least one sentence. Use correct punctuation.

   a. ballet, when, by, well, dancers, go, the, was, are, trained, ballet's, to, performed

   b. lives, where, Oregon, forget, does, write, Portland, in, live, address, her, don't, down, to, call, Gillian

   c. money, class, who, the, sold, will, five hundred, to, for, and, over, tickets, sell, school, make

READING (Dictionary Skills)

▶ 1. Before your child looks up unfamiliar words, review how to use the dictionary. Have your child observe the organization of the entries, including the pronunciation guide , parts of speech, definitions and other features. Turn to the front of the dictionary and have your child skim the guide. Point out guide words at the top of each page.

▶ 2. Have several dictionaries available. Have your child look up some of the unfamiliar words in more than one dictionary. Discuss any differences in the entries.

▶ 3. Compile a list of at least twenty vocabulary words from *The Cay*. For each word, write three pairs of guide words that might appear on a page in a dictionary.

Example: 1. *woolly*   wooden/wordy   with/wonky   which/wild

Have your child circle the correct pair of guide words for each vocabulary word. Once your child has done this, have him/her alphabetize the list of vocabulary words. Finally, have your child write three sentences using some of the new vocabulary words.

MATH (Division)

▶ 1. Explain to your child that division can be viewed as repeated subtraction. The division sentence $28 \div 4 = 7$ can be demonstrated with small counters as $28 - 4 - 4 - 4 - 4 - 4 - 4 - 4$. Start with 28 counters. Take away a group of 4 counters seven times. Twenty-eight can be divided into seven groups of four.

▶ 2. When you have a large dividend, think of the number in thousands, hundreds, tens and ones.

Example: 375 has 3 hundreds, 7 tens and 5 ones. It also can be seen as having 37 tens and 5 ones or 375 ones.
Divide 375 by 5.

| | | | | *Since 5 x 5 is 25, place the 5 in* |
| *Try dividing 3 by 5. The number in the hundreds place is too small.* | *Try dividing 37 tens by 5. Since 5 x 7 is 35, place the 7 over the tens place, muliply and subtract 35 from 37.* | *You have 2 tens left.* | *Bring down the 5 ones. Now you have 25 ones. How many groups of 5 are there in 25?* | *the ones place, muliply and subtract 25 from the problem. You are left with zero remaining.* |

```
                    7                75              7              75
 5 ⌐375         5 ⌐375          5 ⌐375        5  375⌐        5 ⌐375
                  - 35            - 35          - 35            - 35
                                    2             25              25
                                                                - 25
                                                                   0
```

     Learn At Home, Grade 5

Check your solution with a calculator. Multiply the quotient (75) by the divisor (5). If the product is equal to the dividend (375), the solution is correct.

▶ 3. Here is another method for division. In this method, your child may multiply the divisor by easy numbers and slowly reduce the dividend. The quotient is determined by adding all the numbers on the right.

Try dividing 8 by 9. The number in the hundreds place is too small. Estimate how many groups of 9 are in 87 tens.	*Try 60. Place the 60 to the right of the equation and multiply 60 x 9. Subtract 540 from the dividend.*	*Continue to estimate and subtract products until you reach zero. Add the numbers on the right to get the*	*The solution is not affected by the numbers you try on the right.*

$$9\overline{)873}$$

$$
\begin{array}{r}
9\overline{)873} \\
-540 \quad 60 \\
\hline
333
\end{array}
$$

$$
\begin{array}{r}
9\overline{)873} \\
-540 \quad 60 \\
\hline
333 \\
-270 \quad 30 \\
\hline
63 \\
-63 \quad 7 \\
\hline
0
\end{array}
$$
total = **97**

$$
\begin{array}{r}
9\overline{)873} \\
-720 \quad 80 \\
\hline
153 \\
-135 \quad 15 \\
\hline
18 \\
-18 \quad 2 \\
\hline
0
\end{array}
$$
total = **97**

SCIENCE (Plant Kingdom)

BACKGROUND

There are about 500,000 known types of plants on Earth. They grow in all climates and on all continents. Plants provide oxygen, food, clothing, shelter and numerous products for life on Earth. Sixteen groups or phyla of plants make up the plant kingdom. Explore this botanical diversity with your child over the next several weeks.

▶ 1. Have your child begin a plant glossary with the following terms: *botany, bud, chlorophyll, cotyledon, flower, fruit, herb, leaf, ovule, photosynthesis, pollen, roots, seed, spore, stem* and *vegetable.* Have your child write the words in alphabetical order and write a definition for each. Encourage your child to leave space in the glossary to add other plant-related terms that he/she may encounter in research.

▶ 2. Botanists classify plants into groups to make them easier to study. They look for characteristics that make plants similar or different. Some important plant categories include *vascular* and *nonvascular, spore-producing* and *seed-producing.* Have your child do research to discover the meanings of these terms. Other identifiable characteristics of plants include type of root system, type of stem or trunk, type of leaf, biome in which they live, how quickly they grow, types of fruit produced and the amount of light needed to grow.

▶ 3. Remove an entire plant from the soil. Lay the plant on a paper towel or piece of newspaper for your child to examine. Have your child identify the main parts of the plant: roots, stem and leaves. On a growing plant, identify the flower, seed and fruit. Have your child read about the functions and uses of each part of a plant. Read about and discuss photosynthesis and plant reproduction.

▶ 4. Ask your child to name some foods and identify which part of the plant each comes from: *roots*—carrots and beets, *stem*—celery and asparagus, *leaves*—lettuce and cabbage, *flower*—broccoli and artichokes, *seeds*—peanuts and peas, *fruit*—apples and grapes.

▶ 5. You will need the following materials to build a plant press: two 1' x 1' x $\frac{1}{2}$" boards, pieces of corrugated cardboard, plain paper towels, 3- to 4-inch-long bolts and nuts. Drill a hole in each corner of the two boards. Insert the bolts in the drilled holes. Cut several pieces of cardboard to fit between the boards as you fasten the nuts on the bolts. See the illustration at right.

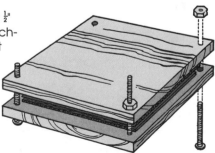

Kinds of Sentences

There are four kinds of sentences.

A **declarative** sentence makes a statement.
Tuesday was a chilly day.
An **interrogative** sentence asks a question.
Was Tuesday a chilly day?
An **imperative** sentence gives a command or makes a request.
Be at my house at 11 o'clock.
An **exclamatory** sentence expresses excitement or strong feeling.
What a terrible storm!

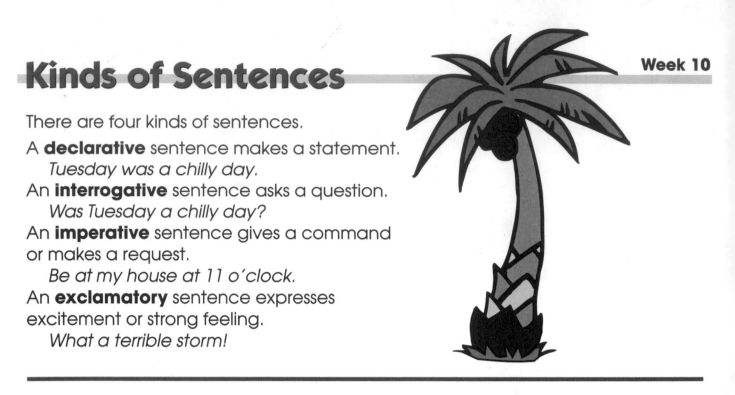

Identify each type of sentence.

1. The Hawaiian Islands are really mountaintops. _____

2. Were those mountains once active volcanoes? _____

3. Read the article in the magazine that Sid brought. _____

4. What beautiful pictures that article has! _____

5. Hawaii is made up of a chain of 132 islands in the Pacific Ocean.

   _____

6. Bring your lei to school tomorrow. _____

7. Which island has the most people living on it? _____

8. I just can't believe that the small island of Oahu does! _____

9. I'm astonished that the average temperature is 75° F! _____

Rewrite each sentence as the type suggested in parentheses.

10. Were the Polynesians the first people on Hawaii? (declarative)

    _____

11. An English explorer, Captain Cook, named the islands the "Sandwich Islands."
    (interrogative) _____

    _____

12. Will you bring me a present from Hawaii? (imperative)

    _____

114

Managing Short a

Say each word. Listen for the **short a** sound(s) and the number of syllables. Then, complete the graphic organizer.

additive
badge
chapter
daffodil
dragon
fraction
gathering
kangaroo
magazine
pasture
patches
rapid
sassafras
standard
tacks
thankful
transplant
traveler

One syllable

Two syllables

Three syllables

Short a words

Words containing two **short a** sounds.

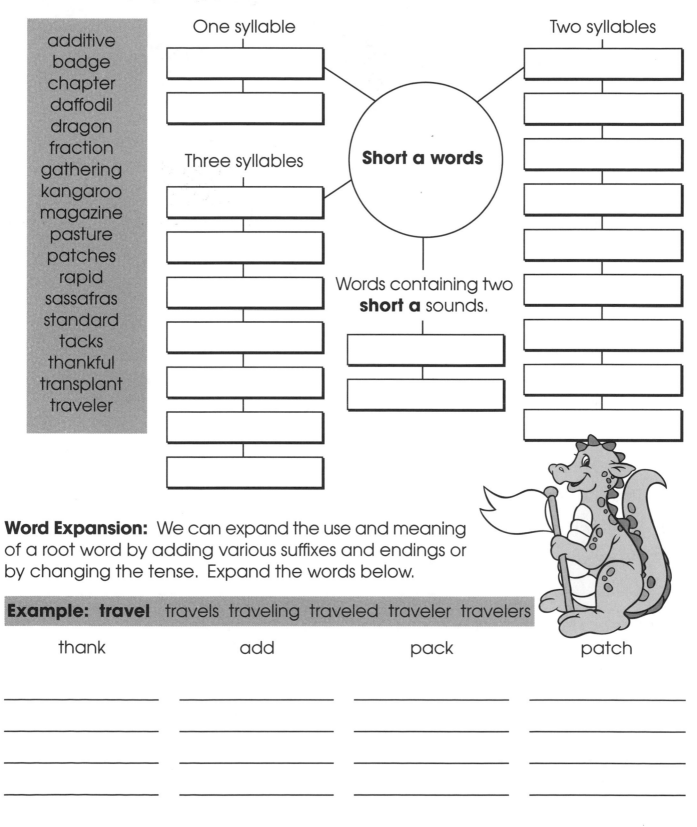

Word Expansion: We can expand the use and meaning of a root word by adding various suffixes and endings or by changing the tense. Expand the words below.

Example: travel travels traveling traveled traveler travelers

thank   add   pack   patch

_____   _____   _____   _____

_____   _____   _____   _____

_____   _____   _____   _____

_____   _____   _____   _____

To Know and Understand

A **fact** is something that is proven to be true. An **opinion** is what someone believes. People hold differing opinions, some of which are unfair or untrue.
Use the code to **label** each statement below.

F = Fact   **PO** = Phillip's opinion   **MO** = Phillip's mother's opinion   **TO** = Timothy's opinion

1. Black people were odd because they ate raw fish. _____

2. Timothy's nose was flat and his face was broad. _____

3. Timothy should have let Phillip stay in the water. _____

4. Phillip was nearly twelve years old. _____

5. The cat brought bad luck. _____

6. Timothy was saving all the water for himself. _____

7. It was safer to leave Curacao than stay. _____

8. In Virginia, blacks and whites lived in different parts of town. _____

9. Timothy was strange because he didn't know his parents. _____

10. White children should not play near black workers. _____

11. Timothy could be a very stubborn person. _____

Discussion: In your neighborhood, what are some opinions people hold that are unfair? Is it fair to tease or ignore people who are different from you? Talk about how the following types of people are treated in your neighborhood.

- physically handicapped people
- people who speak other languages
- awkward people
- poor/rich people
- popular/unpopular people

- younger/older people
- people of other cultures
- mentally impaired people
- attractive/unattractive people
- girls/boys

116

Division Facts

3⟌24	9⟌81	8⟌40	4⟌4	9⟌90	8⟌56	6⟌24
7⟌14	7⟌49	5⟌20	6⟌36	9⟌72	4⟌16	3⟌27
8⟌64	9⟌36	5⟌25	9⟌45	2⟌18	4⟌24	8⟌8
3⟌9	2⟌14	6⟌54	7⟌21	8⟌32	5⟌30	1⟌6
2⟌4	9⟌81	6⟌30	4⟌8	5⟌50	5⟌15	2⟌20
1⟌10	7⟌7	2⟌16	3⟌15	7⟌49	1⟌4	9⟌63
8⟌16	2⟌12	8⟌72	3⟌30	9⟌63	3⟌18	7⟌56
9⟌9	7⟌63	2⟌8	8⟌80	7⟌28	6⟌12	3⟌6
7⟌42	3⟌12	7⟌35	9⟌27	6⟌42	5⟌10	5⟌45
2⟌10	9⟌54	4⟌20	8⟌48	9⟌18	6⟌6	2⟌6

Artifact Facts

Help the archaeologist find the artifact. First, **solve** the division problems. Then, connect the quotients in numerical order, starting at 795, to make his path.

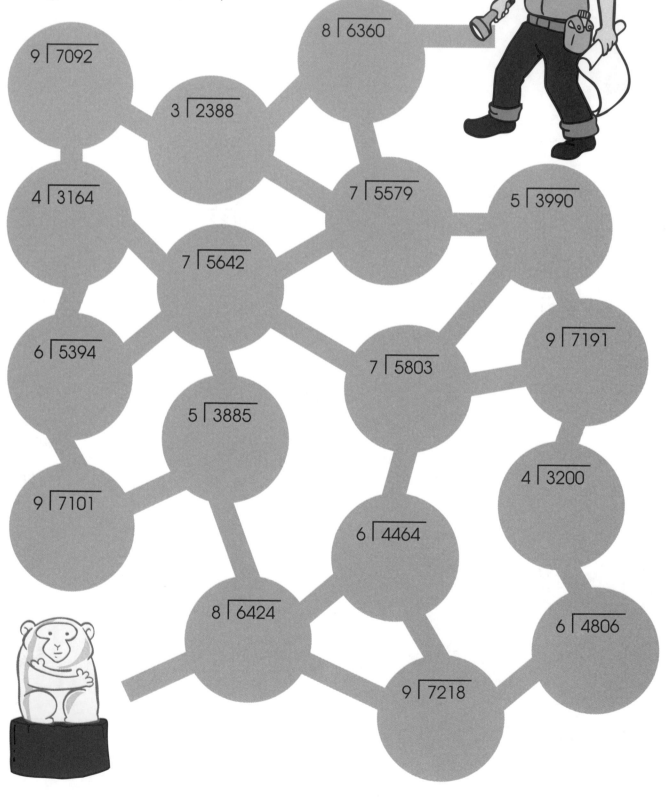

$8 \overline{)6360}$

$9 \overline{)7092}$

$3 \overline{)2388}$

$4 \overline{)3164}$

$7 \overline{)5579}$

$5 \overline{)3990}$

$7 \overline{)5642}$

$6 \overline{)5394}$

$7 \overline{)5803}$

$9 \overline{)7191}$

$5 \overline{)3885}$

$9 \overline{)7101}$

$4 \overline{)3200}$

$6 \overline{)4464}$

$8 \overline{)6424}$

$6 \overline{)4806}$

$9 \overline{)7218}$

118

Learn At Home, Grade 5

Zeros in the Quotient

Zero holds a place in the quotient.

Example:

$$
\begin{array}{r}
1 \\
5\overline{)545} \\
-5 \\
\hline
04
\end{array}
$$
Five goes into 4 zero times.

$$
\begin{array}{r}
10 \\
5\overline{)545} \\
-5 \\
\hline
45
\end{array}
$$
Five goes into 45 nine times.

$$
\begin{array}{r}
109 \\
5\overline{)545} \\
-5 \\
\hline
45 \\
-45 \\
\hline
0
\end{array}
$$

1. $4\overline{)420}$

2. $6\overline{)636}$

3. $9\overline{)963}$

4. $9\overline{)945}$

5. $9\overline{)963}$

6. $8\overline{)816}$

7. $3\overline{)312}$

8. $3\overline{)9,021}$

9. $7\overline{)1,386}$

Do Plants Need Light?

Once a plant germinates, artificial or natural light is essential in the growth of the plant. Some plants need full sunlight while others need only indirect light. Most garden plants will grow best in full light. As long as the moisture and soil mixture are kept constant, the growth of the plants will be determined by the light conditions.

You will need: 6 bean seeds, metric ruler, 2 germination pots, water, green and yellow markers, potting soil, tables, metric measuring cup

Directions: Fill each pot about $\frac{3}{4}$ full with potting soil. Plant three bean seeds in each pot about 1 cm below the surface of the soil. Add 50 ml of water to each pot. Label one pot **Light** and the other **Dark**. The **Light** pot should be placed in a well-lit area and the **Dark** pot in a dark area. When the beans begin to sprout, make a daily measurement of the height of the tallest plant in each pot. Record the plant heights on a graph similar to the one shown here. Use a different color for each plant. Record the heights for five days.

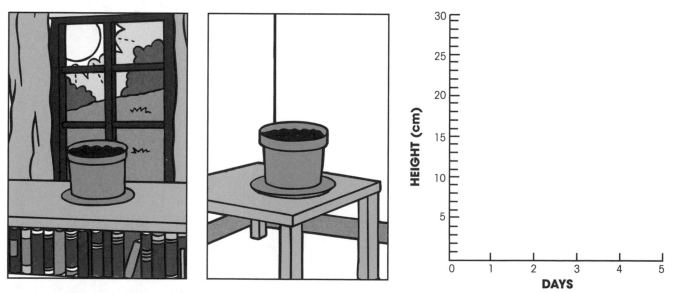

Discuss the results of the activity. How tall did the plants grow in the light? How tall did the plants grow in the dark? Did the amount of sunlight make a difference? Do you think the plants will continue to grow at the same rate?

Learn At Home, Grade 5

Photosynthesis

Photosynthesis is a food-making process that occurs in green plants. It is the main function of the leaves. With the help of page 131, a science book or other source, **complete** the puzzle below.

Across

1. Small green bodies that contain the green pigment chlorophyll
4. Gas that is released into the air as a by-product of photosynthesis
6. The escaping of water vapor from a leaf
7. Liquid obtained through the roots
8. Source of energy to power photosynthesis
9. Simple food made by photosynthesis

Down

2. The process by which green plants make food
3. One of the raw materials for photosynthesis is _____ dioxide.
5. Opening in the underside of a leaf

	Language Skills	**Spelling**	**Reading**
Monday	Review the elements of a newspaper article (*see* Reading, Week 7). Discuss the writing style used in articles. Have your child write an article as if he/she were a sportswriter. Help your child write a headline for the article after it is completed. *See* Language Skills, Week 11, number 1.	Pretest your child on these spelling words: ancestor, attempt, central, definition, enforce, festival, generally, genuine, legend, medicine, necessary, pedal, reference, residence, section, sentence, temperature, tennis. Have your child correct the pretest. Add personalized words and make two copies of this week's study list.	Review the events so far in *The Cay*. Discuss how Phillip has changed. Does your child think Phillip has changed in a positive way? Have him/her predict what might happen next. Have your child read chapters 10 and 11 of *The Cay*.
Tuesday	**Sentences:** Have your child write five statements about what he/she is studying in social studies. Then, have him/her write related questions using most of the words in the statements. Have your child write five questions about something he/she is curious about in science. Then, have him/her write an answer to each question. (Some questions may require some research.)	Review this week's spelling words. Have your child complete **Effective Short e** (p. 126).	**Vocabulary:** Review the vocabulary your child has collected so far while reading. Write out some of these words using diacritical spellings. Explain that *diacritical spellings* guide pronunciation. Have your child try to match each word's diacritical spelling to its traditional spelling. Have your child read chapters 12 and 13 of *The Cay*.
Wednesday	Watch part of a favorite videotape. Have your child listen carefully to the dialogue and write down exactly what he/she hears. Have your child sort the sentences into statements, questions, commands and exclamations.	Have your child use each of this week's spelling words correctly in a sentence.	Have your child read chapters 14 and 15 of *The Cay*. Have your child write about how he/she thinks Phillip will survive without Timothy. Write a list of unfamiliar words for your child to look up and rewrite phonetically with diacritical marks. Have your child read each word aloud, write the definition of the word and use it in a sentence.
Thursday	Review subjects and predicates. Explain that every sentence is made up of a subject and a predicate. The *complete subject* is all the words that tell whom or what the sentence is about. The *complete predicate* is all the words that tell what the subject is or does. The *simple subject* is the main word in the complete subject. The *simple predicate* is the main word in the complete predicate. *See* Language Skills, Week 11, number 2.	Have your child study this week's spelling words.	Have your child read chapters 16 and 17 of *The Cay*. Have your child describe the work of Phillip that will allow him to survive on the island. Is he careless in any way? Write words that are familiar to your child using diacritical spellings. Have your child use the diacritical spelling to read each word aloud, then write the word using traditional spelling.
Friday	Have your child combine subjects and predicates to form original sentences. *See* Language Skills, Week 11, number 3. Have your child use some of his/her original sentences to make a story. He/she may add other sentences as necessary.	Give your child the final spelling test. Have your child record pretest and final test words in his/her Word Bank.	Have your child read chapters 18 and 19 of *The Cay*. Choose a final project that will allow your child to communicate his/her reaction to the book. For project ideas, see page 13.

Learn At Home, Grade 5

Math	Science	Social Studies
Teach your child how to divide by a multiple of ten. This step is a bridge between one-digit divisors and two-digit divisors. *See* Math, Week 11, number 1. Have your child rewrite and solve the following equations: 560 ÷ 10 3,690 ÷ 10 880 ÷ 20 723 ÷ 30 965 ÷ 40 8,260 ÷ 50 420 ÷ 60 893 ÷ 80 9,685 ÷ 80	Have your child record observations from the bean plant experiment from Week 10. Have your child look up and define the term *biome*. What are some biomes? Have your child research the different biomes on Earth. Encourage your child to use a variety of sources and to identify the continents and countries where each biome is found. Have your child use these resources to complete **Biomes of the Earth** (p. 129).	**The Constitution** There is a picture that hangs in the U.S. Capitol of the signing of the Constitution. If possible, show your child a copy of that picture. Identify some of the delegates shown. *See* Social Studies, Week 11, numbers 1 and 2. Have your child read *Shh! We're Writing the Constitution* by Jean Fritz.
Teach your child to round the divisor in order to estimate the quotient. Estimating can help your child determine if his/her answer is reasonable. **Example:** 428 ÷ 37. Round 37 to 40 and 428 to 430. Think 430 ÷ 40. The estimated quotient is 10. Have your child rewrite and estimate the following equations: 1,050 ÷ 35 6,720 ÷ 84 1,638 ÷ 26 523 ÷ 36 918 ÷ 48 8,060 ÷ 52 420 ÷ 61 165 ÷ 38 4,239 ÷ 69	**Forests and Trees:** Provide books and other resources on trees, shrubs and herbs for your child's reference. Discuss with your child the characteristics that distinguish trees from shrubs and bushes. *See* Science, Week 11, number 1. Have your child take notes on trees and shrubs in his/her Science Log, including some illustrations.	Have your child read the Preamble to the Constitution. The Preamble lists six reasons explaining why the Constitution was written. Have your child write out these six reasons. *How were each of these goals achieved? Can you cite any examples?*
Teach your child how to do two-digit division. *See* Math, Week 11, number 2. Give your child 10–15 problems to practice division with two-digit divisors. Have your child estimate then solve each problem and check his/her answers using multiplication.	Obtain a field guide of trees and a dictionary. Have your child use these resources to define the terms *tropical rainforest, deciduous forest, coniferous forest* and *boreal forest*. Based on his/her research, have your child identify on a map areas in North America and throughout the world where each type of forest may be found.	Have your child read about the three branches of government established by the Constitution. Discuss why the founding fathers felt that the three branches were necessary. Have your child research the phrases "separation of powers" and "checks and balances." *See* Social Studies, Week 11, number 3. Have your child complete a chart of the three branches of government, including the titles of the leaders and their duties.
Practice division with two-digit divisors. Have your child complete **Wisconsin's Nickname** (p. 127).	If possible, plan a field trip to a nearby park or forest. Collect leaves or flowers for use in the plant press. *See* Science, Week 11, number 2. Have your child complete **A Study of the Forest Floor** (p. 130).	Play a game that will teach your child about how the Constitution controls government and how the three branches of government check one another. You will need a copy of **Game Cards** (p. 132) and **Government at Work** (p. 133) to play the game. *See* Social Studies, Week 11, number 4.
Practice division with two-digit divisors. Have your child complete **Octopus Crossword** (p. 128).	Discuss the parts of a tree and their functions, using **Parts of a Tree** (p. 131). Have your child identify the shapes of the leaves collected during yesterday's field trip, then sort them into different categories. Help your child press some of the leaves and flowers with the press made in Week 10. *See* Science, Week 11, number 3. Have your child write a poem about a specific type of tree. *See* Science, Week 11, number 4.	Arrange for your child to perform some community service.

123

TEACHING SUGGESTIONS AND ACTIVITIES

LANGUAGE SKILLS (Sentences)

▶ 1. Observe the writing style of various newspaper articles. Give your child time to look through the sports section and read several articles. Point out that the important facts generally show up in the first few paragraphs of an article. Have your child consider how writers begin their articles, what information they include in the article, any visuals that accompany the article and the descriptiveness of the writing. Then, have your child choose a game or sports event to watch on television, taking notes on the players, coaches, highlights of the contest and the final outcome. Have your child use these notes to write an article.

▶ 2. Write these sentences on the chalkboard: *The calico cat/ ran up the tree.*
   My sister Julia/ went to New York for the summer.

   Explain that everything to the left of each slash is the complete subject and everything to the right of each slash is the complete predicate. The simple subjects and predicates have been underlined. Give your child twelve sentences. Have your child draw a slash between the complete subject and complete predicate in each sentence, then circle the simple subject and underline the simple predicate.

▶ 3. Copy each subject below onto a white index card. Copy each predicate onto a colored index card. Put all the cards in a shoe box and mix them up. Have your child combine subject cards with predicate cards to create complete and coherent sentences.

   Subjects:
the demanding captain	three mysterious characters
the afternoon before graduation	several brilliant scientists
the glorious sunset	our class
prickly cacti in the desert	early European explorers
Kris and Rachel	Marie's dog
everyone in Miss Brown's class	the crumbling mansion

   Predicates:
returned after being gone three days	do not need much water
had many scheduled activities	searched for gold in America
ordered the men to cast off	play ball every day after school
slipped behind the old Smith cottage	belonged to an old miser
worked on developing nuclear energy	wore red on Tuesday
went to the art and science museums	made the western sky look like it was on fire

MATH (Division)

▶ 1. To divide by a multiple of ten, follow the same procedure as for single-digit divisors. The only difference is that the quotient moves one digit to the right.

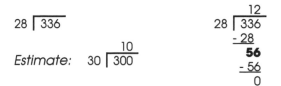

   Try dividing 9 by 40. Then try dividing 96 by 40. Since 40 x 2 = 80, write 2 over the tens place, multiply and subtract 80 from 96.

   $$40\overline{)960}$$

   $$40\overline{)960} \\ \underline{-\ 80} \\ 16$$

   Bring down the zero and divide 160 by 40. Since 40 x 4 = 160, you have no remainder.

   $$40\overline{)960} \\ \underline{-\ 80} \\ 160 \\ \underline{-160} \\ 0$$

▶ 2. Have your child estimate the solution to every problem before working it out. This will make it easier for your child to determine where to place the quotient and decide if the final solution is reasonable. From the estimate and by comparing the divisor (28) to the 33 tens, your child can determine that there is one ten in the quotient. Remind your child to check his/her work after completing a problem (28 x 12 = 336).

   $$28\overline{)336}$$

   Estimate: $30\overline{)300}$

   $$28\overline{)336} \\ \underline{-\ 28} \\ 56 \\ \underline{-\ 56} \\ 0$$

Learn At Home, Grade 5

SCIENCE (Forests and Trees)

▶ 1. Plants may be classified by the form they take:

    trees—plants with tall, woody stems or trunks; usually at least 8 feet tall
    shrubs—plants that grow close to the ground with many branching stems
    herbs—plants with tender juicy stems and less woody tissue

▶ 2. Before your trip, explain to your child some of the rules about picking wildflowers. If you are visiting a nature center or park, find out their policies on picking flowers. If wildflowers are abundant or weedy, you may be allowed to pick a few. Have your child collect a variety of leaves as well.

▶ 3. Have your child select certain leaves and flowers to place in the plant press. Place a layer of paper towels and cardboard between the layers of leaves and flowers. Tighten the boards with the nuts and bolts and set aside. The plants will dry and preserve over several weeks.

▶ 4. Have your child select a favorite tree and write an acrostic poem about it. Each line of the poem should contain information from observations and readings or feelings about the topic.

    Aromatic blossoms, white as the snow,
    Plentiful fruits come in red, green and yellow.
    Pies, cider, juice and jellies,
    Luscious desserts to fill our bellies.
    Everyone loves apples!

Social Studies (The Constitution)

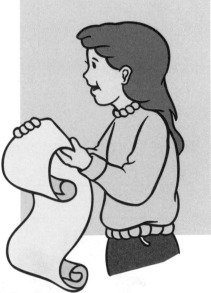

▶ 1. Many people worked together to create the Constitution. After reading about these men, have your child make a chart of information about several of the men. The chart could include headings such as *Name, State* and *Contribution to the Constitution.* Some names to get started: Benjamin Franklin, Alexander Hamilton, George Mason, Robert Morris, Elbridge Gerry, Gouverneur Morris, Roger Sherman and James Madison, Jr.

▶ 2. Have your child title a column on the chart of famous Americans *Creators of the Constitution.* Have your child add the names of the men read about this week. *See* Social Studies, Week 7, number 4.

▶ 3. Have your child read the first three Articles of the Constitution, which lay out the framework for a three-branched government. Discuss the functions of each branch of government. In what ways do their duties overlap? Have your child identify some individuals who currently serve in each branch of government.

▶ 4. While playing this game, your child will gain some understanding of how the Constitution controls government and how the three branches of government check one another. Make copies of **Game Cards** (p. 132) and **Government at Work** (p. 133). Glue each copy onto cardboard and laminate when dry. Cut apart the game cards, shuffle and put a rubber band around them. Copy the rules below onto an index card. Store all the game components in a manila envelope.

Rules: This game may be played with two to four players. The youngest player goes first. Play proceeds clockwise. The first player draws a game card, reads it and moves the number of spaces indicated. Return the card to the bottom of the stack. If a player lands on a White House, Capitol or Supreme Court space, the player must do as indicated on that space. The first player to reach "Finish" wins the game.

Effective Short e

Use the code to decipher some of the words from the spelling list.

ancestor
attempt
central
definition
enforce
festival
generally
genuine
legend
medicine
necessary
pedal
reference
residence
section
sentence
temperature
tennis

Code

A = 1	E = 5	I = 9	M = 13	Q = 17	U = 21	X = 24
B = 2	F = 6	J = 10	N = 14	R = 18	V = 22	Y = 25
C = 3	G = 7	K = 11	O = 15	S = 19	W = 23	Z = 26
D= 4	H = 8	L = 12	P = 16	T = 20		

1. 12-5-7-5-14-4 _____

2. 18-5-19-9-4-5-14-3-5 _____

3. 1-14-3-5-19-20-15-18 _____

4. 14-5-3-5-19-19-1-18-25 _____

5. 3-5-14-20-18-1-12 _____

6. 20-5-13-16-5-18-1-20-21-18-5 _____

7. 4-5-6-9-14-9-20-9-15-14 _____

8. 5-14-6-15-18-3-5 _____

9. 6-5-19-20-9-22-1-12 _____

Write the nine remaining words using the code.

10. _____

11. _____

12. _____

13. _____

14. _____

15. _____

16. _____

17. _____

18. _____

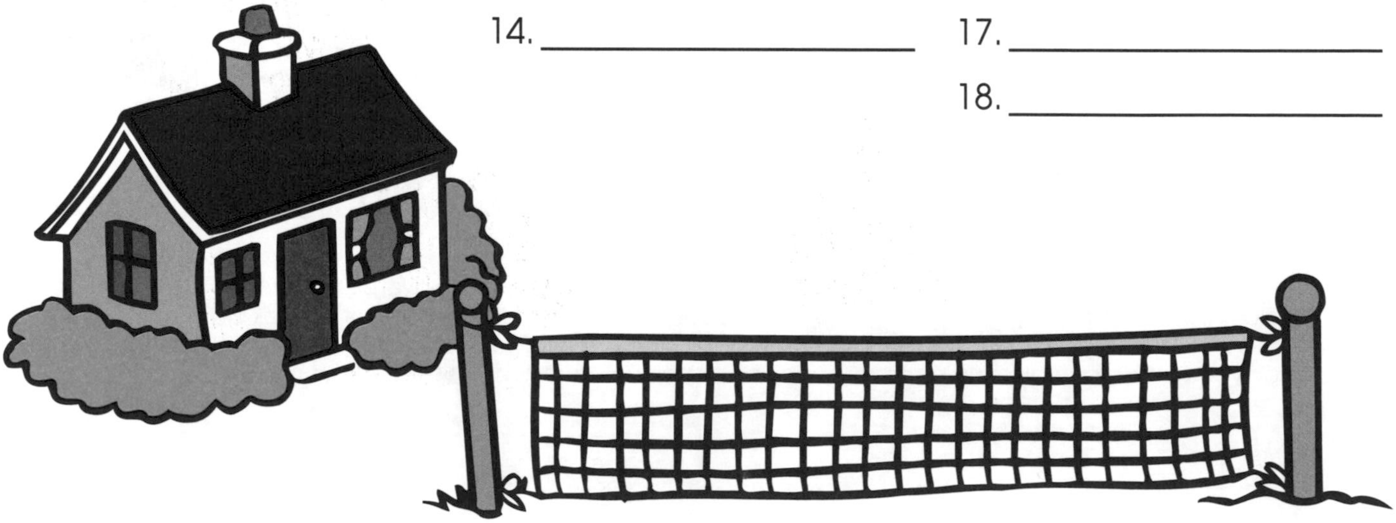

Wisconsin's Nickname

What is Wisconsin known as? To find out, **solve** the division problems below. Then, find the answers at the bottom of the page and **write** the corresponding letter on the line above the answer.

T. 14⟌1218   E. 23⟌1633   S. 53⟌2756

A. 38⟌1596   A. 61⟌5185   E. 18⟌1764

T. 22⟌1628   R. 40⟌2520   D. 55⟌4400

G. 31⟌1364   B. 12⟌780

___ ___ ___ ___ ___ ___   ___ ___ ___ ___ ___
65   85   80   44   71   63   52   74   42   87   98

127

Octopus Crossword

Solve the division problems. **Write** the remainders in word form to complete the puzzle.

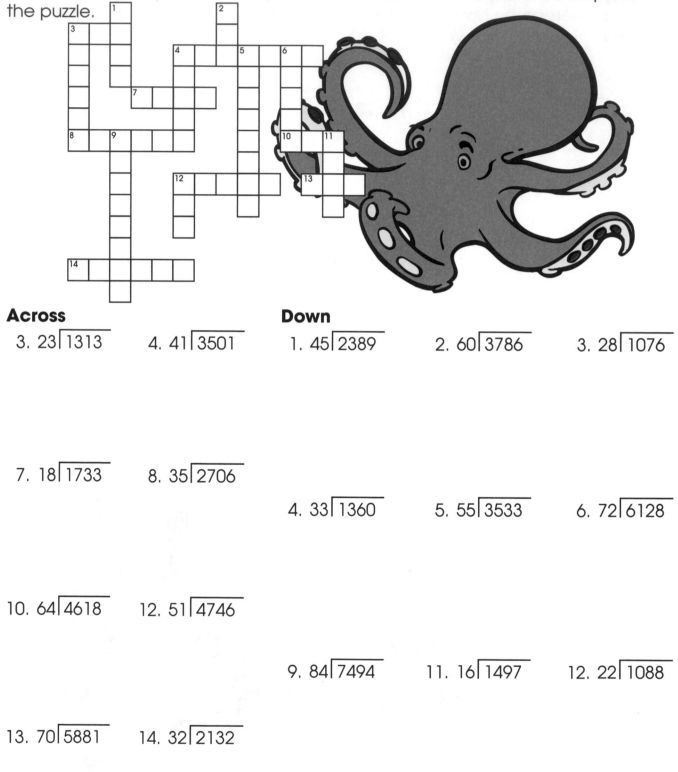

Across

3. 23 ⟌ 1313

4. 41 ⟌ 3501

7. 18 ⟌ 1733

8. 35 ⟌ 2706

10. 64 ⟌ 4618

12. 51 ⟌ 4746

13. 70 ⟌ 5881

14. 32 ⟌ 2132

Down

1. 45 ⟌ 2389

2. 60 ⟌ 3786

3. 28 ⟌ 1076

4. 33 ⟌ 1360

5. 55 ⟌ 3533

6. 72 ⟌ 6128

9. 84 ⟌ 7494

11. 16 ⟌ 1497

12. 22 ⟌ 1088

Learn At Home, Grade 5

Biomes of the Earth

Using a world map, a globe, an atlas, an encyclopedia and other resources, **complete** the chart below to get a better understanding of some biomes and their characteristics.

Biome	Continents and Countries	Animals	Plants
Coniferous Forest			
Deciduous Forest			
Grassland			
Tropical Rainforest			
Desert			
Tundra			
Marine			

A Study of the Forest Floor

A forest habitat is generally cool, damp and shady. At first glance, it might seem that plant life is less abundant than in a pond or grassland area, but as you look more closely, you will see many kinds of species that love shade, such as horsetails, mosses, ferns and fungi. The soil of a forest floor is rich in decaying matter. Its acidity will depend upon whether it contains fallen evergreen needles (which increase the acidity) or leaves from deciduous trees. This rich soil is home to many kinds of animals, including earthworms, centipedes, snails and beetles.

You are going to study a forest floor, either on your own or on a field trip. You will need a wire hanger. Bend it into a circle and toss it onto the ground in a forest. Answer these questions and complete the activities as you examine the living things in your own tiny forest plot.

What is the temperature inside your plot? _____ Is it dry or moist? _____
Identify and describe all the plants that are in your plot. _____
_____
_____

Sketch the ones you cannot identify in the boxes below.

Look for animals. Look under any leaves, evergreen needles or twigs. Identify and describe the different animals that you find. _____
_____
_____

Sketch the ones you cannot identify in the boxes below.

Pick up the hanger and toss it on your lawn or in a field near your home. Compare that habitat to the forest habitat.

Learn At Home, Grade 5

Parts of a Tree

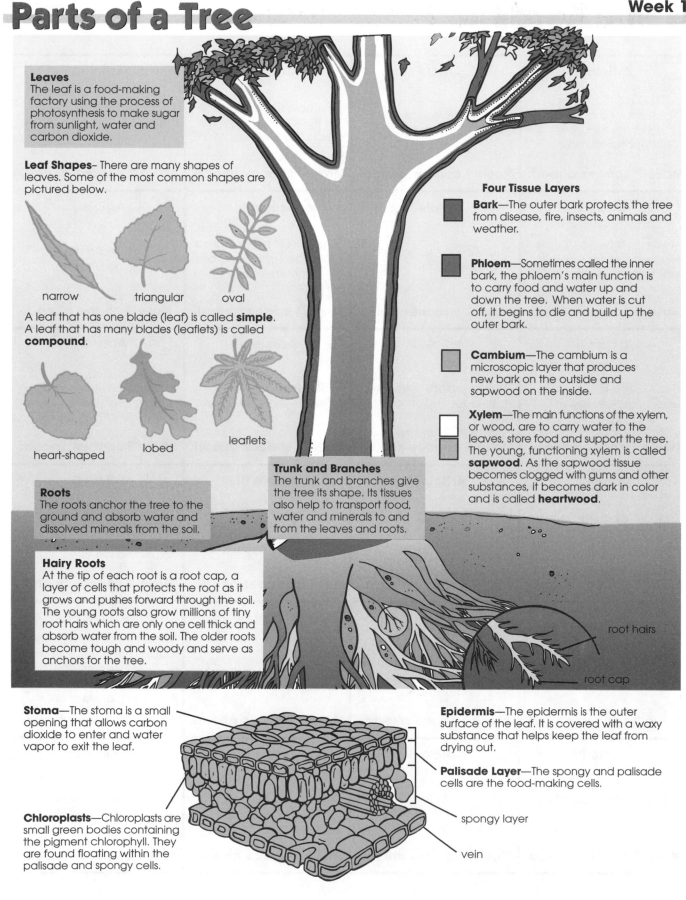

Leaves
The leaf is a food-making factory using the process of photosynthesis to make sugar from sunlight, water and carbon dioxide.

Leaf Shapes– There are many shapes of leaves. Some of the most common shapes are pictured below.

narrow   triangular   oval

A leaf that has one blade (leaf) is called **simple**. A leaf that has many blades (leaflets) is called **compound**.

heart-shaped   lobed   leaflets

Roots
The roots anchor the tree to the ground and absorb water and dissolved minerals from the soil.

Hairy Roots
At the tip of each root is a root cap, a layer of cells that protects the root as it grows and pushes forward through the soil. The young roots also grow millions of tiny root hairs which are only one cell thick and absorb water from the soil. The older roots become tough and woody and serve as anchors for the tree.

Trunk and Branches
The trunk and branches give the tree its shape. Its tissues also help to transport food, water and minerals to and from the leaves and roots.

Four Tissue Layers

Bark—The outer bark protects the tree from disease, fire, insects, animals and weather.

Phloem—Sometimes called the inner bark, the phloem's main function is to carry food and water up and down the tree. When water is cut off, it begins to die and build up the outer bark.

Cambium—The cambium is a microscopic layer that produces new bark on the outside and sapwood on the inside.

Xylem—The main functions of the xylem, or wood, are to carry water to the leaves, store food and support the tree. The young, functioning xylem is called **sapwood**. As the sapwood tissue becomes clogged with gums and other substances, it becomes dark in color and is called **heartwood**.

root hairs

root cap

Stoma—The stoma is a small opening that allows carbon dioxide to enter and water vapor to exit the leaf.

Chloroplasts—Chloroplasts are small green bodies containing the pigment chlorophyll. They are found floating within the palisade and spongy cells.

Epidermis—The epidermis is the outer surface of the leaf. It is covered with a waxy substance that helps keep the leaf from drying out.

Palisade Layer—The spongy and palisade cells are the food-making cells.

spongy layer

vein

131

Article I The U.S. Congress consists of the Senate and the House of Representatives. **Move 3 spaces ahead.**	**Article I** Legislative Acts are enacted by congress. **Move 2 spaces ahead.**	**Article I** Members of the House of Representatives are elected every two years. **Move 3 spaces ahead.**	**Article I** Every state elects a representative for every 30,000 residents. **Move 2 spaces ahead.**
Article I There are two senators elected from every state each for a six-year term. **Move 3 spaces ahead.**	**Article I** The Vice President is the President of the Senate. **Move 2 spaces ahead.**	**Article I** Bills passed by Congress must be approved by the President. **Move 1 space ahead.**	**Article I** The Senate tries all impeachments. **Move 1 space ahead.**
Article II The President has Executive power. **Move 1 space ahead.**	**Article II** The President is elected to a four-year term. **Move 2 spaces ahead.**	**Article II** The President is the Commander-in-Chief. **Move 2 spaces ahead.**	**Article II** All civil officers of the U.S. will be removed from office for reasons of treason, bribery and other high crimes. **Move 3 spaces ahead.**
Article III Congress has the power to declare the punishment of treason. **Move 3 spaces ahead.**	**Article III** The trial of all crimes except impeachment shall be by jury. **Move 1 space ahead.**	**Article III** The judicial power of the U.S. is vested with the Supreme Court and inferior courts. **Move 2 spaces ahead.**	**Article III** The U.S. guarantees a republican form of government and protection to every state. **Move 3 spaces ahead.**
Article IV New states may be admitted to the Union by Congress. **Move 2 spaces ahead.**	**Article IV** A fugitive from one state, found in another, may be delivered to the first state on demand. **Move 1 space ahead.**	**Article IV** Citizens in every state have the same rights. **Move 3 spaces ahead.**	**Article IV** When $\frac{2}{3}$'s of both Houses approve and $\frac{3}{4}$'s of the states ratify an amendment, it is added to the Constitution. **Move 1 space ahead.**
Article IV All federal and state officials are bound by oath to support the Constitution. **Move 3 spaces ahead.**	**Article IV** All laws and treaties made under the authority of the U.S. are the supreme law of the land. **Move 2 spaces ahead.**	**Article IV** Congress may admit new states into the country. **Move 1 space ahead.**	**Article IV** It would take nine states to ratify the Constitution. **Move 2 spaces ahead.**

Learn At Home, Grade 5

Government at Work

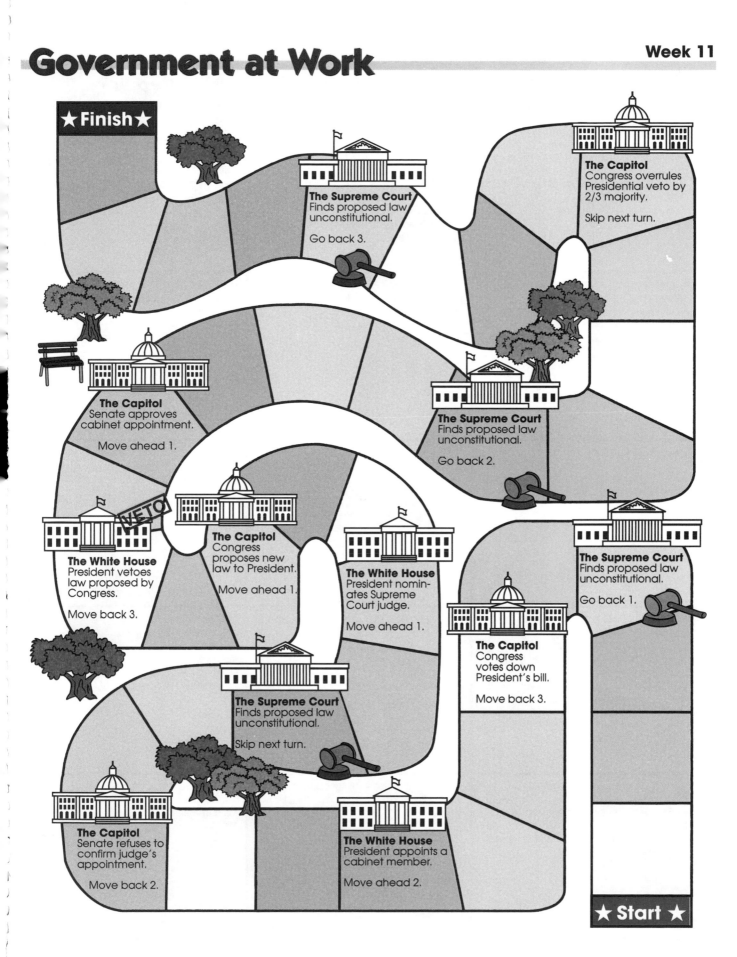

★ Finish ★

The Supreme Court
Finds proposed law unconstitutional.

Go back 3.

The Capitol
Congress overrules Presidential veto by 2/3 majority.

Skip next turn.

The Capitol
Senate approves cabinet appointment.

Move ahead 1.

The Supreme Court
Finds proposed law unconstitutional.

Go back 2.

The White House
President vetoes law proposed by Congress.

Move back 3.

The Capitol
Congress proposes new law to President.

Move ahead 1.

The White House
President nominates Supreme Court judge.

Move ahead 1.

The Supreme Court
Finds proposed law unconstitutional.

Go back 1.

The Capitol
Congress votes down President's bill.

Move back 3.

The Supreme Court
Finds proposed law unconstitutional.

Skip next turn.

The Capitol
Senate refuses to confirm judge's appointment.

Move back 2.

The White House
President appoints a cabinet member.

Move ahead 2.

★ Start ★

	Language Skills	**Spelling**	**Reading**
Monday	Introduce your child to the concept of expository writing. Guide your child as he/she writes an expository writing piece. Have your child choose a topic, make a plan for writing and start working on a rough draft. *See* Language Skills, Week 12, number 1.	Pretest your child on these spelling words: activities, citizen, difference, difficulties, exit, fiction, hippopotamus, individual, instrument, interesting, kitchen, listening, miniature, miserable, officer, principal, prisoner, shipment. Have your child correct the pretest. Add personalized words and make two copies of this week's study list.	**Story Elements** Review the elements of a story. Then, introduce *Mr. Popper's Penguins* by Richard and Florence Atwater. Have your child read chapter 1. Have your child list the story's characters, setting and problem so far.
Tuesday	**Sentences:** Review capitalization rules and ending punctuation. Have your child complete **Proofreading for Punctuation** (p. 138).	Review this week's spelling words. Have your child complete **Itty-Bitty i** (p. 140).	Have your child read chapters 2 and 3 of *Mr. Popper's Penguins*. Discuss any difficult words in the text. Have him/her look up the following words in the dictionary: *calcimine, debris, expanses, expedition, faint, heathen, inquisitive, missionary* and *pompous*.
Wednesday	Discuss conjunctions with your child. A *conjunction* joins two simple sentences to form a compound sentence. *See* Language Skills, Week 12, numbers 2–4.	Have your child use each of this week's spelling words correctly in a sentence.	Have your child read chapters 4 and 5 of *Mr. Popper's Penguins*. Have your child do some research on penguins and record the information on **Mr. Popper's Penguins** (p. 141).
Thursday	Review the use of commas in direct address and with introductory words. *See* Language Skills, Week 8, number 2. Give your child 10–15 sentences that contain direct address and introductory words. Omit all commas. Have your child determine where commas are needed and add them accordingly.	Have your child study this week's spelling words.	Discuss the plot of the story. *What is the problem that drives the plot and what are the events that carry it along? Can predict the climax of the plot?* Have your child read chapters 6 and 7 of *Mr. Popper's Penguins*.
Friday	Review the many uses of commas, including with an appositive, in a series and to set off an interrupting word or phrase. Have your child complete **Using Commas** (p. 139).	Give your child the final spelling test. Have your child record pretest and final test words in his/her Word Bank.	Have your child read chapters 8 and 9 of *Mr. Popper's Penguins*. Then, have your child imagine that he/she is interviewing Mr. Popper. Have your child write the questions he/she would ask, as well as Mr. Popper's probable responses.

Learn At Home, Grade 5

Math	Science	Social Studies
Explain to your child that there are three ways to write the same division problem. Your child has already worked with two ways: 6 ÷ 3 and 3⟌6. A third way is to write the equation as a fraction. In this case, the dividend is written on the top and the divisor is written on the bottom. **Example:** $\frac{6}{3} = 2$ Have your child complete **Division in Three Ways** (p. 142).	**Flowering Plants** Provide books and other resources on flowering plants for your child's reference. Have your child take notes on flowering plants in his/her Science Log. Have him/her describe the characteristics that distinguish *annuals, biennials* and *perennials. See* Science, Week 12, number 1.	**Bill of Rights** Some states refused to sign the Constitution unless some individual rights were clarified. The first ten amendments to the Constitution are known as the Bill of Rights. Discuss why the Bill of Rights was so important to the early Americans after their experiences with Britain. Are they important to your child? Have him/her prioritize the first ten amendments. Can he/she eliminate any that are not important?
Teach your child how to perform division when there is a decimal in the dividend. *See* Math, Week 12, number 1. Have your child complete **Decimal Dividends** (p. 143).	Use **Flowering Plants** (p. 144) to teach your child about the parts of the flower. Explain the function of each of these parts. Bring in several real flowers for your child to examine. *See* Science, Week 12, number 2. Have your child sketch and label the parts of a flower in his/her Science Log.	Read the rest of the amendments with your child. Work together to group the amendments into the following categories: gives you the right to do something, gives you the right to have something, gives you rights when you are accused of something, gives you the right to be something. Alternately, your child may wish to make up his/her own categories.
Using division, have your child find the price per item for things sold in groups. Use real items and real prices, if possible. You may even want to go to a store with paper and pencil. **Examples:** 3 pairs of socks for $5.97 or 1 pair for ___ 1 dozen eggs for $1.92 or 1 egg for ___ 8 apples for $2.48 or 1 apple for ___ 3 pairs of jeans for $95.55 or 1 pair for ___ 1 dozen pencils for $2.40 or 1 pencil for ___	Have your child complete the activity on **Flower Fun** (p. 145).	Discuss ways that you hear (on the news) the Constitution at work today. Listen for evidence that the branches of government are carrying out the ideals and laws of the Constitution. Have your child write about one instance that proves the Constitution remains a powerful document.
Teach your child how to find averages. **Example:** *Marta earned the following scores on her last eight math tests: 97, 85, 95, 99, 100, 84, 88 and 96. What was her average score?* Add the numbers to obtain a total, then divide by the number of groups. You may wish to round your answer to the nearest whole number. *See* Math, Week 12, numbers 2–4.	The function of a flower is to make seeds. Seeds can take many shapes and may range in size from microscopic to quite large. The form a seed takes is related to how the plant spreads itself. For instance, some seeds are light so they may be carried by the wind. Have your child observe the seeds in a variety of flowering plants. Have your child draw illustrations of the seeds he/she observes.	Discuss the actions of George Washington, America's first leader of the executive branch. *See* Social Studies, Week 12, numbers 1–3. The Cabinet is part of the executive branch. Have your child read about the current Cabinet. *What are the positions and who currently occupies them?* Have your child read the poem "Alexander Hamilton" by Rosemary and Stephen Vincent Benet. It may be found in *A Book of Americans.*
Have your child find the averages of numbers in several real-life situations. **Examples:** Find the average of 5 grades (percentages). Find the average high temperature for a week. Find the average low temperature for a week. Find the average height of your friends. Find the average number of cars that get through a green light. Find the average number of people in cars.	Some seeds are surrounded by the fruit of the plant. *See* Science, Week 12, number 3. The word *fruit* usually refers to an edible treat, such as an apple, a banana, an orange or a berry. Identify and discuss the two main classifications of fruits: fleshy and dry. *See* Science, Week 12, number 4. Have your child examine some fruits, locating the seed(s) in each. Have him/her observe the fruitlets of compound fruits, such as raspberries.	Arrange for your child to perform some community service.

TEACHING SUGGESTIONS AND ACTIVITIES

LANGUAGE SKILLS (Sentences)

▶ 1. To plan for expository writing, it is helpful to draw a concept map. Have your child choose a familiar topic and write it in the center of a page. Write subtopics and details on spokes radiating out from the center topic. Have your child use the concept map as a guide in writing a first draft.

▶ 2. Write the following two simple sentences on the chalkboard:

> *The cows knew it was milking time.*
> *They walked slowly toward the barn.*

These sentences can be joined with a conjunction to form one sentence, called a compound sentence. Use a conjunction such as *and, but, or, nor* or *yet* as the joining word. Have your child combine the two sentences and write out the new sentence:
The cows knew it was milking time, and they walked slowly toward the barn.
Circle the comma. Explain that when two sentences are joined, a comma is always placed before the joining word or conjunction.

▶ 3. Write the following sentences on the board. Have your child make a ✓ next to each compound sentence.

> *Jack enjoyed the book, but he didn't enjoy the movie.*
> *Mary took out the garbage. The garbage collector did not take it.*
> *Juan likes to walk, but Nancy prefers to run.*
> *The weather turned warm, and the ice began to melt.*
> *Kim and Lauren will arrive this afternoon.*

▶ 4. Give your child the following sets of sentences. Have him/her combine each set into a compound sentence, using a different conjunction each time.

> *Greg unpacked the groceries. Sue put them away.*
> *You can go to the store today. You can go early tomorrow.*
> *He turned the key. The door would not open.*
> *The dog did like the cat. He did not like the bird.*

MATH (Division)

▶ 1. This lesson introduces decimals in division. Decimals will be taught more thoroughly in a few weeks. At this time, the decimal is in the dividend only. your child will divide a decimal number (e.g., money) by a whole number. This is done in the same way as division with whole numbers, except that the decimal point is moved up to the quotient.

Move the decimal directly up into the quotient.

$$9 \overline{\smash{)}19.98}$$

Divide as usual.

$$
\begin{array}{r}
2.22 \\
9 \overline{\smash{)}19.98} \\
-18 \\
\hline
1\,9 \\
-1\,8 \\
\hline
18 \\
-18 \\
\hline
0
\end{array}
$$

▶ 2. Help your child visualize averages with the following activity. Have your child build several block towers of different heights, then count how many blocks there are in all. Discuss ways to make all of the towers the same height, using only the existing blocks. Keeping the same number of towers, have your child move the blocks around until there are (nearly) the same number of blocks in each tower. Count the total number of blocks and divide this total by the number of towers. Help your child see that this division resulted in the same answer as the physical rearrangement.

Learn At Home, Grade 5

3. Encourage your child to listen and watch for everyday uses of averages, such as average speed, average yards per carry in a football game, average points per game for a basketball player, average rainfall, average temperature, average height, average weight and average grades.

4. Have your child find the average of each group of numbers. Answers (some are rounded to the nearest whole number) are provided in parentheses.

202, 85, 172 (153)   987, 1003, 1111, 1013, 1011 (1025)   622, 645, 601, 604, 635 (621)
34, 56, 49, 52 (48)   121, 143, 162, 101, 159 (137)   90, 100, 123, 89 (101)

SCIENCE (Flowering Plants)

1. Obtain pictures of a variety of flowering plants from seed catalogs or field guides.

   Annuals complete their life cycle in just one year. Some common annuals include snapdragons, sweet peas, petunias, pansies, impatiens, marigolds, sunflowers, larkspurs, cosmos, zinnias and nasturtiums.

   Biennials complete their life cycle in two years. Some common biennials include Canterbury bells, foxglove, hollyhocks and Iceland poppies.

   Perennials live for more than two years. Some common perennials include peonies, irises, phlox, daffodils, tulips, hyacinths and flowering shrubs and trees. Many perennials die down during the winter, but their underground roots and stems survive. Flowering shrubs and trees lose their leaves and flowers during the winter, but new ones grow each year.

2. Select a few flowers, such as a rose, an iris, a daffodil and a tulip, for your child to examine. Have him/her locate the flower parts shown on **Flowering Plants** (p. 144). Provide your child with a cutting board and a cutting instrument, such as a razor-blade knife. Supervise your child as he/she cuts a cross section of the selected flowers. Direct your child to locate and name the parts of each flower. Discuss the function of the *sepals, petals, receptacle, stigma, style, ovary, anther* and *filament.*

3. A fruit supplies protection for the seed, as well as nourishment for the sprouting seedling. Many fruits are edible. When an animal (or human) eats a fruit, its seed(s) may be deposited in a new location where a new plant will grow. Have your child read more about the functions of fruits.

4. Explain that fruits may be classified as fleshy or dry.

   Fleshy—The tissue surrounding the seed is fleshy. This group includes berries, oranges, lemons, melons, gourds, cucumbers, squash, apples and pears.

   Dry—The tissue surrounding the seed is dry. This group includes nuts, grains, milkweed and chestnuts.

   Provide some samples of each type of fruit for your child to examine. Supervise him/her in cutting or breaking open some of the fruits to examine the seeds and pits.

SOCIAL STUDIES (Bill of Rights)

1. Have your child draw a three-column chart for organizing facts about George Washington. Have your child use the following headings: *Early Life, Soldier-Statesman* and *President.* Have your child list facts that fit each category as he/she reads about Washington. *How was Washington elected? How many terms did he serve? Who was in his cabinet? Where was the first capital?* Have your child include the dates of Washington's presidency on the American history time line.

2. John Jay, Henry Knox, Edmund Randolph, Thomas Jefferson and Alexander Hamilton were members of Washington's cabinet. They were people he could trust to advise him. Two of his cabinet members had very different ideas about how government should be run. The arguments between Thomas Jefferson and Alexander Hamilton led to the beginning of political parties.

3. Have your child read about the early history of the nation's permanent capital, Washington, D.C. Ask your child to find out who chose the site, why it was selected, on what river it was located and why it was not part of any state. Discuss the planning of the capital and the people involved, when it was completed and who was the first president to live there.

Proofreading for Punctuation

Anna is running for class president. She has written her last campaign speech before the election but has not done a very good job of punctuating it. Read her speech. Write in capital letters where needed and add correct punctuation.

tomorrow you will choose one of five candidates as your class president i want to be the one you choose. why should you vote for me As class president I will collect twenty-five cents a month from every class member The money will be used for a party at the end of the school year I will listen to your suggestions and try to do something about them As president of our class I will go to teachers' meetings I will try to have homework assignments over weekends reduced Vote for me I know I will make the next year the best one for you and our class. it will be a year to remember thank you for your support

Anna did not win the election, but she was a good sport. She wrote a message to Kim, the winner, in the school newspaper. The editor did not proofread Anna's message, and it got published just as she wrote it. Correct Anna's work once more.

I want to congratulate Kim i know she will make a fine class president i am sorry I did not win, but I want Kim and everyone else to know I support her Now that the election is over and the class showed their preference, let's all join together and support Kim congratulations Kim

Using Commas

Use commas to set off an **appositive**, a noun
or phrase that explains or identifies the noun it follows.
Example: *Jack, the janitor, walked down the hall.*

Use commas to separate words or phrases in a **series**.
Example: *He ate the apple, the peach and the plum.*

Use commas after **introductory** words or phrases.
Examples: *Yes, I'm going to the fair.*
By the way, did you bring a camera?

Use commas to set off a **noun of address**, the name
of the person being addressed or spoken to.
Example: *Caroline, will you come with me?*

Use commas to set off **interrupting** words or phrases.
Example: *He was, as you know, an actor before he was elected.*

Add commas to the sentences where they are needed. On each line, explain why
you added the comma by writing **appositive**, **series**, **introductory**, **noun of
address** or **interrupting**.

1. Maryanne the new girl in school is a very good cook. _____

2. My favorite snacks are red apples pretzels and popcorn. _____

3. My skills however do not include cooking. _____

4. I know Sally that you love to cook. _____

5. That was in my opinion the best meal ever served. _____

6. After they finished the books Tom and Larry wrote the report. _____

7. Thomas Edison an inventor had failures before each success. _____

8. Pete our best soccer player won't be here for the big game. _____

9. No I won't be seeing the movie. _____

10. The coating on the pecans was sweet sugary and crisp. _____

11. That is if I'm not mistaken my yellow and green pencil._____

12. Sam would you please pass me my pen? _____

Itty-Bitty i

activities
citizen
difference
difficulties
exit
fiction
hippopotamus
individual
instrument
interesting
kitchen
listening
miniature
miserable
officer
principal
prisoner
shipment

Write the spelling word that best completes each sentence.

1. We received a _____ of new books for our library.
2. Our family usually eats dinner in the _____.
3. When we subtract one number from another, we find the _____.
4. A story which is not true is _____.
5. We all have special talents and gifts because we are _____ people.
6. Pay close attention by _____ carefully to the directions.
7. The _____ was released on parole.
8. A violin is considered a stringed _____.
9. My sister collects _____ teapots.
10. Friends can be especially helpful when one is experiencing _____.
11. What kinds of _____ do you do after school?
12. Find the _____ sign so we can leave the building.
13. That movie had a very _____ plot.
14. The _____ is a friend to both teachers and students.
15. As a _____ of the U.S., I respect the American flag.
16. The police _____ spoke kindly to the little child.
17. The head cold made my brother feel _____.
18. It would be difficult to have a _____ for a pet.

Each word below is hidden in a list word. **Write** that spelling word on the blank.

1. on _____
2. son _____
3. act _____
4. kit _____
5. pal _____
6. pot _____
7. me _____
8. miser _____
9. ties _____

Learn At Home, Grade 5

Mr. Popper's Penguins

Complete this sheet with factual information about penguins.

1. Where do penguins live? _____

2. How many species of penguins are there? _____

   Name two types: _____ and _____

3. Describe the general appearance of penguins, including body covering, height and weight ranges. _____

   _____

   _____

4. How do penguins move? _____

5. What do penguins eat? _____

6. Describe penguins' breeding habits: _____

7. Describe a newly hatched penguin. _____

Draw an emperor penguin in the space below.

141

Division in Three Ways

The equation $12 \div 3$ can also be written as $3\overline{)12}$ or $\frac{12}{3}$.

Write each equation in the three forms.
The first one has been done for you.

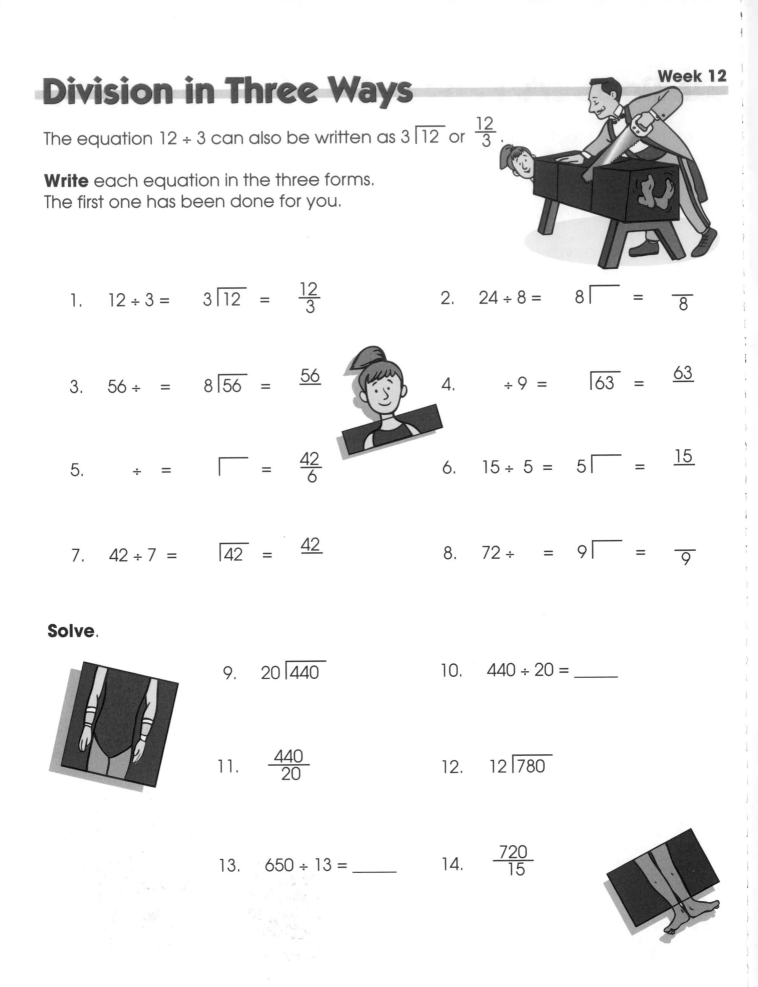

1. $12 \div 3 =$ $3\overline{)12}$ $=$ $\frac{12}{3}$

2. $24 \div 8 =$ $8\overline{)}$ $=$ $\frac{}{8}$

3. $56 \div =$ $8\overline{)56}$ $=$ $\frac{56}{}$

4. $ \div 9 =$ $\overline{)63}$ $=$ $\frac{63}{}$

5. $ \div =$ $\overline{)}$ $=$ $\frac{42}{6}$

6. $15 \div 5 =$ $5\overline{)}$ $=$ $\frac{15}{}$

7. $42 \div 7 =$ $\overline{)42}$ $=$ $\frac{42}{}$

8. $72 \div =$ $9\overline{)}$ $=$ $\frac{}{9}$

Solve.

9. $20\overline{)440}$

10. $440 \div 20 =$ _____

11. $\frac{440}{20}$

12. $12\overline{)780}$

13. $650 \div 13 =$ _____

14. $\frac{720}{15}$

142

Decimal Dividends

Bring the decimal to the quotient. **Solve**.

1. $8\overline{)13.84}$

2. $12\overline{)27.96}$

3. $\dfrac{36.63}{11}$

4. $71.4 \div 51 =$

5. $93.09 \div 87$

6. $\dfrac{99.52}{32}$

7. Mandy wants to buy one bottle of soda pop. The advertised price is 3 bottles for $2.58. How much is one bottle? _____

8. Youngen and her 5 friends went to a movie together. Youngen paid $31.50 for all of the tickets. How much did each ticket cost? _____

9. Sang and Jon ate lunch for $12.58. They each had a turkey sandwich, fries and milk. How much did each boy pay? _____

143

Flowering Plants

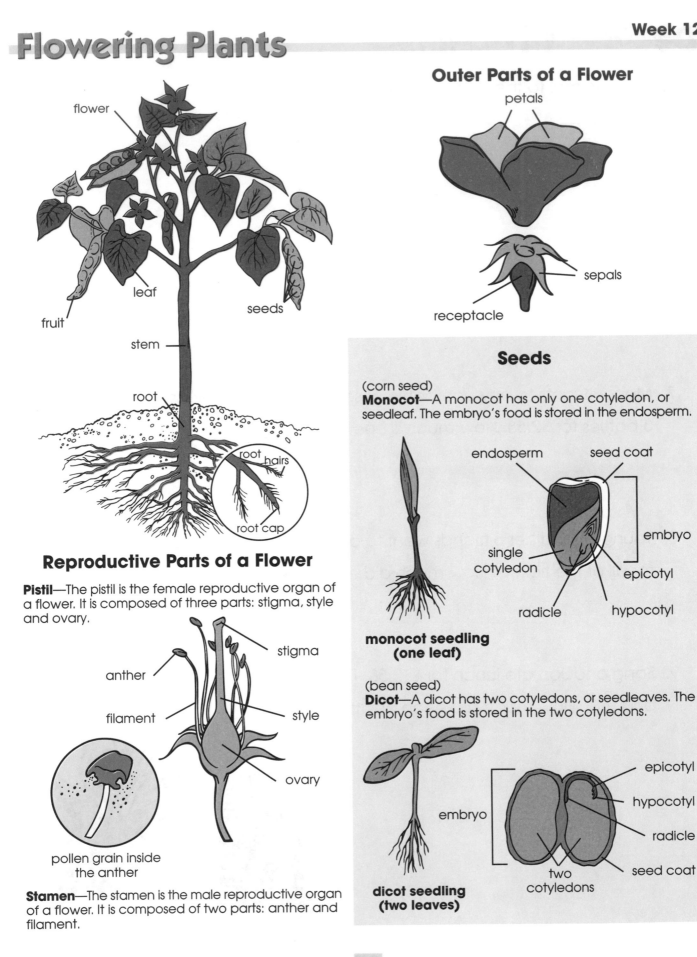

flower

leaf

fruit

seeds

stem

root

root hairs

root cap

Outer Parts of a Flower

petals

sepals

receptacle

Reproductive Parts of a Flower

Pistil—The pistil is the female reproductive organ of a flower. It is composed of three parts: stigma, style and ovary.

anther

filament

stigma

style

ovary

pollen grain inside the anther

Stamen—The stamen is the male reproductive organ of a flower. It is composed of two parts: anther and filament.

Seeds

(corn seed)
Monocot—A monocot has only one cotyledon, or seedleaf. The embryo's food is stored in the endosperm.

endosperm

seed coat

single cotyledon

embryo

epicotyl

radicle

hypocotyl

monocot seedling (one leaf)

(bean seed)
Dicot—A dicot has two cotyledons, or seedleaves. The embryo's food is stored in the two cotyledons.

embryo

epicotyl

hypocotyl

radicle

seed coat

two cotyledons

dicot seedling (two leaves)

Learn At Home, Grade 5

Flower Fun

Fill in the label for each plant part.

1. ___ ___ ___ **F**
2. ___ ___ **L** ___ ___ ___ ___ ___
3. ___ **O** ___ ___
4. ___ ___ ___ **W** ___ ___
5. ___ **E** ___ ___ ___ ___
6. ___ ___ ___ **R** ___
7. ___ **I** ___ ___ ___ ___
8. ___ ___ ___ ___ **N** ___
9. ___ ___ ___ **G** ___

10. ___ ___ ___ ___ **P** ___ ___ ___ ___ ___
11. ___ ___ ___ ___ **L** ___
12. ___ ___ **A** ___ ___ ___
13. ___ **N** ___ ___ ___ ___
14. ___ **T** ___ ___
15. **S** ___ ___ ___

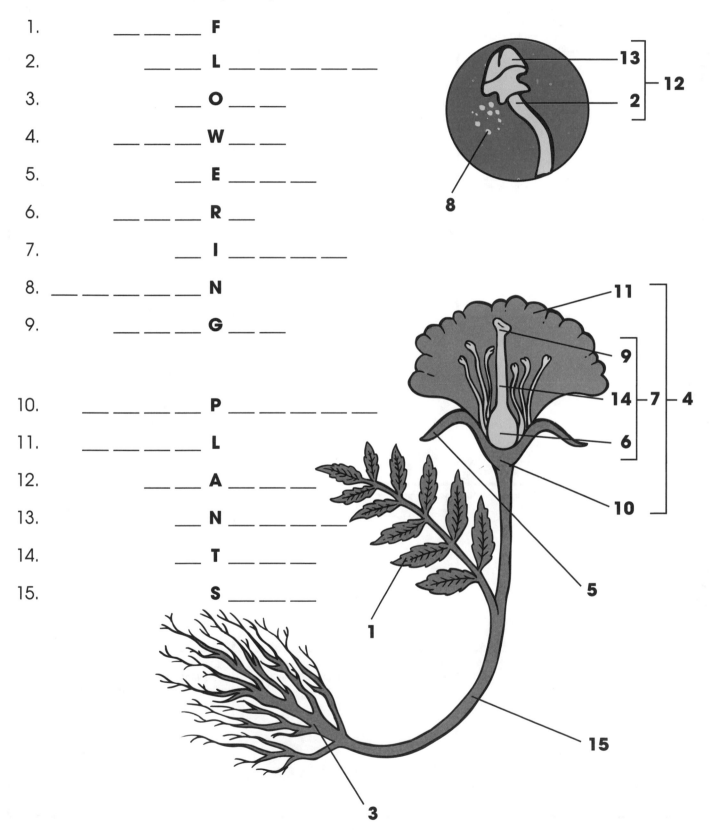

Learn At Home, Grade 5

© 1999 Tribune Education. All Rights Reserved.

Language Skills	Spelling	Reading
Monday **Friendly Letter** Review the format of a friendly letter. Discuss proper punctuation in letters, such as in addresses and dates. *See* Language Skills, Week 13, number 1.	Pretest your child on these spelling words: blocked, honor, product, bother, model, promise, column, monster, robberies, common, octopus, soccer, dodge, oxen, toboggan, gossip, problem, wobble. Have your child correct the pretest. Add personalized words and make two copies of this week's study list.	Have your child read chapters 10–11 of *Mr. Popper's Penguins*. Have your child list four adjectives to describe each of the following characters: Mr. Popper, Mrs. Popper and Captain Cook.
Tuesday Have your child write a friendly letter to a friend or relative. Stress proper form and punctuation. Encourage your child to describe recent events and to ask questions in his/her letter.	Review this week's spelling words. Have your child complete **Hidden o's** (p. 151).	Have your child read chapters 12–14 of *Mr. Popper's Penguins*. Have him/her summarize the main idea of each chapter with a single sentence.
Wednesday Teach your child the proper way to address an envelope. *See* Language Skills, Week 13, number 2.	Have your child use each of this week's spelling words correctly in a sentence.	Discuss the type of information that is displayed on a time line. Show your child several examples of time lines. Have your child read chapters 15–16 of *Mr. Popper's Penguins*. Have your child make a time line of events in the story, adding to the time line as he/she completes the book this week.
Thursday Make a chart of capitalization rules. Keep it posted for your child's reference. *See* Language Skills, Week 13, number 3.	Have your child study this week's spelling words.	Have your child read chapters 17–18 of *Mr. Popper's Penguins*. Have your child make a chart of the cities that the performers visit. Then, have him/her estimate how much money they are making on tour.
Friday Have your child complete **Capitals** (p. 150).	Give your child the final spelling test. Have your child record pretest and final test words in his/her Word Bank.	Have your child finish reading *Mr. Popper's Penguins*. Have your child write in his/her Reading Journal about the book. How does your child feel about Mr. Popper's choice?

Learn At Home, Grade 5

Math	Science	Social Studies
Have your child complete **Multiplication Table** (p. 152). Make two copies of the completed table. On one copy, have your child circle all the even numbers in red. These are all numbers divisible by 2. On the same copy, have your child lightly shade every fifth number in blue. These are numbers divisible by 5. Finally, have your child draw a green **X** over every tenth number. These are all numbers divisible by 10. Study the patterns and discuss.	**Seed Dispersal** Discuss the importance of seed dispersal in a plant's propagation. Why must seeds disperse rather than drop directly beneath the plant? Obtain books and other resources on seed dispersal for your child's reference.	**Early Presidents** Have your child read about America's second president, John Adams. Discuss his good and bad qualities, as well as the highlights of his term in office. *What were his greatest accomplishments as president?* Have your child add the dates of Adams's presidency to the time line. Abigail Adams is a well-known first lady. Have your child write a short biography detailing her influence and accomplishments.
Teach your child how to find the numbers divisible by 3 and 9. On the second copy of the completed **Multiplication Table** (p. 152), have your child color every third number yellow. These are all numbers divisible by 3. Then, have your child draw an orange **X** over every ninth number (every third colored square). These are all numbers divisible by 9. Study the patterns and discuss. **Option:** Repeat this activity with numbers divisible by 4, 6, 7 and 8.	Some seeds are dispersed to different locations while still inside the fruit. Have your child name an example. Later, the fruit may split open and release the seed(s). Ask your child to consider how a fruit might be dispersed to a new location.	Have your child read about America's third president, Thomas Jefferson. Discuss his good and bad qualities, as well as the highlights of his term in office. *What were his greatest accomplishments as president?* Have your child add the dates of Jefferson's presidency to the time line. Introduce and discuss the Louisiana Purchase. *See* Social Studies, Week 13, numbers 1–3.
Quiz your child on division. Have your child complete **Division** (p. 153). Reteach concepts if necessary.	Some seeds are carried by animals. Birds and other animals eat fruits containing seeds. The seeds are not digested and the animal deposits the seeds elsewhere as part of its body waste. Other seeds are dispersed by sticking to an animal's fur or body or to clothing. Have your child sketch some of the seeds that stick to an animal's fur (with barbs or sticky coats) in his/her Science Log.	**Lewis and Clark Expedition:** Introduce your child to the explorations of Meriwether Lewis and William Clark. Provide several resources on the expedition for your child's reference. Set aside some time for your child to read about the expedition and learn some of the details of their travels. *See* Social Studies, Week 13, number 4. Have your child read about Sacagawea and draw a picture of her with the expedition.
Geometry: Teach your child how to use a protractor to measure angles. Have your child place the straight edge of the protractor along one ray of the angle to be measured. Ask your child to identify the number, in degrees, to which the other ray points. *See* Math, Week 13, numbers 1–3. Teach the following terms: *ray, angle, vertex, acute angle, right angle* and *obtuse angle.* Have your child complete **Angle Measurement** (p. 154).	Some seeds are dispersed by the wind. These seeds may have structures that enable them to ride the wind for long distances. Study a maple leaf seed and dandelion seeds. What structures enable these seeds to be carried by the wind? Have your child illustrate seeds traveling in the wind and landing (and sprouting) in new spots.	Have your child trace the journey of the Lewis and Clark expedition on a map. From this, have your child make a list of some of the geographic features the expedition encountered.
Review the following geometry terms: *point, line, line segment, ray* and *plane.* Show your child examples of each. Have your child complete **Geometric Figures** (p. 155).	Help your child plant a variety of seeds and label them carefully. Have your child observe and care for the plants daily, then predict which seeds will sprout first. Have your child record his/her observations and analysis in the Science Log. Remove the pressed plants from the plant press. *See* Science, Week 13.	Arrange for your child to perform some community service.

Week 13

TEACHING SUGGESTIONS AND ACTIVITIES

LANGUAGE SKILLS (Friendly Letter)

▶ 1. In a letter, commas are used to separate the day from the date and the date from the year.

Saturday, April 12, 1999   February 14, 2002

Demonstrate the format for writing the address. Discuss where commas are used. Point out the comma after the salutation or greeting. Point out that the closing is always followed by a comma before the signature on a letter. Teach your child to indent each paragraph in the body of a friendly letter.

▶ 2. Show your child some envelopes that you have received in the mail. Ask what information is necessary to mail a letter (mailing address with zip code). Observe the punctuation. Have your child point out everything that is capitalized and where commas are used. Point out the use of periods after abbreviations of titles (Mr., Dr., Mrs.) and streets (St., Ave.). Give your child three envelopes to address. Have your child address one to him/herself, one to you and one to a relative or friend.

▶ 3. Have your child brainstorm when to use a capital letter. Then, group the list into categories. Have your child write examples for each category. Here is a sample chart of categories and examples:

abbreviations: titles (Mr., Ms., Dr., Jr., Sr.)
business (Co., Corp., Ltd., Inc.)
days (Mon., Tues., Wed., Sat.)
months (Jan., Feb., Sept., Dec.)
addresses (St., Ave., Blvd., Apt., P.O.)
states (AR, CA, NY, PA, RI, TX)

first word in a sentence: It rained all day.
We will spend this summer at our camp.

greeting and closing in a letter: Dear Sir, Dear Julie, Yours truly, Sincerely

outlines: first word of each main topic and subtopic

    I. Types of nutrients
      A. Minerals
      B. Vitamins
      C. Proteins
      D. Carbohydrates

pronoun I: I will read ten books this month.
When will I read more than ten books?

proper nouns: Thomas A. Edison
Alexander the Great (most important words)
Golden Gate Bridge

proper adjectives: Picasso was a Spanish painter.
She is learning to speak the Japanese language.
We are reading Native American folktales.

holidays: Easter, May Day, Fourth of July, Labor Day

buildings: Empire State Building, Chrysler Building

companies: Good Art Company, Better Bread Company

148

© 1999 Tribune Education. All Rights Reserved.   *Learn At Home*, Grade 5

MATH (Geometry)

▶ 1. The most common type of protractor used by children is shaped like a D, but this is actually only one-half of a protractor. A protractor represents a circle divided into 360 parts. Each of these parts is called a degree. When measuring an angle, you are actually measuring how much of a circle an angle includes.

▶ 2. Help your child make and use a giant protractor. Draw a large (3' radius) circle on the ground or on a large sheet of butcher paper. Use a string compass to make this circle. Tie a string to a piece of chalk and cut the string to the length of the radius. Hold the end of the string at the center point while your child draws the circle with the chalk. Draw a straight line across the circle through the center point. Label one side 0° and the other side 180° where the line meets the circle. Use a small protractor to help draw the 90° angle. Write the numbers along the circle as on the protractor.

▶ 3. Have your child stand at the center point of the giant protractor, facing 0°. Name an angle measurement such as 45°. Have your child point with one arm to 0° and with the other to the named measurement. Repeat with several different angle measurements so your child gains a sense of the relative size of different angles. Also ask your child to identify each angle as right, obtuse or acute. Have fun with this by having your child spin around 360° or 720°.

SCIENCE (Seed Dispersal)

Help your child open the plant press, carefully removing the layers of paper and cardboard to expose the pressed leaves or flowers. If the plants seem to be nicely pressed and preserved, have your child think of ways to use these specimens. The pressed leaves or flowers could be used to make note cards or assembled together in a leaf booklet. Provide construction paper, glue, ring binders and clear, self-adhesive shelf paper. To make the booklet, have your child glue each leaf onto a sheet of paper, label the leaf and protect the page with a piece of the shelf paper. Then, bind together the leaf collection as a booklet with the ring binders.

SOCIAL STUDIES (Early Presidents / Lewis and Clark Expedition)

▶ 1. When Thomas Jefferson was president, the United States purchased a piece of land from France. This deal was called the Louisiana Purchase and effectively doubled the size of the United States. The parcel of land lay west of the Mississippi River and was 827,987 square miles in size. Jefferson authorized the government to buy the land for $15 million. Write those figures on the chalkboard. Ask your child if that was a lot of money. Have your child figure out how much it cost per square mile. Then, have your child compare that figure with current prices of real estate to determine whether the Louisiana Purchase was a "good deal."

▶ 2. Use a map to show your child the stretch of land acquired with the Louisiana Purchase. Have your child trace over the area. Have him/her write the names of the states and parts of states that were part of the purchase.

▶ 3. Have your child read about the Louisiana Purchase in an encyclopedia. Discuss. Ask your child the date of the purchase. Have him/her add the date to the time line. *Was the Louisiana Purchase a good acquisition? Why or why not?* Ask your child to imagine that Jefferson had not made the purchase. *How big might America be today? What language(s) would probably be spoken in what is now known as the United States?*

▶ 4. President Jefferson was anxious to map an all-water route to the Pacific Ocean across the continent. He sent Meriwether Lewis, his private secretary, to lead the expedition along with William Clark, who had traveled in the West and knew how to communicate with Native Americans. Clark was also an excellent cartographer and artist. Clark mapped and drew animals and plants he saw on the expedition.

Capitals

Always remember to capitalize the following:

- first word in a sentence
- first word in a direct quotation
- first word in every line of poetry
- pronoun **I**
- initials
- proper nouns
- proper adjectives

Underline each word that should begin with a capital letter.

one summer night, seth and tony noticed a bat flying overhead.
"did you know that bats help control insects?" remarked tony.
seth replied, "somehow i always think of dracula when i see a bat."
"long ago, people of slavic countries believed in vampires, but a bat isn't
really scary," laughed tony. "a brown bat weighs only about half an ounce."
"i haven't seen one up close," admitted seth.
"a good place to see bats is carlsbad caverns in new mexico. a colony of
mexican free-tailed bats lives in one of the caves. at dusk, hundreds of
thousands of bats fly out to hunt. many american tourists visit there to see
this amazing sight."

edwin gould studied the eating habits of bats in cape cod, massachusetts.
donald r. griffin photographed bats eating. one tiny bat caught 175 mosquitoes
in fifteen minutes of hunting! fredric a. webster discovered that bats catch
insects with their tail membranes.

most north american bats hibernate during december, january and february.
when early insects come out in march or april, the bats awaken.

Bats

Bats come out at night,
Catching insects in their flight.
Furry little mammal brown,
Found in country, village and town.

Learn At Home, Grade 5

Hidden o's

blocked
bother
column
common
dodge
gossip
honor
model
monster
octopus
oxen
problem
product
promise
robberies
soccer
toboggan
wobble

Circle the spelling words in the word search. Look horizontally, vertically and diagonally. **Write** each word below when you find it.

r	e	c	c	o	s	b	h	i	k	y	a
x	m	w	o	s	p	r	o	d	u	c	t
v	o	i	m	q	d	b	n	t	x	v	e
g	d	u	m	n	o	h	o	l	h	j	f
e	e	b	o	g	d	a	r	d	n	e	o
l	l	n	g	g	e	p	r	e	u	r
b	s	o	v	t	e	n	r	d	q	f	o
b	p	c	m	o	c	t	o	p	u	s	b
o	r	k	o	b	r	o	b	x	e	l	b
w	o	e	n	o	m	g	l	n	e	r	e
f	m	d	s	g	f	t	e	u	q	n	r
n	i	f	t	g	x	a	m	g	m	s	i
s	s	e	e	a	n	w	n	t	h	n	e
b	e	v	r	n	g	o	s	s	i	p	s

Write the number of syllables in the parentheses (   ).

1. _____ (   )   10. _____ (   )

2. _____ (   )   11. _____ (   )

3. _____ (   )   12. _____ (   )

4. _____ (   )   13. _____ (   )

5. _____ (   )   14. _____ (   )

6. _____ (   )   15. _____ (   )

7. _____ (   )   16. _____ (   )

8. _____ (   )   17. _____ (   )

9. _____ (   )   18. _____ (   )

Multiplication Table

X	0	1	2	3	4	5	6	7	8	9	10	11	12
0													
1													
2													
3													
4													
5													
6													
7													
8													
9													
10													
11													
12													

Learn At Home, Grade 5

Division

Solve.

1. 9) 3,654

2. 8) 835

3. 6) 618

Estimate.

4. 36) 660

5. 23) 4,280

6. 158 ÷ 21

Solve.

7. 24) 228

8. 1298 ÷ 37

9. $\frac{703}{41}$

10. What is the cost for 1 golf ball?

_____

**On Sale
Today Only**

One dozen golf balls

Only $3.36

Learn At Home, Grade 5

Angle Measurement

The **degree** is the unit used to measure angles.
Measure the following angles using a protractor.

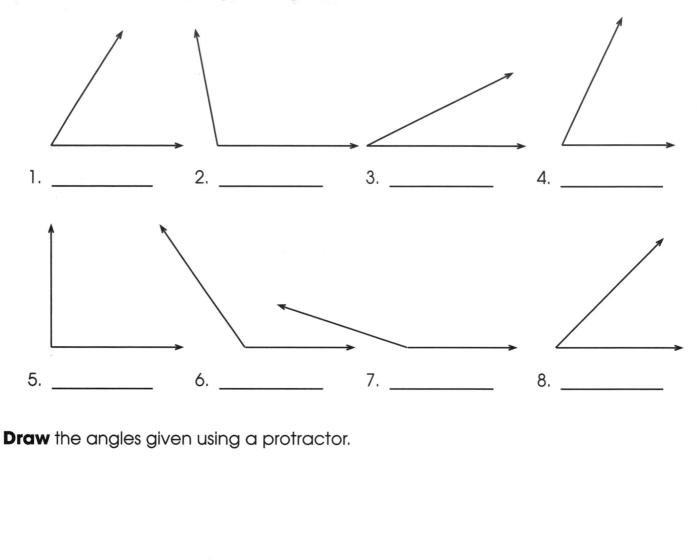

1. _____

2. _____

3. _____

4. _____

5. _____

6. _____

7. _____

8. _____

Draw the angles given using a protractor.

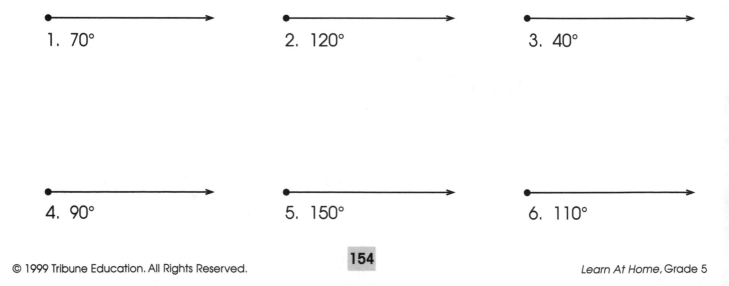

1. 70°

2. 120°

3. 40°

4. 90°

5. 150°

6. 110°

154

Learn At Home, Grade 5

Geometric Figures

Write the correct letter in the box next to each figure.

Point S = •S   Ray XY = $\overrightarrow{XY}$
Line CD = $\overleftrightarrow{CD}$ Line segment BC = $\overline{BC}$

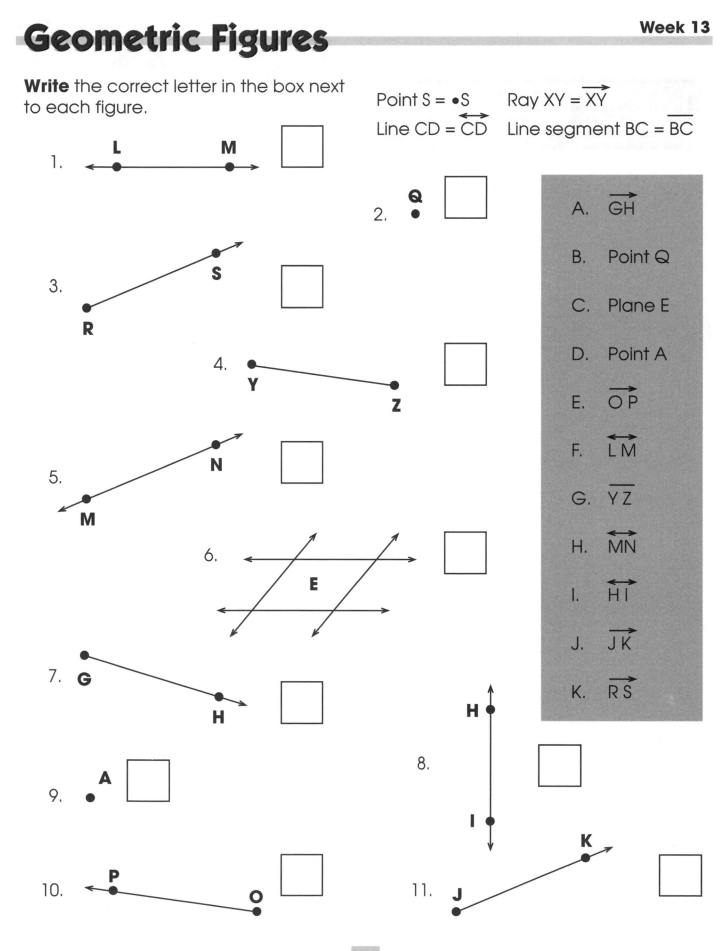

A. $\overrightarrow{GH}$

B. Point Q

C. Plane E

D. Point A

E. $\overrightarrow{OP}$

F. $\overleftrightarrow{LM}$

G. $\overline{YZ}$

H. $\overleftrightarrow{MN}$

I. $\overleftrightarrow{HI}$

J. $\overrightarrow{JK}$

K. $\overrightarrow{RS}$

	Language Skills	**Spelling**	**Reading**
Monday	Discuss the genre of science fiction. Help your child plan a science fiction short story. *See* Language Skills, Week 14, number 1. Have your child make a plan for writing and start working on a rough draft.	Pretest your child on these spelling words: bucket lucky struck button public subject crunchy refund thunder dusk ruffle trust guppies skunk ugly judges spun umbrella Have your child correct the pretest. Add personalized words and make two copies of this week's study list.	Introduce *Hang Tough, Paul Mather* by Alfred Slote. The first chapter in this book is not the beginning of the story. Discuss how the author gets Paul to tell his own story. Have your child read chapters 1 and 2 of *Hang Tough, Paul Mather*.
Tuesday	**Capitalization:** Book, magazine and newspaper titles are traditionally underlined (now, often italicized) and capitalized in running text. Help your child find examples in book reviews and magazine articles. *See* Language Skills, Week 14, number 2.	Review this week's spelling words. Have your child complete **Utterly Upbeat u** (p. 160).	Have your child read chapters 3 and 4 of *Hang Tough, Paul Mather*. Discuss the importance of reading carefully. Some words may have more than one meaning. Reading too quickly may leave a reader with a false understanding of a word or passage. If a sentence doesn't make sense, have your child look up the key words in a dictionary. Have your child complete **Double Trouble** (p. 161).
Wednesday	Review proper nouns. Proper nouns are names of specific persons, places, things and ideas. *See* Language Skills, Week 14, number 3.	Have your child use each of this week's spelling words correctly in a sentence.	**Charts and Diagrams:** Have your child read chapters 5 and 6 of *Hang Tough, Paul Mather*. Teach your child how to read a diagram. A diagram combines pictures and labels to communicate information. *See* Reading, Week 14, numbers 1–3. Have your child complete **Take Me out to the Ball Game** (p. 162).
Thursday	Have your child revise, edit and improve this week's science fiction story, focusing on capitalization and punctuation when proofreading. Have your child prepare the piece for publication. For ideas on how to publish your child's work, see page 6.	Have your child study this week's spelling words. For activity ideas, see pages 9–10.	Have your child read chapters 7 and 8 of *Hang Tough, Paul Mather*. Review metaphors. Compare and contrast with similes. Have your child think of similes and metaphors to describe Paul's behavior and/or pitching.
Friday	Help your child compile and edit his/her best written work (poems, stories, essays, etc.) so far into a literary magazine. For more information on producing a literary magazine, see page 6.	Give your child the final spelling test. Have your child record pretest and final test words in his/her Word Bank.	Show your child examples of charts from a newspaper or magazine. Ask your child questions about the information presented in the charts. *See* Reading, Week 14, number 4. Have your child read chapters 9 and 10 of *Hang Tough, Paul Mather*. Have him/her create a line graph that shows Paul's changing emotions in chapters 8 and 10.

Learn At Home, Grade 5

Math	Science	Social Studies
Introduce the terms *intersecting, parallel* and *perpendicular*. Draw a simple street map. Have your child study the map to answer questions: *Which street runs parallel to Main Street?* *Which two streets does Lewis Street intersect?* *Which streets are perpendicular to Park Road?* *Which streets are parallel to the Big River?*	**Plants and Their Needs** Have your child look up and read about *geotropism, hydrotropism* and *phototropism* in plants. Have your child complete **Plant Movements** (p. 166).	Have your child continue to read about the Lewis and Clark expedition. Guide your child's reading with the following questions: *How high is Pike's Peak? What plants and animals did Clark sketch? How did Lewis and Clark and their crew spend the winter? How long was their journey?* Have your child complete **What a Trip!** (p. 167).
The sum of the angles in any triangle is 180°. *See* Math, Week 14, number 1. Teach your child about the different types of triangles: *equilateral, isosceles, scalene* and *right*. Have your child look around your house to find examples of each type of triangle.	Use the bean plants from the **Do Plants Need Light?** activity (p. 120) in Week 10 to demonstrate geotropism. *See* Science, Week 14.	On their expedition, Lewis and Clark encountered the Mandan tribe. Have your child read the Mandan legend of their origins. *See* Social Studies, Week 14, number 1. After reading, have your child draw a picture to illustrate the legend.
A quadrilateral is a four-sided figure. There are five variations of the quadrilateral: *square, trapezoid, rhombus, rectangle* and *parallelogram*. There is some overlap between them. For example, a square is also a rectangle and a rhombus. *See* Math, Week 14, number 2 for definitions and illustrations of each type of quadrilateral. Have your child complete **Identify the Quadrilateral** (p. 163).	Use any houseplant to demonstrate phototropism. Choose a plant that is growing near a window. Turn the plant 180°. Observe the change in the plant over the next day or two. Have your child sketch the plant just after it is turned. Have him/her draw the plant again after one or two days. Be sure your child includes the window in the drawings.	Have your child paint four panels depicting Lewis and Clark's journey. *See* Social Studies, Week 14, number 2. Have your child read *Winged Moccasin* by Frances Joyce Farnsworth. Have him/her keep an "anecdotal record" of the events in each chapter. After completing the book, have your child summarize the story using these records for reference.
Teach your child about other polygons. *Pentagon:* five sides and five angles *Hexagon:* six sides and six angles *Octagon:* eight sides and eight angles *Decagon:* ten sides and ten angles Regular polygons are polygons whose sides are all the same length and whose angles all have the same measurements. Have your child complete **Shapes in Hiding** (p. 164).	Use one of the bean plants to demonstrate the importance of leaves in the growth and success of a plant. Pinch off all of the leaves (or all except one) from a bean plant. Continue to care for it by providing sun and water. Have your child predict what will happen to the bean plant with no leaves. Have your child observe the health of the plant over several days. Discuss the results of the experiment.	**Pioneers:** Introduce your child to the pioneers and to the pioneer lifestyle. *See* Social Studies, Week 14, numbers 3 and 4. Have your child look up the word *pioneer* in the dictionary. Have your child rewrite the definition in his/her own words.
Test your child's critical thinking skills and knowledge of geometry. Have your child complete **Lines Across a Triangle** (p. 165).	Provide resources on photosynthesis for your child's reference. Have your child explain photosynthesis in his/her Science Log. Ask your child to include a diagram as well. Pose the following question: *What is the purpose of a plant's leaves?*	Arrange for your child to perform some community service.

157

TEACHING SUGGESTIONS AND ACTIVITIES

LANGUAGE SKILLS (Capitalization)

▶ 1. Science fiction typically deals with technological advances that have not yet been realized. Science fiction speculates on the future. Submarines, helicopters, laser beams, robots, space travel and advanced communication devices are all science fiction topics of the past. Today, these technological advances are real. Ask your child to project what scientific achievement might occur in the next 100 years. Have your child select one of these projections and use it to write a story that takes place in the future. **Sample story starter:** *The spaceship was in trouble and had to make an emergency landing. The pilot of the ship called NASA. The engineers advised the pilot she was closest to Saturn and that she should land there.* (Notice the combination of existing technology with futuristic.)

▶ 2. Write the following book, magazine and newspaper titles on the chalkboard. Have your child capitalize and alphabetize the titles. If the title starts with *a, the* or *an,* your child should alphabetize the title by the first letter in the second word.

how to train your dog	family circle	time
the cincinnati reporter	mystery of the fat cat	fortune
where the red fern grows	treasure island	the delaware times
summer of the swans	the call of the wild	popular mechanics
seventeen	san francisco monitor	albuquerque journal

▶ 3. The names of mountains, lakes, rivers, seas, oceans and other geographic terms (proper nouns) begin with capital letters. **Examples:** Hudson River, Pacific Ocean. Have your child draw a five-column chart. At the head of each column, have your child write a geographic term, such as *Rivers, Mountains, Lakes, Seas* and *Deserts.* Have your child use an encyclopedia or atlas to locate at least five examples of each geographic term and write their names in the appropriate columns.

READING (Charts and Diagrams)

▶ 1. Look at a weather map with your child. Discuss the different symbols used and their meanings. Ask your child to explain why he/she thinks symbols are used instead of words.

▶ 2. Explain that a time line is a kind of diagram. Create a time line of events for the next month. Leave room for your child to fill in events as they occur. Have him/her label the time line with dates and events.

▶ 3. Have your child draw a diagram of a baseball player, labeling each part of his/her uniform and equipment.

▶ 4. Collect tables and charts (movie timetables, bar graphs, pie charts, television viewing guide, etc.) from newspapers and magazines for your child to examine. Ask questions that require your child to process the information presented in the tables and charts. Ask why tables and charts might be included in articles. How is a chart better at presenting data than a paragraph?

MATH (Geometry)

▶ 1. Triangles always have three angles. The three angle measurements always add up to 180°. Illustrate this concept by placing the three angles together. Have your child draw any triangle using a straight edge. Cut out the triangle and mark each angle with a colored mark. Cut off each corner and place the vertices together with the sides touching. Your child will see that the three angles make a straight angle of 180° (a semicircle). Repeat with other triangles. The angles of any triangle will add up to 180°, no matter what the configuration of the triangle.

Learn At Home, Grade 5

▶ 2. Encourage your child to become familiar with the following quadrilaterals:

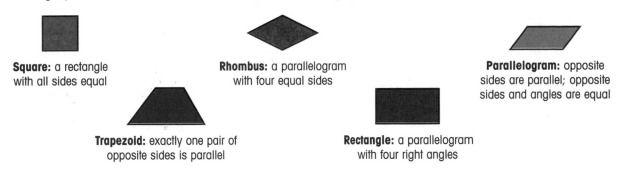

Square: a rectangle with all sides equal

Rhombus: a parallelogram with four equal sides

Parallelogram: opposite sides are parallel; opposite sides and angles are equal

Trapezoid: exactly one pair of opposite sides is parallel

Rectangle: a parallelogram with four right angles

SCIENCE (Plants and Their Needs)

For this demonstration, you will need small plastic bags, soil and masking tape. Have your child remove some of the bean plants, placing one plant in each of the plastic bags. (save one or two plants for a later experiment.) Add soil to cover the roots and water lightly. Close the top of the bag around the stem, allowing most of the bean plant to remain outside of the bag, and seal with masking tape. Have your child find different places in your classroom where the bags can be suspended with more masking tape. Leave some bags upright, turn some on their sides and turn some upside down. Have your child observe the changes in the plants over the next week. This experiment will demonstrate the nature of geotropism: the tendency of plants to grow upward, no matter which way they are turned. Conversely, the roots will always grow downward.

SOCIAL STUDIES (Lewis and Clark Expedition / Pioneers)

▶ 1. This is the story of the origins of the Mandan tribe as told to Lewis and Clark in the winter of 1804. Copy the following Mandan legend for your child to read:

It was believed long, long ago that the Mandan tribe lived under the earth near a lake. They could see daylight through the openings made by the roots of a grapevine that grew down into their underground residence. With the help of several animals, some of the Mandans were able to reach the grapevine and climb above ground. When they emerged, they explored the land on which they found themselves.

They liked what they saw—land with lots and lots of buffalo and many trees full of different kinds of fruits. Word of these riches got back to those who had stayed below, and many of them decided to come see for themselves. About half the men, women and children in the tribe had reached the surface when the vine broke under the weight of a very fat woman. The rest of the tribe was not able to climb out from under the ground. Those that made it to the top were taught how to survive in their new surroundings by their leader, Good Fur Robe. They believed the name of their tribe came from the Indian word, minatarees, which means "people of the willow."

▶ 2. Have your child divide Lewis and Clark's expedition into four parts: *Setting Out, Indian Contact, Crossing the Rockies* and *On the Columbia River.* Give your child four pieces of paper, each measuring 18" x 24". Have your child paint pictures to represent the four aspects of the journey on the four pieces of paper. When the paint dries, have your child use a black marker to write the title on each picture.

▶ 3. Discuss the characteristics a pioneer needed to possess in order to survive. Ask your child to recall information about the following pioneers or pioneer trails: Daniel Boone, the Oregon Trail, the Santa Fe Trail and the Lewis and Clark expedition. Give your child an opportunity to talk about movies or television programs that are about the journeys westward in wagon trains and on riverboats.

▶ 4. Find books of American songs and poems that tell of the "pioneer spirit" and life on the frontier. Have your child read these, then draw or paint an image that symbolizes the pioneering spirit.

Complete each phrase with a spelling word.

bucket
button
crunchy
dusk
guppies
judges
lucky
public
refund
ruffle
skunk
spun
struck
subject
thunder
trust
ugly
umbrella

1. chewing sometimes makes a _____ sound
2. books from the _____ library
3. from dawn to _____
4. return it for a _____
5. _____ your instincts
6. my _____ number
7. lightning _____ the pole
8. math is my favorite _____
9. the _____ duckling
10. the top _____ rapidly
11. the _____ in my aquarium
12. water poured from the _____
13. _____ and lightning
14. open the _____
15. sew on the _____
16. annoying _____ spray
17. nine _____ on the court
18. added a _____ to the curtain

Fill in the missing letters to complete the spelling words.

j___dges   ___unk   um___ella
gu___ies   ___fund   ___under
___gly   bu___on   ___sk
bu___et   ru___le   ___uck
tr___st   c___nchy   pub___ic
sp___n   su___ect   lu___y

Learn At Home, Grade 5

Double Trouble

Fill in the blanks with the correct definition number for each underlined word.

Example: __3__ I was covered with <u>pitch</u> after climbing the pine tree.

winding	1. having bends or curves
	2. the act of turning something around a central core
wolf	1. to gulp down
	2. a large carnivorous member of the dog family
pitch	1. to sell or persuade
	2. to throw a ball from the mound to the batter
	3. a resin that comes from the sap of pine trees

GULP!

_____ 1. Do girls' clubs <u>pitch</u> cookies?

_____ 2. We are <u>winding</u> the top's string tightly.

_____ 3. The adult <u>wolf</u> returned to her lair.

_____ 4. Red didn't <u>pitch</u> after the fourth inning.

_____ 5. The Mather family had a <u>winding</u> driveway.

_____ 6. The young ball player <u>wolfed</u> down his lunch and left.

choke	1. to strangle
	2. to bring the hands up on the bat
hitch	1. obstacle
	2. to fasten or tie temporarily
windup	1. the swing of the pitcher's arm just before the pitch
	2. a concluding part

_____ 1. We <u>hitched</u> the mule to the cart.

_____ 2. Tip would not <u>choke</u> up on his bat.

_____ 3. Paul wished to play, but there was just one <u>hitch</u>.

_____ 4. The program's <u>windup</u> was filled with more of Joe's record hits.

_____ 5. Mom was afraid the dog would <u>choke</u> itself on its leash.

_____ 6. He has a great <u>windup</u> and curve ball.

161

Take Me out to the Ball Game

Use the diagram to answer the questions.

1. Who plays left field? _____

2. How far is it from first to second base? _____

3. Does Monk Lawler play the outfield? _____

4. How many innings are played in Little League? _____

5. If a batter hits a triple, how many feet will he run? _____

6. What position does Cliff Borton play? _____

7. How far is Paul Mather from home plate? _____

8. Can a 10-year-old child play Little League ball? _____

9. How long may a bat be? _____

10. What position does Jim Hakken play? _____

11. Is Stu closer to Monk or Kenny? _____

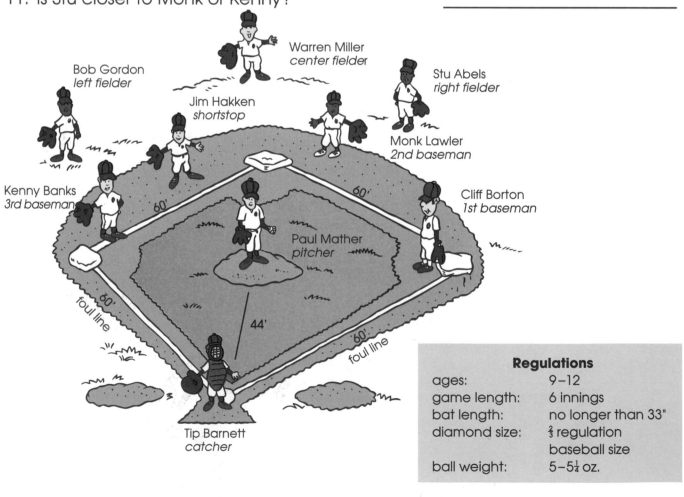

Warren Miller
center fielder

Bob Gordon
left fielder

Stu Abels
right fielder

Jim Hakken
shortstop

Monk Lawler
2nd baseman

Kenny Banks
3rd baseman

Cliff Borton
1st baseman

Paul Mather
pitcher

60'

60'

60'

60'

44'

foul line

foul line

Tip Barnett
catcher

Regulations	
ages:	9–12
game length:	6 innings
bat length:	no longer than 33"
diamond size:	$\frac{2}{3}$ regulation baseball size
ball weight:	5–5$\frac{1}{4}$ oz.

Learn At Home, Grade 5

Identify the Quadrilateral

Cut out and sort the shapes. Make your own categories and name them.

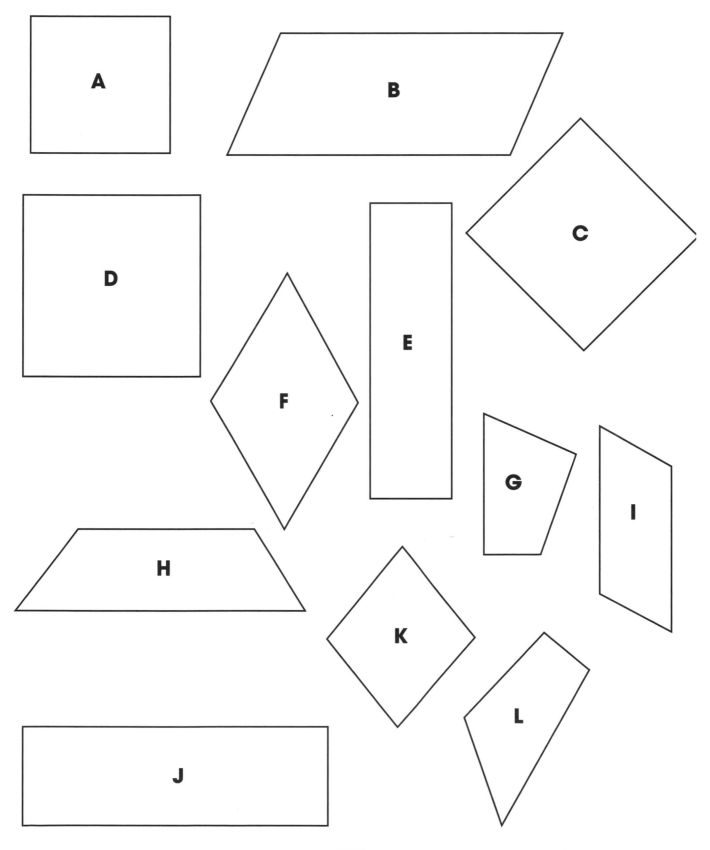

Shapes in Hiding

Shade triangles to make each shape.

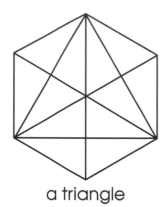

a triangle

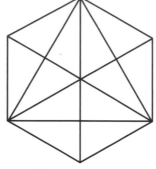

a different triangle

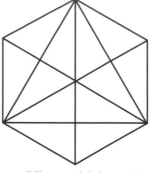

a different triangle

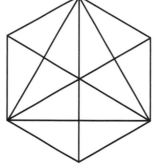

a different triangle

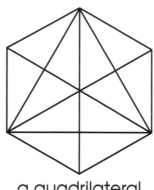

a quadrilateral

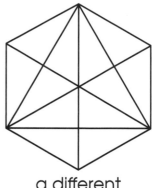

a different
quadrilateral

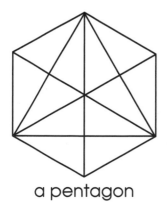

a pentagon

a hexagon

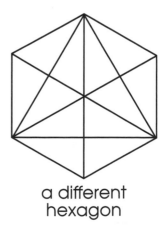

a different
hexagon

Learn At Home, Grade 5

Draw the given number of straight lines to divide each triangle into the shapes listed. The first one has been done for you.

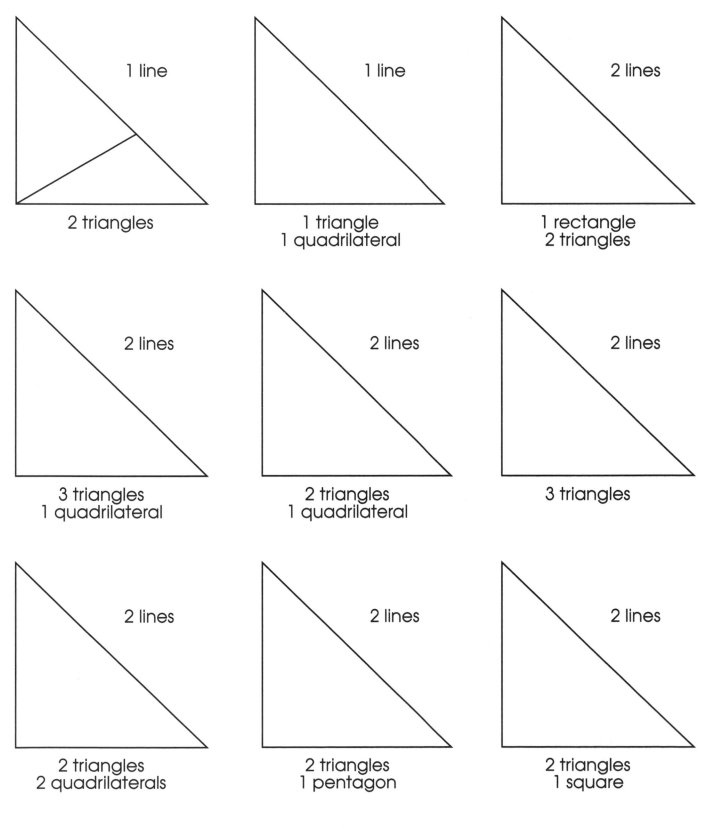

1 line

2 triangles

1 line

1 triangle
1 quadrilateral

2 lines

1 rectangle
2 triangles

2 lines

3 triangles
1 quadrilateral

2 lines

2 triangles
1 quadrilateral

2 lines

3 triangles

2 lines

2 triangles
2 quadrilaterals

2 lines

2 triangles
1 pentagon

2 lines

2 triangles
1 square

Plant Movements

After a seed germinates and anchors itself by its roots in one place, it can still show some movement. These movements are called **tropisms**. Tropisms are a plant's response to stimuli such as light, gravity and water.

Geotropism, **hydrotropism** and **phototropism** are three tropisms that are easily demonstrated with bean seedlings. Research these three types of tropisms using an encyclopedia, science textbook or other source. Study the pictures of the three experiments. Name the kind of tropism. Explain what is happening in each picture.

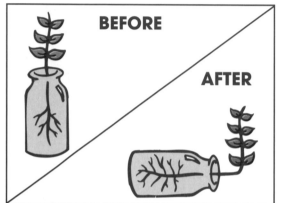

Kind of Tropism: _____

What happened? _____

_____

_____

_____

_____

_____

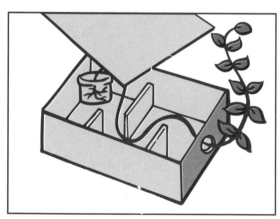

Kind of Tropism: _____

What happened? _____

_____

_____

_____

_____

_____

Kind of Tropism: _____

What happened? _____

_____

_____

_____

_____

Learn At Home, Grade 5

What a Trip!

Read the paragraphs about Meriwether Lewis and William Clark's journey to the Pacific Coast. Then, **plot** their journey on the map below.

Lewis and Clark led the first expedition across our country's vast northwestern wilderness. It began in 1804 and lasted more than two years. The expedition covered almost 7,700 miles.

President Thomas Jefferson chose Lewis to lead the expedition. Then, Jefferson and Lewis selected Clark to be second in command. Lewis and Clark and their group of about 45 people set out on May 14, 1804, and traveled up the Missouri River. In October, they reached a village of friendly Mandan Indians in what is now North Dakota. They built Fort Mandan near there and stayed for the winter.

On April 17, 1805, the journey resumed. By summer, the group made the hardest part of the trip—they crossed the Rocky Mountains. This took them about a month. From there, they reached the Clearwater River in what is now Idaho. They built new canoes and then paddled toward the Columbia River which they reached in October. The expedition continued on in hopes of reaching the Pacific Coast. They ultimately succeeded, arriving at the coast in November of 1805.

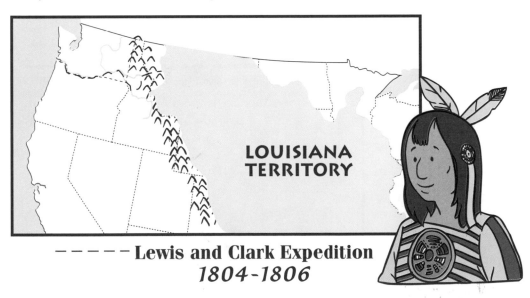

LOUISIANA TERRITORY

– – – – – – **Lewis and Clark Expedition**
1804-1806

1. Label the areas that are now states through which Lewis and Clark journeyed.
2. Label the rivers on which the expedition traveled.
3. Label the Rocky Mountains.
4. Label the Pacific Ocean.
5. Put a star where the group met the Mandan Indians.

	Language Skills	**Spelling**	**Reading**
Monday	This week, have your child write a tall tale. Have your child think of a main character who possesses a unique trait, such as great intelligence or incredible speed. Have your child exaggerate the character's traits to make him/her "larger than life." Also encourage your child to include some dialogue or quotations in the story. Have your child make a plan for writing, then start working on a rough draft.	Pretest your child on these spelling words: afford forlorn perfume carton further refer curtain girth starch departing harbor sturdy directions observe temper emergency origin thirst Have your child correct the pretest. Add personalized words and make two copies of this week's study list.	Have your child plot the excitement level of *Hang Tough, Paul Mather* by chapter. Have him/her rate the excitement of each chapter as *dull, somewhat interesting, interesting, getting tense* or *exciting.* Have your child plot the chapter ratings on a line graph (with excitement levels along the vertical axis) in chronological order to see a plot profile. Discuss chapters 11 and 12 of *Hang Tough, Paul Mather.*
Tuesday	**Quotations:** Write several sentences containing quotation marks on the chalkboard. Teach your child the proper way to punctuate each sentence. Focus today on the placement of commas. *See* Language Skills, Week 15, number 1. Give your child several sentences containing dialogue to punctuate correctly. **Examples:** I'm going to the store said Jim. Tom replied I'll go with you.	Review this week's spelling words. Have your child complete **"R" You Listening?** (p. 172).	Have your child read chapters 13–14 of *Hang Tough, Paul Mather.* Have your child complete **Throwing Too Many Curves** (p. 173).
Wednesday	Final commas are omitted in quotations when a question mark or an exclamation point is required. **Examples:** "When is the plane due?" asked Ned. "Watch your step!" shrieked Father. Give your child a list of sentences containing quotations. Include punctuation, some correct and some incorrect. Have your child read each sentence and make any necessary changes in punctuation.	Have your child use each of this week's spelling words correctly in a sentence.	Have your child read chapters 15–17 of *Hang Tough, Paul Mather.* Have your child complete **Day of Reckoning** (p. 174).
Thursday	Every quotation begins with a capital letter. **Examples:** "This is my brother," said John. Mark asked, "How old is he?" When a direct quotation is interrupted, however, the second part is not capitalized. **Example:** "He is only three," replied John, "but he is big for his age." Give your child several sentences containing quotations. Write in all lower-case letters and without punctuation. Have your child rewrite each sentence correctly.	Have your child study this week's spelling words.	Give your child three or four choices for a book project. For project ideas, see page 13. Let your child choose a project. Have him/her work to complete the project today and tomorrow.
Friday	Help your child avoid always using the word "said" with quotations. Brainstorm a list of alternative signal words, such as *screamed, demanded, admitted, wailed, shouted, argued, growled, whined, bellowed, stammered, screeched, accused, replied, snapped, stuttered, shrieked, answered, bragged, laughed, muttered, inquired, argued, hollered* and *whispered.* *See* Language Skills, Week 15, numbers 2 and 3.	Give your child the final spelling test. Have your child record pretest and final test words in his/her Word Bank.	Give your child time to complete his/her book project begun yesterday.

Learn At Home, Grade 5

Math	Science	Social Studies
Teach your child to recognize congruent shapes, angles and lines. *Congruent* figures are identical in size and shape but may be in different positions. Draw several pairs of angles, polygons and line segments on the chalkboard. Have your child determine if each pair is congruent.	**Plant Identification** Explain how a key can be used in the identification of a flower, shrub or tree. *See* Science, Week 15, number 1. Have your child complete **Name That Tree** (p. 176).	**Pioneer Life** Help your child construct a concept map on the topic of pioneer life in America. *See* Social Studies, Week 15, number 1.
Discuss the concept of *symmetry*. *See* Math, Week 15, number 1. Have your child find objects around the house and in the neighborhood that are symmetrical. Have your child write the upper- and lower-case letters of the alphabet neatly on a sheet of paper. Have him/her draw the line of symmetry in each symmetrical letter and circle the letters that are not symmetrical.	Teach your child how to use a field guide to identify leaves, flowers or trees. Discuss how the book is organized to help you identify the name of the plant. Have your child bring along a field guide as you walk through the woods, a park or a garden. Have your child try to identify the plants you see and write down the names of all the plants he/she can identify.	Have your child begin to answer some of yesterday's questions by doing some research. Have your child read books about pioneers and study the varied aspects of pioneer life. *See* Social Studies, Week 15, numbers 2–4.
Introduce perimeter. The *perimeter* of a polygon is determined by adding together the length of each of its sides. Discuss some practical applications of perimeter, such as measuring for a fence, making a picture frame or putting trim on a bulletin board. Teach your child to estimate the perimeter of your yard by pacing the measurement.	**How Trees Grow:** Study **How a Tree Grows** (p. 177) with your child. Discuss the information presented there. What kinds of information can be gathered just by looking at a tree's rings?	Discuss pioneer travel. *See* Social Studies, Week 15, numbers 5–8. Have your child make a travel poster. Have your child imagine that he/she is selling covered wagons and wants to attract the attention of pioneers. Alternately, ask your child to imagine that he/she is selling land out west and wants to convince people to move there.
Area is the amount of space covered by a flat figure. Area is measured in square units. Use centimeter (or inch) grid paper to help teach this concept. Draw different-sized rectangles on the grid paper. Ask your child to count the number of squares in each figure and identify the area. **Example:** a rectangle with 24 squares would have an area of 24 square centimeters (or square inches). *See* Math, Week 15, number 2.	Take a walk with your child in a nearby park or wooded area. Try to locate a stump. Have your child study the tree's annual rings. Have him/her count back to find the ring that represents the year he/she was born. Can he/she tell what kind of year that was—rainy or dry? *See* Science, Week 15, number 2.	Have your child read about the men and women of the pioneer movement. Important figures include Daniel Boone, Davy Crockett, John Frémont, Johnny Appleseed, Mike Fink, Noah Webster, Jim Bridger, Mary Jemison, Kit Carson and Jedediah Smith. Have your child write a brief biography of one of these people. Have your child add a column entitled *Pioneers* to the chart of famous Americans, then add the above names to it.
The area of a triangle can also be determined by counting the number of squares contained by the figure. This is difficult, though, because many of the squares inside the triangle are cut in half. It is easier to use the formula for finding the area of a triangle. *See* Math, Week 15, number 3. Have your child complete **I'm Hungry!** (p. 175).	Help your child generate a list of 10–15 trivia questions about trees. Then, have him/her do some research to find the answers to the questions. Ask your child to choose his/her favorite tree. *Don't let him/her tell you what it is!* Have your child write a riddle about the tree, including clues about its identity. Have your child give the finished riddle to you or a friend to solve.	Arrange for your child to perform some community service.

TEACHING SUGGESTIONS AND ACTIVITIES

LANGUAGE SKILLS (Quotations)

▶ 1. Commas separate who is speaking from what is said. Write the following examples on the chalkboard.

Examples: "Come on, Jane," urged her mother.
"But I don't want to go to the park," Jane answered.
Mother continued, "It's a beautiful day, and Karen will be there."
"Just a minute," Jane called, "I want to take my jump rope."

Write the commas in colored chalk for emphasis. Point out how the speaker is separated from the quotation by a comma. Two commas are required if the reference to the speaker is inserted within the quotation, as in the final example.

▶ 2. Encourage your child to think of the tone of a quotation. Provide a list of subject/signal word pairs (e.g., *Mother yelled*) and have your child complete the imagined quotations.

Examples: Mother yelled, " <u>I told you to clean up your room!</u> "
Mother yelled, "<u>Come here this instant!</u>"

▶ 3. Do the opposite of #2 above. Write the spoken words (the words in quotation marks) and have your child supply the speaker's name and an appropriate signal word to indicate the tone of the speaker.

Examples: <u>Monique</u> <u>called</u>, "Hey, come back here with the ball!"
<u>George</u> <u>sighed</u>, "I've been grounded for three days."

MATH (Geometry)

▶ 1. Symmetry is an exact correspondence of size, shape and position on opposite sides of a dividing line. The line that divides an object into symmetrical parts is called a *line of symmetry*. It is helpful to think of symmetry as a mirror image or reflection. Place a ruler edge perpendicular to an image. If the figure on one side of the ruler is a mirror image of the figure on the other side, the ruler lies on the line of symmetry. A line of symmetry may be vertical, horizontal or diagonal. One shape may have several lines of symmetry. A square, for example, has four lines of symmetry.

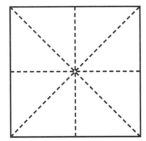

▶ 2. After your child has identified the area of a rectangle by counting squares, show him/her how to multiply the length times the width. Compare the measurements obtained by counting and by multiplying. Then, have your child determine the area of several rectangles by measuring their lengths and widths with a ruler.

▶ 3. Have your child cut out a rectangle drawn on the grid paper in yesterday's lesson. Have him/her draw a diagonal across the rectangle and cut it into two triangles. Help your child discover that the area of each triangle is one-half the area of the rectangle. To determine the area of one triangle, simply divide the area of the original rectangle by two. For example, if the area of the original rectangle was 24 square centimeters, the area of the triangle would be 12 square centimeters.

As a formula, the area of a triangle is equal to **base x height ÷ 2** or **A = $\frac{1}{2}$ (b x h)**

SCIENCE (Plant Identification / How Trees Grow)

▶ 1. A key is a list of identifiable characteristics of a group of plants or animals that can be used to identify a given plant or animal. The characteristics are listed in a particular order. To arrive at the correct identification of the plant or animal, its features must be identified in the specific order laid out in the key.

▶ 2. Back at home, have your child draw a cross section of a tree trunk showing its rings. The tree should be as old as your child. Have your child do research and write down an important event for each year represented by the tree's rings. Each event can be important personally, locally or internationally. If one year saw particularly bad (or good) weather, your child may want to represent that in his/her drawing of the rings.

SOCIAL STUDIES (Pioneer Life)

▶ 1. Have your child write the words *Pioneer Life in America* in the center of a large sheet of paper, then circle the words. Brainstorm questions about pioneer life to write around the central topic.

Why settle in a new land?
What were their occupations?
What foods did they grow and eat?
What was their life expectancy?
What were their houses like?
What did they wear?
How did they travel?

What dangers were there?
What was their entertainment?
What did they read?
How were the children educated?
How did they govern themselves?
How large were the communities?
How close were neighbors?

▶ 2. Throughout this week, have your child add answers and details to the concept map as he/she reads about the lives of the pioneers. At the same time, have your child read a fictional account of pioneer life. Look for books by such authors as Laura Ingalls Wilder and Patricia MacLachlan. Discuss the meaning of historical fiction as it compares to nonfiction.

▶ 3. Ask your child to imagine the types of homes in which the early settlers and pioneers might have lived. The early pioneers built a variety of homes, but most of them were simple and small. If possible, show your child the video *Digging for Data,* produced by the National Livestock and Meat Board, Chicago, Illinois. This video compares the lives of Native Americans and European settlers—their heights, their tools, their homes, the foods they ate and the way they preserved them. Look for the special features of the log cabin described in the film. The book *Prairie Songs,* written by Pam Conrad, describes another type of pioneer house, the sod house. Discuss why people living on the prairie would want to live in sod houses.

▶ 4. With your child, read *A Pioneer Sampler: The Daily Life of a Pioneer Family in 1840* by Barbara Greenwood. This book follows the life of a pioneer family for one year. The book also contains some activity suggestions. Try making cheese, creating dyes or making a water carrier with your child.

▶ 5. Discuss how long it takes to fly from New York to Los Angeles or how long it takes to drive across your state. Compare this to travel in pioneer days. Travel was much slower then. Discuss means of transportation then and now. What were the roads like? How did weather affect travel? How did travelers cross rivers?

▶ 6. Help your child find resources on pioneer travel. What were some of the most common modes of transportation available at the time? (sailing boats, prairie schooners, horses, pack animals, keelboats, canoes, rafts, Conestoga wagons, sleds, stagecoaches)

▶ 7. Have your child read about two of the famous trails to the west: the Santa Fe Trail and the Oregon Trail. Have your child trace each trail on a map. Discuss the length of each trip, the hardships encountered and points of interest along each trail. Have your child mark the dates of each trail on the time line.

▶ 8. Show your child a picture of the painting *The Oregon Trail* by Albert Bierstadt. Discuss the images presented. What sort of mood does the artist create with the painting?

"R" You Listening?

When the letter **r** comes after a vowel, it sometimes changes the vowel sound. **Write** each spelling word under the category with the same spelling pattern.

afford
carton
curtain
departing
directions
emergency
forlorn
further
girth
harbor
observe
origin
perfume
refer
starch
sturdy
temper
thirst

ir
_____

_____

_____

or
_____

_____

_____

er
_____

_____

_____

_____

_____

ur
_____

_____

_____

ar
_____

_____

_____

_____

Write the spelling words that fit in the appropriate categories.

1. Can be used as an adverb, adjective or verb. _____

2. Can be used as a noun or verb. _____

_____ _____ _____

3. Used only as an adjective. _____ _____

4. Used as a verb. _____ _____

_____ _____

Learn At Home, Grade 5

Throwing Too Many Curves

Interpret these quotations from *Hang Tough, Paul Mather* and **write** them in your own words.

Chapter 2

"The world begins and ends with basketball for the punk . . ."

_____

_____

Chapter 4

"I grinned. I knew what the punk was planning. I had to hand it to him. He was maneuvering with a straight face."

_____

_____

_____

Chapter 8

"That night they didn't notice that I had stopped bugging them about calling Dr. Kinsella. Either that or they decided to let sleeping dogs lie."

_____

_____

_____

Chapter 8

"I wasn't (sure of myself), but I wasn't going to tell him that. When you've spent months in a hospital bed, you learn to play things close to the vest."

_____

_____

_____

Chapter 13

"Tom and my father got along carefully. Dad thought Tom was young."

_____

_____

_____

Day of Reckoning

Use the time line to answer the questions.

At what time does Paul ask for his mirror? _____

Which happens earlier? Do Red and Paul shake hands or does Paul greet Toddy?

_____

What is the earliest time shown on the time line? _____

Which happens later? Does Brophy give Paul his medication or does the game begin? _____

What is the final score of the game? _____

At what time does the game end? _____

When do Brophy and Paul's dad get Paul back into bed?_____

How many Dairy players walk in the fourth inning? _____

What happens first in the fourth inning? _____

_____

How many hours does this time line cover? Be careful! _____

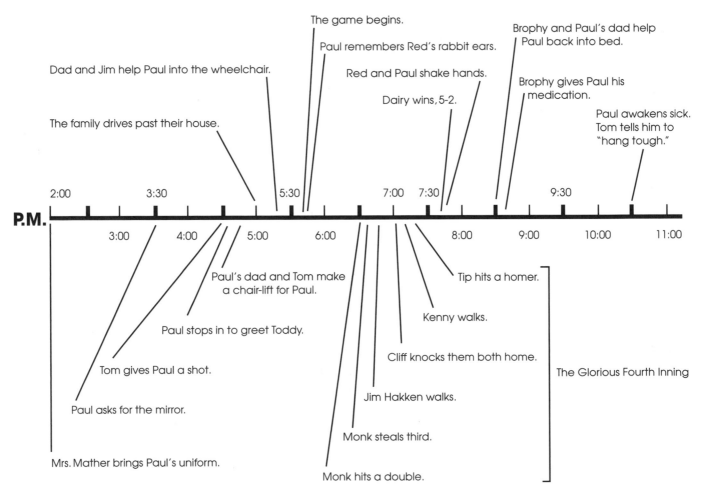

Learn At Home, Grade 5

I'm Hungry!

Someone has already found the area for each triangle, but some are incorrect. Check each problem. Connect the problems with correct areas to make a path for the giraffe to the tree. Then, correct each wrong area.

Name That Tree

Trees can be identified by their shape, bark, buds and leaves. A key is a valuable tool that can be used to identify a tree by its leaves. The key on this page was designed to identify the leaves pictured below.

Use the key to identify the leaves. Write the name of each leaf on the space provided.

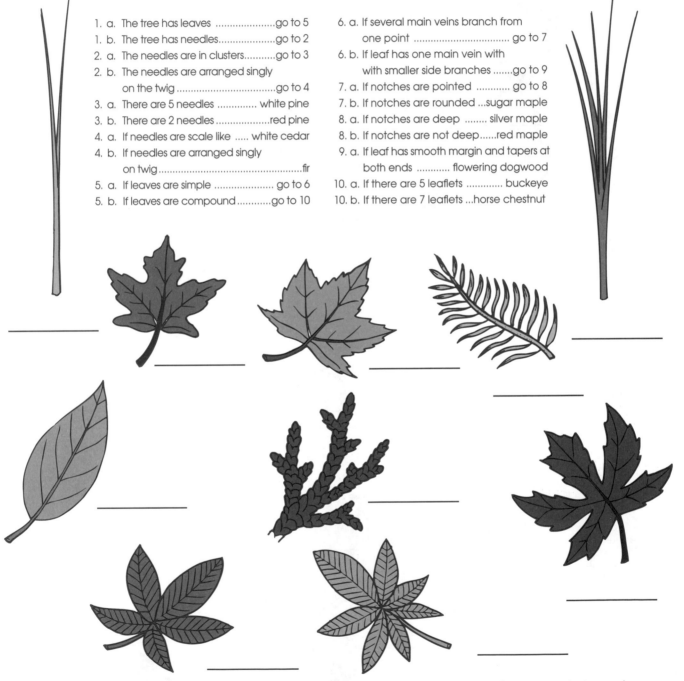

1. a. The tree has leaves ....go to 5
1. b. The tree has needles......................go to 2
2. a. The needles are in clusters...........go to 3
2. b. The needles are arranged singly on the twig ....go to 4
3. a. There are 5 needles .... white pine
3. b. There are 2 needles ....red pine
4. a. If needles are scale like ..... white cedar
4. b. If needles are arranged singly on twig ....fir
5. a. If leaves are simple .... go to 6
5. b. If leaves are compound...........go to 10

6. a. If several main veins branch from one point .... go to 7
6. b. If leaf has one main vein with with smaller side branches ....go to 9
7. a. If notches are pointed .... go to 8
7. b. If notches are rounded ...sugar maple
8. a. If notches are deep .... silver maple
8. b. If notches are not deep......red maple
9. a. If leaf has smooth margin and tapers at both ends .... flowering dogwood
10. a. If there are 5 leaflets .... buckeye
10. b. If there are 7 leaflets ...horse chestnut

Please note that the key on this page was made for the leaves pictured here. It may not work for the trees in your area.

Learn At Home, Grade 5

How A Tree Grows

Trees Grow Taller

The end of each twig has a terminal bud with special cells that divide and make the twig grow longer. Each year's growth comes from a bud that contains the beginnings of a twig, leaves and flowers.

Inside a Bud

bud scales

immature leaves

immature stem

Scale leaves cover and protect young flowers, leaves and stems inside the bud.

lateral bud

leaf bud

leaf scar

One-year-old side shoot formed by a lateral bud.

Terminal Bud
The terminal (leading) bud is protected from weather by thick, overlapping scales.

Terminal buds produce a hormone called auxin that prevents the growth of lateral buds. If the terminal bud dies or is removed, the lateral bud develops.

Last Year's Growth
Last year's growth extends from the terminal bud back to the scale scar.

Scale Scar
The scale scar, or growth rings, consists of lines around the twig that show where last year's terminal bud was located.

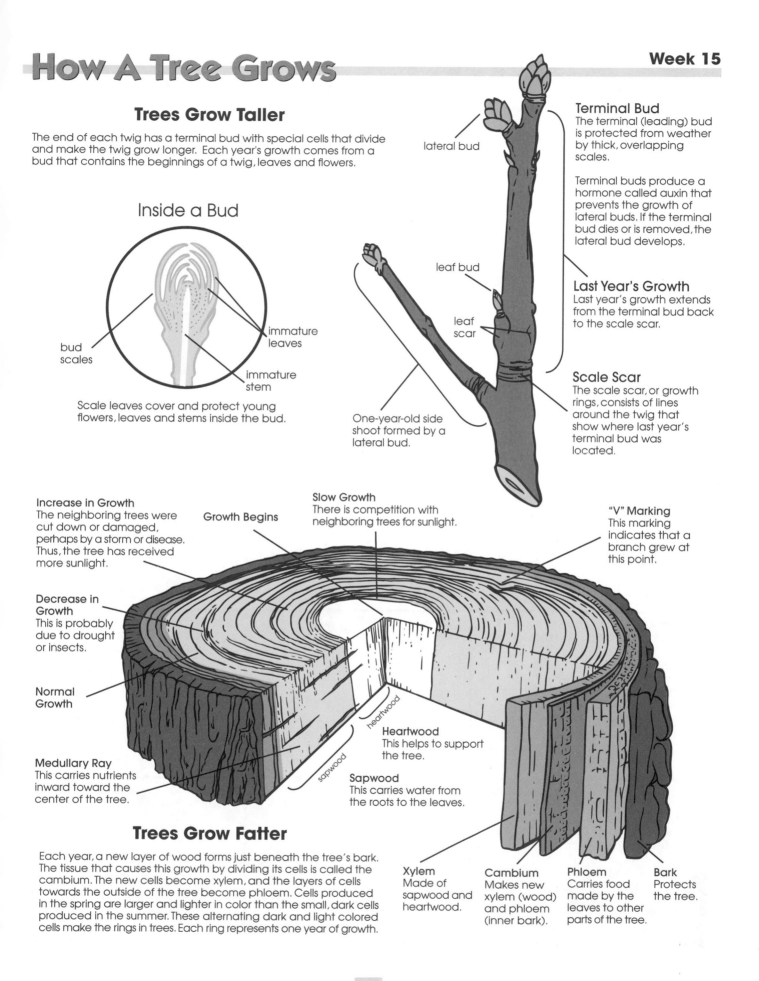

Increase in Growth
The neighboring trees were cut down or damaged, perhaps by a storm or disease. Thus, the tree has received more sunlight.

Growth Begins

Slow Growth
There is competition with neighboring trees for sunlight.

"V" Marking
This marking indicates that a branch grew at this point.

Decrease in Growth
This is probably due to drought or insects.

Normal Growth

Medullary Ray
This carries nutrients inward toward the center of the tree.

heartwood

sapwood

Heartwood
This helps to support the tree.

Sapwood
This carries water from the roots to the leaves.

Trees Grow Fatter

Each year, a new layer of wood forms just beneath the tree's bark. The tissue that causes this growth by dividing its cells is called the cambium. The new cells become xylem, and the layers of cells towards the outside of the tree become phloem. Cells produced in the spring are larger and lighter in color than the small, dark cells produced in the summer. These alternating dark and light colored cells make the rings in trees. Each ring represents one year of growth.

Xylem
Made of sapwood and heartwood.

Cambium
Makes new xylem (wood) and phloem (inner bark).

Phloem
Carries food made by the leaves to other parts of the tree.

Bark
Protects the tree.

	Language Skills	Spelling	Reading
Monday	**Poetry** Introduce your child to different forms of poetry this week and next week. *See* Language Skills, Week 16, number 1. Have your child choose a topic and write an acrostic poem on that topic.	Pretest your child on these spelling words: although chiffon sheriff another chocolate shovel athlete choir Thursday birth chrome whether channel exchange whiskers chauffeur radish whisper Have your child correct the pretest. Add personalized words and make two copies of this week's study list.	**Biography** Define biography. Brainstorm with your child the types of things that might be included in a biography. Make a list for reference. Help your child choose an appropriate biography to read this week. Encourage your child to check out other related books at the same time. Teach your child to take notes on the biography as he/she reads and to organize this information in an outline. *See* Reading,
Tuesday	**Subjects and Predicates:** Teach your child the difference between a compound sentence and a sentence containing a compound subject. A compound sentence has two subjects and two predicates. A sentence with a compound subject has two subjects but only one predicate. *See* Language Skills, Week 16, numbers 2–3.	Review this week's spelling words. Have your child complete **Dynamic Digraphs** (p. 182).	Talk with your child as he/she reads the biography. Discuss the reading periodically to check your child's understanding.
Wednesday	A sentence containing a compound predicate has a single subject and two predicates. These two sentences have the same subject but different predicates: *Sally packed too many clothes. Sally could not close her suitcase.* These two sentences can be combined into one sentence with a single subject and a compound predicate: *Sally packed too many clothes and could not close her suitcase. See* Language Skills, Week 16, number 4.	Have your child use each of this week's spelling words correctly in a sentence.	Guide your child as he/she reads more about the subject of the biography. Teach your child to skim through nonfiction. Have your child write three questions he/she has about the subject of the biography, then do some research to answer them.
Thursday	Teach your child the difference between a subject and an object. *See* Language Skills, Week 16, number 5. Have your child choose or create a character and write a limerick about him/her. After the limerick is written, have your child go back through the poem, circling each subject and underlining each object.	Have your child study this week's spelling words.	Have your child write a creative report based on the subject of the biography.
Friday	Show your child how to use personal pronouns in the subject and predicate. Teach him/her to use the correct form of the personal pronouns. *See* Language Skills, Week 16, number 6.	Give your child the final spelling test. Have your child record pretest and final test words in his/her Word Bank.	Once the report is finished, have your child present the information to an audience (just you, family or friends).

Learn At Home, Grade 5

Math	**Science**	**Social Studies**
Explore the relationship between area and perimeter. Provide several sheets of centimeter grid paper. Challenge your child to make all the possible figures that contain 24 square centimeters. (This is not limited to rectangles.) Confirm that all the figures contain 24 squares. Have your child predict the perimeter of each figure, then measure. Have your child use this information to make a statement about the relationship between area and perimeter.	**Roots** The three main parts of a plant are the stem, leaves and roots. All vascular plants have roots. The roots have several jobs. Have your child read about roots in an encyclopedia or other resource book. What are the key functions of a plant's roots? Have your child list three important functions of roots in his/her Science Log.	**The War of 1812** Discuss the War of 1812. *Who was president at that time? Why was war declared? How long did it last? How were messages sent in those days?* Have your child draw a diagram showing how the British announcement might have traveled across the ocean. Have your child add the dates of the war to the time line.
Show your child how to use a compass. Have him/her use the compass to practice drawing circles. For today, have your child draw circles of different sizes. Have your child create designs and pictures using only circles. The goal for today is for your child to gain confidence using a compass.	Have your child read about the two different types of root systems, then test his/her understanding. *See* Science, Week 16, number 1. Have your child list several foods that come from roots. Have your child complete **Root Systems** (p. 184).	Continue your discussion of the War of 1812. *Did most Americans want another war? Which regions were most in favor of the war? Where were the chief battles fought? What happened on August 12, 1814, in Washington, D.C.? Were the initial causes of the war settled? Who were the War Hawks?* Discuss the Treaty of Ghent. Have your child read the lyrics to "The Star-Spangled Banner" and write a paragraph about what it meant at the time it was written.
Teach your child to identify and measure the diameter and radius of a circle. Draw a circle with the compass. Draw an **X** over the center point. Draw a straight line across the circle through the center point. Lead your child to discover that the radius of any circle is half the length of its diameter. Draw several circles. Have your child measure the diameter and radius of each, then record the measurements.	Provide resources for your child to read about the different parts of a root and the function of each part. Have your child label the parts of a root on the diagram **Inside a Root** (p. 185). Then, have your child write a sentence in his/her Science Log about each part.	Play a strategic game in which your child will come to realize the toll the War of 1812 took on both the Americans and the British. You will need a copy of **Who Won?** (p.187). *See* Social Studies, Week 16.
Introduce your child to solids. Three-dimensional shapes can be found in many common objects. Have your child look for and identify examples of *cubes, cones, cylinders, spheres, pyramids* and *rectangular prisms. See* Math, Week 16 for illustrations and definitions of these solids.	Help your child learn to distinguish bulbs, rhizomes and tubers from roots. Bulbs, rhizomes and tubers are actually underground stems. These underground stems still have roots that protrude into the soil. Have your child do some research to define these three types of underground stems. Have your child write these definitions in his/her own words in the Science Log. Ask your child to list 2 or 3 examples of each type of stem and draw a picture of each as well.	Have your child read about America's fifth president, James Monroe. Discuss. *What was Monroe's experience with government before becoming president? Why were his years in office called "The Era of Good Feeling"? What was interesting about the number of votes he received his second term? What land acquisitions were made during his terms in office? What was the Missouri Compromise? What is the Monroe Doctrine? How does it affect American foreign policy today?*
Have your child complete **The Rocketangular Puzzle** (p. 183).	Nutrients from the soil are carried from the roots, up the stem and to the leaves. The nutrients travel through a vascular system. Have your child read about the "tubes" that transport nutrients up and down the stem. Help your child conduct an experiment to observe the vascular system at work. *See* Science, Week 16, number 2. Have your child complete **Plant Pipelines** (p. 186).	Arrange for your child to perform some community service.

179

TEACHING SUGGESTIONS AND ACTIVITIES

LANGUAGE SKILLS (Poetry / Subjects and Predicates)

▶ 1. Collect an assortment of poetry anthologies for your child to examine. There are all sorts of anthologies available, ranging from the classic to the ridiculous. Have your child write some original poems mimicking the style of other poems or using some standard formats such as acrostic, limerick or haiku. Provide plenty of examples of each type of poem.

▶ 2. The following two sentences have the same predicate: *Joan helps mother fix dinner. Barbara helps mother fix dinner.* These sentences can be joined to form one sentence with a compound subject: *Joan and Barbara help mother fix dinner.* Be careful to make the subject and verb agree.

▶ 3. Write ten pairs of sentences on the chalkboard with identical predicates but different subjects. Have your child rewrite each pair of sentences as one sentence.

▶ 4. Write ten pairs of sentences on the chalkboard with identical subjects but different predicates. Have your child rewrite each pair of sentences as one sentence.

▶ 5. Write the following sentences on the chalkboard. Ask your child to underline all the nouns.

The <u>fifth-grader</u> caught a <u>fish</u>.   <u>Bees</u> make <u>honey</u>.   The <u>ants</u> were building an <u>anthill</u>.

Have your child determine which part of each sentence is the subject and which part is the predicate. Subject nouns (fifth-grader, bees and ants) are found in the subject. Object nouns (fish, honey and anthill) are found in the predicate. The object nouns in the given sentences are recipients of the action of a verb. They are called *direct objects.* A direct object is used with an action verb.

▶ 6. Personal pronouns can be divided into subject and object pronouns. Subject pronouns include *I, you, he, she, it, we* and *they.* Object pronouns include *me, you, him, her, it, us* and *them.* Write the following groups of sentences on the chalkboard. Have your child fill in the missing personal pronoun in each sentence and explain his/her choice.

    a. Bob wants to go on a ride. _____ has ten cents. Bob needs ten cents more. _____ sees his father and asks _____ for another dime.

    b. After school, Sarah and her mom went shopping. _____ first went to a shoe store. A woman waited on _____. _____ sold Sarah a pair of brown shoes.

    c. Monday was warm. _____ was sunny. Today _____ is cold and windy. _____ never know what to wear.

READING (Biography)

Encourage your child to use the following format to outline the main ideas in the biography.

    I. Chapter title
      A. One main point of chapter
        1. detail
        2. detail
      B. One main point of chapter
        1. detail
        2. detail
        3. detail
    II. Chapter title
      A. One main point of chapter
        1. detail
        2. detail
      B. One main point of chapter
        1. detail
        2. detail

Learn At Home, Grade 5

MATH (Geometry)

Encourage your child to become familiar with the following geometric solids:

Cube: six faces of
congruent squares

Cylinder: two parallel
bases that are congruent circles

Rectangular prism: all
six faces are rectangles

Cone: shaped like a
pointed ice-cream cone

Sphere: all points are
equidistant from the center

Pyramid: square base with triangular
faces meeting at a common vertex

SCIENCE (Roots)

▶ 1. Read the following scenario to test your child's understanding of root systems:

   It has been a long, hot, dry summer. Mr. Warren's grass is turning brown, but the dandelions are bright green.

   Ask your child the following questions: *What kind of root system does the grass have? What kind of root system do the dandelions have? Why do the dandelions stay green while the grass turns brown?*

▶ 2. Flowering plants are divided into two main groups: *dicotyledons* and *monocotyledons*. The main difference between them is that "monocot" seeds have one cotyledon, or food part, and "dicot" seeds have two cotyledons. See **Plant Pipelines** (p. 186) for more on monocot and dicot plants.

SOCIAL STUDIES (The War of 1812)

The game "War of 1812" is designed for two players: one player will represent America, the other will represent England. Players must answer questions about the war in order to win the game.

You will need: one copy of **Who Won?** game board (p. 187), a die, a penny, a dime and 12 cardboard circles.

Preparation: Glue the copy of the game board onto a piece of cardboard and laminate for durability. Next, cut out 12 cardboard circles—6 red and 6 blue—to mark victories on the board. (You may also use a crayon or wipe-off marker to mark victories on a laminated board.) Each player must write 12 questions about the War of 1812 for his/her opponent to answer during the game.

Play: Each player places his/her marker (use a penny and a dime, markers from another game or simple, colored cardboard squares) on the appropriate start space and rolls the die. Whoever rolls the higher number goes first. Player 1 rolls the die again and moves his/her marker that number of spaces in any direction—players can move horizontally and vertically, but not diagonally. Movement is blocked or redirected by the British blockade, the U.S. embargo or the opponent's marker. The British can pass through the blockade, but the Americans must go around it; the Americans can pass through the embargo, but the British must go around it. The object of the game is to be the first player to win six victories. A victory is achieved by landing on a colored square (red for the British, blue for the Americans) with a victory number (1–6) and answering an opponent's question correctly. Each victory should be marked in the box on the game board. A player must answer a question correctly at each victory site in order to win the game.

This game can be played again and again to review events of the War of 1812. The game changes each time as the players write different questions.

Dynamic Digraphs

Consonant digraphs consist of two letters that represent one sound. Consonant digraphs may be found anywhere in a word.

although
another
athlete
birth
channel
chauffeur
chiffon
chocolate
choir
chrome
exchange
radish
sheriff
shovel
Thursday
whether
whiskers
whisper

- The digraph **sh** usually has the sound heard in **sharp** and **fish**.
- The digraph **wh** usually has the sound heard in **white** and **wheel**.
- The digraph **th** has two common sounds: **th** as in **this** and **th** as in **thin**.
- The digraph **ch** has three different sounds: **ch** as in **chair**, **ch** (like **k**) as in **chorus** and **ch** (like **sh**) as in **chef**.

Write each spelling word under the appropriate category.

ch as in **reach**

_____

_____

_____

— — — — — — — — — —

sh as in **dish**

_____

_____

_____

— — — — — — — — — —

wh as in **whale**

_____

_____

_____

— — — — — — — — — —

th as in **thimble**

_____

_____

_____

— — — — — — — — — —

th as in **this**

_____

_____

_____

— — — — — — — — — —

ch as in **chorus**

_____

_____

— — — — — — — — — —

ch as in **chef**

_____

_____

— — — — — — — — — —

Now, think of one additional word for each category and write it on the dotted line.

Learn At Home, Grade 5

Take an 8½" x 11" piece of paper. Fold it in half, half again, half again and half again. Open it up. It should look like this:

Draw in the two diagonals using a ruler and fold on them. Trace over all the fold lines on both sides. Cut on the dashed lines.

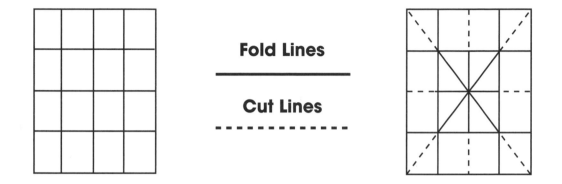

Fold Lines

Cut Lines

Fold the piece of paper flat to make each shape below. Calculate the area of each shape and write it on the blank.

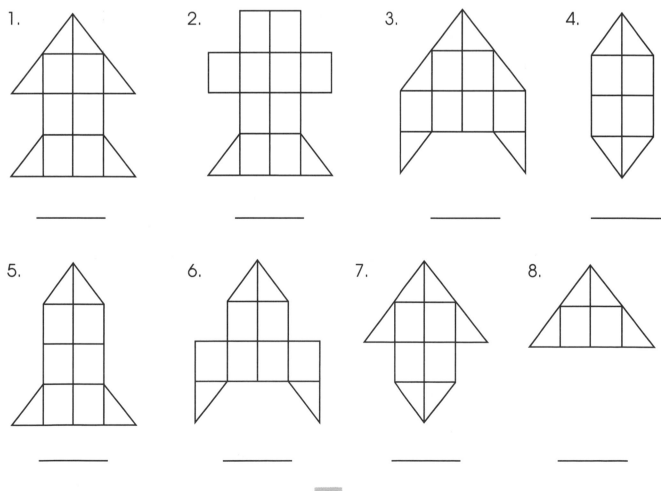

1.

2.

3.

4.

5.

6.

7.

8.

Root Systems

Label the two root systems pictured below. Use the terms in the Word Box.

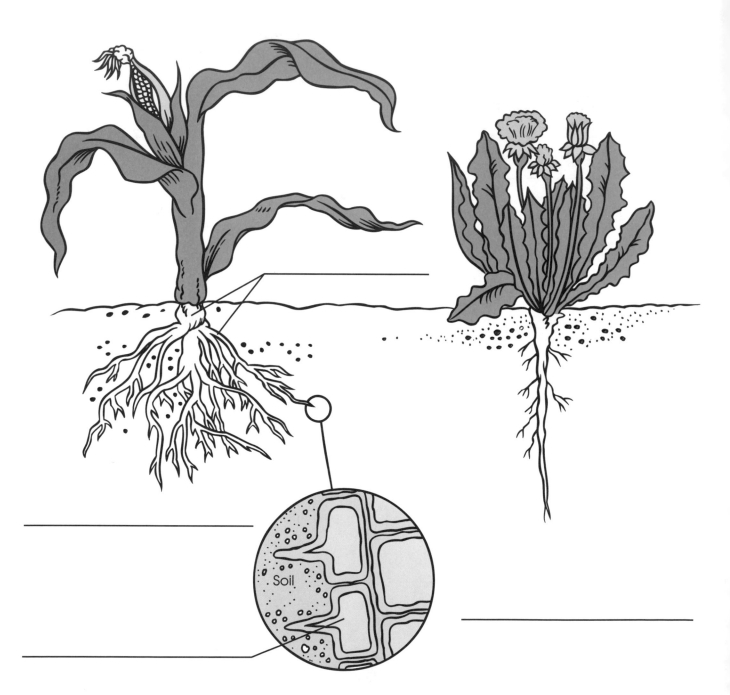

Soil

Word Box	
fibrous root system	root hair cell
taproot system	prop roots

Learn At Home, Grade 5

Inside a Root

Study the two views of a root shown below. **Label** the parts in both the top cross section and side cross section. Use the terms in the Word Box.

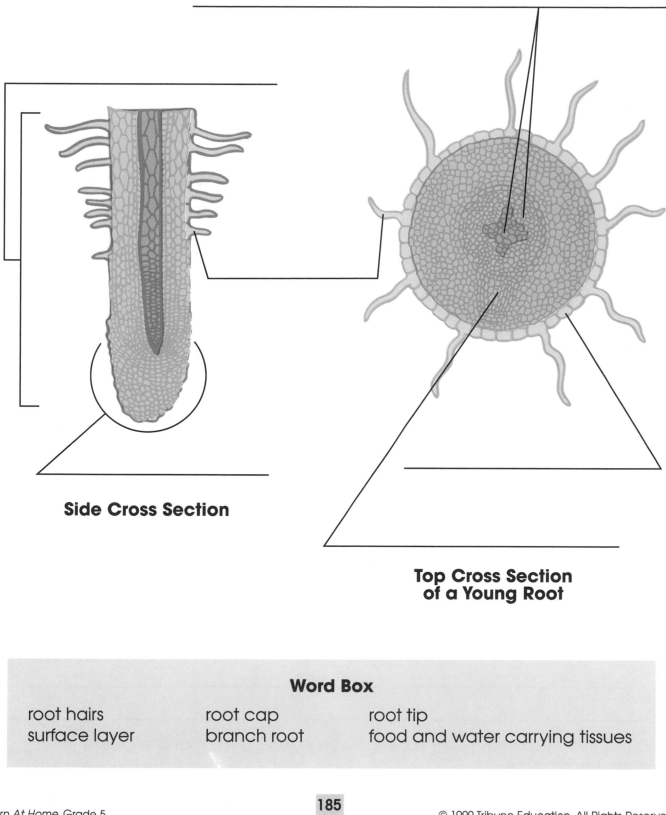

Side Cross Section

**Top Cross Section
of a Young Root**

Word Box		
root hairs	root cap	root tip
surface layer	branch root	food and water carrying tissues

Plant Pipelines

How does the plant get its food? Thin tubes in the stem carry food from the leaf to the rest of the plant. Other tubes carry water and minerals from the roots to the leaves. Both kinds of tubes are found in bundles in the stem.

The tube bundles are arranged in two ways. A **monocot** plant has bundles scattered throughout the stem. A **dicot** plant has bundles arranged in a ring around the edge of the stem.

Dicot or monocot stem?
Label the two pictures above.

Observing Plant Pipelines

You will need: a drinking glass, water, food coloring, an eyedropper, a knife and a stalk of celery

Directions:
Put a few drops of food coloring in a glass of water. Trim off the bottom inch of the celery stalk. Place the celery in the water. Let it sit for 3–4 hours.

Analysis:

1. Describe what you see. _____

_____

2. Cut the stalk crosswise. Look at the cut end. What do you see?

_____

3. What carried the water up the stalk?_____

4. What would happen if the stem of a plant were broken? Why?

_____

_____

Repeat this experiment using a white carnation in place of the celery. Watch what happens!

Learn At Home, Grade 5

Who Won?

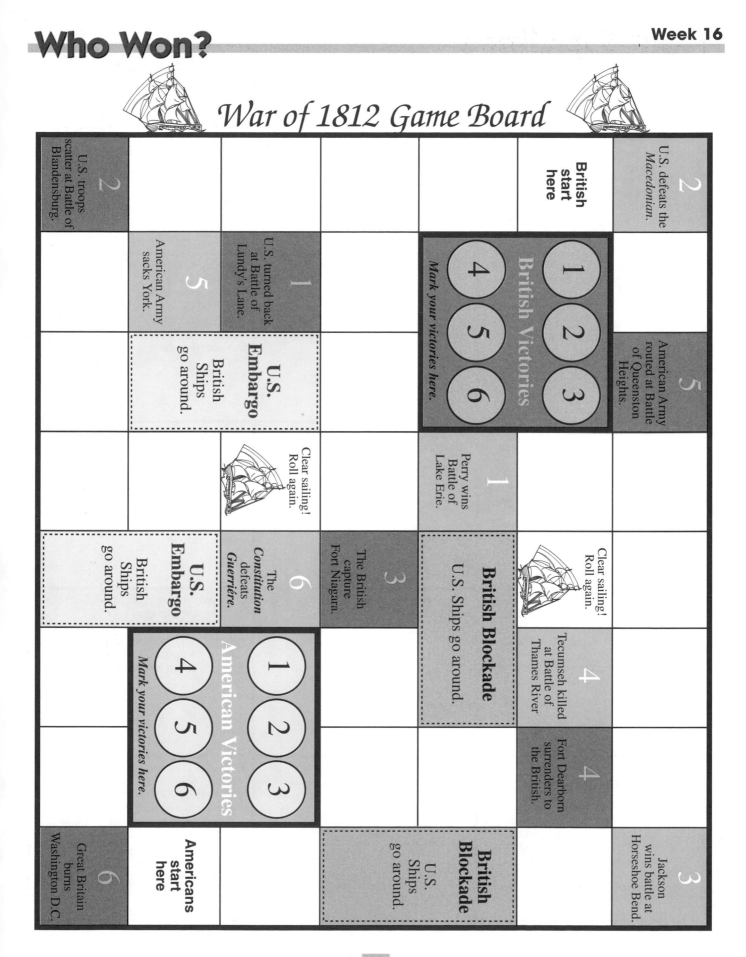

War of 1812 Game Board

British start here

Mark your victories here.

British Victories 1 2 3 4 5 6

Mark your victories here.

American Victories 1 2 3 4 5 6

Americans start here

U.S. defeats the *Macedonian*. 2

American Army routed at Battle of Queenston Heights. 5

Jackson wins battle at Horseshoe Bend. 3

U.S. troops scatter at Battle of Bladensburg. 2

American Army sacks York. 5

U.S. turned back at Battle of Lundy's Lane. 1

U.S. Embargo British Ships go around.

Clear sailing! Roll again.

Perry wins Battle of Lake Erie. 1

Clear sailing! Roll again.

Tecumseh killed at Battle of Thames River. 4

U.S. Embargo British Ships go around.

The *Constitution* defeats *Guerrière*. 6

The British capture Fort Niagara. 3

British Blockade U.S. Ships go around.

Fort Dearborn surrenders to the British. 4

Great Britain burns Washington D.C. 6

British Blockade U.S. Ships go around.

Learn At Home, Grade 5

	Language Skills	**Spelling**	**Reading**
Monday	Continue to discuss different forms of poetry. Have your child write a definition poem about one of this week's spelling words. **Example: word = marionette** *Wooden marionette, hanging by your strings, Waiting for your master to make you sing, As stiff as a board and motionless, Until a show when you bring happiness To audiences of every age, When your master gives you life on stage.*	Pretest your child on these spelling words: blind, plate, speak, blue, plump, spin, climb, sleep, swarm, close, slow, sweep, frog, small, track, fruit, smell, trap. Have your child correct the pretest. Add personalized words and make two copies of this week's study list.	Introduce *The War with Grandpa* by Robert Kimmel Smith. Have your child read chapters 1–3. Discuss the descriptive paragraphs about Peter's room in chapter 3. Point out the vivid adjectives used to describe the room. Have your child write a descriptive paragraph about his/her own room, describing not only the physical elements but also the emotions the room inspires. Have your child draw a floor plan and illustration as well.
Tuesday	**Pronouns and Nouns:** Review the concept of possession. To show possession, use a possessive pronoun or add *'s* to the noun. *See* Language Skills, Week 17, numbers 1 and 2.	Review this week's spelling words. Have your child complete **Beguiling Blends** (p. 192).	Have your child read chapters 4–8 of *The War with Grandpa*. Peter is writing what is "true and real" that happened to him. Have your child write about something that happened to him/her. Have your child use short sentences and use quotation marks.
Wednesday	Teach your child how to form the possessive of singular and plural nouns. *See* Language Skills, Week 17, number 3. Write several sentences with singular possessive nouns on the chalkboard. Have your child rewrite the sentences, changing each singular possessive to a plural possessive. **Example:** The boy's parents are here. *The boys' parents are here.*	Have your child use each of this week's spelling words correctly in a sentence.	Help your child edit and revise his/her writing from yesterday. Discuss aspects of your child's writing that are very good and at least one area that still needs work. Have your child read chapters 9–12 of *The War with Grandpa*. Have your child predict in his/her Reading Journal how Peter and his friends will fight Grandpa to get back Peter's room.
Thursday	Introduce your child to collective nouns. *See* Language Skills, Week 17, number 4. Have your child use each of the following collective nouns in a sentence: *committee, jury, troop, team, herd, club, class, audience, army, orchestra, band, flock* and *family.*	Have your child study this week's spelling words.	Have your child read chapters 13–16 of *The War with Grandpa*. Discuss *homographs*, words that sound alike and are spelled alike but have different meanings. Have your child complete **Watch for Grandpa's Watch** (p. 193).
Friday	Have your child read color poems in *Hailstones and Halibut Bones* by Mary O'Neill. Have your child write his/her own color poem, modeled on the poems in O'Neill's book. First, have your child choose a color. Then, have him/her brainstorm a list of things that are that color. From this list, have your child write the poem. Encourage your child to use metaphors and rhymes to add interest to the poem.	Give your child the final spelling test. Have your child record pretest and final test words in his/her Word Bank.	Have your child read chapters 17–20 of *The War with Grandpa*. Copy the **Story Organizer** (p. 33), and have your child complete as much of the sheet as possible at this point. He/she may need to write more events on the back of the page. Have your child leave the solution section blank for now; he/she can fill it in next week after completing the book. Discuss possible solutions to the war.

188

Math	Science	Social Studies
Graphing Use **From Here to There** (p. 194) for an exercise in grids and directions. Make one copy for yourself and one for your child. Give your child verbal directions to follow. **Example:** *Start at your home. Go one block west. Then, go five blocks north. Turn and go east one and a half blocks.* Have your child trace the path, then read back the directions. Did he/she follow the directions correctly? Repeat, then switch roles.	**Not in the Plant Kingdom** Provide your child with resource materials on algae, fungi and molds. Have your child read about these unique organisms. *See* Science, Week 17, number 1. Have your child write in his/her Science Log about algae, fungi and molds. What kinds of organisms rely on these non-plants as a food source?	Have your child read about America's sixth president, John Quincy Adams. *See* Social Studies, Week 17, number 1. Have your child add Adams's presidency to the time line.
Play a game with your child to practice graphing and plotting skills. Each of you will plot a rectangular shape on a grid and, like in the game of "Battleship," try to locate the position of your partner's rectangle. This game provides fun practice in using a two-dimensional grid. *See* Math, Week 17, number 1.	Take your child on a walk through a nearby forest or park. Ask your child to be on the lookout for lichens. You may need a field guide to identify lichens. *See* Science, Week 17, number 2. Have your child answer the following questions about any lichens you find: *Is the lichen growing in the sun or in the shade? Where is the lichen growing? How is the lichen attached? Are there any plants growing near the lichen?*	Have your child read about America's seventh president, Andrew Jackson. *See* Social Studies, Week 17, number 2. Have your child read about the government's policies regarding the Indians and the infamous Trail of Tears. Have your child add Jackson's presidency to the time line.
Graphs are used to display information visually in a format that is easy to read and understand. Reading graphs and interpreting the data in a meaningful context is an important skill. Look for examples of different types of graphs in newspapers, magazines, ads and other informational sources. Define *range* and review how to read bar graphs and double-bar graphs. Have your child complete **Dog and Jog Graphs** (p. 195).	Help your child prepare an experiment to cultivate the growth of bread mold. *See* Science, Week 17, number 3.	**Westward Movement:** Trace the Oregon Trail on a map. Ask your child: *What kind of terrain did the pioneers cross?* Have your child do research to discover why people left their homes and risked this difficult journey to resettle in the West. Ask your child to imagine that he/she is traveling the Oregon Trail. Have your child write a letter to a friend back home describing all he/she sees and experiences.
Gather examples of circle graphs (also called pie charts) for your child to examine. Review how to read a circle graph. Choose two circle graphs to look at in greater depth. Give your child four or five questions pertaining to each graph that require him/her to analyze the information presented. Discuss other types of graphs. *See* Math, Week 17, number 2.	Explain to your child how to monitor the bread mold experiment. Have your child examine the bags every day for the next seven days and create a chart to record any observations and changes. *See* Science, Week 17, number 4. Have your child predict what he/she thinks will happen in each bread bag after seven days. Have your child record these predictions in his/her Science Log.	Have your child read about the Texas revolution. Who fought in this war? What instigated the war? Discuss the battle at the Alamo. Who won? What is the significance of the battle cry, "Remember the Alamo!"? What was the outcome of Texas's battle for independence? Have your child draw a picture of the flag of the Republic of Texas.
Have your child collect data and present the results in an appropriate graph. Possible topics include favorite ice cream flavors, daily high temperatures for a week or the number and types of birds visiting a bird feeder in one hour. *See* Math, Week 17, number 3.	People often confuse lichens and mosses. Explain to your child the differences between these two types of organisms. Unlike lichens, mosses are plants. They are nonvascular plants, so they do not have leaves, stems or roots. They reproduce by means of spores. Have your child look for and identify mosses in your area. Look for the same patch of moss later in the year. Note any changes. Many mosses can withstand severe temperatures.	Arrange for your child to perform some community service.

189

TEACHING SUGGESTIONS AND ACTIVITIES

LANGUAGE SKILLS (Pronouns and Nouns)

▶ 1. Read the following sentence to your child: *I rode Brian's bicycle around the park.* Ask your child what pronoun would replace Brian in this sentence. (his) Since the noun is possessive in the sentence, the pronoun must also be possessive. Possessive pronouns include *mine, yours, his, her(s), its, our(s)* and *their(s).* Call attention to the possessive pronoun *its.* Stress that there is no apostrophe. The word *it's* is a contraction for *it is.*

▶ 2. Give your child the following sentences. Have him/her substitute a possessive pronoun for each possessive noun. For additional practice, make up more of your own sentences.

  Remember to return Elena's book by Friday. (her)
  Mario brought fresh flowers to Mario's mother. (his)
  I found Robert's hat under the couch. (his)
  The dinner is Greg's, Dave's and Terry's. (theirs)
  The runaway puppy is my sister's, my brother's and mine. (ours)
  Fluffy cleans Fluffy's fur with Fluffy's rough tongue. (its)

▶ 3. If a plural noun ends in *s,* simply add an apostrophe to show possession.
  Example: *I returned all of my friends' books yesterday.*

  Do not confuse this with singular nouns that end in *s.* In that case, add *'s* to the singular.
  Example: *Bill wore Travis's jacket at the football game.*

  If a plural noun does not end in *s,* add *'s* to show possession.
  Example: *your children's mittens were all wet.*

▶ 4. Collective nouns name groups of people or things. They most often take a singular verb.
  Examples: My family lives in Wisconsin.
      The team has come in second place for three years.

  When you use a collective noun to mean the individuals in the group, use a plural verb.
  Examples: The committee vote for different objectives.
      The orchestra are turning in their parts.

MATH (Graphing)

▶ 1. On graph paper, draw two grids with coordinates from 0–10 along both axes. Copy for each player. Keeping the paper hidden from the opponent, each player draws a rectangular shape with an area of 12 square units on the first grid. Players take turns trying to locate the opponent's rectangle by calling out ordered number pairs (e.g., (5, 7)). Ordered pairs are always counted across the bottom first and then up. After the player names a point, the opponent must tell if he/she hit the perimeter of the rectangle. Each player keeps track of the points he/she names on the second grid. Use a red marker to indicate a hit and a pencil to show a miss. Continue playing until one player has located and identified all the points on his/her opponent's rectangle.

▶ 2. Discuss the different types of graphs and how they are used. Gather examples to show your child.
  Bar graph: used to show and compare differences in amounts or sizes, such as rainfall or height.
  Line graph: used to show changes in one item, usually over time, such as stock prices or heart rate.
  Pictograph: same as a bar graph, but with representative pictures or symbols replacing the bar.
  Circle graph: used to show different parts of a whole, such as family monthly expenses or use of time in a day.

▶ 3. Be sure that your child includes the following elements in his/her graph.
  Title: The title should convey the information displayed on the graph.
  Labels: The horizontal and vertical axes should be labeled clearly on a bar, picture or line graph. The reader should be able to see at a glance what is being compared.
  Key: A key is necessary to explain different colors or patterns on a circle or double-bar graph.

Learn At Home, Grade 5

SCIENCE (Not in the Plant Kingdom)

▶ 1. Algae, fungi and molds are not in the plant kingdom. Many people mistakenly call these living things plants. Have your child read about the varieties of algae. Where is algae generally found? Have your child read about fungi. There are many different kinds. You may have some fungi growing in your own refrigerator.

▶ 2. Ask your child if he/she has ever noticed what seemed to be greenish white paint smeared on rocks or tree trunks. That probably wasn't paint at all, but a kind of lichen (LIE-ken)—an organism that is a combination of an alga and a fungus, living together. The alga makes food, while the fungus absorbs moisture and minerals and provides an anchor for the plant. Lichens can grow in places where plants cannot. Lichens produce a weak acid that can break up hard rock and turn it into soil. The soil then provides an environment in which other plants can start growing.

▶ 3. For this bread mold experiment you will need the following materials: 6 slices of white bread, 6 plastic sandwich bags, water and vinegar. Have your child follow these directions for each bag:

    a. Put one slice of dry bread in a bag and place in a sunny location.

    b. Put one slice of dry bread in a bag and place in a dark location.

    c. Sprinkle one slice of bread with water, put it in a bag and place in a sunny location.

    d. Sprinkle one slice of bread with water, put it in a bag and place in a dark location.

    e. Sprinkle one slice of bread with vinegar, put it in a bag and place in a sunny location.

    f. Sprinkle one slice of bread with vinegar, put it in a bag and place in a dark location.

▶ 4. Have your child create a chart to record observations of the bread bags over the next seven days. Encourage your child to use a magnifying glass to make careful observations.

Bag	Day 1	Day 2	Day 3	Day 4	Day 5	Day 6	Day 7
a							
b							
c							
d							
e							
f							

SOCIAL STUDIES (Early Presidents)

▶ 1. Follow up your child's reading with some of the following questions:

    What was unusual about John Quincy Adams's election to the presidency?

    Who was his father? mother?

    What were some of the things he did in Monroe's cabinet?

    What did he do after he was president?

    Why wasn't he elected to a second term?

    Why was he nicknamed "Old Man Eloquent"?

▶ 2. Follow up your child's reading with some of the following questions:

    What are some of the "firsts" that Jackson experienced as president? (first president born in a log cabin, first president born in the U.S., first from the frontier, first to ride a train)

    In what wars had Jackson participated? Discuss his role in them.

    Explain the reasons behind Jackson's split with Vice President Calhoun.

    What was the "spoils system" that Jackson started?

    Explain how Jackson acquired the nickname Old Hickory.

    Discuss Jackson's attitude toward Indians.

    What political party began during Jackson's presidency?

Beguiling Blends

Use the clues to **fill in** the blanks with the correct consonant blend to complete each spelling word.

Consonant Blends

sp   bl   tr   sl   cl

1. nearby ___**ose**
2. close your eyes and ___**eep**
3. used to catch lobsters ___**ap**
4. what a top does ___**in**
5. cannot see ___**ind**
6. not very fast ___**ow**
7. to go up a hill ___**imb**
8. a pretty color ___**ue**
9. to utter something ___**eak**
10. trains run on it ___**ack**

Consonant Blends

pl   sm   fr   sw

1. an amphibian ___**og**
2. not big or large ___**all**
3. food is placed on this ___**ate**
4. do it with a broom ___**eep**
5. one of the food groups ___**uit**
6. bees do this ___**arm**
7. you do this with your nose ___**ell**
8. a little chubby ___**ump**

blind
blue
climb
close
frog
fruit
plate
plump
sleep
slow
small
smell
speak
spin
swarm
sweep
track
trap

Write the spelling word that rhymes with each word below.

1. creep _____
2. find _____
3. stack _____
4. peak _____
5. grate _____
6. twin _____
7. throw _____
8. jeep _____
9. dwell _____

10. jute _____
11. storm _____
12. strap _____
13. chump _____
14. flog _____
15. mime _____
16. dose _____
17. stall _____
18. glue _____

Learn At Home, Grade 5

Watch for Grandpa's Watch

Each "watch" in the title of this activity sheet has a different meaning. One means "to look for," and the other means "timepiece." **Write** two meanings for each of the words below.

	Meaning 1	**Meaning 2**
1. spring	_____	_____
2. run	_____	_____
3. ruler	_____	_____
4. duck	_____	_____
5. suit	_____	_____
6. cold	_____	_____
7. fall	_____	_____
8. tire	_____	_____
9. rose	_____	_____
10. face	_____	_____
11. train	_____	_____
12. play	_____	_____
13. foot	_____	_____
14. pen	_____	_____
15. box	_____	_____
16. dice	_____	_____
17. fly	_____	_____
18. seal	_____	_____
19. bowl	_____	_____
20. ride	_____	_____

Choose some of the above words and illustrate both meanings on another sheet of paper.

From Here to There

Use the map below for an exercise in following and giving directions. Give verbal directions to a partner from one location to another, using the compass and counting the number of blocks. Switch places and follow directions given by your partner. Repeat several times, beginning and ending at different locations.

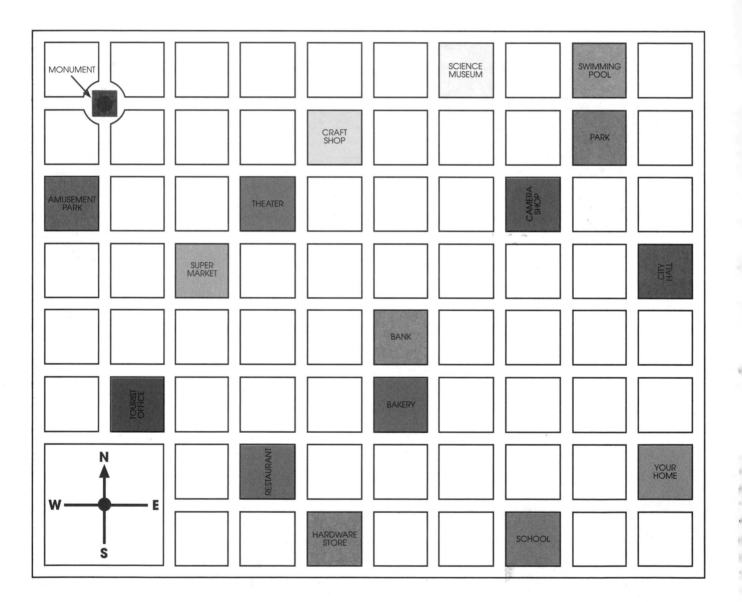

Learn At Home, Grade 5

Dog and Jog Graphs

Answer the questions using the graphs indicated.

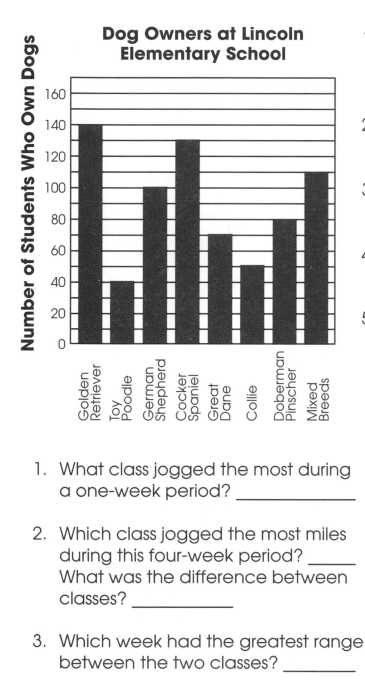

Dog Owners at Lincoln Elementary School

1. How many students own Great Danes at Lincoln Elementary School? _____

2. Which breed of dog is owned by the fewest students? _____

3. Which breed is owned by the most students? _____

4. How many students own Doberman pinschers? _____

5. How many more students own German shepherds than collies? _____

1. What class jogged the most during a one-week period? _____

2. Which class jogged the most miles during this four-week period? _____ What was the difference between classes? _____

3. Which week had the greatest range between the two classes? _____

4. Which week had the smallest range? _____

5. What was the range for Mr. Halverson's class during these four weeks? _____

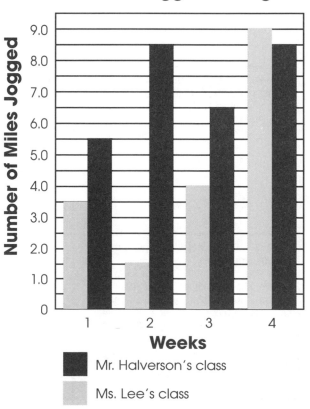

Distance Jogged During P.E.

■ Mr. Halverson's class
□ Ms. Lee's class

Language Skills	Spelling	Reading
Monday Teach your child how to write a diamante poem. *See* Language Skills, Week 18, number 1. Have your child choose two topics as the subjects of an original diamante poem. If there is time, have your child write a second poem or illustrate the first one.	Select words from the past eight weeks for this week's pretest. Have your child correct the pretest. Add personalized words and make two copies of this week's study list.	**Using Resources** Have your child read chapters 21–24 of *The War with Grandpa*. In chapter 24, Peter's friend shows off his vocabulary. Have your child look up the definition of each big word the friend uses. Then, have your child look up other words to increase his/her own vocabulary. This week, explore different types of reference materials with your child. *See* Reading, Week 18, number 1.
Tuesday **Building Vocabulary:** Provide your child with a list of words that are often misused. *See* Language Skills, Week 18, number 2. Have your child make an alphabetical glossary of these words. Each glossary entry should include a definition that sets the word apart from a similar word. This project may take several days.	Have your child sort spelling words from the past eight weeks by parts of speech. Ask your child to list all nouns, verbs, adjectives and so on.	Have your child read parts of *The War with Grandpa* out loud. Have him/her choose passages that contain dialogue. Does your child read with much expression? If not, encourage him/her to try. Have your child read chapters 25–29 of *The War with Grandpa*. *See* Reading, Week 18, numbers 2 and 3.
Wednesday Have your child continue working on the glossary of confusing words. Choose three word pairs that your child has already entered into the glossary. Have your child use each word correctly in a sentence.	Scramble the letters of several spelling words from the past eight weeks. Then, ask your child to unscramble the letters in each word and spell out the word correctly.	Have your child read chapters 30–34 of *The War with Grandpa*. Have your child write in his/her Reading Journal about Peter's reaction to losing the war. Explore geographical resources with your child. Have your child look at and compare maps, atlases, globes and road maps. *How are these resources different? How are they alike? What might you use each reference to find?*
Thursday Have your child continue working on his/her glossary of confusing words. Have your child complete **Troublesome Verb Pairs** (p. 200).	Have your child look at the words from the past eight weeks. Can he/she find any words *within* those words (e.g., sen**ten**ce, refe**r**ence)? How many can he/she find?	Have your child read chapters 35–37 of *The War with Grandpa*. Discuss the alliteration in the words "Pete's Place." Have your child design a doorknob tag to hang on his/her bedroom door. Have him/her write an alliterative phrase on the tag and decorate it. **Examples:** Rachel's Room, Carl's Cavern, Letrisha's Lodge. Discuss how a table of contents compares to an index. *See* Reading, Week 18, number 4.
Friday Have your child complete his/her glossary of confusing words. Have your child publish his/her favorite poems from the last few weeks in a personal poetry anthology. Have him/her create an appropriate cover for the book, including a title and the poet's (your child's) name.	Give your child the final spelling test.	Discuss the main idea of *The War with Grandpa*. Then, discuss the book as a whole. Have your child express an opinion about the actions of the characters. Discuss glossaries. *See* Reading, Week 18, number 5. Review reference materials. Have your child complete **The Right Stuff** (p. 201).

Learn At Home, Grade 5

Math	Science	Social Studies
Teach your child how to make a double-line graph. A double-line graph compares two related events over the same period of time. *See* Math, Week 18.	Have your child research the work of Gregor Mendel. *See* Science, Week 18, number 1. Have your child take notes on Mendel and his work in his/her Science Log.	**Westward Expansion** Continue last week's discussion of Texas. *Why might Texans have wanted statehood?* (for protection) *Why were some people in the U.S. in favor of annexation?* (desire for land) *Why were more Southern states in favor of annexation than Northern states?* (slavery) *How do you think the Mexicans felt about Texas becoming a state? See* Social Studies, Week 18, numbers 1 and 2.
Review the different types of graphs and how to read them. Have your child complete **Circle Graph** (p. 202).	Have your child complete a research project based on his/her research on Gregor Mendel. Have your child write a report or create a poster that demonstrates his/her understanding.	Have your child read about the presidents (up to Lincoln) and social reform in the nineteenth century. Have your child make a list of facts about the presidents. *See* Social Studies, Week 18, numbers 3 and 4.
Review place value and the basic mathematical operations: addition, subtraction, multiplication and division. Does your child understand regrouping? Review estimation and rounding. Repeat any activities that your child still finds difficult.	Have your child use the plant glossary begun in Week 10 and other related terms to write riddles or a story. *See* Science, Week 18, number 2.	Have your child continue reading about America's early presidents.
Review concepts of geometry with your child. Does your child know the difference between a line, a line segment and a ray? Review angles. Determine whether your child can recognize different geometric shapes and solids. Reteach any concepts, if necessary. Repeat some of the exercises from previous weeks on topics your child finds most difficult.	Observe the bread mold experiment from Week 17. Discuss the results. *Under what conditions does the bread mold seem to develop and grow the fastest? What do you think commercial bakers do to retard mold growth in their products? What chemicals are added to bread products to prevent molding?* (look at a label) Review plants, flowers and trees. Have your child complete **What Am I?** (p. 204). Reteach any concepts if necessary.	Make a copy of **United States Map** (p. 205). Have your child color the successive expansions of the country in different colors: Thirteen Colonies (1776), Post-Revolution (1783), Louisiana Purchase (1803), British Cession (1818), Florida (1819), Texas (1845), Oregon Country (1846), Mexican Cession (1848), Gadsden Purchase (1853), Alaskan Territory (1867) and Hawaii Territory (1898). Then, have your child add these dates to the time line.
Quiz your child on the material covered so far this year. Have your child complete **Second Quarter Test** (p. 203).	Discuss jobs that are related to plants, such as botanist, horticulturist, forest ranger and farmer. Have your child write a job application and cover letter to apply for an imaginary job related to plants. In the application and cover letter, have your child demonstrate his/her understanding of plants and describe in detail his/her skills that pertain to the chosen job.	Arrange for your child to perform some community service.

TEACHING SUGGESTIONS AND ACTIVITIES

LANGUAGE SKILLS (Poetry / Building Vocabulary)

▶ 1. A diamante poem follows a strict grammatical format and looks like a diamond when completed. A diamante covers two (often contrasting) subjects. Lines 1–3 and the first two nouns of line 4 describe the first topic; the remainder of the poem describes the second topic. The example shown here contrasts the city and the country. Have your child follow the pattern shown to write his/her own diamante poem. (A *participle* is a verb form that is used as an adjective.)

Pattern:	**Example:**
noun	*Country*
adjective, adjective	*Quiet, green*
participle, participle, participle	*Planting, growing, harvesting*
noun, noun, noun, noun	*Barns, meadows, skyscrapers, factories*
participle, participle, participle	*Hustling, bustling, hurrying*
adjective, adjective	*Big, busy*
noun	*City*

▶ 2. Give your child the following list of word pairs that are often misused. Encourage your child to use grammar books, dictionaries and other resources to clarify the correct usage of each word.

bring, take	affect, effect	alright, all right	can, may
ascent, assent	your, you're	who, whom	sit, set
counsel, council	very, vary	accept, except	its, it's
principal, principle	imply, infer	learn, teach	lie, lay
immigrate, emigrate	farther, further	fewer, less	than, then
continual, continuous	pore, poor, pour	good, well	bad, badly
altogether, all together	miner, minor	capital, capitol	later, latter
complement, compliment	among, between	all ready, already	let, leave

READING (Using Resources)

▶ 1. Explore the wealth of resources that can be found at the library. Dictionaries and encyclopedias are just two of the many different types of reference materials available. If possible, arrange a trip to a local library sometime this week. Allow your child to browse through the reference section. Point out the many types of resources found there. Have your child compare and contrast some of the materials. Incorporate some of the following activities (2–5) into this week's lesson plan. Try to connect the activities to topics or questions that arise from the reading of *The War with Grandpa*.

▶ 2. Discuss which type of resource might contain the answer to the following question: *Where is the jaeger's nesting grounds?* Guide your child to the correct resource and the answer to the question. Teach your child how to find the correct volume of an encyclopedia by looking at the spine. Provide other questions for your child to answer. Some suggestions: *What land masses are found along the Chukchi Sea? How is peat created and what is it used for? What materials are used to construct a kayak? What plants are found in the tundra?*

▶ 3. Have your child compare the information about a particular bird found in an encyclopedia entry with the information found in a bird book. Ask your child why the information is presented so differently.

▶ 4. Have your child look at a table of contents and an index in the same book. Ask how the two are alike and different. Ask your child to locate various things in the same book using one or the other guide.

▶ 5. Explain to your child the purpose of a glossary. Name some examples of books that might have glossaries. List the following words on the chalkboard. This list contains words that might be found in the glossaries of certain types of reference books. Have your child name the type of book that might contain each word.

Example: the word *robin* might appear in the glossary of a bird book.

triceratops	gulls	coniferous	longitude	plateau
constellation	cumulus	herbivorous	skeleton	sedimentation
insulated	cold front	elephant	light bulb	triangle
satellite	similes	aorta	Navajo	byte

Learn At Home, Grade 5

MATH (Graphs)

Have your child make a line graph showing the outside temperature twice a day. Have him/her write the dates for one week along the horizontal axis and a range of temperatures along the vertical axis. Have your child post a thermometer outside and record the temperature at the same times (9:00 A.M. and 4:00 P.M.) each day for a week. Have your child record each morning temperature in blue and each afternoon temperature in red along the same vertical line (same date). After seven days, have your child connect the dots of the same color. Ask your child to compare the two lines and make any observations.

SCIENCE (Plant Review)

▶ 1. Have your child find the answers to the following questions about Gregor Mendel:

Where did he conduct his experiments?
Which plant did he use in his experiments?
Why do you think he selected this plant?
Why was Mendel's work so important to the field of genetics?
What does the term recessive *mean?*
What does the term dominant *mean?*
What is a hybrid?

▶ 2. Have your child look at the terms in the unit's glossary and add other important words related to plants that have been studied. Then, have your child use these words to compose a series of riddles. Provide your child with index cards on which to write the riddles. Use the following riddle as an example:

I grow from bulbs.
I bloom in the spring.
I have thick green leaves.
I have large, beautiful petals.
I am the national flower of the Netherlands.
What flower am I?   **Answer: a tulip**

SOCIAL STUDIES (Westward Expansion)

▶ 1. Have your child read about the Mexican-American War. Guide your discussion with the following questions:

What events led to the war?
What were the dates? (add to the time line)
Who was the American president at the time?
Where did the battles take place and under whose leadership?

Who were the American generals?
Who was the Mexican president at the time?
What was the outcome of the war?

▶ 2. Discuss the concept of Manifest Destiny. Americans thought it was their right to expand their territory across the continent to the Pacific Ocean. What does your child think of such an attitude?

▶ 3. During the 1800s, settlers continued moving west, establishing new states and territories. As new areas developed, so did the need for social policies. The women's rights movement began to grow as women saw their roles changing. Many people also spoke out against slavery or demanded better schools for everybody—not just for the elite.

▶ 4. Have your child research the following presidents: Martin Van Buren, William Henry Harrison, John Tyler, James K. Polk, Zachary Taylor, Millard Fillmore, Franklin Pierce and James Buchanan. As your child reads about each president, have him/her take notes on an index card. Notes should include the president's name, the dates he held office and at least three facts about his presidency or public life. Discuss each president and have your child add dates to the time line.

199

Troublesome Verb Pairs

Don't confuse verbs that have similar meanings.

Lay means *put* or *place*.
Lie means *rest* or *recline*.

Teach means *show how*.
Learn means *find out*.

Set means *put something somewhere*.
Sit means *sit down*.

Lend means *give to someone*.
Borrow means *get from someone*.

Let means *allow*.
Leave means *allow to remain*.

Write the correct verb on each blank below.

"Mark, did you _____ (set, sit) the saddle on the fence?" David asked.

"Yes, David. I was going to _____ (let, leave) it in the barn, but it was heavy."

Did you _____ (teach, learn) how to throw the saddle onto your horse's back yet?" Mark asked.

"Yes, and then I needed to _____ (lay, lie) down and rest," David answered.

"I was going to _____ (lend, borrow) you a hand, but I was too busy trying to _____ (teach, learn) how to rope," David remarked.

"Will you _____ (let, leave) me _____ (lend, borrow) your horse tomorrow morning?" Mark inquired.

"Sure, Mark. I'm going to just _____ (set, sit) under a tree and read a book tomorrow morning," David responded.

Write the correct verb from the parentheses for each sentence.

1. Tell your dog to _____ (lay, lie) down in front of the barn.
2. Please, _____ (lay, lie) that saddle down in front of the stall and _____ (set, sit) the bridle on the table.
3. _____ (Set, Sit) on that bale of hay and rest your tired legs.
4. Will you _____ (let, leave) me wear your boots tomorrow?
5. Don't _____ (let, leave) those oats there.
6. I want to _____ (teach, learn) how to trim my horse's hooves.
7. We will certainly be happy to _____ (teach, learn) you.

200

Learn At Home, Grade 5

The Right Stuff

Circle the resource book you would use to find . . .

1. A recipe for baking homemade bread.

   encyclopedia   cookbook   *The Life of a Beaver*

2. A description of how beavers make dams.

   almanac   *The Life of a Beaver*   *The Guinness Book of World Records*

3. Another word for "route."

   thesaurus   math textbook   world atlas

4. A map of the United Kingdom.

   thesaurus   world atlas   *The Guinness Book of World Records*

5. The difference between a muffler and a mantle.

   dictionary   science textbook   cookbook

6. Information about the author, C. S. Lewis.

   almanac   encyclopedia   *Guidebook for Art Instructors*

7. Which is the world's most massive dam.

   The Guinness Book of World Records   dictionary   thesaurus

8. The oldest words in the English language.

   almanac   atlas   *The Guinness Book of World Records*

9. Why a beaver slaps its tail.

   dictionary   *The Life of a Beaver*   atlas

10. The pronunciation of "courtier."

    The Hobbit   dictionary   almanac

11. What camphor is used for.

    dictionary   *The Life of a Beaver*   thesaurus

12. The average snowfall for December 25th.

    almanac   cookbook   spelling workbook

Circle Graph

Ned earns an allowance of $10.00 each week. He created this circle graph on his computer to show his parents how he spends the money. Refer to the graph to answer each question below.

Ned's Allowance

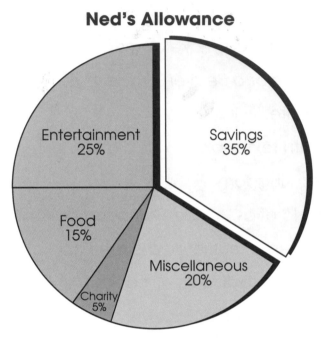

1. Ned highlighted the savings segment of the circle graph because his family believes that having a savings account is very important.
   If Ned saves $3.50 each week, how much will he have left for other things?

   _____

2. Ned spends all of his entertainment allowance on movies. How much does he spend each week on movies?

   _____

3. How much does Ned spend each week on miscellaneous expenses? Name some things he might buy which would fall into this category.

   _____

4. If you have an allowance, create your own circle graph detailing your spending habits. If you don't have an allowance, write two sentences describing how you would spend $10.00 differently than Ned.

   _____

   _____

202

Add or **subtract**.

1. $87 + 36{,}542 + 3 =$ _____

2. $22 +$ _____ $= 39$

3.
$$\begin{array}{rr} 7 \text{ ft.} & 3 \text{ in.} \\ + \; 2 \text{ ft.} & 9 \text{ in.} \\ \hline \end{array}$$

4.
$$\begin{array}{rr} 3 \text{ wks.} & 2 \text{ days} \\ - & 3 \text{ days} \\ \hline \end{array}$$

5. $103 -$ _____ $= 45$

6. $89 - 27 = x$
   $x =$ _____

Estimate.

7.
$$\begin{array}{r} 29{,}365 \\ + \; 7{,}850 \\ \hline \end{array}$$

8. $87 \times 4 =$ _____

9. $22 \overline{)3{,}849}$

Multiply or **divide**.

10. $9 \overline{)736}$

11. $76 \times 30 =$ _____

12. $\dfrac{529}{31} =$ _____

13. What is the change from $5 for a purchase of $1.87? _____

14. Identify each angle as acute, right or obtuse.

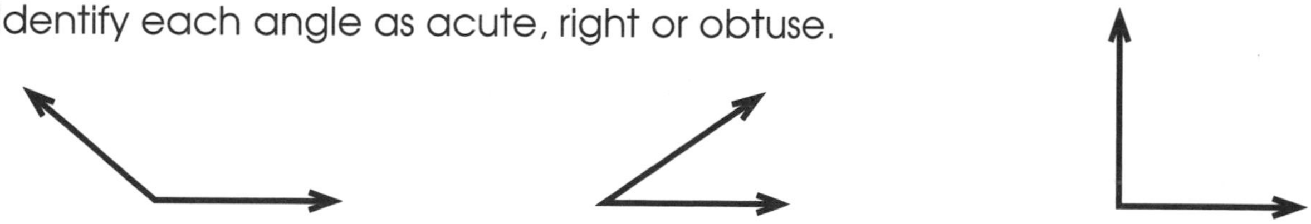

_____ _____ _____

15. Draw a 60° angle.

16. Draw 2 parallel lines.

17. Label each polygon.

_____ _____ _____ _____ _____

What Am I?

Find the answers to the riddles in the word search. **Circle** them and **write** them on the blanks provided. Use pages 131, 144 and 177 to help you. **Hint:** Words may be found horizontally, vertically, diagonally and backwards.

1. I am made of sapwood and heartwood. What am I?

   _____

2. I am a seed with two cotyledons. What kind of seed am I? _____

3. I carry food made by the leaves to other parts of the tree. What am I? _____

4. A monocot has only one of me. What am I?_____

5. Every year, I produce a new layer of bark. What am I?

   _____

6. I am the female reproductive part of the flower. What am I?

   _____

```
T H E T C G I T N E C D N M M
E E S T A M E N A W B Z O E S
R P R I M I W H H I O B D D E
M I O M B R A S S T W S B U P
I D O D I C O T D D R B O L A
N E T M U N L S N N V Y T L L
O R S E M L A A A U E O A A R
P M P A Y W L L E O N Y L R G
A I R T M A I P G P S R D Y E
R S Y A P H L O E M D B O R T
T T L L E N N R A O E M O A S
C O T Y L E D O N C E E W Y A
X Y L E M T A L I T S I P K T
Y L T H M S V H G H I B A A S
A L E T I T O C A A N M S C R
```

7. I am the male reproductive part of the plant. What am I? _____

8. We absorb water and minerals from the soil. What are we? _____

9. I am a leaf with many blades. What kind of leaf am I? _____

10. Animals and wind can disperse us. What are we? _____

11. My food is stored inside two cotyledons. What am I? _____

12. I carry water from the roots to the leaves. What am I? _____

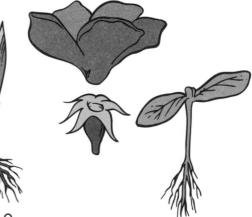

Can you find other plant terms hidden in the puzzle?

Learn At Home, Grade 5

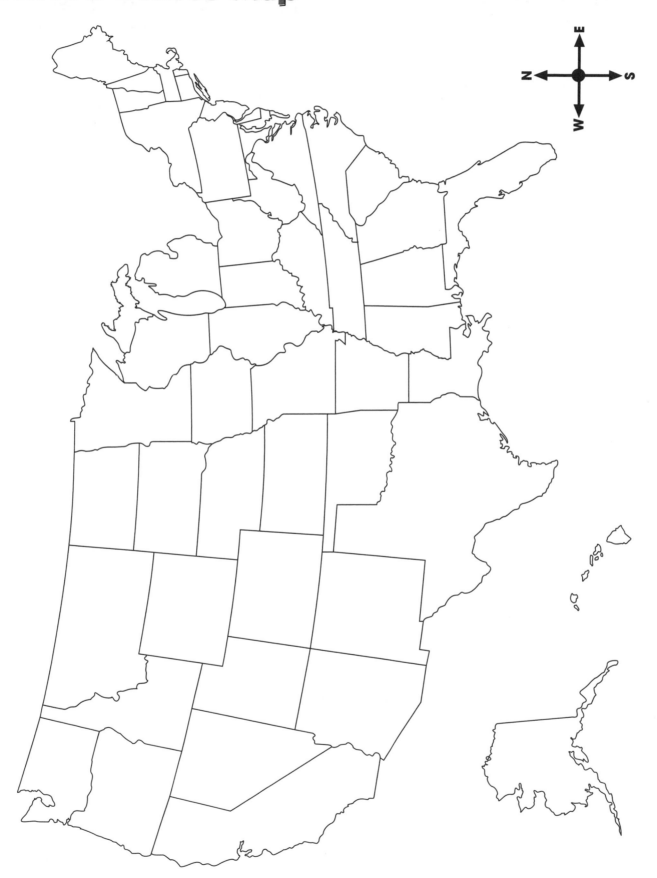

	Language Skills	**Spelling**	**Reading**
Monday	**Business Letters** Discuss the reasons for writing a business letter. Compare the purpose of a business letter with the purpose of a friendly letter. Have your child start working on a rough draft of a business letter that he/she will actually send. Your child may wish to request information, voice an opinion or call attention to a mistake. Do not worry about format at this point.	Pretest your child on these spelling words: cactus convoy gopher celebrate cumbersome gurgle cement cyclone gypsum certain dangerous Gypsy citizen gallery magic citrus gesture region Have your child correct the pretest. Add personalized words and make two copies of this week's study list.	**Affixes** Introduce *Tuck Everlasting* by Natalie Babbitt. Have your child read the prologue and chapters 1 and 2. Have your child respond to this question in his/her Reading Journal: *What do you find mysterious about woods and forests?* Review and reteach the use of prefixes and suffixes this week. Have your child list words from today's reading that contain prefixes and suffixes.
Tuesday	Teach your child the proper format of a business letter. *See* Language Skills, Week 19. Have your child revise the first draft of the business letter, focusing today on format.	Review this week's spelling words. Have your child complete **Double Trouble** (p. 210).	Ask your child about the characters in the book. Ask questions that require your child to make inferences. Have your child read chapters 3 and 4 of *Tuck Everlasting*. Write a list of words that contain prefixes and suffixes on the chalkboard. Have your child underline the root words. Then, have him/her look up the meaning(s) of each prefix and suffix used.
Wednesday	Help your child revise and edit the business letter. Ask your child the following questions: *Have you included the important facts and details? Is your letter easy to read? Have you followed the business letter format?* Then, have your child check for proper punctuation, capitalization, spelling and grammar. Have your child type a final copy of the letter to send.	Have your child use each of this week's spelling words correctly in a sentence.	Have your child read chapters 5–7 of *Tuck Everlasting*. Discuss how to recognize the mood of a speaker even if it is not stated directly in the text. Have your child complete **How's It Said?** (p. 211). Letters that are prefixes in some words may not be prefixes in others. Give examples. Have your child look up these words: *untie, under, republish, require, inside, invent, sublet, substitute, disapprove, distant, misspell, mister.* Discuss which have prefixes.
Thursday	Review the proper way to address an envelope. Explain that the post office prefers all capital letters and no punctuation, but the traditional form with upper- and lower-case letters and punctuation is also accepted. **preferred:** DIRECTOR OF QUALITY CONTROL ANIMAL GRAPHICS 9876 RAINFOREST DRIVE RIVERSIDE CA 91090	Have your child study this week's spelling words.	Have your child read chapters 8 and 9 of *Tuck Everlasting*. Discuss whether the man in the yellow suit will tell the world about the spring. Review your discussion of reference materials from Week 18. Have your child complete **Help Me!** (p. 212).
Friday	Review run-on sentences. Write several run-on sentences on the chalkboard for your child to rewrite. Then, give your child the following sentence to rewrite: *Mother went to the store and she saw our neighbor, Mrs. Gold, there, they talked about what they were having for dinner and Mother finally bought chicken, broccoli and milk, when she got home I helped her fix dinner.*	Give your child the final spelling test. Have your child record pretest and final test words in his/her Word Bank.	Discuss whether the events in *Tuck Everlasting* could really happen or not. Have your child read chapters 10 and 11. Have your child write in his/her Reading Journal about the importance of the Tuck family keeping their secret.

Learn At Home, Grade 5

Math	**Science**	**Social Studies**
Fractions Your child will learn to identify fractional parts while creating a tangram set. Have your child complete **Making a Tangram Set** (p. 213). Have your child manipulate the tangram pieces until he/she can name what fraction of the whole square each piece represents.	**Earth Science** Introduce your child to the scientific study of the earth and its varied formations. Provide lots of resource materials for your child's reference. Add the following terms to the weekly spelling lists: *cleavage, crystal, facet, fracture, gem, hardness, inorganic, lapidary, luster, mineral, Mohs hardness scale, mineralogy, quarry, streak* and *streak plate*. Have your child make a glossary of these terms in his/her Science Log.	Have your child read about the California Gold Rush. Discuss how it started, the type of person that searched for gold and what his life was probably like. *How did the gold rushes help settle the West?* Have your child write a newspaper article about the California Gold Rush. Have your child imagine that he/she writes for a paper back east. The article should include events from history and boast a catchy headline.
Have your child manipulate the tangram pieces to create figures. Have your child complete **Totally Tangram!** (p. 214).	**Minerals:** Provide resources on minerals for your child's reference. Display some samples of minerals. Have your child examine the minerals and note the color, shape and mass of each. Explain that a mineral is an inorganic substance that occurs naturally on Earth. Discuss minerals. *See* Science, Week 19, number 1. Have your child take notes on minerals in his/her Science Log.	**Slavery:** The life of a slave was very unpleasant. Discuss the conditions in which black slaves lived and worked. Compare the lives of African-Americans today to the lives of slaves in the 1800s. Have your child imagine that he/she is a black slave working on a cotton plantation and write a dialogue he/she might have with a brother or sister about the work, working conditions or life as a slave.
Use manipulatives to compare fractions. Fraction models can be purchased, but they are also easy to create. Use modeling clay or graph paper to make physical representations of fractions. Lead your child to understand concepts such as $\frac{1}{4}$ is equivalent to $\frac{2}{8}$ and $\frac{4}{16}$. *See* Math, Week 19, number 1.	Introduce your child to Mohs hardness scale and other tests used to identify minerals. Have your child conduct some of these identification tests on your own mineral specimens. *See* Science, Week 19, number 2. Have your child answer these questions in his/her Science Log: *What is a common use of talc because of its softness? Why are many cutting instruments made from diamond dust?*	Discuss the history of opposition to slavery. *Does the Declaration of Independence or the Constitution mention slavery?* Have your child look up the words *slave* and *slavery*, then state their meanings in his/her own words. Show your child a map that illustrates how the states were divided over the issue of slavery in 1820. Discuss this division. *Why was slavery more important to the Southern states?*
Teach your child to create equivalent fractions by multiplying the numerator and denominator by the same factor. **Example:** $\frac{3}{4} = \frac{9}{12}$ (3 x 3 = 9, 4 x 3 = 12) Have your child use manipulatives to show that these two fractions are indeed equivalent. Have your child complete **Equivalent Fractions** (p. 215).	Read about gemstones and their uses. Visit a gemologist or jeweler, if possible. *See* Science, Week 19, number 3. Have your child write about the different ways the value of a gem is determined.	Have your child read about the Missouri Compromise, the Compromise of 1850 and the Kansas-Nebraska Act. *How were these acts related? What was the impact of these decisions?* Have your child add these events to the time line. Have your child consider what the United States might have been like had each state been allowed to establish its own rules about slavery. Have your child write a paragraph on the topic.
Teach your child how to identify common factors of two numbers. *See* Math, Week 19, number 2. This is an important skill in simplifying fractions to lowest terms. Simplifying will be taught in Week 20. Ask your child: *If you multiply the numerator and denominator of a fraction by the same number, you have an equivalent fraction. Will you have an equivalent fraction if you divide the numerator and denominator by the same number?*	Have your child grow crystals using the following common household items: salt, alum and sugar. Introduce this experiment by asking your child to think of where crystals grow naturally and how quickly they grow. *See* Science, Week 19, number 4.	Arrange for your child to perform some community service.

TEACHING SUGGESTIONS AND ACTIVITIES

LANGUAGE SKILLS (Business Letters)

A business letter may be a letter of request, a letter of complaint or a letter to an editor or official. Teach your child either the full block or semiblock form. The full block form is shown here.

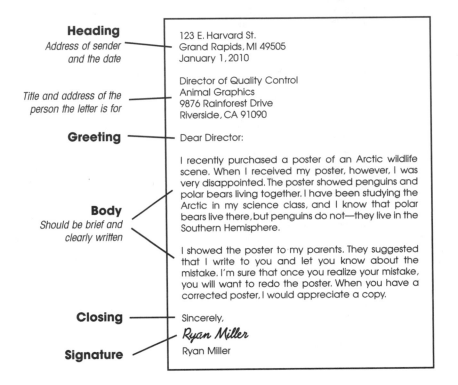

Heading
Address of sender and the date

123 E. Harvard St.
Grand Rapids, MI 49505
January 1, 2010

Title and address of the person the letter is for

Director of Quality Control
Animal Graphics
9876 Rainforest Drive
Riverside, CA 91090

Greeting

Dear Director:

Body
Should be brief and clearly written

I recently purchased a poster of an Arctic wildlife scene. When I received my poster, however, I was very disappointed. The poster showed penguins and polar bears living together. I have been studying the Arctic in my science class, and I know that polar bears live there, but penguins do not—they live in the Southern Hemisphere.

I showed the poster to my parents. They suggested that I write to you and let you know about the mistake. I'm sure that once you realize your mistake, you will want to redo the poster. When you have a corrected poster, I would appreciate a copy.

Closing

Sincerely,

Ryan Miller

Signature

Ryan Miller

MATH (Fractions)

▶ 1. In the tangram lesson, your child saw that two of the one-sixteenth triangles made up one of the one-eighth squares. Also, two of the one-fourth triangles made up one of the one-half triangles. Review this concept with the tangrams. Further reinforce the idea of equivalent fractions with other manipulatives and in practical situations which arise.

▶ 2. On a chart, have your child list all the factors of each of the following numbers: 2, 3, 4, 5, 6, 8, 12, 16, 18, 24, 36, 38, 42 and 50.

Examples:

number	factors
2	1, 2
8	1, 2, 4, 8
24	1, 2, 3, 4, 6, 8, 12, 24

Next, have your child list the *common* factors of pairs of numbers, such as 2 and 16 or 18 and 42. Have your child circle the greatest common factor of each pair.

Examples: The common factors of 2 and 16 are 1 and 2. The greatest common factor (GCF) is 2.
The common factors of 18 and 42 are 1, 2, 3 and 6. The GCF is 6.

Learn At Home, Grade 5

SCIENCE (Earth Science / Minerals)

▶ 1. Guide your discussion of minerals with some of the following questions:

Is coal a mineral? Why or why not?   *What is another name for table salt?*
Can you name some common minerals?   *What is "fool's gold"? How did it get its name?*
Why are many minerals found in the oceans?   *What are some minerals prized for their beauty?*

▶ 2. Some simple tests using simple equipment are used to help identify minerals. Have your child read about each test. The tests look at the following attributes of the minerals:

color   the mineral may be colorless, white or very distinctive in color; color can be misleading

cleavage the tendency to split along smooth, flat surfaces

fracture the characteristic appearance of the broken mineral

luster   refers to the amount of light reflected; the mineral may be glassy, metallic, non-metallic, waxy, pearly or dull

streak   a mineral is rubbed on a piece of white tile called a streak plate; color of streak is noted

hardness ability to be scratched; Mohs hardness scale (shown here) guides the mineralogist in determining the hardness of a mineral

Hardness	Example	Description
1	talc	scratched by fingernail
2	gypsum	scratched by fingernail
3	calcite	scratched with a penny
4	fluorite	scratched with a knife blade
5	apatite	scratched with a knife blade
6	feldspar	scratches a knife blade or glass
7	quartz	scratches a knife blade or glass
8	topaz	scratches a knife blade or glass
9	corundum	scratches a knife blade or glass
10	diamond	scratches all common materials

▶ 3. Gemstones may be found naturally or made artificially. Some common gems include amethyst, aquamarine, diamond, emerald, garnet, jade, onyx, opal, ruby, sapphire, topaz, tourmaline, turquoise and zircon. A *lapidary* is a person who cuts and polishes minerals and gemstones. If possible, visit a lapidary, gemologist or jewelry designer to view their techniques and learn more about their art. Have your child ask the expert to explain how the value of a gem is determined.

▶ 4. *You will need:* 3 glass jars, hot water, heavy cotton string, scissors, 3 wooden stirring sticks, table salt, alum (found in the spice section of a grocery store), sugar, magnifying glass and newspaper to catch any spills

Directions:

a. Fill a jar two-thirds full of hot water. Add one chemical slowly to the water, stirring until no more will dissolve.

b. Tie a piece of string to the middle of the stirrer. Lay the stirrer across the top of the jar so that the end of the string barely touches the bottom of the jar.

c. Label the jar with the chemical used and set the jar (with the string) where it will not be disturbed for several days.

d. Repeat steps a–c for the other two chemicals.

e. Each day, observe the three jars to see the crystals begin to grow.

f. After several days, lift the strings out of the jars and place them on newspapers or paper towels. Examine the crystals more closely with a magnifying glass.

Double Trouble

cactus
celebrate
cement
certain
citizen
citrus
convoy
cumbersome
cyclone
dangerous
gallery
gesture
gopher
gurgle
gypsum
Gypsy
magic
region

The letters **c** and **g** each make two distinctly different sounds, depending on the letters following them within a word. Both **c** and **g** can make a hard sound or a soft sound.

Hard **c** sounds like **k** when followed by **a**, **o** or **u**.
Examples: cake, cobra, cut

Soft **c** sounds like **s** when followed by **e**, **i** or **y**.
Examples: cent, city, cycle

Hard **g** carries its regular sound when followed by **a**, **o** or **u**.
Examples: gate, goat, gurgle

Soft **g** sounds like **j** when followed by **e**, **i** or **y**.
Examples: gem, giant, gym

Say each of the spelling words carefully while listening for the hard and soft sounds of **c** or **g**. Then, **write** each word under the appropriate heading.

hard **c** as in **carton**

1. _____
2. _____
3. _____

hard **g** as in **gutter**

1. _____
2. _____
3. _____

soft **c** as in **center**

1. _____
2. _____
3. _____
4. _____
5. _____
6. _____

soft **g** as in **gerbil**

1. _____
2. _____
3. _____
4. _____
5. _____
6. _____

Learn At Home, Grade 5

How's It Said?

Circle the word which best describes the mood or tone of the person speaking.

1. When Winnie's grandmother heard the little melody in the woods, she said, "That's it! That's the elf music I told you about."

    resentful   eager   anxious

2. Winnie spied on Jesse in the woods and watched as he drank from the spring. When he saw her, Jesse cried, "What're *you* doing here?"

    stern   hopeless   joyful

3. When Jesse told her not to drink from the spring, Winnie questioned, "Why not? It's mine, anyway, if it's in the wood."

    stubborn   reluctant   worried

4. Winnie cried when she realized she was being kidnapped. Seeing this, Mae exclaimed, "Please don't cry, child! We're not bad people, truly we're not."

    angry   reluctant   dismayed

5. When Winnie was calmed, everyone relaxed. Jesse began to explain the family's story. "We're friends, we really are. But you got to help us."

    persuasive   happy   helpless

6. Miles recalled how his family reacted when he didn't age. "My wife, she left me. She went away and she took the children with her."

    stern   sad   stubborn

What might you say if . . .

1. . . . you were angry at your parents for not letting you go outside?_____

    _____

2. . . . you were hopelessly unprepared for your spelling test?_____

    _____

Help Me!

Circle the reference source you would use to answer each question below.

1. Which source would you use to learn how to make pancakes?

   dictionary   atlas   cookbook

2. Which source might show where Treegap is?

   dictionary   atlas   thesaurus

3. Which source would describe the peacock?

   book on insects   encyclopedia   newspaper

4. Which source would describe the sounds a cricket makes?

   book on insects   thesaurus   atlas

5. Which source would give the meaning of "constable"?

   newspaper   dictionary   atlas

6. Which source would describe the most recent world events?

   newspaper   encyclopedia   thesaurus

7. Which source would tell how to divide "accommodations" into syllables?

   thesaurus   book on insects   dictionary

8. Which source could give a synonym for "push"?

   thesaurus   cookbook   encyclopedia

9. Which source might best forecast tomorrow's weather?

   encyclopedia   atlas   newspaper

Use references to answer the following questions:

Which countries border Nepal?

Answer: _____

Source: _____

Page #: _____

What are the headlines in today's paper?

Answer: _____

Source: _____

Page #: _____

Learn At Home, Grade 5

Making a Tangram Set

You will need: a piece of tagboard, a ruler, a pencil and scissors

Directions: Using the ruler to measure precisely, cut the tagboard into a 5" square. Cut the square according to the pattern below.

For a challenge, identify each shape and each type of angle.

Laminate the finished pieces (or cover with clear shelf paper). Save the tangram set for future use.

213

Totally Tangram!

Use the Tangram pieces from page 213 to create the shapes below.

Now, use the tangram pieces to create your own pictures, shapes and designs. **Trace** around each image you make. Save the outlines and try to recreate the images another day.

Learn At Home, Grade 5

Equivalent Fractions

Match the pairs of equivalent fractions to find which line is longest—**A**, **B** or **C**.

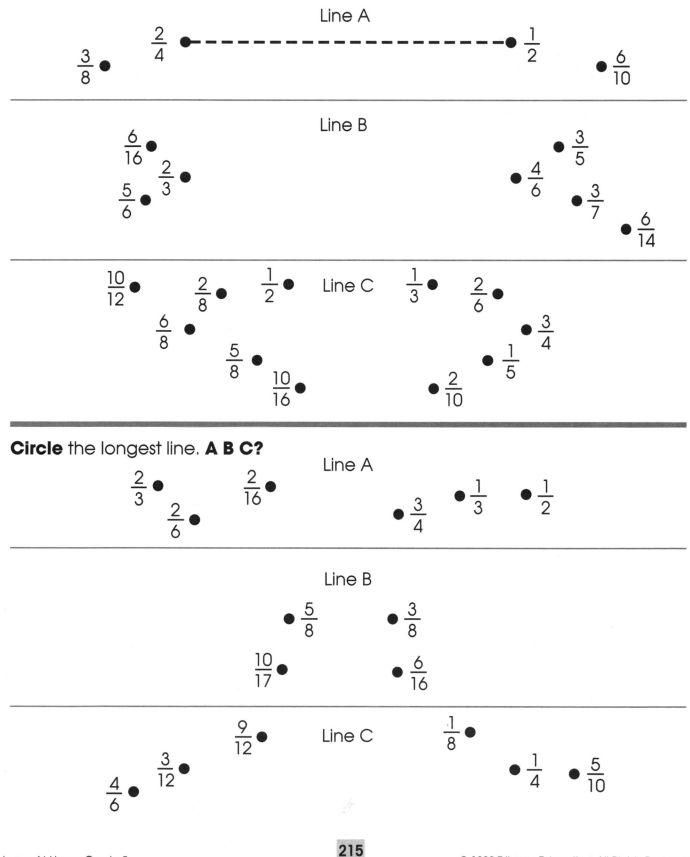

Line A

$\frac{3}{8}$ $\frac{2}{4}$ $\frac{1}{2}$ $\frac{6}{10}$

Line B

$\frac{6}{16}$ $\frac{2}{3}$ $\frac{5}{6}$ $\frac{3}{5}$ $\frac{4}{6}$ $\frac{3}{7}$ $\frac{6}{14}$

Line C

$\frac{10}{12}$ $\frac{2}{8}$ $\frac{1}{2}$ $\frac{1}{3}$ $\frac{2}{6}$ $\frac{6}{8}$ $\frac{3}{4}$ $\frac{5}{8}$ $\frac{10}{16}$ $\frac{1}{5}$ $\frac{2}{10}$

Circle the longest line. **A B C?**

Line A

$\frac{2}{3}$ $\frac{2}{16}$ $\frac{2}{6}$ $\frac{3}{4}$ $\frac{1}{3}$ $\frac{1}{2}$

Line B

$\frac{5}{8}$ $\frac{3}{8}$ $\frac{10}{17}$ $\frac{6}{16}$

Line C

$\frac{9}{12}$ $\frac{1}{8}$ $\frac{3}{12}$ $\frac{4}{6}$ $\frac{1}{4}$ $\frac{5}{10}$

Language Skills	Spelling	Reading

Monday

Creative Writing
The most natural story to write is one based on a real experience. This week, use this story starter: *Write about the time…* Model this type of writing for your child by writing about a shared experience such as a camping trip or a walk along a beach. Then, talk with your child about how you came up with your idea.

Pretest your child on these spelling words:
affection   frequent   philosophy
autograph   furniture   physical
cough   geography   raffle
enough   laughter   slough
familiar   muffler   stuff
foreign   paragraph   tough
Have your child correct the pretest. Add personalized words and make two copies of this week's study list.

Parts of Speech
Have your child read chapters 12–14 of *Tuck Everlasting.*
Discuss how some words can act as either a noun or a verb. Have your child locate some words in the reading book that may be used both ways. Have your child read the sentences and tell how each word is used.
Have your child complete **A Whale of an Activity** (p. 221).

Tuesday

Have your child write a story about a personal experience. Encourage your child to try to convey the mood of the experience and his/her feelings by including vivid details and descriptions.

Review this week's spelling words. Have your child complete **Fussing About f** (p. 220).

Have your child read chapters 15–17 of *Tuck Everlasting.*
Have your child read part of the story aloud. Guide him/her to read with lots of expression.

Wednesday

Have your child write a story about a personal experience. Have your child read the story to a friend and ask for feedback. Have your child ask the friend questions such as these: *Does my story interest you? Could you tell how I felt when…? Are there any parts of the story that are confusing? Is there anything else you would like to know about this experience?*

Have your child use each of this week's spelling words correctly in a sentence.

Have your child read chapters 18–20 of *Tuck Everlasting.*
Review the concepts of cause and effect. Have your child complete **Because…** (p. 222).

Thursday

Have your child imagine that he/she is telling his/her story to someone special. Encourage your child to include words that will engage the reader. The story should sound natural, not forced.

Have your child study this week's spelling words.

Have your child read chapters 21–23 of *Tuck Everlasting.*
After reading, have your child identify several pronouns in the story and the people or things to which each refers.

Friday

Have your child write a story about something that happened to someone he/she knows. Have your child write the story in the third person.

Give your child the final spelling test. Have your child record pretest and final test words in his/her Word Bank.

Have your child finish reading *Tuck Everlasting,* including the epilogue. Follow up the story with an activity that requires critical thinking skills as well as creativity. *See* Reading, Week 20.

Learn At Home, Grade 5

Math	Science	Social Studies
Simplifying fractions makes them easier to work with and to visualize. The simplified fraction is equivalent to the original fraction. To simplify a fraction, divide the numerator and denominator by their greatest common factor. *See* Math, Week 20, numbers 1 and 2.	**Mountains** Point out the major mountain ranges of the world on a map or globe. Introduce your child to the different types of mountains: *volcanic, fold, fault-block, dome* and *erosion.* Have your child read about how these mountains are formed. Have your child add a glossary page on mountains to his/her Science Log. *See* Science, Week 20, number 1. Add the glossary words to this week's spelling list.	**Slavery** Have your child read about and discuss the Dred Scott case. Dred Scott was a slave who moved with his master to a free state. He sued for his freedom when his master died. The Supreme Court ruled that he was still a slave. *Was the outcome fair? What impact did the Supreme Court's decision have on the slavery issue?* Have your child add the date of the Dred Scott decision to the time line.
Have your child explain in a paragraph why it is easier to work with fractions that have been simplified or reduced.	Ask your child what mountain peaks he/she has heard of or seen. Can he/she locate them on a map? Have your child locate major mountains on a map or in a world atlas. *See* Science, Week 20, numbers 2 and 3. Have your child make a bar graph comparing the heights of eight of these (or other) famous mountains. Then, ask your child questions that require him/her to analyze the information presented on the graph.	Discuss the events leading up to the Civil War. Have your child read about some famous people of the time. *See* Social Studies, Week 20, number 1.
Have your child complete **Conversion** (p. 223). After completing the page, have your child describe the best strategy for solving the problems.	Inspire your child to read books set in the mountains. Some suggestions include *Grandpa's Mountain* by Carolyn Reeder, *Rip Van Winkle* by Washington Irving, *Heidi* by Johanna Spyri and *The Last of the Mohicans* by James Fenimore Cooper.	Have your child read about the organization called the Underground Railroad. *What was the Underground Railroad? What were the goals of this organization? Who were some of the key figures in its operation?* Have your child write some imaginary diary entries as a conductor on the Underground Railroad.
Since it can be difficult to understand which of two fractions is greater, teach your child to count with fractions. Cut an apple into eighths. Count the pieces: one eighth, two eighths, three eighths, four eighths, five eighths, etc. It is easy to see that five eighths is greater than one eighth. *See* Math, Week 20, numbers 3 and 4. Give your child several fraction pairs to compare using these methods.	Have your child compare the Rocky Mountains to the Appalachian Mountains. Have your child compile the information from the comparison into a chart or diagram.	Have your child imagine that he/she is a slave on a plantation and has decided to run away. Have your child write a plan for his/her escape. *See* Social Studies, Week 20, number 2 for some of the factors your child will have to consider in making this plan.
Rather than asking your child to memorize several rules for comparing fractions, encourage your child to come up with his/her own strategies. Make sure your child sees a purpose in comparing fractions by putting the fractions in a meaningful context. **Example:** Which is a larger part of a candy bar: $\frac{4}{5}$ or $\frac{6}{7}$? *See* Math, Week 20, number 5.	Have your child study a mountain biome. *What plants and animals live at different altitudes?* Have your child choose one mountain range to study. Ask him/her to write about the variety of life (both plant and animal) that can be found on that mountain range. Have your child include illustrations or photos (from magazines) as well.	Arrange for your child to perform some community service.

217

TEACHING SUGGESTIONS AND ACTIVITIES

READING (Critical Thinking)

Ask your child to imagine that he/she is the author of *Tuck Everlasting*. Give your child the following list of events, and ask him/her to imagine how the story might have ended had each of these events occurred. Have your child write a summary of the story's ending for each case.

Winnie drank the spring water.

Mae was hung from the gallows.

The toad was attacked by the dog.

Mae did not kill the man in the yellow suit.

The constable discovered Winnie in the prison immediately.

The wood and the spring were not bulldozed.

MATH (Fractions)

▶ 1. A fraction is in lowest terms when 1 is the only common factor of the numerator and denominator. To reduce a fraction, divide both the numerator and denominator by their GCF, or greatest common factor.

Example: $\frac{6}{8}$ 2 is the largest number (GCF) that goes into both 6 and 8.

$$\frac{6 \ (\div 2)}{8 \ (\div 2)} = \frac{3}{4}$$

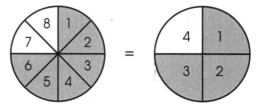

▶ 2. Write these fractions on the chalkboard. Have your child reduce each fraction to lowest terms.

$\frac{20}{25}$ $\frac{12}{18}$ $\frac{2}{11}$ $\frac{16}{20}$ $\frac{7}{21}$ $\frac{6}{9}$ $\frac{14}{49}$ $\frac{30}{50}$ $\frac{27}{63}$ $\frac{40}{64}$ $\frac{5}{13}$ $\frac{36}{96}$

▶ 3. Comparing $\frac{13}{15}$ (thirteen fifteenths) and $\frac{11}{15}$ (eleven fifteenths) is the same as comparing 13 cakes and 11 cakes. Thirteen cakes is more, just as $\frac{13}{15}$ is more. Think of the denominator as a common object. Using this method, your child will see the numerator as the number of something, or in this case, the number of parts of the whole. This method is appropriate only when comparing fractions with the same denominators.

▶ 4. When your child compares fractions with different denominators, have him/her draw a model of both fractions. Ask your child to compare the models. As an alternative, ask your child to visualize the models of the fractions. Your child should be able to estimate whether each fraction is closer to zero, one half or the whole. Based on the estimations, have your child decide which fraction represents a larger number.

▶ 5. Have your child develop strategies for determining the larger of two fractions. There are different challenges with different types of comparisons. See the following examples of different types of comparisons:

a. Same numerators but different denominators:

$\frac{3}{5}$ and $\frac{3}{7}$ $\frac{1}{2}$ and $\frac{1}{7}$

b. Different numerators but same denominators:

$\frac{2}{5}$ and $\frac{4}{5}$ $\frac{5}{9}$ and $\frac{2}{9}$

c. Mixed numerators and denominators:

$\frac{2}{3}$ and $\frac{5}{6}$ $\frac{1}{4}$ and $\frac{4}{9}$

SCIENCE (Mountains)

▶ 1. Have your child look up the following words in a dictionary or science resource. Discuss the meanings. Have your child make a glossary of these words, arranging the entries in alphabetical order and writing a definition for each word. You might also ask your child to include illustrations where applicable.

fault	metamorphic	subduction	crust
sedimentary	erosion	timberline	mantle
igneous	plateau	plate tectonics	altitude

▶ 2. Give your child the following list of mountain peaks to locate on a world map or in an atlas.

Aconcagua, Argentina	Mont Blanc, France-Italy-Switzerland border
Chimborazo, Ecuador	Mount Elbrus, Russia
Mount Everest, Tibet-Nepal border	Mount Fuji, Japan
Jungfrau, Switzerland	K2, Kashmir
Kilimanjaro, Tanzania	Mount Kosciusko, Australia
Mount Logan, Canada	Mount McKinley, Alaska
Mauna Kea, Hawaii	Matterhorn, Switzerland-Italy border
Mount Washington, New Hampshire	Mount Whitney, California

▶ 3. Can your child name the highest mountain on Earth?
Mauna Kea, Hawaii is actually the highest mountain on Earth, because it is measured from the seafloor! It stands 33,476 feet tall.

SOCIAL STUDIES (Slavery)

▶ 1. Your child should recognize the following names and understand each person's historical significance:

John Brown	Frederick Douglass	Harriet Tubman
Henry Clay	James Forten	Nat Turner
Stephen Douglas	Sojourner Truth	Harriet Beecher Stowe

Have your child add the following to the time line: Harpers Ferry, *Uncle Tom's Cabin* and Nat Turner's rebellion.

▶ 2. Have your child consider the following questions when planning his/her escape:

Where are you starting (what state)?
What states will you pass through and why?
You may take only the clothes on your back and a pocketknife wrapped in a handkerchief.
Will you take your family?
How will you travel (by foot, boat or horse)?
How will you get food and drink?
What time of day will you travel?
How long do you expect it to take?
What is your final destination?
How will you support yourself once you get there?

Fussing About f

affection
autograph
cough
enough
familiar
foreign
frequent
furniture
geography
laughter
muffler
paragraph
philosophy
physical
raffle
slough
stuff
tough

The **f** sound can be made using the following letter combinations:

f as in **afternoon**   **ff** as in **staff**
gh as in **rough**   **ph** as in **photo**

Write each spelling word in the appropriate category.

f

1. _____
2. _____
3. _____
4. _____

ff

1. _____
2. _____
3. _____
4. _____

gh

1. _____
2. _____
3. _____
4. _____
5. _____

ph

1. _____
2. _____
3. _____
4. _____
5. _____

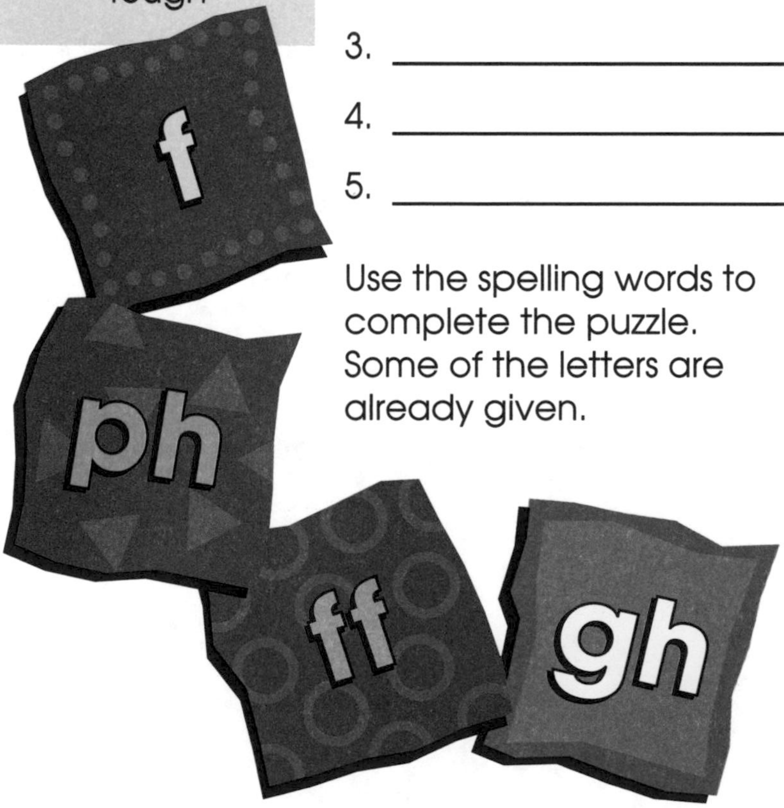

Use the spelling words to complete the puzzle. Some of the letters are already given.

Learn At Home, Grade 5

A Whale of an Activity

Some words may be used as either nouns or verbs.

Example: Fish
Fish are good to eat. (noun)
We **fish** every Saturday in the summer. (verb)

Read the paragraphs below. Decide if each bold word is
used as a noun or as a verb. **Write** your answers on the lines below.

A whale is a mammal that does not live on **land**[1]. It would be impossible
to **land**[2] a whale with ordinary fishing gear. A whale would not **attack**[3] a boat
unless the whale was injured. However, an **attack**[4] by an injured whale could
be very dangerous. Whales can **dive**[5] in the sea to a depth of more than
one-half of a mile. Their powerful tails make such a **dive**[6] possible. Whales do
not **fight**[7] among themselves. A **fight**[8] with a whale would be a losing battle!
The skeleton of a whale is not strong enough to **support**[9] the whale's weight.
Water provides the extra **support**[10] needed to hold up such huge bodies.
Whales **swim**[11] across entire oceans searching for food. Such a long **swim**[12] is
not unusual for a whale.

Whalers **hunt**[13] for whales in many countries of the world. In the old days,
sailing ships might stay at sea for 2 to 3 years on a whale **hunt**[14]. Men would
race[15] to get into small boats. It was a **race**[16] to see who could get to the whale
first. Now, whaling boats may **catch**[17] just a few whales each year. Their **catch**[18]
may not include mother whales with calves. Whalers have had to **part**[19] with
old ways. They may no longer catch whales in every **part**[20] of the ocean.

1. _____
2. _____
3. _____
4. _____
5. _____
6. _____
7. _____

8. _____
9. _____
10. _____
11. _____
12. _____
13. _____
14. _____

15. _____
16. _____
17. _____
18. _____
19. _____
20. _____

Because . . .

Remember:
The **cause** is the reason for the action or **why** something happened. The **effect** is the result of the action **what** actually happened.

Underline the causes.
1. Because she knew her face so well, Mae didn't need a mirror.
2. Because the Tucks had drunk water from the spring, they could not age.
3. Mae went into town, because her two boys were returning home.
4. The Tucks kidnapped Winnie, because she had discovered the spring.
5. Because Miles and Winnie brought no fish home for breakfast, the Tucks had flapjacks instead.

Circle the effects.
1. The Tuck boys never worked in the same place for long because their employers would become suspicious.
2. Because the stranger wished to obtain the property in the woods, he offered to return Winnie to her parents.
3. Because the stranger planned to sell the secret, Mae clubbed him.
4. The constable couldn't charge the Tucks with kidnapping because Winnie declared that she had gone with them of her own free will.
5. Winnie's grandmother ordered her to enter the house soon, because the heat was intense that day.

What do you think caused the most problems in the story?

a. The Tucks' discovery of the spring
b. The stranger's greed
c. Winnie's discovery of Jesse Tuck
d. Other: _____

_____

Explain your answer. _____

_____

Learn At Home, Grade 5

Conversion

Find the number of units in each fraction described.

1. If there are 12 eggs in a dozen, how many eggs are in . . .

   $\frac{1}{2}$ dozen? _____

   $\frac{1}{4}$ dozen? _____

   $\frac{1}{3}$ dozen? _____

2. If there are 100 centimeters (cm) in a meter, how many cm are in . . .

   $\frac{1}{2}$ meter? _____

   $\frac{1}{4}$ meter? _____

   $\frac{1}{10}$ meter? _____

3. If there are 16 ounces in a pound, how many ounces are in . . .

   $\frac{1}{2}$ pound? _____

   $\frac{1}{4}$ pound? _____

   $\frac{3}{8}$ pound? _____

4. If there are 4 quarts in a gallon, how many quarts are in . . .

   $\frac{1}{2}$ gallon? _____

   $\frac{1}{4}$ gallon? _____

   $\frac{3}{4}$ gallon? _____

5. If there are 60 seconds in a minute, how many seconds are in . . .

   $\frac{1}{2}$ minute? _____

   $\frac{1}{4}$ minute? _____

   $\frac{3}{4}$ minute? _____

6. If there are 1,000 meters in a kilometer, how many meters are in . . .

   $\frac{1}{10}$ kilometer? _____

   $\frac{1}{2}$ kilometer? _____

   $\frac{1}{4}$ kilometer? _____

7. If there are 30 days in most months, how many days are in . . .

   $\frac{1}{3}$ month? _____

   $\frac{1}{6}$ month? _____

   $\frac{1}{10}$ month? _____

8. If there are 24 hours in a day, how many hours are in . . .

   $\frac{1}{3}$ day? _____

   $\frac{2}{3}$ day? _____

   $\frac{1}{4}$ day? _____

9. If there are 36 inches in a yard, how many inches are in . . .

   $\frac{2}{3}$ yard? _____

   $\frac{1}{4}$ yard? _____

   $\frac{1}{2}$ yard? _____

10. If there are 2,000 pounds in a ton, how many pounds are in . . .

    $\frac{1}{2}$ ton? _____

    $\frac{1}{4}$ ton? _____

    $\frac{1}{20}$ ton? _____

	Language Skills	**Spelling**	**Reading**
Monday	**Creative Writing** This week, encourage your child to write an imaginative story. Getting started will probably be the hardest part, so teach your child how to make a story plan. • Decide *who* is in the story. • *Where* does the story take place? • What *activity* are the characters involved in? • What *conflict* needs to be resolved?	Pretest your child on these spelling words: ballet knight thumb castle known weight crumb knuckle wreck doubt listen wren height plumber wrench knack soften wrestle Have your child correct the pretest. Add personalized words and make two copies of this week's study list.	Introduce the book *Circle of Gold*, written by Candy Dawson Boyd. Before reading each day, discuss vocabulary from the book. Have your child read chapters 1 and 2 of *Circle of Gold*. **Vocabulary:** *superintendent, fierce, beret, jolt, anticipation, double-dutch, taunt, monitor, ghoul, irritate, sputter, grimace, accept.* After your child looks up the vocabulary words, have him/her use each in a new sentence.
Tuesday	Have your child sketch out a plan for a creative story and begin working on a rough draft today. It is okay for your child to start with only a couple parts of the plan complete. Your child's ideas are likely to change and develop as he/she writes.	Review this week's spelling words. Have your child complete **Silent Knight** (p. 228).	Have your child read chapters 3 and 4 of *Circle of Gold*. **Vocabulary:** *resist, urge, employ, rueful, wary, dole, precede, revolve, enrapture, hasty, filigree, anxious, console.* Review synonyms and antonyms. Have your child give a synonym for some of the vocabulary words. Teach your child to look in a thesaurus or dictionary for ideas. Then, have your child name antonyms for some of the vocabulary words.
Wednesday	Have your child read the rough draft of his/her story to a friend. At this point, your child may choose to revise and edit the story or write a plan and rough draft for a second story.	Have your child use each of this week's spelling words correctly in a sentence.	Have your child read chapters 5 and 6 of *Circle of Gold*. **Vocabulary:** *collide, deposit, vow, lacquer, croon, insure, grudge, interrupt.* Review similes and metaphors. Have your child complete **Like...a Simile!** (p. 229).
Thursday	Have your child read through his/her story. *Are the characters interesting? Is the conflict believable?* Encourage your child to do his/her best. If your child enjoys the story, so will the reader!	Have your child study this week's spelling words.	Have your child read chapter 7 of *Circle of Gold*. **Vocabulary:** *self-conscious, incident, tormentor, psychology, genuine.* Discuss how punctuation affects how you read with expression. Use passages from the book as examples.
Friday	Have your child read several books by good authors for inspiration. Have your child write a story using the characters and setting from a favorite book. Have your child change the characters' activities as well as the conflict they face.	Give your child the final spelling test. Have your child record pretest and final test words in his/her Word Bank.	Have your child read chapter 8 of *Circle of Gold*. **Vocabulary:** *concern, deliberate, saunter, retort, brood, grim.* Ask your child if the story is believable or not. Could it really happen? Discuss.

Learn At Home, Grade 5

Math	Science	Social Studies
Adding and Subtracting Fractions Teach your child how to add fractions with the same denominator. Use manipulatives or models to show how it is done. **Example:** $\frac{1}{4} + \frac{2}{4} = \frac{3}{4}$ Have your child make models of addition problems using fractions with like denominators. *See* Math, Week 21, number 1 for practice problems. With these models, show your child how to rename improper fractions as mixed numbers.	**Volcanoes** Have your child read about some of the major volcanoes on Earth. Discuss the Ring of Fire. *Why do so many volcanoes appear around this ring?* Watch a video on this phenomenon if possible, or look through a book with lots of photographs. Have your child add a glossary page on volcanoes to his/her Science Log. *See* Science, Week 21, number 1.	**Civil War** Abraham Lincoln came from humble beginnings and went on to become one of the greatest presidents of the U.S. Have your child read about the significant events in Lincoln's life. *See* Social Studies, Week 21, number 1. Have your child present his/her findings about the life of Abraham Lincoln.
Continue to practice addition with fractions. Have your child complete **A Trip to the Ocean** (p. 230).	Have your child arrange the names of volcanoes in order of elevation. *See* Science, Week 21, number 2.	The Civil War began after the South seceded from the Union. Lincoln's wish throughout the war was that the Southern states would return to the Union. Have your child write an expository paragraph explaining why the South refused to be part of the U.S. in 1860.
Teach your child how to subtract fractions with the same denominator. Use manipulatives or models to show how it is done. **Example:** $\frac{3}{4} - \frac{2}{4} = \frac{1}{4}$ Have your child make models of subtraction problems using fractions with like denominators. *See* Math, Week 21, number 2 for practice problems.	Have your child research a famous volcanic eruption. Have your child write a magazine article about the eruption as if he/she were an eyewitness. The article should include the volcano's location, date of eruption and other important facts. Have your child use colored pencils to draw a picture of the eruption to accompany the article.	On February 4, 1861, the Confederacy was formed. *See* Social Studies, Week 21, numbers 2 and 3. Have your child imagine that he/she is a poor farmer in a Southern state who does not own slaves and believes that the Union should not be split. Have your child write a persuasive paragraph against secession.
Continue to practice subtraction with fractions. Have your child complete **Tic-Tac-Toe Fractions** (p. 231).	Have your child match facts about volcanoes with their names. *See* Science, Week 21, number 3.	Many soldiers in the Civil War kept diaries about the battles, living conditions and their families. Have your child imagine that he/she is a soldier fighting in the Civil War. your child may choose which side he/she is fighting for. Have him/her write an entry in the soldier's diary (from early in the war). *See* Social Studies, Week 21, number 4.
Show your child an addition problem in which the fractions have different denominators. **Example:** $\frac{1}{3} + \frac{3}{10}$. Ask your child: *Can we add the numerators to solve this equation?* Lead your child to see the need for finding a common denominator when adding or subtracting fractions. *See* Math, Week 21, numbers 3 and 4. Give your child several problems to solve using the LCM as a common denominator.	Have your child read about other eruptions from beneath the surface of the earth. Then, have your child answer some questions about hot springs, geysers and fumaroles. *See* Science, Week 21, number 4.	Arrange for your child to perform some community service.

TEACHING SUGGESTIONS AND ACTIVITIES

MATH (Adding and Subtracting Fractions)

▶ 1. Have your child model the following addition problems:

$\frac{4}{9} + \frac{8}{9}$ $\frac{11}{15} + \frac{7}{15}$ $\frac{3}{10} + \frac{1}{10}$ $\frac{9}{20} + \frac{8}{20}$

$\frac{7}{9} + \frac{5}{9}$ $\frac{12}{24} + \frac{11}{24}$ $\frac{6}{12} + \frac{4}{12}$ $\frac{4}{15} + \frac{6}{15}$

$\frac{3}{4} + \frac{1}{4}$ $\frac{10}{16} + \frac{3}{16}$ $\frac{1}{5} + \frac{3}{5}$ $2\frac{9}{20} + \frac{8}{20}$

▶ 2. Have your child model the following subtraction problems:

$\frac{8}{9} - \frac{5}{9}$ $\frac{12}{15} - \frac{7}{15}$ $\frac{3}{10} - \frac{1}{10}$ $\frac{19}{20} - \frac{8}{20}$

$\frac{2}{3} - \frac{1}{3}$ $\frac{12}{24} - \frac{10}{24}$ $\frac{6}{12} - \frac{3}{12}$ $\frac{14}{15} - \frac{5}{15}$

$\frac{9}{10} - \frac{4}{10}$ $\frac{11}{15} - \frac{6}{15}$ $\frac{11}{12} - \frac{8}{12}$ $1\frac{5}{9} - \frac{4}{9}$

▶ 3. Ask your child to explain why adding tenths and thirds is a little more difficult than adding thirds and thirds. (Thirds and tenths are not the same parts of the whole.) Lead your child to understand that he/she must first find an equivalent fraction for one or both of the fractions so the denominators are the same. When the denominators are the same, your child may add or subtract the numerators as usual to solve the problem.

▶ 4. Finding the least common multiple is a step used in adding or subtracting fractions with different denominators. You may teach it as a separate lesson as shown here.

   a. Remember that multiples are the products shown on a multiplication table.
      The first six multiples of 4 are 4, 8, 12, 16, 20 and 24.
      The first five multiples of 6 are 6, 12, 18, 24 and 30.

   b. The numbers 12 and 24 are common multiples of 4 and 6.

   c. The lowest of the common multiples is 12. The least common multiple (LCM) is 12.

   Have your child list multiples and find the LCM of several pairs of numbers, such as 2 and 3, 4 and 5, 3 and 6, 3 and 5, 4 and 8, 4 and 7, 9 and 6.

SCIENCE (Volcanoes)

▶ 1. Add the following words to your child's weekly spelling list. Have your child look up each word in a dictionary or science resource. Discuss the meaning. Have your child make a glossary of terms related to volcanoes. Have your child arrange the entries in alphabetical order and write a definition for each word.

caldera	eruption	hot springs	stratovolcano
cinder cone	extinct	lava	vent
crater	fumarole	magma	volcano
dormant	geyser	shield volcano	vulcanism

▶ 2. Have your child print the names and elevations of the following volcanoes on index cards. Then, have him/her arrange the volcanoes in order of elevation from highest to lowest.

Volcano	Elevation (feet)	Volcano	Elevation (feet)
Kilimanjaro	19,340	Cameroon	13,353
Mauna Kea	13,796	Mauna Loa	13,677
Fuji	12,388	Aconcagua	22,831
Krakatoa	2,667	Rainier	14,410
Etna	11,122	El Chichón	3,478
Stromboli	3,031	Pinatubo	4,875
Thira	1,850	Tambora	9,350
Surtsey	568	Shasta	14,162
St. Helens	8,364	Nevado del Ruiz	17,717

Learn At Home, Grade 5

▶ 3. Copy the following facts and names of volcanoes on the chalkboard. Have your child draw a line to match each fact with the correct volcano. Then, have your child write out the facts in complete sentences.

world's largest volcano	El Chichón
volcanic dust from 1982 eruption in Mexico encircled the earth	Tambora
1980 eruption in the state of Washington	Etna
eruption was 6 million times more powerful than an atomic bomb	Vesuvius
famous A.D. 79 eruption destroyed Pompeii	Krakatau
famous 1883 explosion produced 130 ft. waves	Mauna Loa
destructive 1669 eruption on Sicily	Thira
may be cause of the lost continent of Atlantis	St. Helens
underwater eruption formed island of same name	Surtsey

▶ 4. Volcanoes emit molten matter, ashes, rock and gases. Hot springs, geysers and fumaroles, on the other hand, emit only gases and water. Have your child read from a variety of resources to answer the following questions:

Where in the United States are hot springs found?

Which states contain cities named Hot Springs?

Why do people like to bathe in and drink water from hot springs?

How does the water become hot underground?

What is a geyser? What makes "Old Faithful" unique?

How does a thermal spring differ from a geyser?

Where are geysers found?

How is a fumarole different from a geyser?

Why can fumaroles be dangerous to people and animals?

What are some of the gases given off by fumaroles?

SOCIAL STUDIES (Civil War)

▶ 1. Divide Lincoln's life into six periods: *Childhood, New Salem, Springfield, Political Career, Presidency* and *Death.* Have your child read about Lincoln's life during each period. Then, help your child devise a way to present these facts and anecdotes in a meaningful way.

▶ 2. Give your child a copy of **United States Map** (p. 205). Have your child label the states involved in the Civil War, coloring the slave states red and the free states blue. Teach your child to label (give a title to) a map accurately and to make a key or legend.

▶ 3. Not only did the South disagree about slavery in the territories, they also believed that states had the right to leave the Union. The Southern states did not agree with Lincoln's policies on prohibiting slavery in the territories, so they did secede. They formed the Confederate States of America and elected Jefferson Davis as their president.

▶ 4. Stephen Crane's novel, *The Red Badge of Courage,* deals with the Civil War as seen through the eyes of a young soldier. You may wish to choose descriptive passages from the book to read with your child or find a version of the book on audio tape and play a passage for your child. Discuss the passage and its description of the war. *What was it like to be a soldier in the Civil War?*

227

Silent Knight

ballet
castle
crumb
doubt
height
knack
knight
known
knuckle
listen
plumber
soften
thumb
weight
wreck
wren
wrench
wrestle

Many words contain one or more letters that are silent. Say each spelling word aloud. **Write** each spelling word in the appropriate silent letter category. (Some words may fit into more than one category.)

silent w

1. _____
2. _____
3. _____
4. _____

silent k

1. _____
2. _____
3. _____
4. _____

silent gh

1. _____
2. _____
3. _____

silent b

1. _____
2. _____
3. _____
4. _____

silent t

1. _____
2. _____
3. _____
4. _____
5. _____

Answer the following questions with other silent **b** words.

What . . .

1. is a part of a tree? _____
2. followed Mary to school? _____
3. means no feeling? _____
4. smooths your hair in place? _____
5. is a destructive force? _____

Like . . . a Simile!

Underline the two being compared in each sentence.
On the blank, write if the comparison is a simile
or a metaphor. Remember, a simile uses
like or as; a metaphor does not.

1. Angel was as mean as a wild bull. _____

2. Toni and Mattie were like toast and jam. _____

3. Mr. Ashby expected the students to be as busy as beavers. _____

4. The pin was a masterpiece in Mattie's mind. _____

5. The park's peacefulness was a friend to Mattie. _____

6. The words came as slow as molasses into Mattie's mind. _____

7. Mrs. Stamps's apartment was like a museum. _____

8. Mrs. Benson was as happy as a lark when Mattie won the contest.

    _____

9. Mr. Phillip's smile was a glowing beam to Mattie and Mrs. Benson.

    _____

10. Mattie ran like the wind to get her money. _____

11. Angel's mean words cut through Charlene like glass. _____

12. Mr. Bacon was a fairy godmother to Mattie. _____

13. The gingko tree's leaves were like fans. _____

Complete the following similes.

1. Matt was as artistic as _____

2. Hannibal's teeth were like _____

3. Toni's mind worked fast like _____

4. Mattie was as sad as _____

5. Mrs. Stamps was like _____

A Trip to the Ocean

Maria's girls' club earned enough money from their cookie sale to go on a camping trip by the ocean. Read about their trip. **Write** your answers in complete sentences.

1. The bus started with $6\frac{1}{2}$ gallons of gasoline. When the driver added $9\frac{1}{2}$ more gallons of gasoline, how much gasoline did the bus have in it?

    _____

2. The girls and their leaders stopped for a picnic after driving $58\frac{1}{5}$ miles. After the picnic, they drove another $43\frac{4}{5}$ miles before reaching the ocean. How far were they from home?

    _____

3. Before leaving home, the girls made sandwiches for their lunch. They had $7\frac{1}{2}$ tuna sandwiches, $4\frac{1}{4}$ cheese sandwiches, $2\frac{3}{4}$ peanut butter sandwiches and $5\frac{1}{2}$ beef sandwiches. How many total sandwiches did they bring?

    _____

4. The leader cut a watermelon into 16 slices for lunch. The girls ate 8 of the slices. What fraction of the watermelon did they eat?

    _____

5. When they arrived, they took $1\frac{1}{3}$ hours to set up the tents. They spent another $\frac{2}{3}$ hour getting their bedrolls ready. How long did they work before they could play in the ocean?

    _____

6. The girls swam and played in the water for $1\frac{3}{4}$ hours. Then, they sat in the sun for $\frac{3}{4}$ hour. How many hours did they play and sunbathe?

    _____

7. After dinner, they had a campfire. First, they sang for $1\frac{1}{3}$ hours. Then, they told ghost stories for $\frac{2}{3}$ hour. If they put out the fire and went to sleep at 10:30 P.M., what time did they begin the campfire?

    _____

8. The next morning, $\frac{3}{8}$ of the girls went fishing. The rest of the girls hunted for shells. If there were 8 girls altogether, how many hunted for shells? _____
    How many went fishing? _____

230

Learn At Home, Grade 5

Solve each problem. Then, look in the boxes below for the answers to the problems. **Draw** an **X** over each correct answer. **Circle** the other numbers.

1. $\dfrac{7}{8} - \dfrac{5}{8}$

2. $\dfrac{8}{10} - \dfrac{3}{10}$

3. $2\dfrac{1}{2} - \dfrac{1}{2}$

4. $\dfrac{7}{9} - \dfrac{4}{9}$

5. $\dfrac{5}{3} - \dfrac{4}{3}$

6. $\dfrac{6}{7} - \dfrac{3}{7}$

7. $\dfrac{4}{5} - \dfrac{2}{5}$

8. $\dfrac{9}{11} - \dfrac{5}{11}$

9. $\dfrac{11}{12} - \dfrac{5}{12}$

10. $\dfrac{11}{6} - \dfrac{7}{6}$

11. $\dfrac{3}{4} - \dfrac{1}{4}$

12. $\dfrac{3}{3} - \dfrac{1}{3}$

$\dfrac{5}{8}$	$\dfrac{1}{7}$	$\dfrac{1}{3}$
$\dfrac{2}{4}$	$\dfrac{5}{10}$	$\dfrac{3}{4}$
2	$\dfrac{3}{5}$	$\dfrac{2}{9}$

$\dfrac{4}{5}$	$\dfrac{3}{7}$	$\dfrac{1}{9}$
$\dfrac{5}{6}$	$\dfrac{1}{2}$	$\dfrac{3}{11}$
$\dfrac{2}{5}$	$\dfrac{2}{3}$	$\dfrac{4}{6}$

$\dfrac{1}{5}$	$\dfrac{6}{7}$	$\dfrac{2}{8}$
$\dfrac{3}{8}$	$\dfrac{4}{11}$	$\dfrac{6}{12}$
$\dfrac{2}{7}$	$\dfrac{1}{10}$	$\dfrac{3}{9}$

Language Skills	Spelling	Reading
Monday **Writing Dialogue** Dialogue can really liven up a story. Give your child tips on writing interesting dialogue, such as avoiding dialogue that doesn't reveal something about the character or move the action along. Have your child practice writing dialogue. Have him/her write a dialogue between a boy and a girl who both want to buy the last baseball on a store shelf.	Pretest your child on these spelling words: accounts couches indexes adventures decisions larynxes arches dresses syllables blouses erasers telescopes classes eyelashes toothbrushes compasses inches walruses Have your child correct the pretest. Add personalized words and make two copies of this week's study list.	Discuss Mattie and Toni's plan. *Was it an honest or good plan?* Have your child read chapters 9 and 10 of *Circle of Gold*. Then, have your child express his/her opinion about what happened to the bracelet in an organized paragraph.
Tuesday Have your child write a dialogue between two good friends. Ask your child to imagine that one of the friends just lost a very valuable possession.	Review this week's spelling words. Have your child complete **Plentiful Plurals** (p. 236).	Before your child reads today, discuss how the girls' teacher might be able to get the truth from the meeting. Have your child read chapter 11 of *Circle of Gold*. Have your child write about the meeting. *Was the problem solved? Explain.*
Wednesday Have your child write a dialogue between an 8-year-old and a 12-year-old. The younger child is frightened to go on a tour of a cave. The older child is eager to go on the tour.	Have your child use each of this week's spelling words correctly in a sentence.	Have your child read chapter 12 of *Circle of Gold*. Discuss. Review proper nouns. *See* Reading, Week 22, numbers 1–3.
Thursday Have your child write a story that includes some dialogue. The story may be entirely fictional or based on a personal experience.	Have your child study this week's spelling words.	Have your child finish reading *Circle of Gold*. Discuss. Have your child write in his/her Reading Journal about the story's climax.
Friday Have your child read his/her story to a friend. Then, have him/her revise and edit the story, making sure the dialogue is realistic and interesting. Help your child publish the story for others to read.	Give your child the final spelling test. Have your child record pretest and final test words in his/her Word Bank.	Discuss the meaning of the title, *Circle of Gold*. *Is it an appropriate title? To what does the title refer?* Choose a book project for your child to complete that will demonstrate his/her reaction to and understanding of the book. For project ideas, see page 13.

Learn At Home, Grade 5

Math	Science	Social Studies
Have your child find equivalent fractions with given denominators. **Remember:** To find an equivalent fraction, you must multiply the numerator and denominator by the same number. *See* Math, Week 22 for practice problems.	**Caves** Introduce your child to the study of caves. Have your child read about how caves are formed. A *solution cave* is formed when water dissolves rock underground. Many of the beautiful formations are created by the effects of the minerals in the water. Have your child create a glossary of terms related to caves. *See* Science, Week 22, number 1.	Discuss the significance of the colors blue and gray during the Civil War. The Union Army wore blue uniforms, while the Confederate Army wore gray uniforms. Have your child read about the leaders of both sides in the Civil War. Have your child write a biographical sketch about each of the following leaders: Ulysses Grant, William Tecumseh Sherman, Robert E. Lee and Stonewall Jackson.
Show your child how to find the least common denominator before adding fractions. **Example:** $\frac{3}{8} + \frac{5}{12}$ *What is the smallest multiple that 8 and 12 have in common? (24)* *Determine the equivalent fractions with the common denominator:* $\frac{3}{8} = \frac{9}{24}, \frac{5}{12} = \frac{10}{24}$ Solution: $\frac{9}{24} + \frac{10}{24} = \frac{19}{24}$ Give your child several problems with unlike denominators to practice this concept.	Has your child ever been in a cave before? Have your child read about the dangers of spelunking. Discuss the protective gear and equipment that a spelunker should have in order to explore caves safely. Have your child draw and label a diagram showing what a spelunker must wear and carry to be safe. Then, have your child write in his/her Science Log about the hobby of spelunking. What are your child's thoughts on this activity?	Have your child read about some of the famous battles of the Civil War. *See* Social Studies, Week 22, number 1. Have your child make a chart summarizing information about these battles. The chart should include the following headings: *Battle, Location, Dates* and *Winner.*
Play a simple game to help your child memorize multiples. The game is called "Multiples Race." Name a number. Your child must respond by quickly citing the multiples of that number up to 50. **Example:** You say "Five." Your child responds, "5, 10, 15, 20, 25, 30, 35, 40, 45, 50." Repeat the game several times, naming a different number each time.	Have your child read about a famous cave or group of caves, such as Lascaux Cave, Carlsbad Caverns or Mammoth Cave. Encourage your child to learn about the features that make the cave(s) unique. Then, have your child write a travelogue presentation on that cave, including pictures. *See* Science, Week 22, number 2.	Have your child read about the battle at Gettysburg, the most famous battle of the Civil War. Have your child find Gettysburg on a current map of the U.S. Have your child create a time line of events at Gettysburg, Pennsylvania, from July 1 to July 3, 1863. Discuss the Gettysburg Address. *See* Social Studies, Week 22, number 2.
Play "Multiple Match." Write two numbers on the chalkboard. Working quickly, your child must write all the multiples (in order) of the larger number up to 50. Every time your child writes a number that is also a multiple of the smaller number, he/she must shout "Match!" and circle the number. Repeat several times, each time with a different pair of numbers.	Let your child continue working on his/her cave research and presentation.	The Emancipation Proclamation was a document that stated all slaves in the Confederacy were free. This greatly influenced the outcome of the war. Have your child read about the end of the war. *See* Social Studies, Week 22, number 3. Have your child write a newspaper account of the assassination of President Lincoln. The article should include who, what, when, where, why and how.
Have your child complete **Adding Unlike Fractions** (p. 237). To solve these problems, your child must first find the least common denominator, then create equivalent fractions and finally add the fractions.	Have your child read about cave dwellers and cave paintings. *See* Science, Week 22, number 3. Then, discuss animals that make their homes in caves. Have your child write about his/her findings in the Science Log.	Arrange for your child to perform some community service.

TEACHING SUGGESTIONS AND ACTIVITIES

READING (Proper Nouns)

▶ 1. Ask your child to define a *common noun*, then a proper noun. A *common noun* is a person, place or thing. A *proper noun* is a *particular* person, place or thing. Have your child cite examples of each. Then, have him/her page through *Circle of Gold* to find more examples.

▶ 2. Write the following sentences on the chalkboard. Ask your child to circle the noun(s) in each sentence. Then, above each noun, have your child write whether the noun is common or proper.

a. Mrs. Benson worked late each night.

b. The pin was made very elegantly.

c. The bracelet was an expensive gift.

d. Mother's Day was an important event to the children.

e. The telephone rang in the living room.

f. Mr. Phillips worked at the *South Side Daily*.

g. The children worked hard at school.

h. The envelope had extra money in it.

i. Hannibal was her dog.

▶ 3. Dictate the following paragraph to your child. Have him/her write the paragraph on a sheet of paper, checking it over for proper capitalization and punctuation.

> Mattie and Toni took the Jackson Park El to downtown Chicago one Saturday. They found a beautiful pin in Stern's. Mattie knew it was perfect for her mother. She began to work on an essay for the *South Side Daily*, hoping to win the prize money so she could buy the pin.

Have your child underline all of the proper nouns in the paragraph. Then, have him/her think of a common noun that could substitute each proper noun. Have your child rewrite the paragraph using the common nouns. Ask your child to compare the two sentences. Which one does he/she like better? Which is more vivid?

MATH (Fractions)

Have your child calculate the following equivalent fractions:

$\frac{1}{4} = \frac{}{20}$ $\frac{2}{3} = \frac{}{15}$ $\frac{3}{5} = \frac{}{25}$ $\frac{3}{8} = \frac{}{32}$

$\frac{5}{9} = \frac{}{27}$ $\frac{1}{2} = \frac{}{8}$ $\frac{3}{4} = \frac{}{12}$ $\frac{3}{4} = \frac{}{16}$

$\frac{7}{8} = \frac{}{32}$ $\frac{3}{7} = \frac{}{28}$ $\frac{1}{10} = \frac{}{50}$ $\frac{1}{6} = \frac{}{48}$

$\frac{1}{5} = \frac{}{30}$ $\frac{5}{6} = \frac{}{24}$ $\frac{4}{7} = \frac{}{14}$ $\frac{2}{3} = \frac{}{21}$

Learn At Home, Grade 5

SCIENCE (Caves)

▶ 1. Add the following words to your child's weekly spelling list. Have your child look up each word in a dictionary or science resource. Discuss the meaning. Have your child make a glossary of terms related to caves. Have your child arrange the entries in alphabetical order and write a definition for each word. Encourage your child to include illustrations where they might be most helpful.

cavern	guano	limestone	sea caves	speleothems	stalactites
column	lava caves	porous	speleology	spelunker	stalagmites

▶ 2. If possible, arrange for a trip to visit some nearby caves. Check with your local or state tourism office to learn about any caves or cave systems in your area. If it is not possible for you and your child to visit a cave, have your child write a letter requesting brochures and other information on a cave or cave system that is of particular interest to him/her.

▶ 3. Caves have been used by people for hundreds of thousands of years. Archaeologists are scientists who study the cultural remains—structures, drawings, tools and other artifacts—left behind by humans. Although cave drawings and paintings have been discovered in caves throughout the world, it is believed that very few people have actually lived in caves since they are so dark, cold and damp.

SOCIAL STUDIES (Civil War)

▶ 1. Important Civil War battle sites include Bull Run, Gettysburg, Vicksburg, Atlanta, Chattanooga, Antietam, Chancellorsville, Fort Sumter, Mobile Bay and Appomattox Court House.

▶ 2. The Gettysburg Address is one of the best-known speeches in American history. Find a copy of Lincoln's famous speech for your child to read. Discuss its significance. Then, have your child memorize part of the speech—at the very least, the opening lines. Have your child recite (with expression!) the memorized parts on Thursday or Friday.

▶ 3. When Petersburg, Virginia, fell to the Union Army, General Lee knew that the end of the war was near. The North overpowered the South one last time in North Carolina, and Lee surrendered to Grant. Grant and Lee met in a home in Appomattox Court House, Virginia. Grant fed the starving Confederate soldiers and sent them home to plant their crops. The South faced many hardships after the war and harbored bitter feelings toward Lincoln.

235

Plentiful Plurals

accounts
adventures
arches
blouses
classes
compasses
couches
decisions
dresses
erasers
eyelashes
inches
indexes
larynxes
syllables
telescopes
toothbrushes
walruses

The plural form of most words is formed by adding **s** to the singular form. **Example:** horse + s = horses

Singular words ending in **x**, **ss**, **sh** or **ch** usually form the plural by adding **es** to the singular.
Examples: tax + es = taxes   church + es = churches

Write the singular form of each spelling word.

1. telescopes _____
2. inches _____
3. adventures _____
4. blouses _____
5. toothbrushes _____
6. arches _____
7. decisions _____
8. erasers _____
9. classes _____

10. indexes _____
11. walruses _____
12. compasses _____
13. eyelashes _____
14. couches _____
15. larynxes _____
16. dresses _____
17. accounts _____
18. syllables _____

Read the following clues. **Write** the word that matches each clue.

1. these protect your eyes _____
2. used to indicate direction _____
3. used to clean teeth _____
4. used to view the heavens _____
5. unit of measurement _____

Learn At Home, Grade 5

Adding Unlike Fractions

Solve the problems. **Shade** in your answers on the pizzas below to show which pieces have been eaten.

$$\frac{1}{10}$$
$$+\ \frac{4}{5}$$

$$\frac{3}{12}$$
$$+\ \frac{1}{6}$$

$$\frac{1}{2}$$
$$+\ \frac{1}{3}$$

$$\frac{3}{4}$$
$$+\ \frac{1}{5}$$

$$\frac{1}{5}$$
$$+\ \frac{1}{3}$$

$$\frac{2}{3}$$
$$+\ \frac{1}{4}$$

$$\frac{5}{12}$$
$$+\ \frac{1}{6}$$

$$\frac{2}{5}$$
$$+\ \frac{9}{20}$$

$$\frac{1}{3}$$
$$+\ \frac{2}{9}$$

$$\frac{3}{5}$$
$$+\ \frac{1}{10}$$

$$\frac{1}{10}$$
$$+\ \frac{1}{5}$$

$$\frac{2}{3}$$
$$+\ \frac{1}{5}$$

$$\frac{1}{8}$$
$$+\ \frac{1}{3}$$

$$\frac{3}{8}$$
$$+\ \frac{1}{5}$$

$$\frac{1}{5}$$
$$+\ \frac{1}{9}$$

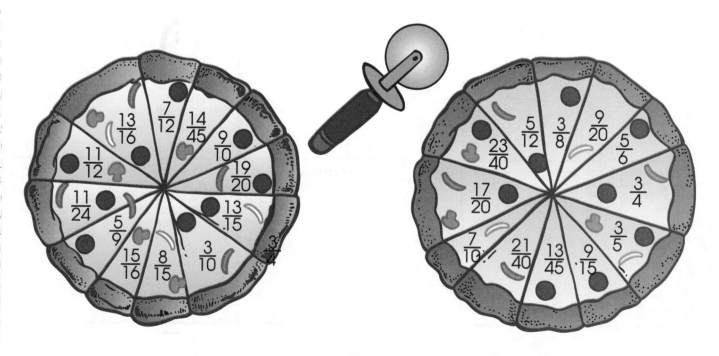

	Language Skills	**Spelling**	**Reading**
Monday	**Paragraphs** A topic sentence clearly states the subject of a paragraph. Sometimes the topic sentence also expresses a feeling about the subject. **Examples:** *The Northtown Gerbils are a really bad team. One of my favorite people in the world is my Aunt Alice.* Have your child write a topic sentence that states a subject and expresses feelings about that subject.	Pretest your child on these spelling words: anniversary highway quantity beauty holiday salary birthday industry strawberry chimney monkey survey decoy mortuary turkey dictionary party valley Have your child correct the pretest. Add personalized words and make two copies of this week's study list.	**Syllables** Review the rules of syllabication and accenting this week. Today, help your child make a chart of these rules. *See* Reading, Week 23, number 1. Introduce *Baseball Saved Us*, a picture book by Ken Mochizuki. Have your child read the book. Then, have your child write in his/her Reading Journal about the meaning of the book's title.
Tuesday	The topic sentence is often the first sentence in a paragraph. The rest of the paragraph is made up of sentences that relate back to the topic sentence. Have your child write several sentences that support the topic sentence written yesterday. Encourage your child to use both simple and compound sentences to add variety and interest to the paragraph.	Review this week's spelling words. Have your child complete **Persistent Plurals** (p. 243).	Ask questions to assess your child's comprehension of *Baseball Saved Us*. Have your child imagine what Shorty's life was like after camp and write a paragraph about it.
Wednesday	A paragraph should contain related sentences. Explain to your child that when he/she is ready to move to a new idea, he/she should start a new paragraph. Have your child read a story and determine where new paragraphs should begin. *See* Language Skills, Week 23.	Have your child use each of this week's spelling words correctly in a sentence.	Write several words with three, four and five syllables on the chalkboard. **Examples:** *admissible, communication, elaborate, fictitious, liveliest, sufficient.* Teach your child to use the same rules as discussed Monday to divide these words. **Example:** opportunity op•por•tu•ni•ty *See* Reading, Week 23, number 2 for a related activity.
Thursday	Teach your child how to identify the topic sentence in a given paragraph. Have your child complete **Dolphins** (p. 242).	Have your child study this week's spelling words.	Discuss accented syllables. Tap out a rhythm: **1**-2-3, **1**-2-3, **1**-2-3 or 1-2-**3**-4, 1-2-**3**-4, 1-2-**3**-4. Have your child tell which beat is accented. Explain to your child that words, like music, have stressed syllables. Words that contain more than one syllable have one or more accented or stressed syllables. *See* Reading, Week 23, numbers 3 and 4.
Friday	Have your child use proofreading symbols to edit a piece of his/her own writing (*see* Reading, Week 30, number 2). Have him/her also look for topic sentences and add them where necessary.	Give your child the final spelling test. Have your child record pretest and final test words in his/her Word Bank.	Write events from the story, *Baseball Saved Us*, on strips of paper. The events should range from the beginning of the story to the end. Cut out the sentences. Have your child arrange the events in order. Then, have your child illustrate each sentence.

Learn At Home, Grade 5

Math	Science	Social Studies
Show your child a subtraction problem in which the fractions have different denominators. **Example:** $\frac{1}{3} - \frac{3}{10}$. Ask your child if you can subtract the numerators to solve this equation. Lead your child to see the need for finding a common denominator when subtracting fractions. Have your child complete **Sandwich Solutions** (p. 244).	**Canyons and Waterfalls** Ask your child to define *canyon* and *gorge*. In an encyclopedia or other resource, have your child read about how canyons and gorges are formed. Have your child add a glossary page on canyons and gorges to his/her Science Log. *See* Science, Week 23, numbers 1 and 2.	**Geographic Regions** Introduce the regions of the United States. *See* Social Studies, Week 23. Then, have your child compare the maps supplied in this book with a physical map of the U.S. *See* Social Studies, Week 23, number 1.
Teach your child to see fractions such as $\frac{2}{2}$ or $\frac{4}{4}$ as "wholes." Use several models to demonstrate this concept. $\frac{2}{2}$ $\frac{4}{4}$	Have your child locate the major canyons and gorges of the world in an atlas. Are there any found in the Mountain States? Look at pictures of these sites in an encyclopedia or other resource. *See* Science, Week 23, number 3. Have your child write a descriptive paragraph or poem inspired by the appearance of one of the canyons.	Introduce a regional map activity that will take several days to complete. Copy the maps on pages 247–249 for this week. Provide your child with resources such as maps, a globe, an atlas, encyclopedias and other reference books. *See* Social Studies, Week 23, numbers 2–4. Have your child label and add features to **Mountain States** (p. 247). Save for Week 25.
Mixed Numbers and Improper Fractions: Use models to demonstrate improper fractions and mixed numbers. **Example:** The mixed number $1\frac{2}{3}$ is also known as the improper fraction $\frac{5}{3}$. Have your child model the mixed numbers below to rename them as improper fractions: $1\frac{1}{4}$ $3\frac{1}{2}$ $2\frac{3}{8}$ $6\frac{1}{2}$ $1\frac{11}{12}$ $2\frac{2}{5}$ $1\frac{2}{3}$ $1\frac{4}{7}$ $2\frac{3}{4}$ $3\frac{3}{10}$ $1\frac{7}{8}$ $4\frac{3}{5}$ $5\frac{1}{3}$ $3\frac{4}{5}$ $4\frac{5}{8}$	Have your child compose "Who-Am-I?" riddles about famous canyons and gorges. **Example:** I am in the state of Utah. I am up to half a mile wide. My steep walls are up to 3,000 feet high. I am known for my beautiful colors. What am I? (Answer: *Zion Canyon*)	Have your child label and add features to **North Central States** (p. 248). Save this page for Week 25.
Teach your child to convert an improper fraction to a mixed number without using models. *Divide the numerator by the denominator. If there is a remainder, the remainder is the fractional part of the divisor.* **Example:** $\frac{7}{2}$ Divide: $7 \div 2 = 3$ R1 *Place the remainder over the original denominator:* $3\frac{1}{2}$ Have your child complete **Fractions: Improper to Mixed** (p. 245).	Have your child read about, then define, waterfalls. Discuss how they are created. Can your child explain the difference between a cascade and a cateract? Have your child gather some facts about waterfalls, such as the highest falls, the falls with the greatest volume of water and the longest falls. Have him/her use this information to create a small fact sheet on waterfalls.	Have your child label and add features to **South Central States** (p. 249). Save this page for Week 25.
Teach your child to convert a mixed number to an improper fraction without using models. The multiplication method is shown here. *Multiply the whole number by the denominator.* **Example:** $2\frac{3}{4}$ $2 \times 4 = 8$ *Add that number to the numerator.* $8 + 3 = 11$ *Maintain the original denominator.* $\frac{11}{4}$ *See* Math, Week 23 for the addition method. Have your child complete **Fractions: Mixed to Improper** (p. 246).	Ask your child to choose a famous waterfall. Have your child write about the waterfall's appearance, location and other interesting facts.	Arrange for your child to perform some community service.

TEACHING SUGGESTIONS AND ACTIVITIES

LANGUAGE SKILLS (Paragraphs)

Give your child a copy of the following story, as written. Have your child read the story and mark any corrections using proofreading symbols (*See* Reading, Week 30, number 2 for a list of proofreading symbols). Have your child look for proper capitalization, subject/verb agreement and correct pronouns. Teach your child how to use the paragraph symbol (¶) to show where a new paragraph should begin. Have your child rewrite the story with corrections, then add an illustration of Skooter.

How Skooter Got Her Stripes

Late one night, a baby skunk named Skooter wandered away from her mother's side. the mother skunk were not worried about her daughter when she noticed she had leaved. skooter was an independent little skunk who wanted to go off to explore the world for himself. skooter roamed through the woods, grumbling and complaining to herself because the terrain and protruding roots hurt her tired, tender feet. At the edge of the woods, skooter happened upon a cool, flat strip of black surface (known to humans as a road). it soothed her pounding paws. exhausted, she lay down in the center of the road to take a little snooze. As Skooter slept, a road crew came by to paint the white line down the center of the road. them never seen skooter as her black fur blended in with the black asphalt of the road. they painted right over him. from that night on, skooter has had a white stripe down the center of her back. her friends liked it so much that they all begged their mothers for a stripe like skooter's.

READING (Syllables)

▶ 1. Have your child make a chart of the following rules for dividing words into syllables. Remind your child that the number of vowel sounds heard is the same as the number of syllables in a word. Help your child come up with examples for each rule. Post the chart for reference.

   a. Compound words divide between the two root words.

   b. Two-syllable words with two consonants in the middle are divided between the consonants.

   c. Two-syllable words with a consonant and a blend in the middle are divided between the consonant and the blend. A blend is *never* divided.

   d. Two-syllable words with one consonant in the middle are divided *before* the middle consonant. **Exception:** If the first vowel sound is short, divide *after* the middle consonant.

   e. Two-syllable words that end with a consonant + *le* are divided in front of the consonant.

   f. When a vowel is followed by *r*, divide the syllables after the *r*.

▶ 2. Have your child divide the following words into syllables. He/she may use a dictionary if necessary.

amusement	evasive	reverently
antagonistic	extricate	ruthless
antiquated	gingerly	self-respecting
blimey	horrendous	suspect
conservatory	incidentally	unshod
conversation	minute	vanished
creatures	remotely	varmint

   Next, have your child write a brief story using as many of these words as possible. The story may be serious or silly.

▶ 3. Show your child what an accent mark looks like. Look in the dictionary at words that have accent marks. Point out that some accent marks are darker than others. Explain that the darker mark denotes the primary accent while the lighter mark shows the secondary accent. In some dictionaries, the primary accent mark is set higher than the secondary accent. **Example:** 'pen-men-,ship. Teach your child to read the words with the accents.

▶ 4. Say some words that contain three or more syllables. Ask your child to listen carefully, clapping out the word if necessary, and tell which syllable is accented.

MATH (Mixed Numbers and Improper Fractions)

There are two methods of converting a mixed number to an improper fraction. Teach your child both methods and let him/her decide which one makes more sense. The multiplication method is shown in the lesson plan.

Here is the addition method:

Mixed number: $2\frac{3}{4}$

Think of the whole number as a fraction with the given denominator: $2 = \frac{8}{4}$

Add the "whole number" to the fraction to convert to the improper fraction: $\frac{8}{4} + \frac{3}{4} = \frac{11}{4}$

SCIENCE (Canyons and Waterfalls)

▶ 1. The word *canyon* comes from a Spanish word meaning "tube." Canyons are deep valleys with steep sides cut through the land by the erosive forces of water and wind. A narrow canyon with steep sides is called a *gorge*.

▶ 2. Add the following words to your child's weekly spelling list. Have your child look up each word in a dictionary or science resource. Discuss the meaning. Have your child make a glossary of words related to canyons. Have him/her arrange the entries in alphabetical order and write a definition for each word.

canyon	fiords	gorge	stream velocity	waterfall
erosion	glacier	rapids	valley	whitewater

▶ 3. Have your child locate these canyons and gorges on a map. Then, have your child look at photographs of these magnificent land formations.

Bryce Canyon	Zion Canyon	Yellowstone
Grand Canyon	Kings Canyon	Royal Gorge

SOCIAL STUDIES (Geographic Regions)

BACKGROUND

The United States is often divided into seven regions. The regions are defined by common features, such as landforms, climate and natural resources. In this book, the regions will be referred to as Mountain States, North Central States, South Central States, Northeastern States, Southeastern States, Midwest States and Pacific States.

▶ 1. Look at a physical map of the U.S. with your child. The colors of the map divide the country into natural regions. Have your child look at the regions outlined on pages 247–249 and 256–259. Then, have him/her compare the seven regions on the worksheets to the naturally occurring regions shown on the physical map. *Where are the boundaries similar?*

▶ 2. Review landforms and bodies of water. Have your child give a brief definition of each of the following physical features and name an example of each: *mountain, island, volcano, river, ocean, bay, peninsula, coast, delta* and *plain.*

▶ 3. Have your child look at the keys, or legends, of several maps before designing a legend for the regional maps. Have your child make a list of the features he/she would like to include on the regional maps, then design symbols to represent each of those features. For example, mountains may be represented by zigzags, state boundaries may be represented by solid black lines and the fishing industry may be represented by a picture of a fish. These symbols may be developed as your child reads more about each region.

▶ 4. Using a pencil, felt-tip markers and colored pencils, have your child fill in each regional map with features. The following is a list of suggestions for your child:

   a. Write each state's name within that state's boundaries.

   b. Use a symbol to indicate the location of each state's capital. Label the capital.

   c. Research each state. Add features to the map, such as natural resources found in the state, as well as land and water forms. Use the symbols in your key. (See number 3, above.)

   d. Represent the major industries of each state with different symbols.

241

Dolphins

Underline the topic sentence of each paragraph. Add the missing punctuation.

Dolphins are among the most intelligent animals on Earth. They are playful as well as smart and are easily trained for zoo and aquarium shows. They jump through hoops and fetch and grab objects from the trainer's hands Dolphins communicate with each other in a variety of ways using clicking whistling and slapping sounds.

Dolphins can locate objects easily under the water through a system called *echolocation* This is like a built-in sonar system. The dolphin makes a series of clicking sounds then listens for the sounds as echoes bounce back from the underwater object.

Many dolphins are caught and killed. These friendly mammals are killed by hunters of several nations for their meat and oils and are often caught in fishing nets intended to catch tuna cod and other fish. Steps have been taken to try to limit the number of dolphins killed

Learn At Home, Grade 5

Persistent Plurals

anniversary
beauty
birthday
chimney
decoy
dictionary
highway
holiday
industry
monkey
mortuary
party
quantity
salary
strawberry
survey
turkey
valley

Words ending in **y**, preceded by a vowel, form the plural by adding **s** to the singular. **Example:** boy → boys

Words ending in **y**, preceded by a consonant, form the plural by changing the **y** to **i** and adding **es**.
Example: bunny → bunnies

Using the rules above, **write** the **singular** and **plural** forms of each spelling word in the appropriate category.

vowel **y** = add **s**

1. _____ _____
2. _____ _____
3. _____ _____
4. _____ _____
5. _____ _____
6. _____ _____
7. _____ _____
8. _____ _____
9. _____ _____

consonant **y** = change **y** to **i** + **es**

1. _____ _____
2. _____ _____
3. _____ _____
4. _____ _____
5. _____ _____
6. _____ _____
7. _____ _____
8. _____ _____
9. _____ _____

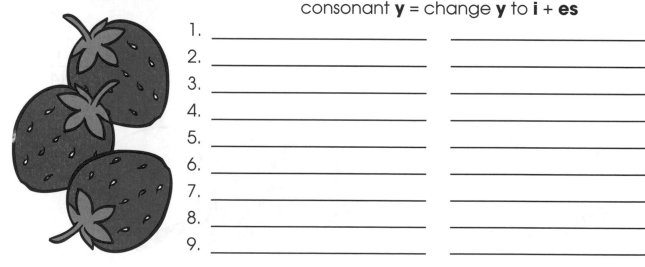

On the lines below, **rewrite** the two rules above in your own words.

_____

_____

_____

Sandwich Solutions

Solve the following subtraction problems to find out who invented the sandwich.
Write the letter next to each problem above its answer at the bottom.

A. $\dfrac{3}{5} - \dfrac{1}{4}$ A. $\dfrac{5}{6} - \dfrac{1}{3}$ E. $\dfrac{9}{16} - \dfrac{1}{4}$

I. $\dfrac{7}{10} - \dfrac{3}{5}$ D. $\dfrac{1}{2} - \dfrac{5}{12}$ C. $\dfrac{7}{8} - \dfrac{3}{4}$

W. $\dfrac{13}{18} - \dfrac{1}{6}$ N. $\dfrac{2}{3} - \dfrac{1}{12}$ H. $\dfrac{19}{20} - \dfrac{4}{5}$

F. $\dfrac{18}{25} - \dfrac{2}{5}$ L. $\dfrac{8}{9} - \dfrac{1}{6}$ R. $\dfrac{5}{8} - \dfrac{3}{16}$

O. $\dfrac{4}{5} - \dfrac{2}{3}$ S. $\dfrac{1}{7} - \dfrac{1}{14}$

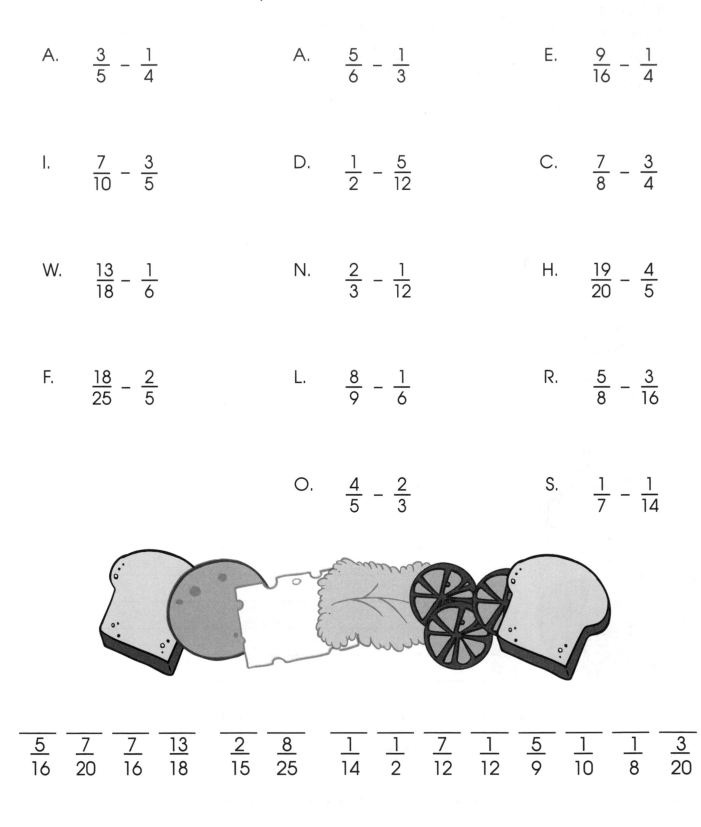

$\dfrac{5}{16}$ $\dfrac{7}{20}$ $\dfrac{7}{16}$ $\dfrac{13}{18}$ $\dfrac{2}{15}$ $\dfrac{8}{25}$ $\dfrac{1}{14}$ $\dfrac{1}{2}$ $\dfrac{7}{12}$ $\dfrac{1}{12}$ $\dfrac{5}{9}$ $\dfrac{1}{10}$ $\dfrac{1}{8}$ $\dfrac{3}{20}$

Learn At Home, Grade 5

Fractions: Improper to Mixed

Change the fractions to mixed numbers. **Shade** in each answer to find the path to the pot of gold.

1. $\dfrac{11}{9}$ =   2. $\dfrac{8}{3}$ =   3. $\dfrac{8}{7}$ =   4. $\dfrac{11}{6}$ =

5. $\dfrac{7}{3}$ =   6. $\dfrac{7}{6}$ =   7. $\dfrac{9}{4}$ =   8. $\dfrac{8}{5}$ =

9. $\dfrac{4}{3}$ =   10. $\dfrac{7}{2}$ =   11. $\dfrac{3}{2}$ =   12. $\dfrac{6}{5}$ =

13. $\dfrac{7}{4}$ =   14. $\dfrac{9}{2}$ =   15. $\dfrac{11}{8}$ =   16. $\dfrac{5}{2}$ =

17. $\dfrac{9}{7}$ =   18. $\dfrac{11}{4}$ =   19. $\dfrac{17}{12}$ =   20. $\dfrac{13}{12}$ =

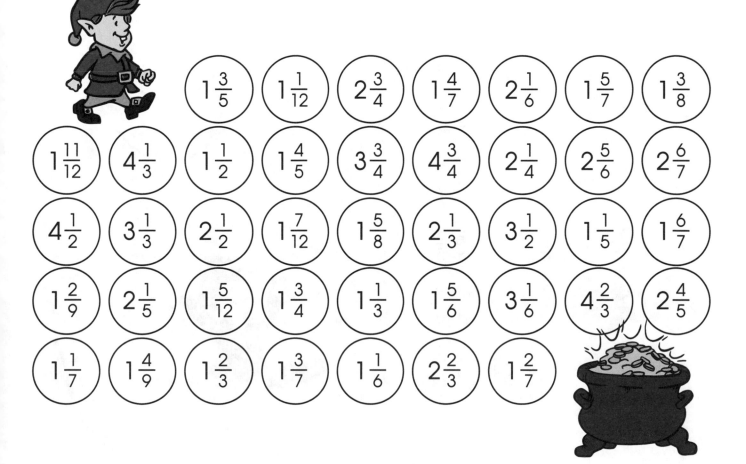

245

Fractions: Mixed to Improper

Solve the problems. **Connect** the dots in the order of the answers.

1. $1\frac{2}{5} = \frac{}{5}$ 2. $1\frac{1}{3} = \frac{}{3}$

3. $1\frac{5}{7} = \frac{}{7}$ 4. $2\frac{2}{3} = \frac{}{3}$

5. $2\frac{5}{8} = \frac{}{8}$ 6. $2\frac{1}{2} = \frac{}{2}$

7. $1\frac{5}{6} = \frac{}{6}$ 8. $1\frac{1}{5} = \frac{}{5}$

9. $2\frac{4}{5} = \frac{}{5}$ 10. $1\frac{1}{16} = \frac{}{16}$

11. $1\frac{1}{2} = \frac{}{2}$ 12. $3\frac{1}{5} = \frac{}{5}$

13. $1\frac{11}{12} = \frac{}{12}$ 14. $1\frac{7}{8} = \frac{}{8}$

15. $1\frac{6}{7} = \frac{}{7}$ 16. $2\frac{1}{4} = \frac{}{4}$

17. $1\frac{7}{12} = \frac{}{12}$ 18. $1\frac{3}{7} = \frac{}{7}$

19. $6\frac{2}{3} = \frac{}{3}$ 20. $3\frac{3}{5} = \frac{}{5}$

21. $1\frac{5}{21} = \frac{}{21}$ 22. $1\frac{7}{36} = \frac{}{36}$

23. $1\frac{9}{20} = \frac{}{20}$ 24. $1\frac{13}{24} = \frac{}{24}$

Learn At Home, Grade 5

Mountain States

Learn At Home, Grade 5

Learn At Home, Grade 5

Language Skills	Spelling	Reading
Monday		
Main Idea Guide your child as he/she plans a report on a historical person. your child's plan should include the topic sentence (or main idea) of each paragraph. Have your child begin writing a rough draft of the report based on his/her plan. Have your child fill in each paragraph with details to support the topic sentence.	Pretest your child on these spelling words: calves heroes thieves echoes leaves tomatoes elves moose wives geese potatoes wolves halves scarves women handkerchiefs shelves yourselves Have your child correct the pretest. Add personalized words and make two copies of this week's study list.	**Outlining a Story** Introduce *Stone Fox* by John Reynolds Gardiner. Teach your child how to outline the story as he/she reads. *See* Reading, Week 24. Have your child read chapters 1 and 2 of *Stone Fox*. **Vocabulary:** *examination, harmonica, churns, imagination.*
Tuesday		
Show your child a picture from a magazine or book. Ask your child to study the picture, describe several details and tell the main idea of the picture. Have your child write a paragraph describing the main idea of the picture. The paragraph should begin with a topic sentence and include supporting details.	Review this week's spelling words. Have your child complete **Perplexing Plurals** (p. 254).	Have your child select descriptive paragraphs from the book to read aloud. Discuss what each paragraph is describing. Ask your child to identify any metaphors or similes used by the author. Have your child read chapters 3 and 4 of *Stone Fox*. Have your child answer these questions in his/her Reading Journal: *Can a ten-year-old live on his/her own in your town? How long could Willy continue without help?*
Wednesday		
Read aloud the following related phrases: *honking horns, screaming people, policeman's whistle.* Ask your child to name how the phrases are all related or to state the main idea. There is more than one correct answer. For example, these things are all noisy, but they are also things you might hear in a city. Have your child name other words or phrases that fit under this particular main idea.	Have your child use each of this week's spelling words correctly in a sentence.	Explain the reasons for taxes and discuss the types of things that are taxed. Have your child read chapters 5 and 6 of *Stone Fox*. Have your child write about Stone Fox's dream for his people and how he helped them achieve that dream.
Thursday		
Copy paragraphs from a book, magazine or newspaper. Eliminate the topic sentence in each paragraph, but leave a space where it was written. Have your child read each paragraph and write an appropriate topic sentence.	Have your child study this week's spelling words.	Call on your child to recall details from the story. Have your child locate and read aloud a sentence that tells something funny about the main character, something scary that happened or something about the setting. Have your child read chapters 7 and 8 of *Stone Fox*. **Vocabulary:** *investigate, treacherous, abrupt, jagged.*
Friday		
Have your child look at a group of details to generate a possible topic sentence. *See* Language Skills, Week 24. Have your child choose one of the topic sentences to turn into a descriptive paragraph. Encourage your child to use specific language, vary the length of sentences and add adjectives to make the paragraph interesting. Have your child illustrate the paragraph if time allows.	Give your child the final spelling test. Have your child record pretest and final test words in his/her Word Bank.	Have your child read chapters 9 and 10 of *Stone Fox*. Have him/her summarize the book in outline form. Watch the movie *Iron Will* (Walt Disney Productions, 1994). Have your child compare the movie to Gardiner's book using a Venn diagram. *How are the book and the movie similar? How are they different?*

250

    Learn At Home, Grade 5

Math	Science	Social Studies
Measuring with a ruler is a natural application for fractions. All the lines on an inch ruler can be confusing (less confusing on a centimeter ruler). Help your child see the lines as logical divisions of the unit (one inch). Guide your child to see that each inch is divided into 2 halves, 4 fourths, 8 eighths and 16 sixteenths. Draw several 2-inch sections for your child to label. Have your child write the appropriate fractions at each line on the ruler.	**River Systems** Have your child read about the major rivers of the world. Have him/her locate the following rivers on a map or globe: Nile, Amazon, Niger, Mississippi, Missouri, Yangtze, Yenisei, Congo, Huang He, Lena, Mekong, Amur, Mackenzie, Ob and Volga. Have your child add a glossary page on river systems to his/her Science Log. *See* Science, Week 24, number 1.	Have your child label and add features to **Northeastern States** (p. 256). Save for Week 25.
Watch your child as he/she measures at least ten small items (each under 6 inches in length). Assess your child's ability to measure accurately to the sixteenth of an inch. Does he/she place the zero of the ruler at the edge of the item being measured? Does your child name the fraction or mixed number accurately? Does your child write the accurate measurement correctly on paper? Reteach if necessary.	Have your child read about the Mississippi, Nile and Amazon river systems. Discuss the different parts of a river system. Have your child complete **River System** (p. 255).	Have your child label and add features to **Southeastern States** (p. 257). Save for Week 25.
Demonstrate addition with mixed numbers. Use models with the same fractional parts for each equation (all fourths or all thirds). First, ask your child to model the numbers $2\frac{3}{4}$ and $3\frac{1}{4}$. Then, have him/her move the two models together to determine the sum. Write down the equation as your child works. Repeat several times, each time with different fractions. Let your child try writing the equations as well.	Have your child construct a bar graph comparing the approximate lengths of the world's fifteen longest rivers. *See* Science, Week 24, number 2.	Have your child label and add features to **Midwestern States** (p. 258). Save for Week 25.
Introduce addition of mixed numbers with different denominators. Ask your child to propose a procedure for solving the equation $\frac{4}{5} + 1\frac{3}{4}$. Try out your child's suggestion to see if it works. If it does, then continue to use it. If your child's suggestion does not work well, try another method. *See* Math, Week 24. Have your child try solving these problems: $5\frac{5}{6} + 7\frac{3}{4}$ $9\frac{1}{2} + \frac{7}{8}$ $10\frac{1}{7} + 3\frac{2}{3}$ $8\frac{1}{4} + 17\frac{3}{10}$	Teach your child about how a river delta forms. Have your child locate the world's major river deltas in an atlas or on a globe. *See* Science, Week 24, numbers 3 and 4.	Have your child label and add features to **Pacific States** (p. 259). Save for Week 25.
Demonstrate subtraction with mixed numbers. Use models with the same fractional parts for each equation (all fourths or all thirds). First, ask your child to model the number $2\frac{3}{4}$. Then, have him/her remove the fraction $1\frac{2}{4}$ and determine the difference. Write down the equation as your child works. Repeat several times, each time with different fractions. Let your child try writing the equations as well.	Have your child read about the major rivers and tributaries in your state and locate these rivers on a state map. *See* Science, Week 24, number 5 for a series of questions about your state's rivers. Have your child research the answers to these questions. Discuss with your child, then have him/her write the questions and answers in his/her Science Log.	Arrange for your child to perform some community service.

Learn At Home, Grade 5

TEACHING SUGGESTIONS AND ACTIVITIES

LANGUAGE SKILLS (Main Idea)

Write each group of details below on a separate index card. Have your child write a possible topic sentence on the back of each card. Keep the cards for future reference for writing activities.

good smell, hot steam, dirty dishes
dark clouds, bent trees, people running
peas, cauliflower, turnips, asparagus
people cheering, ball flying, players running
cool drinks, beaches, shady spots, fans

long distances, highways, cities, towns
bathing, feeding, petting, barking
fingers, calculator, abacus
pencils, eraser, paper, crayons, notebook
dance lesson, hockey practice, dentist appointment

READING (Outlining a Story)

Teach your child how to outline a story. Write the following skeleton outline on the chalkboard and discuss.

I. Introduction
   A. Setting
      1. Where
      2. When
   B. Characters
II. Problem
   A. Mini-plots
      1. Briefly describe the events.
      2. Number these events in order.
   B. Climax
III. Ending
   A. Solution
   B. Wrap-up

MATH (Fractions)

The following is one method of adding mixed numbers.

1. Find the LCM (least common multiple) of the denominators.
2. Multiply the numerator and denominator of each fraction by a number to reach the LCM.
3. Add the whole numbers.
4. Add the fractions.
5. Convert an improper fraction to a mixed number.
6. Reduce the fraction to lowest terms.

$2\frac{4}{5} + 1\frac{1}{2}$ The LCM of 5 and 2 is 10.

$2\frac{4}{5}^{(\times 2)}_{(\times 2)} + 1\frac{1}{2}^{(\times 5)}_{(\times 5)}$

$2\frac{8}{10} + 1\frac{5}{10} = 3\frac{13}{10}$

$3\frac{13}{10} = 4\frac{3}{10}$

Learn At Home, Grade 5

SCIENCE (River Systems)

▶ 1. Add the following words to this week's spelling list. Have your child look up each word in a dictionary or science resource. Discuss the meaning. Have your child make a glossary of words related to rivers. Have him/her arrange the entries in alphabetical order and write a definition for each word.

alluvial fan	gradient	oxbow lake	tributary
channel	headwaters	rapids	valley
delta	lake	runoff	velocity
flood plain	meander	silt	waterfall

▶ 2. Have your child construct a bar graph comparing the approximate lengths of the fifteen longest rivers in the world. Your child will need to do some research to find the lengths (in miles and in kilometers) of each of these rivers: Nile, Amazon, Mississippi, Missouri, Yangtze, Yenisei, Congo, Huang He, Lena, Mekong, Amur, Mackenzie, Niger, Ob and Volga. Help your child set the scale of the bar graph to fit the large numbers.

▶ 3. Have your child read about how river deltas are formed. Explain that the Greek letter *delta* is a triangle. Herodotus, an ancient Greek, first used the word *delta* to describe the triangular formation of land at the mouth of a river. Find a map of Egypt and point out the Nile delta and its shape. Deltas are formed when clay, gravel, sand, sediment and silt are deposited at the mouth of a river. Can your child name a major delta located in the United States?

▶ 4. Have your child look in a world atlas at the mouths of the following rivers in search of deltas: Mississippi, Mekong, Ganges-Brahmaputra, Rhine, Orinoco and Niger. Ask your child to ponder the following questions. Discuss your child's answers.

Why are large cities often located near large river deltas?
Why are deltas such good areas for agriculture?
What are the dangers from flooding in a delta region?
Why do the river channels through a delta have to be dredged for ship traffic?
Why is the Mississippi delta called a "bird-foot" delta?
Why do deltas keep getting larger?

▶ 5. Have your child read about the major rivers in your state. Have him/her research the answers to the following questions:

Are any of the rivers used for hydroelectric power supply?
Are any of the rivers used for commercial traffic?
Are any of the rivers used for recreation?
Do any of the rivers continue into neighboring states?
Are any of the rivers used for fresh water supplies?
Are any of the rivers used for agricultural irrigation?
Have any of the rivers flooded towns and cities in recent years?

253

Perplexing Plurals

calves
echoes
elves
geese
halves
handkerchiefs
heroes
leaves
moose
potatoes
scarves
shelves
thieves
tomatoes
wives
wolves
women
yourselves

Some plurals involve changes in vowels or even consonants. These are called irregular plurals. Here are some common rules for spelling plurals.

Most words ending in **f** or **fe** form the plural by changing the **f** or **fe** to **v** and adding **es**. **Example:** wolf–wolves

A few words ending in **f** just add **s**. **Example:** chief–chiefs

Words ending in **o** add **s** or **es**. **Example:** buffalo–buffaloes

Some plurals involve changes within the word.
Examples: foot–feet   mouse–mice

Some singular and plural forms have the same spelling.
Examples: deer–deer   sheep–sheep

Write the plural form of each spelling word in the appropriate category.

f to **v**, add **es**

_____   _____
_____   _____
_____   _____
_____   _____
_____

same singular and plural   add **s** only

_____   _____

vowel change   end in **o**, add **es**

_____   _____   _____
_____   _____   _____

Complete the following analogies using the spelling words.

1. **Snow** is to **shovel** as _____ are to **rake**.

2. **Boys** are to **men** as **girls** are to _____ .

3. _____ are to **neck** as **belts** are to **waist**.

4. **Lives** are to **life** as **calves** are to _____ .

5. **Mouse** is to **mice** as **goose** is to _____ .

Learn At Home, Grade 5

River System

Using resource materials and the terms below, **label** the parts of the river system.
Write a description of each word in the space provided.

waterfall _____

_____

_____

meander _____

_____

_____

rapids _____

_____

_____

flood plain _____

_____

_____

delta _____

_____

_____

oxbow lake _____

_____

_____

tributary _____

_____

_____

lake _____

_____

_____

Northeastern States

Learn At Home, Grade 5

	Language Skills	**Spelling**	**Reading**
Monday	**Paragraphs** Have your child write an article about a scientist. Have him/her plan the article by forming a topic sentence and several supporting sentences for each paragraph. *See* Language Skills, Week 25, number 1.	Pretest your child on these spelling words: conserve impure recharge constructed prearrange reclaim impatient prepaid redecorate imperfect preview redeem impersonate react relate impractical recall retain Have your child correct the pretest. Add personalized words and make two copies of this week's study list.	**Life Skills** This week, engage your child in practical, everyday reading exercises. Today, focus on the phone book. Have your child look at your local telephone directory. Discuss how it is arranged. Have your child look up your family's listing and the listings of your doctor, city hall, friends and relatives. Prepare an activity sheet for your child to complete independently. *See* Reading, Week 25, numbers 1 and 2.
Tuesday	Each supporting sentence in a paragraph should relate to the topic sentence. *See* Language Skills, Week 25, number 2. Have your child write a paragraph using one of the following topic sentences. Make sure each sentence in your child's paragraph supports the topic sentence. *The Yankees are the best ball team in history.* *My mother is an excellent cook.* *My brother taught me how to use a yo-yo.*	Review this week's spelling words. Have your child complete **Preparing for Prefixes** (p. 264).	Today, focus on the newspaper. Using the index as a guide, have your child find the score of last night's game, a weather report and the time the news is on tonight. When your child seems familiar with the paper, prepare a worksheet of questions, such as these: *Who came to visit the city yesterday and gave a speech in the town square? What movie is playing at the local theater? Who wrote letters to the editor? See* Reading, Week 25, number 3.
Wednesday	Teach your child to develop a paragraph by answering these six questions: who, what, when, where, why and how. Use the following topic sentence to demonstrate how answering these six questions can fill out a paragraph: *Stu's family went on a two-week vacation.* Have your child write a paragraph by first choosing a topic and asking some questions, then developing a topic sentence and supporting sentences.	Have your child use each of this week's spelling words correctly in a sentence.	Today, focus on using maps. Look at a city map with your child. Establish your location and have your child find other familiar spots. Ask your child specific questions: *How many blocks is it from the court house to the library? In what direction would you walk to get to the hospital? What is located just east of the fire station? See* Reading, Week 25, number 4. Have your child plan a route between two places and write out the directions.
Thursday	Have your child write an expository paragraph on a nonfiction topic of his/her choice. Have your child research the topic and take notes before organizing the information into an interesting paragraph.	Have your child study this week's spelling words.	Plan a scavenger hunt. Hide clues around your house and neighborhood. Draw a map and give your child the first clue. When your child gets to the place described, he/she should look to find a second clue. Arrange for your child to find a special prize or arrive at a special place at the end of the hunt.
Friday	Allow your child time to edit and revise his/her expository paragraph. Depending on the topic, your child may want to add an illustration or photograph to accompany the paragraph.	Give your child the final spelling test. Have your child record pretest and final test words in his/her Word Bank.	Show your child labels on medicines, cleaners, food and other household items. Discuss the importance of reading labels. Teach your child to look for and read warnings, expiration dates, ingredients, directions, uses and nutritional values on labels. Have your child look at a variety of labels to see what type of information is given on each. *See* Reading, Week 25, numbers 5 and 6.

Learn At Home, Grade 5

Math	Science	Social Studies
Introduce subtraction of mixed numbers with different denominators. Ask your child to propose a procedure for solving the equation $2\frac{4}{5} - 1\frac{3}{4}$. Try your child's suggestion to see if it works. If it does, then continue to use it. If your child's suggestion does not work well, try another method. *See* Math, Week 25, number 1. Have your child solve the following problems: $9\frac{1}{5} - 3\frac{3}{4}$ $8 - 5\frac{2}{9}$ $12\frac{1}{2} - 5\frac{2}{3}$ $7\frac{1}{3} - 2\frac{5}{6}$ $10 - 4\frac{3}{7}$ $15\frac{1}{20} - 4\frac{1}{4}$	**Oceans and Seas** Provide books and other resource materials for your child's reference on the world's oceans and seas. *See* Science, Week 25, number 1. Have your child add a glossary page on oceans and seas to his/her Science Log. *See* Science, Week 25, number 2.	Have your child cut out and paste the labeled regions of the United States (pgs. 247–249 and 256–259) onto a large sheet of paper or poster board. Have your child label the map and draw a key, or legend, in the corner. Then, have your child make a chart comparing the current populations of the regions. Have him/her add the chart to the corner of the map.
Review addition and subtraction of fractions. Review and reteach concepts from Week 19 through today.	Guide your child to read about the minerals and salts found in the oceans. Help your child complete the experiment described on **The Salty Seas** (p. 266).	Have your child find the land area of each state, then add the areas together to determine the area of each region. Have your child compile this information into a chart and add to the corner of the map. Help your child analyze the results of his/her research. Look at the population and area of each region. Discuss the meaning of population density. *Which region has the highest population density? Which has the lowest? Why is this so?*
Test your child on addition and subtraction of fractions. Have your child complete **Fractions: Addition and Subtraction** (p. 265). Reteach any concepts your child missed on the test.	Have your child draw a food web of ocean-dwelling plants and animals.	Discuss the climate of your region. How would your child describe it? Introduce some terms related to climate: *alpine, steppe, tundra, mediterranean, desert, continental, subtropical, marine, tropical* and *subarctic*. Have your child look up and define each of these terms. Ask him/her to name examples of each type of climate. **Example:** mediterranean—Greece. Have your child complete **U.S. Climate Zones** (p. 267).
Multiplication of Fractions: The procedure for multiplication of fractions is simple—multiply the numerators, then the denominators, and reduce to lowest terms—but performing the procedure does not mean your child understands the concept. Use models to demonstrate this operation. Show that the same answer is produced with the models as with multiplying the numerals. Repeat with several problems. *See* Math, Week 25, number 2.	Have your child study two islands (or groups of islands) from the following list: Madagascar, Greenland, British Isles, Crete, Hawaii, Ireland, Cuba, Aleutian Islands, Sicily, New Zealand, Iceland, Cyprus. Have your child write some interesting facts about the two islands, then compare the islands to each other. *What features do they have in common? (language, location, origin, natural resources, size, population, landforms, plants, animals)*	Have your child read about some of the natural wonders found in the United States. *See* Social Studies, Week 25, number 1. Have your child choose one natural wonder to write about in a poem. *See* Social Studies, Week 25, number 2.
Provide your child with several problems to solve using multiplication of fractions. Encourage your child to use different models and procedures to solve the problems. Ask your child to explain what he/she is doing along the way.	Underwater exploration is considered by some to be the final frontier. Much of the oceans has yet to be explored. Have your child read in scientific journals about current undersea explorations. Discuss special underwater vehicles and equipment. Have your child read about the fascinating ocean floor. If possible, have your child interview a person whose hobby is scuba diving. Have your child record notes and draw illustrations in his/her Science Log.	Arrange for your child to perform some community service.

Learn At Home, Grade 5

TEACHING SUGGESTIONS AND ACTIVITIES

LANGUAGE SKILLS (Paragraphs)

▶ 1. To prepare for writing the article, have your child read about a scientist in an encyclopedia or biography. Have your child list facts in note form. Each fact should be written on a separate index card. Help your child organize the cards by grouping related concepts. The introductory paragraph should include the person's name, when he/she lived (or was born) and why your child selected this person. Have your child use each group of index cards to write a supporting paragraph.

▶ 2. Copy the following paragraph on the chalkboard. Have your child delete the sentence that does not belong. Discuss the fact that a supporting sentence should support the idea expressed in the topic sentence.

My aunt and uncle's new baby is the smartest baby I have ever known. She is only four months old, but she already rolls over both ways. She is making many new sounds, such as "ba-ba-ba," "ma-ma-ma" and delighted squeals. She is very cute. What I find most impressive is that she looks carefully at the pictures when I read her a book.

READING (Life Skills)

▶ 1. The activity sheet should contain a series of questions that will familiarize your child with the phone book.

Examples: *On what page is William Harrigan's listing?* *What is J. P. Oshman's telephone number?*
What are the guide letters on page 178? *What is Harry Rappaport's zip code?*

▶ 2. Have your child do a similar search through the yellow pages.

▶ 3. Another newspaper activity involves reading the want ads and answering questions about specific ads.

Examples: *What does the first ad under Homes for Sale offer?* *What kinds of pets are for sale?*
Under what heading would you look to buy a bike? *What is the cheapest used car for sale?*

▶ 4. Following directions is a skill your child will use throughout life. Write some directions for your child to follow on a map. Have your child use a yellow highlighter to mark the route he/she would take.

Example: *Start at the corner of Main Street and Fourth Avenue. Walk two blocks north. Turn left. Go three blocks to Spruce Street. Cross the street and turn right. In the middle of the block, turn left. Where are you?*

▶ 5. Select several labels for your child to read. Prepare a worksheet with questions about the information presented on those labels.

Examples: *What warning is given on the cough medicine bottle?*
How often should a dose of the cold medicine be taken and in what amount?
Which food should you not serve because it has over 20% fat content?
Which item will make your shoes waterproof?

▶ 6. Obtain a list of home safety rules from your local fire department. Have your child read the rules carefully. Tell your child to use these rules as a checklist and to go through the house to see that the rules are being observed.

MATH (Fractions)

▶ 1. **Method 1 (Whole Number–Mixed Number)**

    a. Write the whole number as a mixed number ($3 = 2\frac{6}{6}$).

    b. Subtract the fractions.

    c. Subtract the whole numbers.

    d. Reduce the answer to lowest terms.

$$3 - 2\frac{1}{6}$$

$$2\frac{6}{6} - 2\frac{1}{6} = \frac{5}{6}$$

Learn At Home, Grade 5

Method 2 (Mixed Number–Mixed Number)

a. Find the LCM of the denominators.

$2\frac{1}{4} - 1\frac{3}{8}$ The LCM of 4 and 8 is 8.

b. Multiply the numerator and denominator of each fraction by a number to arrive at the LCM.

$2\frac{1}{4} \,^{(\times 2)}_{(\times 2)} - 1\frac{3}{8} =$

c. When necessary, borrow a whole number and make an improper fraction ($2\frac{2}{8} = 1\frac{10}{8}$).

$2\frac{2}{8} - 1\frac{3}{8} =$

d. Subtract the fractions.

$1\frac{10}{8} - 1\frac{3}{8} = \frac{7}{8}$

e. Subtract the whole numbers.

f. Reduce the answer to lowest terms.

▶ 2. Remind your child that 4 x 5 means four sets of five each. The meaning is the same with fractions. The problem $\frac{2}{3} \times \frac{4}{5}$ means two thirds of a set of four fifths. The confusing part to your child may be that the product is smaller than the factors. Ask your child to explore why that is true.

Model the problem $\frac{2}{5} \times \frac{1}{4}$:

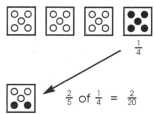

a. Have your child restate the problem as $\frac{2}{5}$ of a set of $\frac{1}{4}$.

b. Draw or build a model of one fourth.

c. Divide the area designated as one fourth into fifths.

d. Shade or indicate two of the fifths to show the product.

$\frac{1}{4}$

$\frac{2}{5}$ of $\frac{1}{4} = \frac{2}{20}$

Repeat with other problems. Then, have your child model the problems.

SCIENCE (Oceans and Seas)

▶ 1. The earth is a unique planet—water covers three fourths of its surface. This vast supply of water provides the world with food, energy, minerals and medicines, as well as a means of transportation.

Name the four oceans.   *What role did the oceans play in early explorations?*
Name some of the major seas.   *What are some of the resources we obtain from the oceans?*
How do the oceans affect the climate?   *What do we call the study of the oceans?*
Why are the oceans salty?

▶ 2. Add the following words to this week's spelling list. Have your child look up each word in a dictionary or science resource. Discuss the meaning. Have your child make a glossary of words related to oceans and seas. Have him/her arrange the entries in alphabetical order and write a definition for each word.

bay	currents	island	oceanography	sea level	trench
coral reef	gulf	marine biology	sea	tide	waves

SOCIAL STUDIES (Geographic Regions)

▶ 1. List some of the natural wonders of the United States. Have your child research where each is located and write a description of each. Have your child make a mark and label where each natural wonder is found on the regional maps. Here are some natural wonders to get you started:

Appalachians	Lake Superior	Kilauea	Niagara Falls
Grand Canyon	Devil's Tower	Great Plains	Everglades
Mount McKinley	Carlsbad Caverns	Great Salt Lake	Mount St. Helens

▶ 2. Have your child write a diamante poem about a natural wonder, using the following guidelines.

Line 1: one noun telling where the natural wonder is located   *Alaska*
Line 2: two adjectives describing the natural wonder   *Great, tall*
Line 3: three participles telling what it is known for   *Freezing, climbing, sightseeing*
Line 4: four nouns related to the natural wonder   *Denali, High One, mountain, range*
Line 5: three participles telling what it is known for   *Soaring, scraping, peaking*
Line 6: two different adjectives describing it   *High, northern*
Line 7: the name of the natural wonder   *Mount McKinley*

Preparing for Prefixes

A **prefix** is a word part that is added to the beginning of a root word to make a new word. Every prefix has a meaning and alters the meaning of the root word.

Prefixes

pre—before   **con**—with, together
im—not   **re**—again, back

Complete each sentence with a word containing the prefix **im**.

1. Be careful! Don't drink that _____ water.
2. It is _____ to own five automobiles.
3. Don't be so _____ —this takes time to complete.
4. The comedian will _____ the president.
5. It was not a very good mold; it was _____.

Match each clue with a word containing the prefix **re**.

1. call again _____
2. energize the battery _____
3. to pay off, buy back _____
4. to decorate again _____
5. to tell or narrate _____
6. to respond _____
7. win in competition after losing title _____
8. to hold onto _____

conserve
constructed
impatient
imperfect
impersonate
impractical
impure
prearrange
prepaid
preview
react
recall
recharge
reclaim
redecorate
redeem
relate
retain

Complete the passage with words containing the prefixes **pre** or **con**.

Last week, a group of teachers was asked to _____ a science-fiction TV program. We had to _____ a specific time and date with the producers. When everyone was settled, the producers described how they had _____ creatures for the program. They discussed how they tried to _____ time, money and materials by planning every detail in advance. They even _____ for all materials to take advantage of discounts. We all felt the production was informative as well as entertaining.

264

Learn At Home, Grade 5

Fractions: Addition and Subtraction

Identify the shaded part.

1. 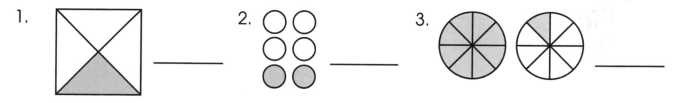 _____

2. _____

3. _____

Complete.

4. $\dfrac{2}{3} = \dfrac{}{15}$

Reduce to lowest terms.

5. $\dfrac{9}{12} = $ ___

6. $\dfrac{18}{54} = $ ___

Compare using > or <.

7. $\dfrac{13}{27} \qquad \dfrac{12}{27}$

8. $\dfrac{5}{6} \qquad \dfrac{3}{4}$

9. $2\dfrac{3}{4} \qquad \dfrac{13}{4}$

Add or **subtract**.

10. $\dfrac{1}{5} + \dfrac{2}{5} = $ ___

11. $\dfrac{3}{8} - \dfrac{2}{8} = $ ___

12. $\dfrac{3}{4} + \dfrac{1}{2} = $ ___

13. $\dfrac{7}{8} - \dfrac{3}{4} = $ ___

14. $5\dfrac{1}{2} + 2\dfrac{1}{2} = $ ___

15. $2\dfrac{1}{8} - 1\dfrac{5}{8} = $ ___

16. $\dfrac{21}{5} - \dfrac{21}{10} = $ ___

17. $5\dfrac{1}{6} + 3\dfrac{2}{4} = $ ___

18. $\dfrac{5}{3} + \dfrac{2}{5} = $ ___

Draw a model to show each fraction.

19. $3\dfrac{1}{4}$

20. $\dfrac{10}{3}$

The Salty Seas

Swimming in the sea is easier than swimming in a lake. This is because seawater contains salty material that helps a swimmer float. Three-fourths of a sea's salty material is the same as the salt we use in our food. Seawater contains 55.2% chlorine, 30.5% sodium, 7.6% sulfate, 3.7% magnesium, 1.2% calcium, 1.1% potassium and other elements. All these ingredients are found in rocks and soil around the world. When seawater evaporates, most of the salt is left behind. When it rains, the rivers continually wash in more soil and rocks (and, therefore, more salt). But the seas do not get more salty, because the salt gets trapped with the mud and sand that builds up on the seafloor. Did you know that if all the salt was taken out of the seas and spread over the land surface of Earth, there would be a layer 500 feet thick? To learn more about evaporation, try the experiment below.

You will need: pie pan or saucer, water, salt, teaspoon

Experiment:

1. Fill the pie pan halfway with water.
2. Pour as much salt in the water as will dissolve. Stir with the teaspoon.
3. Place the salt water in a warm, dry place until the water has evaporated.

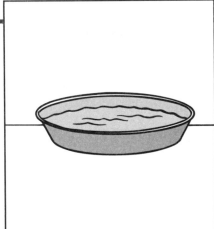

Predict:

1. What do you think will happen to the water? _____

2. How long do you think this will take? _____

3. What do you think will happen to the salt? _____

Analyze:

1. On another sheet of paper, make a chart to record the daily water level.

2. What has happened to the water? _____

_____

3. How long did it take? _____

U.S. Climate Zones

The word **climate** is used to describe the weather in a particular place over a long period of time. Because the United States covers such a large area, it has a number of different climate zones. Some areas have long, cold winters and short, cool summers, while other areas are warm in both summer and winter.

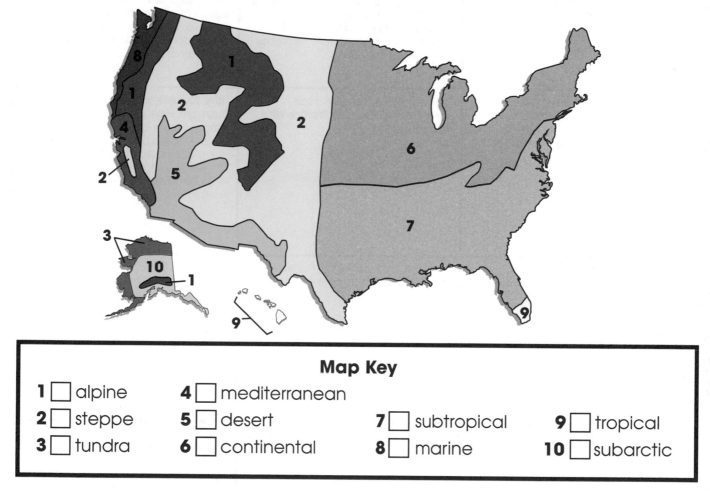

Map Key

1 ☐ alpine	4 ☐ mediterranean		
2 ☐ steppe	5 ☐ desert	7 ☐ subtropical	9 ☐ tropical
3 ☐ tundra	6 ☐ continental	8 ☐ marine	10 ☐ subarctic

Choose colors to color-code the Map Key and the climate zone map. Then, determine the . . .

climate zone you live in. _____

climate zone of the Northeast. _____

climate zones of the Rocky Mountains. _____

three climate zones found in Alaska. _____

climate zones found in Texas. _____

climate zones of Florida. _____

climate zone of Michigan. _____

Language Skills	**Spelling**	**Reading**
Monday		
Topics for Writing Brainstorm ideas for writing topics with your child. Have your child make lists of special people, special events, hobbies, pets, things he/she is good at, unusual characters and other creative inspirations.	Pretest your child on these spelling words: administer derail export advantage disagree external adventure disappeared extricate defog dishonest unequal dehumidify disinterested unprepared depart explode untrue Have your child correct the pretest. Add personalized words and make two copies of this week's study list.	Introduce the humorous book *Bunnicula: A Rabbit-Tale of Mystery* by Deborah and James Howe. Read aloud the editor's note at the beginning of the book and discuss whether the story could be true. Have your child read chapter 1 of *Bunnicula*. **Vocabulary:** *admonition, bereaved, compromise, dazed, decipher, dialect, digress, hysteria, mongrel, plaintively, reverie, tranquil, traumatized, unison.*
Tuesday		
Have your child follow the steps in the writing process as he/she writes independently this week. For more information on the writing process, see page 6.	Review this week's spelling words. Have your child complete **Practice With Prefixes** (p. 272).	Have your child read chapter 2 of *Bunnicula*. Have your child design a hanging mobile to display the story elements (setting, characters, problem, events and solution). Have your child continue to work on the mobile as he/she reads this week. *See* Reading, Week 26, number 1.
Wednesday		
Let your child continue to work independently on his/her writing project.	Have your child use each of this week's spelling words correctly in a sentence.	Discuss the following: *Why do you think Chester is able to read? How would the story be different if he could not read?* Have your child read chapters 3 and 4 of *Bunnicula*. Have your child write a descriptive paragraph about one of the "unusual goings-on." Explain what is meant by "smart but not scholarly."
Thursday		
Let your child continue to work independently on his/her writing project.	Have your child study this week's spelling words.	Have your child read chapters 5 and 6 of *Bunnicula*. **Vocabulary:** *blight, dolt, grimace, inexplicable, interjected, organic, emanated, emits, immobile, inert, pendant, renders, shrivel, strewn.* Review adjectives with your child. *Which of the vocabulary words are adjectives?* Have your child search through *Bunnicula* to locate adjectives used with certain nouns. *See* Reading, Week 26, numbers 2 and 3.
Friday		
Have your child do a final edit and revision of his/her writing project.	Give your child the final spelling test. Have your child record pretest and final test words in his/her Word Bank.	Some of the characteristics given the animals in the story could not happen in real life. Ask your child to name four things about each pet: two that are possible and two that are not. Have your child read chapters 7–9 of *Bunnicula*. Have your child complete the story mobile.

Learn At Home, Grade 5

Math	Science	Social Studies
Give your child several word problems to solve that involve fractions. Have your child illustrate each situation before solving the problem. *See* Math, Week 26, number 1.	**Deserts** Have your child draw a picture of a desert. Then, ask him/her to define the term *desert*. *See* Science, Week 26, number 1. How accurate is your child's drawing? Are there any elements missing? Have your child add a glossary page on deserts to his/her Science Log. *See* Science, Week 26, number 2.	**Maps** Explore different types of maps with your child. Find examples of maps for several different purposes. *See* Social Studies, Week 26, number 1.
Teach your child three different ways to multiply a whole number by a fraction. *See* Math, Week 26, number 2. Have your child complete **Puzzling Fractions** (p. 273).	Have your child begin research of one major desert today. Over the course of this week, have your child read about that desert and take notes for a final report. Ask your child to create a model of the desert as well. Encourage him/her to be creative.	With your child, read *Anno's Journey* by Mitsumasa Anno. Ask your child to join the traveler on his journey eastward across the United States. *See* Social Studies, Week 26, number 2.
Discuss with your child how to multiply with mixed numbers. Explain how and why to cancel numbers in fractions. Walk through the steps as shown on **Multiplication With Mixed Numbers** (p. 274). Model the sample problem. Walk your child through a second and third problem before assigning independent work. Have your child complete the problems at the bottom of the page on **Multiplication With Mixed Numbers**.	Allow time for your child to continue his/her research on the chosen desert area.	Look at a map of the U.S. Have your child plan an imaginary trip across the country. Have your child write about the route he/she would take, estimate how far he/she would travel each day and write down what sights he/she would see. Provide resource books so that your child may get accurate information.
Use models to teach your child how to divide with fractions. *See* Math, Week 26, number 3. Have your child draw models of the following division problems: $\frac{7}{8} \div \frac{3}{4}$ $\frac{7}{8} \div \frac{1}{2}$ $\frac{5}{4} \div \frac{2}{3}$ $\frac{4}{5} \div \frac{1}{2}$ $\frac{7}{5} \div \frac{2}{5}$ $\frac{3}{4} \div \frac{2}{4}$ $\frac{1}{2} \div \frac{1}{3}$ $\frac{3}{5} \div \frac{1}{4}$	Help your child perform an experiment to observe the effects of wind on sand. *See* Science, Week 26, number 3. Have your child sketch the formation and movement of the sand dunes in his/her Science Log.	Have your child make flash cards to help learn the state capitals. Have your child use the flash cards for several weeks until he/she has memorized the capitals.
Teach your child the "invert and multiply" method for dividing fractions. Use the examples on **Dividing Fractions** (p. 275). Have your child complete the independent practice problems at the bottom of the page. Have your child use the "invert and multiply" method to check his/her work from yesterday.	Have your child complete his/her desert project and present it to an audience.	Arrange for your child to perform some community service.

READING (Story Elements / Adjectives)

▶ 1. Use a heavy stock of paper for the mobile. Have your child cut the paper into various shapes and sizes. While reading the story, have your child write about the major events and characters. Have him/her include pictures as well. These may be drawn on both sides of the paper shapes. Have your child number the events in the order they happened. When the reading and drawings are completed, give your child a paper punch, colored yarn and a metal coat hanger. Have your child lay out the shapes in a sequential order, keeping in mind that the mobile needs to balance. Punch a hole at the top and bottom of the paper shapes. You can punch holes off-center to help balance the shapes on the mobile. Use bits of yarn to attach the cards. Teach your child to attach the top shapes to the coat hanger and suspend it from the ceiling. He/she may need to trim some paper shapes, add paper clips or add other shapes to balance the mobile.

▶ 2. Have your child scan *Bunnicula* for the adjectives used to describe the following nouns.

Chapter 4	Chapter 5
_____ crackers	_____ cream
_____ cupcakes	_____ beans
_____ _____ sandwich	_____ blight
_____ book	_____ Department
_____ _____ _____ teeth	_____ glass
_____ tomato	_____ bite
_____ rooms	_____ beings
_____ handkerchiefs	_____ sweater
_____ zucchini	_____ _____ mice

▶ 3. Have your child choose three or four of the above phrases to illustrate. Your child may want to include these pictures in the story mobile.

MATH (Multiplication and Division With Fractions)

▶ 1. Give your child the following word problems to solve. Have your child illustrate the situation presented in each case before solving the problem.

   a. After the party, Jesse put $\frac{1}{2}$ of his birthday cake in the refrigerator. Later, he ate $\frac{1}{8}$ of the remaining cake. What fraction of the whole cake did he just eat?

   b. Greg finished his math assignment in $\frac{5}{8}$ of an hour. Shauna finished her assignment in $\frac{2}{5}$ of that time. What fraction of an hour did it take Shauna to finish her assignment?

   c. Robyn read $\frac{1}{2}$ of her library book aloud. Then, she silently read $\frac{1}{4}$ of the part she had left. What fraction of the book did Robyn read silently?

   d. Carlos ran $\frac{3}{4}$ of the way to the park before he rested. He then walked $\frac{1}{2}$ of the remaining distance before he got a ride from Arne. What fraction of the total distance did Carlos walk?

   e. Two thirds of the adults in George's town were registered to vote. Only $\frac{3}{5}$ of those registered actually voted on the library expansion issue. What fraction of the adults in George's town actually voted on this issue? Is that a majority of the adults?

▶ 2. There are three ways to multiply whole numbers and fractions. All three methods will arrive at the same answer.

   a. **Method 1:** Think of the whole number as a fraction. The whole number becomes the numerator with 1 as the denominator. **Example:** $4 \times \frac{3}{5} = \frac{4}{1} \times \frac{3}{5} = \frac{12}{5} = 2\frac{2}{5}$

   b. **Method 2:** Think of $4 \times \frac{3}{5}$ as four sets of $\frac{3}{5}$. Draw or build a model of $\frac{3}{5}$. Repeat the model four times. Count the total number of fifths ($\frac{12}{5}$).

   c. **Method 3:** Reverse $4 \times \frac{3}{5}$ to $\frac{3}{5} \times 4$. The product is $\frac{3}{5}$ of 4 wholes. Draw four whole units. Divide that drawing into fifths and identify three-fifths.

Learn At Home, Grade 5

▶ 3. When working with division of fractions, refer to the concept of division with whole numbers. Given a number of items, how many sets of *x* things are there?

Example: $1\frac{1}{2} \div \frac{3}{4}$ How many sets of $\frac{3}{4}$ are in a set of $1\frac{1}{2}$? (2)

SCIENCE (Deserts)

▶ 1. A desert is a region that can support little plant life because of low amounts of moisture. Some people picture a desert as nothing but barren stretches of sand, but the world's deserts have varied landscapes and types of soil. The people, animals and plants that live in the desert have adapted to the dry climate. Provide materials so your child can read about some of the following deserts:

Sahara	Kalahari	Arabian	Gobi	Syrian
Great Victoria	Australian	Great Basin	Patagonian	Mojave

▶ 2. Add the following words to this week's spelling list. Have your child look up each word in a dictionary or science resource. Discuss the meaning. Have your child make a glossary of terms related to deserts. Have him/her arrange the entries in alphabetical order and write a definition for each word.

abrasion	arid	dune	saguaro
adobe	blowout	dust bowl	semiarid
alluvial fan	dromedary	oasis	wash

▶ 3. Have your child conduct an experiment that simulates the movement of sand in a desert and the creation of dunes. Locate an outdoor site that is about one square meter in size and cover the area with builder's sand. Have your child blow onto the sand through a cardboard tube or use a small fan to represent wind. Ask your child to describe and sketch the patterns of sand movement and the creation of dunes. Add rocks to the sand and repeat the experiment. Observe what happens.

SOCIAL STUDIES (Maps)

▶ 1. Teach your child about the different types of maps that are available. Look at a variety of maps in textbooks and other resources. Discuss the purpose of each kind of map. A *political map* shows state and country boundaries and the locations of cities. A *physical map* shows geographic features, such as mountains and rivers. A *road map* shows roadways and streets and is used to guide motorists while traveling. A *precipitation map* shows the amount of rainfall (as well as snow, sleet and hail). Maps can also show natural resources, industry, election results or historic routes and battles.

▶ 2. Have your child tell the story of America's history, culture and geography orally as he/she "rides" with the traveler eastward across the United States. Along the way, the traveler sees a variety of physical features that should be familiar to your child. Spend time observing and discussing each page with your child. When your child has completed the story, have him/her trace the journey on a large map. Compare the journey in the book with a journey that might be taken today along the same route.

Practice With Prefixes

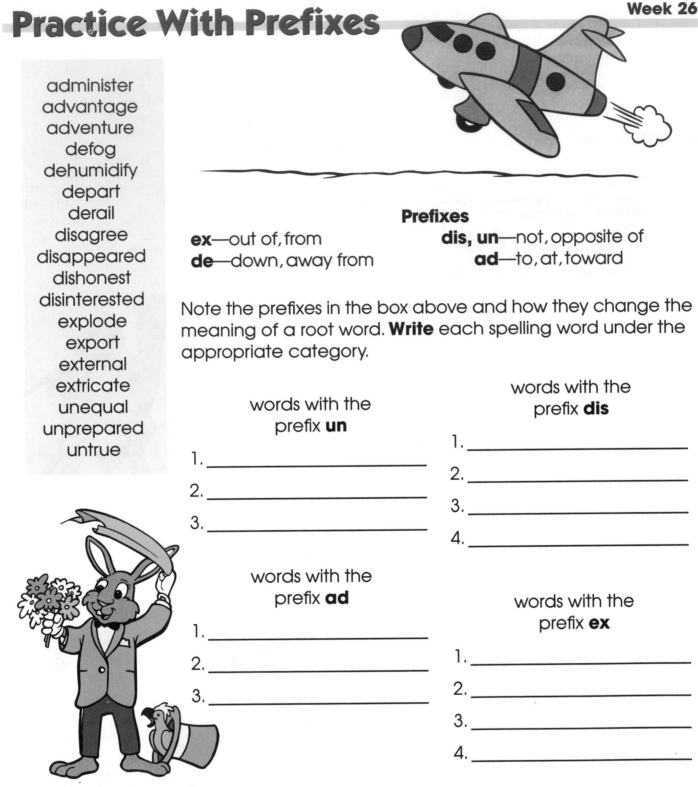

administer
advantage
adventure
defog
dehumidify
depart
derail
disagree
disappeared
dishonest
disinterested
explode
export
external
extricate
unequal
unprepared
untrue

Prefixes

ex—out of, from
de—down, away from

dis, un—not, opposite of
ad—to, at, toward

Note the prefixes in the box above and how they change the meaning of a root word. **Write** each spelling word under the appropriate category.

words with the
prefix **un**

1. _____
2. _____
3. _____

words with the
prefix **dis**

1. _____
2. _____
3. _____
4. _____

words with the
prefix **ad**

1. _____
2. _____
3. _____

words with the
prefix **ex**

1. _____
2. _____
3. _____
4. _____

Add the prefix **de** to each of these root words. Say each word to yourself as you write it on the line.

humidify   **part**   **fog**   **rail**

_____   _____   _____   _____

272

Learn At Home, Grade 5

Puzzling Fractions

Multiply to solve the problems.

$7 \times \dfrac{1}{5} = $ _____

$9 \times \dfrac{1}{10} = $ _____

$8 \times \dfrac{1}{8} = $ _____

$8 \times \dfrac{1}{7} = $ _____

$7 \times \dfrac{1}{11} = $ _____

$9 \times \dfrac{1}{3} = $ _____

$3 \times \dfrac{1}{6} = $ _____

$12 \times \dfrac{1}{5} = $ _____

$\dfrac{1}{5} \times 4 = $ _____

$\dfrac{1}{3} \times 9 = $ _____

$\dfrac{1}{5} \times 20 = $ _____

$\dfrac{1}{6} \times 12 = $ _____

$\dfrac{1}{10} \times \dfrac{1}{100} = $ _____

$\dfrac{1}{6} \times \dfrac{1}{10} = $ _____

$\dfrac{1}{12} \times \dfrac{1}{3} = $ _____

$\dfrac{1}{6} \times \dfrac{1}{6} = $ _____

$\dfrac{1}{9} \times \dfrac{1}{8} = $ _____

$\dfrac{1}{9} \times \dfrac{1}{10} = $ _____

$\dfrac{1}{10} \times \dfrac{1}{10} = $ _____

$\dfrac{1}{20} \times \dfrac{1}{5} = $ _____

$8 \times \dfrac{1}{10} = $ _____

$\dfrac{1}{5} \times \dfrac{1}{8} = $ _____

$\dfrac{1}{6} \times \dfrac{1}{7} = $ _____

$\dfrac{1}{100} \times \dfrac{1}{100} = $ _____

$\dfrac{1}{9} \times 9 = $ _____

$\dfrac{1}{8} \times 7 = $ _____

$\dfrac{1}{7} \times 6 = $ _____

$12 \times \dfrac{1}{4} = $ _____

$\dfrac{1}{15} \times \dfrac{1}{13} = $ _____

$\dfrac{1}{3} \times \dfrac{1}{7} = $ _____

$\dfrac{1}{8} \times 3 = $ _____

$\dfrac{1}{7} \times 21 = $ _____

Multiplication With Mixed Numbers

When multiplying by a mixed number, change the mixed number to an improper fraction. Cancel if possible. Multiply the numerators, then the denominators. **Write** the improper fractions as mixed numbers.

Example A: $\dfrac{3}{4} \times 1\dfrac{1}{2} = \dfrac{3}{4} \times \dfrac{3}{2} = \dfrac{9}{8} = 1\dfrac{1}{8}$

multiply

multiply

Example B: $2\dfrac{4}{7} \times \dfrac{5}{9} = \dfrac{\overset{2}{\cancel{18}}}{7} \times \dfrac{5}{\underset{1}{\cancel{9}}} = \dfrac{10}{7} = 1\dfrac{3}{7}$

multiply

multiply

Multiply.

1. $\dfrac{1}{2} \times 8\dfrac{3}{4} = \dfrac{1}{2} \times \dfrac{35}{4} =$

2. $5\dfrac{1}{3} \times \dfrac{6}{7}$

3. $\dfrac{11}{12} \times 11\dfrac{1}{3}$

4. $7\dfrac{1}{2} \times \dfrac{8}{9}$

5. $\dfrac{2}{5} \times 2\dfrac{1}{12}$

6. $8\dfrac{2}{3} \times \dfrac{1}{4}$

274

Dividing Fractions

When dividing fractions, change the problem to multiplication. Invert the divisor. Cancel if possible. Multiply the numerators, then the denominators. **Write** improper fractions as mixed numbers.

Example A: $\dfrac{3}{10} \div \dfrac{4}{5} = \dfrac{3}{10} \times \dfrac{5}{4} = {}_2\dfrac{3}{\cancel{10}} \times \dfrac{\cancel{5}^{1}}{4} = \dfrac{3}{8}$

multiply

multiply

Example B: $\dfrac{5}{12} \div \dfrac{3}{8} = \dfrac{5}{12} \times \dfrac{8}{3} = {}_3\dfrac{5}{\cancel{12}} \times \dfrac{\cancel{8}^{2}}{3} = \dfrac{10}{9} = 1\dfrac{1}{9}$

multiply

multiply

Divide.

1. $\dfrac{1}{2} \div \dfrac{3}{10} = \dfrac{1}{2} \times \dfrac{10}{3} =$

2. $\dfrac{3}{8} \div \dfrac{1}{4}$

3. $\dfrac{4}{9} \div \dfrac{2}{3}$

4. $\dfrac{3}{8} \div \dfrac{5}{12}$

5. $\dfrac{1}{10} \div \dfrac{2}{5}$

6. $\dfrac{5}{6} \div \dfrac{11}{12}$

7. $\dfrac{14}{15} \div \dfrac{2}{3}$

8. $\dfrac{4}{5} \div \dfrac{3}{10}$

275

Language Skills	**Spelling**	**Reading**
Monday Use music as an inspiration for a story. Play a recording of Prokofiev's *Peter and the Wolf*. Allow your child to listen to and enjoy the entire musical recording. Discuss the story and the music. Leonard Bernstein narrates a version for children in which he explains the story and the use of different instruments to portray characters. Have your child make an outline of the story, then tell the story in his/her own words. *See* Language Skills, Week 27, number 1.	Select words from the past eight weeks for this week's pretest. Have your child correct the pretest. Add personalized words and make two copies of this week's study list.	**Using a Dictionary and a Thesaurus** Introduce *Number the Stars* by Lois Lowry. Help your child identify the setting of the story and locate the place on a map. Then, have your child read chapters 1 and 2. **Vocabulary:** *contempt, crocheting, intricate, mourned, outdistanced, sabotage, scurried, sneering, solemn, trousseau.* Review the use of dictionaries and thesauri this week. *See* Reading, Week 27, numbers 1 and 2.
Tuesday Have your child piece together sentence fragments to form complete sentences. *See* Language Skills, Week 27, number 2. Have your child read through his/her version of the story of "Peter and the Wolf." Have your child edit the story, then proofread for proper capitalization, punctuation and paragraph breaks.	Have your child look up spelling words in a dictionary. Have him/her write down the proper pronunciation(s) on the back of each card from the Word Bank.	Have your child read chapters 3 and 4 of *Number the Stars*. **Vocabulary:** *belligerently, carousel, curfew, dawdled, disdain, dubiously, flowering, haughtily, rationed, sprawled, swastika, synagogue.* See Reading, Week 27, numbers 3 and 4.
Wednesday Review grammar and parts of speech. *See* Language Skills, Week 27, number 3.	Have your child once again look up spelling words in a dictionary. This time, have him/her write a sentence using each word correctly. Record on the appropriate index cards from the Word Bank.	Have your child read chapters 5 and 6 of *Number the Stars*. **Vocabulary:** *distorted, holstered, imperious, intoned, massive, peered, probed, tentatively, unwavering.* Discuss the following questions: *What happened to Lise? Why won't Lise's parents talk about her? Why was it significant that the soldier destroyed Lise's picture? How would the story have been different if Annemarie had forgotten about Ellen's necklace?*
Thursday Discuss what makes a good paragraph. Have your child study a paragraph from a book. Ask him/her to state the main idea of the paragraph. *What words does the author use to help the reader picture the main idea? See* Language Skills, Week 27, number 4.	Provide your child with art supplies such as paints and markers. Have him/her write out each spelling word from the past eight weeks in an artistic manner. Encourage your child to be creative, adding flourishes, pictures or other unique touches.	Ask your child to predict the outcome of the story. Have your child read chapters 7 and 8 of *Number the Stars*. **Vocabulary:** *apparently, appliqued, bobbing, distracted, relocate, Scandinavian, specter, tidier.* Have your child make a detailed drawing of the house by the sea. Have your child complete **Radical Referents** (p. 280).
Friday Have your child choose his/her best and favorite pieces of writing so far to publish in a personal literary magazine. For more information on publishing your child's work, see page 6.	Give your child the final spelling test.	Have your child read chapters 9 and 10 of *Number the Stars*. **Vocabulary:** *condescending, deftly, poised, psalm, splintery, staccato, wail, wryly.* Ask your child: *Is it ever all right to tell a lie? Offer examples to support your answer.*

Math	Science	Social Studies
Review the four basic mathematical operations with fractions. Have your child complete **Stump the Teacher** (p. 281).	**Glaciers** Provide books and other resources on glaciers for your child's reference. *See* Science, Week 27, number 1. Have your child add a glossary page on glaciers to his/her Science Log. *See* Science, Week 27, number 2.	**Famous Americans** This week, introduce your child to famous Americans of all kinds. Discuss the men and women who have shaped and who continue to shape the history of our nation. Consider all kinds of Americans, from the fields of politics, science, society, literature, the arts and sports. Have your child try to guess famous Americans based on riddles. *See* Social Studies, Week 27, number 1.
Review and reteach multiplication and division with fractions.	Explain how glaciers move and how they shape the land as they move. If there is any glacial erosion (or glacial deposits) near your home, go see it. If not, find pictures in science resources.	Have your child study American inventors, their inventions and their impact on American life. *See* Social Studies, Week 27, numbers 2 and 3.
Test your child on multiplication and division of fractions. Have your child complete **Fractions: Multiplication and Division** (p. 282). Reteach any concepts missed on the test.	Discuss well-known glaciers. Have your child choose a famous glacier and write about how it was formed, where it is located and other interesting facts.	Have your child continue the research from yesterday's lesson. When your child is finished with the research, discuss his/her findings. Ask your child to rank the most important inventions to Americans. Have your child imagine what America (or the world) might be like today if the _____ had never been invented. Have your child write about a day in the life of an average American living without that invention.
Review the concepts taught over the past nine weeks. Repeat activities that your child found most difficult. Show your child more practical applications of fractions.	Review the different features of the earth studied over the past nine weeks. Have your child create an imaginary island filled with striking geological features. Have your child draw a picture of the island and label each of its unique features. Your child may also want to name these features (e.g., Forgotten Canyon, Mount Juniper) as well as the island itself.	Discuss the work of Thomas Edison. Have your child research Edison's life and write a one-page biography of the inventor.
Test your child's understanding of fractions. Have your child complete **Third Quarter Test** (p. 283).	Have your child plan an imaginary vacation in which you will visit many of the incredible sites studied this quarter. Have your child plan the route on a map. Ask him/her to include a time line (or itinerary) of the trip and explain what you will see.	Arrange for your child to perform some community service.

TEACHING SUGGESTIONS AND ACTIVITIES

LANGUAGE SKILLS (Review)

▶ 1. Help your child complete the following story frame for *Peter and the Wolf*. Using the story frame as a guide, your child will then retell the story of Peter and the wolf in his/her own words.

There once was a _____ named _____ who _____.
The story takes place _____.
A problem occurs when _____.
First, _____.
Then, _____.
The action continues when _____.
The problem is solved when _____.
The story ends when _____.

▶ 2. Write several complete sentences on 18" x 2" strips of construction paper. Cut each sentence into two or three parts: cut between the complete subject and complete predicate, and separate any prepositional phrases from the rest of the sentence. Mix up the parts. Have your child arrange the sentence parts to make sensible sentences.

▶ 3. Copy a paragraph from a book or magazine. Have your child identify given parts of speech by following these (and more of your own) directions.

Draw a box around all prepositional phrases.
Read all of the third person, present tense verbs aloud.
*Draw an **X** on collective nouns.*
Circle each action verb and draw an arrow to the receiver of its action (direct object).
Underline all proper nouns.

▶ 4. Find a well-written paragraph in a book your child is reading or has read recently. Copy the sentences from the paragraph onto index cards (one sentence per card). Mix up the cards and have your child arrange the sentences in an order that makes sense. Have your child copy the sentences on paper in paragraph form and read the paragraph aloud. Compare to the original paragraph. Repeat with a second paragraph.

READING (Using a Dictionary and a Thesaurus)

▶ 1. Compare and contrast a dictionary and a thesaurus. Have your child look up the same words in both resources. Discuss the differences in the entries. Assess your child's understanding of the purpose of each book by asking him/her to find a word that means the same as _____ . Your child should know to look in the thesaurus.

▶ 2. Write a sentence using a vocabulary word. Underline the new vocabulary. Have your child find a similar word to use in its place. Ask your child to judge which word creates a clearer image in the sentence.

▶ 3. Have your child identify what part of speech each vocabulary word is (noun, adjective, verb, etc.).

▶ 4. Before reading, have your child look up the vocabulary words and use each one in a sentence. After reading, have your child compare the meanings of the words in the sentences with the words as used in the story.

SCIENCE (Glaciers)

▶ 1. A glacier is a large mass of flowing ice found in cold regions of the world. A glacier may be found in high mountains where snow builds up until it turns to ice. There are two types of glaciers: *continental glaciers* and *valley glaciers*. Have your child read about the differences in an encyclopedia or other resource.

▶ 2. Add the following words to this week's spelling list. Have your child look up each word in a dictionary or science resource. Discuss the meaning. Have your child make a glossary of words related to glaciers. Have him/her arrange the entries in alphabetical order and write a definition for each word.

bedrock	continental glacier	drumlins	firn	moraine
cirque	crevasse	eskers	kettle	till

Learn At Home, Grade 5

SOCIAL STUDIES (Famous Americans)

▶ 1. Play a game in which you give clues about a selected famous American and your child tries to guess who it is. Begin with broad clues, then gradually get more specific. Say one clue at a time, giving your child the chance to look in an encyclopedia or other resource to narrow the search. Encourage your child to guess the famous American with as few clues as possible. For a variation, have your child research a famous American and write his/her own riddle for *you* to guess! Here are four riddles to get you started.

    a. As the daughter of Quaker abolitionists, she often spoke against slavery.
        She was a good friend of Elizabeth Cady Stanton.
        The Nineteenth Amendment to the Constitution was passed 14 years after her death.
        She helped form the National Woman Suffrage Association.
        She was the first woman to be pictured on a U.S. coin.
        Answer: *Susan B. Anthony*

    b. This man was one of America's most accomplished scientists.
        He taught farmers more productive agricultural practices.
        He was named the head of the Department of Research at Tuskegee Institute in 1910.
        He is especially famous for his experiments with a type of legume.
        He developed more than 300 products from the peanut.
        Answer: *George Washington Carver*

    c. He was one of the original seven astronauts chosen for the Mercury program.
        His historic flight took place in a spacecraft called *Friendship 7.*
        In 1974, he won election to the U.S. Senate from the state of Ohio.
        In 1998, he become the oldest human ever to travel in space.
        He was the first American to orbit the earth.
        Answer: *John Glenn*

    d. This famous American was part of an expedition exploring the Northwestern States.
        This famous American belonged to the Shoshone tribe.
        She married Toussaint Charbonneau, a French-Canadian fur trader.
        Her name means "Bird Woman."
        She and her husband were guides for Lewis and Clark.
        Answer: *Sacagawea*

▶ 2. Have your child look up the words *invention* and *discovery*. Ask your child to give examples illustrating the difference between the two words: *Columbus* <u>discovered</u> *America.* (It existed but was not known to the Europeans.) *Edison* <u>invented</u> *the light bulb.* (It did not exist before.) Discuss why things are invented. Have your child explain the meaning of the saying, "Necessity is the mother of invention." Inventions may arise out of economic, military or social needs.

▶ 3. Make a list of several inventions developed by Americans. Here is a list to get you started.

adding machine	harvester	sleeping car
air conditioning	incandescent lamp	steamboat (commercial)
airplane with motor	laser	submarine
camera (Kodak)	microphone	telegraph (magnetic)
camera (Polaroid)	pen (ballpoint)	telephone
carpet sweeper	pin (safety)	television
cash register	polio vaccine	trolley car
cotton gin	reaper	typewriter
elevator	rocket engine	vacuum cleaner
frozen food	rubber (vulcanized)	washing machine

Have your child make a chart of at least ten of these inventions. The chart should have the following headings: *Inventor, Invention, Date, Function* and *Social Impact.* Have your child fill in the chart.

Radical Referents

Write the name of the person or thing to which the **bold** words refer.

1. Mama took Ellen's hand and told **her she** had beautiful hair. _____
2. After discussing the girls, Papa and Mama decided that **they** should be taken to Henrik's house. _____
3. Papa reached for the phone to call Henrik, hoping that **he** would still reach **him** at home. _____
4. Papa promised Mama and the children **they** would be safe. _____
5. A soldier on the train asked Mama where **she** was going. _____
6. Kirsti told the soldier, "**I** am going to visit **my** Uncle Henrik!" _____
7. Annemarie was surprised when Ellen said **she** had never seen the sea. _____
8. Henrik named his fishing boat the *Ingeborg* after Mama, who was **his** sister. _____

    In the morning, Annemarie awoke and stumbled
downstairs where **she** found her chatterbox sister _____
feeding a kitten. Kirsti named **it** after the God _____
of Thunder and **she** was attempting to give it water. _____

    When Kirsti laughed, the kitten scurried off to be
alone and soon **it** rested on a windowsill out _____
of **her** reach. There it sat, licking its paws. _____

    Ellen was still sleeping while Mama prepared
oatmeal for **her** and the others. Mama's brother _____
Henrik no longer grew vegetables but **he** was able to _____
provide cream and butter because of Blossom, **his** cow. _____

Underline the character's name hidden in each of the following sentences.
The first one has been done for you.

1. May Mary B<u>eth or</u> Betty Ann play the game in the blizzard?
2. The fakir stirred his cauliflower soup with a spatula and a dowel.
3. The party's success was certain when Sam amazed his audience.
4. Matilda foolishly flipped and fell entirely into a foaming filth.
5. The Fieldings figured the top apartment was the best of the lot.
6. My winsome sister could shop eternally for chartreuse stockings.

Learn At Home, Grade 5

Stump the Teacher

The students in Ms. Davidson's class were playing "Stump the Teacher." See if you can solve their problems.

1. If baseball cards are worth $\frac{1}{10}$ of a dollar each, how much are Brad's 54 cards worth? _____

2. If $\frac{6}{8}$ of Sally's 8 puppies are female and $\frac{1}{2}$ of the female puppies have been sold, how many female puppies have been sold?_____

3. Felipe used $\frac{2}{3}$ cup of cheese for each pizza. If he made 4 pizzas, how much cheese did he need to buy? _____

4. Francis bought $\frac{15}{16}$ of a yard of fabric. She used $\frac{1}{2}$ of it to make a dress for her doll. What fraction of a yard did she use? _____

5. If a lot is $\frac{5}{8}$ of an acre, and the house covers $\frac{1}{2}$ of it, what fraction of an acre is covered by the house?_____

6. At the track meet, Rick entered 5 sprint contests. If each race was $\frac{1}{4}$ mile long, how many miles did Rick sprint in all?_____

7. The class had $\frac{1}{4}$ of an hour to take a math quiz. Nate used only $\frac{1}{3}$ of the time. What fraction of an hour did Nate use for the quiz?

_____

8. Lisa and Kim live $\frac{3}{8}$ of a mile apart. If they each walked $\frac{1}{2}$ of the way and met in the middle, what part of a mile did each walk?

_____

9. This year's summer vacation was $\frac{1}{6}$ of the year. How many months long was the summer vacation this year?_____

10. Paul's dog was asleep $\frac{2}{3}$ of the day. How many hours was it awake?

_____

Fractions: Multiplication and Division

Solve.

1. $\dfrac{7}{9} \times \dfrac{1}{4} =$ _____

2. $\dfrac{5}{6} \times \dfrac{1}{10} =$ _____

3. $\dfrac{9}{10} \times \dfrac{2}{3} =$ _____

4. $8 \times \dfrac{1}{4} =$ _____

5. $\dfrac{1}{3} \times 15 =$ _____

6. Jaime sat in his chair for $\dfrac{5}{6}$ of an hour. For $\dfrac{1}{3}$ of this time, he worked on this assignment. What fraction of an hour did he work on this assignment?

7. $\dfrac{1}{2} \div \dfrac{1}{5} =$ _____

8. $\dfrac{1}{5} \div \dfrac{1}{2} =$ _____

9. $\dfrac{3}{4} \div \dfrac{3}{8} =$ _____

10. $\dfrac{7}{16} \div \dfrac{4}{7} =$ _____

Learn At Home, Grade 5

Third Quarter Test

Identify the shaded fraction and simplify to lowest terms.

1. _____

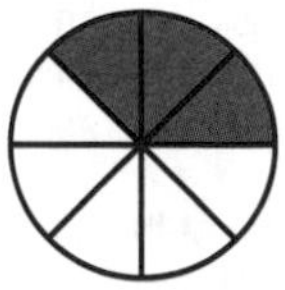

2. _____

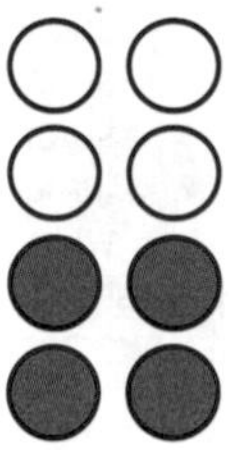

3. _____

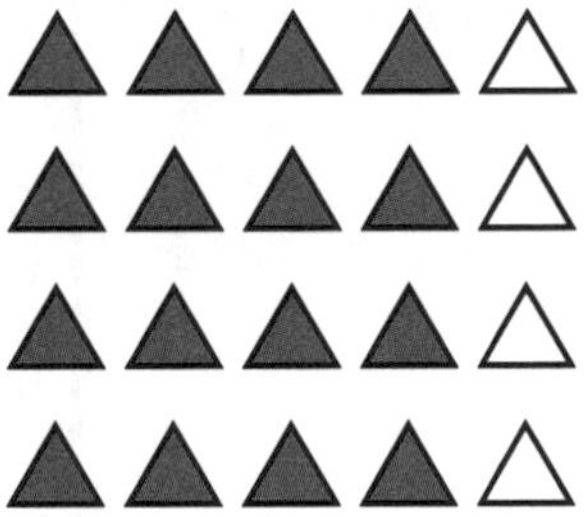

Compare using > or <.

4. $\dfrac{3}{5}$ $\dfrac{4}{5}$

5. $\dfrac{5}{8}$ $\dfrac{5}{11}$

6. 1 $\dfrac{7}{8}$

Add or **subtract**.

7. $\dfrac{1}{9} + \dfrac{5}{9} = $ _____

8. $\dfrac{2}{5} + \dfrac{1}{10} = $ _____

9. $\dfrac{3}{8} + \dfrac{1}{6} = $ _____

10. $3\dfrac{1}{4} + 2\dfrac{1}{3} = $ _____

11. $\dfrac{7}{9} - \dfrac{2}{3} = $ _____

12. $11\dfrac{7}{8} - 4\dfrac{5}{12} = $ _____

13. Change $\dfrac{17}{4}$ into a mixed number. _____

14. Change $3\dfrac{2}{5}$ into an improper fraction. _____

Multiply or **divide**.

15. $\dfrac{3}{4} \times \dfrac{1}{2} = $ _____

16. $\dfrac{11}{12} \times \dfrac{4}{5} = $ _____

17. $\dfrac{2}{3} \div \dfrac{1}{3} = $ _____

18. $\dfrac{1}{2} \div \dfrac{1}{4} = $ _____

	Language Skills	**Spelling**	**Reading**
Monday	**Different Kinds of Writing** Have your child write an imaginative story about how a constellation came to be. *See* Language Skills, Week 28, number 1.	Pretest your child on these spelling words: arrange dance reduce bore divide shake capture explore strange compare give surprise create mend tame crowd promise write Have your child correct the pretest. Add personalized words and make two copies of this week's study list.	**Library Skills** Have your child read chapters 11 and 12 of *Number the Stars*. Ask your child to define *neutrality*. Then, have your child list five topics about which his/her feelings are neutral. Review the organization of the card catalog or the computer index at the library. *See* Reading, Week 28, number 1.
Tuesday	Have your child write a narrative about a personal experience, describing the events in sequential order. Let your child choose whether to write in the first person or in the third person.	Review this week's spelling words. Have your child complete **Serving up Suffixes** (p. 288).	Have your child read chapters 13 and 14 of *Number the Stars*. Then, have him/her write about the symbolic use of the story, "Little Red Riding Hood." Review the Dewey decimal system and call numbers. *See* Reading, Week 28, number 2.
Wednesday	Have your child think of his/her favorite place or favorite thing to do. Then, have him/her write a descriptive paragraph about it. Encourage your child to use all five senses in his/her description.	Have your child use each of this week's spelling words correctly in a sentence.	Have your child read chapters 15 and 16 of *Number the Stars*. Take your child to the library to research Sweden's history of neutrality or to look up the training of guard dogs. While at the library, continue your discussion of the Dewey decimal system. Have your child use the card catalog or computer index to identify call numbers for given topics. **Examples:** koalas, gardening, limericks, organic chemistry, eastern religions, soccer, tangrams, Latin.
Thursday	Have your child write a paragraph that gives detailed directions. Encourage your child to use clear language and to keep the directions simple. *See* Language Skills, Week 28, number 2.	Have your child study this week's spelling words.	Have your child read chapter 17 and the afterword of *Number the Stars*. Have your child complete **You Be the Judge** (p. 289). Return to the library. Design an activity sheet for your child to complete using the card catalog or computer index. Questions should require your child to find books by a certain author, books on a particular subject and specific titles. Then, give your child several books to shelve.
Friday	Have your child write a persuasive paragraph in which he/she tries to convince someone to believe or do something. First, have your child decide whom he/she is trying to persuade and what he/she wants the person(s) to think or do. Then, have your child write a persuasive argument with supporting details to convince the intended audience.	Give your child the final spelling test. Have your child record pretest and final test words in his/her Word Bank.	Choose a final project for your child to complete that will demonstrate his/her understanding of the book *Number the Stars*. See page 13 for book project ideas.

Math	Science	Social Studies
Decimals Decimals are very similar to fractions. *See* Math, Week 28. Demonstrate that decimals are simply fractions with 10, 100 or 1000 in the denominator. Teach your child how to read decimals. *See* Math, Week 28, numbers 1 and 2. Have your child read about decimals in an encyclopedia. Then, have your child look for numbers in the newspaper that are written as decimals.	**Force, Motion and Work** Introduce the science of force, motion and work. A *force* may be a push or pull on an object. Forces create *motion*, which can be used to accomplish *work*. The rate of motion can be affected by friction, gravity and other forces. *See* Science, Week 28, number 1. Have your child add a glossary page on force, motion and work to his/her Science Log. *See* Science, Week 28, number 2.	**Famous Inventors** In addition to being great politicians, Thomas Jefferson and Benjamin Franklin were also creative inventors. Have your child read about their inventions. Have your child draw a picture of Monticello, the home that President Jefferson designed and built. Then, have your child write a paragraph describing some of the unique features of the house.
Make several copies of **Base-Ten Squares** (p. 290). Teach your child how to shade the boxes to represent given decimals. Each base-ten square represents 1, or the whole. The square is then divided into 100 little squares. Each little square represents one hundredth (0.01). Ten little squares (or a bar) make up one tenth (0.1). your child should recognize that this is the same concept as fractions. *See* Math, Week 28, number 3.	Have your child begin a concept map of force, motion and work. Have your child write "force, motion and work" in the center of a large piece of paper and circle it. Then, have him/her draw lines radiating out from the circle for subheadings. Fill in the subheadings and details as you study them in the unit. Key terms might include *gravity, speed, friction, pressure, laws of motion, simple machines* and *compound machines*.	Have your child choose one major invention and write a report about it. The report should include information about the life of the inventor, the need for this invention, how it was conceived, what impact it had and any improvements that have been made on the invention since its inception.
Teach your child to read decimals to the thousandths place. Discuss how large a thousandth would be in the base-ten squares. Ask your child to imagine the size of a thousandth of an inch or a thousandth of a football field. Have your child read aloud some decimals with thousandths: 0.008, 0.032, 0.215, 0.875. Lead your child to discover that digits appearing far to the right of the decimal point represent smaller and smaller numbers.	Have your child look for a definition of *force* in a science textbook or another resource. Demonstrate force and motion with a simple activity. Discuss the different types of force. *See* Science, Week 28, numbers 3 and 4.	Discuss today's inventions. *What sorts of things are people inventing today?* Discuss the fields (science, medicine, etc.) that generate most of today's inventions. *How has the nature of inventing changed since the time of Thomas Edison?* Ask your child to think of a need that is not being met. Have your child design (on paper) an invention that will fill that need. If time permits, your child may even want to try and build his/her invention.
In baseball, batting averages are expressed in decimals to the thousandths place. A batting average is the number of hits divided by the number of times at bat. Gather the batting averages of some of the greatest baseball players of all time. Have your child arrange the averages in order from highest to lowest. Then, ask your child questions that require him/her to add and subtract the averages. This will provide great practice with decimals.	Have your child read about and define the force of gravity. Discuss the contributions of Sir Isaac Newton. The force of *gravity* pulls objects toward the center of the earth. It acts upon objects in motion, causing a change in the object's trajectory. If you throw a ball into the air, the force of gravity pulls the ball downward. Have your child name other examples of the force of gravity (waterfalls, parachuting, skydiving, jumping off a diving board, seesawing).	Discuss the history of transportation. *How have people moved from one location to another over time?* Ask your child to choose one form of transportation (boat/plane/train/car) and research its history. *What did the earliest form look like? When was it invented? Who were the key inventors in its development?* Have your child draw pictures to show the progression of the form of transportation. *What will cars (boats/planes/trains) look like in 20 years?*
Dictate 10–15 number words to your child. Have him/her write each number in decimal form. Use a variety of numbers. **Examples:** *one thousand and eleven hundredths* (1000.11) *seven thousand fifteen and six hundred twenty-five thousandths* (7015.625) *eight tenths* (0.8) Review your child's work immediately and reteach, if necessary.	Investigate gravity with your child. Help him/her perform the experiment described in **Egg Drop** (p. 291). Have your child read about the lack of gravity in space. *Why is this so?*	Arrange for your child to perform some community service.

Learn At Home, Grade 5

 TEACHING SUGGESTIONS AND ACTIVITIES

LANGUAGE SKILLS (Different Kinds of Writing)

▶ 1. Look at pictures of constellations with your child. Name some of the constellations. Stargazers, since the beginning of time, have made pictures by connecting the stars with imaginary lines. Many of the constellation names are accompanied by imaginative stories that explain their origins.

Copy the constellation at right for your child to study. Have your child name the constellation and write an imaginative story about the group of stars.

▶ 2. Have your child follow written directions to complete a drawing.

Example: *Draw a five-inch square in the center of the paper. In the upper right corner of the square, make a circle with a one-inch diameter. Draw a second circle just like it in the upper left corner of the square. Color the circles green. Color the square orange. Write your name below the square.*

Next, have your child write a paragraph giving simple directions. Discuss how to make the directions clear and concise. Follow your child's directions and see if you create the desired results. If your results are different than your child expected, discuss which steps could be written more clearly.

The Constellation Orion

READING (Library Skills)

▶ 1. Spend some time at the library this week. Libraries use a cataloging system to keep track of books and to help you locate books easily. A card catalog contains three sets of cards: subject, title and author cards. Each book in the library is represented by these three cards. A computer index allows you to access books through the same three categories.

▶ 2. The Dewey decimal system is used in many libraries. Call numbers in this system are made up of numbers and letters. The number tells you where in the library the book is found and the letters represent the author's last name. Call numbers are arranged first by number, then by letters. **Example:** 92.1 Ab comes before 92.1 Tr.

000–099	General works (encyclopedias, bibliographies, periodicals, journals)
100–199	Philosophy and related disciplines (philosophy, psychology, logic)
200–299	Religion
300–399	Social Sciences (economics, sociology, law, civics, education, vocations, customs)
400–499	Language (languages, grammar, dictionaries)
500–599	Pure sciences (biology, botany, zoology, chemistry, physics, mathematics, astronomy, geology, paleontology)
600–699	Technology and applied sciences (medicine, engineering, agriculture, home economics, radio, television, aviation, business)
700–799	The arts (painting, music, photography, recreation, architecture, sculpture)
800–899	Literature (novels, plays, poetry, criticism)
900–999	Geography, history and related disciplines

MATH (Decimals)

BACKGROUND

Decimals and fractions are both systems for naming parts of a whole. Use the same models to teach decimals as fractions, but stress that decimal fractions are always a power of 10. Just as numbers to the left of the decimal have place value, so do numbers to the right. The first place to the right of the decimal is the *tenths* place (0.5 = five tenths). The second place to the right is the *hundredths* place (0.03 = three hundredths). The third place to the right is the *thousandths* place (0.008 = eight thousandths). Place value to the right increases infinitely just as it does to the left.

▶ 1. One slice of a pizza that is cut into ten pieces can be represented as $\frac{1}{10}$. This same quantity can be represented in decimal form as 0.1 (read "one tenth"). Five slices of the same pizza can be written as $\frac{5}{10}$ or 0.5 (read "five tenths"). Fractions with 100 parts, such as pennies, are written with a denominator of 100. Seventy-five pennies is $\frac{75}{100}$ of a dollar in fraction form and 0.75 in decimal form. Eight pennies can be written as $\frac{8}{100}$ or 0.08. The placement of the 8 is very important. A misplaced decimal point could change 0.08 ($\frac{8}{100}$) to 0.8 ($\frac{8}{10}$).

Learn At Home, Grade 5

▶ 2. Always read a decimal as a fraction. Read 3.14 as "three and fourteen hundredths," not as "three point fourteen" or "three point one four." Reading the decimal as a fraction reinforces its meaning. Since all decimals are to be read as fractions, they will all end in a *th* sound, as in tenth, hundredth and thousandth. The word *and* is used to separate the whole number from the decimal fraction. Read 214.37 as "two hundred fourteen *and* thirty-seven hundredths." Finally, to reinforce the idea that a decimal is part of a whole, always include a value in the ones place to the left of the decimal point (0.4, not .4).

▶ 3. Have your child color a base-ten square to represent a decimal fraction.

Examples:

0.3 (three tenths)

0.62 (sixty-two hundredths)

Now, have your child try shading these decimals.

0.4	0.7	0.2	0.5	0.43	0.59
0.20	0.54	0.73	0.11	0.99	0.05

SCIENCE (Force, Motion and Work)

▶ 1. Collect pictures of the following for your child to observe: tools, machines, playground equipment, amusement park rides, cars, airplanes, boats, exercise equipment, athletic events and people working. Ask your child to name what is in motion in each picture. Ask your child to name the force that set it in motion. Have your child classify the pictures into those with a strong force and those with a weak force.

▶ 2. Add the following words to this week's spelling list. Have your child look up each word in a dictionary or science resource. Discuss the meaning. Have your child make a glossary of force, motion and work words. Have him/her arrange the entries in alphabetical order and write a definition for each word.

acceleration	gravity	machine	pressure	wedge
force	inclined plane	motion	pulley	weight
friction	laws of motion	pendulum	screw	wheel and axle
fulcrum	lever	power	speed	work

▶ 3. Place a block on a table and push it gently across the surface. Ask your child whether the motion was caused by a push or a pull. Continue pushing until it falls off the table and hits the floor. *What force caused the motion this time?* (pull by gravity to the floor) Have your child then pick up the block from the floor and explain the force used to do this task. Explain that a force can be either a push or a pull. Have your child name the type(s) of force at work in the following situations:

What force is used to throw a baseball? (push)
What force is used to open a door? (pull or push)
What force is used to paddle a boat? (push and pull)
What force is used to raise a window? (push)
What force is used to cut an apple? (push)
What force is used to cut paper with scissors? (push and pull)

▶ 4. Discuss the motion caused by natural forces such as wind, water, ice, volcanoes, earthquakes, tornadoes and hurricanes. What type of motion occurs with these forces? Can the forces be singled out as either pushes or pulls?

Serving up Suffixes

A **suffix** is a group of letters added to the end of a root word to form a new word. When the root word ends in silent **e**, you usually drop the final **e** before adding the suffix.

arrange
bore
capture
compare
create
crowd
dance
divide
explore
give
mend
promise
reduce
shake
strange
surprise
tame
write

Examples: trade **+ ed** = traded
move **+ er** = mover
surprise **+ ing** = surprising

Use the spelling words to **write** the correct root word.

1. comparing _____

2. surprising _____

3. promised _____

4. captured _____

5. dancer _____

6. writing _____

7. stranger _____

8. creating _____

9. shaker _____

10. taming _____

11. arranged _____

12. giving _____

13. bored _____

14. reducing _____

15. divided _____

16. exploring _____

Write the two spelling words you have not used. Then, **write** each one, adding the **ed** and the **ing** endings.

1. _____ _____ _____

2. _____ _____ _____

Brainstorm and list more words to fit the rule.

_____

_____

_____

Learn At Home, Grade 5

You Be the Judge

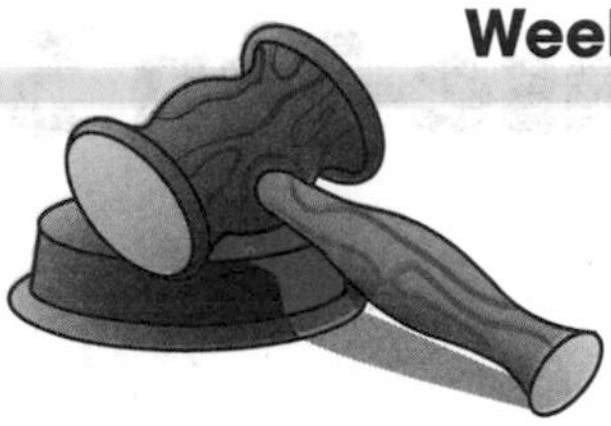

1. Rank these people from 1 to 4, with 1 being the bravest. Explain in one paragraph why you ranked them this way.

   _____ Henrik   _____ Mrs. Rosen   _____ Kirsti   _____ Mama

   _____

   _____

   _____

2. How would you compare this book with the last book you read? How is it similar? How is it different?

   Title of last book: _____

Similar	**Different**
1. _____	1. _____
2. _____	2. _____
3. _____	3. _____

3. **Write** three sentences from different chapters in the book that you believe illustrate the emotion of fear.

   Page no. _____ _____

   _____

   Page no. _____ _____

   _____

   Page no. _____ _____

   _____

4. Argue either for or against this statement: *Number the Stars* is a book written especially for girls because its main character is a girl.

   _____

   _____

   _____

   _____

Egg Drop

Gravity is the force which pulls all objects toward Earth. Some materials can insulate and cushion an object from the impact of gravity. Paper, foam cups, cloth and similar materials are good insulators.

You will need:

Collect as many of these materials as possible before beginning the project: newspaper, foam pieces or "peanuts," pantyhose, pieces of cloth and string. You will also need one or more raw eggs and a shoe box or cardboard carton.

Experiment:

The goal of this experiment is to have an egg survive from the highest possible height. Use the collected packaging materials to protect the egg inside the cardboard carton or shoe box. Be as creative as you can when wrapping the egg. Let an adult hold the package as high as possible or use a ladder to stand on. He/she will drop the package. Check your egg. Did it break? _____

If your egg didn't break the first time, have an adult drop it from a higher point. Did it break this time? _____

From how high do you think the egg can be dropped before it breaks? _____

	Language Skills	Spelling	Reading
Monday	Help your child choose a writing topic for this week's writing assignment. Have your child follow the steps in the writing process as he/she writes independently this week. For more information on the writing process, see page 6. Have your child make a plan for writing, then begin work on the rough draft today.	Pretest your child on these spelling words: attached drawing repeated attended enjoying scalding avoiding escorted scooter builder established seller catcher poster spelling concerned prisoner younger Have your child correct the pretest. Add personalized words and make two copies of this week's study list.	Introduce *The Muffin Fiend* by Daniel Pinkwater. Before reading Pinkwater's book, have your child read about Mozart in a nonfiction source. Have your child read *The Muffin Fiend* up to page 25.
Tuesday	Let your child continue to work independently on his/her writing project. Review writing and grammar skills as the need arises.	Review this week's spelling words. Have your child complete **Searching for Suffixes** (p. 296).	Discuss the story elements so far. Have your child identify the characters, setting and problem. Ask your child to predict the solution to the problem before reading further. Have your child read the rest of *The Muffin Fiend*. Discuss the solution to the problem. How accurate was your child's prediction?
Wednesday	Let your child continue to work independently on his/her writing project.	Have your child use each of this week's spelling words correctly in a sentence.	Discuss what type of literature *The Muffin Fiend* is. *Is it an adventure, biography or mystery? How did the author get his idea for the story?* Discuss the style of writing used by the author. *See* Reading, Week 29. Have your child imitate Pinkwater's writing style to write an original story. Have your child place familiar characters in an outrageous situation.
Thursday	Let your child continue to work independently on his/her writing project.	Have your child study this week's spelling words.	Discuss the style of illustrations in *The Muffin Fiend*. *Why do you think the author and publisher chose this style of drawings?* Have your child continue to work on his/her story. Encourage him/her to add illustrations. Then, have your child revise and edit the story with the help of another.
Friday	Have your child do a final edit and revision of his/her writing project.	Give your child the final spelling test. Have your child record pretest and final test words in his/her Word Bank.	Daniel Pinkwater often writes about outrageous characters or situations. Have your child read other books by the author. (Look in the card catalog for other titles.)

    Learn At Home, Grade 5

Math	Science	Social Studies
Review decimal concepts taught so far, including how to read decimal numbers. Have your child complete **More Puzzling Problems** (p. 297).	Have your child read *Why Doesn't the Earth Fall Up?* by Vicki Cobb. As your child reads, he/she will find the answers to the question in the title, as well as to the "not-so-dumb" questions listed in Science, Week 29, number 1.	**Political and Social Reform** Discuss the meaning of *reform*. *What are some of the issues in the past that have caused people to seek political or social reform? What are some issues today in need of reform? See* Social Studies, Week 29, numbers 1 and 2.
Using models, demonstrate that adding zeros to the right of a decimal does not change the size of the decimal fraction. *See* Math, Week 29, number 1. Have your child write equivalent fractions for decimals. *See* Math, Week 29, number 2.	Have your child read about and define *friction*. Like gravity, friction acts on objects in motion and causes a change in motion. Explore friction with the simple activities and questions found in Science, Week 29, numbers 2 and 3. Have your child create a poster that illustrates and explains the concept of friction.	Have your child do some research on American reformers and their causes. *See* Social Studies, Week 29, number 3.
Teach your child to compare decimal fractions using the > and < signs. *See* Math, Week 29, numbers 3 and 4. Have your child compare pairs of decimals. **Examples:** 0.29 1.29 21.23 21.13 3.54 3.541 Then, have your child name the greatest or least number from groups of three decimals. Have your child complete **Missing Train** (p. 298).	Help your child conduct an experiment on friction. *See* Science, Week 29, number 4. You will need a copy of **Exploring Friction** (p. 299).	Discuss reform as it relates to the Amendments to the Constitution. *Which Amendments were the result of a reform movement? Who were the leaders of these movements?* Have your child copy one of the Amendments to the Constitution and read it carefully. Then, have your child explain, in his/her own words, the significance of that Amendment.
Teach your child to round decimals to a given place. Rounding with decimals is like rounding with whole numbers. If the number is 5 or more, round up. If the number is 4 or less, round down. **Example:** *Round 4.78 to the nearest tenth.* Since 78 is nearly 80, round up to 8 tenths = 4.80 *See* Math, Week 29, number 5. Write several decimals on the chalkboard. Have your child round each to a given place.	Introduce the concept of *speed*. Speed is measured by comparing the distance traveled to the time it takes to go that distance. Help your child discover how fast he/she walks. Measure accurately a mile course. Have your child walk the mile and mark the time with a stopwatch. When finished, have your child determine the number of minutes it took to walk the mile. That is your child's speed. Based on that speed, how long would it take your child to walk 3 miles?	Discuss the work of Martin Luther King, Jr. *See* Social Studies, Week 29, number 4. Have your child create a time line of the major events and accomplishments in the life and work of Martin Luther King, Jr.
It is more likely that your child will need to round a decimal to the nearest whole number than to the hundredths place. The number in the tenths place determines whether to round the number up or down. **Examples:** 45.60 is rounded to 46. 29.29 is rounded to 29. 5.7893 is rounded to 6. 100.00001 is rounded to 100.	Have your child research and read about the fastest Olympic runner, car, animal, etc. He/she may want to look at the *Guinness Book of World Records* to find more interesting speed facts. Have your child compile this information into a chart of "fast facts." Have him/her include two or three illustrations or pictures (from magazines) on the chart as well.	Arrange for your child to perform some community service.

TEACHING SUGGESTIONS AND ACTIVITIES

READING SKILLS (Types of Writing)

Review these different types of writing: expository, descriptive and narrative. *Expository* writing explains or presents information. *Descriptive* writing uses words—especially adjectives—to create vivid images. *Narrative* writing tells a story or recounts an experience. A narrative may be told in the first person or in the third person.

MATH (Decimals)

▶ 1. The decimals 0.3, 0.30 and 0.300 each represent 3 tenths.

Give your child a copy of **Base-Ten Squares** (p. 290). Have him/her shade 0.3. In a separate box, have your child shade 0.30. Compare the two models and discuss. Ask your child to predict what 0.300 would look like. (same) Relate this to fractions: $\frac{3}{10}$ represents the same fraction as $\frac{30}{100}$. One fraction is just the simplified (or reduced) version of the other.

▶ 2. Have your child write an equivalent fraction for each of the given decimal fractions.

Example: $0.45 = \frac{45}{100}$ or $\frac{450}{1000}$ or $\frac{9}{20}$

| 0.5 | 0.9 | 0.34 | 0.03 | 0.125 |
| 0.7 | 0.1 | 0.57 | 0.22 | 0.012 |

▶ 3. To compare decimal fractions, look at one digit at a time.

    a. Start with the whole number. The decimal with the larger whole number is the greater number. **Example:** 3.87 > 1.87 If the whole numbers are the same, move right to the tenths place.

    b. Compare the tenths. The decimal with the larger number in the tenths place is the greater number. **Example:** 5.6 > 5.59 (Check your answer using the base-ten squares.) If the tenths are equal, move right to the hundredths place.

    c. Compare the hundredths. The decimal with the larger number in the hundredths place is the greater number. **Example:** 6.37 > 6.368 If the hundredths are equal, move right to the thousandths place.

    d. Compare the thousandths. The decimal with the larger number in the thousandths place is the greater number. **Example:** 4.235 > 4.231

▶ 4. If your child finds this method confusing, try an alternate method. Because 5.6 > 5.59 can look strange to your child, change the first decimal to an equivalent decimal, 5.60. When the decimals have the same number of digits (5.60 > 5.59), your child can see more easily which number is greater. Clearly, 60 hundredths is greater than 59 hundredths.

▶ 5. Use a base-ten square to demonstrate rounding with decimals. Sketch the given decimal fraction. Have your child study the drawing to decide whether the decimal should be rounded up or down to the given place.

Examples:

Round 0.38 to the nearest tenth

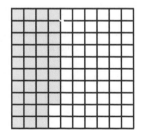

Closer to 0.4

Round 0.22 to the nearest tenth

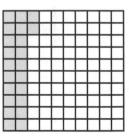

Closer to 0.2

Learn At Home, Grade 5

SCIENCE (Force, Motion and Work)

▶ 1. *Why does a rolling ball stop rolling?*   *Which falls faster, a bowling ball or a marble?*
   Why can't you stand an egg on its end?   *How do we know the Earth is moving when it looks*
   Why doesn't the moon fall to Earth?   *as if the sky is moving?*

▶ 2. Introduce the concept of *friction*. The force of friction causes an object to slow down or stop. Friction can also produce heat. Explore the following examples and ask your child to think of other instances of friction.

     a. Strike a match on a smooth surface, then on a rough surface. Discuss the different reactions.

     b. Have your child examine the soles of different shoes and decide which pair would provide the best traction on a slippery sidewalk.

     c. Collect several advertisements for car and truck tires. Have your child look for statements about the tires that are best for snow or wet roads.

     d. Have your child describe the method of stopping on a bicycle, skateboard or skis.

▶ 3. Discuss the answers to the following questions:

     Could you walk easily without friction?
   How is the heat from friction in an automobile engine controlled?
   Look at stones found in a river or on a lakeshore. What caused the rocks to become smooth and rounded?

▶ 4. Obtain a spring balance that is used to measure force. Have your child explore the amount of force necessary to pull the same object across different surfaces. Discuss why this is a significant experiment in the study of friction. Before the experiment, have your child predict which surface will create the most friction for the object. After completing the experiment described on **Exploring Friction** (p. 299), ask your child to ponder the following questions:

     What else could be done to make the movement of an object across a surface easier?
   Why is the ice on an ice rink scraped and swept after a lot of use?
   Have you ever slid down a water slide or a metal slide? Which slide goes more easily?
   Why is sand spread on icy bridges and roads in the winter?
   Why are ball bearings used in many machine parts?

SOCIAL STUDIES (Political and Social Reform)

▶ 1. The American Revolution was the first American act of political and social reform. The colonists were very unhappy with the influence of Britain. *Who were some of the important reformers of the American Revolution? Who were some of the important reformers of the Civil War?*

▶ 2. Discuss the methods of social and political reform. *What methods are most effective in bringing about change? What are some non-violent methods of protest? What are some violent methods?*

▶ 3. Have your child choose two leaders of social or political reform to research. Using a Venn diagram or other graphic organizer, have your child compare the two leaders. Repeat this exercise with two other leaders.

Jane Addams	Samuel Gompers	Muckrakers (a group)
Susan B. Anthony	Jesse Jackson	Ralph Nader
Amelia Bloomer	Mary Harris Jones	Carry Nation
Carrie Catt	Martin Luther King, Jr.	Rosa Parks
Cesar Chavez	John L. Lewis	Eleanor Roosevelt
Frederick Douglass	Horace Mann	Elizabeth Cady Stanton
W. E. B. Du Bois	Thurgood Marshall	Gloria Steinem
Betty Friedan	Lucretia Mott	Harriet Tubman

▶ 4. Martin Luther King, Jr., is probably one of the best-known American reformers. He led the fight for civil rights in the 1950s and 1960s. His actions were probably the most significant factor in the passage of the Civil Rights Act. Read about the Civil Rights Act of 1964. Discuss the difference between an act and an amendment. Have your child identify amendments to the Constitution that address civil rights.

Searching for Suffixes

This group of spelling words has the same suffixes used in Week 28, but these suffixes were added without any changes to the root words.

attached
attended
avoiding
builder
catcher
concerned
drawing
enjoying
escorted
established
poster
prisoner
repeated
scalding
scooter
seller
spelling
younger

Examples: clean + **ed** = cleaned
clean + **er** = cleaner
clean + **ing** = cleaning

Exception: When a word ends in a single consonant preceded by a short vowel, the consonant is usually doubled before adding a suffix that begins with a vowel.

Examples: sit + **t** + **ing** = sitting
pad + **d** + **ed** = padded

Write each spelling word in the appropriate category.

Root + er	Root + ing
1. _____	1. _____
2. _____	2. _____
3. _____	3. _____
4. _____	4. _____
5. _____	5. _____
6. _____	
7. _____	

Root + ed

1. _____
2. _____
3. _____
4. _____
5. _____
6. _____

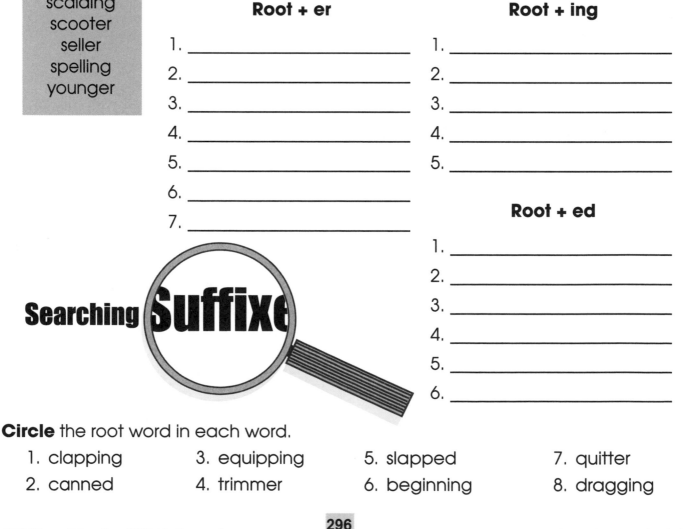
Searching **Suffixe**

Circle the root word in each word.

1. clapping
2. canned
3. equipping
4. trimmer
5. slapped
6. beginning
7. quitter
8. dragging

Learn At Home, Grade 5

Across

3. 7.333 = seven and three hundred thirty-three _____
5. 67.02 = sixty-seven and _____ hundredths
6. 490.1 = four hundred _____ and one tenth
7. 0.512 = five _____ twelve thousandths
9. 8.06 = eight and _____ hundredths
10. 0.007 = _____ thousandths
12. 11.3 = _____ and three tenths
13. 300.12 = _____ hundred and twelve hundredths
15. 62.08 = sixty-two and _____ hundredths
18. 70.009 = _____ and nine thousandths
19. 9.3 = _____ and three tenths
20. 10.51 = _____ and fifty-one hundredths
21. 1,000.02 = one thousand and two __

Down

1. 6.5 = six and five _____
2. 0.428 = four hundred _____ thousandths
3. 8,100.1 = eight _____ one hundred and one tenth
4. 3.02 = three and two _____
8. 0.685 = six hundred _____ thousandths
11. 50. 19 = fifty and _____ hundredths
14. 0.015 = _____ thousandths
16. 430.7 = four hundred thirty and seven _____
17. 73.4 = seventy-three and four _____

Missing Train

Circle the . . .

1.	smallest number	0.31 (A)	0.05 (F)	0.20 (R)
2.	greatest number	0.001 (R)	0.137 (O)	0.100 (A)
3.	greatest number	9.910 (L)	9.010 (C)	9.909 (T)
4.	smallest number	0.110 (A)	0.09 (L)	0.3 (R)
5.	greatest number	0.090 (S)	0.10 (P)	0.12 (O)
6.	smallest number	0.131 (H)	0.2 (T)	0.08 (W)
7.	greatest number	1.310 (E)	1.03 (H)	1.33 (T)
8.	smallest number	2.001 (H)	2.9 (F)	2.010 (A)
9.	greatest number	0.3 (E)	0.03 (A)	0.003 (R)
10.	greatest number	1.01 (U)	1.001 (R)	1.1 (T)
11.	greatest number	3.04 (R)	3.009 (U)	3.039 (N)
12.	smallest number	6.01 (A)	6.11 (C)	6.030 (O)
13.	greatest number	0.001 (T)	0.100 (C)	0.090 (N)
14.	smallest number	1.027 (K)	1.270 (R)	1.207 (P)
15.	smallest number	9.909 (N)	9.09 (G)	9.009 (S)

Fill in the circled letters to solve the riddle below.

How do you search for a missing train?

___ ___ ___ ___ ___ ___ ___ ___ ___   ___ ___ ___ ___ ___ ___
 1   2   3   4   5   6   7   8   9   10 11 12 13 14 15

Learn At Home, Grade 5

Exploring Friction

Friction is the force that keeps some things from moving or slows them down when they do move. Friction is present when surfaces touch one another. The amount of friction depends on the kinds of materials that are touching, how smooth their surfaces are and how much force presses the two surfaces together.

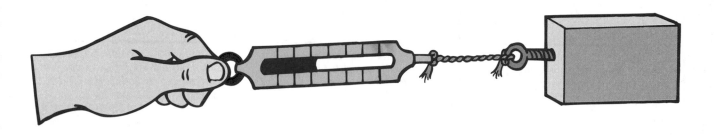

You will need: string, a screw eye, a block of wood and a spring balance

Experiment:

You will measure the amount of force needed to overcome the friction created by the block of wood on different surfaces. You will be measuring in Newtons (N). The greater the amount of friction created by a surface, the greater the force needed to overcome it. Screw the screw eye into the block. Attach one end of the string to the screw eye on the block of wood and the other to the hook on the spring balance. Put the block on its side on a smooth tabletop and pull evenly on your spring balance until the block moves. Keep pulling so that the block of wood moves at the same speed across the table for each surface. Your parent can take a reading from the spring balance. **Write** this quantity in the chart. Repeat the procedure for each surface listed. Hint: When using marbles, place books around the area to keep them from scattering.

Surface	Amount of Force Needed to Overcome Friction (N)
Aluminum foil	
Marbles	
Sandpaper	
Smooth tabletop	

Does sliding or rolling create more friction? _____

	Language Skills	**Spelling**	**Reading**
Monday	Help your child choose a writing topic for this week's writing assignment. Have your child follow the steps in the writing process as he/she writes independently this week. For more information on the writing process, see page 6. Have your child make a plan for writing, then begin work on the rough draft today.	Pretest your child on these spelling words: apply country lily boundary dairy marry canary enemy memory century factory pity city grocery reply company hobby worry Have your child correct the pretest. Add personalized words and make two copies of this week's study list.	Introduce *The Trumpet of the Swan* by E. B. White. Have your child read chapters 1 and 2. Have your child start a daybook of his/her own. After reading each day, have your child write about what he/she read and formulate a question about the story.
Tuesday	Let your child continue to work independently on his/her writing project. Review writing and grammar skills as the need arises.	Review this week's spelling words. Have your child complete **Simplifying Suffixes** (p. 304).	Ask your child to consider the character of Sam. Work with your child to complete a character web for Sam Beaver. *See* Reading, Week 30, number 1. Have your child read chapters 3 and 4 of *The Trumpet of the Swan*. Then, have your child write in his/her daybook.
Wednesday	Let your child continue to work independently on his/her writing project. Have your child proofread what he/she has written so far, using proofreading symbols. *See* Reading, Week 30, number 2.	Have your child use each of this week's spelling words correctly in a sentence.	**Proofreading:** Have your child read chapters 5 and 6 of *The Trumpet of the Swan*. Then, have your child write in his/her daybook. Teach your child formal proofreading symbols. *See* Reading, Week 30, number 2.
Thursday	Let your child continue to work independently on his/her writing project.	Have your child study this week's spelling words.	Have your child read chapters 7 and 8 of *The Trumpet of the Swan*. Then, have your child write in his/her daybook. Give your child a copy of the proofreading symbol chart, as well as a copy of **Tim Burr, Tall Tale Hero** (p. 305). Have your child read the story and mark corrections using the appropriate symbols from the chart. Help your child get started by reviewing the necessary writing skills noted at the top of the page.
Friday	Have your child do a final edit and revision of his/her writing project.	Give your child the final spelling test. Have your child record pretest and final test words in his/her Word Bank.	Have your child read chapters 9 and 10 of *The Trumpet of the Swan*. Then, have your child write in his/her daybook. Ask him/her to answer the following question: *Is Louis's problem solved?*

Math	Science	Social Studies
Teach your child how to convert decimals to fractions and fractions to decimals. *See* Math, Week 30, numbers 1 and 2. Have your child complete **Decimal Delight** (p. 306).	**Laws of Motion** Sir Isaac Newton formulated the laws of motion that inform modern scientific thought. Introduce and explain Newton's first law of motion: *An object at rest tends to remain at rest, and an object in motion tends to remain in motion unless acted on by a force. See* Science, Week 30, number 1. Have your child write about a time he/she experienced Newton's first law of motion first-hand.	Introduce your child to *Bartlett's Familiar Quotations.* Turn to quotations by Martin Luther King, Jr. Have your child read some of the quotations aloud. Discuss the meaning of each quotation and the context in which King was speaking. Have your child choose one of the quotations from Martin Luther King, Jr. to analyze. Have your child describe in writing King's meaning and its significance in today's world.
Review concepts related to decimals discussed so far. Give your child various problems to check his/her understanding of rounding, comparing, writing and reading decimals, as well as converting decimals to fractions.	Introduce and explain Newton's second law of motion: *The acceleration of an object depends upon the size and direction of the force acting on it and the mass of the object. See* Science, Week 30, numbers 2 and 3. Have your child define *acceleration* in his/her Science Log.	**Women Leaders:** Discuss the women's suffrage movement. *See* Social Studies, Week 30, number 1. Have your child write a paragraph explaining why women were not allowed to vote in colonial times.
Quiz your child on his/her understanding of decimals. Have your child complete **Decimals** (p. 307). Reteach any concepts if necessary.	Help your child conduct the experiment described on **Come-Back Can** (p. 309).	Brainstorm a list of famous American women with your child. *See* Social Studies, Week 30, number 2. Provide appropriate resource materials so that your child can look up each woman's name and read about her. Have your child group the women by the type of influence they (have) had on society (musical, social, political, literary, etc.).
Teach your child how to add and subtract decimals. First, line up the decimals. *This is very important!* Then, starting with the decimal place furthest to the right, add or subtract. Add, subtract and regroup just as you would any other addition or subtraction problem. The decimal point carries down into the answer. **Examples:** $\begin{array}{r} 23.678 \\ + 32.356 \\ \hline 56.034 \end{array}$ $\begin{array}{r} 4.89 \\ + 34.2 \\ \hline 39.09 \end{array}$ $\begin{array}{r} 7.0 \\ - 4.68 \\ \hline 2.32 \end{array}$	Introduce and explain Newton's third law of motion: *For every action, there is an equal and opposite reaction. See* Science, Week 30, number 4. Help your child conduct an experiment with a balloon. *See* Science, Week 30, number 5. Have your child explain the third law of motion through a diagram of the balloon experiment.	Have your child write about the life and work of one famous American woman. Encourage your child to explain his/her reasons for choosing that particular woman.
Let your child practice adding and subtracting with decimal fractions. Have your child complete **Blast Off!** (p. 308).	Introduce and demonstrate the concept of a *pendulum.* Help your child design, then carry out, another experiment to investigate the behavior of a pendulum. *See* Science, Week 30, numbers 6 and 7.	Arrange for your child to perform some community service.

TEACHING SUGGESTIONS AND ACTIVITIES

READING (Proofreading)

▶ 1. Help your child make a character web for Sam Beaver. Have your child write Sam's name in the center of a sheet of paper. Then, have your child draw a circle around Sam's name and draw spokes radiating from the circle. At the end of each spoke, have your child write words that describe Sam. From each of those words, your child may write more details about Sam.

▶ 2. Explain that even professional writers often have other people proofread their writing to check for mistakes in grammar, capitalization, spelling and punctuation. Special types of proofreading marks are used to point out mistakes. Discuss the meaning of each symbol shown and when to use it.

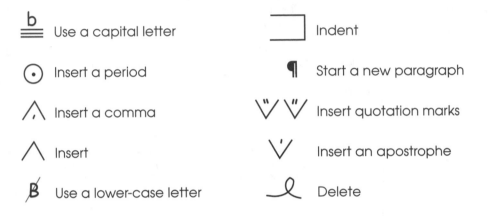

b̲ Use a capital letter	⌐ Indent
⊙ Insert a period	¶ Start a new paragraph
⋏ Insert a comma	∨ ∨ Insert quotation marks
⋀ Insert	∨ Insert an apostrophe
ß Use a lower-case letter	ℓ Delete

MATH (Decimals and Fractions)

▶ 1. To convert a decimal to a fraction, remove the decimal point and write the decimal over a power of 10. If the decimal goes to the tenths place, place it over 10; if the decimal goes to the thousandths place, place it over 1000. Reduce the fraction to lowest terms.
Examples: $0.45 = \frac{45}{100} = \frac{9}{20}$ $0.007 = \frac{7}{1000}$

▶ 2. To convert a fraction to a decimal, divide the numerator by the denominator. Teach your child where to place the decimal. Have your child use a calculator to convert fractions to decimals after practice.
Examples: $\frac{45}{100} = 45 \div 100 = 0.45$ $\frac{3}{8} = 3 \div 8 = .375$

SCIENCE (Laws of Motion)

▶ 1. Have your child look around the classroom and name objects at rest (books, an aquarium, a chair, a table). Those objects will remain at rest until some force acts upon them. Have your child name some forces that could move these objects. Ask your child to recall a time riding in a car when the brakes were applied quickly. Have your child describe what happened and explain how that experience was related to Newton's first law of motion.

▶ 2. Have your child describe the motion of a car on a roller coaster. Discuss the following:
Is the car moving when you board? (No, the engine must *push* it.)
How fast does the car move at first? (It must *accelerate* to start moving.)
Does the car move fast when it first climbs an incline? (The force of gravity pulls in the opposite direction and the car begins to decelerate.)
What happens to the car when it reaches the top of the first incline? (Gravity pulls in the same direction the car is moving so the car accelerates.)
What force finally brings the car to a stop? (Applying brakes creates friction, causing the car to stop.)

Learn At Home, Grade 5

3. Have your child name and describe other examples of Newton's second law of motion, in which objects accelerate or decelerate (skiing, skating, sledding, riding a bicycle, running).

4. Whenever you apply force to an object, the object applies the same amount of force back. When you lift a weight, you are pulling on the weight. The weight is also pulling on you. You can tell it is pulling on you because it feels heavy. When a rifle expels a bullet, the recoil of the gun is the opposite force.

5. Have your child conduct an experiment outside the classroom to investigate Newton's third law of motion. You will need only a balloon.
   a. Inflate the ballon with 5 deep breaths of air.
   b. Pinch the neck of the balloon with your fingers. Hold the balloon over your head and release.
   c. Observe the motion and path of the balloon as it deflates.
   d. Repeat steps a–c, using 10 deep breaths of air to inflate the balloon.
   e. Repeat steps a–c, using 15 deep breaths of air to inflate the balloon.

   Have your child describe the differences in the motion and path of the balloon in each trial. Can he/she describe the force and the opposite force demonstrated in the experiment?

6. Tie a metal washer to a long string. Have your child observe and describe the motion that results when you grasp the string 10 cm from the washer and swing the washer back and forth. Then, have your child observe and describe the differences in the swinging pendulum as you increase the length of the string to 20 cm and 30 cm. *At what length did the pendulum swing the fastest? At what length did the pendulum swing the slowest? What affected the swing of the pendulum?*

7. *You will need:* 5 lengths of string, 5 metal washers, a stopwatch or clock with a second hand and a meterstick
   What to do:
   a. Tie a metal washer to each length of string.
   b. Tie the 5 strings to different positions on the meterstick.
   c. Suspend the meterstick between the backs of two chairs.
   d. Adjust the strings so that no washer touches the floor.
   e. Hold the first washer to one side and release. Note the time or start the stopwatch. Count the number of swings it makes before coming to rest. Record the number of swings on a chart.
   f. Stop the stopwatch or note the time. Record the time on the chart.

Pendulum	Number of swings	Time (seconds)
1		
2		
3		
4		
5		

Repeat steps a–f with the remaining washers. Have your child record each swing count and time on the chart. Have your child write a paragraph analyzing his/her observations. *How did the length of the string affect the number of swings and the time?*

SOCIAL STUDIES (Women Leaders)

1. The women's suffrage movement began in 1848 with Elizabeth Cady Stanton and Lucretia Mott. They held a convention that adopted a *Declaration of Sentiments*. This declaration called for women to have equal rights in education, ownership of property, voting and other areas. Women were not granted the full right to vote in the United States until 1920.

2. Here is a brief list of famous American women:

Madeleine Albright	Helen Hayes	Martina Navratilova
Marian Anderson	Julia Ward Howe	Sandra Day O'Connor
Clara Barton	Billie Jean King	Frances Perkins
Mary McLeod Bethune	Ann Landers	Sally Ride
Elizabeth Blackwell	Belva Lockwood	Cokie Roberts
Mildred Ella Didrikson	Juliette Gordon Low	Eleanor Roosevelt
Amelia Earhart	Barbara McClintock	Betsy Ross

Simplifying Suffixes

When adding a suffix beginning with a vowel to a word that ends in a consonant + **y**, change the **y** to **i** before adding the suffix. An exception to this rule occurs when adding the suffix **ing**.

apply
boundary
canary
century
city
company
country
dairy
enemy
factory
grocery
hobby
lily
marry
memory
pity
reply
worry

Examples:
worry + **es** = worries   copy + **ed** = copied
dry + **ing** = drying   fry + **ing** = frying

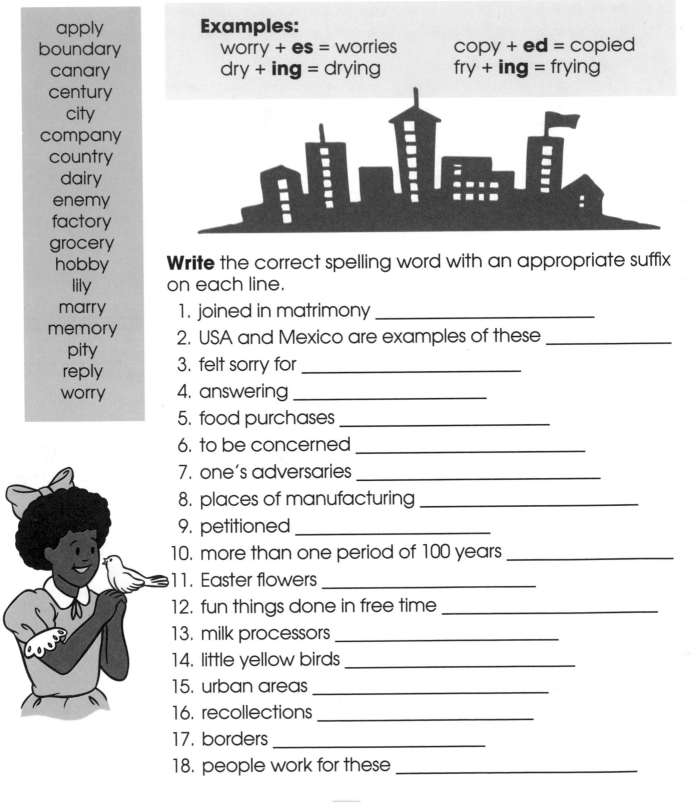

Write the correct spelling word with an appropriate suffix on each line.

1. joined in matrimony _____
2. USA and Mexico are examples of these _____
3. felt sorry for _____
4. answering _____
5. food purchases _____
6. to be concerned _____
7. one's adversaries _____
8. places of manufacturing _____
9. petitioned _____
10. more than one period of 100 years _____
11. Easter flowers _____
12. fun things done in free time _____
13. milk processors _____
14. little yellow birds _____
15. urban areas _____
16. recollections _____
17. borders _____
18. people work for these _____

Learn At Home, Grade 5

Tim Burr, Tall Tale Hero

Read the following tall tale about Tim Burr. Use proofreading marks to edit the paragraphs and correct the sentence fragments. **Write** the quotations correctly. Use proper capitalization and the appropriate homophones.

far up north, in the rugged, wooded regions of canada, their lived the famous lumberjack tim burr. his trusty sidekick, saw mills, lived there to. one day, saw and tim loaded up their axes and set off four the woods. To fell more trees. For the local mill, Log Lagoon. they took along they're pack mules, beauty and beast. they chopped so fast that the trees began falling onto each other. Creating quite a logjam. its knot my fault yelled saw. i can't see where you are cutting.

the problem grew worse. beauty, tim's beloved mule, almost got his tale sliced off. Buy a falling tree trunk. that does it yelled tim angrily when you cut down a tree. call for me. So i no where you are.

saw obeyed tim's wishes. From that day on. as each tree was felled, saw cried "TIM BURR!"

Learn At Home, Grade 5

305

Decimal Delight

Kooky Claude Clod, the cafeteria cook, has some strange ideas about cooking. He does not understand fractions—only decimals. Help Claude convert these measurements to decimals so he can get cooking!

Kooky Soup

Mix together and sauté:

$\frac{9}{20}$ cup minced cat whiskers
$\frac{7}{8}$ cup crushed snails
$\frac{3}{5}$ cup toothpaste
$\frac{3}{4}$ tablespoon vinegar
$\frac{11}{25}$ cup pig slop

Simmer 93$\frac{1}{2}$ days.

Gradually fold in:

$\frac{1}{5}$ teaspoon soot
$\frac{3}{8}$ cup motor oil
$\frac{9}{10}$ tablespoon lemon juice
$\frac{11}{20}$ cup chopped poison ivy
6$\frac{1}{4}$ rotten eggs

Brew for 1,500$\frac{24}{25}$ years. Enjoy!

Mix together and sauté:

_____ cup minced cat whiskers

_____ cup crushed snails

_____ cup toothpaste

_____ tablespoon vinegar

_____ cup pig slop

Simmer _____ days.

Gradually fold in:

_____ teaspoon soot

_____ cup motor oil

_____ tablespoon lemon juice

_____ cup chopped poison ivy

_____ rotten eggs

Brew for _____ years. Enjoy!

Learn At Home, Grade 5

Decimals

1. Write out 36.124 in words. _____

2. Write two hundred thirty-seven and twenty-six hundredths in numerals.

   _____

3. Use > or < to indicate which decimal fraction is greater.

   3.147_____3.205   3.06_____3.059

4. Round 87.658 to the nearest whole number. _____

5. Round 87.658 to the nearest tenth. _____

6. Round 87.658 to the nearest hundredth. _____

7. Write 0.5 as a fraction in lowest terms. _____

8. Write 0.69 as a fraction in lowest terms. _____

9. Write 7.85 as a fraction in lowest terms. _____

10. Draw a model of 0.3.

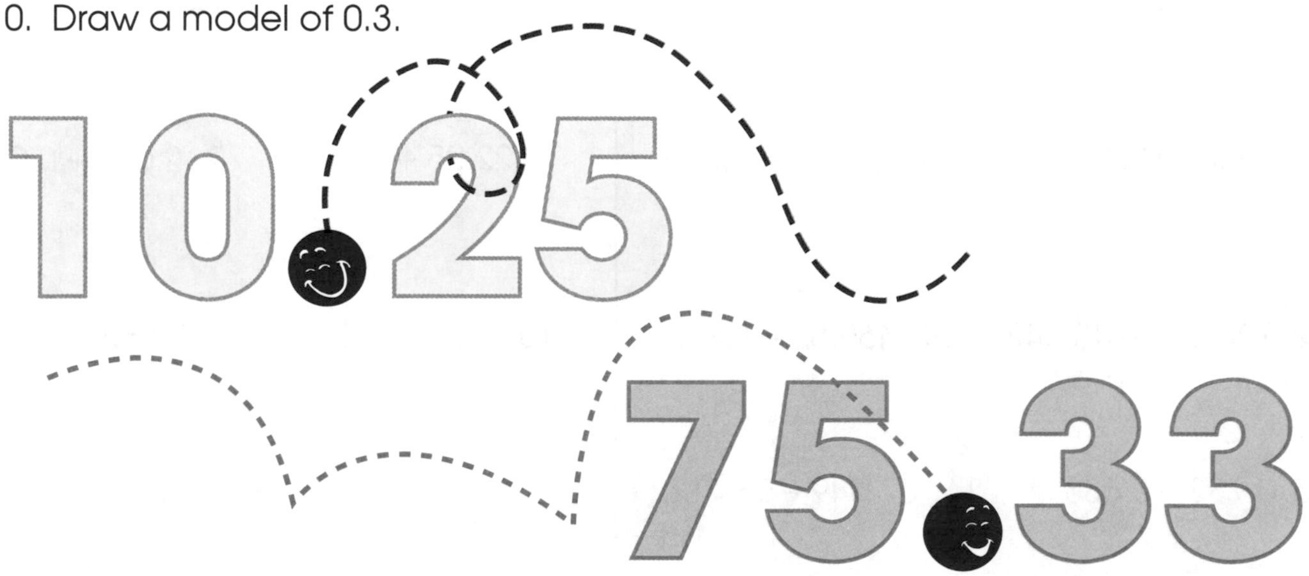

10.25

75.33

Blast Off!

Hint: Decimal points take up their own square. Do not use a zero before the decimal.

Across

3.
   8.237
   − 2.083

4.
   2.23
   − 1.256

5.
   1,376.33
   − 542.13

6. 8.538 − 0.228

8. 3.099 − 2.406

12. 124.107 − 45.642

14. 465.52 − 104.1

15. 0.732 − 0.633

16. 67.549 − 55.412

Down

1.
   33.333
   + 0.896

2.
   2.587
   + 3.191

3.
   5.78
   + 1.09

7. 22.05 + 15.91

9. 2.057 + 0.008

10. 0.531 + .19

11. 7.852 + 1.489

13. 3.012 + 1.025

Learn At Home, Grade 5

Come-Back Can

You will need: a large can with a plastic lid, a compass, 2 long rubber bands, a paper clip, a piece of wire and a bolt

Making the Come-Back Can

With a compass point, punch a hole in the center of the can bottom. Punch another hole in the center of the plastic lid. Feed two long rubber bands through the hole in the bottom of the can. Use a paper clip on the outside of the can to keep the loops of the rubber bands from pulling out. Wrap a piece of wire around a bolt and tie the wire to the center of one of the rubber bands inside the can. Thread the other ends of the rubber bands through the hole in the lid. Use another paper clip to keep these outside loops from pulling out. Snap the lid on the can.

Using the Come-Back Can

Place the can on the floor and roll it away from you. Does it come back? _____

Roll it harder. Does it come all the way back? _____

Roll the can up a ramp or sloping sidewalk.

What happens? _____

Making Hypotheses

Why do you think the can comes back? _____

_____

Can you make the can roll farther, faster or longer? _____

What can you change about the can's design? _____

_____

Try your new design. How does it work? _____

_____

	Language Skills	**Spelling**	**Reading**
Monday	**Research Report** Guide your child through the process of writing a research report this week. First, help your child select a topic. *See* Language Skills, Week 31. Then, take your child to the library to find related research materials. Have your child write a topic sentence to focus the report. The topic sentence is subject to change as your child does more research, but it makes a good place to start.	Pretest your child on these spelling words: approach disagreement groan beaten easel increase blueprint eastern leather boasted feelings needless bread flue peek breath glued reason Have your child correct the pretest. Add personalized words and make two copies of this week's study list.	**Abbreviations** Have your child read chapters 11 and 12 of *The Trumpet of the Swan*. Have your child write in his/her daybook. Teach your child about abbreviations this week. *See* Reading, Week 31, number 1.
Tuesday	Brainstorm questions about the topic with your child. Ask your child what he/she would like to learn about the topic. Have your child write down each question on an index card.	Review this week's spelling words. Have your child complete **Vital Vowel Digraphs** (p. 314).	Send your child searching through the reading book to find answers to these questions: *Who? What? When? Where? Why? How?* Ask your child to find a sentence that answers each question. Have your child read chapters 13 and 14 of *The Trumpet of the Swan*. Ask your child to predict what a night in a hotel will be like for Louis. Have your child write about it in his/her daybook. Continue your discussion of abbreviations. *See* Reading, Week 31, number 2.
Wednesday	Have your child conduct research by looking through the library resources for answers to his/her questions. As your child finds answers, have him/her write them down on the index cards. Remind your child to note which resource contained the answer. If two resources offer conflicting answers, have your child write down both, then look for a third source to confirm one or the other answer.	Have your child use each of this week's spelling words correctly in a sentence.	Have your child read chapters 15 and 16 of *The Trumpet of the Swan*. Have your child write in his/her daybook. Ask your child to name some abbreviations that are commonly used. Then, say a word, such as *road*. Have your child write the abbreviation on the chalkboard. Repeat with other words like *street, negative, mister, doctor, junior, apartment, adverb, corporation, limited, example, ounce, foot, inch, kilometer, teaspoon, quart.*
Thursday	Have your child organize the index cards in a meaningful way. Then, ask your child to think about how he/she will present his/her findings in an interesting report. Have your child begin to make an outline.	Have your child study this week's spelling words.	Have your child read chapters 17 and 18 of *The Trumpet of the Swan*. Have your child write in his/her daybook about the deal the swans make with the zoo. Point to a state on a map. Have your child write its traditional abbreviation and its post office abbreviation. **Example:** Colorado / Colo. / CO Repeat with other states. Can your child list all 50 states' post office abbreviations?
Friday	Following the outline, have your child write a first draft of the research report. Have your child follow the writing process over the next few days, revising, editing and rewriting the report. For more information on the writing process, see page 6.	Give your child the final spelling test. Have your child record pretest and final test words in his/her Word Bank.	Have your child read chapters 17–21 of *The Trumpet of the Swan*. Have your child draw a story map in his/her daybook. The story map should be a detailed list of events from the story. Test your child's knowledge of abbreviations. Have your child write the names of the months and their abbreviations. Then, have him/her write the days of the week and their abbreviations.

Learn At Home, Grade 5

Math	Science	Social Studies
Teach your child how to round decimals to estimate answers to subtraction and addition problems. *See* Math, Week 31, number 1. Write 8–10 addition problems with decimals on the chalkboard. Have your child round each addend to the nearest whole number, then add to estimate the sum of the original problem. Have your child go back and solve the original problems. How accurate were your child's estimates?	**Work** Introduce and explain the term *work*. *See* Science, Week 31, number 1. Your child may think of work simply as a disagreeable task. Make sure your child understands the scientific meaning of work. Have your child list common examples of doing work, such as opening a door, hitting a ball, walking, running, raising a window, flying a kite or pulling a wagon.	**African-American Leaders** Brainstorm a list of famous African Americans with your child. *See* Social Studies, Week 31, number 1. Provide appropriate resource materials so that your child can look up each person's name. Have your child group these Americans by the type of influence they (have) had on society (musical, social, political, literary, religious).
The subtraction sentence $6 - 0.45$ may seem confusing at first. Teach your child to add a decimal point and zeros after the whole number before subtracting a decimal number. **Example:** $6 - 0.45$ $$\begin{array}{r} 6.00 \\ -0.45 \end{array} \qquad \begin{array}{r} \not{5}\ \not{9}\ \not{1}0 \\ 6.00 \\ -0.45 \\ \hline 5.55 \end{array}$$ Have your child complete **Historical Harry** (p. 315).	Have your child create a poster showing different examples of work by animals and people. *See* Science, Week 31, number 2.	Have your child select the famous black musicians from the list generated yesterday. Check out music by these famous Americans from the library. Have your child listen to the music of the different artists. Have your child compare the different types of music. Can he/she hear the influence of earlier musicians on later musicians?
Demonstrate how to multiply two decimal fractions and accurately place the decimal point in the solution. Give your child guided practice with multiplying a 3-digit number by another 3-digit number. *See* Math, Week 31, number 2. Have your child complete **A Multiple Design** (p. 316).	Sports may be fun, but they are also a lot of work. Have your child choose one sport and analyze the different motions involved. Remember that work happens whenever an object is moved. Have your child design a chart or diagram that breaks down the sport into its many distinct motions. *See* Science, Week 31, number 3.	Langston Hughes's poetry is highly visual. Read several of his poems aloud to your child. Ask your child to select one of Hughes's poems to illustrate. Have your child draw a picture inspired by the poem on a 12" x 18" piece of paper. Have your child copy the poem on lined paper and display the drawing with the poem. Ask your child to explain his/her artistic interpretation of the poem.
Show your child how easy it is to multiply a decimal by 10 or 100. To multiply any number by 10, simply move the decimal point one place to the right. **Examples:** $6.3 \times 10 = 63$, $0.29 \times 10 = 2.9$ To multiply any number by 100, move the decimal point two places to the right. **Examples:** $6.3 \times 100 = 630$ $0.29 \times 100 = 29$ Give your child several problems to practice this concept.	Work is measured in *joules*. Force is measured in *newtons*. A newton is the unit of force needed to move one kilogram one meter per second. Have your child push a one-kilogram weight one meter across the floor in one second. your child has moved the weight one newton-meter, or one joule. *See* Science, Week 31, number 4. The *newton* and *joule* were both named after famous scientists. Have your child research these scientists and read about their work.	Obtain U.S. postage stamps that are part of the Black Heritage Series. Each February, a new face is added to the series. Discuss the honor of appearing on a stamp. *See* Social Studies, Week 31, numbers 2 and 3. Have your child design a new stamp to honor and commemorate a famous African American. Have your child write a paragraph telling why he/she chose to honor that person.
Demonstrate how to divide a decimal fraction by a whole number. *See* Math, Week 31, number 3. Have your child complete **The Perfect Sweet-Treat Solution** (p. 317).	Introduce and explain the term *machine*. *See* Science, Week 31, number 5. Have your child name several machines in your home and classroom.	Arrange for your child to perform some community service.

TEACHING SUGGESTIONS AND ACTIVITIES

LANGUAGE SKILLS (Research Report)

Let your child choose a topic for research. Offer your support and suggestions, but let your child decide. If your child is allowed to choose the topic, he/she will have more invested in the research process. Discuss your child's interests. Ask him/her to recall an interesting book. Go to the nonfiction section of your children's library for a wealth of books on any topic. Have fun narrowing the search. Research skills must be taught, so guide your child along the way. It is also important that your child knows who the audience for his/her work will be from the start.

READING (Abbreviations)

▶ 1. Explain that initials are a special kind of abbreviation in which letters represent names of people, businesses, athletic teams, schools, government agencies and publications. Ask your child to name some people, places or things that are often called by their initials rather than their full names. Have your child find examples of initials in books and in the newspaper.

▶ 2. Print the initials and words below on separate index cards. Have your child match each set of initials with the words it represents.

NBA	National Basketball Association	YMCA	Young Men's Christian Association
ABC	American Broadcasting Companies	CNN	Cable News Network
VCR	videocassette recorder	FDA	Food and Drug Administration
FDR	Franklin Delano Roosevelt	GM	General Motors
GE	General Electric	NAACP	National Association for the
BA	Bachelor of Arts		Advancement of Colored People
CPA	Certified Public Accountant	RSVP	répondez s'il vous plaît
USA	United States of America	VFW	Veterans of Foreign Wars
SEC	Securities Exchange Commission	BBC	British Broadcasting Company
BLT	bacon, lettuce and tomato	CD	compact disc
FBI	Federal Bureau of Investigation	UN	United Nations
NAFTA	North American Free Trade Alliance	NFL	National Football League
PO	post office	FCC	Federal Communications Commission

MATH (Decimals)

▶ 1. To estimate addition and subtraction of decimal fractions, first round to the nearest whole number. Then, add or subtract as usual.

Examples:

$$\begin{array}{r} 34.256 \\ + 22.511 \end{array} \qquad \begin{array}{r} \mathbf{34} \\ \mathbf{+ 23} \\ \hline \mathbf{57} \end{array} \qquad \begin{array}{r} 25.68 \\ - 13.22 \end{array} \qquad \begin{array}{r} \mathbf{26} \\ \mathbf{- 13} \\ \hline \mathbf{13} \end{array}$$

▶ 2. The process of multiplying decimals is the same as with multiplication of whole numbers, with the addition of one step. This additional step involves counting the number of decimal places in the problem and including the same number of decimal places in the solution. (The same number of digits follow the decimal point in the solution as follow the decimal points in the problem.)

To help your child understand the placement of the decimal point in the solution, think about how the equation is related to fractions.

Example: $0.\underline{1} \times 0.\underline{1} = \frac{1}{10} \times \frac{1}{10} = \frac{1}{100} = 0.\underline{01}$
(1 place + 1 place = 2 places)

▶ 3. Decimal division is basically identical to whole number division with a few modifications. One modification is that in decimal division, you always place a decimal point in the quotient **before** you begin division. The decimal point in the quotient is placed directly above the decimal point in the divisor. Divide as usual with the decimal in place. Show your child an example on the chalkboard. **Example:** $72.6 \div 3$.

Learn At Home, Grade 5

SCIENCE (Work)

▶ 1. Ask your child to come up with an original definition of *work*. Discuss the many meanings of the term: "work of art," "musical work," one's profession, homework, waterworks, etc. Explain that the scientific definition of work is *the result of a force which moves an object through a distance*. Work happens when an object is moved. The mathematical formula for this is **Work = force x distance**.

▶ 2. Have your child create a poster depicting different examples of work done by animals or people. Provide a large sheet of poster board, glue, scissors and old magazines or catalogs. Have your child collect a variety of pictures, then categorize the pictures into themes or topics, such as animals at work on a farm, animals at work in a circus, sports activities, manual labor, working with tools or machines, working with a hobby, working on an art project, working in a laboratory, working in a medical field, working in the military and working on a television or movie set.

▶ 3. Have your child analyze the work involved in one of the following sports: football, basketball, baseball, volleyball, tennis, bowling, golf, racing, rowing, throwing a shot or javelin, high jumping, skydiving, hang gliding, ice skating, skateboarding, soccer, weightlifting or fishing. Have your child list the forces used and the objects moved through a distance in each sport.

▶ 4. **Work = force x distance.** If an object is moved 5 meters using 4 newtons of force, the amount of work done is 20 joules.

▶ 5. A *machine* is a device that changes the amount of force required to do work. A wheel is a machine—it makes moving objects easier by decreasing the amount of force necessary to move them. Have your child imagine how the wheel was first invented by someone. Have your child look around the classroom and name some devices that would be classified as machines (pencil sharpener, scissors, paper punch, tape dispenser, aquarium pump, water faucet, blind pulls, curtain pulls, vacuum cleaner, computer, printer, paper shredder, etc.). Have your child list the work done by each machine and describe how the work might be done without the help of the machine. Explain the role of electrical energy in the creation and use of many new machines (electric drill vs. manual drill).

SOCIAL STUDIES (African-American Leaders)

▶ 1. Here is a brief list of famous African-Americans:

Henry Aaron	Ralph Bunche	Langston Hughes	Sidney Poitier
Muhammad Ali	George W. Carver	Scott Joplin	Colin Powell
Louis Armstrong	Shirley Chisholm	Michael Jordan	Paul Robeson
Arthur Ashe	Bill Cosby	Coretta Scott King	Jackie Robinson
James Baldwin	Benjamin O. Davis	Spike Lee	Booker T. Washington
Benjamin Banneker	Martin Delany	Joe Louis	Phillis Wheatley
Mary McLeod Bethune	Ella Fitzgerald	James Meredith	Roy Wilkins
Thomas Bradley	Alex Haley	Jesse Owens	Oprah Winfrey

▶ 2. The Black Heritage Series of stamps is called commemorative stamps. Artists submit designs for the stamps. Their designs are carefully studied and a selection is made each year. Show your child a full page of commemorative stamps. Point out the printed information that is sometimes given on the margins or on the backs of the blocks of stamps. Ask at your local post office for the names of people represented in the Black Heritage Series. Have your child draw three stamps (like the sample to the right) and write three facts about the person in the margin.

▶ 3. Have your child find out about the Spingarn Medal—who has received it and why. Have your child look up any names of these medal winners that are unfamiliar and read about their lives and work.

313

Vital Vowel Digraphs

Vowel Digraph are two vowels together that make only one vowel sound. Generally, the vowel digraphs below carry the following sounds:

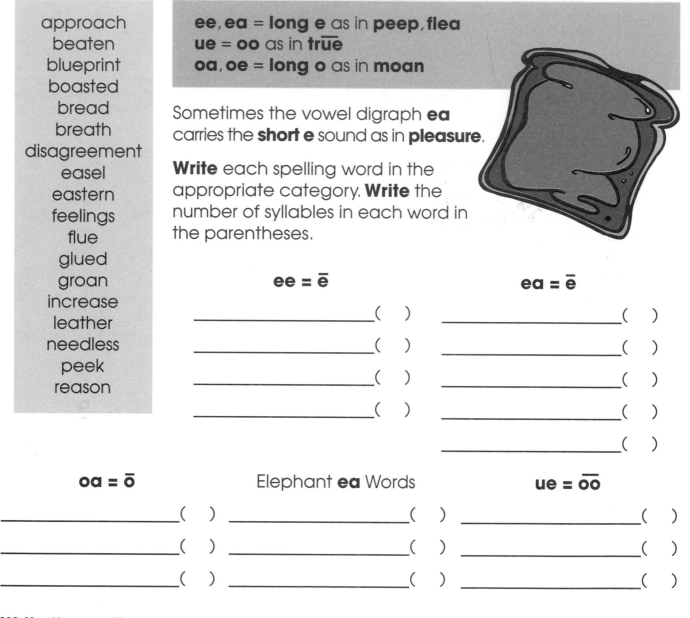

approach
beaten
blueprint
boasted
bread
breath
disagreement
easel
eastern
feelings
flue
glued
groan
increase
leather
needless
peek
reason

ee, ea = long e as in **peep, flea**
ue = oo as in **trūe**
oa, oe = long o as in **moan**

Sometimes the vowel digraph **ea** carries the **short e** sound as in **pleasure**.

Write each spelling word in the appropriate category. **Write** the number of syllables in each word in the parentheses.

ee = ē

_____ ( )
_____ ( )
_____ ( )
_____ ( )

ea = ē

_____ ( )
_____ ( )
_____ ( )
_____ ( )
_____ ( )

oa = ō

_____ ( )
_____ ( )
_____ ( )

Elephant ea Words

_____ ( )
_____ ( )
_____ ( )

ue = oo

_____ ( )
_____ ( )
_____ ( )

Write the spelling word that is a compound.

_____

Write the eight spelling words that contain either a prefix or a suffix.

_____ _____ _____ _____

_____ _____ _____ _____

Historical Harry

What were the large cannons that were used by Germany in World War I?
Solve the following subtraction problems and find the answers in the cannon.
Write the corresponding letter above the problem's number at the bottom of
the page to spell out the answer to this historical trivia question.

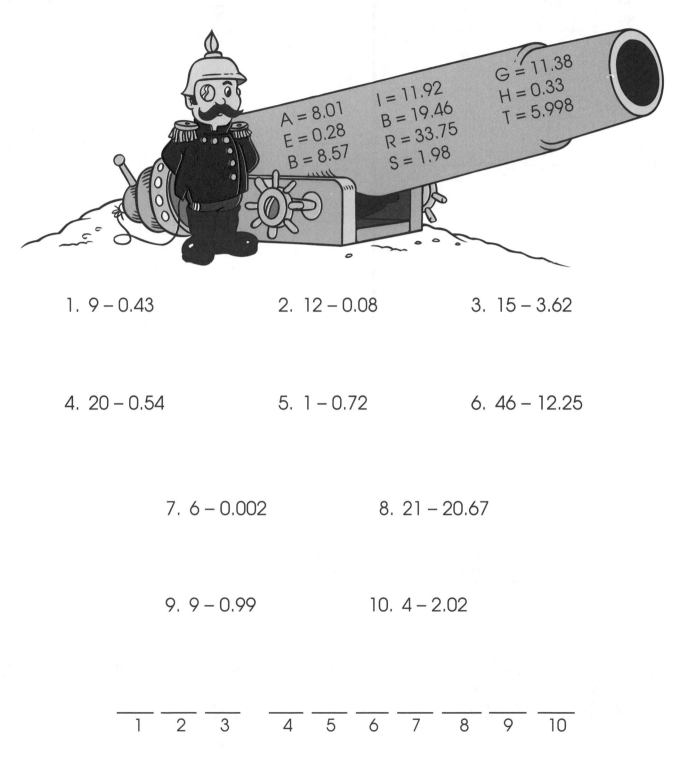

A = 8.01
E = 0.28
B = 8.57
I = 11.92
B = 19.46
R = 33.75
S = 1.98
G = 11.38
H = 0.33
T = 5.998

1. 9 – 0.43

2. 12 – 0.08

3. 15 – 3.62

4. 20 – 0.54

5. 1 – 0.72

6. 46 – 12.25

7. 6 – 0.002

8. 21 – 20.67

9. 9 – 0.99

10. 4 – 2.02

___ ___ ___   ___ ___ ___ ___ ___ ___ ___
 1   2   3   4   5   6   7   8   9   10

Learn At Home, Grade 5

A Multiple Design

Solve the problems on a separate sheet of paper. Find the answers in the design and **color** correctly.

green	blue	red
0.463	28.5	6.51
x 82	x 7.4	x 6.9

yellow	purple	purple
39.2	7.54	0.670
x 0.36	x 0.43	x 0.94

yellow	yellow	purple
64.9	0.592	7.46
x 3.26	x 40.6	x 5.9

Design figure contains the numbers:
80.845, 8.528, 0.8820, 5.42528, 37.966, 3.2422, 14.112, 11.712, 709.878, 163.452, 50.215, 14.2691, 211.574, 0.62980, 22.2180, 44.919, 57.288, 24.0352, 44.014, 2759.88, 24.5802, 2.8560, 210.90, 21.9064

green	blue	blue	green	purple
92.4	32.8	85.1	7.32	6.05
x 0.62	x 0.26	x 0.95	x 1.6	x 8.3

green	blue	yellow	red	red
3.27	5.56	80.5	5.77	95.8
x 844	x 3.94	x 0.276	x 4.26	x 7.41

red	yellow	yellow	yellow	yellow
0.784	2.57	29.3	6.80	0.245
x 6.92	x 63.6	x 0.487	x 0.42	x 3.6

Learn At Home, Grade 5

The Perfect Sweet-Treat Solution

Solve each division problem on a separate sheet of paper. **Draw** a line from the popcorn (problem) to the correct drink (answer).

$3\overline{)7.95}$

6.84

$11\overline{)3.322}$

$5\overline{)0.31}$

2.65

0.905

$9\overline{)2.196}$

0.395

0.302

$2\overline{)0.016}$

$7\overline{)47.88}$

0.063

$5\overline{)11.4}$

0.244

$4\overline{)15.48}$

1.135

$8\overline{)7.24}$

0.008

3.87

2.28

$8\overline{)0.504}$

0.062

$6\overline{)6.81}$

$2\overline{)0.79}$

Learn At Home, Grade 5

	Language Skills	**Spelling**	**Reading**
Monday	Allow your child to continue working on the research report from last week. Once finished, have your child decide how to present the information. He/she could read the report to an audience, build a diorama, make a poster to accompany the report, perform a puppet show, create an illustrated book or even express the information through a poem or song. Let your child decide today how he/she would like to present the information.	Pretest your child on these spelling words: believe, lie, retrieve, brief, perceive, shield, died, piece, shriek, eight, pies, siege, freight, receive, sleigh, leisure, reign, vein. Have your child correct the pretest. Add personalized words and make two copies of this week's study list.	Introduce *Where the Red Fern Grows* by Wilson Rawls. *See* Reading, Week 32, number 1 for a short biography of the author. Have your child read chapters 1 and 2 of *Where the Red Fern Grows*. Have your child locate the Ozark Mountains in northeast Oklahoma and the Illinois River. Have your child imagine how he/she would go about raising $75 for something he/she wanted very badly.
Tuesday	Review the format for a bibliography. Have your child make a bibliography of all the resources used in writing the report. Make arrangements for your child to present his/her research tomorrow. Reserve space if your child wishes to display something or invite people over for a performance. Discuss the arrangements with your child.	Review this week's spelling words. Have your child complete **More Vowel Digraphs** (p. 323).	**Bibliography:** Have your child read chapters 3 and 4 of *Where the Red Fern Grows*. Ask your child: *Is it better to earn something than to have it given to you? Explain your answer.* Have your child read about Daniel Boone in an encyclopedia or other resource. Then, teach your child how to list the book in a bibliography. *See* Reading, Week 32, number 2.
Wednesday	Have your child present his/her research to a "real" audience. You may invite neighbors to a puppet show or display a diorama at the library. Relatives and friends make a natural audience.	Have your child use each of this week's spelling words correctly in a sentence.	Discuss the tone of the book. *How does the author establish the mood of the story?* Have your child read chapters 5 and 6 of *Where the Red Fern Grows*. Why does your child think the townspeople were so cruel to Billy?
Thursday	Have your child write text for a picture book. *See* Language Skills, Week 32. Challenge your child's critical thinking skills. Have your child complete problems 1–4 on **Logic Puzzlers** (p. 322).	Have your child study this week's spelling words.	Help your child compare Billy to a character in another book. Have your child draw a Venn diagram to map out the similarities and differences between the characters. Have your child read chapters 7 and 8 of *Where the Red Fern Grows*. Have your child do some research, then draw a diagram to show how a brace-and-bit trap works. Ask your child to document his/her sources in the form of a short bibliography.
Friday	Review the different purposes for writing. Look at each page of a magazine together with your child. Have your child identify whether the page was written to entertain, inform or persuade. Some things are written to entertain and challenge. Have your child complete problems 5–8 on **Logic Puzzlers** (p. 322).	Give your child the final spelling test. Have your child record pretest and final test words in his/her Word Bank.	Have your child read chapters 9 and 10 of *Where the Red Fern Grows*. Ask your child to read aloud an exciting part of the story. Encourage your child to read with lots of expression.

Math	Science	Social Studies
Demonstrate how to divide with a decimal divisor. Show your child how to move the decimal to the right to create a whole number. To keep the solution accurate, move the decimal in the dividend to the right the same number of spaces. *See* Math, Week 32, number 1. $1.1\overline{)12}\; = \; 11\overline{)120.}$	**Machines** Review and discuss examples of the six simple machines. *See* Science, Week 32, number 1. Ask your child to identify simple machines around the kitchen. Explain that compound machines are made up of two or more simple machines.	**American Business Leaders** Brainstorm a list of famous American businessmen and women with your child. Provide appropriate resource materials so that your child can look up each person's name. *See* Social Studies, Week 32, numbers 1–2. Have your child group the people on the list by the type of work they have done that has brought them fame.
Show your child how to divide a decimal by 10 or 100. *See* Math, Week 32, number 2. Have your child divide a decimal fraction by 10 and compare the quotient to the dividend. Ask your child what would happen if you divided a decimal by 1,000. Give your child several problems to practice dividing decimals by factors of 10.	Ask your child to explain why it is easier to use a hammer to force a nail into a wooden board than to use only one's fingers and hands. Then, have your child name some other tasks that are made easier with the help of a simple machine. **Example:** loading a heavy box onto a truck is easier with the help of a ramp. Have your child make a pattern book based on this concept. *See* Science, Week 32, number 2 for more details.	Have your child choose one person from yesterday's list. Have him/her research, then write about the life and work of that famous American.
Sports statistics, such as batting averages in baseball, are often expressed in decimals. Have your child read the sports statistics published in your local newspaper. Discuss what the statistics actually represent. *See* Math, Week 32, number 3.	Can your child recognize simple machines in common household items? Have your child complete **Simple Machines** (p. 325).	Brainstorm with your child some of the qualities that the famous Americans you have discussed have in common. Discuss the qualities that your child possesses that may bring him/her recognition in the future. Have your child make a list of things he/she is good at. Have him/her make a second list of areas in which he/she would like to improve. Have your child make a plan of action.
Review and reteach the decimal concepts taught in Weeks 28–32. Give your child a sampling of problems for practice.	**Levers:** Introduce and explain the three classes of levers. *See* Science, Week 32, number 3. Have your child draw a tool that is a lever (such as a shovel, can opener or screwdriver) in his/her Science Log. Have your child label the class of lever and its three components.	Collect newspapers over a period of several days. Have your child skim the papers for interesting stories about local or national figures who have done well. Have your child read some of the articles about these people. Then, have your child write a prediction about what those people may accomplish in the future.
Quiz your child on his/her understanding of decimals. Have him/her complete **Working With Decimals** (p. 324). Reteach any concepts your child finds difficult.	Allow your child to explore different tools that are examples of levers. For example, lead your child to discover the best place on the handle to hold a shovel to make digging easiest. Common levers include hammers, scissors, pliers, nutcrackers, car jacks, seesaws, brooms, rakes, baseball bats, tennis rackets and shovels.	Arrange for your child to perform some community service.

```
╔══════════════════════════════════════════════╗
   TEACHING SUGGESTIONS AND ACTIVITIES
╚══════════════════════════════════════════════╝
```

LANGUAGE SKILLS

Find a book that contains only pictures and no text. Have your child look through the book several times and imagine a story line. Affix a stickie note to each page. Have your child write text for each page on the note. Encourage your child to use descriptive language and dialogue.

READING (Bibliography)

▶ 1. Wilson Rawls was born in 1913, in Oklahoma. He had little formal schooling, but his mother taught him to read and write. He and his sisters read and reread books that his grandma bought for them. Wilson Rawls's life was changed forever by Jack London's book, *The Call of the Wild*. One day while working in the fields, Wilson Rawls decided he would write a book like London's. Mr. Rawls admits that this was an ambitious dream for a boy whose family was too poor to afford paper and pencils, but he was encouraged by his father's words: "Son, a man can do anything he sets out to do, if he doesn't give up." Mr. Rawls made several attempts at writing novels. It was his wife who encouraged him to write *Where the Red Fern Grows*, because it was about his own childhood. The book has since been serialized in magazines and newpapers and made into a movie.

▶ 2. Have your child look at several different bibliographies and copy the pattern generally used. Observe the punctuation used in the bibliographies. Entries for books should include the author's name, title, place of publication, publishing company and year published. Entries for articles should include the author's name, title of the article, title of the magazine or periodical, volume number and issue number, date and page numbers.

   Book: Strunk Jr., William. *The Elements of Style.* New York: Macmillan Publishing Co., 1979.
   Article: Fraivillig, Judith. "Listen While They Work." *Creative Classroom* 13, no. 1 (August 1998): 62–64.

MATH (Decimals)

▶ 1. In decimal division, the divisor must be a whole number. The decimal point must be moved to the right until the divisor is a whole number, but you cannot make a change in the decimal divisor without making the same change to the dividend. If you moved the decimal one place to the right, you have multiplied the divisor and dividend by 10. Place the decimal point in the quotient directly above the newly placed decimal point in the dividend. Think of the division problem $3.4 \div 1.2$ as a fraction ($\frac{3.4}{1.2}$). Multiply both the numerator and the denominator by 10 to make an equivalent fraction. The new (equivalent) division problem is $34 \div 12$. Have your child work the following problems:

   $8.4 \div 2.1$ $1.872 \div 0.36$ $0.4712 \div 1.24$ $1.12 \div 8.1$ $17.7 \div 0.3$

▶ 2. To divide any number by 10, simply move the decimal point one place to the left.
   Examples: $63 \div 10 = 6.3$ $0.29 \div 10 = 0.029$

   To divide any number by 100, simply move the decimal point two places to the left.
   Examples: $63 \div 100 = 0.63$ $0.29 \div 100 = 0.0029$

▶ 3. A batting average is always presented as a three-digit decimal fraction.
   Examples: 0.250, 0.333, 0.144. A player's batting average is found by dividing the number of hits by the number of times at bat. As a division problem, this is written as follows: 118 hits ÷ 463 times at bat = 0.255 batting average.

Learn At Home, Grade 5

SCIENCE (Machines)

▶ 1. Review the six types of simple machines. Have your child name one or two examples of each.

lever	hammer, crowbar
wheel and axle	doorknob, wheels on a model car
wedge	chisel, doorstop
pulley	miniblind cord pull, flagpole pulley
inclined plane	ramp or slide
screw	variety of screws

▶ 2. Have your child think of tasks that are made easier with the help of a simple machine. Ask your child to imagine, then draw, how each task would get done without the aid of a simple machine. Have your child compile these drawings to create a book. Each page of the book will show someone doing work without the aid of a machine. At the bottom of each page, have your child write a line that is repeated throughout the book—something like *Wouldn't that be easier with a _____?* The book will essentially be an advertisement promoting the benefits of simple machines.

▶ 3. Introduce and explain the three classes of levers. Explain that every lever has three parts: fulcrum, effort and load (resistance force). Sketch the following illustrations on the chalkboard. Identify the three parts and describe how the lever works. Have your child name examples of each class of lever.

1st class	**2nd class**	**3rd class**
effort fulcrum load	fulcrum load effort	fulcrum effort load

▶ 4. Have your child name and describe some inclined planes (ramps, steps, escalators, roller coasters, winding roads or trails up a mountain, water slides). Visit a factory or machine shop. Have your child look for inclined planes in the machinery. Have your child write a paragraph explaining the usefulness of an inclined plane.

SOCIAL STUDIES (American Business Leaders)

▶ 1. Have your child look up and define the following terms: *businessman/businesswoman, industrialist* and *philanthropist.* Discuss the differences in meaning of these terms.

▶ 2. Here is a brief list of famous American businesspeople:

Mary Kay Ash	Bill Gates	Andrew Mellon	Helena Rubenstein
John Jacob Astor	Katharine Graham	Edward R. Murrow	William H. Seward
Andrew Carnegie	Howard Hughes	H. Ross Perot	Madam C. J. Walker
Walt Disney	Marjorie Child Husted	Joseph Pulitzer	Oprah Winfrey
Debbie Fields	Estée Lauder	John D. Rockefeller	Victoria C. Woodhull
Henry Ford			

Logic Puzzlers

1. Four volumes of an encyclopedia set, Volumes A, B, C and D, are placed on a shelf out of order. Volume A is between B and C. Volume D is not next to Volume C, which is the first volume on the left. From left to right, in what order are the volumes?

2. My cat just tried to eat my telephone book. I cannot find pages 3, 4, 26, 27, 39 and 40. How many sheets of paper did my cat remove from the book?

3. Ken collects balls. Betsy collects postage stamps. Ken thinks 3 balls are as valuable as 2 stamps. If Betsy agrees to swap 14 stamps, how many balls will Ken need to give her?

4. (Do after completing #3.) Amy collects baseball cards. She thinks 5 stamps are worth the same as 1 card. If Amy decides to trade 2 cards, how many stamps should she receive? How many balls would she get?

5. Four people are introduced to one another at a party. Each of the four shakes hands with the other three. How many handshakes are there in all?

6. Four friends meet for dinner. One is a cab driver, one is a carpenter, one is an accountant and one is a fisherman. The four sit at a square table with one person on each side of the table. The carpenter is not sitting next to the cab driver, but the accountant is on the cab driver's left. Draw a square and write where each person is sitting. Put the carpenter at the bottom of your square.

7. James and Esther are brother and sister. Both are married and have children. Carolyn is James's wife. Ryan is Esther's husband. Ron and Gary are cousins in the same family. Gary is not James's son. Who is Ron's mother?

8. At Lee's next birthday he will be three times the age of his son, Robert. Robert is now two and a half times the age of his little sister, Michelle, who is 6. How old is Lee right now?

322

More Vowel Digraphs

The vowel digraphs **ie** and **ei** usually carry the following sounds:

ie = long i as in **tie**	**ie = long e** as in **relief**
ei = long a as in **weigh**	**ei = long e** as in **deceive**

believe
brief
died
eight
freight
leisure
lie
perceive
piece
pies
receive
reign
retrieve
shield
shriek
siege
sleigh
vein

The following rhyme may be helpful to you:

I before *E*
Except after *C*
Or when sounded like *A*
As in *neighbor* or *weigh*.
Either, neither, leisure and *seize*
Are four exceptions,
If you please!

Write each spelling word in the appropriate category.

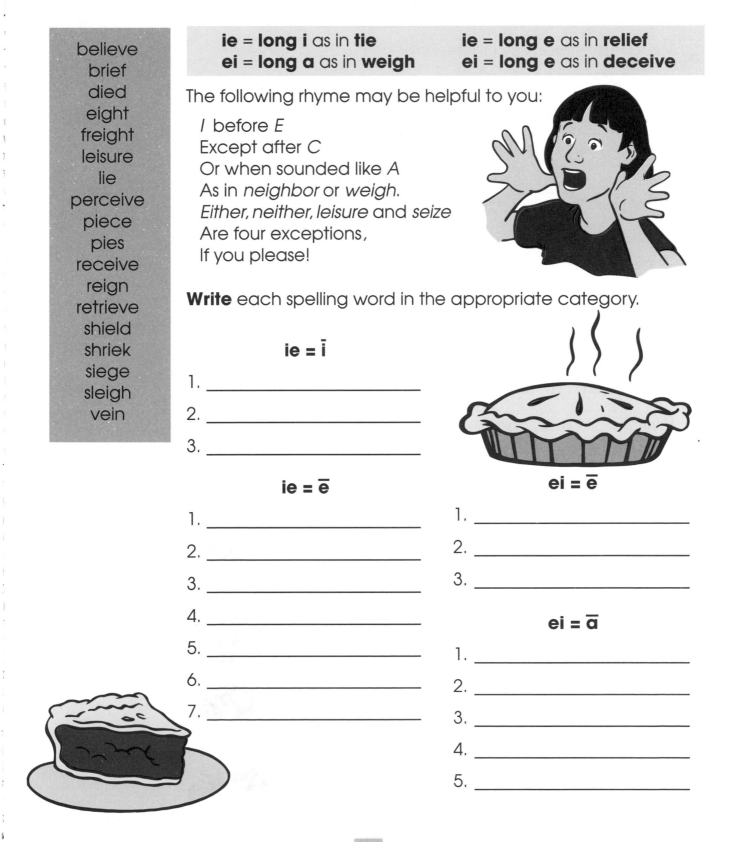

ie = ī

1. _____
2. _____
3. _____

ie = ē

1. _____
2. _____
3. _____
4. _____
5. _____
6. _____
7. _____

ei = ē

1. _____
2. _____
3. _____

ei = ā

1. _____
2. _____
3. _____
4. _____
5. _____

323

Working With Decimals

1. Write 207.426 in words.

   _____

2. Write forty-seven and thirteen thousandths in numerals. _____

3. Use > or < to indicate which decimal fraction is greater.

   17.35_____17.295

Fill in the blanks.

4. Round 12.836 to the nearest whole number. _____

5. Round 12.836 to the nearest tenth. _____

6. Round 12.836 to the nearest hundredth. _____

7. Write 0.36 as a fraction in lowest terms. _____

8. Write 0.25 as a fraction in lowest terms. _____

9. Write $\frac{3}{4}$ as a decimal number. _____

Solve.

10. 36.2 + 27.325 = _____

11. 87.36 − 84.95 = _____

12. 4.6 x 1.2 = _____

13. 3.46 x 10 = _____

14. 11.55 ÷ 7 = _____

15. 39 ÷ 12 = _____

16. 367.52 ÷ 10 = _____

Learn At Home, Grade 5

Simple Machines

There are six simple machines that are the basic units of all complex machines: the lever, the wheel and axle, the wedge, the pulley, the inclined plane and the screw.

Recognizing Simple Machines

Which simple machines can you find in each of the tools listed below?

hammer _____   scissors   _____

doorstop _____   drill   _____

saw _____   screwdriver   _____

crowbar _____   monkey wrench   _____

Bicycle Parts

Study a bicycle carefully. Fill in the blanks with the simple machines you find.

tire _____   kickstand _____

caliper brakes _____   handlebars _____

chain and sprocket _____   gearshift _____

pedal and shaft _____   fork _____

other _____

	Language Skills	**Spelling**	**Reading**
Monday	**Colons and Semicolons** Teach your child about the different uses of the colon. See Language Skills, Week 33, numbers 1–4. Have your child look for examples in books he/she has read. Have your child write his/her own original sentences using the colon.	Pretest your child on these spelling words: auction dawn lawful audience fawns raw autumn flaunt scrawl awkward fraud shawl caught haunt taught cause jaw yawn Have your child correct the pretest. Add personalized words and make two copies of this week's study list.	**Parts of a Book** Have your child read chapters 11 and 12 of *Where the Red Fern Grows*. Have your child define *determination*, then list several ways that Billy shows determination. Review the parts of a book. *See* Reading, Week 33, number 1.
Tuesday	Teach your child about the different uses of the semicolon. *See* Language Skills, Week 33, numbers 5–7. Have your child look for examples in books he/she has read. Have your child write his/her own original sentences using the semicolon.	Review this week's spelling words. Have your child complete **Very Important Digraphs** (p. 331).	Have your child read chapters 13 and 14 of *Where the Red Fern Grows*. Have your child write an imaginary interview with Billy. Encourage your child to recreate Billy's mood and personality through the dialogue. Discuss some of the less familiar parts of a book. *See* Reading, Week 33, number 2.
Wednesday	Write several sentences on the chalkboard that should contain either colons or semicolons, but omit the punctuation. Have your child fill in the correct punctuation as necessary, then explain his/her choices.	Have your child use each of this week's spelling words correctly in a sentence.	Have your child read chapters 15 and 16 of *Where the Red Fern Grows*. Have your child write two questions about tomorrow's reading to give practice with reasonable predictions. Discuss the purpose of an appendix in a book. *See* Reading, Week 33, number 3.
Thursday	Test your child's critical thinking skills. Have your child complete **Falsehood Follies** (p. 330). Your child will have to read *very* carefully in order to solve these riddles!	Have your child study this week's spelling words.	Have your child read chapters 17 and 18 of *Where the Red Fern Grows*. Have your child jot down any unfamiliar words from today's reading, along with the sentence in which each word appears. Can your child guess each word's meaning from its context? Have your child try to guess the meaning, then look up the word in a dictionary. How accurate was your child's guess? Discuss whether his/her questions from yesterday were answered.
Friday	Teach your child to use personification to create a vivid image in the reader's mind. Personification is granting human qualities or abilities to inanimate objects. *See* Language Skills, Week 33, number 8.	Give your child the final spelling test. Have your child record pretest and final test words in his/her Word Bank.	Have your child read chapters 19 and 20 of *Where the Red Fern Grows*. Have your child draw a plot profile showing the range of excitement levels throughout the story. Have your child list events from the story along the horizontal axis and excitement levels along the vertical axis. Discuss the parts of a book. *See* Reading, Week 33, number 4.

Learn At Home, Grade 5

Math	Science	Social Studies
Money Introduce the study of money with a magic trick. Ask your child to put a dime in one pocket and a penny in the other. You are going to guess which coin is in each pocket. *See* Math, Week 33. Discuss with your child the basis of the trick. Challenge your child to make up a similar magic trick using the same basis.	**Inclined Planes** Help your child set up an experiment for exploring variables (height) with a ramp. *See* Science, Week 33, number 1. Have your child graph the results of the experiment. Along the side of the graph, show distance traveled. Along the bottom of the graph, show the height of the ramp. Have your child record the results of each trial. Discuss the results. Ask your child where this phenomenon may be seen in everyday life.	Have your child study a picture of Mount Rushmore. Discuss the famous Americans who are represented there and why they were chosen for the honor. Have your child design a new memorial for four famous Americans (let your child decide who will be honored). Have your child sculpt the memorial out of clay. This may take more than one day to complete.
Play a game that will challenge your child to think of several ways to express the same amount of money. Grab a small handful of change. Do not show the money to your child. Give a series of clues (becoming gradually more specific) until your child guesses exactly what coins you have. **Example:** *The coins add up to 69¢. Three of the coins have a textured edge. Two coins total 50¢. There are eight coins in all.* Repeat, then try switching roles.	Help your child set up a second experiment for exploring variables (friction) with a ramp. *See* Science, Week 33, number 2.	Have your child finish the clay sculpture begun yesterday. Have your child write about the site for this new memorial, as well as the famous Americans it represents.
One helpful problem-solving strategy is organizing data in a systematic way so that you know you have been thorough in your analysis. Ask your child to list every possible coin combination that totals 25¢. Encourage your child to organize the data in a meaningful way, such as a chart. Have your child start with the largest coins and work down to 25 pennies. There are 17 possible combinations.	An inclined plane is a plane set at an angle. It is especially helpful for raising and lowering objects with minimal effort. *See* Science, Week 33, number 3. Arrange a visit to a machine shop or a factory. Have your child look for simple machines in the shop or factory. Some of the simple machines may be found in compound machines.	*For what do (did) famous Americans want to be remembered?* Thomas Jefferson wrote the inscription for his own gravestone. He states three accomplishments, but not that he was president. *What do you know about Thomas Jefferson that might explain that?* Have your child read about the accomplishments and beliefs of one famous American. Using that information, have your child write an appropriate epitaph for the person.
Plan a field trip to the bank. Arrange to speak with a loan officer. Have your child read about our banking system and prepare a list of questions such as these to ask the loan officer: *How does the bank earn money? Where does the money come from to pay interest? How are bank employees paid? Why does the bank loan money? How does a savings account work?*	Demonstrate the similarity between an inclined plane and a screw. A screw is really an inclined plane that raises and lowers wood along its inclined threads. *See* Science, Week 33, number 4. As you turn a screw into a piece of soft wood, have your child observe the wood shavings that travel up the threads of the screw. Ask your child to compare this to an object moving up an inclined plane.	Play "Twenty Questions" with your child. Think of a famous American. Allow your child to ask 20 yes or no questions to find out who it is. Repeat several times, then switch roles.
Take your child to the bank. Have your child open a savings account and, if possible, interview a loan officer.	Help your child experiment with a variety of screws. *See* Science, Week 33, number 5.	Arrange for your child to perform some community service.

TEACHING SUGGESTIONS AND ACTIVITIES

LANGUAGE SKILLS (Colons and Semicolons)

▶ 1. A colon is used when writing digital time. Ask your child to tell exactly where the colon is placed. (between the hour and minutes) Dictate some times for your child to write on the chalkboard.

▶ 2. Use a colon to introduce a list of items, especially after the expression *the following*. Commas are used to separate the items in the list.
Example: The store window displayed the following items: a sled with a bear on it, six wrapped boxes, two young children dressed for winter and snow falling.
Do *not* use a colon if the list directly follows a verb or preposition.
Example: For the picnic, I will bring hot dogs, chips and watermelon.

▶ 3. A colon is used after the greeting in a business letter.
Examples: Dear Ms. Smith: To Whom It May Concern:

▶ 4. Use a colon between two independent clauses when the second clause restates or explains the first clause.
Example: It rained very hard on Saturday: the seedlings in our garden all washed away.

▶ 5. A semicolon is used between two independent clauses that are not joined by a conjunction.
Example: Female sperm whales can grow up to 40 feet in length; males can grow up to 60 feet in length.

▶ 6. To avoid confusion, semicolons are used to separate items in a series when the items contain commas.
Example: Jenny invited the following people to her party: her younger sister, Darla; Laurie, her neighbor; her cousin, Tanya; and me.

▶ 7. Use a semicolon to separate two independent clauses when there are commas within the clauses.
Example: The killer whale typically travels in pods of up to 50 members; and it eats fish, birds, dolphins, penguins, porpoises and sea turtles.

▶ 8. Ask your child to remember a time when he/she had a strong feeling about something inanimate. Was your child frightened? Happy? Excited to see something for the first time? Encourage your child to give an inanimate object a human attribute in order to make a strong impression. Personification is like a metaphor: the object in a metaphor does not literally become what the sentence states, but it helps to create a vivid image.
Examples: *When I opened the garage door, a shiny blue bicycle got up and danced around the room and then smiled at me, saying, "I'm yours!"*

I walked alone to the restroom in the dark campground. My eyes were wide as I looked around at every noise. The tree branches scratched menacingly at the air around me. They laughed with creaky voices at my fear.

READING (Parts of a Book)

▶ 1. Review the parts of a book. Have your child identify the following parts and describe what information each contains: spine, cover, jacket, title page, copyright page, table of contents, glossary, index and bibliography.

▶ 2. Introduce your child to some of the less familiar parts of a book: acknowledgments (recognizes sources and/or people who were helpful in making the book possible), dedication (an inscription to honor someone), preface (a statement usually written by the author that introduces the book and/or its scope, intention or background), foreword (like a preface, but usually written by a person other than the author), appendix (additional material usually at the end of a book).

▶ 3. Have your child look at the appendices in several different books to see what type of material might be included in an appendix.

▶ 4. Ask your child some questions about different parts of a book.
Where in a book can you find the dedication?
What is the difference between a table of contents and an index?
What is the printing date of the book?
Why is the information in an appendix not in the main body of the text?

328

MATH (Money)

Magic trick: "I am going to tell you which coin is in each pocket. Listen carefully to my instructions. I need you to multiply the value of the coin in your right pocket by 15. Add 15 to the value of the coin in your left pocket. Add the numbers together and subtract 36. Now, multiply the difference by 100. What is your answer?" (If the answer is 13,000, the dime is in the right pocket. If the answer is 400, the dime is in the left hand.) The basis of this magic trick is that a dime (10¢) is worth more than a penny (1¢). When you ask your child to multiply, the pocket with the dime produces a greater number.

SCIENCE (Inclined Planes)

▶ 1. Give your child a marble, a ruler (with a groove down the center), a meterstick and three blocks or bricks. Your child will need a bare floor in an open area to conduct this experiment.

   Question: Does the height of the ramp affect the distance a marble travels?

   Directions:

   a. Place one block or brick on the ground. Lean the ruler on the edge of the block (groove side up). Hold the marble at the top of the ruler and let it roll down. Measure the distance the marble traveled and record this distance in meters and centimeters. Repeat for three trials.

   b. Place two blocks on the ground. Lean the ruler on the edge of the blocks and allow the marble to roll down three times. Record the distance of each trial.

   c. Place three blocks on the ground. Lean the ruler on the edge of the blocks and allow the marble to roll down three times. Record the distance of each trial.

   Have your child analyze the results of the experiment. Discuss the answer to the question above.

▶ 2. Repeat yesterday's experiment. This time, use 3 blocks for each trial, but set up the experiment on different surfaces. For the first trial, set the ramp on concrete. For other trials, set the ramp on a thick carpet, sand and a bed sheet. Have your child record the data on a graph like the one shown here.

▶ 3. Explain and demonstrate the relationship of the screw to the inclined plane. Cut a rectangular sheet of paper diagonally. Point out how the paper resembles an inclined plane. Have your child roll the paper, beginning with the shortest side, moving toward the opposite point. After the paper is rolled, ask your child to describe the resulting shape (a screw). Then, ask your child these questions: *Would it be easier to walk straight up the side of a steep mountain or around and around the mountain like the curved paper screw? Why? Which walk would take longer?* Explain that the use of the curved inclined plane (screw) makes the work easier but requires a greater distance. A trail or road winds around a mountain rather than going straight from bottom to top. Have your child compare the use of a screw to a nail in holding an object to a board.

▶ 4. Help your child conduct an experiment with screws.

   You will need: a variety of screws, a soft wooden board, a manual screwdriver, a hammer, a pencil and a nail.

   Directions:

   a. Use the hammer and nail to make some shallow openings in the wooden board. Space the openings across the surface of the wood.
   b. Select one screw and place in one of the openings.
   c. Use the screwdriver and count the number of 360° turns needed to force the screw into the wood until the head is flush with the board.
   d. Select another screw and force it into a different opening, counting the turns.
   e. Repeat with all the screws.
   f. Sort the screws by the number of turns required.
   g. Describe the differences in the force needed for each variety of screw. Explain.

Falsehood Follies

Here are some simple statements that are guaranteed to make you think. Carefully read and solve the first set before going on to the second.

A. Only one of the following statements is true. Find it.

1. One of these statements is false.
2. Two of these statements are false.
3. Three of these statements are false.
4. Four of these statements are false.
5. Five of these statements are false.

Answer: The one true statement is number _____.

B. Now, here is a slightly trickier variation. This time there are *two* true statements. To find them, you will have to **fill in** the blank in sentence number five.

1. One of these statements is false.
2. Two of these statements are true.
3. Three of these statements are false.
4. Three of these statements are true.
5. Four of these statements are _____.
6. Five of these statements are false.

Answer: The two true statements are numbers _____ and _____.

C. Now, find all statements in this set that *could* be true.

1. If one statement is true, then three are false.
2. If two statements are true, then number 1 is one of them.
3. If three statements are false, then three are also true.
4. If one statement is false, then five are true.
5. If four statements are true, then number 4 is false.
6. There are six true statements in this set.

Answer: The statements that could be true are numbers _____.

Learn At Home, Grade 5

Very Important Digraphs

The vowel digraphs **au** and **aw** make the same **ô** sound.
Examples: fa**u**lt, la**w**n

Write each spelling word in the appropriate category in the two inner triangles.
After you have written each word, **circle** the digraph.

Then **write** the spelling words in alphabetical order in the two outer triangles.

auction
audience
autumn
awkward
caught
cause
dawn
fawns
flaunt
fraud
haunt
jaw
lawful
raw
scrawl
shawl
taught
yawn

ô carried by **au**

ô carried by **aw**

au

aw

Learn At Home, Grade 5

	Language Skills	**Spelling**	**Reading**
Monday	**Complex Sentences** Explain the difference between a compound sentence and a complex sentence. A *compound sentence* is made up of two independent clauses joined by a conjunction. A *complex sentence* is made up of a dependent clause and an independent clause. *See* Language Skills, Week 34, number 1. Have your child copy dependent clauses from a book he/she is reading.	Pretest your child on these spelling words: appointed eyebrow power boiling fowl shower county joyous spoiled destroying mountain stout disloyal noises surround employ pronounce thousand Have your child correct the pretest. Add personalized words and make two copies of this week's study list.	**Nonfiction** Help your child choose a nonfiction book to read (cover to cover) this week. Have your child check out other nonfiction books on the same topic, if possible. Use these books to show your child how to scan for information. *See* Reading, Week 34, number 1. Have your child complete **Get the Facts, Max** (p. 337).
Tuesday	A dependent clause often contains a *subordinating conjunction*. This conjunction connects the phrase to the rest of the sentence. *See* Language Skills, Week 34, number 2. Have your child choose five subordinating conjunctions and use each in a sentence.	Review this week's spelling words. Have your child complete **Dynamic Diphthongs** (p. 336).	Teach your child to outline important information while reading nonfiction. *See* Reading, Week 34, number 2. Have your child read from the nonfiction book. Have your child outline the important information as he/she reads.
Wednesday	A complex sentence contains one independent clause and one or more dependent clauses. A comma is generally used between the dependent and independent clauses, especially when the dependent clause comes before or in the middle of the independent clause. **Examples:** *After I watched the movie, I went straight to bed. My mother, after she wakes up, has a cup of coffee.* *See* Language Skills, Week 34, number 3.	Have your child use each of this week's spelling words correctly in a sentence.	Have your child finish reading and outlining the nonfiction book. Then, help your child think of an interesting way to present what he/she has learned. Allow time today, Thursday and Friday for your child to complete a project related to the topic.
Thursday	Prepare a game in which your child must mix and match clauses to form sentences. You may take the clauses from sentences found in familiar books or make up your own. *See* Language Skills, Week 34, number 4.	Have your child study this week's spelling words.	Have your child scan the other nonfiction books he/she checked out from the library. Have your child use these books to gain additional information or to double-check facts for accuracy. Allow time for your child to work on the project started yesterday.
Friday	Consult a grammar book to teach your child about the different parts of speech that dependent clauses may take. Dependent clauses are also known as subordinate clauses.	Give your child the final spelling test. Have your child record pretest and final test words in his/her Word Bank.	Have your child complete and present his/her project on the nonfiction topic of the week.

Learn At Home, Grade 5

Math	Science	Social Studies
Talk about the different categories of spending, such as entertainment, food, clothes, charity and savings. Help your child plan a budget. The budget should show how much money your child takes in (each week/each month/each year) and how he/she would like to spend or save that money. Keep the budget realistic so that your child can maintain the plan. (Option: Have your child make a circle graph that shows how his/her total allowance will be spent.)	**Wheels and Pulleys** Gather at least five wheels of different sizes. You may use any circular object for this activity. Identify each wheel by writing an alphabet letter on masking tape and affixing it to the wheel. Have your child measure the circumference of each wheel in centimeters and record the measurements on a chart. *See* Science, Week 34, number 1.	**Washington, D.C.** Discuss the significance of Washington D.C. *What type of business is conducted there?* *See* Social Studies, Week 34. Study a map of the city with your child. Ask your child to locate major buildings and landmarks, such as the White House, the Capitol Building, the Supreme Court Building, the National Mall, the Pentagon and the Lincoln Memorial.
Teach your child how to maintain a check register. Find an old register or get an extra from your bank. Show your child how to keep track of deposits and withdrawals using addition and subtraction. Remind your child to line up the decimals before adding or subtracting. Have your child complete **Big Bucks for You!** (p. 338).	Have your child study the wheel and axle of a model car. Demonstrate the function of the axle. In his/her Science Log, have your child explain why a wheel cannot operate without an axle. Ask your child to include a labeled diagram with his/her explanation.	Have your child draw pictures of the monuments dedicated to three of our nation's past presidents: Jefferson, Washington and Lincoln.
Review mathematical operations with decimals and money. Have your child complete the problems found in Math, Week 34.	Have your child use a kit of plastic gears to design an interconnected moving model. Ask your child to observe how one gear causes another gear to move. Have your child compare the movement of a larger gear with that of a smaller gear. If you do not have access to gears, you can make gears from corrugated cardboard. *See* Science, Week 34, number 2.	Have your child plan a day or week in the city of Washington, D.C. Ask him/her to make an itinerary of things to see and places to visit. Have your child describe in writing why he/she chose these particular things to do. *What is the significance of each?*
Give your child more practice with decimals and money. Have your child complete **Snails in a Pail** (p. 339).	Provide your child with a set of pulleys and a challenge. Challenge your child to design a system for raising a given object to a given height.	Our nation's capital was a well-planned city. Have your child read about the history of the city and its physical layout. Have your child write twelve facts about the layout of Washington, D.C.
Review and reteach money concepts. Have your child imagine that he/she has exactly $75 to spend. Ask your child to look through a toy catalog and write an itemized order that comes close to $75 without going over. Have your child write three different orders with different combinations of purchases, each order totaling around $75.	Have your child research some of the following inventions and their inventors: wind turbine, elevator, roller coaster, Ferris wheel, steamboat, automobile, motion picture, phonograph, compact disc, copy machine, rotary printing press, sewing machine, jet airplane, calculator, personal computer, vacuum cleaner. Have your child write a one-page report on one of these inventions. *What types of simple machines make up the invention?*	Arrange for your child to perform some community service.

TEACHING SUGGESTIONS AND ACTIVITIES

LANGUAGE SKILLS (Complex Sentences)

▶ 1. An independent clause has a subject and a predicate and can stand alone: *The dog ran after the cat.* A dependent clause has a subject and a predicate but cannot stand alone: *After the dog jumped the fence.* A dependent clause can be combined with an independent clause, however, to form a complex sentence. In this first example, the dependent clause comes before the independent clause: *After the dog jumped the fence, it ran after the cat.* The dependent clause may also come after the independent clause: *The dog ran after the cat after it jumped the fence.*

▶ 2. The following subordinating conjunctions may be used in a dependent clause to link the clause to the rest of the sentence: *after, although, as, because, before, if, in order that, since, so that, though, until, when, whenever, whether, while.*

▶ 3. Write several independent clauses and dependent clauses (in two columns) on the chalkboard. Do not use any punctuation or capitalization. Have your child join the clauses to form complex sentences. Remind your child to add periods, commas and capital letters where needed.
Examples: though the wind blew   everyone cheered
                after the music stopped   the temperature remained high

▶ 4. Write at least ten dependent clauses and ten independent clauses on index cards (one clause per card). Mix the cards together. Put the cards in a box at the language center. Have your child match dependent clauses with independent clauses to make sentences that make sense.

READING (Nonfiction)

▶ 1. Your child will probably not have the time or the desire to read all the nonfiction titles from cover to cover. Nonfiction is often organized with headings and bold print to help you scan or skim through as you search for specific information. Teach your child how to scan for information.

▶ 2. Outlining follows a specific format of Roman numerals, capital letters, numbers and lower-case letters. Your child may not be able to fit everything into these neat categories as he/she is reading. Teach your child to take notes in sentence fragments at first, then clean up the organization later. See Reading, Week 24 for an example of the outline format.

MATH (Money)

Give your child the following pet store problems to solve.

1. Eli has 18 rabbits which he is selling for $2.99 each. How much money will he earn if he sells all 18 rabbits?

2. You bought a parrot for $2.39 and a myna bird for $8.67. What was your total cost?

3. Kim is selling 12 goldfish for $.84 total. How much does she receive for each goldfish?

4. Billie's teacher bought a ribbon snake for the classroom. It cost $4.79. How much change did the teacher receive from a $20.00 bill?

5. Pat is selling a pet python for $9.99. A kitten costs $13.45. What is the difference in their prices?

6. The school principal bought 60 guppies for the school carnival for $23.40. How much did each guppy cost?

7. Myra is selling hamsters for $1.41 each. How much will she receive for 40 hamsters?

8. Jeffrey sold 10 geckos for $2.99 each. How much did he receive for all 10?

9. Your brother loves rodents. He buys a pair of mice for $2.39 and a pair of hamsters for $3.13. How much does it cost him altogether?

10. Marty sold 19 chameleons for a total of $41.04. How much did he charge for each chameleon?

Learn At Home, Grade 5

SCIENCE (Wheels and Pulleys)

▶ 1. Have your child use the information on the chart from Monday's lesson plan to solve the following problems:

a. Compare (by subtracting) the circumference of:

Wheel A and Wheel B	Wheel B and Wheel C
Wheel C and Wheel D	Wheel D and Wheel E
Wheel A and Wheel C	Wheel A and Wheel E

b. How many times must Wheel A rotate to cover the same distance as Wheel C? as Wheel E?

c. How many times must Wheel B rotate to cover the same distance as Wheel D? as Wheel E?

d. How many times must Wheel C rotate to cover the same distance as Wheel A plus wheel E?

▶ 2. The important function of gears is to use a small amount of force to generate a great amount of motion. Explain how a steering wheel works in a car. A combination of gears allows a slight turn of the steering wheel to move the tires a greater distance. If possible, remove the back from a watch or clock to show your child the gear mechanism within. If possible, show your child how a car jack uses a gear mechanism to allow many turns of the handle to raise a heavy weight a small distance.

SOCIAL STUDIES (Washington, D.C.)

BACKGROUND

Every United States president except George Washington has lived and worked in Washington, D.C., while serving his term. Washington, D.C., the nation's capital, is the headquarters of the federal government. The city contains many famous buildings, monuments and museums. For this unit, gather maps and books about Washington, D.C. If possible, take your child to visit this important city.

Use the following questions to lead a discussion about the business of Washington, D.C.

What is Washington, D.C.? Where is it? What forms its borders? Is it well located as the nation's capital? Why or why not? Was it well located when it was originally built?

What is the "main business" in Washington? How does it affect all U.S. citizens?

Name people (office holders) associated with Washington, D.C. In what buildings do they conduct the business of government?

How old is Washington, D.C.? When did it become the capital?

How old is the United States? When did it become a nation?

Dynamic Diphthongs

Diphthongs are two adjacent letters that both contribute to the vowel sound heard. The two vowel sounds are blended. **Examples: oi, oy** as in **coin, joy; ou, ow** as in **hound, flower**

appointed
boiling
county
destroying
disloyal
employ
eyebrow
fowl
joyous
mountain
noises
pronounce
power
shower
spoiled
stout
surround
thousand

Write each spelling word in the appropriate category.

oi

1. _____
2. _____
3. _____
4. _____

oy

1. _____
2. _____
3. _____
4. _____

ou

1. _____
2. _____
3. _____
4. _____
5. _____
6. _____

ow

1. _____
2. _____
3. _____
4. _____

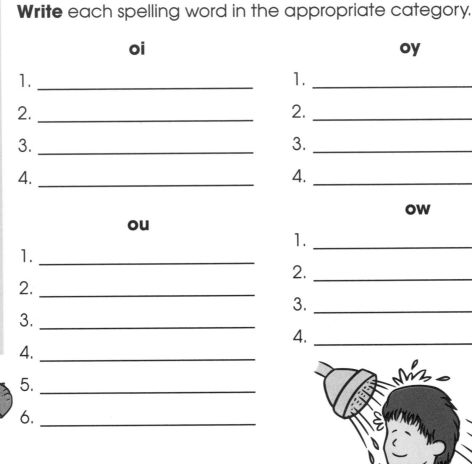

Here come the elephants! Remember that the letters **ow** can also be a vowel digraph carrying the ō sound as in **hollow**. The letters **ou** can carry the ō as in **although**, the ô as in **thought** or the ŭ as in **southern**.

Complete the words within each family by filling in the correct digraph.

ou as in **thought**   **ou** as in **although**   **ow** as in **hollow**   **ou** as in **southern**

f___ght   thor____gh   swall_____   c____ple

br___ght   b____quet   marshmall_____   tr____ble

Learn At Home, Grade 5

Get the Facts, Max

Read the paragraphs to answer the questions below.

The islands of Aruba, Bonaire and Curaçao, sometimes known as the ABC islands, are part of the Netherlands Antilles. They lie 50 miles north off the coast of Venezuela. Three more islands, St. Eustatius, Saba and St. Martin (the northern half of which belongs to France), are approximately 500 miles northeast of the ABC islands.

Until 1949, the islands were known as the Dutch West Indies or Curaçao Territory. In 1986, Aruba separated to become a self-governing part of the Netherlands Realm.

On the island of Curaçao, most food is imported. Because it is so rocky, little farming is possible. The island is the largest and most heavily populated of the Netherlands Antilles. Its oil refineries, among the largest in the world, give its people a relatively high standard of living. Today, most people of Curaçao work in the shipping, refining or tourist industry.

Netherlands Antilles—Other Facts

Area:

Aruba	75 square miles
Bonaire	111 square miles
Curaçao	171 square miles
Saba	5 square miles
St. Eustatius	11 square miles
St. Martin	13 square miles

Capital: Willemstad

Major Languages: Dutch, Paplamento (a mixture of Spanish, Dutch, Portuguese, Carib and English), English, Spanish

1. Name the capital of the Netherlands Antilles. _____
2. What industry gives the people a high standard of living? _____
3. Name the ABC islands. _____
4. What is Papiamento? _____
5. Why must food be imported to Curaçao? _____
6. Which island is smallest? _____
7. Which two islands are the largest? _____
8. Which island belongs in part to France? _____
9. In what year did Aruba become self-governing? _____

Learn At Home, Grade 5

© 1999 Tribune Education. All Rights Reserved.

Big Bucks for You!

Solve the problems on another sheet of paper.

Answer space

1. You receive your first royalty check for $1,000.00 and deposit it in your checking account. You go directly to the music store and spend $234.56 on new CDs. What is your balance?

2. You naturally treat all your friends to pizza, which costs you $47.76. You pay with a check. What is your balance now?

3. You decide to restock your wardrobe and buy $389.99 worth of new clothes. What is your balance?

4. Your next royalty check arrives, and you deposit $1,712.34. You also treat yourself to a new 15-speed bicycle, which costs $667.09. What is your balance?

5. You buy your mother some perfume for a present. You write a check for $37.89. What is your balance?

6. You need a tennis racket and some other sports equipment. The bill comes to $203.45 What is your new balance?

7. You treat your family to dinner at **Snails in a Pail**, where the check comes to $56.17. What is your new balance?

8. You join a health club, and the first payment is $150.90. What is your new balance?

9. You deposit your latest royalty check, which amounts to $4,451.01. What is your new balance?

10. To celebrate this good fortune, you take your entire peewee football team to a professional football game. The bill comes to $4,339.98. What is your new balance?

Learn At Home, Grade 5

Snails in a Pail

Sly Me Slugg, world-famous French chef, has made his fast-food business, **Snails in a Pail**, the most popular restaurant in the whole area. This is his menu:

Slime Soup	$.49
Slugburger	$1.69
Chicken-Fried Snails	$2.99
Slimy Slush	$.89
Snailcream Shake	$1.49
Snailbits Salad	$1.09

Solve the problems on another sheet of paper.

Answer space

1. Sly Me Slugg sold 60 Slimy Slushes and 40 Snailcream Shakes on Friday. How much did he make on drinks that day?

2. A coach treated 15 of his team players to Slugburgers. How much change did he receive from $40.00?

3. Your brother was so hungry that he ordered one of everything on the menu. How much change did he get from a $10.00 bill?

4. Sly Me Slugg sold $43.61 in Slime Soup orders on Wednesday and $38.22 in soup orders on Thursday. How many orders of Slime Soup did he sell in those 2 days?

5. You had a party at **Snails in a Pail** and bought 9 Slugburgers, 3 orders of Chicken-Fried Snails, 2 Snailbits Salads, 5 Snailcream Shakes and 10 Slimy Slushes. What was the total cost for the party?

6. In one week, Sly Me Slugg sold 200 Slugburgers and 79 orders of Chicken-Fried Snails. How much money did he earn from these 2 items?

7. You ordered 10 Slugburgers, 10 Snailcream Shakes and 10 Slimy Slushes. What was your total cost?

8. On Friday, Sly Me earned $1,252. On Saturday, he earned $1,765. On Sunday, he earned $2,998. What was his average daily earnings for those 3 days?

	Language Skills	**Spelling**	**Reading**
Monday	Help your child choose a writing topic for this week's writing assignment. Have your child follow the steps in the writing process as he/she writes independently this week. For more information on the writing process, see page 6. Have your child make a plan for writing, then begin work on the rough draft today.	Pretest your child on these spelling words: answer false question broad freeze reward combine narrow separate council pause thaw cymbal plain true downstairs punish upstairs Have your child correct the pretest. Add personalized words and make two copies of this week's study list.	Have your child read about Theodor Seuss Geisel in a nonfiction book or encyclopedia. Introduce *The 500 Hats of Bartholomew Cubbins* by Dr. Seuss. Have your child read the book aloud. If you cannot read the entire book in one sitting, return to it quickly to maintain the feeling of the story.
Tuesday	Let your child continue to work independently on his/her writing project. Review writing and grammar skills as the need arises.	Review this week's spelling words. Have your child complete **The "Nym" Family** (p. 344).	Finish reading *The 500 Hats of Bartholomew Cubbins*. Have your child retell the story from the point of view of one of the minor characters, such as Sir Alaric.
Wednesday	Let your child continue to work independently on his/her writing project. Have your child proofread what he/she has written so far, using the proofreading symbols discussed in Reading, Week 30, number 2.	Have your child use each of this week's spelling words correctly in a sentence.	Obtain another book by Dr. Seuss. Compare and contrast it with *The 500 Hats of Bartholomew Cubbins*.
Thursday	Let your child continue to work independently on his/her writing project.	Have your child study this week's spelling words.	Have your child imagine what happened when Bartholomew got home that night. Have your child write about that night's events in an epilogue to the story.
Friday	Have your child do a final edit and revision of his/her writing project.	Give your child the final spelling test. Have your child record pretest and final test words in his/her Word Bank.	Have your child choose another book by Dr. Seuss to read for enjoyment. Discuss different reasons for reading. Discuss how we adopt different reading styles when reading different types of books. Have your child compare how he/she would read poetry versus an instruction manual. Have your child complete **Delivery Dilemma** (p. 345). Your child must read the text carefully to gain information to solve the puzzle.

Learn At Home, Grade 5

Math	Science	Social Studies
Percents Introduce your child to the concept of percent. *See* Math, Week 35. Teach your child how to write a fraction as a percentage. If the denominator is 100, the numerator can be written as a percent. If the denominator is not 100, find an equivalent fraction before making the percent. *See* Math, Week 35, number 1. Have your child complete **Percents and Fractions** (p. 346).	**Making Work Easier** Discuss some of the inventions that have made your child's life easier. Then, have your child read *Shoes for Everyone* by Barbara Mitchell. *See* Science, Week 35, number 1.	**Washington, D.C.** Washington, D.C. is not part of any state. Many local residents think it should be considered a state of its own. Have your child read about the local government of Washington, D.C. *See* Social Studies, Week 35, number 1.
Use models to demonstrate the relationships among fractions, percents and decimals. *See* Math, Week 35, number 2. Have your child complete **Models** (p. 347).	Inventions arise out of needs. Brainstorm with your child things that he/she needs. Discuss how a new invention could fill that need. Have your child design on paper an invention to fill one of those needs. Have your child include simple machines in his/her design. *Alternative:* Have your child invent a machine that turns something very simple into a very complicated process. (Think of the game "Mousetrap.")	When the president is elected, he/she chooses a group of advisors, called the Cabinet. Have your child read about the presidential cabinet and list the different departments. Have your child make a list of current cabinet members. *What department does each member represent?*
Have your child present the following information using a circle graph: *Phillippe bought 100 flowers for his garden: 40 petunias, 20 pansies, 10 marigolds, 15 sunflowers and 15 violets.* Have your child label the graph with the percentage of the garden represented by each type of flower.	Have your child read about the work of Rube Goldberg, a cartoonist and sculptor who drew silly inventions. *See* Science, Week 35, number 2.	Read about some of the highlights of Washington, D.C., such as museums, monuments and other buildings. Have your child use a map of the city to locate these places. *See* Social Studies, Week 35, number 2.
Have your child make a circle graph to show how he/she would spend $100. First, have your child divide a circle into 10 equal parts. Each part represents $10 or 10% of the $100. Then, have your child decide how much he/she would spend on different things, rounding each amount to the nearest $10. **Example:** *Shade two sections if you will spend $20 on tapes or CDs.* Have your child shade each section of the graph a different color and label with the correct percentage. The graph should include a key.	Have your child construct a tower that can support a heavy weight. *See* Science, Week 35, number 3. Have your child write a paragraph describing what he/she learned from this experiment. Ask your child to consider the construction of tall buildings. *What issues must engineers who build skyscrapers consider in their designs?*	Have your child write five math word problems related to our nation's capital and the federal government.
Provide practical percent problems for your child to solve. Encourage your child to draw models to help solve the problems. **Example:** *If this square is 80%, draw a shape that could be 100%.* (Think as you did with fractions. Divide the square into eighths. Add two eighths to make the new shape.) *See* Math, Week 35, number 3.	Have your child design a maze for rolling a marble a given distance from a given height. *See* Science, Week 35, number 4.	Arrange for your child to perform some community service.

TEACHING SUGGESTIONS AND ACTIVITIES

MATH (Percents)

BACKGROUND
You have already taught your child that decimals and fractions are two different ways of writing the same number. Now, introduce percents. A percentage is simply another way of expressing hundredths. In a bag of 100 marbles, for example, 25 red marbles represent 25% of the marbles. To demonstrate percents, use the same hundredth models used with fractions and decimals.

▶ 1. The fraction $\frac{35}{100}$ is easily rewritten as a percent: 35%.

The fraction $\frac{4}{25}$ must first be rewritten as an equivalent fraction before it can be written as a percent.
Example: $\frac{4}{25} = \frac{16}{100} = 16\%$

▶ 2. Since percents are fractions of 100, they can be written as decimal fractions to the hundredths place.
Example: $36\% = \frac{36}{100} = 0.36$

▶ 3. Here are some examples of practical percent problems:

a. The company invited its 240 employees to a picnic. If 75% came to the picnic, how many employees showed up? (180 employees)

b. Rob's little league team won 25% of the 16 games they played this year. How many games did they win? (4 games)

c. Of the children enrolled in the summer reading program, 90% reached their reading goals. If 135 children reached their reading goals, how many were enrolled? (150 children)

d. Selena bought a computer at a 30% discount. If the computer originally cost $1200, how much did she pay for it? ($840)

e. If Fiona has read 60% of her 300-page book, how many pages does she have left? (120 pages)

SCIENCE (Making Work Easier)

▶ 1. Locate a copy of Barbara Mitchell's book, *Shoes for Everyone.* The book is about Jan Matzeliger, who invented a shoe-lasting machine in the late nineteenth century. This invention revolutionized the shoe industry. After your child has read the book, ask the following questions:

Where did Jan live as a small boy?
What was his father's occupation?
Why did Jan think that shoes were so special?
When Jan left home at age 19, where did he go and what did he do?
Why did he have trouble finding a job?
Jan moved to which city in 1877?
Which shoe manufacturer hired Jan?
What was the shoe process of lasting?
What machine did Jan invent from cigar boxes and scraps of metal?
Why did he leave his job for a new job at Beal Brothers?
Who provided the money for Jan to build his lasting machine?
When did he finally get his patent?
What effect did his lasting machine have on the shoe industry?
What was the "shoemaker's disease" that killed Jan in 1889, when he was only 37 years old?

▶ 2. Have your child read about the cartoonist Rube Goldberg and his amusing, absurdly complicated devices for accomplishing simple tasks, such as scratching one's back or blowing out a candle. Try to locate some of Goldberg's cartoons in books or magazine articles. Have your child describe each element of the machines he drew and what happens in each step to make the next part work.

Learn At Home, Grade 5

▶ 3. *You will need:* 30 drinking straws, masking tape, scissors, metal washers and a metric ruler.

Directions:

    a. Using only 15 straws and masking tape, design and construct a strong, sturdy tower that stands at least 25 centimeters tall and has a flat surface on top.

    b. Predict how many washers can be placed on the top surface before the tower collapses.

    c. Carefully place the metal washers, one at a time, on the flat surface on top of the tower.

    d. Continue to add metal washers until the tower collapses.

Have your child consider what he/she learned from the first tower. Then, have him/her construct a second tower, using the same materials, and repeat steps a–d. *Was the second tower an improvement over the first?*

▶ 4. Have your child design a device for rolling a marble through a complicated maze of tubes.

You will need: a variety of cardboard tubes, string, tape, a marble and a timer.

Directions:

    a. Tape or suspend one of the tubes to a high place in the room, such as the top of a door or cabinet.

    b. Continue to add tubes by attaching them to each other with tape.

    c. Create turns and dips as you add more tubes to the maze. Use tape or string to help support the maze.

    d. When the tube maze reaches the floor or a table, roll a marble through the maze.

    e. Measure the time that it takes the marble to complete its journey.

    f. Repeat steps d and e.

Was the time the same in each trial? What similar devices, such as a water slide or a museum maze, have you seen? Would a different size marble have a different travel time? Find one and see what happens.

SOCIAL STUDIES (Washington, D.C.)

▶ 1. Use some of the questions below to guide a discussion about the local government of Washington, D.C.

Who is the head of the city of Washington, D.C.?
How does that person get to hold that office?
What other positions are elected city offices?
What powers do the mayor and commissioners have?
Where does the city get its "spending money"?
What power does Congress have over the city?
Have the citizens of the city always been allowed to vote for local offices?
Have they been able to vote for national officials?
What have been some of the different voting laws for residents of Washington, D.C.? What are they now?
What are the restrictions on their one delegate to Congress?
Do you think Washington, D.C. should become a state? Give reasons for your answer.

▶ 2. Here is a partial list of the highlights of Washington, D.C.

    a. The Smithsonian Institution is made up of several museums, each with a different focus. All are free.

    b. The U.S. Holocaust Memorial Museum and the Vietnam Veterans Memorial Wall serve as reminders of two very important moments in history.

    c. The Bureau of Engraving and Printing makes money. Find out whose pictures are on the different denominations of bills and what is on the opposite side.

    d. The Capitol Building houses the Senate and House of Representatives. Visit the offices of your representatives or observe the House or Senate in session.

    e. The Supreme Court Building houses the third branch of the U.S. government. Find out the names of the current justices.

    f. The Library of Congress is the largest library in the world. Find out what books and other important items are housed there.

    g. The National Archives houses important documents in our nation's history. These documents are protected in special fireproof cases.

The "Nym" Family

answer
broad
combine
council
cymbal
downstairs
false
freeze
narrow
pause
plain
punish
question
reward
separate
thaw
true
upstairs

Words that have similar meanings are called **synonyms**.
Examples: trip, journey

Words that have opposite meanings are called **antonyms**.
Examples: hot, cold

Words that sound the same but have different spellings and meanings are called **homonyms**. **Examples:** blue, blew

Use the word list to unscramble the spelling words below. Then, **draw** a line to connect each pair of antonyms.

etusniqo _____   zrefee _____

draiswtson _____   wersan _____

waht _____   woranr _____

nieocbm _____   treapsea _____

odarb _____   riusptas _____

Write a synonym for each of the following.

to chastise _____   faithful _____

a prize _____   erroneous _____

Write the homonym that will complete each pair.

1. plane _____   3. paws _____

2. symbol _____   4. counsel _____

Write twelve sets of homonyms.

1. _____ _____   5. _____ _____   9. _____ _____

2. _____ _____   6. _____ _____   10. _____ _____

3. _____ _____   7. _____ _____   11. _____ _____

4. _____ _____   8. _____ _____   12. _____ _____

Learn At Home, Grade 5

Delivery Dilemma

Dilly's Deliveries is under new management, and the new boss just instructed his top driver to follow a most peculiar route. The driver is to deliver packages to each of the eight businesses shown below, but she is not necessarily meant to visit them in a logical order.

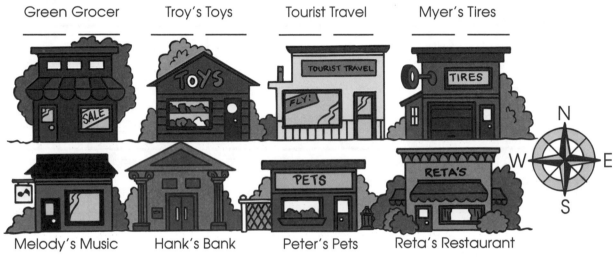

Green Grocer   Troy's Toys   Tourist Travel   Myer's Tires

Melody's Music   Hank's Bank   Peter's Pets   Reta's Restaurant

Help the confused driver plan her route. Number the businesses above in the order in which they should be visited in the first blank. **Write** the number of packages to be delivered in the second blank.

1. The second delivery is directly north of the first delivery and has one fewer package than the first.
2. Melody's Music needs all five packages delivered before 11:00 A.M.
3. By the time the paperwork is completed, the packages are verified and greetings are exchanged between the driver and the recipient, each delivery takes fifteen minutes.
4. The bank is never the last delivery. It always receives four packages.
5. Troy's Toys has the most packages of all. His delivery will contain as many packages as all the others combined.
6. Pete's deliveries are live animals, which need to be unloaded first when the store opens at 9:30 A.M.
7. The fourth delivery is directly east of the first delivery and contains twice the number of packages.
8. The travel agency and the pet store combined are to receive the same number of packages as the music store.
9. The fifth delivery contains three boxes.
10. The third delivery is two stores west of the second.
11. The tire store, the grocery store and the pet store will all receive the same number of packages. They are the only ones to receive this exact amount.

Percents and Fractions

Write the fraction and percent represented in each situation.

Situation	Fraction	Percent
30 marbles out of 100 marbles are red	$\frac{30}{100}$	30%
29 people out of 100 people voted.		
10 fish out of 100 fish are tropical.		
7 cats out of 100 cats live indoors.		
4 turtles out of 100 turtles laid eggs.		
7 out of 10 puppies had spots.	$\frac{7}{10} = \overline{100}$	
5 out of 10 baskets were made.		
6 out of 25 rocks in my yard are igneous.	$\frac{6}{25} = \overline{100}$	
17 out of 25 rulers are metric.		
18 out of 20 goldfish are orange.		
The dress was reduced $5 from $20.		

Learn At Home, Grade 5

Models

Draw the model and **fill in** the missing fraction, percent or decimal.

Draw	Fraction	Percent	Decimal
			0.25
	$\frac{37}{100}$		
		18%	
	$\frac{7}{10}$		
		4%	

	Language Skills	**Spelling**	**Reading**
Monday	**Review** Review parts of speech. Give your child a paragraph from a book. Ask your child to circle the nouns, underline the verbs once, underline the pronouns twice, draw stars above the adjectives and draw boxes around the adverbs. Finally, ask your child to go back and highlight all the conjunctions, prepositions and interjections. Reteach the parts of speech that your child cannot readily identify.	**Review** Select words from the past eight weeks for this week's pretest. Have your child correct the pretest. Add personalized words and make two copies of this week's study list.	**Review** Have your child select the reading book for this week. Ask your child to write a prediction of what he/she expects to learn from the book. Use this book to review the language skills listed each day this week. Discuss new vocabulary from the book.
Tuesday	Review punctuation: commas, periods, colons, semicolons, exclamation marks, question marks and quotation marks. Copy a paragraph from a book, omitting all punctuation. Have your child fill in the correct punctuation. Reteach any punctuation that your child has difficulty using correctly.	Have your child sort the spelling words from the past eight weeks by number of syllables. *Which group (one-syllable words, two-syllable words, etc.) contains the greatest number of words? Which contains the least? What percentage of the words studied have three syllables?*	Have your child write a sentence or two describing the main idea of each chapter as he/she reads.
Wednesday	Review sentence structure. Have your child write a paragraph on a topic related to this week's reading book. Ask your child to include a variety of sentences (simple, compound and complex). Check your child's work for subject/verb agreement and complete sentences. Reteach, if necessary.	Have your child sort the spelling words from the past eight weeks again, this time by parts of speech (nouns, verbs, adjectives, etc.). *In which category does the majority of the words belong? What is the ratio of nouns to verbs?*	Ask your child to identify the problem in the story. Have him/her predict how the problem will be solved.
Thursday	Review the four different kinds of paragraphs. Give your child a newspaper. Have your child locate examples of each type of paragraph: narrative, expository, descriptive and persuasive.	Help your child make a crossword puzzle with spelling words from the past eight weeks. your child should use definitions as clues. Once the puzzle is completed, let your child give it to a friend to solve.	Have your child list phrases from the book that express opinions. Then, have your child list phrases from the book that express facts.
Friday	Have your child write about what he/she has learned this year and what he/she hopes to learn next year.	Give your child the final spelling test.	Have your child analyze his/her predictions about the book. How accurate were they? Have your child write a summary and review of the book.

Learn At Home, Grade 5

Math	**Science**	**Social Studies**
Ratios Ratios, like fractions, compare numbers. Fractions are ratios that compare parts to the whole. Ratios may also compare parts to parts, time to distance, rates and probabilities. *See* Math, Week 36, number 1. Have your child find examples of ratios in the newspaper or in comparisons that you use regularly.	If possible, plan a trip to visit an amusement park. Have your child observe and record (with diagrams) the types of simple machines found on the rides.	**Washington, D.C.** Have your child write twelve sentences related to Washington, D.C.—six about the capital and six about the Capitol.
A ratio of 1:1 means there is the same number of each object. There is a 1:1 ratio of feet to shoes when there are two shoes and two feet. There may be a 1:1 ratio of cars to drivers on the road if all the cars have one driver. Teach your child to simplify ratios. To name equivalent ratios, multiply or divide both numbers by the same number. **Example:** 4:8 = 2:4 = 1:2 Have your child simplify given ratios. *See* Math, Week 36, number 2.	Have your child interview an inventor or read a biography of an inventor.	Washington, D.C. is considered to be a national symbol. Have your child explain why this is so. Then, have your child design a souvenir that might be sold to tourists who visit the capital city.
Review: Review and reteach concepts taught this year. Repeat activities that your child found especially difficult or challenging.	Have your child write "What-Am-I?" riddles about simple and compound machines. Provide your child with a list of machines, or let him/her choose others. The riddle should be made up of clues about the work the machine does and how it is built. The clues should start out broad, then become more specific. *See* Science, Week 36.	Have your child study the interior of the White House. Discuss the purpose of the different rooms. Discuss the influence of different presidents and their spouses. Pose the following question: *If you could live in the White House, which room would you choose to be your own? Explain.*
Give your child a final test on math concepts. Have your child complete **Final Exam** (p. 352).	Review the concept map maintained over the course of this unit. Ask your child to recall information outlined in the concept map. Review pertinent vocabulary.	Have your child compare Washington, D.C. with another city he/she knows. *See* Social Studies, Week 36, number 1.
Reteach any concepts missed on the exam. Then, celebrate the learning that took place this year.	Help your child use tools to construct something out of wood. Discuss the simple machines that make up the tools and other building supplies.	Assess your child's community service experience. Ask your child to choose the services he/she liked best. Have your child write an honest evaluation of his/her performance. Play a game with clues about sights in Washington, D.C. You will need a copy of **See the U.S.A.** (p. 353). *See* Social Studies, Week 36, number 2.

TEACHING SUGGESTIONS AND ACTIVITIES

MATH (Ratios)

▶ 1. In the last few lessons, your child has been working with forms of ratios. *Ratios* are basically comparisons of different units. Percents compare the number of parts to 100. Miles per hour compares miles to hours. Batting averages compare hits to the number of times at bat. Challenge your child to locate ratios encountered in his/her everyday life. Help your child learn to recognize ratios and write them down in two ways.

Examples: children in the family—**3 girls to 2 boys** or **3:2**
red cars to blue cars—**14 red to 23 blue** or **14:23**

Have your child practice this format by naming ratios he/she sees in your home. Have your child compare seats to people, books to boxes, wheels to bicycles, hands to fingers, pounds to ounces and so on.

▶ 2. Write the following ratios on the chalkboard. Have your child simplify each one.

4:6	6:21	2:12	5:25	4:18	7:14	100:1000	90:100
5:15	3:9	12:42	5:100	8:88	34:170	24:36	14:21

SCIENCE (Machines)

Have your child compose a series of riddles about simple or compound machines.
Read the riddle below to your child, as an example.

What Machine Am I?

You may use me every day.
I am made up of several simple machines.
I have a wedge that pierces metal.
I have two levers that come together.
I have some gears that turn around.
If you want soup, I should be found.

What Am I? (Answer: *a can opener*)

Write the following machines on separate index cards. Have your child choose a card, then write a riddle about the device. Repeat with other cards. Write a few riddles for your child to solve as well.

lawn mower	scissors	stapler	fingernail clipper
weed cutter	toaster	spatula	salad spinner
wheelbarrow	car jack	hammer	cookie cutter
pencil sharpener	ramp	broom	lawn sprinkler

Learn At Home, Grade 5

SOCIAL STUDIES (Washington, D.C.)

▶ 1. Have your child use the following questions as guidelines when comparing Washington, D.C. to another city.

What social problems do the cities have?
What are their public transportation systems like?
Do the people participate in the same type of recreational activities?
What kind of work do many of the people do?
What are the downtown areas (shopping areas) like in each city?
What are the backgrounds of the citizens in each community?
What are the major local industries?
Which city has a greater population density?

▶ 2. Play a simple game using the game board pictured on **See the U.S.A.** (p. 353), the clues below and a die. Copy the game board and laminate for durability. Write each of the clues below onto a separate index card. (You may also want to add additional clues on other social studies topics covered this year—historical events and people, geographic regions, etc.) Include the answer at the bottom of each card. Stack the cards facedown next to the board. Roll the die to see who goes first. Player 1 then rolls the die again. His/her opponent draws a card and reads the clue aloud. If Player 1 answers correctly, he/she moves the number shown on the die and rolls again. If Player 1 does not answer correctly, Player 2 takes a turn. The first player to reach "Finish" wins the game.

Clues for the game cards:

It has 897 steps to the top. (Washington Monument)
The constitutionality of laws and government practices are discussed here. (Supreme Court)
An Englishman who had never come to America gave it as a gift. (Smithsonian)
President Madison lived here when the White House was destroyed by fire. (Octagon House)
The nation's documents are preserved here. (National Archives)
The names of over 58,000 men and women are inscribed on its black walls. (Vietnam Veterans Memorial)
It's green and lies between the Capitol and the Lincoln Memorial. (The Mall)
She is on top of the Capitol's dome. (Liberty)
The use of alcohol, tobacco and firearms is controlled by this cabinet department. (Treasury)
U.S. foreign policy originates and is carried out here. (State Department)
It makes our paper money. (Bureau of Engraving and Printing)
John Wilkes Booth fatally wounded President Lincoln here. (Ford's Theater)
It is home to the National Symphony Orchestra. (Kennedy Center for the Performing Arts)
Thirty-six columns around this structure represented the states in the Union at the time. (Lincoln Memorial)
National Parks and Monuments are under this department's jurisdiction. (Department of Interior)
Its circular dome honors the man who stands inside. (Jefferson Memorial)
It is guarded twenty-four hours a day, but it is not in Washington. (Tomb of the Unknown Soldier)
The history of flight is displayed here. (National Air and Space Museum)
It is authorized to investigate federal crimes. (Federal Bureau of Investigation)
It has exactly 100 members. (U.S. Senate)
Its three buildings contain approximately 100 million items written in 470 languages. (Library of Congress)

351

Final Exam

1. Write out 2,645,782.06 in words. _____

_____

Solve.

2. 65 + _____ = 83

3. 13,692 + 78 + 313 = a

a = _____

4. 37 x 30 = y

y = _____

Estimate.

5. 856,311
   − 21,400

6. 33 $\overline{)5,827}$

7. Find the average of these numbers: 7, 12, 29, 15, 18, 15. _____

8. Identify each polygon. ■ _____ ⬡ _____ ▲ _____

9. Find the perimeter and area.

   9 / 5 / 5 / 9   perimeter _____

   7 in. / 7 in.   area _____

10. Write this fraction in lowest terms. _____

11. Use < or > to indicate which fraction is greater. $\frac{7}{9}$ $\frac{4}{9}$ $\frac{5}{12}$ $\frac{5}{9}$

Solve.

12. $\frac{3}{11} + \frac{5}{11} =$ _____

13. $\frac{3}{4} + \frac{1}{8} =$ _____

14. $3\frac{1}{3} + 2\frac{1}{2} =$ _____

15. $12\frac{5}{6} - 1\frac{1}{4} =$ _____

16. $\frac{7}{8} \times \frac{1}{4} =$ _____

17. $\frac{4}{5} \div \frac{2}{3} =$ _____

18. Change $\frac{18}{5}$ into a mixed number. _____

19. Write 3.4 as a mixed number in lowest terms. _____

Add, subtract, multiply or divide.

20. 37.3 + 265.25 = _____
22. 3.654 − 1.7 = _____
24. Write 35% as a fraction. _____

21. 4.8 x 1.3 = _____
23. 37.75 ÷ 100 = _____
25. 17.2 ÷ 8 = _____

© 1999 Tribune Education. All Rights Reserved.

Learn At Home, Grade 5

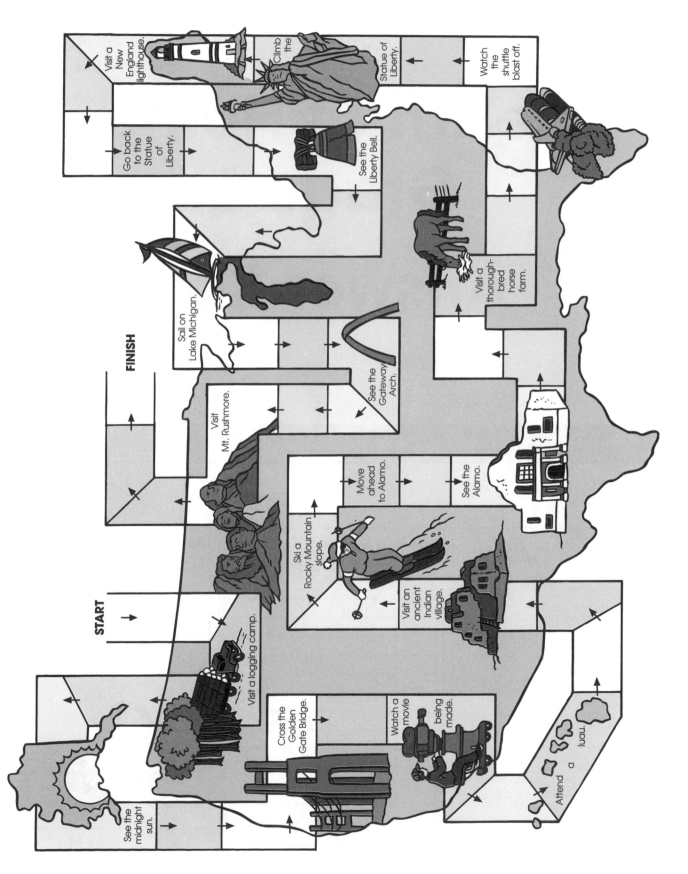

Learn at Home
Grade 5

Answer Key

Homophones

Homophones are words that sound alike but have different spellings and meanings.

Write the correct homophone in the blank.

___Their___ house is around the corner from us. (their, there)

1. We couldn't decide __whether__ to visit Boston or St. Louis. (weather, whether)

2. We chose to visit Boston, the __capital__ of Massachusetts. (capital, capitol)

3. We drove __to__ the city in __two__ days. (to, too, two)

4. Our __route__ was over interstate highways. (route, root)

5. We __read__ many signs along the way. (read, red)

6. My brothers couldn't hide __their__ excitement. (their, there)

7. We found that __it's__ an exciting city. (its, it's)

8. It was interesting to __hear__ the accent of the people. (hear, here)

9. Many people related interesting __tales__ to us about the city's history. (tales, tails)

10. We appreciated the __peace__ and quiet of the parks. (peace, piece)

11. We walked up and down __rows__ of houses in the historic district. (rows, rose)

12. I wore a __hole__ in one of my shoes from __so__ much walking. (whole, hole) (so, sew)

13. Luckily, this caused me __no__ __pain__. (know, no) (pain, pane)

14. I had to have the __sole__ of the shoe repaired. (soul, sole)

page 22

Synonym or Antonym?

Draw a green circle around each word that is a synonym of the first word.
Draw an orange box around each word that is its antonym. Use a dictionary to look up any words you do not know.

forfeit	choose	generous	gain	lose
adjacent	sudden	nearby	clean	remote
pompous	modest	festive	noisy	proud
nosegay	unhappy	bouquet	puncture	weeds
exquisite	careful	beyond	hideous	delightful
impeccable	flawed	perfect	scarce	painful
wary	alert	brittle	unguarded	tired
harry	furry	attract	annoy	soothe
despondently	happily	elegantly	crazily	unhappily
interrogate	cross-examine	dislike	persecute	hush
cull	answer	charge	select	scatter
elude	confront	scold	avoid	frighten

page 23

Amazing a

Write each spelling word in the appropriate spelling pattern category.

Long a

ay	a-e
anyway	amaze
daydream	brace
delay	place
essay	rate
dismay	wage

a	ai
basic	braid
hasten	daisy
matriarch	faint
nature	raisin

amaze
anyway
basic
brace
braid
daisy
daydream
delay
dismay
essay
faint
hasten
matriarch
nature
place
raisin
rate
wage

page 24

Learn at Home, Grade 5

Checks

Fill in each check completely. Invent who you will write it to and why.

Name		
Address		6389A
	Date	

Pay to the Order of _____ $ _____
_____ Dollars

School Bank
5555 Fifth Street
Fifthville, GA 32132

For _____ _____
Signature

Name		
Address		6390A
	Date	

Pay to the Order of _____ $ _____
_____ Dollars

School Bank
5555 Fifth Street
Fifthville, GA 32132

For _____ _____
Signature

Name		
Address		6391A
	Date	

Pay to the Order of _____ $ _____
_____ Dollars

School Bank
5555 Fifth Street
Fifthville, GA 32132

For _____ _____
Signature

page 25

Phyla Match

Scientists separate animals according to their differences and group them according to their likenesses.
Draw a line from the phylum in the first column to the correct picture and then to the related characteristics. The first one is done for you.

Chordates — The bodies of these marine animals have limy plates with spines.

Echinoderms — These animals have a head, thorax, abdomen and three or more pairs of legs.

Mollusks — These animals have a notochord (a rod-like structure) down the middle of their backs.

Arthropods — These radially symmetrical animals contain a jellylike material between two layers of cells.

Coelenterates — These soft-bodied animals are usually covered by a limy shell.

Segmented Worms — These animals have soft, thin, flat bodies made of three layers of cells.

Flatworms — These animals have long bodies divided into many segments.

page 27

Breezing Through e

On the flags, **write** the spelling words according to the **long e** spelling patterns.
Indicate the spelling pattern to the right of each flag.

breathe
breeze
crease
delight
donkey
eager
hockey
kidney
lease
plead
queen
recent
respond
screech
sleeve
squeak
steam
zebra

Spelling Pattern

1. donkey
2. hockey
3. kidney
— **ey**

1. breeze
2. queen
3. screech
4. sleeve
— **ee**

1. breathe   5. plead
2. crease   6. squeak
3. eager   7. steam
4. lease

1. delight
2. recent
3. respond
4. zebra
— **ea**

— **e**

w Answers may include: ords with the **long e** sound.

1. When two e's are together you have a long e sound
2. When there is an ey combination you have a long e sound
3. The combination ea produces a long e sound
4. E alone may produce a long sound, try it out

page 32

Story Organizer

Date _____ Title _____

Vocabulary	Definitions
_____	_____
_____	_____
_____	_____
_____	_____
_____	_____

Setting: _____
Characters: _____
Problem: _____

Answers will vary.

Events: _____
_____
_____
_____

Solution: _____
_____

Did you enjoy this story?   1 2 3 4 5 6
Not   Very
at all   much!

page 33

Dog's Best Friend

Bob the butcher is popular with the dogs in town. He was making a delivery this morning when he noticed he was being followed by two dogs. Bob tried to climb a ladder to escape from the dogs. Solve the following addition problems and shade in the answers on the ladder. If all the numbers are shaded when the problems have been solved, Bob made it up the ladder. Some answers may not be on the ladder.

1. 986,145 621,332 + 200,008 **1,807,485**	2. 1,873,402 925,666 + 4,689 **2,803,757**	3. 506,328 886,510 + 342,225 **1,735,063**
4. 43,015 2,811,604 + 987,053 **3,841,672**	5. 18,443 300,604 + 999,999 **1,319,046**	6. 8,075 14,608 + 33,914 **56,597**
7. 9,162 7,804 + 755,122 **772,088**	8. 88,714 213,653 + 5,441,298 **5,743,665**	9. 3,244,662 1,986,114 + 521,387 **5,752,163**
10. 4,581 22,983 + 5,618,775 **5,646,339**	11. 818,623 926 + 3,260,004 **4,079,553**	12. 80,436 9,159 + 3,028,761 **3,118,356**
13. 25,004 862,010 + 9,302 **896,316**	14. 5,043,666 4,589,771 + 8,711,229 **18,344,666**	15. 432,188 900,000 + 611,042 **1,943,230**

Ladder:
1,319,046
2,803,757
5,743,665
3,118,356
56,597
4,079,553
1,807,485
2,943,230
18,344,666
1,735,063
5,752,163
896,316
3,841,672
5,646,339

Does Bob make it? __No__

page 34

Rounding

Follow these steps to round numbers to a given place.

Example: Round 35,634 to the nearest thousand.

34,000 35,000 36,000 37,000
35,634

a. Locate and highlight the place to which the number is to be rounded. ► Highlight the digit in the thousands place: 3**5**,634

b. Look at the digit to the right of the designated place. If the number is 5 or greater, round the highlighted number up. If the number is 4 or less, round the highlighted number down by keeping the digit the same. ► Six is greater than 5, so round the highlighted number up.

c. Rewrite the original number with the amended digit in the highlighted place and change all of the digits to the right to zeros. ► The rounded number is 36,000.

Example: Round 782 to the nearest 10.

770   780   790   800
782

► Highlight the digit in the tens place: 7**8**2
► Two is four or less, so round down by keeping the tens digit the same. 782
► The rounded number is 780.

Round each number to the given place.

nearest 10:	1. 855	**860**	2. 333	**330**
nearest 100:	3. 725	**700**	4. 2,348	**2,300**
nearest 1,000:	5. 4,317	**4,000**	6. 8,650	**9,000**
nearest 10,000:	7. 25,199	**30,000**	8. 529,740	**530,000**
nearest 100,000:	9. 496,225	**500,000**	10. 97,008	**100,000**

page 35

Number-Line Rounding

Label the endpoints. **Plot** the given number. **Circle** the closer endpoint. The first three have been done for you.

1. Round 87 to the nearest ten.
2. Round 1,322 to the nearest hundred.
3. Round 1,475 to the nearest ten.
4. Round 8,274 to the nearest ten.
5. Round 8,274 to the nearest hundred.
6. Round 1,452 to the nearest thousand.
7. Round 1,452 to the nearest ten.
8. Round 6,937 to the nearest thousand.
9. Round 8,485 to the nearest thousand.
10. Round 25,683 to the nearest ten thousand.

page 36

Estimating Sums

Estimate by rounding before you add.

Nearest Ten	Nearest Hundred	Nearest Thousand
88 → 90	244 → 200	4,566 → 5,000
+ 51 → + 50	+ 776 → + 800	+ 3,320 → + 3,000
139 140	1,020 1,000	7,886 8,000

Actual = 139
Estimated = 140
Difference = 1

Actual = 1,020
Estimated = 1,000
Difference = 20

Actual = 7,886
Estimated = 8,000
Difference = 114

When you do not have to be exact, estimating can be easy and close to the actual sum.

Estimate the sums. Round numbers to the highest place value of the smaller number.

1. 52 → 50 / + 66 → 70 = 118 120
2. 618 → 600 / + 384 → 400 = 1,002 1,000
3. 3,477 → 3,000 / + 8,611 → 9,000 = 12,088 12,000
4. 44 → 40 / + 91 → 90 = 135 130
5. 222 → 200 / + 479 → 500 = 701 700
6. 1,190 → 1,000 / + 7,625 → 8,000 = 8,815 9,000
7. 36 → 30 / + 19 → 20 = 55 50
8. 566 → 600 / + 818 → 800 = 1,384 1,400
9. 4,533 → 5,000 / + 7,498 → 7,000 = 12,031 12,000

page 37

Place Value

Read and solve.

1. Write the number 2,058,763 in words. ___
two million, fifty-eight thousand, seven hundred sixty-three

2. Write the following in numerals: eight billion, two hundred thirty-seven million, eighty-five thousand, three hundred four.
8,237,085,304

3. In the number 9,876,543,210 . . .
which digit is in the hundred thousands place? __5__
which digit is in the ones place? __0__
in what place is the 9? __billions__

4. Add.
3,259 + 32,769 + 305 = __36,333__
8,759,233 + 3,410 + 655,200 = __9,417,843__

5. Round . . .
84,239 to the nearest ten. __84,240__
7,857,355 to the nearest ten thousand. __7,860,000__

6. Estimate the sum.
34,396 → 30,000
+ 5,875 → + 6,000
36,000

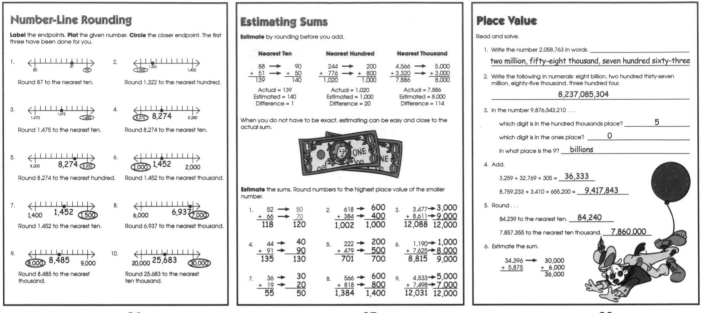

page 38

Sort 'Em Out

Vertebrates are animals with backbones. Animals without backbones are called **invertebrates**. At the bottom of the page are pictures of both kinds of animals. **Write** the name of each animal under the correct heading below.

Vertebrates	Invertebrates
1. dog	1. octopus
2. boy	2. snail
3. turtle	3. starfish
4. frog	4. lobster
5. lizard	5. oyster

Color and **cut out** all the vertebrates. On a separate sheet of paper, make a background using felt-tip markers for your vertebrate animals and **glue** them on it. Label your drawing: **Vertebrates**.

page 39

Good, Bad; Well, Badly

Good and **bad** are adjectives that modify nouns or pronouns. **Well** and **badly** are adverbs that modify verbs.

Examples:
A guitar is a **good** instrument to play on a hayride.
Bringing a piano along would be a **bad** choice.
It's hard to play the accordion **well** while you're dancing.
I played **badly** because my arm was sore.

Complete each sentence below with the correct adjective or adverb found in parentheses. In the blank at the end of the sentence, **write** whether an adjective or adverb has been used.

1. Michele used to play the clarinet __badly__ (bad, badly) when she first started. __adverb__

2. I felt Mark's choice to learn how to play the piano was a __good__ (good, well) one. __adjective__

3. Curt sang very __well__ (good, well) at the graduation ceremony last night. __adverb__

4. Alan made a __bad__ (bad, badly) choice when he quit music class before the session ended. __adjective__

5. Debra made a __good__ (good, well) decision when she brought the music home to practice over vacation. __adjective__

6. Mr. Sutton said that I display __good__ (good, well) rhythm. __adjective__

7. Leaving an expensive instrument out where it can get damaged is a __bad__ (bad, badly) thing to do. __adjective__

8. Gwen performed the trumpet solo __well__ (good, well) because she practiced every day. __adverb__

page 44

Mile-High i

These planes have sighted four spelling patterns for the **long i** sound. **Write** each spelling word in the correct category.

arrive
childhood
chime
climate
delight
digest
fighting
grind
ideal
prize
sight
silence
spying
style
thigh
timing
title
violin

y
spying
style

i-e
arrive
chime
prize

igh
delight
fighting
sight
thigh

i
childhood
climate
grind

digest
ideal
silence

timing
title
violin

page 45

Learn at Home, Grade 5

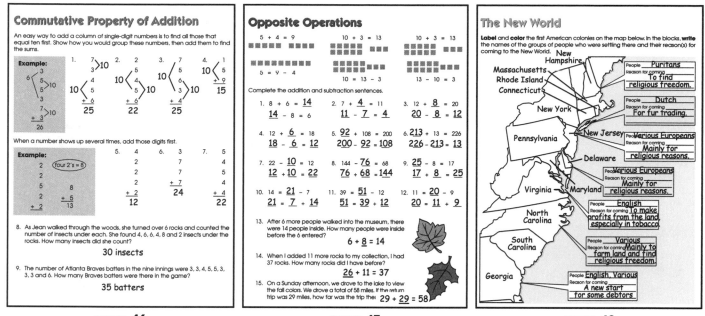

Commutative Property of Addition

An easy way to add a column of single-digit numbers is to find all those that equal ten first. Show how you would group these numbers, then add them to find the sums.

Example:

```
   7
6  3 >10      1. 7 >10   2. 2        3. 7 >10   4. 1
   5             3          2           6          10< 5
10<5          10< 2      10< 4 >10   10< 6 >10      + 9
   3             5          5          3           15
   7 >10       + 6        + 6        + 4
 + 3            25         22         25
   26
```

When a number shows up several times, add those digits first.

Example:

```
   2              5. 4   6. 3   7. 5
 (four 2's = 8)      2      7      4
   2                 2      7      5
   5        8        2    + 7      4
   2      + 5      + 2      24   + 4
 + 2       13       12            22
```

8. As Jean walked through the woods, she turned over 6 rocks and counted the number of insects under each. She found 4, 6, 6, 4, 8 and 2 insects under the rocks. How many insects did she count?

30 insects

9. The number of Atlanta Braves batters in the nine innings were 3, 3, 4, 5, 5, 3, 3, 3 and 6. How many Braves batters were there in the game?

35 batters

page 46

Opposite Operations

Complete the addition and subtraction sentences.

1. $8 + 6 = \underline{14}$
   $\underline{14} - 8 = 6$

2. $7 + \underline{4} = 11$
   $\underline{11} - 7 = \underline{4}$

3. $12 + \underline{8} = 20$
   $\underline{20} - 8 = \underline{12}$

4. $12 + \underline{6} = 18$
   $\underline{18} - \underline{6} = \underline{12}$

5. $\underline{92} + 108 = 200$
   $\underline{200} - 92 = \underline{108}$

6. $\underline{213} + 13 = 226$
   $\underline{226} - \underline{213} = \underline{13}$

7. $22 - \underline{10} = 12$
   $\underline{12} + \underline{10} = 22$

8. $144 - \underline{76} = 68$
   $\underline{76} + \underline{68} = \underline{144}$

9. $\underline{25} - 8 = 17$
   $\underline{17} + \underline{8} = \underline{25}$

10. $14 = \underline{21} - 7$
    $\underline{21} = \underline{7} + 14$

11. $39 = \underline{51} - 12$
    $\underline{51} = \underline{39} + 12$

12. $11 = \underline{20} - 9$
    $\underline{20} = \underline{11} + \underline{9}$

13. After 6 more people walked into the museum, there were 14 people inside. How many people were inside before the 6 entered?
    $6 + \underline{8} = 14$

14. When I added 11 more rocks to my collection, I had 37 rocks. How many rocks did I have before?
    $\underline{26} + 11 = 37$

15. On a Sunday afternoon, we drove to the lake to view the fall colors. We drove a total of 58 miles. If the return trip was 29 miles, how far was the trip there? $29 + \underline{29} = 58$

page 47

The New World

Label and **color** the first American colonies on the map below. In the blocks, **write** the names of the groups of people who were settling there and their reason(s) for coming to the New World.

People **Puritans** — Reason for coming **To find religious freedom.**

People **Dutch** — Reason for coming **For fur trading.**

People **Various Europeans** — Reason for coming **Mainly for religious reasons.**

People **Various Europeans** — Reason for coming **Mainly for religious reasons.**

People **English** — Reason for coming **To make profits from the land, especially in tobacco.**

People **Various** — Reason for coming **Mainly to farm land and find religious freedom.**

People **English, Various** — Reason for coming **A new start for some debtors**

Map labels: New Hampshire, Massachusetts, Rhode Island, Connecticut, New York, Pennsylvania, New Jersey, Delaware, Maryland, Virginia, North Carolina, South Carolina, Georgia

page 49

Proper Adjectives

Adjectives are words that describe nouns. **Proper adjectives** are formed from proper nouns, and they must be capitalized. Other adjectives are called **common nouns**.

Examples:
proper adjectives: **French** toast, **American** flag
common adjectives: **cold** toast, **waving** flag

Circle all the adjectives in the sentences below.

1. Camels have carried loads across (desert) sands for centuries.
2. They were once the (only) means of transporting goods across the (Sahara) Desert and (Middle Eastern) deserts.
3. The (Sahara) Desert is in the (North African) desert region.
4. The (Arabian) camel has (one) hump, while the (Bactrian) camel has (two) humps.
5. The (Bactrian) camel got its name long ago from a (Central Asian) country known as Bactria.
6. Both types of camels are used in (some) (Asian) regions.
7. In wars (fighting) men have ridden the (faithful) camel.
8. The camel Napoleon rode during his (Egyptian) campaign was later put in an exhibit.

Write each circled adjective under the proper heading.

Proper Adjectives	Common Adjectives
1. Sahara	1. desert
2. Middle Eastern	2. only
3. Sahara	3. desert
4. North African	4. one
5. Arabian	5. two
6. Bactrian	6. some
7. Bactrian	7. fighting
8. Central Asian	8. faithful
9. Asian	
10. Egyptian	

page 54

Honing Long o Skills

Write each long o word in the appropriate category.
Answers may vary.

Long o Categories

o	oa	o-e	ow
buffalo	cloak	chose	arrow
burro	foam	chrome	grown
gopher	loan	compose	knowing
solo	loaves	cove	rows
	roast		
	soak		

arrow, buffalo, burro, chose, chrome, cloak, compose, cove, foam, gopher, grown, knowing, loan, loaves, roast, rows, soak, solo

Answers may vary

1. buffalo (N)
2. burro (N)
3. gopher (N)
4. solo (N)
5. cloak (N)
6. foam (N)
7. loan (N)
8. loaves (N)
9. roast (V)
10. soak (V)
11. chose (V)
12. chrome (A)
13. compose (V)
14. cove (N)
15. arrow (N)
16. grown (V)
17. knowing (A)
18. rows (N)

page 55

Adding Inches and Feet

When adding inches, regroup 1 foot for every 12 inches.

Example:

a. 1 ft. 8 in. + 1 ft. 8 in. = 16 in.
   16 in. = 1 ft. 4 in.

b. 1 ft. 8 in. + 1 ft. 8 in. = 4 in.

c. 1 ft. 8 in. + 1 ft. 8 in. = 3 ft. 4 in.

1. 2 ft. 4 in. + 1 ft. 9 in. = **4 ft. 1 in.**
2. 12 ft. 10 in. + 1 ft. 5 in. = **14 ft. 3 in.**
3. 12 ft. 7 in. + 8 ft. 8 in. = **21 ft. 3 in.**
4. 1 ft. 5 in. + 3 ft. 6 in. = **4 ft. 11 in.**
5. 1 ft. 6 in. + 1 ft. 6 in. = **3 ft. 0 in.**
6. 7 ft. 4 in. + 5 ft. 5 in. = **12 ft. 9 in.**
7. 28 ft. 8 in. + 4 ft. 9 in. = **33 ft. 5 in.**
8. 8 ft. 9 in. + 7 in. = **9 ft. 4 in.**
9. 3 ft. 3 in. + 6 ft. 7 in. = **9 ft. 10 in.**

page 56

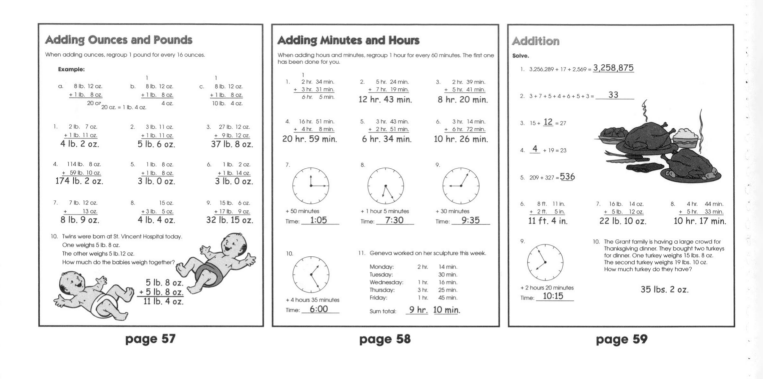

Adding Ounces and Pounds

When adding ounces, regroup 1 pound for every 16 ounces.

Example:

a. 8 lb. 12 oz. + 1 lb. 8 oz. 20 oz 20 oz. = 1 lb. 4 oz.	b. 8 lb. 12 oz. + 1 lb. 8 oz. 4 oz.	c. 8 lb. 12 oz. + 1 lb. 8 oz. 10 lb. 4 oz.

1. 2 lb. 7 oz. + 1 lb. 11 oz. **4 lb. 2 oz.**	2. 3 lb. 11 oz. + 1 lb. 11 oz. **5 lb. 6 oz.**	3. 27 lb. 12 oz. + 9 lb. 12 oz. **37 lb. 8 oz.**
4. 114 lb. 8 oz. + 59 lb. 10 oz. **174 lb. 2 oz.**	5. 1 lb. 8 oz. + 1 lb. 8 oz. **3 lb. 0 oz.**	6. 1 lb. 2 oz. + 1 lb. 14 oz. **3 lb. 0 oz.**
7. 7 lb. 12 oz. + 13 oz. **8 lb. 9 oz.**	8. 15 oz. + 3 lb. 5 oz. **4 lb. 4 oz.**	9. 15 lb. 6 oz. + 17 lb. 9 oz. **32 lb. 15 oz.**

10. Twins were born at St. Vincent Hospital today.
One weighs 5 lb. 8 oz.
The other weighs 5 lb.12 oz.
How much do the babies weigh together?

5 lb. 8 oz.
+ 5 lb. 8 oz.
11 lb. 4 oz.

page 57

Adding Minutes and Hours

When adding hours and minutes, regroup 1 hour for every 60 minutes. The first one has been done for you.

1. 2 hr. 34 min. + 3 hr. 31 min. 6 hr. 5 min.	2. 5 hr. 24 min. + 7 hr. 19 min. **12 hr. 43 min.**	3. 2 hr. 39 min. + 5 hr. 41 min. **8 hr. 20 min.**
4. 16 hr. 51 min. + 4 hr. 8 min. **20 hr. 59 min.**	5. 3 hr. 43 min. + 2 hr. 51 min. **6 hr. 34 min.**	6. 3 hr. 14 min. + 6 hr. 72 min. **10 hr. 26 min.**

7. + 50 minutes Time: **1:05**

8. + 1 hour 5 minutes Time: **7:30**

9. + 30 minutes Time: **9:35**

10. + 4 hours 35 minutes Time: **6:00**

11. Geneva worked on her sculpture this week.

Monday:	2 hr.	14 min.
Tuesday:		30 min.
Wednesday:	1 hr.	16 min.
Thursday:	3 hr.	25 min.
Friday:	1 hr.	45 min.
Sum total:	**9 hr.**	**10 min.**

page 58

Addition

Solve.

1. 3,256,289 + 17 + 2,569 = **3,258,875**

2. 3 + 7 + 5 + 4 + 6 + 5 + 3 = _____ **33**

3. 15 + **12** = 27

4. **4** + 19 = 23

5. 209 + 327 = **536**

6. 8 ft. 11 in. + 2 ft. 5 in. **11 ft. 4 in.**	7. 16 lb. 14 oz. + 5 lb. 12 oz. **22 lb. 10 oz.**	8. 4 hr. 44 min. + 5 hr. 33 min. **10 hr. 17 min.**

9. + 2 hours 20 minutes Time: **10:15**

10. The Grant family is having a large crowd for Thanksgiving dinner. They bought two turkeys for dinner. One turkey weighs 15 lbs. 8 oz. The second turkey weighs 19 lbs. 10 oz. How much turkey do they have?

35 lbs. 2 oz.

page 59

Linking Verbs

Linking verbs link the subject to a word in the predicate. The linking verbs most often used are **am, is, are, was** and **were**.

Example:
*We **were** happy about the outcome.*

A linking verb may be followed by a **predicate noun**, which renames the subject, or a **predicate adjective**, which describes the subject.

Examples:
*Ramy is a **teacher**. (predicate noun)*
...... (verb)

Answers may include:

Complete each sentence with a predicate noun.

1. Sarah is a **skater** .   2. Her best friend is a **swimmer** .

Circle each predicate noun. Underline the noun or pronoun in the subject that is renamed.

1. The <u>children</u> were (actors)
2. The <u>setting</u> of the play was a (garden)
3. <u>Butterflies</u> are (main characters) in the play.
4. <u>Ralph</u> is the (star)

Complete each sentence with a predicate adjective.

1. Today's weather is **sunny** .   2. Tom will be **funny** .

Circle each predicate adjective. Underline the noun or pronoun in the subject that is described.

1. The <u>trap-door spider</u> is (clever)
2. Its building <u>skills</u> are (amazing)
3. The <u>webs</u> covering the walls were (soft and silky)
4. The <u>trap</u> was (invisible)

page 64

Forms of Be, Do and Have

Some forms of the verb **be** can be used as linking or helping verbs. Three forms of **be** cannot be used alone as verbs: **be, being** and **been**. These must always be used with helping verbs.

Examples:
*Polar bears **are** carnivores. (**be** as linking verb)*
*The polar bear **is** hunting the seal. (**be** as helping verb)*
*A polar bear **has been** seen near here. (**be** with helping verb)*
Forms of **be: am, is, are, was, were, be, being, been**

Complete each sentence with the correct form of the verb **be** found in parentheses. Add helping verbs where needed.

1. Polar bears **are** excellent swimmers. (is, are)
2. The polar bear **was** seen running at a speed of 35 miles per hour. (was, being)
3. I **am** sure I saw a polar bear swimming in the water. (am, are)
4. Polar bears **have been** seen swimming many miles from shore. (been, have been)

The verbs **do** and **have** can be used as main verbs or as helping verbs.

Examples:
*I **have** traveled to Canada to see polar bears. (helping verb)*
*I **did** my report on polar bears yesterday. (main verb)*
Forms of **do: do, did, done**   Forms of **have: have, has, had**

Complete the story below using the correct forms of the verbs **do** and **have**.

I **do** believe polar bears are very beautiful. I **have** seen them along the coast of Alaska. I **did** see one come up to our tour bus. By the age of 10 years, a male polar bear **has** grown to its full size. Countries around the Arctic have **done** a very good job of trying to save the polar bear from extinction. Polar bears **have** beautiful coats which **have** attracted hunters. Now the bears **have** protection from hunters by law.

page 65

The Truth About u

argue
blue
confuse
due
duke
dune
excuse
include
issue
museum
plume
ruby
rude
statue
tissue
truth
tube
tulip

The words in the list have the $\overline{oo}$ or $y\overline{oo}$ sound. **Write** each word in the appropriate category.

Classy $\overline{oo}$ Categories

u-e	ue	u
confuse	argue	ruby
duke	blue	truth
dune	due	tulip
excuse	issue	museum
include	tissue	
plume	statue	
rude		
tube		

Oops! We have elephant words. Just like elephants, we must remember that a few words make the $\overline{oo}$ or $y\overline{oo}$ sound spelled with **lew**, as in **review**, **o-e**, as in **lose**, or **eau** as in **beauty. Write** the five elephant words in alphabetical order. Note the number of syllables each word contains in the parentheses ( ).

Elephant Words				
review	whose	beautiful	preview	lose

1. **beautiful** (3)   3. **preview** (2)
2. **lose** (1)   4. **review** (2)
5. **whose** (1)

page 66

Learn at Home, Grade 5

Estimating Differences

To estimate differences, round the numbers and then subtract. This skill can be used daily. An example of this would be when you travel by car. If you have a distance of 862 miles to travel and you've gone 381, you can round in your head—900 – 400 leaves approximately 500 more miles to go.

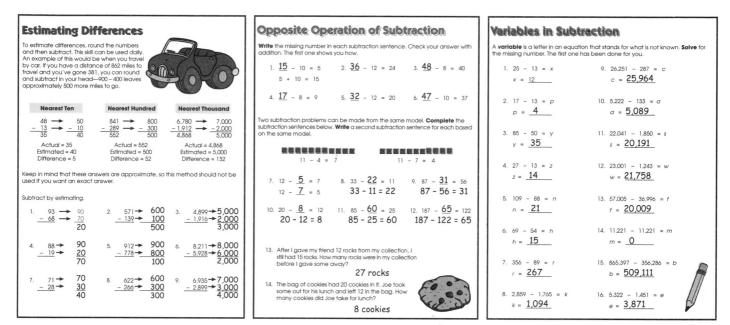

Nearest Ten	Nearest Hundred	Nearest Thousand
48 → 50	841 → 800	6,780 → 7,000
– 13 → – 10	– 289 → – 300	– 1,912 → – 2,000
35 40	552 500	4,868 5,000
Actual = 35	Actual = 552	Actual = 4,868
Estimated = 40	Estimated = 500	Estimated = 5,000
Difference = 5	Difference = 52	Difference = 132

Keep in mind that these answers are approximate, so this method should not be used if you want an exact answer.

Subtract by estimating.

1. 93 → 90
   – 68 → 70
   20

2. 571 → 600
   – 139 → 100
   500

3. 4,899 → 5,000
   – 1,916 → 2,000
   3,000

4. 88 → 90
   – 19 → 20
   70

5. 912 → 900
   – 778 → 800
   100

6. 8,211 → 8,000
   – 5,928 → 6,000
   2,000

7. 71 → 70
   – 28 → 30
   40

8. 622 → 600
   – 266 → 300
   300

9. 6,935 → 7,000
   – 2,899 → 3,000
   4,000

page 67

Opposite Operation of Subtraction

Write the missing number in each subtraction sentence. Check your answer with addition. The first one shows you how.

1. **15** – 10 = 5
   5 + 10 = 15

2. **36** – 12 = 24

3. **48** – 8 = 40

4. **17** – 8 = 9

5. **32** – 12 = 20

6. **47** – 10 = 37

Two subtraction problems can be made from the same model. **Complete** the subtraction sentences below. **Write** a second subtraction sentence for each based on the same model.

11 – 4 = 7   11 – 7 = 4

7. 12 – **5** = 7
   12 – **7** = 5

8. 33 – **22** = 11
   33 – 11 = 22

9. 87 – **31** = 56
   87 – 56 = 31

10. 20 – **8** = 12
    20 – 12 = 8

11. 85 – **60** = 25
    85 – 25 = 60

12. 187 – **65** = 122
    187 – 122 = 65

13. After I gave my friend 12 rocks from my collection, I still had 15 rocks. How many rocks were in my collection before I gave some away?

27 rocks

14. The bag of cookies had 20 cookies in it. Joe took some out for his lunch and left 12 in the bag. How many cookies did Joe take for lunch?

8 cookies

page 68

Variables in Subtraction

A **variable** is a letter in an equation that stands for what is not known. **Solve** for the missing number. The first one has been done for you.

1. 25 – 13 = x
   x = **12**

2. 17 – 13 = p
   p = **4**

3. 85 – 50 = y
   y = **35**

4. 27 – 13 = z
   z = **14**

5. 109 – 88 = n
   n = **21**

6. 69 – 54 = h
   h = **15**

7. 356 – 89 = r
   r = **267**

8. 2,859 – 1,765 = k
   k = **1,094**

9. 26,251 – 287 = c
   c = **25,964**

10. 5,222 – 133 = a
    a = **5,089**

11. 22,041 – 1,850 = s
    s = **20,191**

12. 23,001 – 1,243 = w
    w = **21,758**

13. 57,005 – 36,996 = f
    f = **20,009**

14. 11,221 – 11,221 = m
    m = **0**

15. 865,397 – 356,286 = b
    b = **509,111**

16. 5,322 – 1,451 = e
    e = **3,871**

page 69

Irregular Verbs

Verbs that do not add **ed** to show the past tense are called **irregular verbs**. Irregular verbs change in spelling in the past tense.

Examples:

Present	Past	Past with helpers
begin	began	(has, have) begun
see	saw	(has, have) seen
drive	drove	(has, have) driven

Fill in the blanks on the chart. You may refer to a dictionary.

Present	Past	Past with helpers
speak	**spoke**	**spoken**
take	**took**	taken
ride	**rode**	ridden
choose	**chose**	**chosen**
ring	rang	**rung**
go	went	**gone**
drink	**drank**	**drunk**
drive	**drove**	driven
draw	drew	**drawn**
know	**knew**	**known**
eat	**ate**	eaten
do	**did**	**done**

Underline the correct verb in each sentence below.

1. Martha has (began, <u>begun</u>) her research project.
2. First, she (<u>chose</u>, chosen) the topic.
3. She (<u>drove</u>, driven) many places to locate information.
4. Martha made a list of the interviews she had (did, <u>done</u>).
5. She (<u>spoke</u>, spoken) to people of many ages.
6. Many (<u>knew</u>, known) a great deal about the subject.
7. While interviewing people, Martha had (took, <u>taken</u>) notes.
8. Diagrams were (drew, <u>drawn</u>) for the project.

page 74

Adverbs Modify

You have learned that adverbs modify verbs. An **adverb** can also modify **adjectives** and **other adverbs**. These adverbs usually tell **how much** or **to what degree**.

Examples:
The eagle's descent was **very** steep.
(modifies "steep," an adjective)
The eagle attacked the fish **quite** suddenly.
(modifies "suddenly," an adverb)

Underline only the adverbs in the sentences below that modify an adjective or another adverb. **Draw** an arrow to the word that each modifies. In the blank, **write** if the modified word is an adjective or an adverb.

1. The eagle spread its wings <u>very</u> wide. _adverb_
2. It had to fly <u>quite</u> far to the lake. _adverb_
3. The eagle is an <u>extremely</u> graceful bird. _adjective_
4. It is <u>much</u> larger than most birds. _adjective_
5. Its hooked beak is <u>rather</u> sharp. _adjective_
6. The eagle watched the lake <u>very</u> carefully. _adverb_
7. A large trout is <u>really</u> tasty food for the eagle. _adjective_
8. A beautiful rainbow trout jumped <u>quite</u> suddenly out of the water. _adverb_
9. The eagle has <u>extremely</u> sharp eyesight. _adverb_
10. It swooped <u>almost</u> instantly toward the fish. _adverb_

Answers may include:

1. The eagle flew <u>extremely</u> low over the water's surface.
2. Then, it flew **quite** high into the blue summer sky.
3. It landed in its nest **very** gently.
4. The eagle is a **truly** majestic bird.
5. It has to be **very** patient as it hunts for food.

page 75

Conquering Compounds

barnyard
blastoff
brand-new
chairperson
cupboard
hide-and-seek
homesick
ice skate
jack-o'-lantern
peanut butter
polar bear
post office
seagull
snowstorm
topsy-turvy
town crier
yardstick
zip code

There are three types of compound words: (1) **closed compound**—two separate words joined together, that create a new meaning and written as one word; (2) **open compound**—two separate words create a new meaning, but the two words are not joined together; (3) **hyphenated compound**—two or more words, written separately but connected by a hyphen, create a new meaning.

Add a word or words to each word below to form a compound word from the spelling list.

1. cup **cupboard**
2. snow **snowstorm**
3. home **homesick**
4. barn **barnyard**
5. chair **chairperson**
6. yard **yardstick**
7. sea **seagull**
8. hide- **hide-and-seek**
9. brand- **brand-new**
10. polar **polar bear**
11. ice **ice skate**
12. pea **peanut butter**
13. blast **blastoff**
14. post **post office**
15. topsy- **topsy-turvy**
16. town **town crier**
17. zip **zip code**
18. jack- **jack-o'-lantern**

page 76

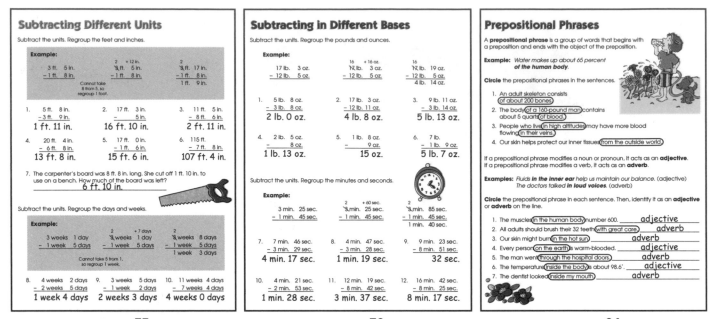

Subtracting Different Units

Subtract the units. Regroup the feet and inches.

Example:

	2 +12 in.	2
3 ft. 5 in.	3 ft. 5 in.	3 ft. 17 in.
– 1 ft. 8 in.	– 1 ft. 8 in.	– 1 ft. 8 in.
	Cannot take 8 from 5, so regroup 1 foot.	1 ft. 9 in.

1. 5 ft. 8 in.
   – 3 ft. 9 in.
   1 ft. 11 in.

2. 17 ft. 3 in.
   – 8 in.
   16 ft. 10 in.

3. 11 ft. 5 in.
   – 8 ft. 6 in.
   2 ft. 11 in.

4. 20 ft. 4 in.
   – 6 ft. 8 in.
   13 ft. 8 in.

5. 17 ft. 0 in.
   – 1 ft. 6 in.
   15 ft. 6 in.

6. 115 ft.
   – 7 ft. 8 in.
   107 ft. 4 in.

7. The carpenter's board was 8 ft. 8 in. long. She cut off 1 ft. 10 in. to use on a bench. How much of the board was left?
   6 ft. 10 in.

Subtract the units. Regroup the days and weeks.

Example:

	2 +7 days	2
3 weeks 1 day	3 weeks 1 day	3 weeks 8 days
– 1 week 5 days	– 1 week 5 days	– 1 week 5 days
	Cannot take 5 from 1, so regroup 1 week.	1 week 3 days

8. 4 weeks 2 days
   – 2 weeks 5 days
   1 week 4 days

9. 3 weeks 5 days
   – 1 week 2 days
   2 weeks 3 days

10. 11 weeks 4 days
    – 7 weeks 4 days
    4 weeks 0 days

page 77

Subtracting in Different Bases

Subtract the units. Regroup the pounds and ounces.

Example:

	16 +16 oz.	16
17 lb. 3 oz.	17 lb. 3 oz.	17 lb. 19 oz.
– 12 lb. 5 oz.	– 12 lb. 5 oz.	– 12 lb. 5 oz.
		4 lb. 14 oz.

1. 5 lb. 8 oz.
   – 3 lb. 8 oz.
   2 lb. 0 oz.

2. 17 lb. 3 oz.
   – 12 lb. 11 oz.
   4 lb. 8 oz.

3. 9 lb. 11 oz.
   – 3 lb. 14 oz.
   5 lb. 13 oz.

4. 2 lb. 5 oz.
   – 8 oz.
   1 lb. 13 oz.

5. 1 lb. 8 oz.
   – 9 oz.
   15 oz.

6. 7 lb.
   – 1 lb. 9 oz.
   5 lb. 7 oz.

Subtract the units. Regroup the minutes and seconds.

Example:

	2 +60 sec.	2
3 min. 25 sec.	3 min. 25 sec.	3 min. 85 sec.
– 1 min. 45 sec.	– 1 min. 45 sec.	– 1 min. 45 sec.
		1 min. 40 sec.

7. 7 min. 46 sec.
   – 3 min. 29 sec.
   4 min. 17 sec.

8. 4 min. 47 sec.
   – 3 min. 28 sec.
   1 min. 19 sec.

9. 9 min. 23 sec.
   – 8 min. 51 sec.
   32 sec.

10. 4 min. 21 sec.
    – 2 min. 53 sec.
    1 min. 28 sec.

11. 12 min. 19 sec.
    – 8 min. 42 sec.
    3 min. 37 sec.

12. 16 min. 42 sec.
    – 8 min. 25 sec.
    8 min. 17 sec.

page 78

Prepositional Phrases

A **prepositional phrase** is a group of words that begins with a preposition and ends with the object of the preposition.

Example: *Water makes up about 65 percent of the human body.*

Circle the prepositional phrases in the sentences.

1. An adult skeleton consists (of about 200 bones).
2. The body (of a 160-pound man) contains about 5 quarts (of blood).
3. People who live (in high altitudes) may have more blood flowing (in their veins).
4. Our skin helps protect our inner tissues (from the outside world).

If a prepositional phrase modifies a noun or pronoun, it acts as an **adjective**. If a prepositional phrase modifies a verb, it acts as an **adverb**.

Examples: *Fluids in the inner ear help us maintain our balance.* (adjective)
The doctors talked in loud voices. (adverb)

Circle the prepositional phrase in each sentence. Then, identify it as an **adjective** or **adverb** on the line.

1. The muscles (in the human body) number 600. **adjective**
2. All adults should brush their 32 teeth (with great care). **adverb**
3. Our skin might burn (in the hot sun). **adverb**
4. Every person (on the earth) is warm-blooded. **adjective**
5. The man went (through the hospital doors). **adverb**
6. The temperature (inside the body) is about 98.6°. **adjective**
7. The dentist looked (inside my mouth). **adverb**

page 84

Puzzling Compounds

baseball	basketball	breakfast	classroom	driftwood	firefly
flagpole	harmless	knickknack	lifetime	motorcycle	paperback
playhouse	railway	switchboard	taxicab	textbook	tiptoe

Write a spelling word that matches each clue. Then, read down the boxed letters to solve the riddle.

1. a place to learn — **c l a s s r o o m**
2. the morning meal — **b r e a k f a s t**
3. not capable of hurting — **h a r m l e s s**
4. game played with a bat and a ball — **b a s e b a l l**
5. to walk softly — **t i p t o e**
6. sometimes called a lightning bug — **f i r e f l y**
7. one's entire period of existence — **l i f e t i m e**
8. it supports Old Glory — **f l a g p o l e**

Riddle: Which tree is the most difficult to get along with?

Answer: _crabtree_

Write a spelling word that belongs in each group.

1. hoop, whistle, **basketball**
2. tracks, railroad, **railway**
3. school, subjects, **textbook**
4. toys, games, **playhouse**
5. wood, ashore, **driftwood**
6. circuit, panel, **switchboard**
7. read, novel, **paperback**
8. 2-wheeled, helmet, **motorcycle**
9. fare, driver, **taxicab**
10. trinket, decoration **knickknack**

page 85

Timed Multiplication

1	9	4	8	2	5	7	12
x 1	x 3	x 10	x 3	x 10	x 7	x 4	x 3
1	27	40	24	20	35	28	36

10	12	10	4	7	11	6	3
x 3	x 9	x 5	x 9	x 5	x 2	x 6	x 2
30	108	50	36	35	22	36	6

5	10	9	3	9	9	8	6
x 8	x 4	x 4	x 3	x 9	x 6	x 5	x 7
40	40	36	9	45	54	40	42

4	11	12	1	7	10	2	4
x 8	x 3	x 5	x 4	x 7	x 6	x 7	x 7
32	33	60	4	49	60	14	28

3	6	9	5	11	3	10	1
x 4	x 8	x 5	x 10	x 9	x 5	x 7	x 5
12	48	45	50	99	15	70	5

2	8	9	4	9	8	7	4
x 6	x 7	x 2	x 6	x 8	x 8	x 9	x 5
12	56	18	24	72	64	63	20

10	3	6	11	9	2	12	7
x 8	x 6	x 10	x 6	x 7	x 5	x 10	x 10
80	18	60	66	63	10	120	70

page 86

Multiplication (One-Digit Multiplier)

Example A (no regrouping)

234
x 2
468

- **Step 1** Multiply ones. 2 x 4 = 8
- **Step 2** Multiply tens. 2 x 3 = 6
- **Step 3** Multiply hundreds. 2 x 2 = 4

Example B (regrouping)

2 1
563
x 4
2,252

- **Step 1** Multiply ones. 4 x 3 = 12 ones = 1 ten 2 ones. Carry the 1.
- **Step 2** Multiply tens. 4 x 6 + 1 = 25 tens = 2 hundreds 5 tens. Carry the 2.
- **Step 3** Multiply hundreds. 4 x 5 + 2 = 22 hundreds = 2 thousands 2 hundreds.

Example C (regrouping and zeros)

7 5
7,086
x 9
63,774

- **Step 1** Multiply ones. 9 x 6 = 54 ones = 5 tens 4 ones. Carry the 5.
- **Step 2** Multiply tens. 9 x 8 + 5 = 77 tens = 7 hundreds 7 tens. Carry the 7.
- **Step 3** Multiply hundreds. 9 x 0 + 7 = 7 hundreds.
- **Step 4** Multiply thousands. 9 x 7 = 63 thousands = 6 ten-thousands 3 thousands.

Multiply.

1. 323
   x 8
   2,584

2. 1,132
   x 2
   2,264

3. 789
   x 5
   3,945

4. 4,008
   x 7
   28,056

5. 2,580
   x 3
   7,740

6. 888
   x 6
   5,328

7. 4,234
   x 4
   16,936

8. 589
   x 9
   5,301

9. 3,211
   x 3
   9,633

page 87

Learn at Home, Grade 5

Conjunctions

A conjunction joins words, groups of words or entire sentences. The most common conjunctions are **and, or,** but.

Examples:
*Christian Huygens **and** Jean Cassini made discoveries about Saturn.* (joins subjects)

*The Italian astronomer Galileo first saw Saturn's rings through a telescope, **but** the rings weren't very clear.* (joins sentences)

*He discovered the rings in the early 1600s **and** thought they were large satellites.* (joins predicates)

Add a conjunction to each sentence below.

1. Did you know that Saturn takes about 29½ Earth-years to orbit the Sun, ___or___ are you still looking up at that fact?
2. Saturn ___and___ Earth have very different day lengths.
3. Earth's day is about 24 hours, ___but___ Saturn's is only about 10½ hours.
4. Saturn has 23 satellites that have been discovered, ___and___ Earth has only one.
5. Saturn's natural satellites all have different names, ___but___ Earth's satellite is just called "the Moon."
6. Saturn has many rings that surround it, ___but___ Earth has none.

Add a conjunction to each phrase below that describes Saturn.

1. beautiful ___and___ majestic
2. far away, ___but___ gigantic
3. larger than Earth, ___but___ lighter in comparison
4. shorter days than Earth ___and___ faster rotation
5. atmosphere of mostly hydrogen ___and___ helium
6. beautiful rings ___but___ not the only planet with them

page 92

Interjections and Direct Address

Strong interjections, which show great feeling, are followed by exclamation points.
Mild interjections, such as **now, well** and **yes,** are set apart by commas.

A comma or commas are used to set apart the name of a person being directly spoken to, or addressed, in a sentence. This is called **direct address.**

Examples:
Ugh! That soup is horrible. (strong interjection)
No, I haven't finished my homework yet. (mild interjection)
Sue, please hand me the pencil. (direct address)
Thank you, **Jean,** for your contribution. (direct address)

Add commas and exclamation points where they are needed in the following sentences.

1. Yes, we will finish the science project soon.
2. Wow! I forgot that it must be completed by Friday.
3. Oh! I forgot that the materials for the experiment are at home.
4. Jim, bring the microscope to the science lab.
5. Now, Leonard, it's your turn to work on the experiment.
6. Will the research for the project be completed soon, Amy?
7. No, Mrs. Clarke, it will take at least another week.
8. Yikes! That was a scary experiment you did, Mark.

Add commas and exclamation points where they are needed in the following sentences. In the blank, **write** the letter of the reason each punctuation mark is used. Some have two answers.

A. Interjection   **B.** Direct Address

1. _B_ Lewis, will you attempt this experiment on air pressure?
2. _A_ No! I need to work on my electricity project Sam.
3. _B_ I need some help, Mr. Johnson, with my electrical circuit.
4. _B_ The science lab is too crowded to set up the project, Ms. Chang.
5. _A_ Cool! I would love to use the other lab.
6. _A/B_ Yes, I'll try to set up the project in that room, Sarah.
7. _A_ Well, that solved my problem.

page 93

Articles

A, an and **the** are special kinds of adjectives called **articles.**

Use **a** before singular nouns that begin with a consonant sound.
Example: *a lizard*

Use **an** before singular nouns that begin with a vowel sound or a silent **h.**
Examples: *an* insect   *an* hour

Use **the** before singular or plural nouns beginning with any letter.
Examples: *the* lizards   *the* branch

Write a, an or **the** in the blanks to complete the paragraph.

There are nearly 3,000 different kinds of lizards. ___The___ lizard may have ___a___ tail that is much longer than its body. ___A___ lizard may even leave its tail behind when escaping from ___an___ enemy. ___The___ lizard then grows ___a___ new tail. Dinosaur is ___a___ word that means "terrible lizard." But ___the___ dinosaur and ___the___ lizard are not in ___the___ same family. Most lizards hatch from ___a___ leathery egg. ___A___ chameleon is ___a___ type of lizard that actually changes color for many different reasons. ___The___ chameleon may change color if it is frightened. It also changes color in response to ___a___ change in temperature or light. ___The___ chameleon gets close enough to shoot out its tongue to capture ___an___ insect to eat. ___A___ chameleon's tongue may be as long as its body. Lizards are truly ___an___ interesting type of animal!

Complete each sentence below using **a, an** or **the.**

1. ___An___ insect would not taste as good to me as it does to lizards!
2. ___A___ lizard could lose its tail while escaping from its enemies.
3. ___The___ chameleon's eyes can move in two different directions at once.
4. Some geckos make ___a___ loud sound.
5. ___The___ claws of some gecko lizards can be drawn in like a cat's.

page 94

Contraction Action

aren't
can't
couldn't
didn't
hasn't
he's
I'd
isn't
let's
shouldn't
they're
they've
wasn't
weren't
we've
wouldn't
you'd
you're

Write the correct contraction for each word pair.

you are	_you're_	should not	_shouldn't_
would not	_wouldn't_	did not	_didn't_
I had	_I'd_	could not	_couldn't_
let us	_let's_	was not	_wasn't_
we have	_we've_	are not	_aren't_
you had	_you'd_	is not	_isn't_
has not	_hasn't_	they have	_they've_
he is	_he's_	can not	_can't_
they are	_they're_	were not	_weren't_

Now, put the contractions into word families.

(n't) not family		('s) is family
wouldn't	wasn't	he's
hasn't	aren't	
shouldn't	isn't	('s) us family
didn't	can't	let's
couldn't	weren't	

('re) are family	('d) would/had family	('ve) have family
they're	I'd	we've
you're	you'd	they've

page 95

Multiplication (Two-Digit Multiplier)

Example A (no regrouping)
```
   21
 x 44
   84
+ 840
  924
```
Step 1 Multiply by ones.
4 x 1 = 4
4 x 2 = 8

Step 2 Multiply by tens.
Add zero in the ones column.
4 x 1 = 4
4 x 2 = 8

Step 3 Add.
84 + 840 = 924

Example B (regrouping)
```
    67
  x 58
   536
+3,350
 3,886
```
Step 1 Multiply by ones.
8 x 7 = 56 (Carry the 5.)
8 x 6 + 5 = 53

Step 2 Multiply by tens.
Add zero in the ones column.
5 x 7 = 35 (Carry the 3.)
5 x 6 + 3 = 33

Step 3 Add.
536 + 3,350 = 3,886

Multiply.

1. 43 x 33 = 1,419
2. 55 x 46 = 2,530
3. 78 x 68 = 5,304
4. 39 x 27 = 1,053
5. 21 x 87 = 1,827
6. 77 x 24 = 1,848
7. 44 x 16 = 704
8. 80 x 71 = 5,680
9. 65 x 49 = 3,185

page 96

Multiplication Maze

These multiplication problems have already been done, but some of them are wrong. Check each problem. **Connect** the problems with correct answers to make a path for Zerpo to get back to his ship. Then, **correct** each wrong answer.

863 x 24 = 21,712 (20,712)
904 x 93 = 85,072 (84,072)
6,520 x 74 = 582,480 (482,480)
663 x 54 = 53,802 (35,802)
392 x 28 = 11,976 (10,976)
485 x 53 = 24,605 (25,705)
199 x 98 = 19,502
566 x 74 = 35,884 (41,884)
2,576 x 92 = 236,992
466 x 18 = 8,388
925 x 68 = 62,900
4,516 x 22 = 98,352 (99,352)
5,568 x 35 = 194,705
719 x 82 = 69,958 (58,958)
239 x 15 = 4,585 (3,585)
1,530 x 93 = 152,290 (142,290)
534 x 34 = 28,156 (18,156)
1,344 x 49 = 65,856
671 x 68 = 45,628
793 x 81 = 64,233
329 x 16 = 5,624 (5,264)
861 x 57 = 50,077 (49,077)
1,524 x 43 = 64,532 (54,033)
651 x 83 = 34,738
819 x 76 = 52,244 (62,244)
2,316 x 27 = 62,532 (65,532)
4,110 x 27 = 125,080 (115,080)

page 97

Puzzling Cross Number

Solve the multiplication problems below. **Write** the answers in the puzzle.

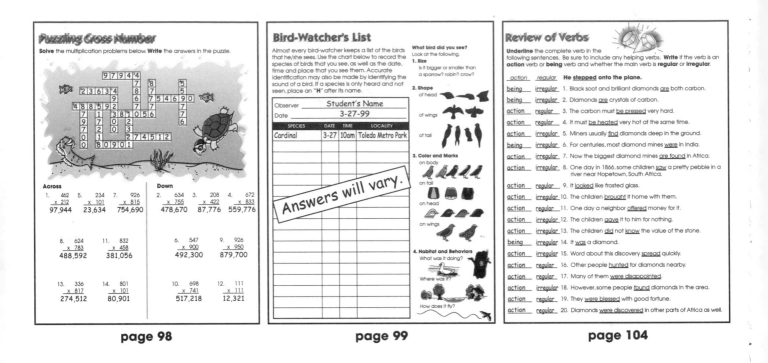

Across

1. 462 × 212 = 97,944
5. 234 × 101 = 23,634
7. 926 × 815 = 754,690
8. 624 × 783 = 488,592
11. 832 × 458 = 381,056
13. 336 × 817 = 274,512
14. 801 × 101 = 80,901

Down

2. 634 × 755 = 478,670
3. 208 × 422 = 87,776
4. 672 × 833 = 559,776
6. 547 × 900 = 492,300
9. 926 × 950 = 879,700
10. 698 × 741 = 517,218
12. 111 × 111 = 12,321

page 98

Bird-Watcher's List

Almost every bird-watcher keeps a list of the birds that he/she sees. Use the chart below to record the species of birds that you see, as well as the date, time and place that you see them. Accurate identification may also be made by identifying the sound of a bird. If a species is only heard and not seen, place an "**H**" after its name.

Observer: Student's Name
Date: 3-27-99

SPECIES	DATE	TIME	LOCALITY
Cardinal	3-27	10am	Toledo Metro Park

Answers will vary.

What bird did you see?
Look at the following.

1. **Size**
Is it bigger or smaller than a sparrow? robin? crow?

2. **Shape**
of head
of wings
of tail

3. **Color and Marks**
on body
on tail
on head
on wings

4. **Habitat and Behaviors**
What was it doing?
Where was it?
How does it fly?

page 99

Review of Verbs

Underline the complete verb in the following sentences. Be sure to include any helping verbs. **Write** if the verb is an **action** verb or **being** verb and whether the main verb is **regular** or **irregular**.

action	_regular_	He <u>stepped</u> **onto the plane.**
being	irregular	1. Black soot and brilliant diamonds <u>are</u> both carbon.
being	irregular	2. Diamonds <u>are</u> crystals of carbon.
action	regular	3. The carbon must <u>be pressed</u> very hard.
action	regular	4. It must <u>be heated</u> very hot at the same time.
action	irregular	5. Miners usually <u>find</u> diamonds deep in the ground.
being	irregular	6. For centuries, most diamond mines <u>were</u> in India.
action	irregular	7. Now the biggest diamond mines <u>are found</u> in Africa.
action	irregular	8. One day in 1866, some children <u>saw</u> a pretty pebble in a river near Hopetown, South Africa.
action	regular	9. It <u>looked</u> like frosted glass.
action	irregular	10. The children <u>brought</u> it home with them.
action	regular	11. One day a neighbor <u>offered</u> money for it.
action	irregular	12. The children <u>gave</u> it to him for nothing.
action	irregular	13. The children <u>did</u> not <u>know</u> the value of the stone.
being	irregular	14. It <u>was</u> a diamond.
action	irregular	15. Word about this discovery <u>spread</u> quickly.
action	regular	16. Other people <u>hunted</u> for diamonds nearby.
action	regular	17. Many of them <u>were disappointed</u>.
action	irregular	18. However, some people <u>found</u> diamonds in the area.
action	regular	19. They <u>were blessed</u> with good fortune.
action	regular	20. Diamonds <u>were discovered</u> in other parts of Africa as well.

page 104

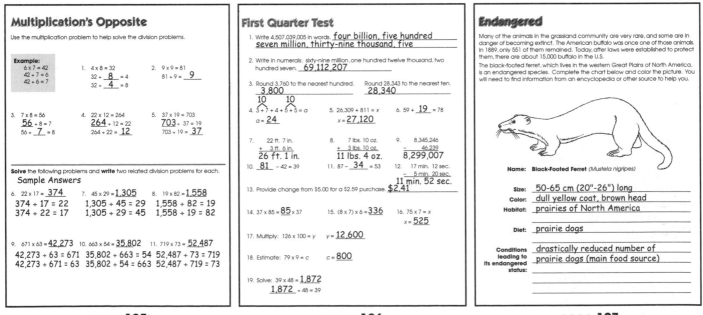

Multiplication's Opposite

Use the multiplication problem to help solve the division problems.

Example:
6 × 7 = 42
42 ÷ 7 = 6
42 ÷ 6 = 7

1. 4 × 8 = 32
32 ÷ **8** = 4
32 ÷ **4** = 8

2. 9 × 9 = 81
81 ÷ 9 = **9**

3. 7 × 8 = 56
56 ÷ 8 = 7
56 ÷ **7** = 8

4. 22 × 12 = 264
264 ÷ 12 = 22
264 ÷ 22 = **12**

5. 37 × 19 = 703
703 ÷ 37 = 19
703 ÷ 19 = **37**

Solve the following problems and **write** two related division problems for each.
Sample Answers

6. 22 × 17 = **374**
374 ÷ 17 = 22
374 ÷ 22 = 17

7. 45 × 29 = **1,305**
1,305 ÷ 45 = 29
1,305 ÷ 29 = 45

8. 19 × 82 = **1,558**
1,558 ÷ 82 = 19
1,558 ÷ 19 = 82

9. 671 × 63 = **42,273**
42,273 ÷ 63 = 671
42,273 ÷ 671 = 63

10. 663 × 54 = **35,802**
35,802 ÷ 663 = 54
35,802 ÷ 54 = 663

11. 719 × 73 = **52,487**
52,487 ÷ 73 = 719
52,487 ÷ 719 = 73

page 105

First Quarter Test

1. Write 4,507,039,005 in words. **four billion, five hundred seven million, thirty-nine thousand, five**

2. Write in numerals: sixty-nine million, one hundred twelve thousand, two hundred seven. **69,112,207**

3. Round 3,760 to the nearest hundred. **3,800**
Round 28,343 to the nearest ten. **28,340**

4. 3 + 7 + 4 + 5 = a
a = **24**

5. 26,309 + 811 = x
x = **27,120**

6. 59 + **19** = 78

7. 22 ft. 7 in. + 3 ft. 6 in. = **26 ft. 1 in.**

8. 7 lbs. 10 oz. + 3 lbs. 10 oz. = **11 lbs. 4 oz.**

9. 8,345,246 − 46,239 = **8,299,007**

10. **81** − 42 = 39

11. 87 − **34** = 53

12. 17 min. 12 sec. − 5 min. 20 sec. = **11 min. 52 sec.**

13. Provide change from $5.00 for a $2.59 purchase. **$2.41**

14. 37 × 85 = **85** × 37

15. (8 × 7) × 6 = **336**

16. 75 × 7 = x
x = **525**

17. Multiply: 126 × 100 = y   y = **12,600**

18. Estimate: 79 × 9 = c   c = **800**

19. Solve: 39 × 48 = **1,872**
1,872 ÷ 48 = 39

page 106

Endangered

Many of the animals in the grassland community are very rare, and some are in danger of becoming extinct. The American buffalo was once one of those animals. In 1889, only 551 of them remained. Today, after laws were established to protect them, there are about 15,000 buffalo in the U.S.

The black-footed ferret, which lives in the western Great Plains of North America, is an endangered species. Complete the chart below and color the picture. You will need to find information from an encyclopedia or other source to help you.

Name: Black-Footed Ferret *(Mustela nigripes)*

Size: 50-65 cm (20"-26") long

Color: dull yellow coat, brown head

Habitat: prairies of North America

Diet: prairie dogs

Conditions leading to its endangered status: drastically reduced number of prairie dogs (main food source)

page 107

Learn at Home, Grade 5

The Prairie Food Web

In complex grassland communities like the prairie, the flow of food and energy cannot be described by a simple food chain. Instead, it is represented by a series of interconnected food chains called a **food web**. The many kinds of producers and consumers in the prairie community provide a wide variety of food sources.

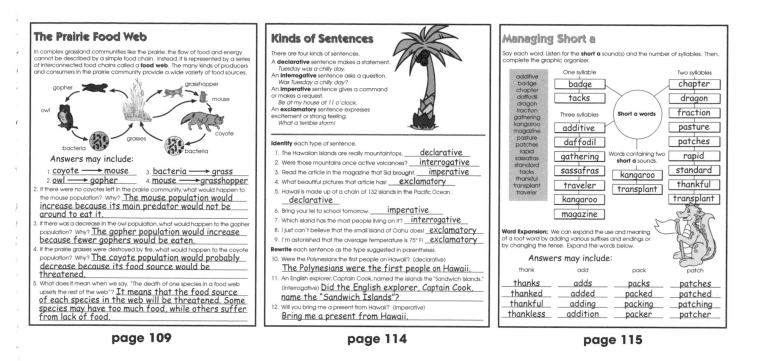

Answers may include:

1. coyote ⟶ mouse
2. owl ⟶ gopher
3. bacteria ⟶ grass
4. mouse ⟶ grasshopper

2. If there were no coyotes left in the prairie community, what would happen to the mouse population? Why? The mouse population would increase because its main predator would not be around to eat it.

3. If there was a decrease in the owl population, what would happen to the gopher population? Why? The gopher population would increase because fewer gophers would be eaten.

4. If the prairie grasses were destroyed by fire, what would happen to the coyote population? Why? The coyote population would probably decrease because its food source would be threatened.

5. What does it mean when we say, "The death of one species in a food web upsets the rest of the web"? It means that the food source of each species in the food web will be threatened. Some species may have too much food, while others suffer from lack of food.

page 109

Kinds of Sentences

There are four kinds of sentences.
A **declarative** sentence makes a statement.
  Tuesday was a chilly day.
An **interrogative** sentence asks a question.
  Was Tuesday a chilly day?
An **imperative** sentence gives a command or makes a request.
  Be at my house at 11 o'clock.
An **exclamatory** sentence expresses excitement or strong feeling.
  What a terrible storm!

Identify each type of sentence.

1. The Hawaiian Islands are really mountaintops. declarative
2. Were those mountains once active volcanoes? interrogative
3. Read the article in the magazine that Sid brought. imperative
4. What beautiful pictures that article has! exclamatory
5. Hawaii is made up of a chain of 132 islands in the Pacific Ocean. declarative
6. Bring your lei to school tomorrow. imperative
7. Which island has the most people living on it? interrogative
8. I just can't believe that the small island of Oahu does! exclamatory
9. I'm astonished that the average temperature is 75° F! exclamatory

Rewrite each sentence as the type suggested in parentheses.

10. Were the Polynesians the first people on Hawaii? (declarative)
The Polynesians were the first people on Hawaii.

11. An English explorer, Captain Cook, named the islands the "Sandwich Islands." (interrogative) Did the English explorer, Captain Cook, name the "Sandwich Islands"?

12. Will you bring me a present from Hawaii? (imperative)
Bring me a present from Hawaii.

page 114

Managing Short a

Say each word. Listen for the **short a** sound(s) and the number of syllables. Then, complete the graphic organizer.

additive, badge, chapter, daffodil, dragon, fraction, gathering, kangaroo, magazine, pasture, patches, rapid, sassafras, standard, tacks, thankful, transplant, traveler

One syllable: badge, tacks
Three syllables: additive, daffodil, gathering, sassafras, traveler, kangaroo, magazine
Short a words
Two syllables: chapter, dragon, fraction, pasture, patches, rapid, standard, thankful, transplant
Words containing two **short a** sounds: kangaroo, transplant

Word Expansion: We can expand the use and meaning of a root word by adding various suffixes and endings or by changing the tense. Expand the words below.

Answers may include:

thank	add	pack	patch
thanks	adds	packs	patches
thanked	added	packed	patched
thankful	adding	packing	patching
thankless	addition	packer	patcher

page 115

To Know and Understand

A **fact** is something that is proven to be true. An **opinion** is what someone believes. People hold differing opinions, some of which are unfair or untrue. Use the code to **label** each statement below.

F = Fact   **PO** = Phillip's opinion   **MO** = Phillip's mother's opinion   **TO** = Timothy's opinion

1. Black people were odd because they ate raw fish. PO
2. Timothy's nose was flat and his face was broad. F
3. Timothy should have let Phillip stay in the water. MO
4. Phillip was nearly twelve years old. F
5. The cat brought bad luck. TO
6. Timothy was saving all the water for himself. PO
7. It was safer to leave Curacao than stay. TO
8. In Virginia, blacks and whites lived in different parts of town. F
9. Timothy was strange because he didn't know his parents. PO
10. White children should not play near black workers. MO
11. Timothy could be a very stubborn person. PO

Discussion: In your neighborhood, what are some opinions people hold that are unfair? Is it fair to tease or ignore people who are different from you? Talk about how the following types of people are treated in your neighborhood.

- physically handicapped people
- younger/older people
- people who speak other languages
- people of other cultures
- awkward people
- mentally impaired people
- poor/rich people
- attractive/unattractive people
- popular/unpopular people
- girls/boys

page 116

Division Facts

8 ÷ 24 ÷ 3	9 ⟌81	8 ⟌40	4 ⟌4	9 ⟌90	8 ⟌56	6 ⟌24

3⟌24 = 8, 9⟌81 = 9, 8⟌40 = 5, 4⟌4 = 1, 9⟌90 = 10, 8⟌56 = 7, 6⟌24 = 4
7⟌14 = 2, 7⟌49 = 7, 5⟌20 = 4, 6⟌36 = 6, 9⟌72 = 8, 4⟌16 = 4, 3⟌27 = 9
8⟌64 = 8, 9⟌36 = 4, 5⟌25 = 5, 9⟌45 = 5, 2⟌18 = 9, 4⟌24 = 6, 8⟌8 = 1
3⟌9 = 3, 2⟌14 = 7, 6⟌54 = 9, 7⟌21 = 3, 8⟌32 = 4, 5⟌30 = 6, 1⟌6 = 6
2⟌4 = 2, 9⟌81 = 9, 6⟌30 = 5, 4⟌8 = 2, 5⟌50 = 10, 5⟌15 = 3, 2⟌20 = 10
1⟌10 = 10, 7⟌7 = 1, 2⟌16 = 8, 3⟌15 = 5, 7⟌49 = 7, 1⟌4 = 4, 9⟌63 = 7
8⟌16 = 2, 2⟌12 = 6, 8⟌72 = 9, 3⟌30 = 10, 9⟌63 = 7, 3⟌18 = 6, 7⟌56 = 8
9⟌9 = 1, 7⟌63 = 9, 2⟌8 = 4, 8⟌80 = 10, 7⟌28 = 4, 6⟌12 = 2, 6⟌6 = 1... 3⟌6 = 2
7⟌42 = 6, 3⟌12 = 4, 7⟌35 = 5, 9⟌27 = 3, 6⟌42 = 7, 5⟌10 = 2, 5⟌45 = 9
2⟌10 = 5, 9⟌54 = 6, 4⟌20 = 5, 9⟌54 = 6, 9⟌18 = 2, 1⟌6 = 6... 2⟌6 = 3

page 117

Artifact Facts

Help the archaeologist find the artifact. First, **solve** the division problems. Then, connect the quotients in numerical order, starting at 795, to make his path.

795 = 8⟌6360
788 = 9⟌7092
796 = 3⟌2388
797 = 7⟌5579
798 = 5⟌3990
791 = 4⟌3164
806 = 7⟌5642
799 = 9⟌7191
899 = 6⟌5394
829 = 7⟌5803
777 = 5⟌3885
789 = 9⟌7101
744 = 6⟌4464
800 = 4⟌3200
803 = 8⟌6424
801 = 6⟌4806
802 = 9⟌7218

page 118

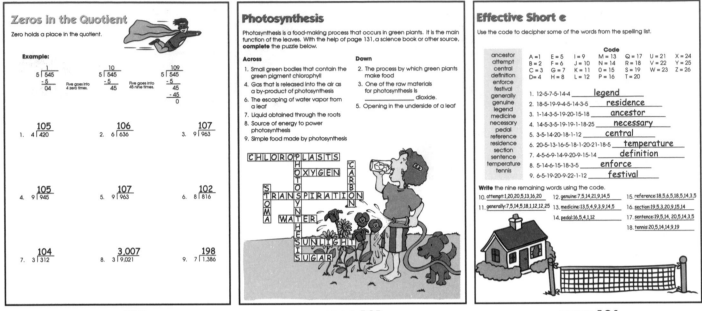

Zeros in the Quotient

Zero holds a place in the quotient.

Example:

$$5\overline{)545} \quad \frac{1}{04}$$ Five goes into 4 zero times.

$$5\overline{)545} \quad \frac{10}{45}$$ Five goes into 45 nine times.

$$5\overline{)545} \quad \frac{109}{45} \\ -5 \\ 45 \\ -45 \\ 0$$

1. $4\overline{)420}$ → 105
2. $6\overline{)636}$ → 106
3. $9\overline{)963}$ → 107
4. $9\overline{)945}$ → 105
5. $9\overline{)963}$ → 107
6. $8\overline{)816}$ → 102
7. $3\overline{)312}$ → 104
8. $3\overline{)9,021}$ → 3,007
9. $7\overline{)1,386}$ → 198

page 119

Photosynthesis

Photosynthesis is a food-making process that occurs in green plants. It is the main function of the leaves. With the help of page 131, a science book or other source, **complete** the puzzle below.

Across
1. Small green bodies that contain the green pigment chlorophyll
4. Gas that is released into the air as a by-product of photosynthesis
6. The escaping of water vapor from a leaf
7. Liquid obtained through the roots
8. Source of energy to power photosynthesis
9. Simple food made by photosynthesis

Down
2. The process by which green plants make food
3. One of the raw materials for photosynthesis is _____ dioxide.
5. Opening in the underside of a leaf

CHLOROPLASTS
OXYGEN
CARBON
TRANSPIRATION
STOMA
WATER
SUNLIGHT
SUGAR
PHOTOSYNTHESIS

page 121

Effective Short e

Use the code to decipher some of the words from the spelling list.

ancestor
attempt
central
definition
enforce
festival
generally
genuine
legend
medicine
necessary
pedal
reference
residence
section
sentence
temperature
tennis

Code

A =1	E = 5	I = 9	M = 13	Q = 17	U = 21	X = 24
B = 2	F = 6	J = 10	N = 14	R = 18	V = 22	Y = 25
C = 3	G = 7	K = 11	O = 15	S = 19	W = 23	Z = 26
D = 4	H = 8	L = 12	P = 16	T = 20		

1. 12-5-7-5-14-4 — legend
2. 18-5-19-9-4-5-14-3-5 — residence
3. 1-14-3-5-19-20-15-18 — ancestor
4. 14-5-3-5-19-19-1-18-25 — necessary
5. 3-5-14-20-18-1-12 — central
6. 20-5-13-16-5-18-1-20-21-18-5 — temperature
7. 4-5-6-9-14-9-20-9-15-14 — definition
8. 5-14-6-15-18-3-5 — enforce
9. 6-5-19-20-9-22-1-12 — festival

Write the nine remaining words using the code.
10. attempt: 1,20,20,5,13,16,20
11. generally: 7,5,14,5,18,1,12,12,25
12. genuine: 7,5,14,21,9,14,5
13. medicine: 13,5,4,9,3,9,14,5
14. pedal: 16,5,4,1,12
15. reference: 18,5,6,5,18,5,14,3,5
16. section: 19,5,3,20,9,15,14
17. sentence: 19,5,14,20,5,14,3,5
18. tennis: 20,5,14,14,9,19

page 126

Wisconsin's Nickname

What is Wisconsin known as? To find out, **solve** the division problems below. Then, find the answers at the bottom of the page and **write** the corresponding letter on the line above the answer.

T. $14\overline{)1218}$ → 87
E. $23\overline{)1633}$ → 71
S. $53\overline{)2756}$ → 52
A. $38\overline{)1596}$ → 42
A. $61\overline{)5185}$ → 85
E. $18\overline{)1764}$ → 98
T. $22\overline{)1628}$ → 74
R. $40\overline{)2520}$ → 63
D. $55\overline{)4400}$ → 80
G. $31\overline{)1364}$ → 44
B. $12\overline{)780}$ → 65

B A D G E R   S T A T E
65 85 80 44 71 63   52 74 42 87 98

page 127

Octopus Crossword

Solve the division problems. **Write** the remainders in word form to complete the puzzle.

TWO FOUR TWELVE SIXTEEN FIVE EIGHT THIRTEEN ELEVEN SEVEN THREE ONE NINE EIGHTEEN TWENTY

Across
3. $23\overline{)1313}$ → 57 R2
4. $41\overline{)3501}$ → 85 R16
7. $18\overline{)1733}$ → 96 R5
8. $35\overline{)2706}$ → 77 R11
10. $64\overline{)4618}$ → 72 R10
12. $51\overline{)4746}$ → 93 R3
13. $70\overline{)5881}$ → 79 R1
14. $32\overline{)2132}$ → 66 R20

Down
1. $45\overline{)2389}$ → 53 R4
2. $60\overline{)3786}$ → 63 R6
3. $28\overline{)1076}$ → 38 R12
4. $33\overline{)1360}$ → 41 R7
5. $55\overline{)3533}$ → 64 R13
6. $72\overline{)6128}$ → 85 R8
9. $84\overline{)7494}$ → 89 R18
11. $16\overline{)1497}$ → 93 R9
12. $22\overline{)1088}$ → 49 R10

page 128

Biomes of the Earth Samples include:

Using a world map, a globe, an atlas, an encyclopedia and other resources, **complete** the chart below to get a better understanding of some biomes and their characteristics.

Biome	Continents and Countries	Animals	Plants
Coniferous Forest	Western US and Canada North America	moose wolves bears birds	needleleaf evergreen trees Aspen trees
Deciduous Forest	Midwestern United States North America	wolves, deer, bears, many small mammals and birds	maple trees oak trees
Grassland	Central North America	prairie dogs foxes grouse reptiles	low-growing flowers grasses
Tropical Rain forest	Brazil South America	reptiles birds monkeys insects	flowers trees
Desert	North Africa Africa	lizards, snakes, rodents, African fennec fox and owls	cacti Joshua trees bunchgrass small scrubs
Tundra	Northern Russia Asia	arctic foxes snowy owls musk-ox insects	reindeer moss grasses sedges
Marine	Atlantic Ocean Pacific Ocean Indian Ocean	whales fish seals	seaweed coral

page 129

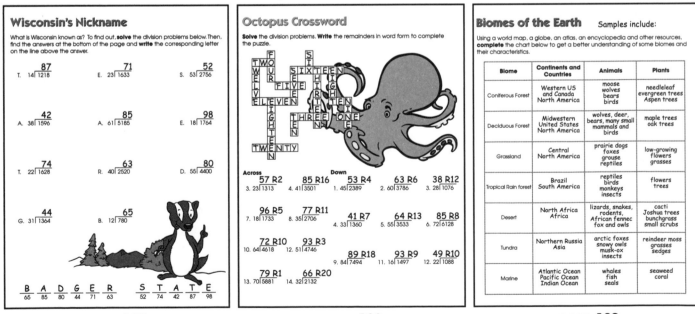

Learn at Home, Grade 5

A Study of the Forest Floor

A forest habitat is generally cool, damp and shady. At first glance, it might seem that plant life is less abundant than in a pond or grassland area, but as you look more closely, you will see many kinds of species that love shade, such as horsetails, mosses, ferns and fungi. The soil of a forest floor is rich in decaying matter. Its acidity will depend upon whether it contains fallen evergreen needles (which increase the acidity) or leaves from deciduous trees. This rich soil is home to many kinds of animals, including earthworms, centipedes, snails and beetles.

You are going to study a forest floor, either on your own or on a field trip. You will need a wire hanger. Bend it into a circle and toss it onto the ground in a forest. Answer these questions and complete the activities as you examine the living things in your own tiny forest plot.

What is the temperature inside your plot? _____ Is it dry or moist? _____
Identify and describe all the plants that are in your plot. _____
_____

Sketch the ones you cannot identify in the boxes below.

Research will vary.	

Look for animals. Look under any leaves, evergreen needles or twigs. Identify and describe the different animals that you find. _____

Sketch the ones you cannot identify in the boxes below.

Pick up the hanger and toss it on your lawn or in a field near your home. Compare that habitat to the forest habitat.

page 130

Proofreading for Punctuation

Anna is running for class president. She has written her last campaign speech before the election but has not done a very good job of punctuating it. Read her speech. Write in capital letters where needed and add correct punctuation.

Tomorrow you will choose one of five candidates as your class president. I want to be the one you choose. Why should you vote for me? As class president, I will collect twenty-five cents a month from every class member. The money will be used for a party at the end of the school year. I will listen to your suggestions and try to do something about them. As president of our class, I will go to teachers' meetings. I will try to have homework assignments over weekends reduced. Vote for me. I know I will make the next year the best one for you and our class. It will be a year to remember. Thank you for your support.

Anna did not win the election, but she was a good sport. She wrote a message to Kim, the winner, in the school newspaper. The editor did not proofread Anna's message, and it got published just as she wrote it. Correct Anna's work once more.

I want to congratulate Kim. I know she will make a fine class president. I am sorry I did not win, but I want Kim and everyone else to know I support her. Now that the election is over and the class showed their preference, let's all join together and support Kim. Congratulations, Kim!

page 138

Using Commas

Use commas to set off an **appositive**, a noun or phrase that explains or identifies the noun it follows.
Example: Jack, the janitor, walked down the hall.

Use commas to separate words or phrases in a **series**.
Example: He ate the apple, the peach and the plum.

Use commas after **introductory** words or phrases.
Examples: Yes, I'm going to the fair.
By the way, did you bring a camera?

Use commas to set off a **noun of address**, the name of the person being addressed or spoken to.
Example: Caroline, will you come with me?

Use commas to set off **interrupting** words or phrases.
Example: He was, as you know, an actor before he was elected.

Add commas to the sentences where they are needed. On each line, explain why you added the comma by writing **appositive**, **series**, **introductory**, **noun of address** or **interrupting**.

1. Maryanne, the new girl in school, is a very good cook. __appositive__
2. My favorite snacks are red apples, pretzels and popcorn. __series__
3. My skills, however, do not include cooking. __interrupting__
4. I know, Sally, that you love to cook. __noun of address__
5. That was, in my opinion, the best meal ever served. __interrupting__
6. After they finished the books, Tom and Larry wrote the re __introductory__
7. Thomas Edison, an inventor, had failures before each succe __appositive__
8. Pete, our best soccer player, won't be here for the big gam __appositive__
9. No, I won't be seeing the movie. __introductory__
10. The coating on the pecans was sweet, sugary and crisp. __series__
11. That is, if I'm not mistaken, my yellow and green pencil. __interrupting__
12. Sam, would you please pass me my pen? __noun of address__

page 139

Itty-Bitty i

activities
citizen
difference
difficulties
exit
fiction
hippopotamus
individual
instrument
interesting
kitchen
listening
miniature
miserable
officer
principal
prisoner
shipment

Write the spelling word that best completes each sentence.

1. We received a __shipment__ of new books for our library.
2. Our family usually eats dinner in the __kitchen__.
3. When we subtract one number from another, we find the __difference__.
4. A story which is not true is __fiction__.
5. We all have special talents and gifts because we are __individual__ people.
6. Pay close attention by __listening__ carefully to the directions.
7. The __prisoner__ was released on parole.
8. A violin is considered a stringed __instrument__.
9. My sister collects __miniature__ teapots.
10. Friends can be especially helpful when one is experiencing __difficulties__.
11. What kinds of __activities__ do you do after school?
12. Find the __exit__ sign so we can leave the building.
13. That movie had a very __interesting__ plot.
14. The __principal__ is a friend to both teachers and students.
15. As a __citizen__ of the U.S., I respect the American flag.
16. The police __officer__ spoke kindly to the little child.
17. The head cold made my brother feel __miserable__.
18. It would be difficult to have a __hippopotamus__ for a pet.

Each word below is hidden in a list word. **Write** that spelling word on the blank.
1. on __fiction/prisoner__
2. son __prisoner__
3. act __activities__
4. kit __kitchen__
5. pal __principal__
6. pot __hippopotamus__
7. instrument/shipment
8. miser __miserable__
9. ties __difficulties__

page 140

Mr. Popper's Penguins

Answers may include:
1. Where do penguins live? __Southern Hemisphere (Antarctic)__
2. How many species of penguins are there? __18__
   Name two types: __Emperor penguin__ and __Rockhopper__
3. Describe the general appearance of penguins, including body covering, height and weight ranges. __white breast, black back and head, short legs, upright posture, wings like flippers, up to 4 feet in height.__
4. How do peng __walk awkwardly on land, swim fast in water__
5. What do peng __fish, cuttlefish, crustaceans, small sea animals__
6. Describe penguins' breeding habits: __They lay eggs in rookeries.__
7. Describe a newly hatched penguin. __little balls of sooty, gray down__

Draw an emperor penguin in the space below.

page 141

Division in Three Ways

The equation $12 \div 3$ can also be written as $3\overline{)12}$ or $\frac{12}{3}$.

Write each equation in the three forms. The first one has been done for you.

1. $12 \div 3 = 3\overline{)12} = \frac{12}{3}$
2. $24 \div 8 = 8\overline{)24} = \frac{24}{8}$
3. $56 \div 8 = 8\overline{)56} = \frac{56}{8}$
4. $63 \div 9 = 9\overline{)63} = \frac{63}{9}$
5. $42 \div 6 = 6\overline{)42} = \frac{42}{6}$
6. $15 \div 5 = 5\overline{)15} = \frac{15}{5}$
7. $42 \div 7 = 7\overline{)42} = \frac{42}{7}$
8. $72 \div 9 = 9\overline{)72} = \frac{72}{9}$

Solve.

9. $20\overline{)440} = 22$
10. $440 \div 20 = 22$
11. $\frac{440}{20} = 22$
12. $12\overline{)780} = 65$
13. $650 \div 13 = 50$
14. $\frac{720}{15} = 48$

page 142

Decimal Dividends

Bring the decimal to the quotient. **Solve.**

1. $8\overline{)13.84} = 1.73$

2. $12\overline{)27.96} = 2.33$

3. $\frac{36.63}{11} = 3.33$

4. $71.4 \div 51 = 1.40$

5. $93.09 \div 87 = 1.07$

6. $\frac{99.52}{32} = 3.11$

7. Mandy wants to buy one bottle of soda pop. The advertised price is 3 bottles for $2.58. How much is one bottle? __$.86__

8. Youngen and her 5 friends went to a movie together. Youngen paid $31.50 for all of the tickets. How much did each ticket cost? __$6.30__

9. Sang and Jon ate lunch for $12.58. They each had a turkey sandwich, fries and milk. How much did each boy pay? __$6.29__

page 143

Flower Fun

Fill in the label for each plant part.

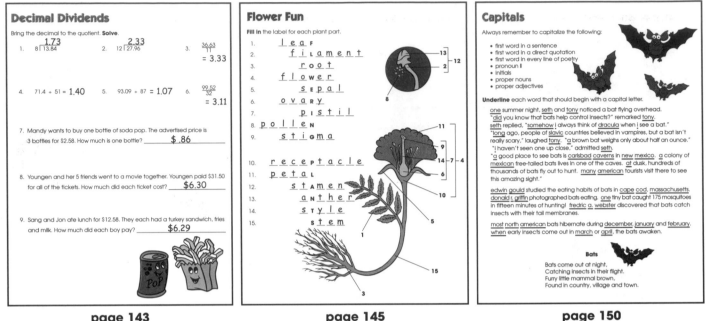

1. l e a f
2. f i l a m e n t
3. r o o t
4. f l o w e r
5. s e p a l
6. o v a r y
7. p i s t i l
8. p o l l e n
9. s t i g m a
10. r e c e p t a c l e
11. p e t a l
12. s t a m e n
13. a n t h e r
14. s t y l e
15. s t e m

page 145

Capitals

Always remember to capitalize the following:
- first word in a sentence
- first word in a direct quotation
- first word in every line of poetry
- pronoun I
- initials
- proper nouns
- proper adjectives

Underline each word that should begin with a capital letter.

<u>one</u> summer night, <u>seth</u> and <u>tony</u> noticed a bat flying overhead. "<u>did</u> you know that bats help control insects?" remarked <u>tony</u>. <u>seth</u> replied, "<u>somehow</u> <u>i</u> always think of <u>dracula</u> when <u>i</u> see a bat." "<u>long</u> ago, people of <u>slavic</u> countries believed in vampires, but a bat isn't really scary," laughed <u>tony</u>. "<u>a</u> brown bat weighs only about half an ounce." "<u>i</u> haven't seen one up close," admitted <u>seth</u>. "<u>a</u> good place to see bats is <u>carlsbad</u> <u>caverns</u> in <u>new</u> <u>mexico</u>. <u>a</u> colony of <u>mexican</u> free-tailed bats lives in one of the caves. <u>at</u> dusk, hundreds of thousands of bats fly out to hunt. <u>many</u> <u>american</u> tourists visit there to see this amazing sight."

<u>edwin</u> <u>gould</u> studied the eating habits of bats in <u>cape</u> <u>cod</u>, <u>massachusetts</u>. <u>donald</u> <u>r</u>. <u>griffin</u> photographed bats eating. <u>one</u> tiny bat caught 175 mosquitoes in fifteen minutes of hunting! <u>fredric</u> <u>a</u>. <u>webster</u> discovered that bats catch insects with their tail membranes.

<u>most</u> <u>north</u> <u>american</u> bats hibernate during <u>december</u>, <u>january</u> and <u>february</u>. <u>when</u> early insects come out in <u>march</u> or <u>april</u>, the bats awaken.

Bats

Bats come out at night,
Catching insects in their flight.
Furry little mammal brown,
Found in country, village and town.

page 150

Hidden o's

Circle the spelling words in the word search. Look horizontally, vertically and diagonally. **Write** each word below when you find it.

blocked
bother
column
common
dodge
gossip
honor
model
monster
octopus
oxen
problem
product
promise
robberies
soccer
toboggan
wobble

Write the number of syllables in the parentheses ( ).

1. product (2)
2. common (2)
3. gossip (2)
4. oxen (2)
5. octopus (3)
6. soccer (2)
7. robberies (3)
8. problem (2)
9. wobble (2)
10. promise (2)
11. monster (2)
12. dodge (1)
13. toboggan (3)
14. column (2)
15. bother (2)
16. blocked (1)
17. honor (2)
18. model (2)

page 151

Multiplication Table

X	0	1	2	3	4	5	6	7	8	9	10	11	12
0	0	0	0	0	0	0	0	0	0	0	0	0	0
1	0	1	2	3	4	5	6	7	8	9	10	11	12
2	0	2	4	6	8	10	12	14	16	18	20	22	24
3	0	3	6	9	12	15	18	21	24	27	30	33	36
4	0	4	8	12	16	20	24	28	32	36	40	44	48
5	0	5	10	15	20	25	30	35	40	45	50	55	60
6	0	6	12	18	24	30	36	42	48	54	60	66	72
7	0	7	14	21	28	35	42	49	56	63	70	77	84
8	0	8	16	24	32	40	48	56	64	72	80	88	96
9	0	9	18	27	36	45	54	63	72	81	90	99	108
10	0	10	20	30	40	50	60	70	80	90	100	110	120
11	0	11	22	33	44	55	66	77	88	99	110	121	132
12	0	12	24	36	48	60	72	84	96	108	120	132	144

page 152

Division

Solve.

1. $9\overline{)3,654} = 406$

2. $8\overline{)835} = 104\ R3$

3. $6\overline{)618} = 103$

Estimate.

4. $36\overline{)660} = 18$

5. $23\overline{)4,280} = 200$

6. $158 \div 21 = 10$

Solve.

7. $24\overline{)228} = 9\ R12$

8. $1298 \div 37 = 35\ R3$

9. $\frac{703}{41} = 17\ R6$

10. What is the cost for 1 golf ball? $3.36 \div 12 = $ .28

On Sale Today Only
One dozen golf balls
Only $3.36

page 153

Learn at Home, Grade 5

Angle Measurement

The **degree** is the unit used to measure angles.
Measure the following angles using a protractor.

1. 60° 2. 100° 3. 30° 4. 65°

5. 90° 6. 120° 7. 160° 8. 45°

Draw the angles given using a protractor.

1. 70° 2. 120° 3. 40°

4. 90° 5. 150° 6. 110°

page 154

Geometric Figures

Write the correct letter in the box next to each figure.

Point S = •S   Ray XY = $\overrightarrow{XY}$
Line CD = $\overleftrightarrow{CD}$ Line segment BC = $\overline{BC}$

1. F
2. B
3. K
4. G
5. H
6. C
7. A
8. I
9. D
10. E
11. J

A. $\overline{GH}$
B. Point Q
C. Plane E
D. Point A
E. $\overrightarrow{OP}$
F. $\overline{LM}$
G. $\overline{YZ}$
H. $\overline{MN}$
I. $\overleftrightarrow{HI}$
J. $\overline{JK}$
K. $\overrightarrow{RS}$

page 155

Utterly Upbeat u

bucket
button
crunchy
dusk
guppies
judges
lucky
public
refund
ruffle
skunk
spun
struck
subject
thunder
trust
ugly
umbrella

Complete each phrase with a spelling word.

1. chewing sometimes makes a __crunchy__ sound
2. books from the __public__ library
3. from dawn to __dusk__
4. return it for a __refund__
5. __trust__ your instincts
6. my __lucky__ number
7. lightning __struck__ the pole
8. math is my favorite __subject__
9. the __ugly__ duckling
10. the top __spun__ rapidly
11. the __guppies__ in my aquarium
12. water poured from the __bucket__
13. __thunder__ and lightning
14. open the __umbrella__
15. sew on the __button__
16. annoying __skunk__ spray
17. nine __judges__ on the court
18. added a __ruffle__ to the curtain

Fill in the missing letters to complete the spelling words.

j_u_dges   _sk_unk   um_br_ella
gu_pp_ies   _re_fund   _th_under
_u_gly   bu_tt_on   _du_sk
bu_ck_et   ru_ff_le   _str_uck
tr_u_st   c_ru_nchy   pub_l_ic
sp_u_n   su_bj_ect   lu_ck_y

page 160

Double Trouble

Fill in the blanks with the correct definition number for each underlined word.

Example: __3__ I was covered with pitch after climbing the pine tree.

winding	1. having bends or curves
	2. the act of turning something around a central core
wolf	1. to gulp down
	2. a large carnivorous member of the dog family
pitch	1. to sell or persuade
	2. to throw a ball from the mound to the batter
	3. a resin that comes from the sap of pine trees

__1__ 1. Do girls' clubs pitch cookies?
__2__ 2. We are winding the top's string tightly.
__2__ 3. The adult wolf returned to her lair.
__2__ 4. Red didn't pitch after the fourth inning.
__1__ 5. The Mather family had a winding driveway.
__1__ 6. The young ball player wolfed down his lunch and left.

choke	1. to strangle
	2. to bring the hands up on the bat
hitch	1. obstacle
	2. to fasten or tie temporarily
windup	1. the swing of the pitcher's arm just before the pitch
	2. a concluding part

__2__ 1. We hitched the mule to the cart.
__2__ 2. Tip would not choke up on his bat.
__1__ 3. Paul wished to play, but there was just one hitch.
__2__ 4. The program's windup was filled with more of Joe's record hits.
__1__ 5. Mom was afraid the dog would choke itself on its leash.
__1__ 6. He has a great windup and curve ball.

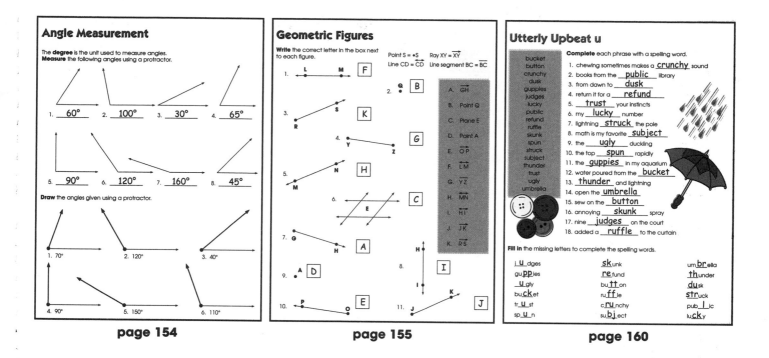

page 161

Take Me out to the Ball Game

Use the diagram to answer the questions.

1. Who plays left field? — Bob Gordon
2. How far is it from first to second base? — 60'
3. Does Monk Lawler play the outfield? — no
4. How many innings are played in Little League? — 6 innings
5. If a batter hits a triple, how many feet will he run? — 180'
6. What position does Cliff Borton play? — 1st base
7. How far is Paul Mather from home plate? — 44'
8. Can a 10-year-old child play Little League ball? — yes
9. How long may a bat be? — no longer than 33"
10. What position does Jim Hakken play? — shortstop
11. Is Stu closer to Monk or Kenny? — Monk

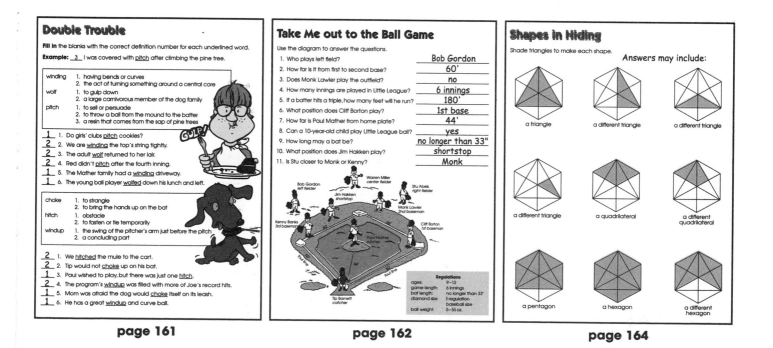

Regulations	
ages:	9–12
game length:	6 innings
bat length:	no longer than 33"
diamond size:	† regulation baseball size
ball weight:	5–5¼ oz.

page 162

Shapes in Hiding

Shade triangles to make each shape.

Answers may include:

a triangle   a different triangle   a different triangle

a different triangle   a quadrilateral   a different quadrilateral

a pentagon   a hexagon   a different hexagon

page 164

Lines Across a Triangle

Answers may include:

1 line	1 line	2 lines
2 triangles	1 triangle 1 quadrilateral	1 rectangle 2 triangles
2 lines	2 lines	2 lines
3 triangles 1 quadrilateral	2 triangles 1 quadrilateral	3 triangles
2 lines	2 lines	2 lines
2 triangles 2 quadrilaterals	2 triangles 1 pentagon	2 triangles 1 square

page 165

Plant Movements

After a seed germinates and anchors itself by its roots in one place, it can still show some movement. These movements are called **tropisms**. Tropisms are a plant's response to stimuli such as light, gravity and water.

Geotropism, hydrotropism and **phototropism** are three tropisms that are easily demonstrated with bean seedlings. Research these three types of tropisms using an encyclopedia, science textbook or other source. Study the pictures of the three experiments. Name the kind of tropis **Sample answers:**

BEFORE / AFTER

Kind of Tropism: __phototropism__
What happened? __When the bottle tipped over, the plant started to grow up toward the light.__

Kind of Tropism: __geotropism__
What happened? __Plant moved toward heat source.__

Kind of Tropism: __hydrotropism__
What happened? __Plant moved toward water source.__

page 166

What a Trip!

Read the paragraphs about Meriwether Lewis and William Clark's journey to the Pacific Coast. Then, **plot** their journey on the map below.

Lewis and Clark led the first expedition across our country's vast northwestern wilderness. It began in 1804 and lasted more than two years. The expedition covered almost 7,700 miles.

President Thomas Jefferson chose Lewis to lead the expedition. Then, Jefferson and Lewis selected Clark to be second in command. Lewis and Clark and their group of about 45 people set out on May 14, 1804, and traveled up the Missouri River. In October, they reached a village of friendly Mandan Indians in what is now North Dakota. They built Fort Mandan near there and stayed for the winter.

On April 17, 1805, the journey resumed. By summer, the group made the hardest part of the trip—they crossed the Rocky Mountains. This took them about a month. From there, they reached the Clearwater River in what is now Idaho. They built new canoes and then paddled toward the Columbia River which they reached in October. The expedition continued on in hopes of reaching the Pacific Coast. They ultimately succeeded, arriving at the coast in November of 1805.

- - - - - Lewis and Clark Expedition
1804-1806

1. Label the areas that are now states through which Lewis and Clark journeyed.
2. Label the rivers on which the expedition traveled.
3. Label the Rocky Mountains.
4. Label the Pacific Ocean.
5. Put a star where the group met the Mandan Indians.

page 167

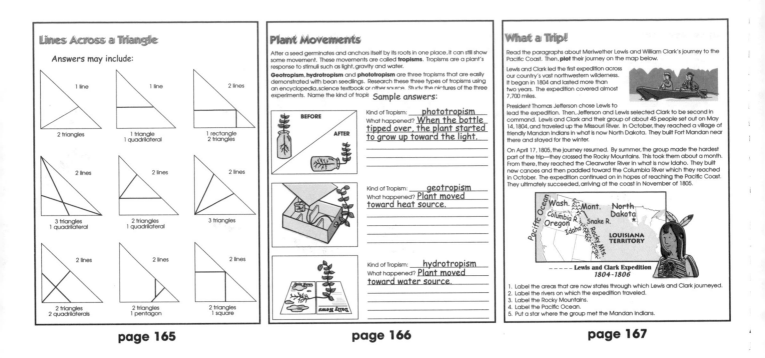

"R" You Listening?

When the letter **r** comes after a vowel, it sometimes changes the vowel sound. **Write** each spelling word under the category with the same spelling pattern.

afford
carton
curtain
departing
directions
emergency
forlorn
further
girth
harbor
observe
origin
perfume
refer
starch
sturdy
temper
thirst

ir	or
directions	afford
girth	forlorn
thirst	origin

er	ur
emergency	curtain
observe	further
perfume	sturdy
refer	
temper	

ar	
carton	
departing	
harbor	
starch	

Answers may include:

Write the spelling words that fit in the appropriate categories.
1. Can be used as an adverb, adjective or verb. __further__
2. Can be used as a noun or verb. __thirst__
   __temper__ __starch__ __harbor__
3. Used only as an adjective. __sturdy__
4. Used as a verb. __afford__ __forlorn__
   __observe__ __refer__

page 172

Throwing Too Many Curves

Interpret these quotations from *Hang Tough, Paul Mather* and **write** them in your own words.

Chapter 2
"The world begins and ends with basketball for the punk ..."

Chapter 4
"I grinned. I knew what the punk was planning. I had to hand it to him. He was maneuvering with a straight face."

Chapter 8
"That night ... bugging them about calling Dr. Kinsella ... sleeping dogs lie."

Answers will vary.

Chapter 8
"I wasn't (sure of myself), but I wasn't going to tell him that. When you've spent months in a hospital bed, you learn to play things close to the vest."

Chapter 13
"Tom and my father got along carefully. Dad thought Tom was young."

page 173

Day of Reckoning

Use the time line to answer the questions.
At what time does Paul ask for his mirror? __3:30__
Which happens earlier? Do Red and Paul shake hands or does Paul greet Toddy? __Paul greets Toddy__
What is the earliest time shown on the time line? __2:00__
Which happens later? Does Brophy give Paul his medication or does the game begin? __Brophy gives Paul his medication__
What is the final score of the game? __5-2__
At what time does the game end? __around 7:45__
When do Brophy and Paul's dad get Paul back into bed? __8:30__
How many Dairy players walk in the fourth inning? __2 players__
What happens first in the fourth inning? __Monk hits a double__

How many hours does this time line cover? Be careful! __9 hrs__

page 174

Learn at Home, Grade 5

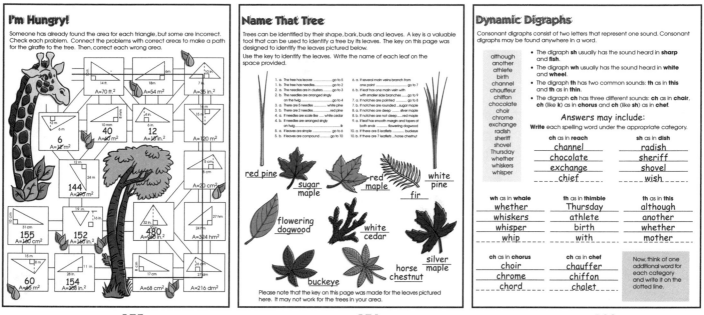

page 175   **page 176**   **page 182**

I'm Hungry!

Someone has already found the area for each triangle, but some are incorrect. Check each problem. Connect the problems with correct areas to make a path for the giraffe to the tree. Then, correct each wrong area.

Name That Tree

Trees can be identified by their shape, bark, buds and leaves. A key is a valuable tool that can be used to identify a tree by its leaves. The key on this page was designed to identify the leaves pictured below.

Use the key to identify the leaves. Write the name of each leaf on the space provided.

red pine, sugar maple, red maple, fir, white pine, flowering dogwood, white cedar, silver maple, buckeye, horse chestnut

Please note that the key on this page was made for the leaves pictured here. It may not work for the trees in your area.

Dynamic Digraphs

Consonant digraphs consist of two letters that represent one sound. Consonant digraphs may be found anywhere in a word.

- The digraph **sh** usually has the sound heard in **sharp** and **fish**.
- The digraph **wh** usually has the sound heard in **white** and **wheel**.
- The digraph **th** has two common sounds: **th** as in **this** and **th** as in **thin**.
- The digraph **ch** has three different sounds: **ch** as in **chair**, **ch** (like **k**) as in **chorus** and **ch** (like **sh**) as in **chef**.

Answers may include:

Write each spelling word under the appropriate category.

ch as in reach	sh as in dish
channel	radish
chocolate	sheriff
exchange	shovel
chief	wish

wh as in whale	th as in thimble	th as in this
whether	Thursday	although
whiskers	athlete	another
whisper	birth	whether
whip	with	mother

ch as in chorus	ch as in chef
choir	chauffer
chrome	chiffon
chord	chalet

Now, think of one additional word for each category and write it on the dotted line.

Word list: although, another, athlete, birth, channel, chauffeur, chiffon, chocolate, choir, chrome, exchange, radish, sheriff, shovel, Thursday, whether, whiskers, whisper

---

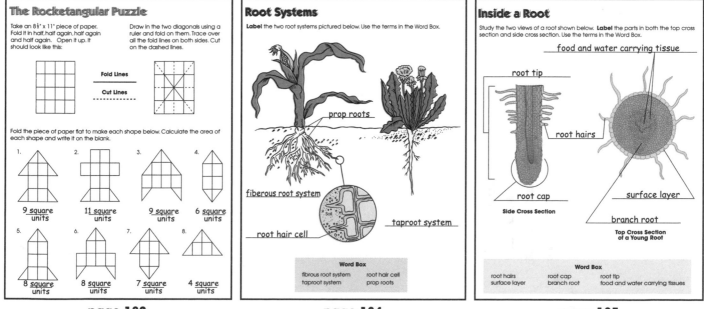

page 183   **page 184**   **page 185**

The Rocketangular Puzzle

Take an 8½" x 11" piece of paper. Fold it in half, half again, half again and half again. Open it up. It should look like this:

Draw in the two diagonals using a ruler and fold on them. Trace over all the fold lines on both sides. Cut on the dashed lines.

Fold Lines

Cut Lines

Fold the piece of paper flat to make each shape below. Calculate the area of each shape and write it on the blank.

1. 9 square units
2. 11 square units
3. 9 square units
4. 6 square units
5. 8 square units
6. 8 square units
7. 7 square units
8. 4 square units

Root Systems

Label the two root systems pictured below. Use the terms in the Word Box.

prop roots, fiberous root system, root hair cell, taproot system

Word Box
fibrous root system, root hair cell, taproot system, prop roots

Inside a Root

Study the two views of a root shown below. Label the parts in both the top cross section and side cross section. Use the terms in the Word Box.

food and water carrying tissue, root tip, root hairs, root cap, surface layer, branch root

Side Cross Section

Top Cross Section of a Young Root

Word Box
root hairs, root cap, root tip, surface layer, branch root, food and water carrying tissues

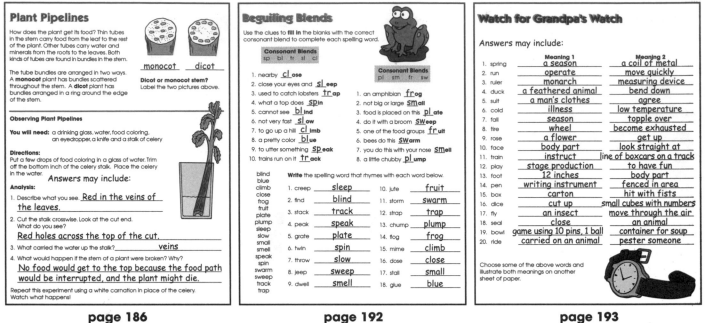

Plant Pipelines

How does the plant get its food? Thin tubes in the stem carry food from the leaf to the rest of the plant. Other tubes carry water and minerals from the roots to the leaves. Both kinds of tubes are found in bundles in the stem.

The tube bundles are arranged in two ways. A **monocot** plant has bundles scattered throughout the stem. A **dicot** plant has bundles arranged in a ring around the edge of the stem.

monocot   dicot

Dicot or monocot stem?
Label the two pictures above.

Observing Plant Pipelines

You will need: a drinking glass, water, food coloring, an eyedropper, a knife and a stalk of celery

Directions:
Put a few drops of food coloring in a glass of water. Trim off the bottom inch of the celery stalk. Place the celery in the water.

Analysis: Answers may include:

1. Describe what you see. __Red in the veins of__ __the leaves.__

2. Cut the stalk crosswise. Look at the cut end. What do you see?
__Red holes across the top of the cut.__

3. What carried the water up the stalk? __veins__

4. What would happen if the stem of a plant were broken? Why?
__No food would get to the top because the food path__ __would be interrupted, and the plant might die.__

Repeat this experiment using a white carnation in place of the celery. Watch what happens!

page 186

Beguiling Blends

Use the clues to **fill in** the blanks with the correct consonant blend to complete each spelling word.

Consonant Blends
sp bl tr sl cl

Consonant Blends
pl sm fr sw

1. nearby __cl__ose
2. close your eyes and __sl__ eep
3. used to catch lobsters __tr__ ap
4. what a top does __sp__in
5. cannot see __bl__ ind
6. not very fast __sl__ ow
7. to go up a hill __cl__ imb
8. a pretty color __bl__ue
9. to utter something __sp__ eak
10. trains run on it __tr__ ack

1. an amphibian __fr__og
2. not big or large __sm__all
3. food is placed on this __pl__ ate
4. do it with a broom __sw__eep
5. one of the food groups __fr__ uit
6. bees do this __sw__arm
7. you do this with your nose __sm__ell
8. a little chubby __pl__ ump

blind
blue
climb
close
frog
fruit
plate
plump
sleep
slow
small
smell
speak
spin
swarm
sweep
track
trap

Write the spelling word that rhymes with each word below.

1. creep __sleep__
2. find __blind__
3. stack __track__
4. peak __speak__
5. grate __plate__
6. twin __spin__
7. throw __slow__
8. jeep __sweep__
9. dwell __smell__

10. jute __fruit__
11. storm __swarm__
12. strap __trap__
13. chump __plump__
14. flog __frog__
15. mime __climb__
16. dose __close__
17. stall __small__
18. glue __blue__

page 192

Watch for Grandpa's Watch

Answers may include:

		Meaning 1	Meaning 2
1.	spring	a season	a coil of metal
2.	run	operate	move quickly
3.	ruler	monarch	measuring device
4.	duck	a feathered animal	bend down
5.	suit	a man's clothes	agree
6.	cold	illness	low temperature
7.	fall	season	topple over
8.	tire	wheel	become exhausted
9.	rose	a flower	get up
10.	face	body part	look straight at
11.	train	instruct	line of boxcars on a track
12.	play	stage production	to have fun
13.	foot	12 inches	body part
14.	pen	writing instrument	fenced in area
15.	box	carton	hit with fists
16.	dice	cut up	small cubes with numbers
17.	fly	an insect	move through the air
18.	seal	close	an animal
19.	bowl	game using 10 pins, 1 ball	container for soup
20.	ride	carried on an animal	pester someone

Choose some of the above words and illustrate both meanings on another sheet of paper.

page 193

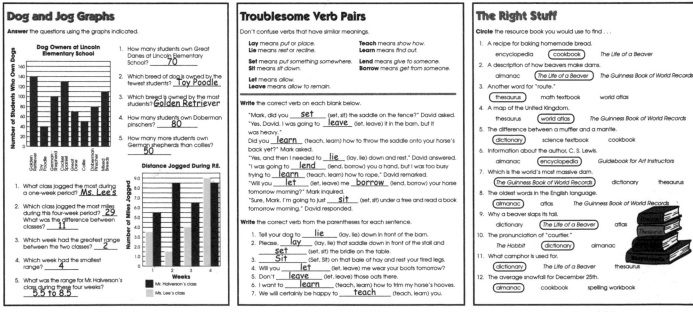

Dog and Jog Graphs

Answer the questions using the graphs indicated.

Dog Owners at Lincoln Elementary School

1. How many students own Great Danes at Lincoln Elementary School? __70__

2. Which breed of dog is owned by the fewest students? __Toy Poodle__

3. Which breed is owned by the most students? __Golden Retriever__

4. How many students own Doberman pinschers? __80__

5. How many more students own German shepherds than collies? __50__

Distance Jogged During P.E.

1. What class jogged the most during a one-week period? __Ms. Lee's__

2. Which class jogged the most miles during this four-week period? __29__ What was the difference between classes? __11__

3. Which week had the greatest range between the two classes? __2__

4. Which week had the smallest range? __4__

5. What was the range for Mr. Halverson's class during these four weeks? __5.5 to 8.5__

■ Mr. Halverson's class
□ Ms. Lee's class

page 195

Troublesome Verb Pairs

Don't confuse verbs that have similar meanings.

Lay means *put or place.*
Lie means *rest or recline.*

Set means *put something somewhere.*
Sit means *sit down.*

Let means *allow.*
Leave means *allow to remain.*

Teach means *show how.*
Learn means *find out.*

Lend means *give to someone.*
Borrow means *get from someone.*

Write the correct verb on each blank below.

"Mark, did you __set__ (set, sit) the saddle on the fence?" David asked.
"Yes, David. I was going to __leave__ (let, leave) it in the barn, but it was heavy."
Did you __learn__ (teach, learn) how to throw the saddle onto your horse's back yet?" Mark asked.
"Yes, and then I needed to __lie__ (lay, lie) down and rest," David answered.
"I was going to __lend__ (lend, borrow) you a hand, but I was too busy trying to __learn__ (teach, learn) how to rope," David remarked.
"Will you __let__ (let, leave) me __borrow__ (lend, borrow) your horse tomorrow morning?" Mark inquired.
"Sure, Mark. I'm going to just __sit__ (set, sit) under a tree and read a book tomorrow morning," David responded.

Write the correct verb from the parentheses for each sentence.

1. Tell your dog to __lie__ (lay, lie) down in front of the barn.
2. Please, __lay__ (lay, lie) that saddle down in front of the stall and __set__ (set, sit) the bridle on the table.
3. __Sit__ (Set, Sit) on that bale of hay and rest your tired legs.
4. Will you __let__ (let, leave) me wear your boots tomorrow?
5. Don't __leave__ (let, leave) those oats there.
6. I want to __learn__ (teach, learn) how to trim my horse's hooves.
7. We will certainly be happy to __teach__ (teach, learn) you.

page 200

The Right Stuff

Circle the resource book you would use to find . . .

1. A recipe for baking homemade bread.
   encyclopedia   (cookbook)   The Life of a Beaver

2. A description of how beavers make dams.
   almanac   (The Life of a Beaver)   The Guinness Book of World Records

3. Another word for "route."
   (thesaurus)   math textbook   world atlas

4. A map of the United Kingdom.
   thesaurus   (world atlas)   The Guinness Book of World Records

5. The difference between a muffler and a mantle.
   (dictionary)   science textbook   cookbook

6. Information about the author, C. S. Lewis.
   almanac   (encyclopedia)   Guidebook for Art Instructors

7. Which is the world's most massive dam.
   (The Guinness Book of World Records)   dictionary   thesaurus

8. The oldest words in the English language.
   (almanac)   atlas   The Guinness Book of World Records

9. Why a beaver slaps its tail.
   dictionary   (The Life of a Beaver)   atlas

10. The pronunciation of "courtier."
    The Hobbit   (dictionary)   almanac

11. What camphor is used for.
    (dictionary)   The Life of a Beaver   thesaurus

12. The average snowfall for December 25th.
    (almanac)   cookbook   spelling workbook

page 201

Learn at Home, Grade 5

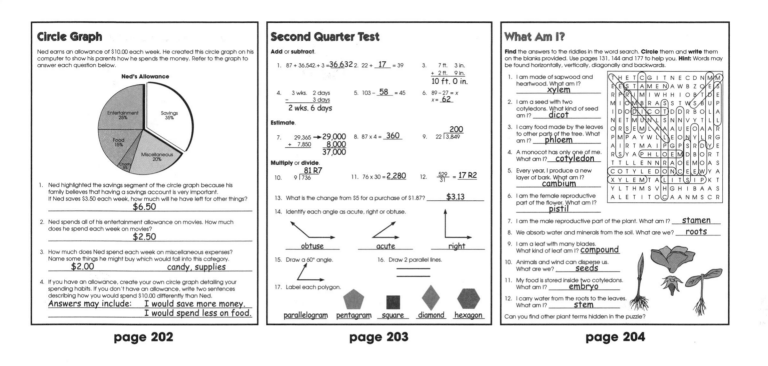

Circle Graph

Ned earns an allowance of $10.00 each week. He created this circle graph on his computer to show his parents how he spends the money. Refer to the graph to answer each question below.

Ned's Allowance

- Savings 35%
- Entertainment 25%
- Food 15%
- Miscellaneous 20%
- Charity 5%

1. Ned highlighted the savings segment of the circle graph because his family believes that having a savings account is very important. If Ned saves $3.50 each week, how much will he have left for other things? **$6.50**

2. Ned spends all of his entertainment allowance on movies. How much does he spend each week on movies? **$2.50**

3. How much does Ned spend each week on miscellaneous expenses? Name some things he might buy which would fall into this category. **$2.00   candy, supplies**

4. If you have an allowance, create your own circle graph detailing your spending habits. If you don't have an allowance, write two sentences describing how you would spend $10.00 differently than Ned. **Answers may include: I would save more money.   I would spend less on food.**

page 202

Second Quarter Test

Add or **subtract**.

1. 87 + 36,542 + 3 = **36,632**
2. 22 + **17** = 39
3. 7 ft.   3 in.
   + 2 ft.   9 in.
   10 ft. 0 in.

4. 3 wks.   2 days
   −   3 days
   2 wks. 6 days
5. 103 − **58** = 45
6. 89 − 27 = x
   x = **62**

Estimate.

7. 29,365 → **29,000**
   + 7,850   **8,000**
              37,000
8. 87 x 4 = **360**
9. 22 ⟌ 3,849   **200**

Multiply or **divide**.

10. 9 ⟌ 736   **81 R7**
11. 76 x 30 = **2,280**
12. $\frac{529}{31}$ = **17 R2**

13. What is the change from $5 for a purchase of $1.87? **$3.13**

14. Identify each angle as acute, right or obtuse.

   obtuse   **acute**   **right**

15. Draw a 60° angle.
16. Draw 2 parallel lines.

17. Label each polygon.

   parallelogram   pentagram   square   diamond   hexagon

page 203

What Am I?

Find the answers to the riddles in the word search. **Circle** them and **write** them on the blanks provided. Use pages 131, 144 and 177 to help you. **Hint:** Words may be found horizontally, vertically, diagonally and backwards.

1. I am made of sapwood and heartwood. What am I? **xylem**
2. I am a seed with two cotyledons. What kind of seed am I? **dicot**
3. I carry food made by the leaves to other parts of the tree. What am I? **phloem**
4. A monocot has only one of me. What am I? **cotyledon**
5. Every year, I produce a new layer of bark. What am I? **cambium**
6. I am the female reproductive part of the flower. What am I? **pistil**
7. I am the male reproductive part of the plant. What am I? **stamen**
8. We absorb water and minerals from the soil. What are we? **roots**
9. I am a leaf with many blades. What kind of leaf am I? **compound**
10. Animals and wind can disperse us. What are we? **seeds**
11. My food is stored inside two cotyledons. What am I? **embryo**
12. I carry water from the roots to the leaves. What am I? **stem**

Can you find other plant terms hidden in the puzzle?

page 204

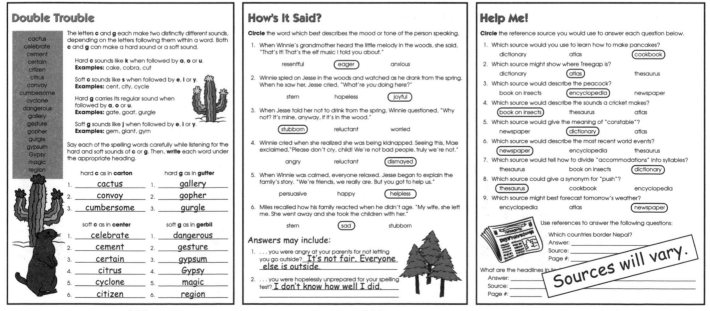

Double Trouble

cactus
celebrate
cement
certain
citizen
citrus
convoy
cumbersome
cyclone
dangerous
gallery
gesture
gopher
gurgle
gypsum
Gypsy
magic
region

The letters **c** and **g** each make two distinctly different sounds, depending on the letters following them within a word. Both **c** and **g** can make a hard sound or a soft sound.

Hard **c** sounds like **k** when followed by **a**, **o** or **u**.
Examples: cake, cobra, cut

Soft **c** sounds like **s** when followed by **e**, **i** or **y**.
Examples: cent, city, cycle

Hard **g** carries its regular sound when followed by **a**, **o** or **u**.
Examples: gate, goat, gurgle

Soft **g** sounds like **j** when followed by **e**, **i** or **y**.
Examples: gem, giant, gym

Say each of the spelling words carefully while listening for the hard and soft sounds of **c** or **g**. Then, **write** each word under the appropriate heading.

hard c as in carton
1. cactus
2. convoy
3. cumbersome

hard g as in gutter
1. gallery
2. gopher
3. gurgle

soft c as in center
1. celebrate
2. cement
3. certain
4. citrus
5. cyclone
6. citizen

soft g as in gerbil
1. dangerous
2. gesture
3. gypsum
4. Gypsy
5. magic
6. region

page 210

How's It Said?

Circle the word which best describes the mood or tone of the person speaking.

1. When Winnie's grandmother heard the little melody in the woods, she said, "That's it! That's the elf music I told you about."
   resentful   **eager**   anxious

2. Winnie spied on Jesse in the woods and watched as he drank from the spring. When he saw her, Jesse cried, "What're you doing here?"
   stern   hopeless   **joyful**

3. When Jesse told her not to drink from the spring, Winnie questioned, "Why not? It's mine, anyway, if it's in the wood."
   stubborn   reluctant   worried

4. Winnie cried when she realized she was being kidnapped. Seeing this, Mae exclaimed, "Please don't cry, child! We're not bad people, truly we're not."
   angry   **dismayed**

5. When Winnie was calmed, everyone relaxed. Jesse began to explain the family's story. "We're friends, we really are. But you got to help us."
   persuasive   happy   **helpless**

6. Miles recalled how his family reacted when he didn't age. "My wife, she left me. She went away and she took the children with her."
   stern   **sad**   stubborn

Answers may include:

1. . . . you were angry at your parents for not letting you go outside? **It's not fair. Everyone else is outside.**

2. . . . you were hopelessly unprepared for your spelling test? **I don't know how well I did.**

page 211

Help Me!

Circle the reference source you would use to answer each question below.

1. Which source would you use to learn how to make pancakes?
   dictionary   atlas   **cookbook**
2. Which source might show where Treegap is?
   dictionary   **atlas**   thesaurus
3. Which source would describe the peacock?
   book on insects   **encyclopedia**   newspaper
4. Which source would describe the sounds a cricket makes?
   book on insects   thesaurus   atlas
5. Which source would give the meaning of "constable"?
   newspaper   **dictionary**   atlas
6. Which source would describe the most recent world events?
   newspaper   encyclopedia   thesaurus
7. Which source would tell how to divide "accommodations" into syllables?
   thesaurus   book on insects   **dictionary**
8. Which source could give a synonym for "push"?
   thesaurus   cookbook   encyclopedia
9. Which source might best forecast tomorrow's weather?
   encyclopedia   atlas   **newspaper**

Use references to answer the following questions:

Which countries border Nepal?
Answer:
Source:
Page #:

What are the headlines in to...

Answer:
Source:
Page #:

Sources will vary.

page 212

Equivalent Fractions

Match the pairs of equivalent fractions to find which line is longest—**A**, **B** or (C).

Line A: $\frac{3}{8}$ • $\frac{2}{4}$ •- - - - - - - • $\frac{1}{2}$ • $\frac{6}{10}$

Line B: $\frac{6}{16}$ • $\frac{2}{3}$ •———• $\frac{4}{6}$ • $\frac{3}{5}$ • $\frac{5}{6}$ • $\frac{3}{7}$ • $\frac{6}{14}$

Line C: $\frac{10}{12}$ • $\frac{2}{8}$ • $\frac{1}{2}$ • $\frac{1}{3}$ • $\frac{2}{6}$ • $\frac{6}{8}$ •———• $\frac{3}{4}$ • $\frac{5}{8}$ • $\frac{10}{16}$ • $\frac{2}{10}$ • $\frac{1}{5}$

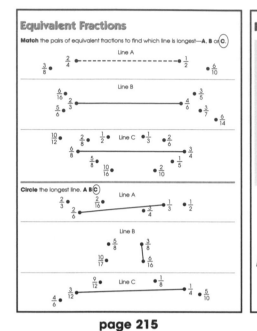

Circle the longest line. A B (C)

Line A: $\frac{2}{3}$ • $\frac{2}{16}$ • $\frac{2}{6}$ •———• $\frac{1}{3}$ • $\frac{3}{4}$ • $\frac{1}{2}$

Line B: $\frac{5}{8}$ • $\frac{3}{8}$ •—• $\frac{6}{16}$ • $\frac{10}{17}$

Line C: $\frac{9}{12}$ • $\frac{1}{8}$ • $\frac{3}{12}$ •———• $\frac{1}{4}$ • $\frac{5}{10}$ • $\frac{4}{6}$

page 215

Fussing About f

affection, autograph, cough, enough, familiar, foreign, frequent, furniture, geography, laughter, muffler, paragraph, philosophy, physical, raffle, slough, stuff, tough

The **f** sound can be made using the following letter combinations:

f as in **afternoon** — **ff** as in **staff**
gh as in **rough** — **ph** as in **photo**

Write each spelling word in the appropriate category.

f	ff
1. familiar	1. affection
2. foreign	2. muffler
3. frequent	3. raffle
4. furniture	4. stuff

gh	ph
1. cough	1. autograph
2. enough	2. geography
3. laughter	3. paragraph
4. slough	4. philosophy
5. tough	5. physical

Use the spelling words to complete the puzzle. Some of the letters are already given.

TOUGH; STUFF; FURNITURE; COUGH; ENOUGH; PARAGRAPH

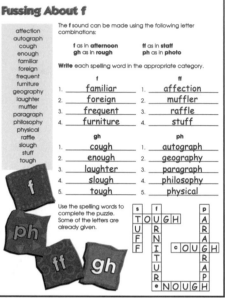

page 220

A Whale of an Activity

Some words may be used as either nouns or verbs.

Example: Fish
Fish are good to eat. (noun)
We ***fish*** every Saturday in the summer. (verb)

Read the paragraphs below. Decide if each bold word is used as a noun or as a verb. **Write** your answers on the lines below.

A whale is a mammal that does not live on **land**[1]. It would be impossible to **land**[2] a whale with ordinary fishing gear. A whale would not **attack**[3] a boat unless the whale was injured. However, an **attack**[4] by an injured whale could be very dangerous. Whales can **dive**[5] in the sea to a depth of more than one-half of a mile. Their powerful tails make such a **dive**[6] possible. Whales do not **fight**[7] among themselves. A **fight**[8] with a whale would be a losing battle! The skeleton of a whale is not strong enough to **support**[9] the whale's weight. Water provides the extra **support**[10] needed to hold up such huge bodies. Whales **swim**[11] across entire oceans searching for food. Such a long **swim**[12] is not unusual for a whale.

Whalers **hunt**[13] for whales in many countries of the world. In the old days, sailing ships might stay at sea for 2 to 3 years on a whale **hunt**[14]. Men would **race**[15] to get into small boats. It was a **race**[16] to see who could get to the whale first. Now, whaling boats may **catch**[17] just a few whales each year. Their **catch**[18] may not include mother whales with calves. Whalers have had to **part**[19] with old ways. They may no longer catch whales in every **part**[20] of the ocean.

1. noun
2. verb
3. verb
4. noun
5. verb
6. noun
7. verb
8. noun
9. verb
10. noun
11. verb
12. noun
13. verb
14. noun
15. verb
16. noun
17. verb
18. noun
19. verb
20. noun

page 221

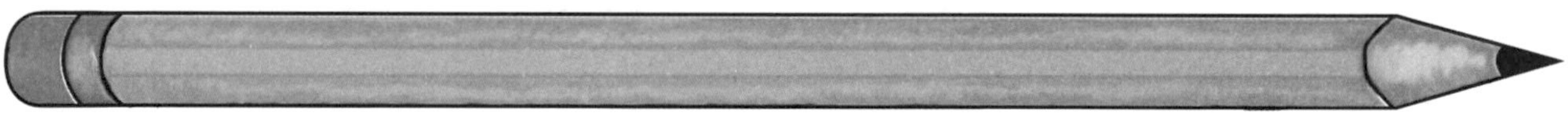

Because . . .

Remember:
The **cause** is the reason for the action or **why** something happened. The **effect** is the result of the action **what** actually happened.

Underline the causes.

1. Because she knew her face so well, Mae didn't need a mirror.
2. Because the Tucks had drunk water from the spring, they could not age.
3. Mae went into town, because her two boys were returning home.
4. The Tucks kidnapped Winnie, because she had discovered the spring.
5. Because Miles and Winnie brought no fish home for breakfast, the Tucks had flapjacks instead.

Circle the effects.

1. The Tuck boys never worked in the same place for long because their employers would become suspicious.
2. Because the stranger wished to obtain the property in the woods he offered to return Winnie to her parents.
3. Because the stranger planned to sell the secret Mae clubbed him.
4. The constable couldn't charge the Tucks with kidnapping because Winnie declared that she had gone with them of her own free will.
5. Winnie's grandmother ordered her to enter the house soon because the heat was intense that day.

What do you think caused the most problems in the story?

a. The Tucks' discovery of the spring
b. The stranger's greed
c. Winnie's discovery of Jesse Tuck
d. Other: ______

Explain your answer. ______

Answers will vary.

page 222

Conversion

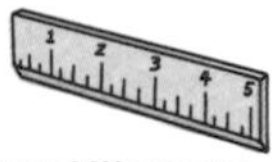

Find the number of units in each fraction described.

1. If there are 12 eggs in a dozen, how many eggs are in . . .
   - $\frac{1}{2}$ dozen? 6
   - $\frac{1}{4}$ dozen? 3
   - $\frac{1}{3}$ dozen? 4
2. If there are 100 centimeters (cm) in a meter, how many cm are in . . .
   - $\frac{1}{2}$ meter? 50
   - $\frac{1}{4}$ meter? 25
   - $\frac{1}{10}$ meter? 10
3. If there are 16 ounces in a pound, how many ounces are in . . .
   - $\frac{1}{2}$ pound? 8
   - $\frac{1}{4}$ pound? 4
   - $\frac{3}{8}$ pound? 6
4. If there are 4 quarts in a gallon, how many quarts are in . . .
   - $\frac{1}{2}$ gallon? 2
   - $\frac{1}{4}$ gallon? 1
   - $\frac{3}{4}$ gallon? 3
5. If there are 60 seconds in a minute, how many seconds are in . . .
   - $\frac{1}{2}$ minute? 30
   - $\frac{1}{4}$ minute? 15
   - $\frac{3}{4}$ minute? 45
6. If there are 1,000 meters in a kilometer, how many meters are in . . .
   - $\frac{1}{10}$ kilometer? 100
   - $\frac{1}{2}$ kilometer? 500
   - $\frac{1}{4}$ kilometer? 250
7. If there are 30 days in most months, how many days are in . . .
   - $\frac{1}{3}$ month? 10
   - $\frac{1}{6}$ month? 5
   - $\frac{1}{10}$ month? 3
8. If there are 24 hours in a day, how many hours are in . . .
   - $\frac{1}{3}$ day? 8
   - $\frac{2}{3}$ day? 16
   - $\frac{1}{4}$ day? 6
9. If there are 36 inches in a yard, how many inches are in . . .
   - $\frac{2}{3}$ yard? 24
   - $\frac{1}{4}$ yard? 9
   - $\frac{1}{2}$ yard? 18
10. If there are 2,000 pounds in a ton, how many pounds are in . . .
   - $\frac{1}{2}$ ton? 1,000
   - $\frac{1}{4}$ ton? 500
   - $\frac{1}{20}$ ton? 100

page 223

Silent Knight

ballet, castle, crumb, doubt, height, knack, knight, known, knuckle, listen, plumber, soften, thumb, weight, wreck, wren, wrench, wrestle

Many words contain one or more letters that are silent. Say each spelling word aloud. **Write** each spelling word in the appropriate silent letter category. (Some words may fit into more than one category.)

silent w	silent k
1. wreck	1. knack
2. wren	2. knight
3. wrench	3. known
4. wrestle	4. knuckle

silent gh	silent b
1. height	1. crumb
2. weight	2. doubt
3. knight	3. plumber
	4. thumb

silent t

1. ballet
2. castle
3. listen
4. soften
5. wrestle

Answer the following questions with other silent **b** words.

What . . .

1. is a part of a tree? limb
2. followed Mary to school? lamb
3. means no feeling? numb
4. smooths your hair in place? comb
5. is a destructive force? listening

page 228

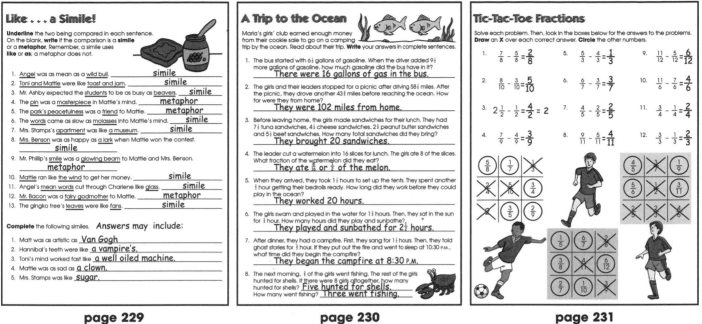

Like . . . a Simile!

Underline the two being compared in each sentence. On the blank, **write** if the comparison is a **simile** or a **metaphor**. Remember, a simile uses **like** or **as**; a metaphor does not.

1. Angel was as mean as a wild bull. simile
2. Toni and Mattie were like toast and jam. simile
3. Mr. Ashby expected the students to be as busy as beavers. simile
4. The pin was a masterpiece in Mattie's mind. metaphor
5. The park's peacefulness was a friend to Mattie. metaphor
6. The words came as slow as molasses into Mattie's mind. simile
7. Mrs. Stamps's apartment was like a museum. simile
8. Mrs. Benson was as happy as a lark when Mattie won the contest. simile
9. Mr. Phillip's smile was a glowing beam to Mattie and Mrs. Benson. metaphor
10. Mattie ran like the wind to get her money. simile
11. Angel's mean words cut through Charlene like glass. simile
12. Mr. Bacon was a fairy godmother to Mattie. metaphor
13. The gingko tree's leaves were like fans. simile

Complete the following similes. Answers may include:

1. Matt was as artistic as Van Gogh
2. Hannibal's teeth were like a vampire's.
3. Toni's mind worked fast like a well oiled machine.
4. Mattie was as sad as a clown.
5. Mrs. Stamps was like sugar.

page 229

A Trip to the Ocean

Maria's girls' club earned enough money from their cookie sale to go on a camping trip by the ocean. Read about their trip. **Write** your answers in complete sentences.

1. The bus started with $6\frac{1}{2}$ gallons of gasoline. When the driver added $9\frac{1}{2}$ more gallons of gasoline, how much gasoline did the bus have in it?
   There were 16 gallons of gas in the bus.
2. The girls and their leaders stopped for a picnic after driving $58\frac{1}{5}$ miles. After the picnic, they drove another $43\frac{4}{5}$ miles before reaching the ocean. How far were they from home?
   They were 102 miles from home.
3. Before leaving home, the girls made sandwiches for their lunch. They had $7\frac{1}{2}$ tuna sandwiches, $4\frac{1}{4}$ cheese sandwiches, $2\frac{3}{4}$ peanut butter sandwiches and $5\frac{1}{2}$ beef sandwiches. How many total sandwiches did they bring?
   They brought 20 sandwiches.
4. The leader cut a watermelon into 16 slices for lunch. The girls ate 8 of the slices. What fraction of the watermelon did they eat?
   They ate $\frac{8}{16}$ or $\frac{1}{2}$ of the melon.
5. When they arrived, they took $1\frac{1}{3}$ hours to set up the tents. They spent another $\frac{2}{3}$ hour getting their bedrolls ready. How long did they work before they could play in the ocean?
   They worked 20 hours.
6. The girls swam and played in the water for $1\frac{3}{4}$ hours. Then, they sat in the sun for $\frac{3}{4}$ hour. How many hours did they play and sunbathe?
   They played and sunbathed for $2\frac{1}{2}$ hours.
7. After dinner, they had a campfire. First, they sang for $1\frac{1}{3}$ hours. Then, they told ghost stories for $\frac{2}{3}$ hour. If they put out the fire and went to sleep at 10:30 P.M., what time did they begin the campfire?
   They began the campfire at 8:30 P.M.
8. The next morning, $\frac{3}{8}$ of the girls went fishing. The rest of the girls hunted for shells. If there were 8 girls altogether, how many hunted for shells? Five hunted for shells.
   How many went fishing? Three went fishing.

page 230

Tic-Tac-Toe Fractions

Solve each problem. Then, look in the boxes below for the answers to the problems. **Draw** an **X** over each correct answer. **Circle** the other numbers.

1. $\frac{7}{8} - \frac{5}{8} = \frac{2}{8}$
2. $\frac{8}{10} - \frac{3}{10} = \frac{5}{10}$
3. $2\frac{1}{2} - \frac{1}{2} = \frac{4}{2} = 2$
4. $\frac{7}{9} - \frac{4}{9} = \frac{3}{9}$
5. $\frac{5}{3} - \frac{4}{3} = \frac{1}{3}$
6. $\frac{6}{7} - \frac{3}{7} = \frac{3}{7}$
7. $\frac{4}{5} - \frac{2}{5} = \frac{2}{5}$
8. $\frac{9}{11} - \frac{5}{11} = \frac{4}{11}$
9. $\frac{11}{12} - \frac{5}{12} = \frac{6}{12}$
10. $\frac{11}{6} - \frac{7}{6} = \frac{4}{6}$
11. $\frac{3}{4} - \frac{1}{4} = \frac{2}{4}$
12. $\frac{3}{3} - \frac{1}{3} = \frac{2}{3}$

$\frac{5}{8}$	$\frac{1}{7}$	~~$\frac{1}{3}$~~
~~$\frac{2}{4}$~~	~~$\frac{5}{10}$~~	$\frac{3}{4}$
~~2~~	$\frac{3}{5}$	$\frac{2}{9}$

$\frac{4}{5}$	~~$\frac{3}{7}$~~	$\frac{1}{9}$
$\frac{5}{6}$	~~$\frac{1}{2}$~~	$\frac{3}{11}$
~~$\frac{2}{5}$~~	~~$\frac{2}{3}$~~	~~$\frac{4}{6}$~~

$\frac{1}{5}$	$\frac{6}{7}$	~~$\frac{2}{8}$~~
$\frac{3}{8}$	~~$\frac{4}{11}$~~	$\frac{6}{12}$
$\frac{2}{7}$	$\frac{1}{10}$	~~$\frac{3}{9}$~~

page 231

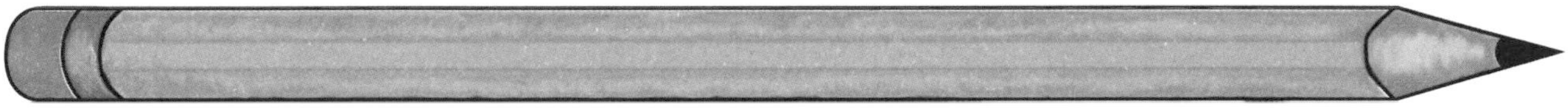

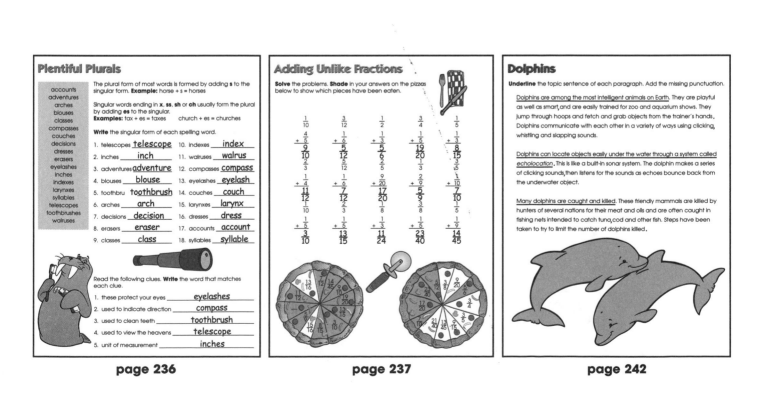

Plentiful Plurals

accounts, adventures, arches, blouses, classes, compasses, couches, decisions, dresses, erasers, eyelashes, inches, indexes, larynxes, syllables, telescopes, toothbrushes, walruses

The plural form of most words is formed by adding **s** to the singular form. **Example:** horse + s = horses

Singular words ending in **x**, **ss**, **sh** or **ch** usually form the plural by adding **es** to the singular.
Examples: tax + es = taxes church + es = churches

Write the singular form of each spelling word.

1. telescopes telescope
2. inches inch
3. adventures adventure
4. blouses blouse
5. toothbru toothbrush
6. arches arch
7. decisions decision
8. erasers eraser
9. classes class
10. indexes index
11. walruses walrus
12. compasses compass
13. eyelashes eyelash
14. couches couch
15. larynxes larynx
16. dresses dress
17. accounts account
18. syllables syllable

Read the following clues. **Write** the word that matches each clue.

1. these protect your eyes eyelashes
2. used to indicate direction compass
3. used to clean teeth toothbrush
4. used to view the heavens telescope
5. unit of measurement inches

page 236

Adding Unlike Fractions

Solve the problems. **Shade** in your answers on the pizzas below to show which pieces have been eaten.

$\frac{1}{10} + \frac{4}{5} = \frac{9}{10}$ $\frac{3}{12} + \frac{1}{6} = \frac{5}{12}$ $\frac{1}{2} + \frac{1}{3} = \frac{5}{6}$ $\frac{3}{4} + \frac{1}{5} = \frac{19}{20}$ $\frac{1}{5} + \frac{1}{3} = \frac{8}{15}$

$\frac{2}{3} + \frac{1}{4} = \frac{11}{12}$ $\frac{5}{12} + \frac{1}{6} = \frac{7}{12}$ $\frac{2}{5} + \frac{9}{20} = \frac{17}{20}$ $\frac{1}{3} + \frac{2}{9} = \frac{5}{9}$ $\frac{3}{5} + \frac{1}{10} = \frac{7}{10}$

$\frac{1}{10} + \frac{1}{5} = \frac{3}{10}$ $\frac{2}{3} + \frac{1}{5} = \frac{13}{15}$ $\frac{1}{8} + \frac{1}{3} = \frac{11}{24}$ $\frac{3}{8} + \frac{1}{5} = \frac{23}{40}$ $\frac{1}{5} + \frac{1}{9} = \frac{14}{45}$

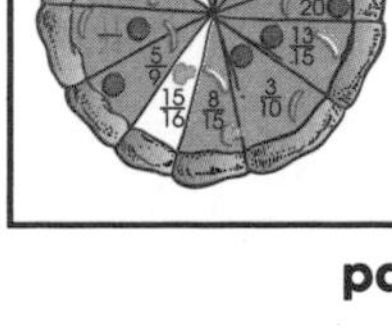

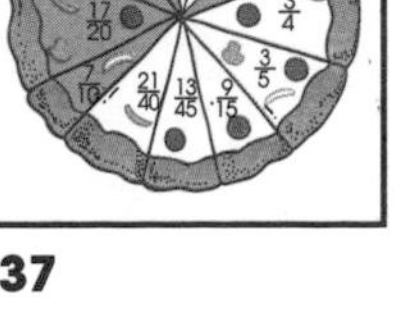

page 237

Dolphins

Underline the topic sentence of each paragraph. Add the missing punctuation.

Dolphins are among the most intelligent animals on Earth. They are playful as well as smart, and are easily trained for zoo and aquarium shows. They jump through hoops and fetch and grab objects from the trainer's hands. Dolphins communicate with each other in a variety of ways using clicking, whistling and slapping sounds.

Dolphins can locate objects easily under the water through a system called *echolocation*. This is like a built-in sonar system. The dolphin makes a series of clicking sounds, then listens for the sounds as echoes bounce back from the underwater object.

Many dolphins are caught and killed. These friendly mammals are killed by hunters of several nations for their meat and oils and are often caught in fishing nets intended to catch tuna, cod and other fish. Steps have been taken to try to limit the number of dolphins killed.

page 242

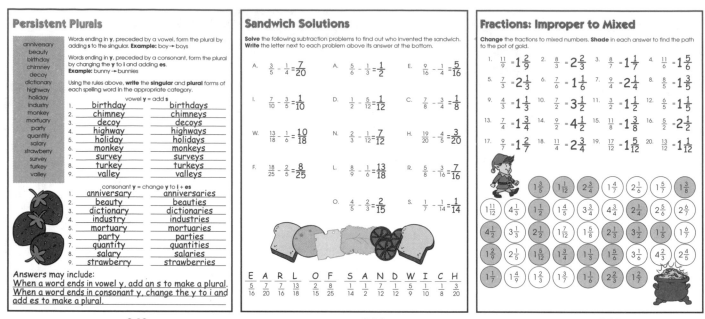

Persistent Plurals

anniversary
beauty
birthday
chimney
decoy
dictionary
highway
holiday
industry
monkey
mortuary
party
quantity
salary
strawberry
survey
turkey
valley

Words ending in **y**, preceded by a vowel, form the plural by adding **s** to the singular. **Example:** boy → boys

Words ending in **y**, preceded by a consonant, form the plural by changing the **y** to **i** and adding **es**. **Example:** bunny → bunnies

Using the rules above, **write** the **singular** and **plural** forms of each spelling word in the appropriate category.

vowel y = add s

1. birthday — birthdays
2. chimney — chimneys
3. decoy — decoys
4. highway — highways
5. holiday — holidays
6. monkey — monkeys
7. survey — surveys
8. turkey — turkeys
9. valley — valleys

consonant y = change y to i + es

1. anniversary — anniversaries
2. beauty — beauties
3. dictionary — dictionaries
4. industry — industries
5. mortuary — mortuaries
6. party — parties
7. quantity — quantities
8. salary — salaries
9. strawberry — strawberries

Answers may include:
When a word ends in vowel y, add an s to make a plural.
When a word ends in consonant y, change the y to i and add es to make a plural.

page 243

Sandwich Solutions

Solve the following subtraction problems to find out who invented the sandwich. **Write** the letter next to each problem above its answer at the bottom.

A. $\frac{3}{5} - \frac{1}{4} = \frac{7}{20}$

A. $\frac{5}{6} - \frac{1}{3} = \frac{1}{2}$

E. $\frac{9}{16} - \frac{1}{4} = \frac{5}{16}$

I. $\frac{7}{10} - \frac{3}{5} = \frac{1}{10}$

D. $\frac{1}{2} - \frac{5}{12} = \frac{1}{12}$

C. $\frac{7}{8} - \frac{3}{4} = \frac{1}{8}$

W. $\frac{13}{18} - \frac{1}{6} = \frac{10}{18}$

N. $\frac{2}{3} - \frac{7}{12} = \frac{7}{12}$

H. $\frac{19}{20} - \frac{4}{5} = \frac{3}{20}$

F. $\frac{18}{25} - \frac{2}{5} = \frac{8}{25}$

L. $\frac{8}{9} - \frac{1}{6} = \frac{13}{18}$

R. $\frac{5}{8} - \frac{3}{16} = \frac{7}{16}$

O. $\frac{4}{5} - \frac{2}{3} = \frac{2}{15}$

S. $\frac{1}{7} - \frac{1}{14} = \frac{1}{14}$

E	A	R	L		O	F		S	A	N	D	W	I	C	H
$\frac{5}{16}$	$\frac{7}{20}$	$\frac{7}{16}$	$\frac{13}{18}$		$\frac{2}{15}$	$\frac{8}{25}$		$\frac{1}{14}$	$\frac{1}{2}$	$\frac{7}{12}$	$\frac{1}{12}$	$\frac{10}{18}$	$\frac{1}{10}$	$\frac{1}{8}$	$\frac{3}{20}$

page 244

Fractions: Improper to Mixed

Change the fractions to mixed numbers. **Shade** in each answer to find the path to the pot of gold.

1. $\frac{11}{9} = 1\frac{2}{9}$
2. $\frac{8}{3} = 2\frac{2}{3}$
3. $\frac{8}{7} = 1\frac{1}{7}$
4. $\frac{11}{6} = 1\frac{5}{6}$
5. $\frac{7}{3} = 2\frac{1}{3}$
6. $\frac{7}{6} = 1\frac{1}{6}$
7. $\frac{9}{4} = 2\frac{1}{4}$
8. $\frac{8}{5} = 1\frac{3}{5}$
9. $\frac{4}{3} = 1\frac{1}{3}$
10. $\frac{7}{2} = 3\frac{1}{2}$
11. $\frac{3}{2} = 1\frac{1}{2}$
12. $\frac{6}{5} = 1\frac{1}{5}$
13. $\frac{7}{4} = 1\frac{3}{4}$
14. $\frac{9}{2} = 4\frac{1}{2}$
15. $\frac{11}{8} = 1\frac{3}{8}$
16. $\frac{5}{2} = 2\frac{1}{2}$
17. $\frac{9}{7} = 1\frac{2}{7}$
18. $\frac{11}{4} = 2\frac{3}{4}$
19. $\frac{17}{12} = 1\frac{5}{12}$
20. $\frac{13}{12} = 1\frac{1}{12}$

page 245

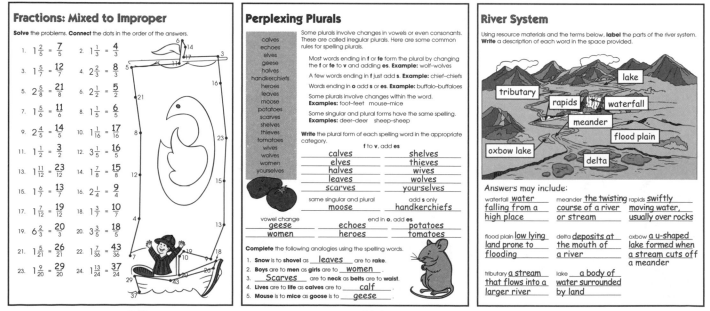

Fractions: Mixed to Improper

Solve the problems. **Connect** the dots in the order of the answers.

1. $1\frac{2}{5} = \frac{7}{5}$
2. $1\frac{1}{3} = \frac{4}{3}$
3. $1\frac{5}{7} = \frac{12}{7}$
4. $2\frac{2}{3} = \frac{8}{3}$
5. $2\frac{5}{8} = \frac{21}{8}$
6. $2\frac{1}{2} = \frac{5}{2}$
7. $1\frac{5}{6} = \frac{11}{6}$
8. $1\frac{1}{5} = \frac{6}{5}$
9. $2\frac{4}{5} = \frac{14}{5}$
10. $1\frac{1}{16} = \frac{17}{16}$
11. $1\frac{1}{2} = \frac{3}{2}$
12. $3\frac{1}{5} = \frac{16}{5}$
13. $1\frac{11}{12} = \frac{23}{12}$
14. $1\frac{7}{8} = \frac{15}{8}$
15. $1\frac{6}{7} = \frac{13}{7}$
16. $2\frac{1}{4} = \frac{9}{4}$
17. $1\frac{7}{12} = \frac{19}{12}$
18. $1\frac{3}{7} = \frac{10}{7}$
19. $6\frac{2}{3} = \frac{20}{3}$
20. $3\frac{3}{5} = \frac{18}{5}$
21. $1\frac{5}{21} = \frac{26}{21}$
22. $1\frac{7}{36} = \frac{43}{36}$
23. $1\frac{9}{20} = \frac{29}{20}$
24. $1\frac{13}{24} = \frac{37}{24}$

page 246

Perplexing Plurals

calves
echoes
elves
geese
halves
handkerchiefs
heroes
leaves
moose
potatoes
scarves
shelves
thieves
tomatoes
wives
wolves
women
yourselves

Some plurals involve changes in vowels or even consonants. These are called irregular plurals. Here are some common rules for spelling plurals.

Most words ending in **f** or **fe** form the plural by changing the **f** or **fe** to **v** and adding **es**. **Example:** wolf–wolves

A few words ending in **f** just add **s**. **Example:** chief–chiefs

Words ending in **o** add **s** or **es**. **Example:** buffalo–buffaloes

Some plurals involve changes within the word. **Examples:** foot–feet mouse–mice

Some singular and plural forms have the same spelling. **Examples:** deer–deer sheep–sheep

Write the plural form of each spelling word in the appropriate category.

f to v, add es

calves	shelves
elves	thieves
halves	wives
leaves	wolves
scarves	yourselves

same singular and plural — moose

add s only — handkerchiefs

vowel change — geese, women

end in o, add es — echoes, heroes, potatoes, tomatoes

Complete the following analogies using the spelling words.

1. **Snow** is to **shovel** as **leaves** are to **rake**.
2. **Boys** are to **men** as **girls** are to **women**.
3. **Scarves** are to **neck** as **belts** are to **waist**.
4. **Lives** are to **life** as **calves** are to **calf**.
5. **Mouse** is to **mice** as **goose** is to **geese**.

page 254

River System

Using resource materials and the terms below, **label** the parts of the river system. **Write** a description of each word in the space provided.

lake
tributary
rapids
waterfall
meander
flood plain
oxbow lake
delta

Answers may include:

waterfall **water falling from a high place**

meander **the twisting course of a river or stream**

rapids **swiftly moving water, usually over rocks**

flood plain **low lying land prone to flooding**

delta **deposits at the mouth of a river**

oxbow **a u-shaped lake formed when a stream cuts off a meander**

tributary **a stream that flows into a larger river**

lake **a body of water surrounded by land**

page 255

Learn at Home, Grade 5

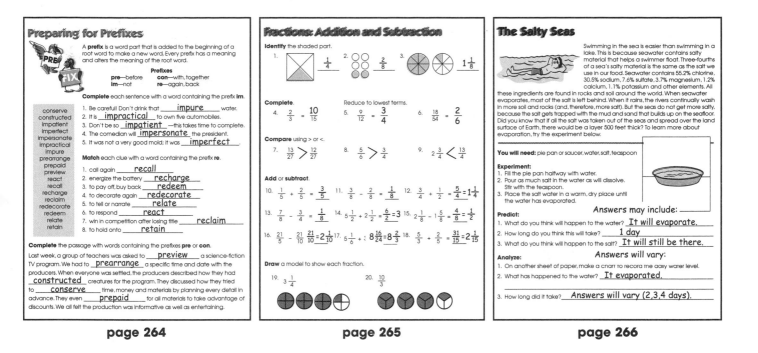

Preparing for Prefixes

A **prefix** is a word part that is added to the beginning of a root word to make a new word. Every prefix has a meaning and alters the meaning of the root word.

Prefixes
pre—before   con—with, together
im—not   re—again, back

Complete each sentence with a word containing the prefix **im**.

1. Be careful. Don't drink that __impure__ water.
2. It is __impractical__ to own five automobiles.
3. Don't be so __impatient__ —this takes time to complete.
4. The comedian will __impersonate__ the president.
5. It was not a very good mold; it was __imperfect__.

conserve
constructed
impatient
imperfect
impersonate
impractical
impure
prearrange
prepaid
preview
react
recall
recharge
reclaim
redecorate
redeem
relate
retain

Match each clue with a word containing the prefix **re**.

1. call again __recall__
2. energize the battery __recharge__
3. to pay off, buy back __redeem__
4. to decorate again __redecorate__
5. to tell or narrate __relate__
6. to respond __react__
7. win in competition after losing title __reclaim__
8. to hold onto __retain__

Complete the passage with words containing the prefixes **pre** or **con**.

Last week, a group of teachers was asked to __preview__ a science-fiction TV program. We had to __prearrange__ a specific time and date with the producers. When everyone was settled, the producers described how they had __constructed__ creatures for the program. They discussed how they tried to __conserve__ time, money and materials by planning every detail in advance. They even __prepaid__ for all materials to take advantage of discounts. We all felt the production was informative as well as entertaining.

page 264

Fractions: Addition and Subtraction

Identify the shaded part.

1. $\frac{1}{4}$ 2. $\frac{2}{8}$ 3. $1\frac{1}{8}$

Complete.

4. $\frac{2}{3} = \frac{10}{15}$

Reduce to lowest terms.

5. $\frac{9}{12} = \frac{3}{4}$ 6. $\frac{18}{54} = \frac{2}{6}$

Compare using > or <.

7. $\frac{13}{27} > \frac{12}{27}$ 8. $\frac{5}{6} > \frac{3}{4}$ 9. $2\frac{3}{4} < \frac{13}{4}$

Add or subtract.

10. $\frac{1}{5} + \frac{2}{5} = \frac{3}{5}$ 11. $\frac{3}{8} - \frac{2}{8} = \frac{1}{8}$ 12. $\frac{3}{4} + \frac{1}{2} = \frac{5}{4} = 1\frac{1}{4}$

13. $\frac{7}{8} - \frac{3}{4} = \frac{1}{8}$ 14. $5\frac{1}{2} + 2\frac{1}{2} = \frac{6}{2} = 3$ 15. $2\frac{1}{8} - 1\frac{5}{8} = \frac{4}{8} = \frac{1}{2}$

16. $\frac{21}{5} - \frac{21}{10} = \frac{21}{10} = 2\frac{1}{10}$ 17. $5\frac{1}{6} + \diamond = 8\frac{16}{24} = 8\frac{2}{3}$ 18. $\frac{5}{3} + \frac{2}{5} = \frac{31}{15} = 2\frac{1}{15}$

Draw a model to show each fraction.

19. $3\frac{1}{4}$ 20. $\frac{10}{3}$

page 265

The Salty Seas

Swimming in the sea is easier than swimming in a lake. This is because seawater contains salty material that helps a swimmer float. Three-fourths of a sea's salty material is the same as the salt we use in our food. Seawater contains 55.2% chlorine, 30.5% sodium, 7.6% sulfate, 3.7% magnesium, 1.2% calcium, 1.1% potassium and other elements. All these ingredients are found in rocks and soil around the world. When seawater evaporates, most of the salt is left behind. When it rains, the rivers continually wash in more soil and rocks (and, therefore, more salt). But the seas do not get more salty, because the salt gets trapped with the mud and sand that builds up on the seafloor. Did you know that if all the salt was taken out of the seas and spread over the land surface of Earth, there would be a layer 500 feet thick? To learn more about evaporation, try the experiment below.

You will need: pie pan or saucer, water, salt, teaspoon

Experiment:
1. Fill the pie pan halfway with water.
2. Pour as much salt in the water as will dissolve. Stir with the teaspoon.
3. Place the salt water in a warm, dry place until the water has evaporated.

Answers may include:

Predict:
1. What do you think will happen to the water? __It will evaporate.__
2. How long do you think this will take? __1 day__
3. What do you think will happen to the salt? __It will still be there.__

Analyze:

Answers will vary:

1. On another sheet of paper, make a chart to record the daily water level.
2. What has happened to the water? __It evaporated.__
3. How long did it take? __Answers will vary (2,3,4 days).__

page 266

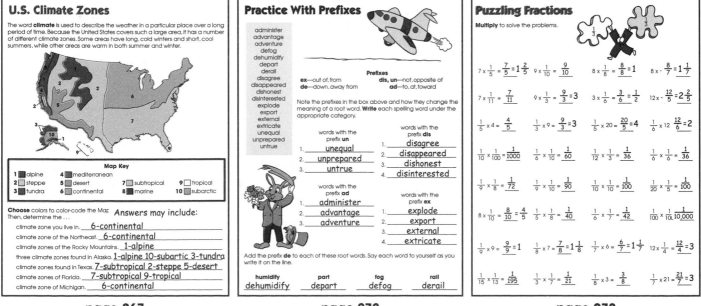

U.S. Climate Zones

The word **climate** is used to describe the weather in a particular place over a long period of time. Because the United States covers such a large area, it has a number of different climate zones. Some areas have long, cold winters and short, cool summers, while other areas are warm in both summer and winter.

Map Key
1 ▨ alpine   4 ▨ mediterranean   7 ▨ subtropical   9 ▢ tropical
2 ▨ steppe   5 ▨ desert   8 ▨ marine   10 ▨ subarctic
3 ▨ tundra   6 ▨ continental

Choose colors to color-code the Map. Then, determine the ...   Answers may include:

climate zone you live in. __6-continental__
climate zone of the Northeast. __6-continental__
climate zone of the Rocky Mountains. __1-alpine__
three climate zones found in Alaska. __1-alpine 10-subartic 3-tundra__
climate zones found in Texas. __7-subtropical 2-steppe 5-desert__
climate zones of Florida. __7-subtropical 9-tropical__
climate zone of Michigan. __6-continental__

page 267

Practice With Prefixes

administer
advantage
adventure
defog
dehumidify
depart
derail
disagree
disappeared
dishonest
disinterested
explode
export
external
extricate
unequal
unprepared
untrue

Prefixes
ex—out of, from   dis, un—not, opposite of
de—down, away from   ad—to, at, toward

Note the prefixes in the box above and how they change the meaning of a root word. **Write** each spelling word under the appropriate category.

words with the prefix **un**
1. __unequal__
2. __unprepared__
3. __untrue__

words with the prefix **dis**
1. __disagree__
2. __disappeared__
3. __dishonest__
4. __disinterested__

words with the prefix **ad**
1. __administer__
2. __advantage__
3. __adventure__

words with the prefix **ex**
1. __explode__
2. __export__
3. __external__
4. __extricate__

Add the prefix **de** to each of these root words. Say each word to yourself as you write it on the line.

humidify   part   fog   rail
__dehumidify__   __depart__   __defog__   __derail__

page 272

Puzzling Fractions

Multiply to solve the problems.

$7 \times \frac{1}{5} = \frac{7}{5} = 1\frac{2}{5}$ $9 \times \frac{1}{10} = \frac{9}{10}$ $8 \times \frac{1}{8} = \frac{8}{8} = 1$ $8 \times \frac{1}{7} = \frac{8}{7} = 1\frac{1}{7}$

$7 \times \frac{1}{11} = \frac{7}{11}$ $9 \times \frac{1}{3} = \frac{9}{3} = 3$ $3 \times \frac{1}{6} = \frac{3}{6} = \frac{1}{2}$ $12 \times \frac{1}{5} = \frac{12}{5} = 2\frac{2}{5}$

$\frac{1}{5} \times 4 = \frac{4}{5}$ $\frac{1}{3} \times 9 = \frac{9}{3} = 3$ $\frac{1}{5} \times 20 = \frac{20}{5} = 4$ $\frac{1}{6} \times 12 = \frac{12}{6} = 2$

$\frac{1}{10} \times \frac{1}{100} = \frac{1}{1000}$ $\frac{1}{6} \times \frac{1}{10} = \frac{1}{60}$ $\frac{1}{12} \times \frac{1}{3} = \frac{1}{36}$ $\frac{1}{6} \times \frac{1}{6} = \frac{1}{36}$

$\frac{1}{9} \times \frac{1}{8} = \frac{1}{72}$ $\frac{1}{9} \times \frac{1}{10} = \frac{1}{90}$ $\frac{1}{10} \times \frac{1}{10} = \frac{1}{100}$ $\frac{1}{20} \times \frac{1}{5} = \frac{1}{100}$

$8 \times \frac{1}{10} = \frac{8}{10} = \frac{4}{5}$ $5 \times \frac{1}{8} = \frac{1}{40}$ $\frac{1}{6} \times \frac{1}{7} = \frac{1}{42}$ $\frac{1}{100} \times \frac{1}{10} = \frac{1}{10,000}$

$\frac{1}{9} \times 9 = \frac{9}{9} = 1$ $\frac{1}{8} \times 7 = \frac{7}{8} = 1\frac{1}{8}$ $\frac{1}{7} \times 6 = \frac{6}{7} = 1\frac{1}{7}$ $12 \times \frac{1}{4} = \frac{12}{4} = 3$

$\frac{1}{15} \times \frac{1}{13} = \frac{1}{195}$ $\frac{1}{3} \times \frac{1}{7} = \frac{1}{21}$ $\frac{1}{8} \times 3 = \frac{3}{8}$ $\frac{1}{7} \times 21 = \frac{21}{7} = 3$

page 273

Multiplication With Mixed Numbers

When multiplying by a mixed number, change the mixed number to an improper fraction. Cancel if possible. Multiply the numerators, then the denominators. **Write** the improper fractions as mixed numbers.

Example A: $\frac{3}{4} \times 1\frac{1}{2} = \frac{3}{4} \times \frac{3}{2} = \frac{9}{8} = 1\frac{1}{8}$

Example B: $2\frac{4}{7} \times \frac{5}{9} = \frac{2\,18}{7} \times \frac{5}{9\,1} = \frac{10}{7} = 1\frac{3}{7}$

Multiply.

1. $\frac{1}{2} \times 8\frac{3}{4} = \frac{1}{2} \times \frac{35}{4} = 4\frac{3}{8}$ 5. $\frac{2}{5} \times 2\frac{1}{12}$ $\frac{5}{6}$

2. $5\frac{1}{3} \times \frac{6}{7}$ $4\frac{4}{7}$ 6. $8\frac{2}{3} \times \frac{1}{4}$ $2\frac{1}{6}$

3. $\frac{11}{12} \times 11\frac{1}{3}$ $10\frac{7}{18}$

4. $7\frac{1}{2} \times \frac{8}{9}$ $6\frac{2}{3}$

page 274

Dividing Fractions

When dividing fractions, change the problem to multiplication. Invert the divisor. Cancel if possible. Multiply the numerators, then the denominators. **Write** improper fractions as mixed numbers.

Example A: $\frac{3}{10} \div \frac{4}{5} = \frac{3}{10} \times \frac{5}{4} = \frac{3}{10} \times \frac{5^1}{4} = \frac{3}{8}$

Example B: $\frac{5}{12} \div \frac{3}{8} = \frac{5}{12} \times \frac{8}{3} = \frac{5}{12} \times \frac{8^2}{3} = \frac{10}{9} = 1\frac{1}{9}$

Divide.

1. $\frac{1}{2} \div \frac{3}{10} = \frac{1}{2} \times \frac{10}{3} = 1\frac{2}{3}$ 5. $\frac{1}{10} \div \frac{2}{5}$ $\frac{1}{4}$

2. $\frac{3}{8} \div \frac{1}{4}$ $1\frac{1}{2}$ 6. $\frac{5}{6} \div \frac{11}{12}$ $\frac{10}{11}$

3. $\frac{4}{9} \div \frac{2}{3}$ $\frac{2}{3}$ 7. $\frac{14}{15} \div \frac{2}{3}$ $1\frac{2}{5}$

4. $\frac{3}{8} \div \frac{5}{12}$ $\frac{9}{10}$ 8. $\frac{4}{5} \div \frac{3}{10}$ $2\frac{2}{3}$

page 275

Radical Referents

Write the name of the person or thing to which the **bold** words refer.

1. Mama took Ellen's hand and told **her** she had beautiful hair.   Ellen
2. After discussing the girls, Papa and Mama decided that **they** should be taken to Henrik's house.   girls
3. Papa reached for the phone to call Henrik, hoping that **he** would still reach **him** at home.   Papa—Henrik
4. Papa promised Mama and the children **they** would be safe.   Mama—children
5. A soldier on the train asked Mama where **she** was going.   Mama
6. Kirsti told the soldier, "I am going to visit **my** Uncle Henrik!"   Kirsti
7. Annemarie was surprised when Ellen said **she** had never seen the sea.   Ellen
8. Henrik named his fishing boat the *Ingeborg* after Mama, who was **his** sister.   Henrik

In the morning, Annemarie awoke and stumbled downstairs where **she** found her chatterbox sister feeding a kitten. Kirsti named **it** after the God of Thunder and **she** was attempting to give it water.   Annemarie / the kitten / Kirsti

When Kirsti laughed, the kitten scurried off to be alone and soon **it** rested on a windowsill out of **her** reach. There it sat, licking its paws.   the kitten / Kirsti

Ellen was still sleeping while Mama prepared oatmeal for **her** and the others. Mama's brother Henrik no longer grew vegetables but **he** was able to provide cream and butter because of Blossom, **his** cow.   Ellen / Henrik / Henrik

Underline the character's name hidden in each of the following sentences. The first one has been done for you.

1. May Mary Beth or Betty Ann play the game in the blizzard?
2. The fakir stirred his cauliflower soup with a spatula and a dowel.
3. The party's success was certain when Sam amazed his audience.
4. Matilda foolishly flipped and fell entirely into a foaming filth.
5. The Fieldings figured the top apartment was the best of the lot.
6. My winsome sister could shop eternally for chartreuse stockings.

page 280

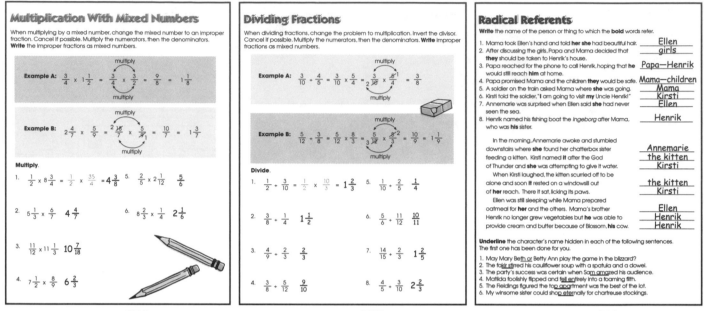

Stump the Teacher

The students in Ms. Davidson's class were playing "Stump the Teacher." See if you can solve their problems.

1. If baseball cards are worth $\frac{1}{10}$ of a dollar each, how much are Brad's 54 cards worth? $5.40

2. If $\frac{6}{8}$ of Sally's 8 puppies are female and $\frac{1}{2}$ of the female puppies have been sold, how many female puppies have been sold?   3 puppies

3. Felipe used $\frac{2}{3}$ cup of cheese for each pizza. If he made 4 pizzas, how much cheese did he need to buy? $2\frac{2}{3}$ cups

4. Francis bought $\frac{15}{16}$ of a yard of fabric. She used $\frac{1}{2}$ of it to make a dress for her doll. What fraction of a yard did she use? $\frac{15}{32}$ yd.

5. If a lot is $\frac{5}{8}$ of an acre, and the house covers $\frac{1}{2}$ of it, what fraction of an acre is covered by the house? $\frac{5}{16}$ acre

6. At the track meet, Rick entered 5 sprint contests. If each race was $\frac{1}{4}$ mile long, how many miles did Rick sprint in all? $1\frac{1}{4}$ mi.

7. The class had $\frac{1}{4}$ of an hour to take a math quiz. Nate used only $\frac{1}{3}$ of the time. What fraction of an hour did Nate use for the quiz? $\frac{1}{12}$ hr.

8. Lisa and Kim live $\frac{3}{8}$ of a mile apart. If they each walked $\frac{1}{2}$ of the way and met in the middle, what part of a mile did each walk? $\frac{3}{16}$ mi.

9. This year's summer vacation was $\frac{1}{6}$ of the year. How many months long was the summer vacation this year?   2 mo.

10. Paul's dog was asleep $\frac{2}{3}$ of the day. How many hours was it awake?   8 hrs.

page 281

Fractions: Multiplication and Division

Solve.

1. $\frac{7}{9} \times \frac{1}{4} = \frac{7}{36}$ 2. $\frac{5}{6} \times \frac{1}{10} = \frac{5}{60} = \frac{1}{12}$ 3. $\frac{9}{10} \times \frac{2}{3} = \frac{18}{30} = \frac{3}{5}$

4. $8 \times \frac{1}{4} = \frac{8}{4} = 2$ 5. $\frac{1}{3} \times 15 = \frac{15}{3} = 5$

6. Jaime sat in his chair for $\frac{5}{6}$ of an hour. For $\frac{1}{3}$ of this time, he worked on this assignment. What fraction of an hour did he work on this assignment?

$\frac{1}{3} \times \frac{5}{6} = \frac{5}{18}$

7. $\frac{1}{2} \div \frac{1}{5} = \frac{5}{2} = 2\frac{1}{2}$ 8. $\frac{1}{5} \div \frac{1}{2} = \frac{2}{5}$

9. $\frac{3}{4} \div \frac{3}{8} = \frac{4}{2} = 2$ 10. $\frac{7}{16} \div \frac{4}{7} = \frac{49}{64}$

page 282

Third Quarter Test

Identify the shaded fraction and simplify to lowest terms.

1. $\frac{3}{8}$ 2. $\frac{4}{8} = \frac{1}{2}$ 3. $\frac{16}{20} = \frac{4}{5}$

Compare using > or <.

4. $\frac{3}{5} < \frac{4}{5}$ 5. $\frac{5}{8} > \frac{5}{11}$ 6. $1 > \frac{7}{8}$

Add or **subtract.**

7. $\frac{1}{9} + \frac{5}{9} = \frac{6}{9} = \frac{2}{3}$ 8. $\frac{2}{5} + \frac{1}{10} = \frac{5}{10} = \frac{1}{2}$ 9. $\frac{3}{8} + \frac{1}{6} = \frac{13}{24}$

10. $3\frac{1}{4} + 2\frac{1}{3} = 5\frac{7}{12}$ 11. $\frac{7}{9} - \frac{2}{3} = \frac{1}{9}$ 12. $11\frac{7}{8} - 4\frac{5}{12} = 7\frac{11}{24}$

13. Change $\frac{17}{4}$ in mixed number. $4\frac{1}{4}$ 14. Change $3\frac{2}{5}$ into improper fraction. $\frac{17}{5}$

Multiply or **divide.**

15. $\frac{3}{4} \times \frac{1}{2} = \frac{3}{8}$ 16. $\frac{11}{12} \times \frac{4}{5} = \frac{44}{60} = \frac{22}{30} = \frac{11}{15}$

17. $\frac{2}{3} \div \frac{1}{3} = 2$ 18. $\frac{1}{2} \div \frac{1}{4} = 2$

page 283

Learn at Home, Grade 5

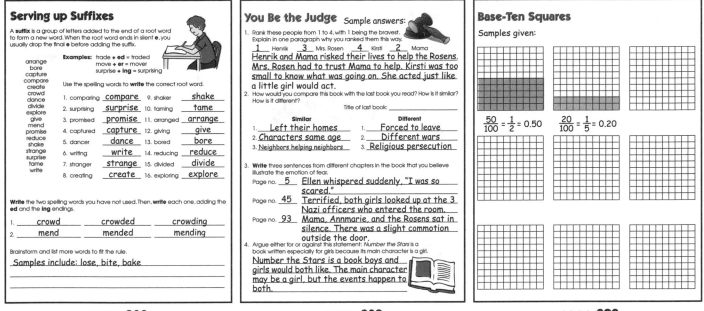

Serving up Suffixes

A **suffix** is a group of letters added to the end of a root word to form a new word. When the root word ends in silent **e**, you usually drop the final **e** before adding the suffix.

Examples: trade + ed = traded
move + er = mover
surprise + ing = surprising

arrange
bore
capture
compare
create
crowd
dance
divide
explore
give
mend
promise
reduce
shake
strange
surprise
tame
write

Use the spelling words to **write** the correct root word.

1. comparing __compare__
2. surprising __surprise__
3. promised __promise__
4. captured __capture__
5. dancer __dance__
6. writing __write__
7. stranger __strange__
8. creating __create__
9. shaker __shake__
10. taming __tame__
11. arranged __arrange__
12. giving __give__
13. bored __bore__
14. reducing __reduce__
15. divided __divide__
16. exploring __explore__

Write the two spelling words you have not used. Then, **write** each one, adding the **ed** and the **ing** endings.

1. __crowd__ __crowded__ __crowding__
2. __mend__ __mended__ __mending__

Brainstorm and list more words to fit the rule.

__Samples include: lose, bite, bake__

page 288

You Be the Judge   Sample answers:

1. Rank these people from 1 to 4, with 1 being the bravest. Explain in one paragraph why you ranked them this way.

__1__ Henrik __3__ Mrs. Rosen __4__ Kirsti __2__ Mama

Henrik and Mama risked their lives to help the Rosens. Mrs. Rosen had to trust Mama to help. Kirsti was too small to know what was going on. She acted just like a little girl would act.

2. How would you compare this book with the last book you read? How is it similar? How is it different?

Title of last book: ____

Similar	Different
1. Left their homes	1. Forced to leave
2. Characters same age	2. Different wars
3. Neighbors helping neighbors	3. Religious persecution

3. **Write** three sentences from different chapters in the book that you believe illustrate the emotion of fear.

Page no. __5__ Ellen whispered suddenly, "I was so scared."

Page no. __45__ Terrified, both girls looked up at the 3 Nazi officers who entered the room.

Page no. __93__ Mama, Annmarie, and the Rosens sat in silence. There was a slight commotion outside the door.

4. Argue either for or against this statement: *Number the Stars* is a book written especially for girls because its main character is a girl.

Number the Stars is a book boys and girls would both like. The main character may be a girl, but the events happen to both.

page 289

Base-Ten Squares

Samples given:

$\frac{50}{100} = \frac{1}{2} = 0.50$ $\frac{20}{100} = \frac{1}{5} = 0.20$

page 290

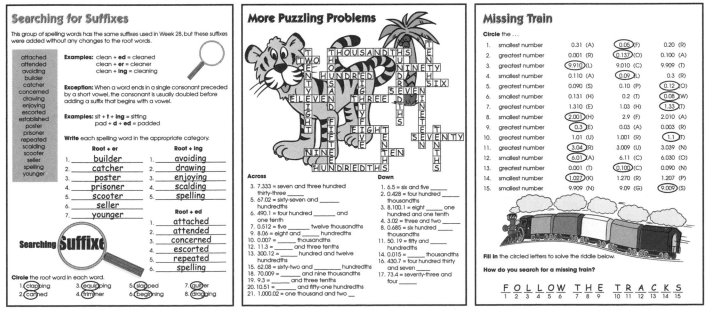

Searching for Suffixes

This group of spelling words has the same suffixes used in Week 28, but these suffixes were added without any changes to the root words.

attached
attended
avoiding
builder
catcher
concerned
drawing
enjoying
escorted
established
poster
prisoner
repeated
scalding
scooter
seller
spelling
younger

Examples: clean + ed = cleaned
clean + er = cleaner
clean + ing = cleaning

Exception: When a word ends in a single consonant preceded by a short vowel, the consonant is usually doubled before adding a suffix that begins with a vowel.

Examples: sit + t + ing = sitting
pad + d + ed = padded

Write each spelling word in the appropriate category.

Root + er
1. __builder__
2. __catcher__
3. __poster__
4. __prisoner__
5. __scooter__
6. __seller__
7. __younger__

Root + ing
1. __avoiding__
2. __drawing__
3. __enjoying__
4. __scalding__
5. __spelling__

Root + ed
1. __attached__
2. __attended__
3. __concerned__
4. __escorted__
5. __repeated__
6. __spelling__

Circle the root word in each word.

1. clapping
2. canned
3. equipping
4. trimmer
5. slapped
6. beginning
7. quitter
8. dragging

page 296

More Puzzling Problems

Across
3. 7.333 = seven and three hundred thirty-three
5. 67.02 = sixty-seven and ____ hundredths
6. 490.1 = four hundred ____ and one tenth
7. 0.512 = five ____ twelve thousandths
9. 8.06 = eight and ____ hundredths
10. 0.007 = ____ thousandths
12. 11.3 = ____ and three tenths
13. 300.12 = ____ hundred and twelve hundredths
15. 62.08 = sixty-two and ____ hundredths
18. 70.009 = ____ and nine thousandths
19. 9.3 = ____ and three tenths
20. 10.51 = ____ and fifty-one hundredths
21. 1,000.02 = one thousand and two ___

Down
1. 6.5 = six and five ____
2. 0.428 = four hundred ____ thousandths
3. 8,100.1 = eight ____ one hundred and one tenth
4. 3.02 = three and two ____
8. 0.685 = six hundred ____ thousandths
11. 50. 19 = fifty and ____ hundredths
14. 0.015 = ____ thousandths
16. 430.7 = four hundred thirty and seven ____
17. 73.4 = seventy-three and four ____

page 297

Missing Train

Circle the ...

1.	smallest number	0.31 (A)	**0.05** (F)	0.20 (R)
2.	greatest number	0.001 (R)	**0.137** (O)	0.100 (A)
3.	greatest number	**9.910** (L)	9.010 (C)	9.909 (T)
4.	smallest number	0.110 (A)	**0.09** (W)	0.3 (R)
5.	greatest number	0.090 (S)	0.10 (P)	**0.12** (O)
6.	smallest number	0.131 (H)	0.2 (O)	**0.08** (W)
7.	greatest number	1.310 (E)	1.03 (H)	**1.33** (T)
8.	smallest number	**2.001** (H)	2.9 (F)	2.010 (A)
9.	greatest number	**0.3** (E)	0.03 (A)	0.003 (R)
10.	greatest number	1.01 (U)	1.001 (R)	**1.1** (T)
11.	greatest number	**3.04** (R)	3.009 (U)	3.039 (N)
12.	smallest number	**6.01** (A)	6.11 (C)	6.030 (O)
13.	greatest number	0.001 (T)	**0.100** (N)	0.090 (N)
14.	smallest number	**1.027** (K)	1.270 (R)	1.207 (P)
15.	smallest number	9.909 (N)	9.09 (G)	**9.009** (S)

Fill in the circled letters to solve the riddle below.

How do you search for a missing train?

$\underset{1}{F}\ \underset{2}{O}\ \underset{3}{L}\ \underset{4}{L}\ \underset{5}{O}\ \underset{6}{W}$ $\underset{7}{T}\ \underset{8}{H}\ \underset{9}{E}$ $\underset{10}{T}\ \underset{11}{R}\ \underset{12}{A}\ \underset{13}{C}\ \underset{14}{K}\ \underset{15}{S}$

page 298

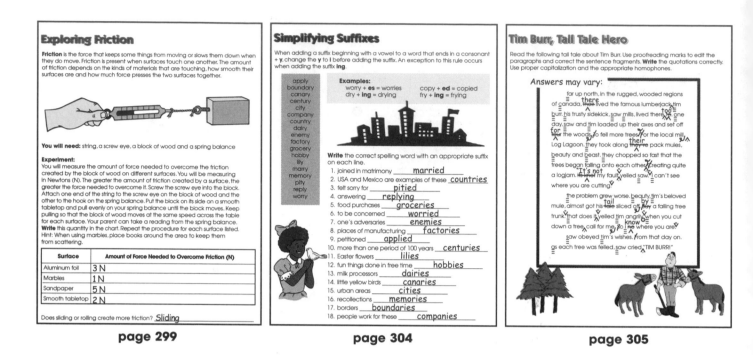

Exploring Friction

Friction is the force that keeps some things from moving or slows them down when they do move. Friction is present when surfaces touch one another. The amount of friction depends on the kinds of materials that are touching, how smooth their surfaces are and how much force presses the two surfaces together.

You will need: string, a screw eye, a block of wood and a spring balance

Experiment:
You will measure the amount of force needed to overcome the friction created by the block of wood on different surfaces. You will be measuring in Newtons (N). The greater the amount of friction created by a surface, the greater the force needed to overcome it. Screw the screw eye into the block. Attach one end of the string to the screw eye on the block of wood and the other to the hook on the spring balance. Put the block on its side on a smooth tabletop and pull evenly on your spring balance until the block moves. Keep pulling so that the block of wood moves at the same speed across the table for each surface. Your parent can take a reading from the spring balance. **Write** this quantity in the chart. Repeat the procedure for each surface listed. Hint: When using marbles, place books around the area to keep them from scattering.

Surface	Amount of Force Needed to Overcome Friction (N)
Aluminum foil	3 N
Marbles	1 N
Sandpaper	5 N
Smooth tabletop	2 N

Does sliding or rolling create more friction? __Sliding__

page 299

Simplifying Suffixes

When adding a suffix beginning with a vowel to a word that ends in a consonant + **y**, change the **y** to **i** before adding the suffix. An exception to this rule occurs when adding the suffix **ing**.

apply
boundary
canary
century
city
company
country
dairy
enemy
factory
grocery
hobby
lily
marry
memory
pity
reply
worry

Examples:
worry + **es** = worries
dry + **ing** = drying
copy + **ed** = copied
fry + **ing** = frying

Write the correct spelling word with an appropriate suffix on each line.
1. joined in matrimony __married__
2. USA and Mexico are examples of these __countries__
3. felt sorry for __pitied__
4. answering __replying__
5. food purchases __groceries__
6. to be concerned __worried__
7. one's adversaries __enemies__
8. places of manufacturing __factories__
9. petitioned __applied__
10. more than one period of 100 years __centuries__
11. Easter flowers __lilies__
12. fun things done in free time __hobbies__
13. milk processors __dairies__
14. little yellow birds __canaries__
15. urban areas __cities__
16. recollections __memories__
17. borders __boundaries__
18. people work for these __companies__

page 304

Tim Burr, Tall Tale Hero

Read the following tall tale about Tim Burr. Use proofreading marks to edit the paragraphs and correct the sentence fragments. **Write** the quotations correctly. Use proper capitalization and the appropriate homophones.

Answers may vary:

far up north, in the rugged, wooded regions of canada, there lived the famous lumberjack, tim burr. his trusty sidekick, saw mills, lived there, too. one day, saw and tim loaded up their axes and set off for the woods, to fell more trees for the local mill, Log Lagoon. they took along their pack mules, beauty and beast. they chopped so fast that the trees began falling onto each other, creating quite a logjam. It's not my fault yelled saw. I can't see where you are cutting.

the problem grew worse. beauty, tim's beloved mule, almost got his tail sliced off, by a falling tree trunk. that does it, yelled tim angrily. when you cut down a tree, call for me, so I know where you are. saw obeyed tim's wishes. from that day on, as each tree was felled, saw cried, "TIM BURR!"

page 305

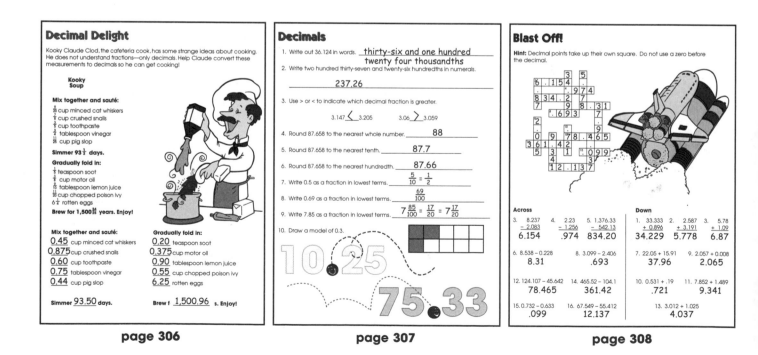

Decimal Delight

Kooky Claude Clod, the cafeteria cook, has some strange ideas about cooking. He does not understand fractions—only decimals. Help Claude convert these measurements to decimals so he can get cooking!

Kooky Soup

Mix together and sauté:
- cup minced cat whiskers
- cup crushed snails
- cup toothpaste
- tablespoon vinegar
- cup pig slop

Simmer 93¼ days.

Gradually fold in:
- teaspoon soot
- cup motor oil
- tablespoon lemon juice
- cup chopped poison ivy
- 6¼ rotten eggs

Brew for 1,500 24/25 years. Enjoy!

Mix together and sauté:
- 0.45 cup minced cat whiskers
- 0.875 cup crushed snails
- 0.60 cup toothpaste
- 0.75 tablespoon vinegar
- 0.44 cup pig slop

Simmer 93.50 days.

Gradually fold in:
- 0.20 teaspoon soot
- 0.375 cup motor oil
- 0.90 tablespoon lemon juice
- 0.55 cup chopped poison ivy
- 6.25 rotten eggs

Brew f 1,500.96 s. Enjoy!

page 306

Decimals

1. Write out 36.124 in words. __thirty-six and one hundred twenty four thousandths__
2. Write two hundred thirty-seven and twenty-six hundredths in numerals.
   __237.26__
3. Use > or < to indicate which decimal fraction is greater.
   3.147 < 3.205   3.06 > 3.059
4. Round 87.658 to the nearest whole number. __88__
5. Round 87.658 to the nearest tenth. __87.7__
6. Round 87.658 to the nearest hundredth. __87.66__
7. Write 0.5 as a fraction in lowest terms. $\frac{5}{10} = \frac{1}{2}$
8. Write 0.69 as a fraction in lowest terms. $\frac{69}{100}$
9. Write 7.85 as a fraction in lowest terms. $7\frac{85}{100} = \frac{17}{20} = 7\frac{17}{20}$
10. Draw a model of 0.3.

page 307

Blast Off!

Hint: Decimal points take up their own square. Do not use a zero before the decimal.

Across
3. $\begin{array}{r} 8.237 \\ -2.083 \\ \hline 6.154 \end{array}$
4. $\begin{array}{r} 2.23 \\ -1.256 \\ \hline .974 \end{array}$
5. $\begin{array}{r} 1,376.33 \\ -542.13 \\ \hline 834.20 \end{array}$

6. 8.538 – 0.228
   8.31
8. 3.099 – 2.406
   .693

12. 124.107 – 45.642
   78.465
14. 465.52 – 104.1
   361.42

15. 0.732 – 0.633
   .099
16. 67.549 – 55.412
   12.137

Down
1. $\begin{array}{r} 33.333 \\ +0.896 \\ \hline 34.229 \end{array}$
2. $\begin{array}{r} 2.587 \\ +3.191 \\ \hline 5.778 \end{array}$
3. $\begin{array}{r} 5.78 \\ +1.09 \\ \hline 6.87 \end{array}$

7. 22.05 + 15.91
   37.96
9. 2.057 + 0.008
   2.065

10. 0.531 + .19
   .721
11. 7.852 + 1.489
   9.341

13. 3.012 + 1.025
   4.037

page 308

Learn at Home, Grade 5

Come-Back Can

You will need: a large can with a plastic lid, a compass, 2 long rubber bands, a paper clip, a piece of wire and a bolt.

Making the Come-Back Can
With a compass point, punch a hole in the center of the can bottom. Punch another hole in the center of the plastic lid. Feed two long rubber bands through the hole in the bottom of the can. Use a paper clip on the outside of the can to keep the loops of the rubber bands from pulling out. Wrap a piece of wire around a bolt and tie the wire to the center of one of the rubber bands inside the can. Thread the other ends of the rubber bands through the hole in the lid. Use another paper clip to keep these outside loops from pulling out. Snap the lid on the can.

Using the Come-Back Can
Place the can on the floor and roll it away from you. Does it come back? __yes__
Roll it harder. Does it come all the way back? __no__
__Rolls farther than the ramp bottom.__

Making Hypotheses
Why do you think the can comes back? __Because the rubber band is unwinding.__
Can you make the can roll farther, (faster) or longer? __Winding the band tighter.__
What can you change about the can's design? __Answer will vary.__

Try your new design. How does it work? __Answer will vary.__

page 309

Vital Vowel Digraphs

Vowel Digraph are two vowels together that make only one vowel sound. Generally, the vowel digraphs below carry the following sounds:

approach
beaten
blueprint
boasted
bread
breath
disagreement
easel
eastern
feelings
flue
glued
groan
increase
leather
needless
peek
reason

> **ee, ea = long e** as in peep, flea
> **ue = oo** as in true
> **oa, oe = long o** as in moan

Sometimes the vowel digraph **ea** carries the **short e** sound as in **pleasure.**

Write each spelling word in the appropriate category. **Write** the number of syllables in each word in the parentheses.

ee = ē		ea = ē	
disagreement	(4)	beaten	(2)
feelings	(2)	easel	(2)
needless	(2)	eastern	(2)
peek	(1)	increase	(2)
		reason	(2)

oa = ō		Elephant **ea** Words		ue = oo	
approach	(2)	bread	(1)	blueprint	(2)
boasted	(2)	breath	(1)	flue	(1)
groan	(1)	leather	(2)	glued	(1)

Write the spelling word that is a compound.
__blueprint__

Write the eight spelling words that contain either a prefix or a suffix.
beaten	needless	eastern	glued
disagreement	boasted	feelings	increase

page 314

Historical Harry

What were the large cannons that were used by Germany in World War I?
Solve the following subtraction problems and find the answers in the cannon. **Write** the corresponding letter above the problem's number at the bottom of the page to spell out the answer to this historical trivia question.

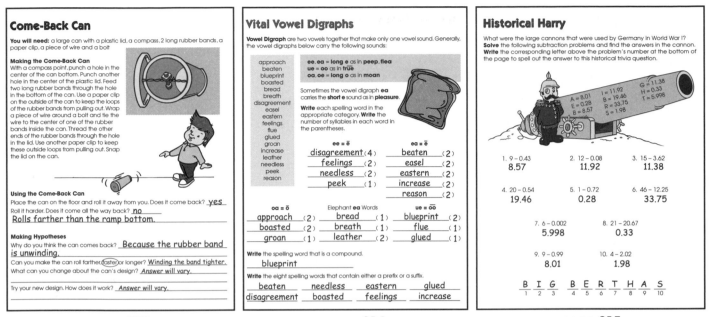

A = 8.01   I = 11.92   G = 11.38
E = 0.28   B = 19.46   H = 0.33
B = 8.57   R = 33.75   T = 5.998
            S = 1.98

1. 9 – 0.43	2. 12 – 0.08	3. 15 – 3.62
8.57	11.92	11.38

4. 20 – 0.54	5. 1 – 0.72	6. 46 – 12.25
19.46	0.28	33.75

7. 6 – 0.002	8. 21 – 20.67
5.998	0.33

9. 9 – 0.99	10. 4 – 2.02
8.01	1.98

B	I	G	B	E	R	T	H	A	S
1	2	3	4	5	6	7	8	9	10

page 315

A Multiple Design

Solve the problems on a separate sheet of paper. Find the answers in the design and **color** correctly.

green	blue	red
0.463	28.5	6.51
x 82	x 7.4	x 6.9
37.966	210.9	44.919

yellow	purple	purple
39.2	7.54	0.670
x 0.36	x 0.43	x 0.94
14.112	3.2422	0.62980

yellow	yellow	purple
64.9	0.592	7.46
x 3.26	x 40.6	x 5.9
211.574	24.0352	44.014

green	blue	blue	green	purple
92.4	32.8	85.1	7.32	6.05
x 0.62	x 0.26	x 0.95	x 1.6	x 8.3
57.288	8.528	80.845	11.712	50.215

green	blue	yellow	red	red
3.27	5.56	80.5	5.77	95.8
x 844	x 3.94	x 0.276	x 4.26	x 7.41
2759.88	21.9064	22.218	24.5802	709.878

red	yellow	yellow	yellow	yellow
0.784	2.57	29.3	6.80	0.245
x 6.92	x 63.6	x 0.487	x 0.42	x 3.6
5.42528	163.452	14.2691	2.856	0.8820

page 316

The Perfect Sweet-Treat Solution

Solve each division problem on a separate sheet of paper. **Draw** a line from the popcorn (problem) to the correct drink (answer).

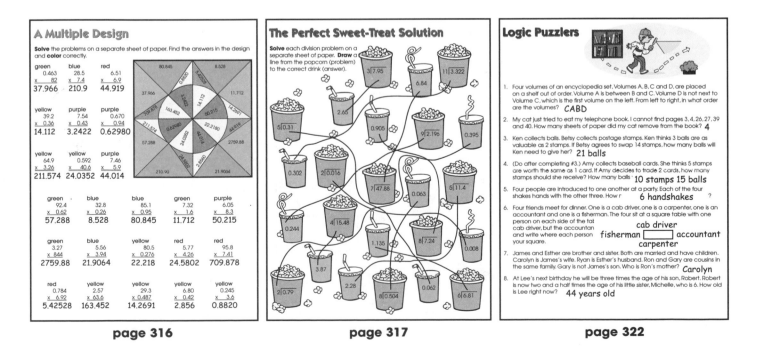

page 317

Logic Puzzlers

1. Four volumes of an encyclopedia set, Volumes A, B, C and D, are placed on a shelf out of order. Volume A is between B and C. Volume D is not next to Volume C, which is the first volume on the left. From left to right, in what order are the volumes? __CABD__

2. My cat just tried to eat my telephone book. I cannot find pages 3, 4, 26, 27, 39 and 40. How many sheets of paper did my cat remove from the book? __4__

3. Ken collects balls. Betsy collects postage stamps. Ken thinks 3 balls are as valuable as 2 stamps. If Betsy agrees to swap 14 stamps, how many balls will Ken need to give her? __21 balls__

4. (Do after completing #3.) Amy collects baseball cards. She thinks 5 stamps are worth the same as 1 card. If Amy decides to trade 2 cards, how many stamps should she receive? __10 stamps   15 balls__

5. Four people are introduced to one another at a party. Each of the four shakes hands with the other three. How r __6 handshakes__ ?

6. Four friends meet for dinner. One is a cab driver, one is a carpenter, one is an accountant and one is a fisherman. The four sit at a square table with one person on each side of the tat. One person is the cab driver, but the accountan and write where each person your square.

__cab driver__
__fisherman__ [ ] __accountant__
__carpenter__

7. James and Esther are brother and sister. Both are married and have children. Carolyn is James's wife. Ryan is Esther's husband. Ron and Gary are cousins in the same family. Gary is not James's son. Who is Ron's mother? __Carolyn__

8. At Lee's next birthday he will be three times the age of his son, Robert. Robert is now two and a half times the age of his little sister, Michelle, who is 6. How old is Lee right now? __44 years old__

page 322

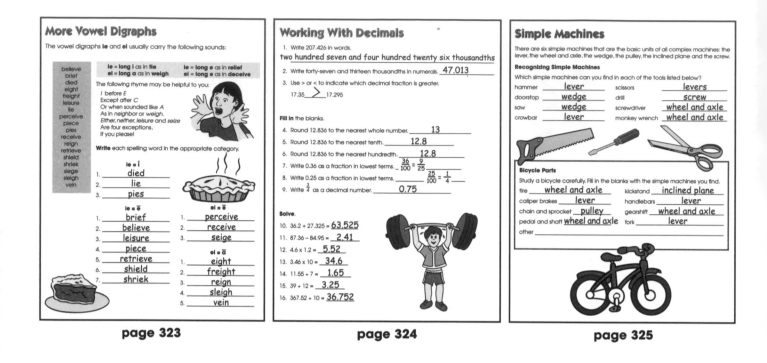

More Vowel Digraphs

The vowel digraphs **ie** and **ei** usually carry the following sounds:

ie = long i as in **tie**	ie = long e as in **relief**
ei = long a as in **weigh**	ei = long e as in **deceive**

believe
brief
died
eight
freight
leisure
lie
perceive
piece
pies
receive
reign
retrieve
shield
shriek
siege
sleigh
vein

The following rhyme may be helpful to you:

I before E
Except after C
Or when sounded like A
As in neighbor or weigh.
Either, neither, leisure and seize
Are four exceptions,
If you please!

Write each spelling word in the appropriate category.

ie = ī
1. died
2. lie
3. pies

ie = ē
1. brief
2. believe
3. leisure
4. piece
5. retrieve
6. shield
7. shriek

ei = ē
1. perceive
2. receive
3. seige

ei = ā
1. eight
2. freight
3. reign
4. sleigh
5. vein

page 323

Working With Decimals

1. Write 207.426 in words.
two hundred seven and four hundred twenty six thousandths

2. Write forty-seven and thirteen thousandths in numerals. __47.013__

3. Use > or < to indicate which decimal fraction is greater.
17.35 __>__ 17.295

Fill in the blanks.

4. Round 12.836 to the nearest whole number. __13__

5. Round 12.836 to the nearest tenth. __12.8__

6. Round 12.836 to the nearest hundredth. __12.8__

7. Write 0.36 as a fraction in lowest terms. $\frac{36}{100} = \frac{9}{25}$

8. Write 0.25 as a fraction in lowest terms. $\frac{25}{100} = \frac{1}{4}$

9. Write $\frac{3}{4}$ as a decimal number. __0.75__

Solve.

10. 36.2 + 27.325 = __63.525__

11. 87.36 − 84.95 = __2.41__

12. 4.6 × 1.2 = __5.52__

13. 3.46 × 10 = __34.6__

14. 11.55 ÷ 7 = __1.65__

15. 39 ÷ 12 = __3.25__

16. 367.52 ÷ 10 = __36.752__

page 324

Simple Machines

There are six simple machines that are the basic units of all complex machines: the lever, the wheel and axle, the wedge, the pulley, the inclined plane and the screw.

Recognizing Simple Machines

Which simple machines can you find in each of the tools listed below?

hammer	lever	scissors	levers
doorstop	wedge	drill	screw
saw	wedge	screwdriver	wheel and axle
crowbar	lever	monkey wrench	wheel and axle

Bicycle Parts

Study a bicycle carefully. Fill in the blanks with the simple machines you find.

tire	wheel and axle	kickstand	inclined plane
caliper brakes	lever	handlebars	lever
chain and sprocket	pulley	gearshift	wheel and axle
pedal and shaft	wheel and axle	fork	lever
other			

page 325

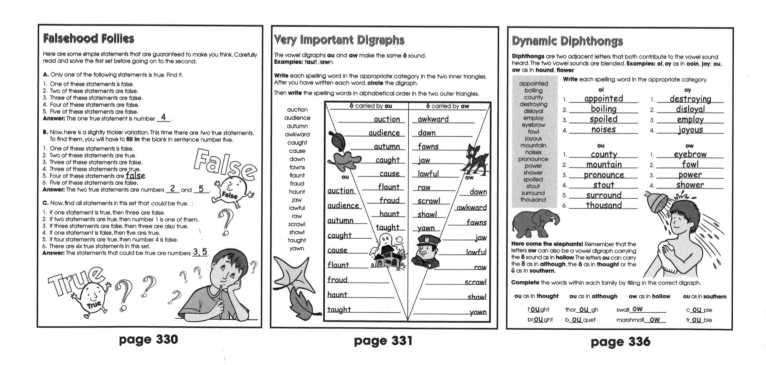

Falsehood Follies

Here are some simple statements that are guaranteed to make you think. Carefully read and solve the first set before going on to the second.

A. Only one of the following statements is true. Find it.

1. One of these statements is false.
2. Two of these statements are false.
3. Three of these statements are false.
4. Four of these statements are false.
5. Five of these statements are false.

Answer: The one true statement is number __4__.

B. Now, here is a slightly trickier variation. This time there are *two* true statements. To find them, you will have to **fill in** the blank in sentence number five.

1. One of these statements is false.
2. Two of these statements are true.
3. Three of these statements are true.
4. Three of these statements are true.
5. Four of these statements are __false__.
6. Five of these statements are false.

Answer: The two true statements are numbers __2__ and __5__.

C. Now, find all statements in this set that *could* be true.

1. If one statement is true, then three are false.
2. If two statements are true, then number 1 is one of them.
3. If three statements are false, then three are also true.
4. If one statement is false, then five are true.
5. If four statements are true, then number 4 is false.
6. There are six true statements in this set.

Answer: The statements that could be true are numbers __3, 5__.

page 330

Very Important Digraphs

The vowel digraphs **au** and **aw** make the same ô sound. **Examples: fault, lawn**

Write each spelling word in the appropriate category in the two inner triangles. After you have written each word, **circle** the digraph.

Then **write** the spelling words in alphabetical order in the two outer triangles.

auction
audience
autumn
awkward
caught
cause
dawn
fawns
flaunt
fraud
haunt
jaw
lawful
raw
scrawl
shawl
taught
yawn

ô carried by **au**	ô carried by **aw**
auction	awkward
audience	dawn
autumn	fawns
caught	jaw
cause	lawful
flaunt	raw
fraud	scrawl
haunt	shawl
taught	yawn

au
auction
audience
autumn
caught
cause
flaunt
fraud
haunt
taught

aw
dawn
awkward
fawns
jaw
lawful
raw
scrawl
shawl
yawn

page 331

Dynamic Diphthongs

Diphthongs are two adjacent letters that both contribute to the vowel sound heard. The two vowel sounds are blended. **Examples: oi, oy** as in **coin, joy; ou, ow** as in **hound, flower**.

appointed
boiling
county
destroying
disloyal
employ
eyebrow
fowl
joyous
mountain
noises
pronounce
power
shower
spoiled
stout
surround
thousand

Write each spelling word in the appropriate category.

oi
1. appointed
2. boiling
3. spoiled
4. noises

oy
1. destroying
2. disloyal
3. employ
4. joyous

ou
1. county
2. mountain
3. pronounce
4. stout
5. surround
6. thousand

ow
1. eyebrow
2. fowl
3. power
4. shower

Here come the elephants! Remember that the letters **ow** can also be a vowel digraph carrying the ô sound as in **hollow**. The letters **ou** can carry the ô as in **although**, the ô as in **thought** or the ŭ as in **southern**.

Complete the words within each family by filling in the correct digraph.

ou as in thought	ou as in although	ow as in hollow	ou as in southern
f**ou**ght	thor**ou**gh	swall**ow**	c**ou**ple
br**ou**ght	b**ou**quet	marshmall**ow**	tr**ou**ble

page 336

Learn at Home, Grade 5

Get the Facts, Max

Read the paragraphs to answer the questions below.

The islands of Aruba, Bonaire and Curaçao, sometimes known as the ABC islands, are part of the Netherlands Antilles. They lie 50 miles north off the coast of Venezuela. Three more islands, St. Eustatius, Saba and St. Martin (the northern half of which belongs to France), are approximately 500 miles northeast of the ABC islands.

Until 1949, the islands were known as the Dutch West Indies or Curaçao Territory. In 1986, Aruba separated to become a self-governing part of the Netherlands Realm.

On the island of Curaçao, most food is imported. Because it is so rocky, little farming is possible. The island is the largest and most heavily populated of the Netherlands Antilles. Its oil refineries, among the largest in the world, give its people a relatively high standard of living. Today, most people of Curaçao work in the shipping, refining or tourist industry.

Netherlands Antilles—Other Facts

Area:
Aruba	75 square miles
Bonaire	111 square miles
Curaçao	171 square miles
Saba	5 square miles
St. Eustatius	11 square miles
St. Martin	13 square miles

Capital: Willemstad

Major Languages: Dutch, Papiamento (a mixture of Spanish, Dutch, Portuguese, Carib and English), English, Spanish

1. Name the capital of the Netherlands Antilles. __Willemstad__
2. What industry gives the people a high standard of living? __oil refinery__
3. Name the ABC islands. __Aruba, Bonaire and Curaçao__
4. What is Papiamento? __a mixture of languages__
5. Why must food be imported to __land is too rocky for farming__
6. Which island is smallest? __Saba__
7. Which two islands are the largest? __Bonaire and Curaçao__
8. Which island belongs in part to France? __St. Martin__
9. In what year did Aruba become self-governing? __1986__

page 337

Big Bucks for You!

Solve the problems on another sheet of paper.

	Answer space
1. You receive your first royalty check for $1,000.00 and deposit it in your checking account. You go directly to the music store and spend $234.56 on new CDs. What is your balance?	$765.44
2. You naturally treat all your friends to pizza, which costs you $47.76. You pay with a check. What is your balance now?	$717.68
3. You decide to restock your wardrobe and buy $389.99 worth of new clothes. What is your balance?	$327.69
4. Your next royalty check arrives, and you deposit $1,712.34. You also treat yourself to a new 15-speed bicycle, which costs $667.09. What is your balance?	$1372.94
5. You buy your mother some perfume for a present. You write a check for $37.89. What is your balance?	$1335.05
6. You need a tennis racket and some other sports equipment. The bill comes to $203.45 What is your new balance?	$1131.60
7. You treat your family to dinner at **Snails in a Pail**, where the check comes to $56.17. What is your new balance?	$1075.43
8. You join a health club, and the first payment is $150.90. What is your new balance?	$924.53
9. You deposit your latest royalty check, which amounts to $4,451.01. What is your new balance?	$5375.54
10. To celebrate this good fortune, you take your entire peewee football team to a professional football game. The bill comes to $4,339.98. What is your new balance?	$1035.56

page 338

Snails in a Pail

Sly Me Slugg, world-famous French chef, has made his fast-food business, **Snails in a Pail**, the most popular restaurant in the whole area. This is his menu:

Slime Soup	$.49
Slugburger	$1.69
Chicken-Fried Snails	$2.99
Slimy Slush	$.89
Snailcream Shake	$1.49
Snailbits Salad	$1.09

Solve the problems on another sheet of paper.

	Answer space
1. Sly Me Slugg sold 60 Slimy Slushes and 40 Snailcream Shakes on Friday. How much did he make on drinks that day?	$113.00
2. A coach treated 15 of his team players to Slugburgers. How much change did he receive from $40.00?	$14.65
3. Your brother was so hungry that he ordered one of everything on the menu. How much change did he get from a $10.00 bill?	$1.36
4. Sly Me Slugg sold $43.61 in Slime Soup orders on Wednesday and $38.22 in soup orders on Thursday. How many orders of Slime Soup did he sell in those 2 days?	167
5. You had a party at **Snails in a Pail** and bought 9 Slugburgers, 3 orders of Chicken-Fried Snails, 2 Snailbits Salads, 5 Snailcream Shakes and 10 Slimy Slushes. What was the total cost for the party?	$42.71
6. In one week, Sly Me Slugg sold 200 Slugburgers and 79 orders of Chicken-Fried Snails. How much money did he earn from these 2 items?	$574.21
7. You ordered 10 Slugburgers, 10 Snailcream Shakes and 10 Slimy Slushes. What was your total cost?	$40.70
8. On Friday, Sly Me earned $1,252. On Saturday, he earned $1,765. On Sunday, he earned $2,998. What was his average daily earnings for those 3 days?	$2005

page 339

The "Nym" Family

Word list:
answer, broad, combine, council, cymbal, downstairs, false, freeze, narrow, pause, plain, punish, question, reward, separate, thaw, true, upstairs

Words that have similar meanings are called **synonyms**. **Examples:** trip, journey

Words that have opposite meanings are called **antonyms**. **Examples:** hot, cold

Words that sound the same but have different spellings and meanings are called **homonyms. Examples:** blue, blew

Use the word list to unscramble the spelling words below. Then, **draw** a line to connect each pair of antonyms.

etusniqo	question	zrefee	freeze
dralswtson	downstairs	wersan	answer
waht	thaw	woranr	narrow
nieocbm	combine	treapsea	separate
odarb	broad	rlupstas	upstairs

Write a synonym for each of the following.

to chastise	punish	faithful	true
a prize	reward	erroneous	false

Write the homonym that will complete each pair.

1. plane __plain__
2. symbol __cymbal__
3. paws __pause__
4. counsel __council__

Answers may include:

1.	son	sun	5.	no	know	9.	sail	sale		
2.	night	knight	6.	there	their	10.	tail	tale		
3.	blew	blue	7.	two	to	11.	bail	bale		
4.	new	knew	8.	so	sew	12.	your	you're		

page 344

Delivery Dilemma

Dilly's Deliveries is under new management, and the new boss just instructed his top driver to follow a most peculiar route. The driver is to deliver packages to each of the eight businesses shown below, but she is not necessarily meant to visit them in a logical order.

Top numbers: 3 3 8 26 2 2 5 3
Bottom numbers: 6 5 7 1 3 4 6

Help the confused driver plan her route. Number the businesses above in the order in which they should be visited in the first blank. **Write** the number of packages to be delivered in the second blank.

1. The second delivery is directly north of the first delivery and has one fewer package than the first.
2. Melody's Music needs all five packages delivered before 11:00 A.M.
3. By the time the paperwork is completed, the packages are verified and greetings are exchanged between the driver and the recipient, each delivery takes fifteen minutes.
4. The bank is never the last delivery. It always receives four packages.
5. Troy's Toys has the most packages of all. His delivery will contain as many packages as all the others combined.
6. Pete's deliveries are live animals, which need to be unloaded first when the store opens at 9:30 A.M.
7. The fourth delivery is directly east of the first delivery and contains twice the number of packages.
8. The travel agency and the pet store combined are to receive the same number of packages as the music store.
9. The fifth delivery contains three boxes.
10. The third delivery is two stores west of the second.
11. The tire store, the grocery store and the pet store will all receive the same number of packages. They are the only ones to receive this exact amount.

page 345

Percents and Fractions

Write the fraction and percent represented in each situation.

Situation	Fraction	Percent
30 marbles out of 100 marbles are red	$\frac{30}{100}$	30%
29 people out of 100 people voted.	$\frac{29}{100}$	29%
10 fish out of 100 fish are tropical.	$\frac{10}{100}$	10%
7 cats out of 100 cats live indoors.	$\frac{7}{100}$	7%
4 turtles out of 100 turtles laid eggs.	$\frac{4}{100}$	4%
7 out of 10 puppies had spots.	$\frac{7}{10}=\frac{70}{100}$	70%
5 out of 10 baskets were made.	$\frac{5}{10}=\frac{50}{100}$	50%
6 out of 25 rocks in my yard are igneous.	$\frac{6}{25}=\frac{24}{100}$	24%
17 out of 25 rulers are metric.	$\frac{17}{25}=\frac{68}{100}$	68%
18 out of 20 goldfish are orange.	$\frac{18}{20}=\frac{90}{100}$	90%
The dress was reduced $5 from $20.	$\frac{5}{20}=\frac{25}{100}$	25%

page 346

Models

Draw the model and **fill in** the missing fraction, percent or decimal.

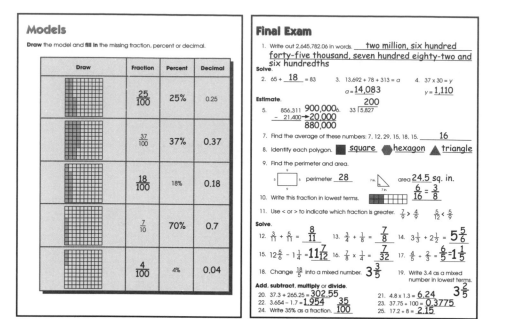

Draw	Fraction	Percent	Decimal
	$\frac{25}{100}$	25%	0.25
	$\frac{37}{100}$	37%	0.37
	$\frac{18}{100}$	18%	0.18
	$\frac{7}{10}$	70%	0.7
	$\frac{4}{100}$	4%	0.04

page 347

Final Exam

1. Write out 2,645,782.06 in words. <u>two million, six hundred forty-five thousand, seven hundred eighty-two and six hundredths</u>

Solve.

2. 65 + <u>18</u> = 83
3. 13,692 + 78 + 313 = a $a = $ <u>14,083</u>
4. 37 × 30 = y y = <u>1,110</u>

Estimate.

5. 856,311 → <u>900,000</u> − 21,400 → <u>20,000</u> = <u>880,000</u>
6. $33\overline{)5,827}$ <u>200</u>

7. Find the average of these numbers: 7, 12, 29, 15, 18, 15. <u>16</u>

8. Identify each polygon. ■ <u>square</u> ⬡ <u>hexagon</u> ▲ <u>triangle</u>

9. Find the perimeter and area.

   perimeter <u>28</u> area <u>24.5</u> sq. in. $\frac{6}{16} = \frac{3}{8}$

10. Write this fraction in lowest terms. $\frac{6}{16} = \frac{3}{8}$

11. Use < or > to indicate which fraction is greater. $\frac{7}{9} > \frac{4}{9}$ $\frac{5}{12} < \frac{5}{9}$

Solve.

12. $\frac{3}{11} + \frac{5}{11} = \frac{8}{11}$
13. $\frac{3}{4} + \frac{1}{8} = \frac{7}{8}$
14. $3\frac{1}{3} + 2\frac{1}{2} = 5\frac{5}{6}$
15. $12\frac{5}{6} - 1\frac{1}{4} = 11\frac{7}{12}$
16. $\frac{7}{8} \times \frac{1}{4} = \frac{7}{32}$
17. $\frac{4}{5} \div \frac{2}{3} = \frac{6}{5} = 1\frac{1}{5}$
18. Change $\frac{18}{5}$ into a mixed number. $3\frac{3}{5}$
19. Write 3.4 as a mixed number in lowest terms. $3\frac{2}{5}$

Add, subtract, multiply or divide.

20. 37.3 + 265.25 = <u>302.55</u>
21. 4.8 × 1.3 = <u>6.24</u>
22. 3.654 − 1.7 = <u>1.954</u>
23. 37.75 ÷ 100 = <u>0.3775</u>
24. Write 35% as a fraction. $\frac{35}{100}$
25. 17.2 ÷ 8 = <u>2.15</u>

page 352

Learn at Home, Grade 5

Write Government Officials

The government needs to hear from kids just like you! Our nation's leaders and the leaders of other countries need to hear our concerns. Most government officials welcome letters and want to know your thoughts.

Write letters that clearly state what you are concerned about and why you are concerned. Using the information that you have learned will help influence the people who make decisions about the laws and funding that govern the safety of our planet.

NO MATTER HOW YOUNG YOU ARE
YOU CAN MAKE A DIFFERENCE.

Here are some addresses of where to write to our government officials.

Representative _____
US House of Representatives
Washington DC 20515

Senator _____
US Senate
Washington DC 20510

(You will need to know the names of your state's Senators and Representatives.)

President _____
The White House
1600 Pennsylvania Ave.
Washington DC 20500
(Begin your letter, "Dear Mr. President.")

If you wish to write to the leaders of other foreign countries, request the proper address from:

(Country's Name) Embassy
The United Nations,
United Nations Plaza
New York, NY 10017

Organizations to Contact

The Acid Rain Foundation
1630 Blackhawk Hills
St. Paul, MN 55122

Acid Rain Information
Clearinghouse Library
Center for Environmental Information, Inc.
33 S. Washington St.
Rochester, NY 14608

Adopt-A-Stream Foundation
P.O. Box 5558
Everett, WA 98201

Air Pollution Control
Bureau of National Affairs Inc.
1231 25th St. NW
Washington DC 20037

Alliance To Save Energy
1925 K St. NW
Suite 206
Washington DC 20036

**American Association of Zoological
Parks and Aquariums**
Oglebay Park
Wheeling, WV 26003

American Wind Energy Association
1730 N Lynn St.
Suite 610
Arlington, VA 22209

Canadian Coalition On Acid Rain
112 St. Clair Ave. West
Suite 504
Toronto, Ontario, Canada
M4V 2Y3

Center for Marine Conservation
1725 DeSales St. NW
Suite 500
Washington DC 20036

Friends of the Earth
530 Seventh St. SE
Washington DC 20003

**Global Releaf, c/o the American
Forestry Association**
P.O. Box 2000
Washington DC 20013

Greenpeace
1436 U Street NW
Washington DC 20009

Household Hazardous Waste Project
901 S. National Ave.
Box 108
Springfield, MO 65804

**National Association of Recycling
Industries**
330 Madison Ave.
New York, NY 10017

National Clean Air Coalition
530 7th St. SE
Washington DC 20003

National Wildlife Federation
1412 16th St. NW
Washington DC 20036

Public Affairs Office
US Environmental Protection Agency
Washington DC 20036

Renew America
1400 16th St. NW
Suite 710
Washington DC 20036

Save the Manatee Club
500 N. Maitland Ave.
Suite 200
Maitland, FL 32751

U.S. Environmental Protection Agency
401 M St. SW
Washington DC 20460

United Nations Environment Programme
North American Office
Room DC2-0803, United Nations
New York, NY 10017